Indian Theatre

INDIAN THEATRE

TRADITIONS OF PERFORMANCE

Edited by

Farley P. Richmond

Darius L. Swann

Phillip B. Zarrilli

University of Hawaii Press

Honolulu

Printed in the United States of America
96 95 94 93 92 90 5 4 3 2 1

Library of Congress Cataloging-in-Publication Data

Indian theatre : traditions of performance / edited by
Farley P. Richmond,
Darius L. Swann, Phillip B. Zarrilli.
p. cm.
Includes bibliographical references.
ISBN 0–8248–1190–9.—ISBN 0–8248–1322–7 (pbk.)
1. Theater—India. 2. Performing arts—India. 3. Sanskrit drama—History and criticism. 4. Folklore—India.
I. Richmond, Farley P., 1938– . II. Swann, Darius L., 1924–
III. Zarrilli, Phillip B., 1947–
PN2881.I53 1990
792'.0954—dc20 89–28699
CIP

Publication of this book has
been assisted by a grant from the
J. Watumull Fund

University of Hawaii Press books are printed
on acid-free paper and meet the guidelines
for permanence and durability of the Council
on Library Resources

CONTENTS

MAPS

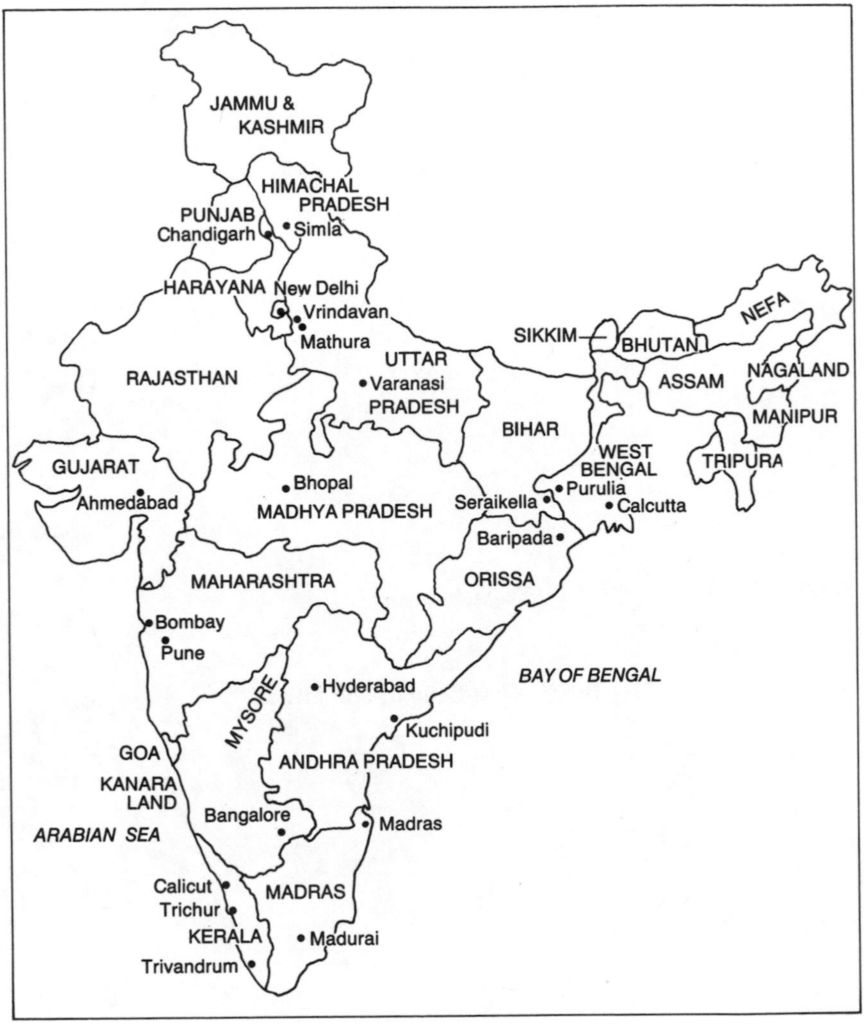
JAMMU &
KASHMIR
HIMACHAL
PRADESH
PUNJAB
Chandigarh
Simla
HARAYANA
New Delhi
Vrindavan
Mathura
RAJASTHAN
UTTAR
Varanasi
PRADESH
SIKKIM
BHUTAN
NEFA
ASSAM
NAGALAND
MANIPUR
BIHAR
WEST
BENGAL
TRIPURA
GUJARAT
Ahmedabad
Bhopal
MADHYA PRADESH
Seraikella
Purulia
Calcutta
Baripada
ORISSA
MAHARASHTRA
Bombay
Pune
MYSORE
Hyderabad
BAY OF BENGAL
Kuchipudi
GOA
ANDHRA PRADESH
KANARA
LAND
Bangalore
Madras
ARABIAN SEA
Calicut
MADRAS
Trichur
KERALA
Madurai
Trivandrum

PREFACE

AS ITS TITLE SUGGESTS, the purpose of this book is to introduce the reader to the multiple dimensions of Indian theatre by presenting a representative sample of the major traditions and genres of performance. Unlike other books of its kind published in recent years, this is a joint effort and, as such, bears the stamp of many hands. It is also the first time that an introduction to Indian theatre has been written by Western scholars from their own perspective. Our primary aim has been to reach students of theatre and all those other readers who may have little or no knowledge of Indian theatre in its manifest variety.

Like the culture from which it springs, Indian theatre holds many intriguing mysteries for foreign writers, prompting them to dig for treasures that are seemingly endless. Initially we set out to write a comprehensive study of Indian theatre. Reason prevailed when we contemplated the sheer enormity of the subject. The vast number and complexity of rural theatre forms alone convinced us to limit the scope of our study.

Our approach to the subject of Indian theatre, while necessarily selective, is not meant to be reductive. We hope that our choice and treatment of topics give some sense of the complexities of the performative field that constitutes the panorama of Indian theatre. The reader will also note that we have pointedly expanded the boundaries of what is usually called "theatre" in the West, since those boundaries (when we literally cross our own in traveling to the third world) can blind us to the possibility of finding something other than our own reflections when we explore that other world.

Each of the contributors to this volume has spent considerable time in India—in villages or cities, in training (and even occasionally, in performance), with neophytes and with masters, with the masses or with connoisseurs or patrons. Field research has hopefully rendered each of us, if nothing else, humbler in the face of mastery, or in the face of the inexhaustible supply of vitality that lingers joyously among performers who crisscross the vast subcontinent doing what they love. And while our point of view is decidedly Western, we hope that it is sympathetic; while descriptive, we trust that it keeps an ear and eye open to what India itself values and how it appreciates its own performance traditions.

Acknowledgments

The authors owe a great deal to many individuals and institutions in North America and India. Although it is not possible to thank them all by name, we would like to express our deep gratitude to all those who gave their kind assistance and support. In addition, we would like to acknowledge the specific debts recorded below.

Tevia Abrams

Of the artists, scholars, journalists, government officials, and others who were consulted in the early 1970s in conjunction with work on my doctoral dissertation, particular mention must be made of Durga Bhagvat, anthropologist and sociologist, who helped me form an intellectual framework for studying *tamāshā;* former Bombay journalist Vinayak Bhave, for his personal guidance and his vast storehouse of knowledge about the cultural history of Maharashtra and the state of *tamāshā;* Shahir (poet) Sable, then a leader of one of the better-known *tamāshā* troupes; and playwrights Vasant Sabnis and Vijay Tendulkar. I would also like to acknowledge the help of G. P. Vaidya, enthusiastic companion on evening rounds of performance in Pune, and of his daughter, Nilima, who served as secretary through most of the research period and who translated many of the Marathi text materials used in the study. Initial research funds were provided by a grant from the Canada Council, and years later a demonstration-workshop in New Delhi on traditional media, sponsored by the United Nations Population Fund, provided the opportunity to update some of the data on the use of *tamāshā* in development programs.

Wayne Ashley

My sincere thanks to the following persons and institutions: Kanan Anthitiriyan; Joe, Lee, and Scott Ashley; V. V. Karunakarran; T. C. Kurian; K. G. Laxmi; Raghavan Payyanad; Richard Schechner; Karen Souza; Phillip Zarrilli; Earthwatch/Center for Field Research; and the Smithsonian Foreign Currency Grant.

Farley P. Richmond

Among the many individuals in India who supported my research, I am particularly grateful to the following: L. S. Rajagopalan, K. Raman Cakyar, Goverdhan Panchal, Ebrahim Alkazi, and Dr. Suresh Awasthi. Supportive family members include Rati and Jimmy Mody, Rashne and Burjor Dubash, and Khursheeda Mody. Without the unfailing support of Yasmin Richmond

I would never have accomplished what I did. Thanks, too, are due the Kerala Kalamandalam, which welcomed me to study *kūṭiyāṭṭam* and introduced me to so many other wonderful art forms; to the National School of Drama of New Delhi, which permitted me to work on modern theatre over two one-year periods; and to the Sangeet Natak Akademi, whose administrators and staff gave me access to its photographic archives and library. I might never have experienced India in the first place without the encouragement of James R. Brandon, William T. and Van Ross, and Anant Negandhi; and without the support of colleagues and friends at Michigan State University and research grants from its Research Initiation Program and Humanities Research Center, I could never have ventured into the field so often. Moreover, without the generous support provided by two Fulbright-Hays grants, the JDR 3rd Fund of New York, the United States Educational Foundation in India, and the New York State Education Resources Center in India, I might not have sustained myself and my family for such long periods of time. I owe a special debt of gratitude for the patience of my extraordinary typists, particularly Joanne Peterson. And finally, my thanks to those who allowed me to use their photographic resources for this book: Kathryn Hansen, John Stratton Hawley, Norvin Hein, Daniel J. Ehnbom, and Niels Roed Sorensen.

Darius L. Swann

I would like to acknowledge the following persons and institutions with special thanks: Shri Ram Narayan Agrawal of Mathura for generous assistance and guidance in research on *rās līlā,* Shri Siddeshwar Prasad Awasthi of Kanpur for assistance in research on *nauṭankī,* and Dr. Suresh Awasthi and the staff of the Sangeet Natak Akademi for assistance in many ways.

Andrew T. Tsubaki

My thanks to the Indo-U.S. Subcommission on Education and Culture for making my trip to Seraikella possible, and to Guru Kedar Nath Sahoo, an excellent teacher and remarkable artist, who patiently taught me *chau.* I am grateful to Dr. Kapila Vatsyayan, an impressive scholar and fine dancer, for her help in untangling a confusion over my status as a student at the Center in Seraikella; without her support my stay there might have proved fruitless. I appreciate, too, the support of Susan Hawks, who helped me learn to enjoy living in India. Dr. Suresh Awasthi is to be thanked for opening my eyes to the joys of Indian performing arts. My thanks also go to Lilly Y. Tsubaki, who gave me constant support and encouragement. The Department of Theatre and Film, University of Kansas, allowed me the time to do my research and training and eventually to stage a Seraikella *chau* in 1981.

Phillip B. Zarrilli

My grateful thanks to Kunju and Vasudevan Namboodiripad for their assistance in studying *Ayyappan tiyatta;* and my gratitude to the Kerala Kalamandalam, the Kottakkal Kathakali Company, the Margi Kathakali School, Sri Muthappan Kathakali Yogam, as well as Kunju and Vasudevan Namboodiripad and M. P. Sankaran Namboodiri for their assistance in my study of *kathakaḷi.*

INTRODUCTION

Farley P. Richmond
Darius L. Swann
Phillip B. Zarrilli

A FOREIGNER LANDING IN INDIA FOR THE FIRST TIME, say in Delhi or Bombay, Calcutta or Madras, is likely to be struck by the incredible color of the landscape, the press of crowds, spilling beyond sidewalks into the streets, the varied modes of transportation—automobiles to elephants—and a host of unfamiliar sensations. At the heart of every city are unique features which set it apart from all the others. But each bears the unmistakable signs of colonial influence—British-style architecture and walled bungalows coexist with the gleaming steel, concrete, and glass skyscrapers that have come to represent the international style of architecture characteristic of our age. Cricket grounds, race courses, polo fields, and immaculate lawns of private clubs dot the cityscape. And everywhere there are people, people, people—strolling the streets, leaning out of windows—school kids in uniforms, hawkers, beggars, petty merchants, the teeming masses that Westerners have come to imagine characterize Asia's great cities.

A visitor is likely to be overwhelmed at first glance and to mistakenly believe that the immediate impressions are representative of the country as a whole. Indeed it is possible to think that India *is* its cities, especially when you do not journey out of them—possible to accept the popular belief that places like Calcutta are harbingers of the dismal future that awaits urbanites everywhere in the world. The truth of the matter is that these giants of modern Indian life are only a small part of the Indian landscape. Beyond the concrete, steel, and glass are other, more characteristic sights—dirt roads, meandering village lanes, open drainage ditches that are washed clean by monsoon rains, simple cottages with cow dung and urine floors, thatched huts, middle-income bungalows surrounded by compound walls in which a cow may leisurely graze on fresh grass, the smoke of hearth fires, tulsi plants strategically placed on the household property to ward off evil spirits, the smell of incense and camphor, the clang of brass and bronze bells in the

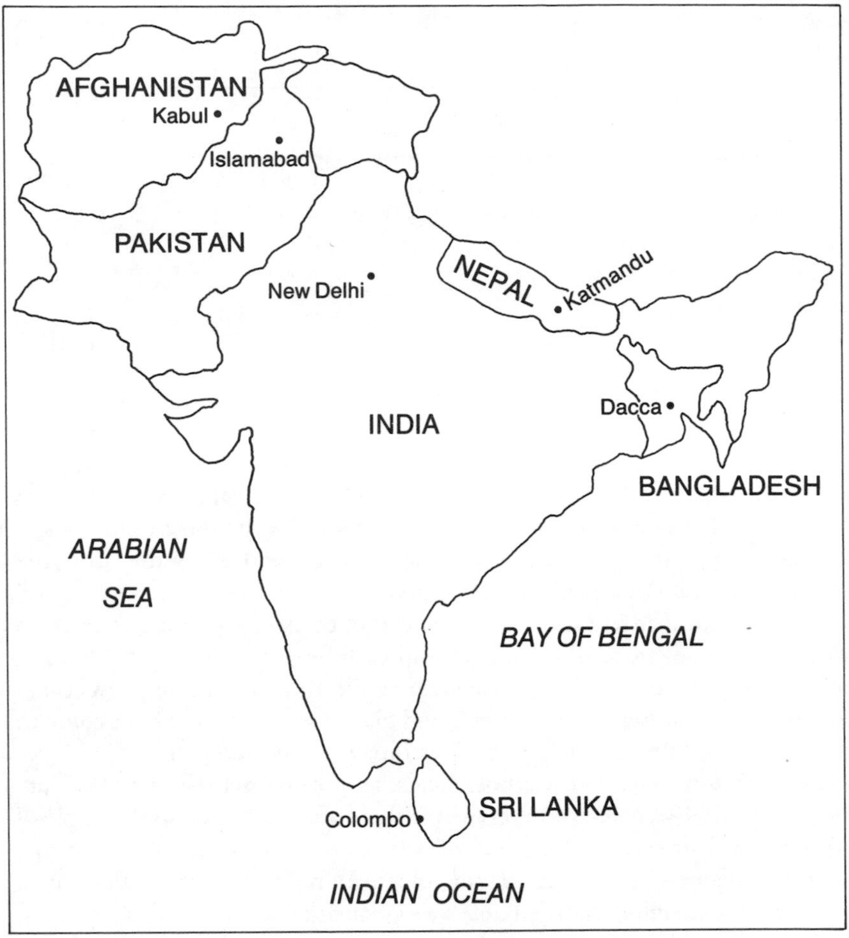

crisp morning air demanding that the gods wake up from their slumber to be propitiated by temple priests, the blare of film music from tiny tea stalls, the clatter of distant bullock carts, or the mournful wail of a coal-driven locomotive winding its way across the country in the dead of night. These too are India, a rural India, perhaps more typical and representative of the present reality of the lives of the vast majority of its people than the sprawling urban giants to which the traveler to India is first exposed.

Contemplating the monuments of the past, one may still conjure up an age when royalty ruled the land, when leisure hours were passed by courtiers whose pleasures consisted of writing and reciting poetry and composing music, when the educated few reveled in elegant silks and brocades and ornaments crafted to perfection in gold and precious jewels, when kings and maharajas assembled at their pleasure to debate the virtues of one religion or philosophy over that of another. Those bygone days witnessed the formation of many of the world's great religions, moral teachings, and ethical principles. India's past is full of events that have shaped the course of the present realities, just as surely as the present realities will dictate the future direction of the nation. The monuments of the past are the tangible evidence of the greatness that was ancient India—Ajanta and Ellora, Sanchi, Fatehpur Sikri, the Red Fort, the Taj Mahal, Khajuraho, Jaipur and Udaipur palaces, Elephanta, Mahabalipuram, Cochin Palace, among hundreds of other magical names.

As we set out to explore the theatre of this fascinating corner of the globe, we must remember the many layers of influence that have shaped India's cultural life: the classical roots, preceded by rites and ritual practices belonging to ancient belief systems, some of which have deep roots in the Middle East; the folk cultures, welded to village settings, as much a part of the land as the land is a part of them; and finally, the modern urban environment, shaped by the continual sense of a global currency quite removed from India's past, with one foot planted in international marketplaces and business and one foot firmly rooted in village soil, bridging two fundamentally different worlds.

Theatre in India, as we see it, speaks with many tongues, has a multitude of patterns, probes a host of issues, mimics no one and, at times, apes the West, pleases the few as well as the many, and serves the rich and the poor alike, man and god. In India it is possible to find those who believe that "theatre is cinema," and that the living theatre of the stage in the village square or in the temple is dead. However, we find Indian theatre very much alive.

And so we launch our readers into this sometimes foreign, sometimes familiar, journey knowing that they may emerge surprised, appalled, thrilled, intrigued, and perhaps every bit as confused and overwhelmed as we have been as we investigated this subject.

Theatre and Performance

Throughout the following pages, the words *theatre* and *performance* are used interchangeably, one for the other, because Indian theatre is not confined to neat, narrow categories. Indeed in this book we pay considerable attention to examples of performance that would not be generally regarded as "theatre" in the West. We note too that this effort to redefine the meaning of theatre and performance is part of a larger rewriting of the history of theatre/performance that is currently under way.

In India performances, except for those of the modern theatre, are known by genre-specific names in their local language—*yakṣagāna, rās līlā, terukkuttu, cavittu nāṭakam*—an endless stream of names, each with its own history and reasons for having been given that name. But it is by these specific names that things are known, not through such large generic categories as theatre or dance. If you are going to a ______, you are going to a ______, and nothing else! Moreover, each genre has its own set of associations. People know what to expect when they go—what type of performance it will be, what functions it will serve, what other types of people will be there, and so on. Especially at the local level, these performances will usually be part of a familiar and friendly world, known since childhood.

By and large it is we Westerners who have the need for clear definitions, for knowing what defines "theatre" versus "dance," or what differentiates "theatre" from "ritual." Most Indians go to performances of whatever type and experience devotion, wonder, and the like. The experience of devotion, for example, is not confined to what we will later define as devotional performances. The devotional experience arises where it will—it can be in witnessing Lord Kṛṣṇa's appearance in a village dance-drama, or even in a cinema hall showing a contemporary movie based on Kṛṣṇa's exploits.

Tradition and the Traditional

India—the name itself suggests a "hoary antiquity," a rich cultural legacy literally thousands of years old. If any culture could be said to be traditional, certainly Indian culture would seem to fit the bill. Before discussing the traditions of Indian performance, we would like to clarify how we are using the words *tradition* and *traditional*.

A tradition of performance, in our nominative use of the word, is virtually synonomous with genre. The word tradition, however, implies something more than genre, which by comparison seems dry and static. Tradition implies movement, action through time. Performance traditions, like religious or literary ones, are best thought of as inherited collections of established ways of feeling, thinking, and doing that are passed down through generations and, just as importantly, consist of the active and often contentious process of transmitting what has been handed down. In other words, a performance tradition is that body of knowledge, including techniques of performance, texts, and aesthetic principles or rules or assumptions, which constitutes and defines what the particular genre is, and it is simultaneously the process of handing that knowledge on from one generation to another. Since most of the performance genres we will be studying in this book are traditional in this sense, it is important to recognize that within Indian culture as a whole traditions from the past are accorded a positive value. It is indeed the passage through generations that gives a tradition its authority.

Even so, an "ancient" performance tradition is not necessarily ossified. To the contrary, what often differentiates one tradition from another, or a group of similar traditions from a group of distinctly different traditions, is the degree of change that is allowable within the limits of the tradition and the extent to which the weight of authority can be flexible in adapting to socioeconomic or artistic change. In the chapters on specific performance traditions in this volume, we have attempted to indicate the degree of change allowable within the tradition.

Features of Traditional Performance

In all the performance traditions discussed in this book, except perhaps that of the modern theatre, there is a convergence or synthesis of music, dance, and drama. As in other traditional forms of Asian performance, the arts are a composite set of skills practiced by a team of artists who, through the creation of verbal, vocal, aural, spatial, and visual patterns, create a total performance.

Given this intermingling of the arts, it is not surprising that many forms of Indian performance do not fit neatly into Western categories. Music and bodily movement are requisite parts of any performance. The individual performer in an ensemble may be a specialist in music or acting-dance, but each specialist also must have an intimate knowledge of the other arts necessary for the successful performance. Actor-dancers will be required to possess as part of their embodied performance knowledge of the rhythmic patterns of the music to which they must perform. Instrumentalists or vocalists will just as assuredly be immersed in the patterns of movement, stage conventions, and methods of character creation used by the actor-dancers. Indian performance is performance created by a total ensemble of artists working together.

The various types of movement that are part of Indian performance were first recorded in ancient times. At that early stage of development, three different facets of movement, all of which are still used in performance today, were recognized. First there is *nṛtta,* or pure, abstract, or decorative dance. Next is *nṛtya,* mime or gesture based on interpretation of the narrative or thematic content of performance. Finally there is *nāṭya,* which is best thought of as a performance in which acting and dance are combined in dramatic form. Specifically *nāṭya* refers to a cataloging of the types of body gestures employed to express various states of the human condition.

Traditional Indian performance genres combine all three types of movement. Variation in forms comes about not through the exclusion of one type of movement but through the degree or proportion of performance that is devoted to a particular type of movement. For example, performance traditions that are usually described as dance forms are those which emphasize a solo performer in whose program *nṛtta* or pure dance plays a primary role.

However, pure dance never constitutes the complete movement vocabulary of a dance form. Equally important are the other facets of Indian movement. For example, in the modern stage concerts of *bhārata nāṭyam,* the major classical dance form of South India, there is an initial emphasis on pure dance. However, as the program develops, the individual performer must also display consummate interpretive abilities in capturing the appropriate mood or flavor of the devotional songs enacted.

At the opposite end of the spectrum from "dance" forms is the contemporary or modern theatre, modeled on Western conventions introduced by the British in the eighteenth and nineteenth centuries. In contrast to traditional forms of performance, the stage deportment in modern performances is limited to the theatrical movement appropriate to individual character depiction, just as in the West.

It is between these two poles of "dance" forms and "modern" theatre that we find the great variety of Indian performance traditions, incorporating all three types of Indian movement in varying degrees. Here we find folk theatre forms in which scripted dramas are enacted and which illustrate and punctuate character portrayal with dance and music inserts intended to enhance both the dramatic action and the mood of particular scenes. Here also we find the dance-dramas, forms which so closely integrate dance (whether pure or interpretive) and drama (either scripted or unscripted) that it is impossible to call them anything other than dance-dramas.

Another characteristic of many forms of traditional Indian performance is the existence of two major styles of movement, *tāṇḍava* and *lāsya. Tāṇḍava* refers to movement that is strong, vigorous, and typically masculine. *Lāsya,* on the other hand, is associated with the feminine and is characterized by a lyrical quality, grace, and fluidity. For many Indian performance genres, no performance is complete without the presentation of roles set in both styles. The coexistence of both styles as the joining of opposites to make a whole is based on Indian mythology. The god Śiva originated the masculine, powerful, *tāṇḍava* style, and just as Śiva is incomplete without his consort, Pārvatī, so must there also exist the feminine, *lāsya* style. Since Śiva is believed to manifest his full power only when conjoined with the sakti *(śakti)* or divine feminine energy represented by Pārvatī, the *tāṇḍava* without the *lāsya* in dance would be incomplete and would create an imbalance in the world.

This mythological basis for the contrasting movement styles found in most traditional forms of Indian theatre is a reflection of the symbiotic relationship between Indian mythology and its performance traditions. The traditional theatre of India relies on an inherited and common set of sources for the majority of its content. The stories and characters of most plays and dance-dramas are taken from the great collections of Hindu epics and stories, the *Mahābhārata, Rāmāyaṇa,* and the Puranas. These stories have been transmitted from generation to generation through the mouths of storytellers, through the medium of puppetry and performing arts, and finally, through written compilations. Even today these stories serve as the most vital source for creative expression in the arts.

The literature of Indian performance genres draws heavily on this epic and puranic literature, and the aesthetics of the theatre are closely linked to the Hindu religious-philosophic base.[1] Therefore, all forms of Hindu performance share common religious-philosophical assumptions. The foremost of these assumptions is that this life is characterized by maya, or illusion, and is part of an endless cycle of birth, death, and rebirth. Only by finding a path to liberation of the soul from bondage will the fetters of attachment and illusion be permanently broken and the soul freed from the cycle of rebirth. Hindus have traditionally recognized three paths that lead to liberation: the way of action, the way of knowledge, and the way of devotion. Each of these approaches contributes to the texture and shape of Indian theatre.

Chronologically the way of action came first. The Aryans who entered India about 1500 B.C. put sacrifice at the center of their religious practice. Accordingly the special skills of a class of people who could manipulate the sacrifice became important—hence the development of ritual specialists. The earliest scriptures of the Indo-Aryans are called the Vedas, and the first three—the *Ṛg,* the *Sāma,* and the *Yajur*—clearly demonstrate this emphasis on sacrificial action. The subsequent literature and development of ritual practice in India are evidence of the continuing centrality of the way of action in Hindu life and worship.

The second path to liberation, the way of knowledge, emerged in the late Vedic period, beginning with the Brāhmaṇas and fully flowering in the Upaniṣads. The fundamental aesthetic principle of *rasa,* or sentiment (discussed in chapter 2), derives from the way of knowledge. The theatre experience was believed to be one way of arriving at the state of blessedness characterized by that *rasa* which eventually was interpreted as subsuming all others, at-onement or peace *(śānta).*

The third path, the way of devotion or bhakti, is associated with the development of popular devotionalism, especially that devotion inspired by and directed toward the popular incarnations of Viṣṇu, Kṛṣṇa, and Rāma. In these forms of devotionalism, religion and theatrical means and ends join in a direct and concrete manner, such as when a male devotee of Kṛṣṇa takes on the persona of his female consort, Rādhā, by adopting female dress and allowing his entire behavior to be guided by Rādhā's loving devotion to her lord. The way of devotion appeals to the affective side of human experience;

[1] Religion has played a significant role in this evolution. In particular Hinduism has dominated and shaped the vast majority of theatre forms with which we deal. Buddhism, Islam, and Christianity, even Jainism and Zoroastrianism, have exerted their own particular influence to a greater or lesser degree depending on the theatre forms concerned.

strong emotion and sometimes ecstatic states are induced through communal singing and dancing.

These three paths to liberation have tended in time to merge into one system. The *Bhagavad Gītā* accommodates all three but seemingly gives the highest place to devotion. The three paths are not mutually exclusive; indeed elements of one are often understood to be helpful in following another. For example, in the practice of classical yoga, devotion to Iśvara and the development of an appropriate devotional attitude are necessary prerequisites for taking up the path. With these precedents it should not be surprising that aspects of all three paths may be found in a number of Indian performance genres today.

Indian Performance: Spheres of Influence

The vast spectrum of performance genres in India is a reflection of its linguistic, cultural, and religious diversity. Both the number and complexity of these genres have been sustained by a remarkably high degree of historical continuity within (and sometimes across) the different regions of India. As suggested earlier, it is impossible to categorize the traditions of Indian performance in any absolute terms, nor is there any need for them to be categorized for the majority of people who attend the performances. Yet for the student of Indian performance, some means of organizing the material must be found.

We have chosen to present our findings under five broad categories, which may be thought of as interlocking spheres of influence: the classical, the ritual, the devotional, the folk-popular, and the modern (as seen in the accompanying chart). The key word here is *interlocking*—none of the spheres is autonomous, and any one performance genre (with the exception of certain aspects of modern theatre) always combines features of at least two or more spheres of influence. A particular genre may thus be *both* devotional *and* folk, or classical and devotional, or ritual and folk-popular and modern. With this degree of complexity, there is clearly room for disagreement over where to locate, as a starting point, certain genres within these five spheres. Throughout this volume the basic principle guiding our classification of genres is the *organizational impetus* that lies behind how and why that genre is performed. By way of introduction to our categories, we will describe the basic features shared by genres within each sphere.

The classical sphere of performance is characterized by a high degree of refinement in performance technique. Genres that are primarily classical in influence are those that follow well-articulated aesthetic principles, most often based on the classical texts of ancient dramaturgy. Classical traditions depend on a high degree of audience knowledge and expertise, so that the elaborations, refinements, and embellishments presented in performance can be appreciated. The classical traditions are thus usually those for which historically there has been continual patronage, allowing the performers the freedom to develop and refine their performance arts. Because classical performances assume a self-consciously articulated aesthetic, shared by performers and patrons alike, the performance system tends to remain relatively closed. Those who control the development of the tradition, and thus the degree of adaptation and change that is permissible, are usually the senior masters of the tradition and the principal patrons.

In contrast to the classical sphere, the folk-popular sphere is characterized by immediate accessibility, by vitality and exuberance, and by readily communicable modes and messages of performance. Folk-popular traditions exhibit three common characteristics: (1) They are regional, belonging to a specific language area, although similar forms may exist in other areas under the same or different names. (2) They are given to profane rather than sacred or devotional ends; while some vestiges of religious practice, such as an opening invocation, may be present, the impact of performance is predominantly secular. (3) The performances appeal to the masses; audience expertise is not required to appreciate the artistry of the performers.[2]

The fact that folk-popular traditions tend toward broad expressive gesture and statement does not mean that the performance techniques are easily acquired. On the contrary, many folk-popular traditions are as complex and difficult to master as classical forms. Because folk-popular performances speak directly to the people, there is less dependence on established aesthetic principles. The performance system is relatively open, with less atten-

---

[2] Along with previous writers on the subject, we have found it difficult to devise a terminology that is adequately descriptive of this category or sphere. Scholars have used a variety of terms, all of which pose some problems. (1) Balwant Gargi (1966) uses the term "folk theatre" to include most of the nonclassical forms covered in this volume. Folk drama should be performed by, for, and through the support of the general populace. While these forms have wide popular appeal, the performers of some are professionals or part-time professionals who receive compensation through contract or sale of tickets. (2) Jagdish Chandra Mathur (1964) implies that these forms are mainly rural. It is probably true that they still have a stronger appeal in the village, but some of these forms are performed in urban settings and attract urban audiences, as well. The largest crowd that one of the authors saw at a *nauṭankī* performance was in a suburb of Delhi. (3) Indian scholars writing in Hindi have commonly used the term "traditional" *(pamparika)* theatre to describe these forms. Since we have used the term in a wider sense, we have avoided it here. (4) James Brandon, writing about roughly parallel forms in Southeast Asia (1967, 81 and 85), uses the category "popular" for forms which are commercial enterprises and performed virtually year-round by specialists for the "semi-literate urban middle class." He sees folk theatre as linked to village life, animistic beliefs and rituals, performed by amateurs who come together periodically, often on special festival occasions, to produce works, free of charge, to the general public. In our view neither single term, folk or popular, accurately describes the genres with which we deal, which are grounded in a specific local context and have such broad, mass appeal, whether in a rural or urban area; therefore, we have linked the two terms together, although we are aware that this is not an altogether satisfactory solution to the problem.

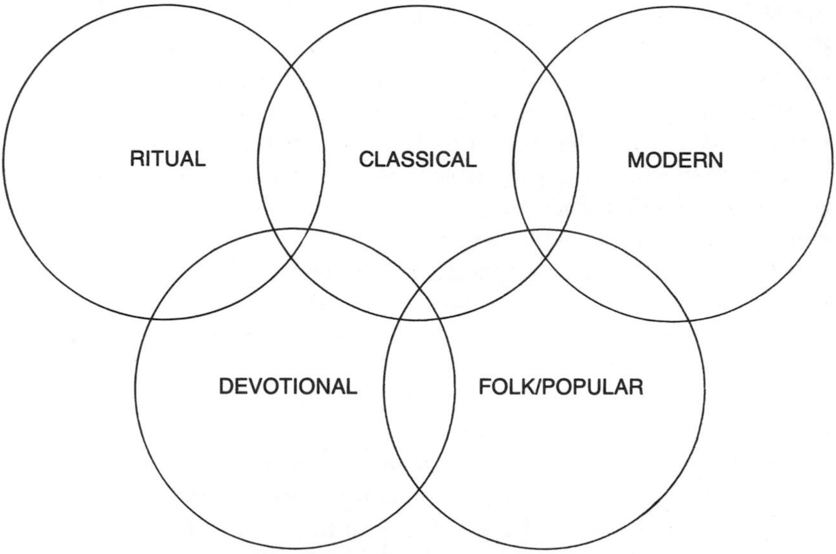

Spheres of performance genre

tion paid to preserving traditional performance techniques. Folk-popular performers may be full-time professionals, but historically they have seldom received patronage from higher castes. Although there are exceptions, most professional folk-popular troupes depend on the vicissitudes of the market —they must keep and hold their audiences to make their living. On the other hand, since many folk-popular performances are seasonal, performers may also be employed in other occupations during the off season.

Ritual performances serve a specific function. The overriding concern is the achievement of a ritual end—the fulfillment of a vow, the granting of a boon, the transformation of an individual, a family, a village, or some other discrete entity from one state of being to another, from illness to health or from a state of unrest and fear to one of repose and confidence. In India rituals may and often do include highly complex and colorful performances that are part of the ritual event. Such performance elements may include the use of makeup or masks, elaborate and colorful costuming, properties used either literally or symbolically to convey appropriate action or to represent a deity, dance or movement patterns set to musical or rhythmic accompaniment, and often the telling of a story associated with the deity. These performance elements serve to highlight and emphasize the achievement of a specific end, often the transformation of the performer into the deity. According to popular belief, this is an actual transformation into the deity, who may then be worshiped by the spectator-participants. Ritual performances, once established, remain relatively closed systems, in which a specific sequence of events must be precisely enacted in order for the efficacy of the ritual to be attained. The guardian of the received tradition is usually a priest or ritual specialist who is responsible for maintaining the purity of the form.

Devotional performances, like those of the ritual sphere, are intended to achieve a desired goal or end. Here, however, the goal is the transportation of the audience into a state of bhakti, or religious devotion. People attend devotional performances hoping to attain at least a glimpse or a vision *(darśana)* of their favorite god. The direct accessibility of devotional performances links them closely with the folk-popular sphere of performance. But it is in the display of the well-known manifestations of the gods, in the revealing of the familiar tableaux, and in the captivating rhythms of the devotional songs that the emotional effect of these performances is to be found.

The final sphere of influence is the modern. Originally imitative of Western models, the environment of modern performances consists of everything from the raised, proscenium stage to the conduct of audiences in the defined space of an enclosed auditorium. The use of modern technology, such as stage lighting, microphones, stage scenery, and machinery for executing scene changes and creating spectacular effects, is one of the obvious characteristics of this environment. Given the structure of the space, the juxtaposition of actor and audience bears its own unique stamp, including the time and duration of performance and the management necessary to control access and use of the space. The acting methods used to accommodate this environment have developed over the last two hundred years, setting it apart from those used by rural performers or those seen at the courts of kings or in religious institutions. Modern performances do not aim at propitiating a deity or transporting the faithful; like the folk-popular traditions, they frankly set out to entertain and frequently also to educate their audiences, as well as to finance the product and, more often than not, to show a profit. Unlike the other influences on Indian theatre, the modern sphere is a product of the urban environment and, consequently, has developed to meet the needs of certain classes of the urban population.

In sum, the major spheres of influence on Indian performance constitute a dynamic field wherein one finds a constant interplay among different traditions of performance. No performance genre is governed exclusively by a single sphere of influence. The classical Sanskrit dramatic tradition, as well as extant regional variations such as the *kūṭiyāṭṭam* of Kerala, is replete with rituals. While *kūṭiyāṭṭam* was nurtured within the temple and was performed as a visual sacrifice to the presiding deity of the temple, nevertheless it existed historically and is performed today primarily as a form of classical theatre for an elite and educated audience. Accordingly when performed outside the temple complex, it has made certain concessions to modern tastes and has even incorporated the use of modern technology to achieve its ends. Recently some contemporary theatre directors have used *kūṭiyāṭṭam* techniques on the contemporary stage. In all traditions of Indian performance, then, multiple functions can and often do coexist without contradiction: entertainment, ritual propitiation, deep devotion, and so on.

While classical performances can include rituals that are part of the total structure of the performance event, the performance exists as its own end, uniting the performers and the audience in a heightened state of aesthetic sensibility. Folk-popular and modern performances are also aimed at the entertainment of their audiences. Ritual and devotional performances, on the other hand, are means to an end not contained within the means, techniques, and interactions of the performance. Ritual performances can be absorbing, fascinating, even entertaining at times, but these modes of audience involvement are momentary steps along the way to the larger goal of the performance.

Chronology

Although we have not set out to write a history, it may be useful to those unfamiliar with the history of theatre to review the timeline of Indian theatre in comparison with that of Western theatre and other forms of Asian theatre.

As seen in the accompanying chart, the earliest form of classical theatre in India was the Sanskrit drama, which came into being well after the development of the classical Greek and Roman theatres and well before the rise of major forms of theatre in other parts of Asia, such as the Yuan *zaju* of China, the No of Japan, and the *wayang kulit* of Java. On the eve of the reemergence of drama in medieval Europe, the Sanskrit drama experienced a sharp decline in activity and importance, and, although plays are still occasionally being written in Sanskrit even today, the classical age has long since ended.

In the sixteenth century, when the kabuki and bunraku of Japan came into being, the drama of Ming China was well under way and the Elizabethan theatre began its ascent to prominence. At about the same time, numerous forms of theatre developed in rural areas of India, some of which are discussed in the introductions to the various parts of this book.

Subsequently as Western theatre began to change its tone and style, the Chinese theatre witnessed the development of *jingxi,* or Beijing Opera (also known in the West as Peking Opera). In India the rural theatre forms continued to develop and grow, and like the kabuki and bunraku today, they still delight appreciative audiences. In recent years some of them have been seen and enjoyed by audiences in the United States, Europe, and other parts of Asia, although the performances have often been modified to suit foreign tastes.

The nineteenth century saw the flowering of modern traditions of theatre throughout the world. And so the development of an urban theatre in India quickly became synchronous with that of its counterparts in other parts of Asia and the West.

For the most part much of the history of Indian theatre is conjectural. It is literally impossible to assign precise dates to most theatre events. However, the overall pattern of development is clear, even if it is not as complete as one might wish.

Structure of the Book

The present work is divided into six parts. Although it does not provide a chronological study of Indian theatre, a glance at the table of contents might suggest that the opposite is the case. Part One focuses on the origins and development of theatre on the subcontinent, and Part Six takes the reader into the modern period, virtually up to the present day. Between the ancient and the modern, however, the intervening four parts are not presented in chronological sequence.

These four parts focus on performances that originated in the villages of India and that still appeal primarily to villagers. In Part Two we investigate the ritual traditions, which have their roots in the religious rituals that have been characteristic of much of the Hindu world from a very early date. Part Three examines the devotional traditions and their origins in classical performances and in ritual. Part Four discusses the folk-popular traditions that accommodate secular concerns and joyously proclaim entertainment as one of their central goals. Part Five deals with the dance-dramas and dramatic dances for which India has become world famous; here while classical materials are linked to ritual and religious origins, the roots of the performances are still firmly lodged in the folk-popular traditions.

In contrast to the rural character of these types of performance, Part One and Part Six reflect the sophisticated taste of urban audiences. Part One represents the court traditions of ancient India and the highly refined culture from which they sprang. Part Six deals with the theatre of modern urbanites who are often more familiar with the symbols of the modern Western world than they are with their own ritual origins. It is this world view that is now being transported back to the villages of India, as we shall see toward the end of this book.

The structure of the individual chapters deserves a word of explanation. Except for the chapter on the origins and characteristics of Sanskrit drama, all the chapters end with a description of an actual performance. These descriptions are intended to provide the reader with a visceral experience of the tradition under discussion. When it seems appropriate, a brief historical survey has been provided at the beginning of the chapter. And when a particular tradition deserves special attention because it possesses some unique

Chronological Chart of Performance Genre

BC AD

600 500 200 100 0 100 200 900 1000 1500 1600 1700 1800 1900 Present

. . . . Development of Sanskrit theatre

Nāṭyaśāstra composed

Earliest surviving Sanskrit plays

Decline of Sanskrit theatre

. . . . *kūṭiyāṭṭam* . . . .

aṇkīya nāṭ . . . .

rās līlā . . . .

nauṭankī . . . .

cavittu nāṭakam . . . .

jātra . . . .

yakṣagana . . . .
bhavāi . . . .
bhamakalapam . . . .
bhāgavata mela . . . .
kuchipudi . . . .
veethi nāṭaka . . . .
tamāshā . . . .
kathakaḷi . . . .
Rām līlā . . . .
seraikella chau . . . .
svāng-khyal . . . .
mayurbhanj chau . . . .
purulia chau . . . .
modern theatre . . . .

Greek theatre. . . . . .
Roman theatre. . . .
Medieval theatre / Elizabethan / Restoration / Modern. . . . .
Yuan *zaju* / Ming *chuanqi* and *kunqu* / Qing *jingxi* (China) / Modern . . . .
No (Japan) . . . .
wayang kulit (Java) . . . .
kabuki / *bunraku* (Japan). . . . .

feature or other, we have stressed that fact. For the most part, we have not presented a detailed or complete study of the individual traditions. Even so the book contains an enormous amount of detail, much of which is new, even to individuals familiar with this field.

ADDITIONAL READING

Indian Culture and Religion

Basham, A. L. 1954.
The Wonder That Was India. London: Sidgwick and Jackson.

deBary, Theodore. 1960.
Sources of Indian Tradition. New York: Columbia University Press.

Kinsley, David R. 1982.
Hinduism. Englewood Cliffs, New Jersey: Prentice-Hall.

Moore, Charles A. Ed. 1967.
The Indian Mind: Essentials of Indian Philosophy and Culture. Honolulu: The University Press of Hawaii.

Singer, Milton. 1972.
When A Great Tradition Modernizes. New York: Praeger.

General Works

Banham, Martin. Ed. 1989.
The Cambridge Guide to World Theatre. New York: Cambridge University Press.

Benegal, Sam. 1968.
A Panorama View of Theatre in India. Bombay: Popular Prakashan.

Brandon, James R. 1967.
Theatre in Southeast Asia. Cambridge, Massachusetts: Harvard University Press.

Gargi, Balwant. 1962.
Theatre in India. New York: Theatre Arts.

Mathur, J. C. 1964
Drama in Rural India. New York: Asia Publishing House.

Rangacharya, Adya. 1971.
The Indian Theatre. New Delhi: National Book Trust.

Richmond, Farley. 1986.
"India." In *Theatre Companies of the World.* Eds. Colby H. Kullman and William C. Young. New York: Greenwood Press.

Scott, A. C. 1972.
The Theatre in Asia. New York: Macmillan.

Vatsyayan, Kapila. 1980.
Traditional Indian Theatre: Multiple Streams. New Delhi: National Book Trust.

Bibliographies and Dictionaries

Awasthi, Suresh. 1956.
"Theatre Collections and Museums in India." *Theatre Research* 7, 1–2:73–76.

Brandon, James R. Ed. 1980.
Asian Theatre: A Study Guide and Annotated Bibliography. Theatre Perspectives, no. 1. Washington, D.C.: University and College Theatre Association.

Patterson, Maureen L. P., and William J. Alspaugh. Eds. 1981.
Asian Civilizations: A Bibliographic Synthesis. Chicago: University of Chicago Press.

Renou, Louis. 1966.
"Research on the Indian Theatre since 1890." *Samskrita Ranga Annual* 4:67–91.

Richmond, Farley. 1975.
"Indian Theatre Materials." *Journal of South Asian Literature* 10, 2:327–376.

Trapido, Joel, with Edward Langhans and James R. Brandon. Eds. 1985.
An International Dictionary of Theatre Language. Westport, Connecticut: Greenwood Press.

van Zile, Judy. 1973.
Dance in India: An Annotated Guide to Source Materials. Providence, Rhode Island: Asian Music Publications.

Zarrilli, Phillip, and Rhea Lehman. 1986.
"Asian Performance: General Introduction" and "South Asian Performance." In *Theatrical Movement: A Bibliographical Anthology.* Ed. Bob Fleshman. Metuchen, New Jersey: Scarecrow Press. Pp. 223–244, 245–348.

PART ONE

THE CLASSICAL TRADITION AND ITS PREDECESSORS

INTRODUCTION

THE LATE PRIME MINISTER JAWAHARLAL NEHRU, struggling to unravel India's mystery, described her as an

> ancient palimpsest on which layer upon layer of thought and reverie had been inscribed, and yet no succeeding layer had completely hidden or erased what had been written previously. . . . Though outwardly there was diversity and infinite variety among our people, everywhere there was that tremendous impress of oneness, which had held all of us together for ages past, whatever political fate or misfortune had befallen us. . . . That essential unity had been so powerful that no political division, no disaster or catastrophe had been able to overcome it. (1960, 27)

Nehru's description might just as well have been applied to the Indian theatre. Viewed in perspective, the Indian theatre, for all its contrasting color and variety, has an underlying and fundamental cohesion. Among the deeper and more important layers of influence is that of the classical period —the Sanskrit drama.

As with other ancient cultures, such as those of Greece and Rome, the plays of the classical period came to be referred to by the language in which they were composed—Sanskrit. The roots of the Sanskrit language are too complicated to explain here. Simply stated, Sanskrit is a member of the Indo-Aryan subgroup of languages belonging to the larger Indo-European language family to which Latin, Greek, German, and French belong. Scholars believe that much of the fundamental character of Sanskrit is derived from the Middle East and colored by changes which occurred over time, as successive invasions of Aryans came into the Indian subcontinent during the second millennium and mixed with the original inhabitants, forming what is now a vast majority of India's population.

It should be remembered that even the classical "Sanskrit" plays were not composed exclusively in Sanskrit. Many use other ancient Indic languages or dialects, known as Prakrits. Today relatively few people speak Sanskrit as their native tongue and the other ancient languages or dialects eventually became the various regional languages of North India. In 1961 only about twenty-five hundred people said that Sanskrit was their native tongue.

Obviously this means that plays in Sanskrit cannot be very popular among the vast majority of the hundreds of millions of people who now live in India. Rather India, with some fifteen different regional languages with literally millions of speakers each, and with over two hundred dialects, is bound to have many different theatre forms, any one of which may claim to be more popular today than the Sanskrit theatre. However, the contribution of Sanskrit drama and theatre to India's cultural heritage has been enormous, particularly since it is one of the earliest, if not the first, significant signs of theatre in Asia.

In Part One of this work I will touch on the origins of theatre in India, if only to indicate how frustrating the search for clear-cut roots may be. My goal is to outline the major characteristics of the Sanskrit theatre, and then to examine in some detail samples of its dramatic literature. Finally Part One concludes with an examination of *kūṭiyāṭṭam* from Kerala, the closest living relative of the ancient Sanskrit theatrical tradition. In form and style of execution it preserves many conventions that are directly related to those of the classical period.

It may first be useful, however, to remember that other forms of traditional theatre also make use of the Sanskrit language and preserve remnants of the Sanskrit theatrical tradition. Among them is the *aṇkīya nāṭ* of Assam, perhaps the next closest relative to the Sanskrit tradition after *kūṭiyāṭṭam*. The form was created by Śankaradeva (1449–1568), an ardent devotee of Lord Kṛṣṇa, who lived in northeastern India along the lush banks of the Brahmaputra River. As an expression of his religious zeal, Śankaradeva instituted the requirement that leaders of religious monasteries compose at least one short play in praise of Lord Kṛṣṇa before their death. The practice helped to promote the spread and maintenance of the Vaiṣṇava faith among the local inhabitants, as well as serve as a means of popularizing *aṇkīya nāṭ* among the Assamese people. *Aṇkīya nāṭ* derives its name from a form of one-act play *(aṅka)* mentioned in the ancient texts of Sanskrit dramaturgy. Sanskrit is used in the invocation at the beginning of the plays and for the composition of the verses strewn throughout the works and, to some extent, as part of the stage directions. Assamese is used for the dialogues among the characters and in the bulk of the stage directions.

Similar to *aṇkīya nāṭ*, the *kuchipudi* of Andhra Pradesh in South Central India focuses on the exploits of Kṛṣṇa's life, and is sustained today as a form of dramatic worship among a small band of devotees in the village of Kuchipudi and neighboring communities. Historical evidence suggests that the form was created in the seventeenth century and popularized by Siddhendra Yogi, an ardent devotee of Lord Kṛṣṇa. Although *kuchipudi* does not enjoy the same popularity in Andhra Pradesh as *aṇkīya nāṭ* does in Assam, it has taken on significance in recent years as a classical dance form. Dance elements, which are so much a part of the drama, have been extracted and performed nationally and internationally. Thus *kuchipudi* is popularly thought of today as a form of classical Indian dance, although its roots are clearly embedded in the dramatic traditions of the region from which it came. Today it is possible for a student to study *kuchipudi* from teachers in many of the large urban centers of India, as well as in the United States and Western Europe. Like *aṇkīya nāṭ,* exponents of *kuchipudi* trace many of the conventions used in the form directly to the Sanskrit drama, and think of the form as a direct descendant. Sanskrit verses are sung in the elaborate pre-

The village barber is the traditional bearer of the torch that lights a *bhavāi* performance in rural Gujarat. (Farley P. Richmond photo)

liminaries to the *kuchipudi* dramas, while Telugu is the language of the verses, dialogues, and stage directions of the main body of the plays. Numerous other forms of traditional theatre have preserved conventions that directly reflect various aspects of the ancient Sanskrit drama: among them the *yakṣagāna* of Mysore, the *jātra* of Bengal, the *bhavāi* of Gujarat, and the *kathakaḷi* of Kerala.

Resonances of the classical Sanskrit theatre are also to be noted today in the various schools and colleges of India, where Sanskrit is studied as a classical language. Production of plays in Sanskrit are occasionally presented so that student actors may better learn to speak the language, as well as to study the unique features of this form of theatre. Also translations and adaptations of Sanskrit plays have been made in various regional languages, offering the general public a means of contact with the ancient past. Many times these productions have served as an excuse for experimenting with unique performance techniques not generally practiced among the contemporary theatre companies in various regions of the country. Sanskrit plays have also inspired contemporary dance-dramas and dramatic dances, although their content has been liberally adapted to suit the particular needs of the dance companies. Even abroad, especially during the nineteenth century in Germany and France and today in various centers of the United States, Russia, Europe, and Asia, Sanskrit plays have been presented, reaching new and nontraditional audiences.

In short the Sanskrit theatre, although ancient in origin, still survives today, if only in a limited and altered way, throughout India and in widely differing parts of the world.

Farley P. Richmond

WORK CITED

Nehru, Jawaharlal. 1960.
The Discovery of India. Ed. Robert I. Crane. Garden City, New York: Anchor.

Chapter One

ORIGINS OF SANSKRIT THEATRE

Farley P. Richmond

Mythological Origins

THE TRADITIONAL LEGEND relating to the origin of drama and theatre serves as a reminder that the ancient Indians were fond of attributing the creation of all important institutions to divine ingenuity. The tale is found in Chapter I of the *Nāṭyaśāstra,* attributed to Bharata (Ghosh 1961 and 1967), and runs as follows:

One day wise sages approached Bharata, an elderly priest, during an interval in his studies and asked him to relate the story of the origin of drama. Bharata commanded them to get themselves "cleansed, be attentive, and hear" (Ghosh 1967, 2). At a time when people were addicted to sensual pleasures, desire and greed, and jealousy and anger, the god Indra along with some of the other gods approached Brahmā, the creator, and requested that he create an object of diversion which would be audible as well as visible. Indra asked that all members of the social order be permitted to hear it: the Brahmans *(brāhmaṇa),* members of the priest caste; the Kshatriyas *(kṣatriya),* members of the warrior caste; the Vaisyas *(vaiśya),* members of the trades caste; and the Sudras *(śūdra),* members of the peasant caste. Brahmā fell into deep meditation and thought on the four books of hymns sacred to the Hindus. He concluded that he should make a fifth Veda and call it drama *(nāṭya).* To do this he took recitation from the *Ṛg Veda,* the oldest book of hymns, song from the *Sāma Veda,* acting from the *Yajuṛ Veda,* and aesthetics from the *Atharva Veda.*

Then Brahmā asked Indra to compose plays based on semihistorical tales and have them acted by the gods. Indra modestly refused on the grounds that it was not proper for the gods to act in plays. Instead he proposed that Brahmā request the priests "who know the mystery of the Vedas and have fulfilled their vows, to maintain and practice the new creation" (Ghosh 1967, 5). Whereupon Brahmā summoned Bharata and asked him and his hundred sons to learn the dramatic art from him. Bharata agreed. The sons were assigned different roles and Bharata set about preparing the first performance. To lend grace to the occasion Brahmā created nymphs to assist in the acting and dancing. Musicians were employed to play and to sing. For the first performance Brahmā chose the occasion of the celebration of Indra's banner pole, which concerned the victory of the gods over the demons. Brahmā and the other deities were so pleased that they gave gifts to the actors as a token of appreciation for undertaking the performance.

But when the show got underway, the demons took offense and caused the actors to forget their lines and physical movements. When Brahmā ascertained that malevolent spirits were responsible for the disturbance, Indra took his banner pole and smashed them to pieces. The gods rejoiced and suggested that henceforth the banner pole should be used as a symbol of the divine protection afforded actors. The performance proceeded but once more the demons attempted to interrupt the show. Bharata requested Brahmā to take some action which would assure the successful completion of the performance.

Brahmā requested Viśvakarmā, the heavenly architect, to construct a theatre structure which would be secure from further disruptions and which would ward off evil spirits. When the building was completed, Brahmā assigned various gods the task of protecting different parts of the structure. Brahmā himself undertook to sanctify and preside over the center of the stage.

In a mood of reconciliation, the gods asked Brahmā to pacify the malevolent spirits. The demons came forward to express their grievances. They contended that the play depicted them in an unfavorable light and showed favoritism toward the gods. In replying to their complaints Brahmā articulated the objective of drama and theatre. He said, "The drama will thus be instructive to all, through actions and states depicted in it, and through sentiments, arising out of it" (Ghosh 1967, 15). Drama is not meant to represent one individual or class of individuals exclusively. "It will [also] give relief to unlucky persons who are afflicted with sorrow and grief or [over]-work, and will be conducive to observance of duty as well as fame, long life, intellect and general good, and will educate people. There is no wise maxim, no learning, no art or craft, no device, no action that is not found in drama" (Ghosh 1967, 15).

In conclusion Brahmā charged the gods to perform a sacred ceremony *(yajña)* in the playhouse and the actors likewise to offer a sacrifice *(pūjā)* to the presiding deity of the stage "which is similar to the (Vedic) sacrifice." Brahmā warned that those who did not offer the sacrifice would be "born as an animal of lower order," and of those who observed the rules and practices of sacrifice, he predicted that they "will attain auspicious wealth and will [in the end] go to heaven" (Ghosh 1967, 17).

This simple tale gives us a wealth of useful information concerning the way the theatre event is regarded in the *Nāṭyaśāstra.* It is obvious that theatre is special, set apart from daily life. It is composed out of material which is considered sacred (namely, the Vedas). It is to be performed by specialists, whose hereditary line may be traced to Bharata himself, a member of the highest social order, the priestly caste. Theatre requires special knowledge above and beyond that required for the performance of other ritual events, including sacrifices. Brahmā makes it plain that the actors were to undergo extensive training before presuming to perform. This training originally came from the creator himself and was passed on to man through Bharata and his hundred sons. It required the development of special skills in dance, music, recitation, and rituals. The theatre fulfilled numerous purposes, not the least of which was to educate and entertain. Like other important ritual events, it was to be performed according to a prescribed order and served as a sacrifice in honor of the gods.

Historical Evidence

The traditional legend offers useful insights into the origins of theatre; history is not quite so generous. From the scant evidence that remains, it is impossible to fix an exact date for the creation of theatre in India. Yet there is good reason to believe it came into being sometime between 200 and 100 B.C. By this period all the elements were present which could have given rise to it. There was a lively tradition of dance, music, and song, all of which were already old and respected branches of the performing arts. Plus there was a rich heritage of myths and legends, historical and semihistorical tales. Also communities of specialists in storytelling and the performing arts may be traced to this and earlier periods. To whom the idea may be attributed and what inspired it are lost to us. We know that the oldest fragments of Sanskrit plays which date from the first century A.D. reveal a dramatic structure already highly developed. The patterns that are evident in these ancient works were to be refined and repeated for nearly twelve hundred years. In the following pages I will explore some of the evidence that leads to the conclusion that Indian theatre originated during the second century B.C.

Early Visual Clues

Indian culture is very old. The Indus Valley Civilization developed a city culture along the Indus river basin in northwestern India about 2300–1750 B.C. Although excavations undertaken at the ancient cities of Mohenjodaro and Harappa reveal a wealth of detail about the early inhabitants, there is nothing to suggest that they knew theatre. However, there are hints of the existence of dance. Small copper and stone figurines of what are obviously nude females have been catalogued in the archaeological record as dancers. If it is true that the figurines depict dancers, music and song may also have been part of the rituals and festivals of the peoples of this civilization.

Sacred Literature

About 1500 B.C. the Indus Valley Civilization came to an abrupt and unexplained halt. Shortly thereafter the country was visited by successive waves of people from the west, people riding on horseback. Their culture initially may have been inferior to that which existed along the Indus river, but it was destined to become the dominant civilization of the region. The new peoples were later called Aryans and a record of their religion and philosophy of life is found in collections of sacred hymns dedicated to supernatural forces. The earliest hymns are found in a collection known as the *Ṛg Veda.* Although an accurate date for the composition of the *Ṛg Veda* is still to be established, scholars generally agree it was composed between 1500 and 1000 B.C. The hymns yield an interesting and perhaps misleading set of clues regarding the formation of theatre. Among the hymns are a few which are short dialogues between two and sometimes three individuals. The following are the concluding verses of one such hymn. The encounter concerns Yami who attempts, without success, to seduce her twin brother Yama.

Yama: Sure there will come succeeding times
When brothers and sisters will do acts unmeet for kinsfolk.
Not me, O fair one,—Seek another husband, and make thine
arm a pillow for thy consort.

Yami: Is he a brother when no lord is left her?
Is she a sister when destruction cometh?
Forced by my love these many words I utter.
Come near, and hold me in thy close embraces.

Yama: I will not fold mine arms about thy body:
They call it sin when one comes near his sister.
Not me,—prepare thy pleasures with another.
Thy brother seeks not this from thee, O fair one.

Yami: Alas! thou are indeed a weakling, Yama;
We find in thee no trace of heart or spirit.
As round the tree the woodbine clings,
Another will cling about thee girt as with a girdle.

Yama: Embrace another, Yami;
Let another, even as the woodbine rings the tree, enfold thee.
Win thou his heart and let him win thy fancy,
And he shall form with thee a blest alliance.

(Griffith 1963, 391–394)

Interesting though it is to speculate that a short exchange such as this might have given rise to the development of full-scale drama, several factors argue against it having done so. A. B. Keith has pointed out that dialogues are unique to the *Ṛg Veda* and died out in the later Vedic literature (1924, 15). Thus it was apparently not popular at this period in time. Also we are unclear as to how the hymns were recited or sung. Possibly two priests impersonated the different roles but this, too, is sheer speculation.

Dramatic Rituals

During the Vedic age (c. 2000–1500 B.C.) ritual practices arose which are highly dramatic in character. In general Vedic rituals include special hymns which are sung or recited in praise of various elemental powers and deities. The ceremonies are complex and include elaborate rites which incorporate symbolic gestures and physical actions often accompanied by percussion and music. In order to carry out the ceremonies, the priest-performers separate themselves from the profane world by rituals, and in so doing, they often take on the role of a personality other than their own. For example, in the death ceremonies conducted in Kerala today by certain sects of Tamil Brahmans, a priest takes the role of a departed family member and converses with the living relatives who have commissioned the rite.

Conflict is the center of some of the rites. The Mahāvrata rite celebrates the strengthening of the sun at the winter's solstice, a contest between Vaiśya (white) and Śūdra (black). Besides bearing the obvious interpretation of the victory of light over darkness, the rite also symbolizes the supremacy of the lighter skinned Aryan race over the darker skinned people whom they encountered during their incursions into northwestern India. Included in the ritual is a comic passage of verbal abuse between a Brahman student and a courtesan, the aim of which may have been to assure fertility. Vedic rituals could have served as the foundation for the emergence of drama and theatre in India in much the same way that the Catholic mass is said to have paved the way for the reemergence of drama in medieval Europe. But it is not possible to ascribe a date to this transformation or to point to a specific event which may have caused it to occur.

Epic Sources

The search for the existence of drama and theatre at some specific date in ancient history inevitably leads to the vast body of literature generated after the composition of the *Ṛg Veda,* in particular to the two great epics composed between about 1000 and 100 B.C. The *Mahābhārata,* the most voluminous of India's epics, often referred to as an encyclopedia of Indian thought, makes reference to performers *(naṭa),* among whom actors may well have been classed. In later history, the word *naṭa* was used to describe dancers and pantomimists, as well as actors. Unfortunately the epic does not describe the precise work of these ancient performers. The *Rāmāyaṇa,*

India's other major epic, also makes reference to *naṭa,* and in addition, it speaks of *nartaka* who speak *nāṭakā.* The latter term is used later to refer to a specific type of drama. Yet there is nothing in the *Rāmāyaṇa* which proves the existence of Sanskrit theatre at this point in time.

Other Texts

In the oldest surviving text of Sanskrit grammar, composed by Pāṇini in approximately the sixth century B.C., reference is made to the *Naṭasūtra,* a textbook for *naṭa,* ascribed to Śilālin and Kṛṣāśva. Unfortunately the *Naṭasūtra* has not survived and Pāṇini does not describe its contents or give us any details about the authors of the work.

Greek Influence

Owing to the diligence of Greek historians, we know that in the early fourth century B.C. Alexander the Great marched into northwestern India, where he encountered and often did battle with numerous Indian kings and princes. It has been argued that troupes of actors normally traveled along to entertain him. Some scholars have argued that Indian monarchs may have seen Greek plays, been impressed, and commissioned their own bards to compose comparable works in Sanskrit. Scraps of evidence have been amassed in support of this so-called Greek influence. To support this argument the following suppositions have been made: The Sanskrit word for curtain *(yavanikā)* seems to have been derived from the word for foreigner *(yavana),* a term the ancient Indians reputedly used to describe Ionian Greeks as well as numerous other foreigners. Keith quotes Windisch, the German Sanskrit scholar, who contends that a curtain took the place of the painted scenery at the back of the Greek stage. He also argues that Greek New Comedy, which flourished about the same time as Alexander's exploits, influenced the plot construction, development of character types, and themes of Indian plays (1924, 57–68).

In particular, *The Little Clay Cart (Mṛcchakaṭikā),* one of the most famous Sanskrit plays, bears a striking resemblance to the Greek New Comedy. But no one has yet been able to prove that actors accompanied Alexander on his Indian campaign. We have no conclusive proof concerning the origin of the word *yavanikā,* nor can we say that *The Little Clay Cart* was derived from one or several Greek New Comedies or even when it was written!

Political Unity Minus Theatre

Drama and theatre are not mentioned during the first great Indian empire, that of King Aśoka (272–232 B.C.). In his public declarations Aśoka condemns the holding of public meetings, which are known from later evidence to have had performers *(naṭa)* as participants. Following this period in India's development, there was a sharp decline in empire and a diffusion of political unity throughout the country. It is during this period that definite signs of the existence of theatre emerge.

Concrete Evidence

To illustrate a grammatical point, Patañjali in his *Mahābhāṣya,* composed approximately 140 B.C., lists various methods by which events such as Kṛṣṇa's slaying of the wicked King Kaṁsa and the binding of Bāli may be described. Patañjali asserts that these dramatic actions could be depicted in one of several ways: (1) by pantomimic action, (2) through pictures which illustrate the story, or (3) through words alone. Although there is nothing in Patañjali's remarks to prove the existence of drama, all the elements are present for its formation: (1) acting in pantomime, if not with words, (2) recitation, (3) *naṭa* who could sing as well as recite, and (4) female dancers. Based on this evidence, Keith has made the point that like the Greek drama, which is said to have had its roots in competition between the forces of good and those of evil, the Indian drama may have arisen from the ritual competition between Kṛṣṇa, the personification of good, and Kaṁsa, the personification of evil. He links this with ancient vegetation rituals in which the outworn spirit (symbolized by Kaṁsa) is destroyed by the new spirit (Kṛṣṇa) (1924, 36–46).

Miscellaneous Views

Diverse other arguments have been advanced concerning the origin of Sanskrit drama and theatre. Sir William Ridgeway theorizes that drama is the outcome of plays in which reverence is paid to the spirits of the dead, and that they were first composed to honor the spirits of the dead heroes who were personified by actors. Other scholars have contended that there were shadow plays and puppet shows in ancient India, and that they dictated the formation of drama. Some suggest that ancient pantomime coupled with epic recitation had a great deal to do with the way the theatre was formed. One proposal claims that the recitation of epic stanzas and the competitions that were held among skilled reciters led to the development of drama. The argument has also been advanced that theatre was first conceived in humble origins, and that plays were first composed in regional languages. When the Aryans came and superimposed their own language—Sanskrit—on the local inhabitants they adopted the regional-language plays and techniques and retained the regional languages (Prakrits) as secondary languages in the drama. Although interesting, the evidence supporting these conjectures is so slight that it is not possible to give them serious consideration here. Suffice it to say that the earliest plays which have been discovered (from about the first century A.D.) indicate that Sanskrit theatre was already fully formed and highly sophisticated. What intervening changes occurred between the first century B.C. and the first century A.D. which resulted in that sophistication are still a mystery.

WORKS CITED

Ghosh, Manmohan. Trans. and ed. 1967.
Nāṭyaśāstra. Ascribed to Bharatamuni. 2nd rev. ed. Vol. 1. Calcutta: Manisha Granthalaya.

———. 1961.
Nāṭyaśāstra. Ascribed to Bharatamuni. Vol. 2. Calcutta: Asiatic Society.

Griffith, Ralph T. H. Trans. 1963
Hymns of the Ṛg Veda. 4th ed. Vol. 2. Varanasi: Chowkhamba Sanskrit Series.

Keith, A. Berriedale. 1924.
The Sanskrit Drama. London: Oxford University Press.

ADDITIONAL READING

Byrski, M. Christopher. 1974.
Concept of Ancient Indian Theatre. Delhi: Munshiram Manoharlal.

Konow, Sten. 1969.
The Indian Drama. Calcutta: General Printers and Publishers.

Shekhar, I. 1977.
Sanskrit Drama: Its Origin and Decline. Delhi: Munshiram Manoharlal.

Chapter Two

CHARACTERISTICS OF SANSKRIT THEATRE AND DRAMA

Farley P. Richmond

WHAT WE KNOW OF THE DRAMATIC COMPOSITION and staging techniques of ancient India is derived primarily from two sources—the extant plays with their stage directions and the numerous dramaturgical texts and books of theory and criticism. Unlike the Greek theatre, whose history relies at least in part on the ruins of theatre monuments, the Indian theatre does not have any surviving theatre buildings which might shed light on its origins and development. Also we are not privy to extensive production records which could help us to understand the performance events of ancient times. Yet a sufficiently large body of information remains from which some basic conclusions may be drawn.

From the plays we learn that Sanskrit theatre was sophisticated, if at times somewhat uneven in quality. Some of the finest poetry of the ancient world may be found in Sanskrit drama, and several of the extant plays compare favorably with dramatic literature elsewhere in the ancient world. A survey of the plays and dramaturgical texts leads us to believe that the theatre was conventional. That is, it called upon on actors and spectators alike to understand and decipher a complex code of gestures, movement patterns, and vocal expressions. Sanskrit theatre also was multidimensional. Dance and music contributed to the overall effect, although the extent of their interaction with dialogue and verse is far from certain. This was a theatre of imagination; costume and makeup were stylized and symbolic, not replicas of those of everyday life or of a particular historical period, and scenery was used sparingly, if ever, in the staging of plays. Special buildings appear to have been constructed for performances. Theatre had a sacred significance. Numerous rituals accompanied the construction of playhouses; the stage was consecrated before performance; and, from all the evidence, theatre served a religious function, as well as being entertaining and educational.

At no other time in India's long history has one genre of theatre been so universally understood and imitated throughout the subcontinent. This was primarily due to the predominance of the Sanskrit language, which was used at court and in religious rituals. As I noted in the introduction to Part One, Sanskrit was not the only language of the plays. Various forms of Prakrits (local languages and dialects) are also found in the surviving works. But Sanskrit was the language of the major male characters; and although the theatre of this period thus had a multilingual character, it is regarded as Sanskrit, rather than Prakrit, theatre. Sanskrit theatre was the national theatre of its day, reflecting the dominance throughout India of the civilization represented in the plays. As a court- and temple-supported art, theatre was exclusive rather than popular in its appeal.

Although Asia boasts many other ancient civilizations, India seems to have been the first country of the region to support an active, sophisticated theatre. And yet theatre in India came into being at a relatively late date, compared to the development of theatre in Greece. However, once theatre finally took shape in India about the second century B.C., it continued virtually uninterrupted for at least twelve hundred years, and when it came to an end it did not disappear overnight. Beginning around the tenth century A.D. no more significant dramatic poets appeared on the scene, but from time to time thereafter, authors tried their hand at writing Sanskrit plays in the style of the acknowledged classics. Even today one may still find dramatic works composed in Sanskrit, but they are either derivative or are modeled on the conventions of Western playwriting.

In the following pages I will explore the characteristics of theatre and drama in ancient India, including the *Nāṭyaśāstra,* the principal text of ancient dramaturgy; the theatre organization; acting; music and dance; the spectators and occasion of performance; the physical theatre, stage, and function; playwrights and their works; and the aesthetics of dramatic composition before concluding the chapter with a brief examination of some of the possible reasons for the decline of the ancient theatre.

Nāṭyaśāstra

The most important text of dramaturgy that ancient India produced is the *Nāṭyaśāstra.* The title literally means "drama science" but a cursory review of the text is all one needs to indicate that this is more than a science of drama; it is a veritable encyclopedia of knowledge concerning Sanskrit drama and theatre, the most comprehensive work of its kind to survive anywhere from ancient times. Without the benefit of the information it contains, we would know relatively little about a number of important issues concerning the Sanskrit theatre. And yet the work is an enigma, prompting a host of questions which have not been and perhaps may never be answered.

Scholars differ on the date of the composition of the *Nāṭyaśāstra.* Based on internal evidence, it is generally believed that it was composed during the period between 200 B.C. and 200 A.D. Although as described in chapter 1 the authorship is traditionally attributed to the sage Bharata, an unevenness of writing styles has led some critics to conclude that it is the work of several hands.

At a glance the *Nāṭyaśāstra* is obviously broader in scope than the other great text of ancient dramaturgy, Aristotle's *Poetics.* The work consists of numerous chapters, beginning with the origins of theatre. Within its scope are a multitude of topics, such as theatre architecture, acting, costuming, makeup, properties, dance, music, play construction, poetic composition, grammar, composition of theatre companies, audiences, dramatic competitions, the actor community, and ritual observances, to name the more important.

The text has exerted a profound influence over the formation and structure of successive theatre genres throughout India. Our understanding of the musical system of ancient India is based almost entirely on the *Nāṭyaśāstra.* Most forms of Indian dance are said to derive their language of gestures, steps, poses, and movement patterns from the *Nāṭyaśāstra.* By comparing the rules of play construction outlined therein with the works of several generations of playwrights, scholars have built a considerable body of dramatic criticism. In attempting to interpret the various aspects of the *Nāṭyaśāstra,* a whole body of theoretical texts has come down to us from ancient times. And debate over the meaning of certain important words and phrases still occupies the attention of scholars throughout the world.

Despite the fact that the *Nāṭyaśāstra* has been the center of scholarly debate and the source of practical information for centuries, the extant manuscripts that are known to exist in private collections and libraries throughout the world have never been compiled into a definitive edition. In preparing the following pages I have consulted Ghosh's 1967 English edition and translation of chapters 1 through 27 (Volume I) and his 1961 publication of chapters 28 through 36 (Volume II). Throughout this work I will make repeated reference to the *Nāṭyaśāstra,* since it sheds light—sometimes the only light—on so many aspects of Indian theatre history.

Theatre Organization

Relatively little is known about theatre companies in ancient India, although there are tantalizing scraps of evidence in the *Nāṭyaśāstra* and various other dramaturgical sources, historical reference works, and plays to suggest a possible hierarchy, composition, and manner in which groups practiced their occupation. As suggested in chapter 1, the first company seems to have been a family affair. The leadership was in the hands of a family elder (Bharata) who received his knowledge and training directly from Brahmā, the creator god, and who in turn passed on his wisdom to his sons (one hundred in all!), the first company of actors. As his contribution to posterity, Bharata gave the world the *Nāṭyaśāstra,* which is reputed to be a record of his teachings as he learned them from Brahmā. Whether theatre continued to be a family affair throughout its long history is unclear. It does appear certain that companies had a group leader, actors of various ranks of importance who received systematic training, numerous assistants and minor functionaries, and perhaps separate categories of musicians and dancers and even playwrights.

After briefly reviewing the activities, means of support, and social status of the group leaders, actors, minor functionaries, and musicians and dancers I shall address the characteristics of ancient acting and what little is known of music and dance of the period.

Leadership

At the head of the company was the troupe leader, who also may have served as producer as well as stage manager *(sūtradhāra).* His major job seems to have been supervisory, although there are references that suggest that he was also an actor, perhaps even the principal actor, of the company and took the roles of the leading male characters.

As leader of the company his responsibilities may have included establishing engagements for the performance of plays with officials of a temple, the court, or wealthy citizens. As stage manager—the original Sanskrit term literally means "holder of the thread or strings"—he may well have been the architect of the ancient theatre buildings. As the producer of the play, the *Nāṭyaśāstra* charges him to "pay attention to the feelings [*bhāva*], gestures [*mudrās*], and the *sāttvas* [perhaps 'feelings'] in representing the psychological states [*bhāva*] through various characters (that may appear in drama)" (Ghosh 1967, 513).[1]

Other evidence suggests that the group leader served a similar function to that of the modern stage director. The *Nāṭyaśāstra* assigns him the job of distributing roles in a play and of teaching the rules which apply to the art and craft of the actors and actresses. It goes further and lays down the characteristics of an ideal leader. He should be a person capable of fulfilling all these diverse and difficult responsibilities, who has an excellent memory and intelligence, and who is versed in music, language, astrology, and physiognomy, as well as theatre. He should be sensitive to human frailty and familiar with the customs of different regions of the subcontinent.

[1] To aid the reader's understanding of this quotation, I have taken the liberty of substituting the word "*bhāva*" for "Durable Psychological states" and "transitory and *sāttvika*" for "other Psychological states," since Ghosh uses these words interchangeably elsewhere in his work.

The troupe leader seems to have presided over a company of actors, singers, dancers, musicians, backstage workers, and playwrights. We know a great deal more about the actors and playwrights than we do about any of the other functionaries.

Actors

The generic term for actor was *bharata,* which seems to be the hereditary group to which they belonged. Actors were also called *naṭa* or *nartaka* and actresses were known as *naṭī* or *naṭakaya.* In the literature of the time, these terms were also used interchangeably to describe dancers and acrobats.

Apparently both men and women could perform in the plays. Roles could be taken by actors who were the approximate age and sex of the characters. However, younger actors could also play older characters and older actors could perform younger roles, and men were permitted to play women and women could act the role of men. There are even records which indicate that entire companies were composed of women. Actresses were usually regarded as better suited than men to sing, but were not thought fit to participate in battle scenes, as actors were regarded as better suited to depict the sentiments of heroism and rage. Men's voices were thought best for recitation, because they were regarded as stronger than those of women.

If the *Nāṭyaśāstra* is correct in its assessment, the knowledge required of an actor must have been considerable. The ideal actor was assumed to have intelligence, strength, physical beauty, knowledge of time and tempo, and appreciation of sentiments and emotions. He must be the proper age to play a role, possess curiosity, be able to acquire knowledge and other arts, and have a retentive memory. He must understand the vocal music that prompts dance, suppress stage fright, and display enthusiasm. He must sing, dance, use complicated, symbolic hand gestures, and be able to recite the text clearly enough to be heard throughout the theatre. Since critics were supposed to judge the merits and faults of his work, he was obviously obliged to pay close attention to the accuracy of his execution.

According to the *Nāṭyaśāstra,* actors could be faulted for the following: (1) unnaturalness in acting, (2) incorrect movement, (3) unsuitability for a role, (4) forgetfulness, (5) improper use of gestures, (6) defect in costume and ornaments, (7) defect in rhythm of execution, (8) improper projection, and (9) excessive laughter or weeping. Like a yogi who is said to possess the power to transfer his soul from his body into that of a person who has recently died, the actor was supposed to think of himself, "I am he" (Ghosh 1961, 216–217).

Procedures for training actors are also established in the mythological origin of the theatre. Instruction came directly to people from god via a wise sage. Thus, a drama teacher is an older person, usually a father, who instructs younger persons, usually his sons. The *Nāṭyaśāstra* seems to have been designed to serve as a guide to the correct procedures. In this way ancient wisdom was preserved and passed down from generation to generation. When the actor had no access to a text or a competent teacher, the text recommends that he observe and imitate the practices of others. Today, many of the same training procedures proposed by the *Nāṭyaśāstra* are practiced by performers of various rural art forms and even by the actors of some urban theatre schools and companies.

The *Nāṭyaśāstra* charges actors to keep physically fit by undergoing a regular routine of exercises. The exercises were to begin with a purgation of the bowels followed by special dietary restrictions during the period of exercise. The body was to be massaged with sesame oil or with barley gruel after exercising. The proper place for exercises was the floor, which was called the "mother" of exercise. The regimen included leaping in the air and stretching, accompanied by special movement patterns, perhaps drawn from those used in the preliminary rituals before the performance of a play. Training must have taken many long years of hard work, starting with the apprenticeship at a very young age of the pupil to a teacher.

Actors may well have specialized in playing specific roles according to set role designations. The hero, heroine, and clown are a few of the more important categories of roles. It is possible that actors who had a natural aptitude, as well as skill and training, gravitated to one of these categories. Such a system encouraged specialization, with the more difficult parts going to the better actors of the troupe and the smaller roles assigned to younger, less experienced players. Given this hierarchy, it is entirely possible that the actors who were senior and more experienced enjoyed a greater share of the profits. Since the society venerated its elders, the practice probably did not seem unfair to highly talented but less experienced younger players.

Other Company Members

The stage manager is thought to have had an assistant whose job was to help in the prologue and recitation of the benediction. He may also have aided in the preparation and construction of the theatre building. References in the prologues of many plays in which actresses appear lead us to believe that the actress and the stage manager were husband and wife, although this has not yet been established as anything more than a theatrical convention. Numerous other assistants seem to have shared in the backstage responsibilities, including makeup artists, dressers, makers of ornaments and garlands, painters and dyers and modelers of effigies, and washermen.

A company may have had musicians at its disposal, but it is also possible that the musicians constituted a separate group of artists who performed with different troupes of players depending on the occasion and the agreements that had been struck. Musical ensembles are thought to have varied in number from small to medium or large, depending on the particular needs of a performance. The ensembles consisted of male and female vocalists, flutists, players of string instruments, drummers, and those who kept time with cymbals and bells.

Theatre companies may also well have included a separate group of dancers, engaged to perform in the complicated preliminary rituals and perhaps between acts or at places undesignated in the extant playscripts. However, it is also possible that the actors were responsible for performing their own dances in the show.

Means of Support and Social Status

Apparently the performers were sustained by payments made by their patrons. This might have been in the form of simple goods, like rice and oil to be used in preparation of the meals, as well as gifts of clothing and precious metals or jewels. When particularly moved by a performance, spectators might show their appreciation by offering material rewards to the players. It does not seem to have been the practice to sell tickets to a play or to take up a collection from the spectators.

The social position of the players does not appear to have been very high. Numerous ancient writers speak of actors in the same breath as prostitutes and bandits. To prevent themselves from being ritually polluted, Brahmans were never to take food from the hands of an actor. It was a common belief that the actors sold their wives as prostitutes, yet some historical authorities indicate that close personal ties existed between some actors and their royal patrons. Most probably acting companies varied widely in terms of their standing in the community and among the various social classes; some probably enjoyed a higher degree of respectability than others.

In the last chapter of the *Nāṭyaśāstra,* Bharata describes the descent of his line from that of high caste Brahmans to lowly Sudras. According to the account, Bharata's sons caricatured the sages in a particular type of drama which caused others to laugh. In retaliation the sages cursed the boys and those born of their line to be Sudras, the lowest rank of the caste system. Fearing that this might mean the end of the dramatic art, Indra and the other gods approached Brahmā. The sages reassured the gods that drama would continue even if the actors were cursed. However, Bharata's sons were so miserable that they threatened to commit suicide. Just then, so the story goes, a king requested that Bharata and his sons descend to earth and perform plays at his court. Thus drama was saved, and consequently it fell within the province of kings, who took it upon themselves to patronize theatre and drama as one of their royal obligations. Bharata's sons married earthly women and drama was sustained and the art passed down from generation to generation.

Acting

The acting techniques that were practiced in ancient India during a major period of its theatre history are lost to us, except for what we may glean from written materials. And yet there is cause for some rejoicing. Compared with the evidence concerning Western acting practices, the body of information in India is vast, though at times it may seem cold, since acting is a temporal art and it is difficult, if not impossible, to place performances within the framework of a civilization thousands of years old and attempt to understand it within that perspective, primarily on the basis of surviving texts. Most of what we know of the Indian system of acting may be found in the pages of the *Nāṭyaśāstra.*

It may be that there were two main schools of acting in ancient India. The *Nāṭyaśāstra* recognizes two styles of representation *(dharmi)* in dramatic performance: the realistic (*lokadharmī,* literally meaning "the popular"), and the conventional (*nāṭyadharmī,* "the theatrical"). To what extent realism as we know it today actually existed on the stage is only a matter of conjecture, for the *Nāṭyaśāstra* almost exclusively emphasizes conventional techniques.

In addition, four styles of performance are identified: the verbal, which probably placed emphasis on speech alone; the grand, which may have emphasized spectacle; the graceful, perhaps referring to an emphasis on feminine movements and music; and the energetic, which may have referred to masculine movement and forceful music.

A tantalizing reference in the *Nāṭyaśāstra* also implies that dramatic performances may have varied from one geographical locale to another. No matter where one went in ancient India, whether north, south, east, or west, there are said to have been local characteristics which prevailed.

The term acting *(abhinaya)* literally means "carrying toward," implying that the actor is one who brings a performance to the spectators. According to the *Nāṭyaśāstra,* the art of acting consists of four major elements: bodily movement, voice, spectacle, and sentiment or emotion. I shall briefly summarize these aspects as they are presented in the text.

Bodily Movement

Five long chapters of the *Nāṭyaśāstra* are devoted to a comprehensive survey of bodily movement, more than is given to any other aspect of acting. For this reason, bodily movement may well have been considered the most important component of the actor's art. Unfortunately the chapters which deal with the subject provide no visual illustrations. Sometimes this leads to a monumental problem of interpretation.

Which one of the several modes of dramatic entertainment the author is referring to is also unclear. At least three models are recognized—pure dance *(nṛtta),* pantomimic dance *(nṛtya),* and drama *(nāṭya).* As indicated in the general introduction to this book, in parlance, pure dance refers to movements, gestures, and facial expressions which are abstract, which do not have a representational context, and in which there is an instrumental accompaniment or abstract syllables recited by a singer. This mode of physical expression glorifies the skill and technique of those who dance in strict patterns, according to the dictates of time and space. Pantomimic dance, as the name implies, stresses the enactment of a story. In many forms of Indian dance today the dancer usually performs a short scene or episode in which gestures and facial expressions rather than dance steps or movements are the important features. A typical example is the dressing and makeup preparations of a beautiful woman waiting for her beloved. One of the musicians usually sings a text to accompany the dancer, who sometimes mouths the words. We are not sure to what extent pure dance and pantomimic dance were combined in the drama. The *Nāṭyaśāstra* seems to recognize several kinds of dramatic expression under the broad category of drama: dance drama, literary drama, and musical drama. Unfortunately it does not distinguish clearly how these differ from one another and how movement and gestures are to be used in each.

Bodily movements are said to be of three kinds: those of the limbs, those of the face, and those of the entire body. The *Nāṭyaśāstra* identifies the major limbs as the head, hands, breasts, sides, waist, and feet. The minor limbs are those of the face—the eyes, eyebrows, nose, lower lip, and chin. Movements of the minor limbs are discussed first in the text and may well have been the more important in communicating the sentiment of a play. Thirteen head positions are itemized and thirty-six glances, each categorized according to the major sentiments and emotions. Movements of the eyes, eyelids, and eyebrows are categorized and identified according to the emotions they convey. The nose, cheeks, lower lip, chin, mouth, and neck are all discussed according to their ability to communicate emotional meaning. In addition to makeup, the *Nāṭyaśāstra* identifies facial color as an important aspect of expressing emotion.

An entire chapter of the text identifies gestures appropriate for one as well as for both hands. It also cites gestures appropriate for use in pure dance. Various meanings are assigned to each gesture. If the gesture language is as complicated as it is in surviving dance and dance-drama forms, then it would require the help of an expert teacher to learn the precise way the gestures were to be executed.

In another chapter precise bodily movements are prescribed to correspond to emotional states. Positions of the breast, side, stomach, waist, thigh, shank, and feet are categorized and discussed at length.

The specific poses and physical reactions of actors in various situations are referred to as *cārī.* Thirty-two *cārī* are identified; approximately half of them are referred to as earthly and the remaining are called aerial. Precise stances are also identified and designated as appropriate for specific situations. The wielding of weapons, such as the shield and bow, are encompassed within the discussion of the poses. In a separate chapter, the *Nāṭyaśāstra* describes the movements which are to accompany the poses. Most of these movements refer to fighting in personal combat.

Chapter thirteen discusses at some length the gaits which are appropriate for various characters, depending on their sex, rank, age, and temperament. It provides a particularly vivid example of the gait appropriate for a blind man or one walking as though in darkness. It says, "The actor's feet glide over the ground and hands grope for the way" (Ghosh 1967, 225). From this description it would appear that this movement was firmly rooted in reality. The extent to which physical movements were conventionalized cannot be determined from the text.

Different eye, head, face, and hand movements are designated for each of the five senses. Provisions are also made for the actors to show three broad categories of reactions to the object of a situation—favorable, unfavorable, or indifferent. Other conventional patterns of movement are discussed with reference to the walking around *(parikramaṇa),* traversing from one locale to another. The stage directions of extant texts provide numerous examples that suggest that acting was highly conventional and yet had a firm basis in reality.

Voice

Five chapters of the *Nāṭyaśāstra* are concerned with language, but relatively little space is devoted to the use an actor should make of his voice in performing a play. Most of what is said applies to the literary composition of a dramatic work. Chapter fifteen begins with a discussion of the human voice, but soon digresses to a consideration of questions of Sanskrit grammar and language. Chapter sixteen identifies the various metrical patterns that should be employed in composing verses, and seventeen deals with the appropriate composition of speech in various dramatic situations, and eventually becomes a linguistic lecture with examples.

The beginning of chapter eighteen concerns Prakrit grammar and language. Some of the more important points about speech in the plays are made shortly thereafter. Plays are said to be composed of two languages: refined *(saṃskṛta)* and vulgar *(prākṛta).* Sanskrit is regarded as appropriate for the dialogue and verses of gods and kings. There is also a common language and even a language for animals and birds. Rules are set forth regarding the kinds of characters that may use various languages to converse with each other. Regional dialects are cited as appropriate for various characters according to their rank and station in life. The point is also made that "the producer of the plays may however at their option use local dialects for plays may be written in different regions [for local productions]" (Ghosh 1967, 329). Chapter nineteen concentrates on the appropriateness of various modes of address as determined by the character's occupation and whom he is addressing. The chapter ends with a brief description of vocal registers, accents, intonations, vocal qualities, enunciation, and the uses of the pause.

Spectacle

The element of spectacle is divided into four component parts: stage properties, decorations, makeup, and "creatures." With reference to properties, realistic objects such as swords, spears, bows and arrows, and the like are considered inappropriate for stage use. Properties resembling these objects were to be fashioned of lightweight material and painted to look like the actual object. Great care was required in the construction of Indra's banner pole, which was used as part of the preliminary rituals.

Among accessories, the *Nāṭyaśāstra* classifies mountains, temples, caves, idols of deities, elephants, horses, aerial vehicles, and houses. It is possible that these objects were used to symbolize an actual place and thereby establish the identity of a certain part of the stage. The items were to be "fashioned in cane frame" and "covered with cloth." This suggests two possible methods of construction. One possibility was that the object was constructed of bamboo and wrapped with cloth, producing an outline of the object. Properties constructed in this manner are found in the No theatre of Japan. The second possibility is that cloth was stretched over a bamboo frame and then painted to resemble the object. This method of construction is used today in the *aṇkīya nāṭ* of Assam. The text also makes reference to the construction of masks.

Elsewhere in the *Nāṭyaśāstra* we find mention of a curtain *(yavanikā)* which may have been held by attendants and then lowered or pulled aside to reveal a character. Some scholars have suggested that curtained entrances from the dressing room or traverse curtains stretched between the stage pillars were regularly in use. The practice of employing a curtained entrance, as in the No of Japan and *jingxi* of China, may have been common in the Sanskrit theatre as well.

The *Nāṭyaśāstra* specifies garlands, ornaments, and costumes as items of decoration for an actor. Specific instructions are given for the decoration of men and women according to the region of the country to which they belonged, their caste, station in life, and the occasion of their appearance on the stage. Headgear, earrings, necklaces, bangles for the arms, wrists, and ankles, and finger and toe rings are also mentioned. These were grouped according to whether they were to pierce the limb, be tied up, hang, or circle the body. From the tops of their heads to the tips of their toes the actors of the Sanskrit theatre were to be profusely and brilliantly ornamented and costumed. Heavy objects such as gold or precious stones were deemed inappropriate because they might easily tire the actor due to their excessive weight. Instead the *Nāṭyaśāstra* advises that they be constructed of light wood and glazed with shellac to resemble the real object.

No clear indication is made in the text concerning the reproduction of historically accurate costumes, ornaments, and properties. Some scholars believe that the actors wore the garb of the particular period in which the play was written. Others think they dressed according to the dictates of the period in which the play was set. Still others regard the decorations as fanciful, conforming to no particular period or style.

The *Nāṭyaśāstra* suggests that makeup be applied to the face and body of the actor according to the region of the country, caste, age, and occupation of the character. Specific colors are designated for specific character types, though it is not clear if the colors prescribed in the text were conventional or realistic.

The meaning of "creatures" *(saṃjīva)* is not made clear in the *Nāṭyaśāstra*. It may be that it refers to actors who portray animals, birds, and superhuman beings, or it may refer to actors who manipulate giant effigies like those used in the *aṇkīya nāṭ* of Assam.

Sentiment and Emotion

Critics have not yet come to an agreement concerning the precise definition of two important aesthetic terms: *sāmānābhinaya,* which seems to be a synonym for *sāttvikābhinaya.* In chapter twenty-four of the *Nāṭyaśāstra, sāttva* is defined as "something invisible" and is said to be the basis of the dramatic production (Ghosh 1967, 442). The whole of the chapter is concerned with the decorous behavior of the characters, particularly the female characters of the plays. Special attention is lavished on the correct speech or gestures appropriate for various occasions. This has led at least one critic to conclude that the term means an "expression in a graceful or charming manner of the various *bhāvas,* i.e. feelings (of a character)" (Rangacharya 1971, 36). Another critic thinks *sāttvika* refers to the psyche of the character. Still another scholar believes that the author of the *Nāṭyaśāstra* meant to introduce a realistic style of acting which depends on correct social behavior as its guide, in contrast to the conventional school of acting mentioned in the majority of the chapters. Whatever the correct definition of the term, the *Nāṭyaśāstra* has presented a notion which requires of a performer more than the external representation of character, such as correct movements, speech, and ornamentation. It implies that the standard of stage performance goes far beyond the mastery of technical considerations, and that the players be believable in order to satisfy the spectators.

Music and Dance

Examining the texts of the extant Sanskrit plays, it is next to impossible to determine how music and dance were integrated into a performance. Indeed from the plays alone, you might well get the impression that Sanskrit drama was dialogue drama without the benefit of music and dance, except for the rare occasion in certain texts in which a character is said to sing or dance or do both. And yet the *Nāṭyaśāstra* tells us something quite different. Songs and dances seem to have been very much a part of the total performance experience.

As indicated earlier, the chapters devoted to music are our earliest source of information about the music of ancient India. Some scholars contend that the music which we now conventionally associate with India is relatively recent in origin and that the *Nāṭyaśāstra* refers to a musical system which was unique and which has undergone considerable changes with the passing of time.

According to the text, melodic sounds were either produced by the human voice or by musical instruments (literally by the *vīṇa,* an ancient stringed instrument). Instruments traditionally associated with the drama are either stringed; covered, namely the various drums; solid, such as the cymbal; or hollow, like the flute. Some scholars contend that the flute was the leading musical instrument, for it provided the pitch from which the singers took their cues and served a similar function to the present-day drone instruments, such as the tambura and harmonium.

I noted earlier that the appropriate place for the musicians to sit was upstage center, between the two doors leading to the dressing room. They may have sat on a rug on the floor and watched the progress of the play from this strategic vantage point. This gave them a full view of the acting area and also provided easy access to the dressing room in case changes in format needed to be made on short notice.

It is apparent from the early chapters of the *Nāṭyaśāstra* that music was essential to the progress of the preliminary rituals and to the consecration of the theatre building. The songs that were sometimes sung by an actress in the prologue probably needed a musical accompaniment, as did the songs referred to on occasion in some of the scripts. A few scholars contend that actors sang some, if not all, of the verses of a play. If this were so, then these too would have required musical accompaniment. According to other scholars, the actors recited or chanted the verses. This controversy has not yet been resolved. Many of the plays indicate that classical and folk dances were to be performed as part of the action. They too would have required a musical accompaniment.

We learn from the *Nāṭyaśāstra* that songs were used extensively throughout a play, for various purposes. The songs were composed by the musicians, and their content was guided by the content of the verses of the play. Songs were used: (1) to introduce a character when he or she first comes on the stage, (2) when a character exits during the middle or at the end of an act, (3) to reinforce a mood already established in the dramatic action, (4) to change the mood of a scene, or when a situation changes, and finally, (5) when some gap occurs in the action due to a mishap, such as the need to adjust or replace a costume or when an overpowering feeling causes great tension.

Apparently, the songs were composed in Prakrit and had a symbolic purpose. It is thought that they were sometimes sung behind a curtain before an entrance, perhaps even by the actor who was preparing to enter. It is also assumed that the melody was rendered completely through at least once, and then was repeated to the accompaniment of the rhythmic pattern of the drums. Since none of the extant plays include references to the songs, nor do they indicate how they were to be incorporated, it is a matter of pure speculation what their effect might have been on the total production.

Although dance is mentioned in a few plays, the details of its execution are also a matter of conjecture. It would seem that its main function was to serve as a part of the preliminary rituals and to heighten the dramatic impact of a particular scene. It is possible that dancelike movements and gestures were used by the actors throughout a performance as part of their acting technique. Practices such as this are still to be seen in the *kūṭiyāṭṭam* of Kerala, which I will discuss in the next chapter. Perhaps these practices provide a clue as to the authentic style of performance practiced at least in the declining years of the Sanskrit theatre.

Spectators and the Occasion of Performance

The *Nāṭyaśāstra* speaks of those who attend the theatre as spectators (*prekṣaka,* literally "those who see"). From this it would seem that the ancient Indian theatre laid particular stress on the visual aspects of performance, and yet there is ample evidence that both sight and sound were to be an effective blend and that the spectators were to be equally cognizant of the importance of both.

Actually very little is known about the individuals and groups that attended plays in ancient India. In the prologues to many of the plays, a stage manager speaks directly to the spectators and flatters them by declaring that they are learned and wise. Perhaps what the stage manager says was true and not just a theatrical convention; however, it is more than likely that those who attended Sanskrit plays varied widely in learning, judgment, and taste. It may be remembered that in the first chapter of the *Nāṭyaśāstra* Indra asked Brahmā to create drama for the amusement and edification of all the color or caste groups *(varṇa),* from the highest caste Brahmans, arbiters of ancient knowledge and wisdom, to the lowly Sudras, simple peasants, as well as for all the occupational groups in between.

Conforming to the general practice of specifying ideal types and classes of individuals and things, the *Nāṭyaśāstra* identifies the characteristics that the ideal spectators should possess. They should be of good character, high birth, quiet and learned, partial, advanced in age, alert, honest, and virtuous. The audience was to be proficient in drama and acting, expert in playing musical instruments, knowledgeable about costumes and makeup, and expert in other branches of the arts and crafts. They should understand the meaning of the sciences *(śāstra)*. Grammar, prosody, sentiment and emotion —all these were to be known and appreciated by the ideal spectator.

Occasion of Performance

The occasion for a theatre performance arose from a desire on the part of an individual, group, or institution to organize a public gathering to celebrate some great occasion; perhaps the first and most important occasion was the celebration of a temple festival. Since theatre architecture was considered a branch of temple architecture, it would appear reasonable that performances in the temple theatre were given on a regular basis when astrological conjunctions favored honoring some deity or other. Indeed the temple deity may well have been the chief guest at such occasions, if not in the form of the temple idol, at least in spirit. After all the *Nāṭyaśāstra* describes the performance of a play as a sacrifice to the gods. The numerous rituals accompanying the building of the theatre, the stages in its construction, its consecration, and the preliminaries preceding the performance of a play strengthen the contention that dramatic events were thought of as sacred affairs.

Other evidence suggests that plays were performed for the coronation of kings, marriages, the birth of a son, the return of a traveler, and the celebration of the confiscation of a town or a state. The *Nāṭyaśāstra* asserts that "of all the duties of the king, this [the performance of a play] has been proclaimed as possessing the best result. Of all kinds of charities, allowing people to enjoy a dramatic show without payment, has been praised most" (Ghosh 1961, 237).

Positive and Negative Critical Responses

The *Nāṭyaśāstra* also recognizes various conventional ways spectators were expected to respond to a production. When the comic sentiment dominated, a spectator was to show a slight smile, a half smile, or perhaps laugh uproariously. If well-acted, moments depicting virtue were to be accorded cries of "excellent." The sentiment of wonder was expected to prompt the spectators to sigh, "How wonderful!" And pathos could cause them to weep and mutter, "How pathetic!" Tumultuous applause greeted astonishing sights and the hair on their arms was to stand on end during moments of fear. In general the spectators were expected to become totally engrossed in the theatrical event and to respond to the acting accordingly. The extent of their involvement seems to have been conventionalized. For example, the stage manager in the prologue to Kālidāsa's *Śākuntala (Abhijñana-śākuntala)* remarks to the actress after she has completed her song, "Charmingly sung, good lady! Look, the entire audience seems like a picture, their souls entranced by your melody" (Kālidāsa 1964, 201).

The *Nāṭyaśāstra* says that a performance was judged to be a success in one of two ways—either it was considered a "human" success, prompting the reactions mentioned above, or it was considered a "divine" success. "Divine" successes seem to have been accorded to performances in which there was no noise, disturbance, or any unusual occurrences to distract from the discriminating depiction of the actor's emotions. Perhaps the *Nāṭyaśāstra* means that divine performances were those in which the spectators showed neither interest nor disinterest, in which they were elevated to a state of supreme bliss akin to that of a yogi who experiences divine revelation.

The *Nāṭyaśāstra* also enumerates the possible disasters that might befall a production. Natural disorders such as wind, fire, rain, lightning, and earthquakes, among others, are categorized as disasters caused by the gods. Manmade calamities which disrupt performances fall into two categories: (1) those brought about by jealous enemies who scream, throw things, and clap loudly; and (2) those caused by the actors, the details of which have already been discussed.

The *Nāṭyaśāstra* takes the sensible view that "nothing can be devoid of merit or free of fault" (Ghosh 1967, 522). And so there are those among the spectators who are recognized as critics and are assigned a place in front of the stage, to evaluate the proceedings and to award prizes. People skilled in any of ten types of activities are fit to be critics. They are: (1) the Brahmans, those expert in performance of sacrifice; (2) experts in acting; (3) prosodists; (4) grammarians; (5) kings; (6) archers; (7) painters; (8) courtesans; (9) musicians; and (10) courtiers. Each expert was assigned to judge the merits and faults of the performance according to his or her own level and area of expertise. For example, the king was to judge the actors who portrayed kings, and so forth. Recorders had the task of keeping score of the faults noted by the critics during a show and tallying the results. Prizes were awarded to the actor who had accumulated the fewest faults. A banner was the usual prize. In case of a tie, the king was to choose between the two contestants, or he was given the privilege of awarding a banner to each, if he happened to be fond of both.

Theatre, Stage, and Function

Unfortunately, none of the theatre structures of ancient India have survived the ravages of time. To make matters worse, we have no visual evidence either—no drawings or floor plans, no sketches made by a diligent visitor, not even the foundations of a building in ruins. Our only substantial source of information regarding the size and shape of the buildings that are said to have housed Sanskrit play productions is the *Nāṭyaśāstra,* and from the discussion it appears to have been written with the intention of laying down rules for the construction of "ideal" models, rather than recording the size and shape of existing structures.

The *Nāṭyaśāstra* attributes Viśvakarmā, the heavenly architect, with conceiving of the first playhouse. As we learned earlier, he did so to accommodate a request made by Brahmā, who wanted a sanctified place where actors might perform a play uninterrupted by malevolent spirits. The text gives no details about the appearance of the "first" theatre except that construction was begun on an auspicious day and that the gods agreed to assist in its protection.

The text prescribes three shapes suitable for playhouses: rectangular, square, and triangular. Each was to come in a small, medium, and large size. Bharata lavishes more of his attention on the medium-sized rectangular building than he does on any other structure. He says that this is the ideal structure because spectators may easily see the facial expressions of the actors and hear their speeches and songs.

Characteristics of the Major Structure

The parameter of the medium-sized rectangular buildings was ninety-six feet by forty-eight feet; and according to directions, it was to be subdivided in half, thus creating two equal squares forty-eight by forty-eight feet. The space of one of the squares was allocated for use by the spectators. The other half was again subdivided and the area closest to the spectators was designated as the acting area and that at the extremity of the building was reserved for the dressing room.

Considering the limited size of the space reserved for the spectators, it would seem that relatively few people could have witnessed a performance of a Sanskrit play at any one time. Perhaps no more than five hundred persons, and possibly only two hundred patrons, comfortably seated, saw plays in the medium-sized rectangular playhouse. This obviously promoted a sense of intimacy between actors and audience inconceivable in the theatre structures of ancient Western cultures, such as those of Greece and Rome or even that of Elizabethan England.

The *Nāṭyaśāstra* specifies that special procedures be followed when selecting the site and clearing the land for construction of a new playhouse. Care was to be taken in laying out the basic divisions of the structure, otherwise disasters might befall the country and those responsible for causing the mistakes. With the sounding of conch shells and the playing of rhythmic instruments the foundation was laid. Undesirables were denied access to this ceremony, probably for fear of casting an evil eye on the proceedings. After the site was marked out on the ground, the gods of the ten directions were honored with ritual ceremonies.

The next step was the raising of the walls and pillars. Four pillars were designated to represent the four castes or color groups. This would seem to support the implication made in the first chapter that drama was created as a form of amusement and edification for all four castes. Symbolically the four castes were the pillars of the theatre.

Considerable disagreement exists among scholars over the meaning of the physical feature of the theatre building that was to be constructed next. Apparently, it had pillars and was higher than the level of the stage. Little more may be said for certain about its shape and function.

The notion that the playhouse was to resemble a mountain cave has led some critics to wonder if the early theatres were actually constructed in caves. Some years ago a cave was found in central India that the Archaeological Survey of India dubbed a theatre, but there is no proof that theatres were ever carved into the sides of mountains. It would seem that if this were a common practice in ancient times, other examples would still remain among the numerous cave sites of the subcontinent. It is more likely that the *Nāṭyaśāstra* meant to imply that the ceiling of the edifice was constructed in such a fashion that it acoustically aided the voices of the actors and the music and drums. Small windows might have been inserted high up in the structure as ventilation and perhaps even to let in some light. The final step in the construction of the structure seems to have been the plastering, whitewashing, and painting of the walls. The paintings were to depict scenes of "creepers, men, women and their amorous exploits" (Ghosh 1956, 30).

We know almost as little about the stage of the ancient Indian theatre as we do about that of Shakespeare's Globe or the Theatre Dionysus of fifth century B.C. Athens. Several points are fairly clear, however. The maximum potential acting area of the ideal structure was twenty-four by forty-eight feet. Two Sanskrit terms used to describe the stage have led some scholars to conclude that the stage was further subdivided in half, the part closest to the audience referred to as the "head of the stage" and the part nearer to the dressing room as the "seat of the stage." The front half is thought to have been slightly lower than the back half. A wall with two doors seems to have separated the dressing room from the acting area. As noted earlier, the space between the doors was reserved for the musicians. The stage seems to have been on a different level from that on which the spectators sat, thus it was clearly demarcated as an acting area. The floor was to be elevated and level as the surface of a mirror, suggesting that it may have been reflective. The *Nāṭyaśāstra* indicates that it was not to be convex or rough, like the back of a tortoise or a fish. Precious stones are said to have been laid in the foundation of the stage, probably for ritual rather than practical purposes. The stage had pillars, which either helped to support the superstructure of the roof of the main building or to support a separate roof which may have been constructed above the acting area. The text is uncertain about the exact number, placement, and function of the pillars. Wooden figures of elephants, tigers, and snakes were to be carved, possibly on the pillars or perhaps on the ceiling above the stage, if the stage had a separate ceiling.

Other Structures

The procedures for the construction of the square theatre are almost identical to those outlined for the construction of the middle-sized rectangular structure. A square was subdivided in half and the area relegated to the actors again subdivided in half, forming a dressing space and stage. Bharata describes a few unique details of this structure worth repeating here, since they may shed light on the features of the ideal structure. He says that the outer walls of the square theatre were to be constructed of bricks. Rows of seats for the spectators were to be made of wood and brick. The seats were to resemble a staircase, in that each successive row was higher than that which preceded it, potentially providing all the spectators with a clear view of the stage. Whether or not the seats were arranged in this manner in the medium-sized rectangular houses is still speculative.

Little of consequence may be said of the triangular theatre. Such a shape is uncommon in the history of architectural units the world over and it seems unlikely that triangular theatres were widely, if ever, constructed in India.

Consecration of the Theatre

Consecration of the newly constructed playhouse was obviously important, for an entire chapter of the *Nāṭyaśāstra* is devoted to ritual prescriptions. Bharata says, "Offering worship to the gods of the stage is as meritorious as a (Vedic) sacrifice." He continues:

> If the stage is properly consecrated it will bring good luck to the king (literally, the master) and to people, young and old of the city as well as of the country. But when the auditorium is not consecrated in proper manner it will be indifferently held by gods, and there will be an end of the dramatic spectacle, and it will likewise bring evil to the king. He who willfully transgresses these rules

> . . . and practices . . . will soon sustain loss and will be reborn as an animal of lower order. (Ghosh 1967, 43–44)

Staging

In chapter fourteen, Bharata says that the stage was divided into different zones and that by walking around from one zone to another, *parikramaṇa,* the actor was understood to have moved from one place of action to another. That this convention was widely accepted may be seen by the ample references that are made to *parikramaṇa* in the extant plays. It is not clear if different parts of the stage were conventionally used over and over again to symbolize the same place, such as a garden or a room in a palace, or whether the whole stage was regarded as a neutral acting area, which did not take on an iconic significance until the actor specified the locale through speeches or actions. Nor may we totally disregard the possibility that scene pieces were employed to designate locales. As mentioned, Bharata classifies, among other things, mountains, temples, caves, aerial vehicles, and houses as stage properties. It may be that these were used in a conventional manner to designate places, as the medieval theatres of Europe designated various locales by employing scene pieces, for the medieval stage was regarded as a neutral acting area *(platea)* until the actors identified themselves with reference to the scenic locales.

Bharata further elaborates on the symbolic use of the stage by suggesting that persons who enter the stage first are regarded as being inside a place or zone and those who enter later are thought to be outside that particular zone and must pass through some barrier, real or imaginary, before they too are regarded as inside the same space. Also in chapter fourteen, Bharata hints that the stage doors may have been used in a conventional manner. Perhaps one was reserved exclusively for entrances and the other for exits. However, it is possible that they may have had a specific symbolic significance, much like that claimed for the doors of the *skene* houses in the ancient Greek theatres.

Playwrights and Their Works

The *Nāṭyaśāstra* categorized playwrights among the members of a theatre company. Although it is possible that playwrights were regularly engaged in the service of a company, it is doubtful that those who achieved great fame and reputation in their profession were ever permanently attached to theatre organizations. Playwrights were generally accorded a much higher social status than the other members of the theatre companies. Many playwrights are known to have been members of the royal court. Even some kings composed plays. While we know relatively little about the lives of the members of the theatre companies, we have a somewhat more vivid picture of the playwrights, in part because they have left their works behind and because they enjoyed a degree of social prestige.

Aśvaghoṣa

With the discovery of fragments of three plays found in Turfan, Russia, and subsequently published in 1911, we have the earliest examples of Sanskrit drama now in our possession. The title and author of one of the works is certain—*The Story of Śāriputra (Śāriputraprakaraṇa)* of Aśvaghoṣa. Although the precise date for the playwright has not yet been established, Aśvaghoṣa was probably a member of the court of Kaniṣka, a great patron of Buddhism in northern India, who ruled the western half of North India at least as far as Varanasi, and held dominions in central Asia as well. Historians are still not certain of the date Kaniṣka ascended to the throne but the most convincing arguments place it sometime between 78 A.D. and 144 A.D. So Aśvaghoṣa probably lived sometime between the first and second centuries A.D.

The two manuscripts found with *The Story of Śāriputra* do not bear a title or the signature of their author. One of the fragments is unusual in that it makes use of allegorical characters. The other work is humorous in tone and has a courtesan as one of its central figures. All three plays were obviously intended for religious edification, since they espouse Buddhist teachings.

The plays are important not so much in themselves, but because they show that their author (or authors) had abundant precedents as a guide. By this period in history the dramatic form was firmly fixed. The fragments abide by the various rules laid down in the *Nāṭyaśāstra* for dramatic composition.

Thus by the first century A.D. and certainly no later than the second century, Sanskrit drama had established the basic form that it was to follow for more than a thousand years. It is obvious from what little evidence we have about Aśvaghoṣa that he was not the father of Sanskrit drama. In fact, no name comes to mind who can claim that title. Unlike the ancient Greeks who could point with pride to Thespis as the first actor and Aeschylus as the first major playwright, the Sanskrit theatre has no clear historical personalities and events which link the early drama with the formative drama after the first century.

Bhāsa

Bhāsa is the earliest significant dramatist of ancient India. He is unique in that a large body of work has been assigned to his hand. Under the supervision of the late Ganapati Sastri, thirteen plays attributed to Bhāsa were collected and published in 1912.

Virtually nothing is known about Bhāsa. It is not even certain that he

Malayalam script of the original Sanskrit plays of Bhāsa incised on palm leaves. (Farley P. Richmond photo)

wrote all thirteen works ascribed to him. The only clear reference to his authorship of one of the works is a tenth century verse by Rājaśekhara which proclaims that "critics cast on the fire, to test it, the discus composed of the dramas of *bhāsa;* the *The Vision of Vāsavadattā (Svapnavāsavadattā)* did not succumb to the flames" (Keith 1924, 91–92). Modern critics uniformly agree that *The Vision of Vāsavadattā* is by far Bhāsa's finest work and that it was unmistakably composed by him. Attribution of the authorship of the other twelve plays to Bhāsa rests primarily on stylistic grounds.

Not only are we uncertain about the personality of Bhāsa or precisely which plays he wrote, but we do not know the exact period in which he lived. Kālidāsa, the acknowledged master of Sanskrit playwriting, proclaims Bhāsa as one of his major predecessors, along with Saumilla and Kaviputra, for whom we have no surviving works. If Kālidāsa lived around the fourth century A.D., it is possible that Bhāsa practiced his art between the time of Aśvaghoṣa in the first century A.D. and the fifth century, a span of four hundred years! Based on careful internal analysis of the Prakrits in the plays, Keith places Bhāsa no later than 350 A.D. and no earlier than 300 (Keith 1924, 93 and 95). Considering that there is no substantial evidence to disprove Keith's analysis, we may safely assume that Bhāsa lived about 400 A.D.

His place of residence is also uncertain. Some scholars assign him to the ancient city of Ujjain in North Central India. Others suggest that he may have lived somewhere in the south, perhaps in modern Kerala, where actors of the *kūṭiyāṭṭam* still perform plays attributed to him.

The range of Bhāsa's work is wide. He experimented with most of the dramatic forms mentioned in the *Nāṭyaśāstra.* His subject matter is also drawn from a wide variety of sources—from the *Rāmāyaṇa,* the *Mahābhārata,* the

Scene from Bhāsa's *Karnabharam* directed by K. N. Pannikar in 1984. (K. N. Pannikar photo)

Puranas, from semihistorical tales, and from his own imagination. Like so many other writers of this period he took liberties with his subject matter, deviating where he saw fit to strengthen the plot, to draw a unique view of a mythological or historical character or to stress an emotion. Unlike the work of later writers his plays are simple, direct, and dramatic. They are not excessively poetic and florid. Reading his works without considering their manner of presentation, they leave one with the feeling that this was a man of the theatre and not just a gifted poet.

Śūdraka

What we know of Śūdraka is found primarily in the prologue of the only work which bears his name, *The Little Clay Cart (Mṛcchakaṭikā),* one of the half dozen acknowledged masterpieces of Sanskrit dramatic literature. The passage is worth quoting as a basis for the following discussion. Of the poet, the Stage Manager says,

> He was renowned under the name of Śūdraka; he had the dignity of an elephant, the eye of a chakora (a kind of partridge which according to mythology drinks moonbeams), a face like the full moon, and a body harmoniously pro-

> portioned; he was the most distinguished of all men of the superior castes; and the profundity of his wisdom was unfathomable.

Indeed,

> He knew the *Ṛg-Veda,* the *Sāma-Veda,* mathematics, the science of erotics, and the art of training elephants. By the grace of Śiva, the veil of ignorance was lifted from Śūdraka's eyes, so that after he had witnessed the coronation of his son and had performed the incomparable Horse-Sacrifice, he, having attained the age of one hundred years and ten days, cast himself into the flames.

Moreover,

> Śūdraka was a monarch valiant in war, yet endowed with great prudence. He excelled all those who are learned in the *Vedas;* he attained great merit by his austerities; and, in battle, he delighted in assailing with his own arm the elephant on which his enemy was mounted. (Śūdraka 1964, 45–46)

From the prologue we deduce that Śūdraka was a king, that he was a learned man, valiant in war but prudent in tactics. He was reported to be accomplished in mathematics, the science of erotics, and the art of training elephants. He was endowed with great physical beauty and extraordinary prowess. Śūdraka performed austerities appropriate to a monarch. He was the devotee of Lord Śiva. He performed the horse sacrifice, a difficult and expensive rite which assured his sovereignty over kings of other lands. All these things were conventionally attributed to monarchs of ancient India. It was the style then for a poet to flatter his ruler. However, it must be remembered that it was the practice for the poet himself to write the prologue. So Śūdraka seems to be complimenting himself, unless the passage was composed by some other author. One passage supports this contention. Śūdraka is said to have cast himself into the flames shortly after his hundredth birthday. Although many men in India are said to have had prior knowledge of the day of their death, it seems unlikely that Śūdraka would have spoken of it so freely in this verse before it had actually taken place. It may be that this particular part of the prologue was revised upon the death of the king so that future generations would remember him and his exploits.

Nevertheless there are other problems which further confuse the issue of Śūdraka's identity. History has not left us any record of a king called Śūdraka. In fact, the name itself is quite inappropriate for a monarch—it means "little servant." There is also a question of plagiarism. The first four acts of *The Little Clay Cart* virtually duplicate those of Bhāsa's unfinished play *Cārudattam.* One scholar has gone so far as to suggest that the poet found Bhāsa's play and, out of respect for his work, continued where Bhāsa left off, styling himself the "little servant" of Bhāsa.

Various critics after the eighth century mention Śūdraka as the author of *The Little Clay Cart,* but give no details about his personality or the kingdom over which he ruled. A fourteenth century text attributes the play to a pair of collaborators, Bhartrimentha and Vikramāditya. The former was reported to have been one of the great poets living in the city of Ujjain about the time of Kālidāsa, and the latter may have been none other than King Chandragupta II of the Gupta dynasty. However, these references are so far removed from the probable date of the composition of *The Little Clay Cart* that considerable doubt is cast on their validity.

The general consensus is that Śūdraka was a mythical figure who had no place in history. Thus, unless we take the prologue at face value and the possibility that it was revised after the death of the king, we must assume that Śūdraka never lived and the authorship of one of the most famous plays of ancient India is uncertain!

The date of the work is also in doubt. It was probably written after the works of Aśvaghoṣa and, if we assume that Bhāsa's *Cārudattam* was composed before *The Little Clay Cart,* then the play must have been been written sometime after 350 A.D. If it was in existence before Kālidāsa wrote his prologue honoring his predecessors, then it seems strange that the author of so excellent a play as *The Little Clay Cart* would not have been mentioned therein. The number and age of Prakrits in the work places it considerably earlier than the eighth century, when Śūdraka is mentioned for the first time.

Some scholars have simply thrown up their hands in dismay and refused to assign any date to the work. Others have placed it about the fifth century or a little earlier, which corresponds roughly with Kālidāsa's dates.

Since *The Little Clay Cart* is a major example of Sanskrit drama, we will briefly explore selected aspects of the play. In design and scope it is one of the most ambitious works of Sanskrit dramatic literature. It paints a vivid picture of life in the ancient and culturally important city of Ujjain, in North Central India. To what extent Śūdraka actually captured the true spirit and splendor of the city has yet to be determined. So much of what was written in ancient times idealizes life rather than mirrors it.

His characters are drawn from the lower echelons of street life, as testified by the variety of languages and regional dialects spoken in the play. What he pictures is probably exaggerated to suit his dramatic purpose. The moral lessons which he draws suggests that he was no social critic in the modern sense of the term. But by reading the play we may learn a great deal from this idealized picture of life in an ancient urban setting. Each and every character emerges with a lively and distinct personality. Thanks to Śūdraka's keen sense of humor the play is one of the easiest and best to stage in the Western world. In fact, it reminds one of the more delightful comedies of Plautus. However, its essential moorings remain in Indian philosophy, religion, and social life.

A summary of the complicated plot does not do justice to the rich use of language and carefully contrived characters. However, it does clarify the basic objectives of the play. The play opens with a traditional benediction in praise of Śiva, which is followed by an extensive preliminary scene, including flattering remarks about the audience, details concerning the author, which we have already mentioned, and a witty bit of patter between the stage manager and his pert wife concerning their poverty. The plot proceeds to expand upon the theme of material poverty and spiritual wealth.

At the beginning of Act I, the hero of the piece is disconsolate. Due to his excessive generosity Cārudatta, a Brahman merchant-prince, is penniless. As he scatters offerings to the household gods, he observes, "In bygone days the swans and innumerable cranes instantly devoured the offerings which I strewed over the terrace of my house; but now the handful of poor grain that I scatter about falls unheeded into the tangled grass and the worms slaver it" (Śūdraka 1964, 50). His unfortunate state of affairs causes him to observe,

> Assuredly my dejection springs not from the mere loss of material possession, for riches come and go as turns the wheel of Destiny; nay what pains me is that friends desert the man whose sometime wealth has taken flight. . . . Poverty makes a man timid; and timidity destroys self-confidence. And when a man has lost assurance, he finds himself scorned; and from humiliation is born despair. Then despair stuns and enfeebles the mind; and a turpid mind can but await utter ruin. Alas! Poverty is the source of all evil. . . . Poverty is for man an unfailing source of afflictions. It exposes him to the insolence of his enemies and makes him the enemy of all mankind; it makes his friends despise him, and his servants hate him, and it fills him, who reads contempt in his wife's eyes, with desire to flee to the solitude of the forest. It places within the heart a flame of sorrow that tortures but does not kill. (Śūdraka 1964, 51)

In sharp contrast to Cārudatta's mood of despair, on another part of the stage Vasantasenā, the heroine, enters hurriedly fleeing from Saṁsthanāka, the king's wicked brother-in-law, and two of his cronies. The pursuers argue that it is out of character for a courtesan, such as herself, to repel their advances. One of them pleads, "Your body, your caresses, are merchandise that may be bought with gold; you should, therefore, sell to all alike, and open your arms with equal abandon to the man who pleases you and to him who displeases you" (Śūdraka 1964, 55). Vasantasenā's behavior assures us that she heartily disapproves of such ruffians and does not intend to be persuaded by their arguments. Under cover of darkness she slips unseen into Cārudatta's house. By mistake the rogues catch Cārudatta's maidservant. Discovering their mistake Saṁsthanāka shouts,

> Tell the pauper called Cārudatta that a hetaera named Vasantasenā, covered with golden ornaments and brilliant jewels, like a leading lady at the premiere

> of a new play, has been in love with him ever since she saw him in the garden of the temple of Kāma; and that now, just as we were about to overcome her with violence, she has escaped into his house. If he consents to deliver her into my hands immediately and without lawsuit, I shall be grateful for his prompt obedience, and I shall reward him with my friendship; if, on the other hand, he should refuse, I shall swear against him undying hatred. (Śūdraka 1964, 62)

Cārudatta offers the frightened Vasantasenā refuge, and thus begins an intense love affair which gradually reaches its climax in a thunderstorm in Act V. It also forebodes trouble for the already unfortunate Brahman, in that Saṁsthanāka sets about constructing a web of deceit which brings Cārudatta to the very brink of death in the last act. As a reward for protecting her from Saṁsthanāka's advances, Vasantasenā leaves her jewels with Cārudatta for safekeeping. In one of the most brilliant of comic monologues, the jewels are stolen by an artful thief who pantomimes breaking and entering Cārudatta's house, guided by the rules of kleptology outlined in a pocket manual. Fearing that her husband's reputation will be ruined, Cārudatta's wife bestows on him through Maitreya, his Brahman friend, her only possession, a necklace of pearls. Unwillingly, Maitreya sets out to deliver the necklace to Vasantasenā with a fabricated story that Cārudatta has lost her jewels in a gambling house and offers to replace them with the necklace. But before he arrives at the courtesan's house the thief returns the stolen jewels to Vasanta-

Bahorupee's version of *The Little Clay Cart* directed by Kumar Roy in Calcutta. (Bahorupee photo)

senā to buy the freedom of her slave girl with whom he is in love. When Maitreya arrives, Vasantasenā is already aware that the gambling house story is false and that the pearl necklace belongs to Cārudatta's wife. Nevertheless she takes the jewels and tells Maitreya that she will come to Cārudatta's house in the evening. Her slave girl warns, "See, my lady—see the storm that is gathering suddenly." In a magnificent verse, Vasantasenā replies,

> Let the clouds pile high; let the rain fall; let the rain pour down unintermittently! My heart yearns for the one whom I love, and I shall not stop for any obstacle. (Śūdraka 1964, 108)

The union of the lovers in Act V is surely one of the most beautiful of poetic scenes in all of Sanskrit literature. As Vasantasenā approaches the house of Cārudatta, accompanied by her retinue of servants and slave girls, umbrella held high above her head, her slave exclaims:

> At this hour, when the earth is adorned by incandescent clouds and perfumed by the flowering cadamba and spice trees, this woman, exalted by love, joyful, and with long hair drenched by the rain, has come to the house of her beloved. Frightened by the flashing lightning and roaring thunder, she sighs for him, even while she is washing from her feet and ankles the mud that clings to the encircling bracelets. (Śūdraka 1964, 118)

The symphony of love reaches its crescendo with Cārudatta's poetic conclusion to the act:

> Let the storm rage for a hundred years, let the rain fall and the lightning flash incessantly, for now I enjoy the embraces of my beloved and the pleasures that are rarely known by men like me. Happy is the life of man whose mistress has come to him, and who may warm with his limbs her limbs that are drenched and chilled by the water of the clouds. . . . See, beloved, see, the rainbow: Is it not as though the sky were yawning? It vibrates its tongue, the lightning; it throws out its gigantic arms, the rainbow; and it opens its vast jaws, the clouds. Come, let us go into the house. The rain as it throbs on the leaves of the palm trees, as it sighs in the branches, as it beats on the rocks, as it hisses in the pools, resounds harmoniously like the tones of a *vīṇa* that is skillfully played and accompanied by cymbals. (Śūdraka 1964, 122–23)

The delicate strains of love that conclude Act V fade into the more ponderous mood of pathos in Act VI. The play takes its name from an incident early in the act. Cārudatta's little son weeps over the loss of his golden cart, which was sold to pay his father's debts. His only remaining toy is a little clay cart. Seeing the child's bitterness, Vasantasenā is moved to tears and out of pity fills the little clay cart with her magnificent jewels.

Shortly thereafter Cārudatta's driver, who is sent to take Vasantasenā to the public garden, mistakenly delivers Āryaka, an escaped prisoner who is destined to overthrow the king. In Act VII, Āryaka arrives at the garden after narrowly escaping his guards. He throws himself on the mercy of Cārudatta, who unhesitatingly extends his protection and pledges his support for Āryaka's noble cause. Meanwhile Vasantasenā is delivered by mistake to the evil Saṁsthanāka elsewhere in the public garden, after she mistakes his coach for that of Cārudatta. When she discovers her grave error she begs to be released. In an unusual act of violence for a Sanskrit play, Saṁsthanāka strangles her and buries her body under a pile of dead leaves. The act ends as a Buddhist friar finds Vasantasenā, revives her and takes her to a Buddhist cloister where she may be attended by the nuns. Determined to pin the blame of Vasantasenā's murder on Cārudatta, Saṁsthanāka brings a court case against him. The judge is inclined to believe Cārudatta until Saṁsthanāka's political pressure and circumstantial evidence seems to point conclusively to Cārudatta's guilt. The mounting gloom of Act IX continues in Act X as Cārudatta is paraded through the streets of the city by his executioners, who proclaim aloud his guilt. In a moment of extreme pathos, Cārudatta's little son begs that he be executed in his father's stead. As Cārudatta is about to be impaled upon the stakes, Vasantasenā enters and saves his life. Like a deux ex machina the thief who stole the jewels from Cārudatta's house enters, having just come from slaying the wicked king and placing Āryaka on the throne. He bears the news that Cārudatta has been made the viceroy of the neighboring city. In a grand gesture of compassion Cārudatta orders the release of Saṁsthanāka, when all the others advise that he be tortured and killed. Cārudatta compassionately says, "When an enemy, however malevolent he may have been, throws himself at your feet and implores your protection, you should not put him to the sword, for the punishment that he deserves is kindness" (Śūdraka 1964, 192–93).

The thief proclaims that Āryaka has released Vasantasenā from her obligations as a courtesan and given her the right to marry Cārudatta. The play ends with the promised union of Cārudatta and Vasantasenā and the restoration of good. It is evident from the brief highlights of the plot that the two main sentiments of the play are love and pathos. However, the play is often thought of as a farce, primarily because of the humorous incidents involving Cārudatta's Brahman friend Maitreya, the townspeople, and servants who appear throughout the story. However, there can be little doubt that the two chief characters in the piece are Cārudatta and Vasantasenā and that the outcome of their love affair is central to the play.

The element which distinguishes this play from all the previous works is conflict. Besides a hero and a heroine, we have a villain, one of the few in all of Sanskrit dramatic literature. Saṁsthanāka is not the totally evil figure that he might have been because he behaves in an utterly ridiculous and absurd manner. He speaks malapropisms throughout the play and confuses classical references to such an extent that a knowledgeable spectator cannot help but laugh when he speaks. To the main characters, however, he is a formidable threat to be reckoned with.

An appealing feature of the play is the use of a courtesan as the heroine. With the exception of the *Cārudattam* of Bhāsa, this is the only serious play in Sanskrit dramatic literature in which a courtesan is a heroine. Vasantasenā is an idealized woman. She is ample testimony that the behavior of an individual's character is not always determined by their occupation. If Vasantasenā behaved according to her occupational role, she should be immoral but instead she is virtuous in much the same way as the other heroines of Sanskrit drama. Indeed, she shines above the creations of Bhāsa, for she has a code of behavior which is antithetical to her occupational role. In Act VI we cannot help but compare Vasantasenā to the jewels which she bestows in the little clay cart. She is the "jewel" inside Saṁsthanāka's cart. Symbolically we are to think of his cart as a thing of clay, a poor thing indeed despite its exterior opulence. By contrast Cārudatta's cart, which is probably designed to reflect his declining fortunes, proves to be a cart of gold in which Āryaka, the "jewel" of the kingdom, hides. Āryaka probably wears the rags and chains of a prisoner, although he is destined to don the robes and ornaments of state. Vasantasenā is eventually bestowed on Cārudatta as a just reward for his high moral character, which stands far above the station to which he has fallen as a result of poverty. Vasantasenā is a fitting partner for him at the triumphant end of this magnificent play.

Kālidāsa

Unquestionably one of India's greatest playwrights is Kālidāsa, whose dates and life are still uncertain. Scholars hold widely differing views about the period in which Kālidāsa lived and worked. There are those who place him as early as 150 B.C., others place him in the late fifth century A.D., a span of more than five hundred years! A widely held belief is that he was one of the nine "jewels" of the court of King Vikramāditya Maurya, who is thought to have reigned around the midfirst century B.C. Keith places Kālidāsa in the early to midfifth century A.D. at the court of Chandragupta II of Ujjain.

Very little is known of this great literary figure. He is thought to have settled in Ujjain, although his work reflects a wide knowledge of Indian geography and familiarity with terrain that one might have acquired only through travel. He is thought to have been a Brahman by caste and a worshipper of Śiva, whom he honors in the benedictions to his plays.

As we have indicated earlier, the poet wrote only three plays. His poetry in these works and in various poetic compositions is justly celebrated. *Śākuntala (Abhijñanaśākuntala)* is regarded as his masterpiece. His other plays, the *Mālavikāgnimitra* and *Vikramurvaṣīya,* are both named after their central characters.

In discussing dramatic composition later in this chapter we will focus our attention on *Śākuntala* and, therefore, not discuss Kālidāsa's other works here.

Bhavabhūti and Later Writers

Bhavabhūti holds a place of honor among the more distinguished playwrights of ancient India. Some scholars go so far as to characterize *The Latter History of Rama (Uttararāmacarita),* his major work, as the best dramatic play of the period. Bhavabhūti wrote three plays in all. His dates are relatively certain, around 700 A.D., and he was probably a member of the court of a North Indian king.

Among the other important playwrights of Sanskrit literature are Harṣa, a king who composed three works about the seventh century A.D., Viśākhadatta, whose *The Minister's Seal (Mudrārākṣasa)* is one of the few decidedly political plays of Sanskrit dramatic literature, and Mahendra Vikrama Varman, a southern king who is credited with composing several short plays with humorous and moral content, also around the seventh century A.D.

Dramatic Composition

The casual reader who examines a Sanskrit play in translation for the first time is likely to be somewhat puzzled by what he finds there, unless he has a reader's guide. In this section I will focus on some of the general characteristics of dramatic composition, including plot, time, place, character, and the purpose of the drama, as well as some special factors, such as a brief examination of fate, duty, illusion, nature, and the language of the play. A consideration of the all-important role of aesthetics in the Sanskrit theatre will be discussed in the next subsection.

As a background, it will be useful to have an illustration around which to focus the discussion. To that end I have chosen to quote extensively from the opening section of Act I of Kālidāsa's *Śākuntala* (1964, 200–201). The play opens as follows:

BENEDICTION

May he whose presence is made manifest
To mortals in these eight embodiments:
The Water, earliest of created things;
The Fire, which, ascending, bears on high
The offering of the holy sacrifice;
The Sun and Moon, distributors of time;

The all-pervading Ether, realm of sound;
The Earth, "producer of all beings" named;
And last the Air, respiring creatures' life; May he, the Lord, be gracious unto you!

PROLOGUE

Stage-Manager (looking toward the scenes). Lady, if you have arranged your costume, please come forward!

Actress (entering). Here I am, sir. Command me. What shall be done?

Stage-Manager. This is for the most part a refined audience, my lady. We must now represent the new play by Kālidāsa called *The Recognition of Śākuntala.* May each actor endeavor to do his best!

Actress. Thanks to your judicious arrangement, sir, nothing will go amiss.

Stage-Manager. I will, good lady, tell you a truth:

> Not till it please enlightened taste
> I find perfection in our art.
> Even those of a commanding skill
> Are unpretending in their heart.

Actress (modestly). That is true. And now command what shall be done.

Stage-Manager. What else than to please this audience by a song.

Actress. Well, then, about which season shall I sing?

Stage-Manager. Sing by all means about this enjoyable summer season just set in. For these are days

> With grateful baths in rippling waves,
> And sylvan breezes carrying on
> The trumpet-flower's fragrant balm,
> And gentle slumbers in the shade,
> And evenings full of sweetest calm.

Actress. I will. (Sings.)

> Fair loving maidens wreathe their heads
> With blossoms of acacia trees,
> Whose slender, graceful pollen threads
> Are gently kissed by humming bees.

Stage-Manager. Charmingly sung, good lady! Look, the entire audience seems like a picture, their souls entranced by your melody. Now then, what play shall we select to preserve their favour?

Actress. Why, surely, we must play the new drama already announced by your honour, *The Recognition of Śākuntala.*
Stage-Manager. I am rightly reminded, good lady. For the moment, indeed, I had forgotten it.

Transported was my soul with force
By the enchanting melody of your song,
As King Duṣyanta here is lured
By that swift-speeding deer along.
(Exeunt)

(Kālidāsa 1964, 200–201)

Opening Verse and Prologue

Just prior to the main body of *Śākuntala,* and for that matter most Sanskrit plays, there is a short benediction and a prologue. The benediction is composed in verse to honor a deity, Brahman, king, or the like. The prologue usually praises the audience, announces the name of the play and its author, and gives details regarding the content of the work. Obviously the benediction and the prologue serve both a ritual and a practical function. The benediction adds a touch of formality and sanctity necessary to insure that the evil eye is not cast on the proceedings. The information that the stage manager imparts takes the place of some of the essential information found in modern theatre programs. It usually sets the tone for the opening scene and thus is vital to the work. It serves as a bridge between the world of the audience and the world of the play. By having a more important member of the acting company, and not one of the characters of the play, address the audience directly, as a storyteller might do, the two worlds are linked, making the theatre event special and distinct from everyday life.

Preliminaries

According to the *Nāṭyaśāstra,* the benediction and prologue are features of a much more extensive set of introductory items. It may be that the procedures outlined in the *Nāṭyaśāstra* were no longer in vogue when many of the important plays were composed or that some authors took great liberty with the rules and composed prologues according to their own needs. Whatever the case, chapter five lists eighteen different stages of preliminaries (*pūrvarañga,* which literally means "before the stage"). The first nine were to be executed on the stage behind a curtain. Each had as its objective to gain the favor of some deity or other. The nine steps are:

1. Arrangement of musical instruments.
2. The singers enter and take their seats.

3. Beginning of vocal exercises.
4. Adjustment of musical instruments.
5. Rehearsal of the different styles of playing.
6. Adjustment of the stringed instruments.
7. The dancers enter and rehearse.
8. The drums and strings are played in unison.
9. Complicated rhythmic passages are practiced.

After a curtain was removed the remaining preliminary items were executed.

10. Songs are sung in praise of the gods.
11. The stage manager raises the banner pole of Indra.

According to the *Nāṭyaśāstra,* this "is considered by some to be the beginning (of the performance)" (Ghosh 1967, 79).

12. The stage manager walks around the stage and offers praise to the guardian deities of the stage.
13. The benediction is recited.
14. The meaning of this item is unclear in the text. Keith believes that it was the recitation by the stage manager of a verse in honor of the god, king, or Brahman whose festival was being celebrated (Keith 1924, 339–340).
15. Keith also explains this item as "the beginning of the dramatic action *(abhinaya),* the Sūtradhāra reciting another verse and bowing before the banner of Indra" (339–340).
16. Patterns of movement are performed depicting the erotic and then the furious sentiment. [Perhaps this indicates the performance of dance movement which are predominately female *(lāsya)* and male *(tāṇḍava)* in character.]
17. Then a conversation ensues between the stage manager, the clown, and the attendant which is referred to as the three men's talk.
18. Finally, the stage manager announces the content of the drama and appeals for its success, after which he makes an exit and brings the preliminaries to a close.

Objectives

It would seem that several objectives were served by the lengthy preliminaries. First, they provided the musicians with an opportunity to tune their instruments and warm up before the show began. For the dancers it offered an opportunity to practice their dances and gestures. Second, once the curtain was removed the formal songs and dances in praise of the deities were sung in accordance with the general ritual character of the event. Third, the stage manager could offer praise to the banner pole of Indra, which symbolically protected the actors from harm. He begged protection from various gods and thus sanctified the acting area. Fourth, speech began to assume greater importance than physical action and music in the events, and the preliminaries blend into the prologue which serves as the final bridge into the beginning of the drama proper. The *Nāṭyaśāstra* even makes provisions for truncating the preliminaries and also expanding them, which suggests that the author was aware of a need to make compromises to suit any occasion.

Types of Plays

The *Nāṭyaśāstra* identifies ten major types of plays: *nāṭakā, prakaraṇa, aṅka, vyāyoga, bhāṇa, saṃvakāra, vīthī, prahasana, ḍima,* and *īhāmṛga.* This list is apparently not exhaustive, for other ancient writers mention the existence of additional dramatic types. Ten so-called minor *(uparūpaka)* types of drama are discussed in the ancient literature, although the *Nāṭyaśāstra* mentions only one of these in passing. It would seem that there was a wide range of dramatic types within which a writer might choose to compose a play. Yet the *Nāṭyaśāstra* chooses to focus almost exclusively on two of the ten types—the *nāṭaka* and *prakaraṇa.* A number of *nāṭaka* and only two *prakaraṇa* survive to aid us in understanding the differences between these two important dramatic types. Among the extant *nāṭaka* are three of the finest examples of Sanskrit drama—Bhavabhūti's *The Latter History of Rāma,* Bhāsa's *The Vision of Vāsavadattā,* and the play under discussion here, Kālidāsa's *Śākuntala.*

The chief characteristics of the *nāṭaka* are that it has as its subject matter a well-known story concerning the exploits of a hero who is either a royal sage or a king; the dominant sentiment of the work should be either love or heroism; and the extant *nāṭaka* normally have no fewer than five and no more than seven acts each. In contrast the *prakaraṇa,* of which *The Little Clay Cart* is the finest example, has a story which is invented by the author, a hero who is either a Brahman, a minister, or a merchant, a heroine who is a courtesan, and the sentiment of love predominates. The *prakaraṇa* should have no less than five and no more than ten acts.

As a prelude to the following discussion, it is useful to have a point of reference. Therefore nearly half of Act I of *Śākuntala* is quoted here from Edgren's translation (Kālidāsa 1964, 201–05):

ACT FIRST

Scene-A forest

King Duṣyanta, with bow and arrow in his hand pursuing an antelope, appears with his Driver in a chariot.

CHARIOTEER (looking at the King and the deer).

When I behold, great king, yourself
With well-strung bow, and that black deer,
I think I see the bow-armed god,
As he pursued the deer, revealed.

KING. We have drawn far away, my charioteer, by that antelope. See him now.

With graceful curving of his neck,
He gazes on the chasing car,
And, to escape the falling dart,
Contracts his frame with shrinking dread.
His path is strewn with half-chewed grass
That drips from his wide-gaping mouth.
Look, by his bounding, in the air
Far more than on the earth he flies! (Amazed.)
What now! Though I follow closely I hardly can see the antelope.

CHARIOTEER. Sire, the ground is very uneven; I have drawn the rein and slackened the speed of the chariot. So the antelope has left us behind. But now that you are on level ground he will easily be overtaken.

KING. Slacken the reins, then!

CHARIOTEER. As Your Grace commands. (Drives the chariot at full speed.) My prince,

Behold again, with slackened rein,
Incited by the speeding deer,
Untouched even by the floating dust
Which they themselves have raised,
The chariot horses dash along,
Their necks with eager vying stretched,
Their cresting plumelets floating stiff,
Their ears erect and motionless.

KING (joyously). Indeed, these spirited horses excel even Indra's steeds and the sun's.

What to my view appeared as small
Suddenly grows to magnitude;
What was divided into two
Seems blending fast into one whole;
What was uneven in its form
Turns to my gaze a perfect line;
So swift the car nothing appears
An instant even, far nor near.

Charioteer, now see how the deer will be laid low!

A VOICE (behind the scenes). King! King! this antelope belongs to the hermitage. Do not kill him! Do not kill him!

CHARIOTEER (listening and looking). Noble prince, some hermits have indeed thrown themselves between that black antelope and your arrow.

KING (hastily). Check the horses, then!

CHARIOTEER. It's done. (Stopping the chariot. Enter a Hermit followed by two others.)

HERMIT (raising his hand). O King, pray, do not kill this antelope, which belongs to the hermitage!

> No, no, let not your arrow strike
> The tender body of this deer
> As a spark falls on softest down!
> How is that right, his gentle life
> And your sharp, adamantine dart?
> Then, pray, withhold your well-aimed shaft.
> Your weapon should defend the weak
> And not assail the innocent.

KING. It is withdrawn! (Replacing the arrow into its quiver.)

HERMIT. This action is worthy of a prince, the light of Puru's race.

> Yes, it befits you well, indeed,
> You scion of a noble race!
> Your guerdon be a virtuous son,
> The mighty ruler of a world!

THE OTHER TWO HERMITS (raising their hands). Yes, may you be rewarded with a world-commanding son!

KING (bowing). Your benediction is reverently received.

HERMIT. Noble prince, we are here to gather fuel. There, on the banks of the Malini, you can see the hermitage of Kaṇva, the great saint. If you are not prevented by other duties, enter and accept our hospitable attention. And then,

> When you have seen the pleasing rites
> That unmolested hermits perform there,
> You must know how well your arm,
> That arm with bowstring marks, protects.

KING. Is the head of your community now at home?

HERMIT. For the present, indeed, he is on a pilgrimage to Soma-tirtha to propitiate Destiny, turned inauspicious to his daughter Śākuntala. But in the meantime he has enjoined on her the functions of hospitality.

KING. Good! I will see her. When she has learned my veneration for the great saint, she will report my homage.

HERMIT. Then we will complete our task. (Exit with companions.)

KING. Charioteer, urge the horses on. We will purify ourselves by the view of this sacred hermitage.

CHARIOTEER. As Your Majesty commands. (Drives the chariot rapidly.)

KING (looking around). It is evident, even without being told, that these are the precincts of a sacred grove.

CHARIOTEER. How so?

KING. Why, just observe

The rice is strewn below the trees
From hollow trunks that parrots fill;
There lie the oily stones that serve
To bruise the fruit of Ingudi;
The antelopes, taught here to trust,
Unstartled hear the human voice;
And fountain paths are marked by lines
Of falling drops from clothes of bark.

And see:

The rootlets of the trees are laved
By waters trembling in the breeze;
Their budding splendor is obscured
By smoke from sacrificial oil;
And slowly the confiding fawns
Roam near by on the well-mown lawns.

CHARIOTEER. All is as you say.

KING (after a short advance). Let us not disturb the dwellers of this hermit grove. Stop the chariot so that I may alight.

CHARIOTEER. The reins are drawn in. Your Majesty may descend.

KING (alighting). On entering a penance grove it is right, my charioteer, to lay aside all ornament. So take this. (Reaching him his bow and ornaments.) Until I return from visiting the dwellers of this hermitage, see that the horses are refreshed.

CHARIOTEER. It shall be done. (Exit.)

KING (walking and looking around.) Here is the gate of the hermitage. Well, then, I will enter. (Entering. Evincing a tremour of the right arm.)

This hermit home is placid, calm,
Yet my arm feels a sudden throb.
What can it mean? Ah, everywhere,
The Gates of Things To Be are found.

VOICE (behind the scenes). Here, this way, my friends!

KING (listening). I hear a conversation to the right of that grove. I must go there. (Walking on and looking about.) Ah, there some hermit maidens are approaching to sprinkle the young shrubs from watering pots suited to their strength. (Gazing at them.) Their appearance is indeed charming!

If hermit maidens' forms like these
In queenly halls are rarely seen,
It is because the forest vines
Excel the garden vines in charm.

I will conceal myself in that shade and watch them.

(Enter Śākuntala with two friends, employed in the manner described.)

ŚĀKUNTALA. Here, this way, my friends!

ANASŪYĀ. Dear Śākuntala, I think father Kaṇva must love these hermitage shrubs even more than yourself. How else could he enjoin on you, yourself as delicate as the fresh-blown jasmine flower, to fill their trenches with water?

ŚĀKUNTALA. Dear Anasūyā, it is, indeed, not only by my father's command I do this task. I feel a sisterly love for these plants. (Watering the shrubs.)

KING. How? Is she the daughter of Kaṇva? That venerable descendant of Kaśyapa does not appear very wise in imposing on her the rigorous duties of a hermitage.

The saint who would to penance train
This lovely, charming, guileless form
Indeed attempts to cut the stem
Of an acacia with the edge
Of only a blue lotus leaf.

Well, concealed among these trees, I can see her without rousing her suspicion.

Composition

The smallest unit of composition of any play is an act *(aṅka)*. The *Nāṭyaśāstra* lays down numerous rules which govern the composition of acts of plays (Ghosh 1967, 344). For example, an act should portray the change in the hero's basic situation and thus cause the plot to develop. It is made up of a series of incidents directly related to the exploits of the hero, heroine, or a person of similar importance and not to the minor characters. Certain events should not be depicted, such as the pronouncement of a curse, a marriage ceremony, a battle, loss of a kingdom, or death. The *Nāṭyaśāstra* goes on to say that "a wise playwright should not put in (too) many events in one act" (Ghosh 1967, 356).

By putting restrictions on the events that may be depicted in the drama, the rulemakers forced the playwrights to focus on scenes which at first glance seem inconsequential or even trivial. The first three acts of *Śākuntala* are a case in point. In Act I the king meets and instantly falls in love with Śākuntala, learns that she is a suitable match for him and determines to win her for his bride. In Act II he reasserts his determination to remain at the hermitage in order to wed Śākuntala, despite pressing business at the palace. In Act III, the high point of this part of the play, the king secretly overhears Śākuntala imply that she loves him. By the end of the act we assume that they will be married, although she makes no promises to him. In contrast the events that happen between Act III and Act IV are of major consequence—Śākuntala and Duṣyanta are married by mutual consent; she becomes pregnant; he departs for the city and her foster father returns to the hermitage, approves of her marriage and determines to send her to the palace where he assumes she will become queen. In the first three acts the playwright has chosen to focus on seemingly minor incidents in the lives of the chief characters and only mentions the major events in the prologue to Act IV. In Sanskrit drama the plot usually stresses the means to the end rather than the end itself. In *Śākuntala* Kālidāsa is more interested in showing the subtle and delicate human emotions of the central characters.

Plot

According to the *Nāṭyaśāstra* the principal objective of the plot is to show the hero struggling for and finally attaining the object of his desire. Subsidiary incidents may contribute to this aim but should not divert attention from it. The realization of the goal relates to the three ends of Hindu life—duty, pleasure, and wealth.

The plot or subject matter is regarded as the "body" of the drama (Ghosh 1967, 355). The anthropomorphic analogy is extended throughout the discussion of this subject. To begin with there are five stages in the development of the action. The first or "beginning" stage refers to the planting of a seed or germ—the desire on the part of the hero to obtain his objective. In *Śākuntala* the king's objective is to wed Śākuntala and to get an heir to his throne. Both of these goals are clearly implied in the excerpt quoted from Act I. Second, there is a determined effort to achieve the object of desire. Duṣyanta's determination in Act II clearly exemplifies his desire to take Śākuntala as his wife. Third, there is hope of success. In Act III Duṣyanta is confident of winning Śākuntala, although she does not commit herself to fulfilling his wishes. Fourth, success is assured if only a difficulty may be overcome. In Acts IV, V, and VI Duṣyanta's original desires are thwarted and delayed. In Act IV we learn that Śākuntala is cursed to be forgotten by the king. In Act V, as a result of the curse, he does not recognize her when she comes to court and in her humiliation she is whisked away by a heavenly nymph to an undisclosed sanctuary. In Act VI, when the king's keepsake ring that he gave Śākuntala in the hermitage is found, his memory is immediately restored and he bemoans the loss of his beloved. The fifth stage in the development of the action occurs when the hero attains the object of his desire. In the final act of *Śākuntala,* Duṣyanta is reunited with Śākuntala and discovers that he is the father of a fine son and heir to the throne.

Corresponding to the five stages of the action are five elements. The first and principal element is the seed. After the seed is planted the incidents expand like a drop of oil on water (Ghosh 1967, 355 and 381). It is this step which sustains the continuity of the action throughout the play. Step three is

Final scene of *Śākuntala* produced by the Goa Hindu Association of Bombay in 1985. (Rajdatt Arts Photos)

the intervention of the major subplot and step four is that of the minor subplot. Step five is the denouement in which one of the three objectives of human existence is achieved.

Resulting from the conjunctions of the five stages with the five elements are junctures or links in the plot. The *Nāṭyaśāstra* makes clear that these do not necessarily coincide with a single act but may well overlap several acts. The junctures are: (1) opening, (2) progression, (3) development, (4) pause, or a stage in which the hero deliberates the seed, his desire, and (5) conclusion. The last juncture corresponds to the state of release from pleasure and pain by union of the individual soul with the divine soul. Each of the segments has corresponding limbs without which the play is said to be "unfit for production" (Ghosh 1967, 386). Details regarding the manner in which these are to be employed are wanting in the text. In general it is fair to say that each limb relates to some action or emotion of the hero in each of the stages of the junctures.

The profusion of details regarding the plot of a *nāṭakā* or *prakaraṇa* may seem unnecessarily confusing. But in essence the approach is simple. Sanskrit plays of these two major types were to be created with a definite end in mind. This end was to satisfy the fulfillment of a desire of a hero or chief character in the piece and, by association, his counterpart, the heroine. The play was to end happily, as one of the limbs of the concluding junctures implies. There is no place here for plays which raise controversies that cannot be resolved or that leave the mind disturbed at the end. The process by which the hero attains the object of his desire is steady, starting gradually and progressing rapidly to the conclusion. Unnecessary diversions have no place in Sanskrit plays. Only those diversions which relate in some way to the principal plot are admitted. Rules for the formation of the plot are far more specific in the *Nāṭyaśāstra* than those outlined by Aristotle for Greek drama. This specificity might well have resulted in works which were cold, calculated, and uninteresting, but for nearly a thousand years writers came to grips with the rules and, in many cases, managed to write original and sometimes brilliant theatre fare.

Time

The *Nāṭyaśāstra* clearly states that the events of an act should take place in the course of a single day. But obviously some events take longer than twenty-four hours to complete and are of such magnitude (battles, for example) that they demand accommodation be made for them in the drama. The Sanskrit playwright was given considerable latitude to digress, through a clever device, the introductory scene. Minor or secondary characters, for example, maidservants or the clown, may report the events which have intervened between the previous act and the events that are about to take place, and in this way compress time and avoid depicting subjects which are taboo and, at the same time, make use of them for furthering the dramatic action (Ghosh 1967, 357–58).

Time is often compressed radically within an act. An act may begin at sunrise and end at sunset. Also actions which would normally take a great deal of time to complete in real life, such as the plaiting of a garland, are accomplished in record time on stage. Coupled with the conventional changes of locales, both time and space assumed broad theatrical significance.

Place

Unlike the rules that were laid down for neoclassical French and English drama, rules for establishing and changing locales in a Sanskrit play were quite flexible and conventionalized. An act might begin in one spot and simply by performing a symbolic movement, such as walking around, the actors indicated that they had moved to another locale. The excerpt just quoted from *Śākuntala* contains numerous transitions of locale. At the beginning of the play, the king and his charioteer are traveling in the sky on a magic chariot in pursuit of a deer. The description of the landscape below during the chase, and perhaps some conventional movements, help the spectators to imagine the rapid change of place. Suddenly they halt outside the hermitage compound, where the king agrees not to kill the helpless creature which has taken refuge within. It is presumed that the spectators have to imagine the boundaries of the compound. This section of the scene ends as the king commands the charioteer to enter the hermitage. As the act proceeds the locale becomes even more specific until finally we end with the king in a particular spot in the hermitage garden engaged in conversation with the friends of Śākuntala. So we have moved from a broad generalized locale in the air to a very specific locale on the hermitage, all in the space of one short act. Sanskrit playwrights were fond of using this convention of changing locales to further the aim of the play. As we have noted earlier the stage seems to have been regarded as a neutral acting area and given symbolic significance through dialogue and conventional actions—the ancient equivalent to the focusing techniques used in cinema.

Character

In the Sanskrit plays, most characters are types: the just, powerful, handsome, benevolent hero and his equivalent, the beautiful and virtuous heroine; the witty, proverbially hungry clown-companion; trusted and loyal ministers; charming and witty servants; and so on. In *The Little Clay Cart,* there are a host of rogues, wags, a foolish villain, an intimidated judge, a doting mother, a reformed gambler turned Buddhist monk, a thief turned patriotic reformer—all somewhat unusual in the cadre of characters of the major plays. Character portrayal in Sanskrit drama is not based on realism but on the presentation of universal characteristics, emphasizing the typical. This sets Sanskrit theatre apart from much of Western theatre, in which characters are prized for their individuality of spirit and uniqueness of personality, such as Hamlet, Macbeth, Oedipus, or Hedda Gabler.

The tradition of using character types in the theatre may be understood within the framework of three traditions: the literary, the social, and the theatrical. The literary tradition stems principally from the epics, such as the *Rāmāyaṇa* and *Mahābhārata,* and from books of law and those dealing with social behavior. In the epics, characters such as Rāma and Arjuna are idealized. They exhibit certain superhuman character traits. Indeed Rāma is the god Viṣṇu reincarnated in the image of a man. Their regard for propriety and strict codes of behavior in given situations easily marks them as idealized heroic types. They are more alike than they are dissimilar. According to the law books and codes of social behavior, men of certain rank and station in life were expected to behave in a particular way; to do otherwise would be improper, unthinkable. The ritual of social behavior seems to have stemmed from the original separation of men into occupation groups—priests, warriors, tradesmen, and peasants. Each group had particular duties to fulfill and a particular behavior pattern was expected of men in these categories. Perhaps the priests had the most rigid taboos surrounding their daily existence and, as such, refrained from certain social interactions and participated in sacred acts which would be unthinkable for those at the other levels of society.

The broad patterns of behavior are clearly seen in the drama. Despite the caricature of the clown-priest who is the sidekick of the hero, he is always treated with the utmost respect by all those who owe deference to him. The duty of the warrior-hero, such as Duṣyanta, is to protect the Brahmans so that they may make sacrifices to the gods, acts which symbolically sustain the life and power of the heavenly beings. The gods are weakened when offerings cannot be made to them by the Brahmans and thus evil is permitted to gain the upper hand on earth. The social order is sustained when members of every caste fulfill their correct social function. To do otherwise would weaken the social order and wreck the system.

One may well ask, "How does this system permit creativity and individual expression?" In many instances the playwrights have succumbed to slavish perpetuation of the rules of the *Nāṭyaśāstra,* producing lifeless characters. But a number of characters are subtle, fresh, and very much alive. We might even describe them as three dimensional. Śākuntala is one of those. When we first meet her she is a child of nature. Her swelling bosom proclaims that she is a maiden on the verge of blossoming into a charming young woman.

It is this sweetness and innocence that initially attracts Duṣyanta to her. She exchanges no words with her suitor during their first encounter, yet her glances give him hope that she is equally attracted to him. In Act III in the flower arbor she freely and playfully confides to her friends that she is attracted to the king and yet she shyly withdraws into silence when he comes out of hiding and protests his love for her. Here she is growing more daring and on the verge of maturing into a woman. The end of the act is a virtual repeat of the end of Act I when she delays her departure in order to steal a glimpse of the king, confirming that she is attracted to him. In Act IV, generally regarded as the best act of the play by Indian and Western critics alike and some say the most beautiful act of all Sanskrit dramatic literature, Śākuntala must part from all that she loves in the forest hermitage—the plants, deer, her childhood friends, her foster father. She must venture out into the world, to the sophisticated court where she expects her husband to receive her as his wife and queen. The pathos of this act of parting is a high point of the play and offers the spectators an insight into another side of this innocent, trusting girl. When she is rejected in Act V, her retorts and tears give us yet another side of her. In Act VI she is reported to be emaciated with grief, longing for her beloved Duṣyanta who unwittingly has deceived her. When we meet her again in the final act, she is mature, the mother of a handsome and proud little son. Her tenderness and humility are still intact. But she has made a transition from that of a playful, innocent forest dweller to a mature woman, devoted to her husband and their child.

In the personality of Śākuntala, Kālidāsa has painted one of the most striking portrayals of womanhood in all of Indian literature. Certainly he has conformed to the rules of character development outlined in the *Nāṭyaśāstra,* but the character of Śākuntala is imaginatively and creatively constructed by a master, of that there may be no doubt.

Purpose of Drama

Given the multitude of theatrical conventions and character types it is doubtful that Sanskrit theatre was meant to be a reflection of life in ancient India. Rather it was a model of human behavior and in this it served a very definite educational function. To us today there is a great deal to be learned about Indian civilization by examining the plays of this culture. It gives us a perspective of the pervading views of Hindu philosophy and religion, and to some degree those of Buddhism. It tells us a great deal about human behavior and social interaction. The values and mores of the culture are encapsulated in the plays and should be carefully scrutinized for what they teach us about ancient Indian life, and even for what they say about the continuity between ancient and modern life.

When approaching the plays it is well to remember that the wider the students read the better the plays will fit into their cultural framework. A quick reading cannot do justice to intricacies of customs, philosophies, and behavior radically different from our own. Indian drama, like Indian literature in general, has many complicated and subtle nuances. Probing the poetry, epics, and law books of ancient India will inevitably lead to a more comprehensive grasp of the place of drama within the whole fabric of the social setting.

Fate, Duty, Illusion, and Nature

A word or two must be said about several important features of the plays which characterize them as uniquely Indian. In the plays, people are but part of a larger universal order. An individual plays an important part, but when he or she neglects some duty the system is threatened. In *Śākuntala* all seems well at the end of Act III. Śākuntala and Duṣyanta seem destined to lead a long and happy life together. And yet Śākuntala makes one small error. In the prologue to Act IV, her friends report that she has been so engrossed in thinking of her absent lover that she neglects to offer the proper respects to a hotheaded sage who comes as a guest to the hermitage. He curses her to forget the person of whom she is thinking. Not realizing the consequences of her oversight, Śākuntala is doomed to spend many long years away from her beloved.

Fate thus plays a significant role in *Śākuntala* and in most Sanskrit plays. Usually in the opening act we are specifically told, or at least it is alluded to, that the object of desire will be achieved at the end of the play. During the path to the goal, however, the hero and the heroine usually experience some setback, often separation. This tests their love and devotion to each other. And after a period of suffering, the system returns to normal, the wheel of fortune completes its revolution. In our excerpt from Act I of *Śākuntala,* Duṣyanta is blessed by the hermits to have a son who is destined to be a universal ruler. Often the prophesy of success is foretold in this manner.

The characters then are ruled by duty—duty to their people, to their caste obligations, to their social obligations. By neglecting her duty to show utmost respect to a prominent sage, Śākuntala is fated to be punished. The social contract is so great that the slightest infringement of it will bring about serious consequences. The plays seem to have been written to demonstrate the virtue of performing one's duty properly.

The characters are often beset by maya, or illusion. Like the concept of duty, this term is a great deal more complicated to explain than we may allow space for here. However, on a very simple level, maya refers to the notion that the temporal world seems to be permanent, and yet we know that it is constantly changing. The tree that was a sapling yesterday will be a powerful banyan tomorrow and is eventually destined to die or be destroyed. Nothing ever remains the same. Nothing is permanent. People, then, are caught in the eternal web of illusion, thinking they are permanent, when in fact they are constantly changing.

There is a charming illustration of the effects of maya in Act I of *Śākuntala,* when the king chases a bee away from Śākuntala's face. The bee is reported to treat Śākuntala as though she were a flower. The king wishes he were the bee that he might taste the sweet nectar of her loveliness. In Act VI, a picture of the incident is shown to the king and he immediately thinks that the incident depicted in the painting is just happening. He addresses the painted bee as though it were a real bee actually attacking Śākuntala. His companion points out that this is only a picture and that he has temporarily lost his sense of reality. Indeed, the king suffers from maya. He also does so when he forgets Śākuntala as a result of the curse, but with far more serious consequences. The plays then are a subtle example of the workings of maya in the world. The only absolute reality, according to Hindu philosophy, is God who is permanent and who dreams the world. We are but figures in God's dreams.

Finally a word must be said about nature. In *Śākuntala* nature plays a very important part. The hermitage is vividly portrayed. Śākuntala's relationships with the plants, which are as much alive to her as her beloved animals and birds and the people of this idyllic spot, suggest that humans and nature are one and inseparable. It is no accident that Duṣyanta meets Śākuntala and is reunited with her in a hermitage. Śākuntala's haven in the final act is none other than the home of the mother and father of the gods. Court life, city life in general, seems a great deal more contrived and artificial in the plays than does the life in the pleasure gardens of the palace or the hermitages of the forest. Sanskrit theatre paints a vivid picture of the intimate relationship between people and nature, one that places it firmly within the great traditions of dramatic literature of other Asian cultures.

Language

The example taken from *Śākuntala* is typical of Sanskrit plays, in general. Verses are mixed with prose passages. Critics have acknowledged that some of the most beautiful passages of Sanskrit literature are found in the drama, and several passages of *Śākuntala* and *The Little Clay Cart* serve as excellent examples.

It is impossible for a layman to understand much about the subtlety of the Sanskrit language from an English translation, however. Sanskrit is a telegraphic language, full of innuendo. Compressed into a short passage are a multitude of ideas and meanings which are not always possible to translate into another language. Translations cannot distinguish between the levels of Sanskrit spoken by the different characters, nor may we see the fine distinctions between the Prakrits spoken by the heroine and the lofty Sanskrit of the hero. Translations are not capable of rendering the subtle differences among the various regional languages and dialects that must have made Sanskrit theatre a great pleasure and an intellectually challenging art to the ears of ancient listeners.

Aesthetics

The *Nāṭyaśāstra* outlines a theory of theatre performance that is an original contribution to the field of aesthetics and a major distinguishing feature that separates Indian theatre from all other forms of world theatre. Initially it was applied to theatre performance and subsequently it was borrowed and applied to dramatic literature and expanded to include other forms of Sanskrit literature and other performing arts, as well. Although seemingly simple in its basic outline, it is deceptively so, for critics from a very early date up to the present age have wrestled with the precise meaning of the major terms of the theory and the import of their application.

The theory of *rasa,* or sentiment, attempts to explain how a spectator perceives the performance of a play. This can only be accomplished when he or she interprets what is seen, as well as what is heard and responds to both stimuli as one composite whole. As we have seen earlier, the *Nāṭyaśāstra* emphasizes that a performance may best be understood in its proper context by those who are learned, wise, skilled in the arts, and sensitive. We have also noted that theatre appears to have been designed for the elite few rather than for the masses. At one point in the text, the aesthetic experience is equated with that of tasting and eating fine foods. Indeed, some scholars have translated *rasa* as "taste." Let us examine this analogy for a moment.

In France haute cuisine is regarded as a high point of cultural experience, engaged in by experts. The permutation and combination of delicately flavored dishes sensitively presented in an appropriate atmosphere is said to delight expert palates, gently leading them through a gastronomical garden of delights to the ultimate conclusion of a meal. The experience is tantamount to a state of exaltation. There are two separate aspects of this aesthetic journey which are intertwined and yet may be viewed separately—the meal itself and the context in which it is served. On the one hand, dishes are chosen to complement and contrast with each other, each dish is prepared with the correct ingredients, combined with care by an expert chef, and presented in a manner which is appealing and conventional. On the other hand, major contributing factors to the total experience are the environment, mood of the participant, time, and place. All these conspire to influence the outcome of the gastronomical event.

The meal is savored by a connoisseur who recognizes the difference between haute cuisine prepared by an expert chef, served in a quiet dining room of a four star restaurant on a quiet summer evening with friends, and meat and potatoes dished up by a harried cook in a steamy kitchen on a Saturday night.

If we equate the theatre experience described in the *Nāṭyaśāstra* to that of an expert dining on haute cuisine, we may more easily follow the basic aspects of the theory. The spectators are like the connoisseurs of cooked food (called bhaktas, literally the "devotees" of god) and the performers may be equated both with the chef and the meal. The actors, musicians, dancers, playwrights, and other functionaries are all expected to prepare and train themselves according to the rules and conventions, for the moment when they will offer their lavish feast for the spectators to savor. Like the priests who officiate at the temple sacrifices, the performers are obliged to perform with seriousness and care so that they do not cause the evil eye to be cast on the whole affair, spoiling and polluting the proceedings and causing the judicious to find fault. In this respect, the theatre event was no ordinary event but a special occasion. It was expected that it would be executed on a very high plane, in a similar vein to that of a religious sacrifice.

The *Nāṭyaśāstra* divides human experience into eight basic sentiments: erotic, comic, pathetic, furious, heroic, terrible, odious, and marvelous. It is these which the spectators savor in various permutations and combinations as they observe the work in performance. And yet to give focus to the experience, just as a meal has a dominant flavor, one sentiment should dominate all others in the total context of the performance. The most common dominant sentiment of the extant plays is love. And yet all the plays, even the short one-act works, employ varieties of feelings and emotions which provide the needed variety and texture.

Corresponding to the eight sentiments are eight emotions or feelings *(bhāva)*. They are expressed by the actor in the process of laying his or her bouquet of experiences derived from the play before the spectators. They are correspondingly love, mirth, anger, sorrow, energy, terror, disgust, and astonishment.

In addition there are thirty-three transitory feelings: despondency, weakness, apprehension, envy, intoxication, weariness, indolence, depression, anxiety, distraction, recollection, contentment, shame, inconstancy, joy, agitation, stupor, arrogance, despair, impatience, sleep, epilepsy, dreaming, awakening, indignation, dissimulation, cruelty, assurance, sickness, insanity, death, fright, and deliberation. And eight *sāttvika* states (although the exact meaning of the word has not yet been satisfactorily translated into English, we have used both "emotion" and "feeling," as a definition elsewhere in this chapter) which are paralysis, perspiration, horripilation, change of voice, trembling, change of color, weeping, and fainting. This makes forty-nine different feelings in all. However, the *Nāṭyaśāstra* clearly states that "just as a king is superior to other men, and the preceptor is superior to his disciples, so the *bhāva* are superior to the transitory and *sāttvika* states" (Ghosh 1967, 122).

The emotions are perceived by the spectators in the actors and evoke a corresponding sentiment in the spectators. At one point in the *Nāṭyaśāstra,* the emotions and sentiments seem to refer to the same thing. Indeed it is somewhat difficult to distinguish between them.

It is said that every play has a dominant emotion just as it has a dominant sentiment. The dominant emotion may be easily determined by the expert spectator (or reader) from among various transitory feelings, for a play performed with only one emotion would be like consuming a meal in which all the food tasted exactly the same.

It is said an actor produces an emotion and causes a sentiment to be perceived through the union of the determinants, the consequents, and the transitory feelings. Perhaps this may be best understood by citing a simple illustration. Rāma, the epic hero of the *Rāmāyaṇa,* acts as though he sees the beauty of the forest (determinant) which causes his eyes to widen and his shoulders to tremble with pleasure (consequent). He stands stunned and overjoyed (transitory feeling). Thus the actor portrays this emotion of astonishment. If the actor has portrayed the emotion correctly and with feeling, the experienced and sensitive spectator will savor the sentiment of wonder.

Within the context of an act of a play this example may be but a tiny part of a much broader pattern in which wonder becomes a minor factor. Indeed, the act of the play from which the illustration was taken emphasizes the dominant emotion of love. And the entire work lays particular stress on astonishment *(vismaya).*

According to the dramatic theory, the play is always the touchstone of the actor's portrayal, and the character will dictate to what extent the actor should depict the emotions of the play and the general rules governing his preparation. It would seem that the system just outlined leaves virtually nothing to chance. In actuality a great deal of latitude is provided. Obviously not all actors are equally capable of portraying emotions. Some are brilliant technicians but lack a well-developed ability to portray emotions. Others are highly emotional but lack the skill and technique to depict feelings within the framework of a set of rules and conventions. There are others who are both brilliant in their craft and artists. If the *Nāṭyaśāstra* served as the actor's text, it is safe to assume that ancient Indian performers possessed at least an adequate set of conventional techniques, even if they lacked the necessary emotional base to lift the performance from the ordinary to the sublime. In this regard, the theory of sentiment is a practical guide to a performer in developing his or her craft, as well as being a useful tool in realizing the maximum potential of the art.

Decline of Sanskrit Theatre

The decline of Sanskrit drama cannot be attributed to any one cause but to a combination of factors. It is certain that it did not die suddenly. The signs of decay are evident as early as the ninth century, and it is generally believed that the tenth century marks the end of the Sanskrit theatre as a creative force in Indian theatre. In practice its influence is still being felt, as we shall see at various points in the remainder of this book. A major factor in its decline may be the successive invasions of Mahmud of Ghazni and successive waves of invasions of other plunderers from kingdoms to the west of India. At this time India was divided into small princely states, each vying with the other for supremacy. The armies of Ghazni were well organized and tactically superior to those of the kings of the subcontinent, and so the old court life of Hindu India began to crumble under the pressure of warrior lords that plundered, looted, sacked, and razed cities and temples with only one objective in mind—to confiscate the wealth of India.

By one scenario, during these harsh times courts and temples could ill afford the luxury of supporting the performance of a Sanskrit play, so this put the actors on foot trying to eke out a living by touring from village to village. But there too they met with little success, for Sanskrit was not a language that was widely spoken by the people of the rural areas. Except for the Brahman priests very few people outside the courts could understand the texts of the plays. The players had very few options—either they reverted to performing in a regional language of the locality or they gave up their hereditary occupation. The practice of performing Sanskrit plays was doomed to disappear over a period of centuries, in all but a few isolated pockets around the country.

Another reason for the decline of Sanskrit drama lay in the trends in composition which appear as early as the plays of Bhāsa. Greater and greater emphasis was placed on the poetry and less and less on the dramatic action and the dialogue. Kālidāsa and later poets, especially Bhavabhūti, laid heavy stress on the lyrics, often at the expense of the progress of the story. This made the works seem more like long poems than plays. Strict adherence to the rules of the *Nāṭyaśāstra* also may have contributed to the downfall of this form of aesthetic expression.

It is rare that talented individuals had the imagination and the daring to create plays outside the strict rules. True, the rules often served merely as guidelines but when critics were harsh to judge the merits of a play according to the rules, the playwrights must have succumbed to authority and composed according to form to win approval.

Thus, a form of theatre which represents a high water mark in the history of world theatre began to pass from the scene. In the next chapter I shall examine at some length a form of theatre that preserves the essence of the ancient drama, the *kūṭiyāṭṭam* of Kerala.

WORKS CITED

Bharata. 1967, 1961.
Nāṭyaśāstra. Trans. and ed. Manmohan Ghosh. 2nd rev. ed. Vol. 1. Calcutta: Manisha Granthalaya, 1967; and Vol. 2. Calcutta: Asiatic Society, 1961.

Kālidāsa. 1964.
Śākuntala, or the Recovered Ring. Trans. A. Hjalmar Edgren. In Wells 1964. Pp. 195–281.

Keith, A. Berriedale. 1924.
The Sanskrit Drama. London: Oxford University Press. 1971.

Rangacharya, Adya. 1971.
The Indian Theatre. New Delhi: National Book Trust.

Śūdraka. 1964.
The Little Clay Cart. Trans. Revilo Pendleton Oliver. In Wells 1964. Pp. 39–193.

Wells, Henry W. Ed. 1964.
Six Sanskrit Plays. Bombay: Asia Publishing House.

ADDITIONAL READING

Baumer, Rachel Van M., and James R. Brandon. Eds. 1981.
Sanskrit Drama in Performance. Honolulu: The University Press of Hawaii.

Bhat, G. K. 1959.
The Vidūṣaka. Ahmedabad: The New Order Book Co.

Chaudhury, Pravas Jivan. 1952.
"The Theory of Rasa." *Journal of Aesthetics and Art Criticism* 11, 2:147–150.

Coulson, Michael. Trans. 1981.
Three Sanskrit Plays. New York: Penguin.

Dace, Wallace. 1963.
"The Concept of Rasa in Sanskrit Dramatic Theory." *Educational Theatre Journal* 15:249–254.

Dhanaṃjaya. 1962.
The Daśarūpa: A Treatise on Hindu Dramaturgy. Trans. George C. O. Haas. Delhi: Motilal Banarsidass.

Gerow, Edwin. 1977.
"Indian Poetics." In *A History of Indian Literature.* Ed. Jan Gonda. Vol. V. Wiesbaden: Otto Harrassowitz. Pp. 217–301.

Kale, Pramod. 1974.
The Theatric Universe. Bombay: Popular Prakashan.

Levi, Sylvain. 1978.
The Theatre of India. Vols. I and II. Trans. Narayan Mukherji. Calcutta: Writers Workshop.

Nandikesvara. 1975.
Abhinayadarpaṇam. Trans. Manomohan Ghosh. 3rd ed. Calcutta: Manisha Granthalaya.

Raghavan, V. 1958.
"The Aesthetics of Ancient Indian Drama." *Indian Literature* 1, 2:67–74.

———. 1967.
"Sanskrit Drama: Theory and Performance." *Comparative Drama* 1, 1:36–48.

Rangacharya, Adya. 1967.
Drama in Sanskrit Literature. 2nd revised ed. Bombay: Popular Prakashan.

Stoler Miller, Barbara. Ed. 1984.
Theater of Memory: The Plays of Kālidāsa. New York: Columbia University Press.

Swann, Darius L. 1969.
"Indian and Greek Drama: Two Definitions." *Comparative Drama* 3, 2:110–120.

Van Buitenen, J. A. B. 1968.
Two Plays of Ancient India. New York: Columbia University Press.

Vatsyayan, Kapila. 1968.
Classical Indian Dance in Literature and the Arts. Delhi: Sangeet Natak Akademi.

Wells, Henry W. 1963.
The Classical Drama of India: Studies in Its Value for the Literature and Theatre of the World. New York: Asia Publishing House.

———. Trans. 1968.
Sanskrit Plays from Epic Sources. Baroda: Maharaja Sayajirao University of Baroda.

Winternitz, M. 1963.
History of Indian Literature. Delhi: Motilal Banarsidass.

Zarrilli, Phillip B. 1987.
" 'Where the Hand is [. . .].' " *Asian Theatre Journal* 4, 2:205–214.

Chapter Three

KŪṬIYĀṬṬAM

Farley P. Richmond

FOR HUNDREDS OF YEARS a tradition of performing Sanskrit plays along the lines indicated in the *Nāṭyaśāstra* has remained alive but very much out of the limelight of Indian theatre history. Only within the last decade or so have the unexplored riches of this unique art form begun to receive serious scholarly attention.

Kūṭiyāṭṭam is one of the oldest continuously performed theatre forms in India, and it may well be the oldest surviving art form of the ancient world.

Mādhavan Cākyār as the clown performs a prayer as part of his entrance in a *kūṭiyāṭṭam* production in the Trichur Temple theatre. (Murali Photo)

Although the precise links between it and the ancient Sanskrit theatre have not yet been determined, *kūṭiyāṭṭam* is probably a regional derivation of the pan-Indian classical tradition, a bridge between the past and the present. No one knows exactly when *kūṭiyāṭṭam* came into being. Records of the tenth century A.D., attributed to King Kūlaśekhara Varman, indicate that it was already at an advanced stage of its development by this date. Other evidence suggests it may be far older.

Kūṭiyāṭṭam is found exclusively in Kerala, a narrow stretch of land running along the Arabian seacoast in southwestern India (see map). In the early years of its existence it may have been performed in areas of what is now the state of Tamil Nadu. *Kūṭiyāṭṭam* is complex in structure and execution. It is performed by actors and musicians in theatres constructed in the compounds of less than half a dozen Hindu temples. Until this century it was confined to the temples, particularly in the north and central regions of the state.

As a result of its close association with temple life and rituals *kūṭiyāṭṭam* first serves a religious function as a visual sacrifice to the temple deity. Its acting style is conventional, composed of an elaborate blend of symbolic gesture, stylized physical movements, and chanted dialogue and verses. Like its acting style, the costumes and makeup are also conventional. Its repertory consists of plays written and acted in Sanskrit and Prakrit. Malayalam, the regional language, is also used, particularly in improvised passages spoken by humorous characters.

In the old days the chief spectators were Kerala Brahmans and those of royal blood. Today men and women of all castes and communities may witness *kūṭiyāṭṭam* when it is performed outside the confines of an orthodox temple. *Kūṭiyāṭṭam* appeals to the taste of intellectuals and rarely to those of the untutored. Since few contemporary spectators understand the Sanskrit and Prakrit languages, its appeal is further limited. As far as we know it was never meant to be a popular art form or designed to be witnessed by large numbers of people of different educational, social, and cultural backgrounds.

With the declining fortunes of the Kerala temples in recent years, patronage has waned. Performances are now rarely commissioned. Most performers are forced to seek alternative means of livelihood and often to perform outside the sanctified quarters of the temple theatres, and to make changes in the form, cutting and adapting their work to meet the current taste for short, concise performances. How long *kūṭiyāṭṭam* will withstand the severe pressures to make more radical changes in its formal style of presentation, or even if it will survive to the end of this century, is uncertain.

In the following pages I will examine some of the characteristics of *kūṭiyāṭṭam:* the community of performers and the training of the actors, the plays and staging manuals, the purpose of performances, the audience, theatre buildings, costumes and makeup, music, and the current state of the

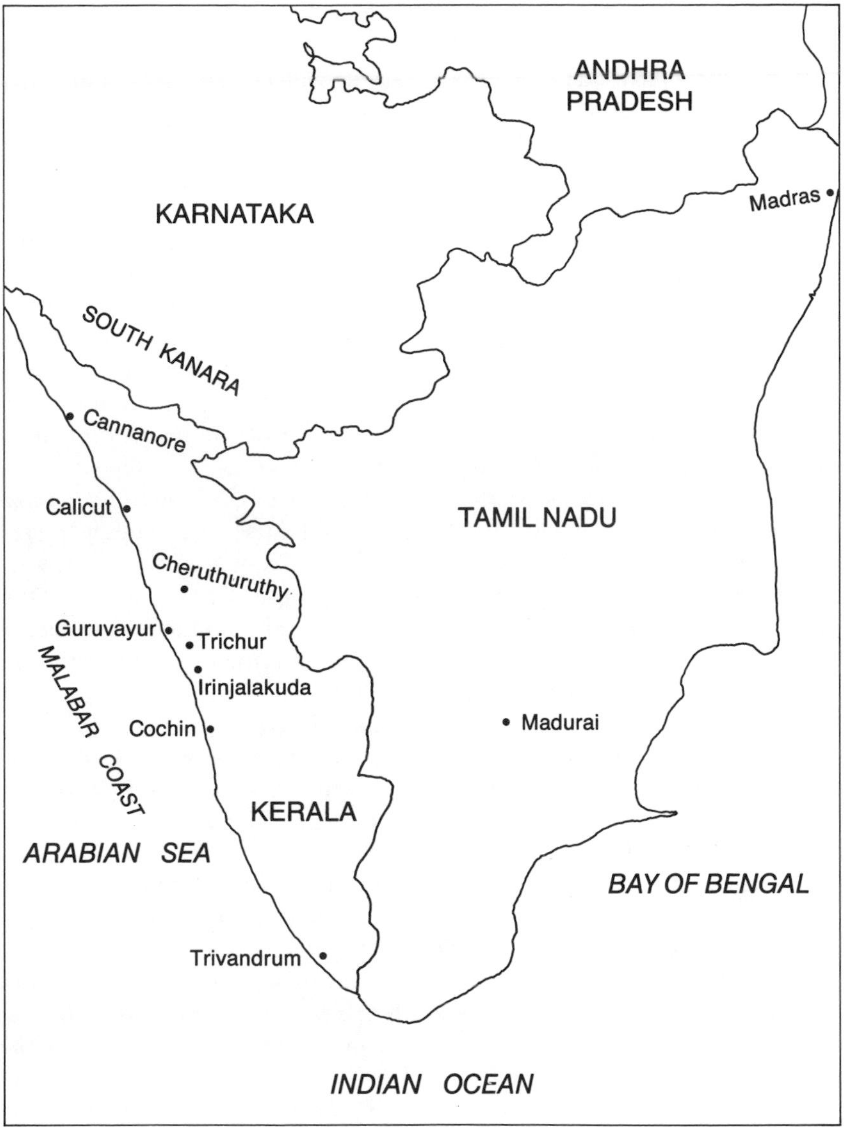

art. A selected play in performance will be described at the end of this section to provide something of the flavor of this unique art form.

Performers and Training

According to tradition, families of actors and musicians, belonging to particular castes of temple servants, hold the exclusive right to perform in the

Kerala temples. In some temples performers of one and only one family maintain the right to perform *kūṭiyāṭṭam.* The following pages will focus on the actors and actor training and only touch briefly on the role that the musicians serve in performance.

The story is told that the *kūṭiyāṭṭam* performers descend from a line of court bards who drove the battle chariots of kings. When the Perumāḷs, the ancient rulers of Kerala, settled in this region of South India, they are said to have brought with them a family of actors who were charioteers by caste. The father was childless and so to carry on his line he implored the king to allow him to adopt children who were born outside the orthodox confines of the caste system, specifically those who were born of the union of a Brahman woman and a non-Brahman man. The king agreed and a line of performers came into being called Cakyar, literally those who are half Brahman and half non-Brahman. Sometime in the distant past a further refinement occurred. The male children who had been initiated into this community by undergoing the investiture of a sacred thread[1] were known as Cakyar and preserved the right to act the male roles in the plays. Children who had not undergone the thread ceremony, even though also born of a Brahman mother, were known as Nambyar. The Nambyar could not wear the sacred thread and were not permitted to act in the Sanskrit plays. The women of the Cakyar caste also were restricted from participating in performances. The women of the Nambyar households (Naṅgyar) were permitted to perform, however.

By the tenth century A.D., the Cakyar, Nambyar, and Naṅgyar were engaged in the ritual observances in the Kerala temples. Today they are recognized as a subcaste of a larger caste of temple servants who have the sole right to perform specific duties in the temples, then and now a place of extreme ritual purity.

If you think of the temple deity as the center of the temple's purity, the various castes of servants form concentric circles of purity around the deity. Those with the highest ritual purity are permitted close contact with the effigy in the sanctum sanctorum and those who are less ritually pure must remain farther away from the deity. The performers of *kūṭiyāṭṭam* do not have the right to perform the most sacred and intimate sacrifices close to the deity, as do the Nambūdiri Brahmans, but they do have the right to perform plays as a "visual sacrifice" in honor of the deity. It is not our intention to examine the complex notion of purity and pollution in the Kerala temples and what is obviously a complicated system of caste interrelationships,

[1] Ordinarily, only Brahmans who are initiated into their community wear a sign such as this. In this instance, the Cakyar have adopted the ways of those of a higher caste, but as I have indicated, they may not participate in the same acts of ritual purity as the Brahmans. The thread is worn at all times and is normally changed every year in a special ceremony. It is worn across the chest from the left shoulder to the right side and is thought to correspond to a vein that runs through the body.

rights, and responsibilities. It is enough to know that the *kūṭiyāṭṭam* performers occupy a relatively high status in the caste hierarchy and, at least as far as the Kerala temples are concerned, are respected members of society.

Today only a few actors have the knowledge and skill to perform *kūṭiyāṭṭam*. Little more than a dozen people regularly act Sanskrit plays in the *kūṭiyāṭṭam* form. The eldest male member of a family of actors is regarded as the head of a family. He is responsible for keeping the traditions alive by teaching the rudiments and eventually the secrets of the art to the younger generation of his family. Now only two senior actors conduct formal training programs in *kūṭiyāṭṭam*. They are Padma Shri M. M. Cākyār of the village of Lakkadi and Mādhavan Cākyār of the town of Iriñjālagada. It was a deep loss to the art when Paiṅkulam Rāma Cākyār, a senior member of the Cakyar families and head of the training program of the state academy, passed away in 1980. *Kūṭiyāṭṭam* has survived centuries of struggle precisely because men such as these have transmitted their knowledge to the members of their families. In this respect the tradition of training and method of preservation is similar to that described in the *Nāṭyaśāstra*.

According to tradition, acting is an hereditary occupation. A child's profession was determined by birth, not through choice. As a consequence training literally begins at birth. Today formal instruction of a fledgling actor begins when a child is between eight and ten years old. Besides undergoing the formal instruction, the child is intimately involved in the procedures of performance by assisting his elders in the dressing room and on the stage. By growing up with *kūṭiyāṭṭam* he absorbs vast quantities of complicated material in a casual, unhurried way. As in most fields of endeavor

Mani Madhava Cākyār. (M. M. Cākyār photo)

Mādhavan Cākyār. (Mādhavan Cākyār photo)

some actors distinguish themselves and others do not. The history of *kūṭiyāṭṭam* is highlighted with stories concerning the lives and exploits of well-known performers.

Although training practices differ from one teacher to another, the student is instilled with a sense of selflessness and absolute devotion to the teacher and to his art. Even if the teacher does not happen to be the student's parent, he pays his teacher the same respect he would his own father.

Formal training is conducted in a family compound, the *kaḷari,* a small gymnasium of mud walls and earthen floor which is well ventilated by large windows. A simple wooden roof covered with tile shingles protects the structure from the heavy monsoon rains. In former times the roof was made of palm thatch and replaced every year during the dry season between March and May.

In his fascinating study of *kūṭiyāṭṭam,* M. M. Cākyār describes a typical day in the life of student apprentices (1975).[2] The day begins between three and four in the morning with rigorous physical exercises. The morning hours are regarded as sacred to Sarasvatī, the goddess of learning; therefore, they are considered to be the appropriate and auspicious time for study. A slight chill hangs in the morning air in this tropical climate. Recitation of verses from the plays and practice of various stylized movements follow the physical routines. Work continues until around eight A.M. when the students bathe, pray, and eat a hearty breakfast of rice porridge and pickled mangoes dipped up with leaf spoons. During the mid-part of the day the students rehearse Sanskrit verses from the plays, entrances of characters, and sections of physical movement mentioned in the staging manuals. The evening is devoted to the practice of various eye exercises and stylized facial expressions that indicate the mood and temperament of various characters. In addition they rehearse sections of plays, which must be learned entirely by heart. Although the routine may differ somewhat from one teacher to another, the content of the training is essentially the same.

During the long years of study a student is expected to develop a thorough knowledge of the subtleties of Sanskrit and Malayalam poetry, rhetoric, logic, and grammar. A sense of the complicated rhythmic patterns which accompany all the movements, stylized gestures, facial expressions, and patterns of speech is instilled in the actor through constant contact with the theatre. In short the actor must be both an artist and a scholar. Over the years several actors have distinguished themselves for their wit and wisdom and continue to be spoken of with respect and affection by devoted supporters.

[2] An English translation of the work was completed by the late Narayana Subrahmaniam but has not yet been published.

Plays and Staging Manuals

Kūṭiyāṭṭam is unusual in that plays are performed not in whole but in part. On any given occasion only one act or part of an act of a play is presented. Although this practice may seem somewhat odd to us, it is not really so, for in *kūṭiyāṭṭam* it may take from five to twenty nights to complete the complicated preliminaries, elaborations of the story, and the dramatic action of a single act. To produce a whole play would probably require the better part of several months! The spectators speak of the performance by referring to the title of the act rather than the title of the play.

Very few Sanskrit plays from which acts are produced are known widely outside Kerala. Bhāsa's *The Vision of Vāsavadatta (Svapnavāsavadattam)* and Harṣa's *The Delight of Snakes (Nāgānanda)* are exceptions. The repertory also includes acts from the following plays: *Subadhrādhanañjayam* and *Tapatīsaṃvaraṇam* by King Kūlaśekhra Varman; *The Wonderful Crest Jewel (Aścaryacūḍamaṇi)* by Śaktibhadra; *Bālacaritam, The Minister's Vow (Pratijñāyaugandharāyaṇa)* and *The Consecration of Rāma (Abhiṣekanāṭakam)* of Bhāsa; and *The Farce of the Drunk Monk (Mattavilāsa),* written by King Mahendra Vikrāma Pallava. The two plays of Kūlaśekhara Varman are thought to have been composed especially for performance in *kūṭiyāṭṭam.* Kālidāsa's *Śākuntala (Abhijñānaśākuntala)* and Bhāsa's *Cārudattam* are among about a dozen other works from which acts were staged but which were eventually dropped from the repertoire.

Like plays of other classical periods in theatre history, Sanskrit plays characteristically do not have elaborate stage directions. While several dozen directions in the texts of the plays serve as useful guides to the actors, they do not provide enough information to stage an act of a play. Perhaps to make up for this deficiency special manuals were composed in old Malayalam to explain the techniques for acting the plays in *kūṭiyāṭṭam* style. It is said that without the aid of these manuals the Cakyar would be unable to perform even one of the acts of a Sanskrit play. Legend has it that the texts were the work of Tolan, Kūlaśekhara Varman's minister. Whether this is true or not, the manuals are probably the work of actors since it requires the insight of an experienced performer to decipher the terminology of the extant texts. The manuals contain indispensable staging instructions concerning the ritual consecration of the stage, properties, costumes, makeup, correct chronology of events to be acted, length of performance in terms of days, specific items of dance and rhythmic accompaniment, the names of melodies to be used when chanting certain verses and dialogue, where and when to move and sit on the stage, and at times, the differences in prevailing performance practices and stated preferences for one or the other alternative. In addition they provide the textual passages which are to be inserted into the scripts and rendered in symbolic gesture, passages not found in the Sanskrit plays.

Context and Support

Kūṭiyāṭṭam is a sacred event, designed as a ritual dedication to the presiding deity of the temple in which it is presented. It has none of the trappings of a commercial venture, none of the associations with the profane world outside the walls of the temple compound. Performances are scheduled to occur on auspicious days in the temple calendar. In recent years, with the declining fortunes of the Kerala temples, fewer and fewer performances have been scheduled. Normally only one performance a year is given in the great Śiva Temple of Trichur, which contains the largest of the temple theatres.

At times no more than a few dozen spectators witness a show. Under such circumstances it would seem that the actors would be disillusioned; and yet they continue to fulfill their ritual duty and obligation, which is to make a visual sacrifice to the presiding deity of the temples in which they perform.

In former times performances were arranged at the request of the temple authorities or a local ruler. Today wealthy or influential citizens and cultural organizations have taken the place of the rulers as patrons of *kūṭiyāṭṭam.* Through their urgings all the heads of the actor families have given performances outside the sacred confines of the temples, exposing *kūṭiyāṭṭam* to a wider potential audience.

Most performances take place at night, usually about nine P.M., shortly after the final rituals have been performed for the deity in the sanctum sanctorum of the temple. Performance segments can finish as late as three A.M., before the morning rituals in the sanctum sanctorum, except on the final day of the *kūṭiyāṭṭam,* when the show usually ends between five and six A.M.

Spectators come from all walks of life. But since only Hindu devotees are allowed to enter the temples, only Hindu spectators see the plays there. It is said that many years ago only Kerala Brahmans and members of the royal family were allowed to see performances. Even then in order to maintain their ritual purity, the Brahmans cordoned off a separate space for the ruler to sit.

Spectators are usually expected to take a bath before entering the temple compound. A casual glance at a typical audience reveals that many spectators wear snow-white cloth pieces around their waists and carry a smaller white cloth over their shoulders, as a sign that they have fulfilled their ritual obligation and purified themselves with water before entering the temple ground.

The space directly in front of the stage is considered the best spot to witness a performance. In the Iriñjālagada temple theatre this space has traditionally been reserved for Brahman men. Non-Brahmans and ladies are obliged to sit or stand in the walkways around the extremities of the interior, another example of the separation of the castes and sexes according to orthodox practices. In current performances in other temple theatres both men and women sit cross-legged on the floor in front of the stage. The women usually sit to the stage-left side of the house and the men sit to the stage-right side. A narrow space normally separates them, thus forming an aisle down the middle of the house. The separation of the sexes in public places is a cultural aspect of traditional social life in many parts of India and is particularly prevalent in Kerala.

As the show progresses it is not mandatory to pay strict attention to the events depicted on stage. If a spectator becomes bored or tired, he or she simply lays down and sleeps. During the early hours of the morning, when a slight chill hangs in the air, even a hard floor may seem inviting.

The environment of a *kūṭiyāṭṭam* performance is rather tame compared to the performances of other forms of theatrical entertainment in the region, in which tea stalls and fast food vendors do a thriving business during the long hours of the night and early morning. The atmosphere of a *kūṭiyāṭṭam* is formal and when the actors perform outside a temple they tend to organize shows away from the hubbub of street life. Certainly the temples do not permit the vendors to do business within the peaceful walled compounds. In this respect *kūṭiyāṭṭam* resembles the solemnity of the No *(nō)* theatre of Japan.

Performance Space

The theatre buildings of *kūṭiyāṭṭam* are unique structures in that they are the only permanent, indigenous theatre architecture that India has produced. At least nine structures survive in the temples of North and South Central Kerala. Two are in an advanced state of ruin and several others border on severe decay. All share common features but each has its own unique details. All the structures are rectangular in shape. The largest, most impressive, and frequently used is that of the famous Śiva Temple of Trichur. The interior of the building is seventy-two by fifty-five feet. Next in size and importance is the theatre of the Iriñjālagada Temple, which has an interior approximately sixty-seven by fifty-four feet. The smallest structure still in use is that of the famous Kṛṣṇa Temple of Guruvāyur, which is a mere thirty-two by twenty-four feet. The Trichur Temple theatre holds approximately five hundred spectators, and in size it resembles the "ideal" rectangular theatre described in the *Nāṭyaśāstra.*

As indicated earlier, the area in front of the stage is the best place to see and hear a performance. In some theatres it is slightly raised and bordered

Exterior of the Iriñjālagada Temple theatre. To the left of the building is the sanctum sanctorum. The pole behind is the golden flagstaff near the building from which the deity may be viewed during prayers. (Farley P. Richmond photo)

by a row of pillars supporting the high, central roof of the building. The aisles running between the pillars and the outer edge of the interior of the building are also used by the spectators.

The space reserved for the actors in the temple theatres of Kerala is considerably smaller and different in shape from that described for the rectangular theatres in the *Nāṭyaśāstra*. For one thing the stage is square rather than rectangular. The Trichur Temple stage is approximately twenty-one and a half feet square, the Iriñjālagada Temple stage is fourteen feet square, and that of the Guruvāyur Temple is nine and a half feet square. All of the stages of the temple theatres are raised approximately one foot above the audience area. The front of the stage touches a point approximately half the distance of the total length of the building. Except for the Trichur Temple, which has twelve pillars supporting the stage roof, all the stages have four pillars which support a roof above the stage. The underside of the roof in most theatres is ornately decorated with wood carvings or paintings. Due to the smoke from the oil lamps which illuminate the stages these rich and often exquisitely carved and painted figures are covered with a thick layer of soot. In any case the decorations are barely visible to the spectators and seem to have been meant to fulfill ritual purposes rather than to be admired during a performance.

Although there is room for spectators to sit or stand in the space to the left and right of the square stage, the actors play exclusively for the spectators sit-

Stage of the Iriñjālagada Temple theatre. (Farley P. Richmond photo)

ting in front of the stage. The oil lamp, which is the only means of illuminating a traditional performance, is located downstage center. The stage is so arranged in all the theatres that the actors perform facing in the direction of the temple deity. Thus *kūṭiyāṭṭam* has been designed as a frontal art form for religious as well as for practical purposes.

The dressing room is a small room adjacent to the rear of the stage. Two doors connect it with the acting area. The door upleft is normally used for entrances and the door upright is used for exits. The size of the acting area is somewhat reduced by the presence of two large pot-shaped drums, which lie in stands situated between and sometimes awkwardly in front of the doors leading to the dressing room.

The surface of the stage in all but a few of the theatres is convex. The center is slightly higher than the extremities. This unusual shape is designed to facilitate quick drainage after the stage has been washed. In temples where care has been taken to maintain the appearance of the theatre, the surface of the stage is slick and shiny to permit ease in dancing.

The area between the lamp downstage center and the drums tends to be the most frequently used acting area. *Kūṭiyāṭṭam* actors are not concerned with picturization. Scenery has no place in *kūṭiyāṭṭam*. The actors conjure up the place and time of the action through words, gestures, and movements. The stage remains a neutral platform until the actors invest it with symbolic significance. Through conventional movement patterns the actors convey the idea that they have traversed great distances. In this respect they

Rāma confronts Surpanakha disguised as a beautiful woman. Young Brahman boys sit on the edge of the stage to watch this Trichur Temple production. (Mādhavan Cākyār photo)

use the stage in an identical manner to that described in the *Nāṭyaśāstra.* A simple stool symbolizes a throne, a garden bench, and so on. Swords, spears, bows, and arrows are constructed of wood and painted to resemble the actual object. A simple red curtain is used for special entrances by characters.

Costumes and Makeup

Since settings and adjustable stage lighting are not used in *kūṭiyāṭṭam,* the visual spectacle depends on the costumes and makeup. Designs and colors of

The actor playing Lakṣmaṇa challenges Surpanakha dressed as a demoness. They prepare to fight. (Mādhavan Cākyār photo)

costumes, ornaments, and headdresses have symbolic meaning and significance, meant to reveal the identity of the characters to the spectators.

Careful attention is paid to every detail. For example, the elaborate beards of white paper worn by certain characters, cut and shaped to fit the individual actor's face, are applied with meticulous care with layer on layer of a white gluelike substance. The ornaments of wood are painstakingly hand-carved by traditional craftsmen and decorated with mirrors and tinsel paper. The costumes are washed by a particular caste of launderers to assure their ritual purity.

Kūṭiyāṭṭam costumes are tied rather than buttoned, sewn, snapped, zippered, or velcroed. The process of preparing some of the garments starts several days prior to a show and takes many hours to complete. For example, the bustlelike skirt of the heroic characters is one of the most difficult and time-consuming costumes to prepare. Usually an apprentice is assigned the three-hour task of carefully folding more than twenty yards of starched fabric in complicated patterns, using his hands and feet in preparation for the simple act of tying the bustle around an actor's waist. At first glance *kūṭiyāṭṭam* costumes resemble those of other traditional theatre forms of the region, such as *kathakaḷi* and *Kṛṣṇanāṭṭam*. But on close inspection they have their own unique characteristics.

Music

Without rhythm there would be no *kūṭiyāṭṭam*. Every movement, every gesture, and the pace of each verse and bit of dialogue is governed by one of six specific different rhythmic patterns. The only time rhythm does not guide the action is when a clown or demon is improvising dialogue. During these intervals no musical accompaniment is required.

Kūṭiyāṭṭam begins and ends with the sound of the pot-shaped drum. Two are required for a performance. These unusual instruments, measuring

The *mizhāvŭ* drummer at left sits on the wooden drum stand and accompanies the action. The drummer at right stands on the stage and beats time. Two enthralled spectators stand behind. (Murali Photo)

approximately three feet in diameter at their midsection, provide the basic time frame for the action. Their deep, sonorous tones are aided by the resonance of the low wooden ceiling above the stage, the heavy wooden cases in which they are suspended, and the elaborate wooden beams of the temple theatres. They are consider sacred. Should one be taken out of the temple compound, special rituals must be performed to cleanse it before its return; otherwise it is said to pollute the entire temple. As indicated earlier, these pot-shaped drums are played by the Nambyar, who have the exclusive right to perform on the instrument.

A second, less important, instrument is a small bell metal cymbal, played traditionally by the women of the drummer community. Normally two are played during a show but actually only one is needed. The purpose of the cymbals is to keep a steady beat to help guide the pace of the drumming.

Several other instruments have a place in the *kūṭiyāṭṭam* ensemble, albeit they are far less important to the major action. They are a small hourglass-shaped drum struck with a curved stick, a wind instrument resembling an oboe, and a conch shell. All five instruments are played simultaneously as a five piece orchestra at auspicious moments in the action, such as the entrance of the first character from behind the curtain on the first day of performance.

The only instrument which has the potential of carrying a melody is the wind instrument. But the art of playing melodies appropriate to the dramatic action has somehow been lost. So the temple musician normally engaged to play the wind instrument during a performance uses his own discretion and selects from among the melodies in his repertory those which he believes are appropriate.

The human voice is also considered a melodious instrument. Melodies have been developed for chanting dialogues and verses with various emotional content. Twenty melodies are now recognized by the actors. These are rendered with extreme care, only after long years of training under the guidance of an older teacher, and tend to be among the most difficult tasks an apprentice must master. The sound of the Sanskrit and Prakrit dialogue chanted in the appropriate melody is reminiscent of Gregorian chants or the chant of the Buddhist monks of Japan.

According to tradition the musicians sit on the stage in prescribed positions. The drummers sit upstage center on the large stands behind their drums. To the right of the drummers and slightly downstage the female cymbal players sit on plain white cloth pieces laid out on the floor. They normally face stage left. A space is left between the drums and the cymbal players to permit actors to enter and exit from the dressing room. To the stage left side of the drummers the other musicians stand throughout the sections in which they are required to play. Usually their job does not entail the long hours of intense playing that is demanded of the drummers and cymbal players, so they retire to the dressing room or stand amid the spectators and watch the show until they are needed.

Performance Structure

The structure of a *kūṭiyāṭṭam* performance is radically different from the structure of a typical Western play production, irrespective of whether the performance is viewed in the orthodox confines of a temple theatre or on the concert stage. Before examining the individual elements in detail it may be useful to review the general performance pattern. The following model provides a means of doing so.

Hypothetical Performance Model

Night	*Event*
First	a. Enactment of elaborate rituals. b. Entrance of the First Character (Actor A) who relates abbreviated details about the story based on the first few lines or verses of the text of the act to be performed. c. Brief concluding rituals.
Second	a. Abbreviated opening rituals. b. First Character (Actor B) elaborates on the events related to the story and its major characters. c. Brief concluding rituals.
Third	a. Brief introductory rituals. b. Further elaboration of the story by the First Character (Actor B). c. Brief concluding rituals.
Fourth	a. Short introductory rituals. b. Entrance of the Second Character (Actor C) and introduction of events from the story as seen from his perspective. c. Brief concluding rituals.
Fifth	a. Abbreviated introductory rituals. b. Elaboration of events of the story performed by the Second Character (Actor B). c. Abbreviated concluding rituals.
Sixth	a. Brief introductory rituals. b. Performance of the act of the play beginning at the point in the script where the characters in the previous day's procedures left off and continuing all chronological sequence to the end, with all the necessary characters (Actors A, B, C, and so on) or their symbolic substitutes appearing on the stage. c. Concluding rituals performed by the chief actor of the company.

Kūṭiyāṭṭam structure lays stress on the introduction of characters and elaboration of details of the story not found in the act of the play as it is written or published. This type of information is normally drawn from the staging manuals discussed earlier and not from the script itself. Thus *kūṭiyāṭṭam* performance departs radically from the text of a play. The structure also lays stress on an actor's individual performance rather than on ensemble playing, as is so often the case in Western theatre. It is not until the sixth night in our hypothetical model that the act is performed in its entirety with several characters appearing on the stage at once. It is only then that *kūṭyāṭṭam* resembles what we characteristically think of as a theatre performance. Another unique structural feature of *kūṭiyāṭṭam* is that it permits several actors to perform the same role on different occasions. Actors A and B portray the first character on the first two nights and on the sixth night Actor B performs a different character altogether. Such shifting of roles among different actors permits them an opportunity to develop tour de force performances, depending on the level of their skill and imagination.

Besides deemphasizing ensemble playing, this particular structure of performance also deemphasizes the notion of the play as a total, integrated, artistic unit. Rather it focuses on peripheral events which relate to the central issues and characters of one act, a small portion of the play. It does all this within the framework of ritual, no matter where a performance takes place,

It is traditional that the entrance of the disfigured demoness Surpanakha, accompanied by torches, is made through the audience from the south gate of the temple theatre. (Mādhavan Cākyār photo)

be it in the temple or on the concert stage. With this basic overview in mind we will now proceed to discuss the various units of performance in more detail.

Rituals

Kūṭiyāṭṭam begins and ends with rituals. Well before a temple performance starts the drummer goes to the sanctum sanctorum of the temple, where a priest lights a small oil lamp from the flame burning before the temple deity. Returning to the theatre with the lamp, the drummer lights the lamp in the dressing room and eventually lights the large stage lamp which illuminates the show. Thus the fire which presides over the sacrifices made to the temple deity illuminates the world of the play, extending the realm of the sacred to the performance.

The actor ties a red cloth around his head and offers silent prayers facing the oil lamp in the dressing room, after having dotted his face in a special pattern with coconut oil. From this point on he enters the world of the play, gradually and cautiously obliterating his own personality and taking on the personality of the character he is to portray. The dressing room is a quiet place. The actors speak in whispers. It usually takes several hours to prepare an actor for his entrance. During this period he has ample time to focus his attention on the role and its intricacies.

As the moment draws near for the show to begin, the drummer lights one wick of a bell metal stage lamp. A special pattern of drumming is played. When the first actor is ready for his entrance, the other wicks are ceremoniously lighted and a drummer offers flowers and water at the center of the stage, in honor of Brahmā, the creator, and to sanctify the stage space. He recites verses in Sanskrit and in some cases he recites a summary of the plot in old Malayalam.

A special pattern of drumming signals the first actor to enter. A red curtain is held up behind the oil lamp downstage and the actor performs a special pattern of movement as a sign of respect for the musical instruments and as an extension of the rituals. Finally he purifies himself by sprinkling holy water on his face. Then he takes his place behind the curtain, which is quickly removed to the accompaniment of the drums. The first character is finally revealed.

Entrance

The entrance of a character is called *purapad.* The first evening of the performance is devoted to the entrance of the first character and usually reveals something about the story and his personality. It normally takes little more than an hour to complete. The elements of the entrance are prescribed in the stage manuals of the actors and are not found in the texts of the plays.

Elaboration

The next evening a similar preparation pattern is followed. The lamp is lighted. The drums are played. The same character enters once again, though a different actor may play the role, this time without the accompanying elaborate preliminary ceremonies, and proceeds to expand the story through verses and actions also prescribed by the stage manuals. This section is known as the elaboration *(nirvahaṇa)* and may continue for several days. Two to three hours are generally required each evening to perform the elaboration.

Second Entrance and Elaboration of the Story

Depending on the play, during the third or fourth day, another major character is introduced and performs his entrance. This may be followed by a day or two in which he performs his elaboration.

Concluding Day

On the final day of the show the actual *kūṭiyāṭṭam* takes place. *Kūṭi* means "together" and *aṭṭam* means "play." Thus when two or more characters perform together on the stage a *kūṭiyāṭṭam* is said to take place. This usually requires a long period of time to complete, longer than any of the previous days of performance. During the *kūṭiyāṭṭam* the act is played in its entirety with the required number of characters making an appearance on the stage to chant the dialogue and verses of the dramatic action. Since the last day is normally the high point of the show it usually draws a large and enthusiastic crowd. During plays in which a clown *(vidūṣaka)* is required, the theatre is invariably packed from the day of his entrance through his elaboration and the performance of the act. The clown is permitted to speak and improvise in the local language and elaborate on the story, digressing as he sees fit to criticize the audience or offer sage advice about all sorts of matters; the spectators are always delighted with his antics and seem to enjoy themselves thoroughly.

Concluding Rituals

At the end of the final day a special ritual is performed, usually by the leading actor on behalf of all the other actors. This restores the stage to its original state through the extinction of the flames of the oil lamp. The actor symbolically bathes, obliterating all traces of his character, and returns to the profane world. His final act is to lie prone, face down on the stage, with his hands above his head in prayer, facing the direction of the temple deity for whom the performance was dedicated.

Length of Performance

A *kūṭiyāṭṭam* performance may take as few as five days or as many as eleven days to complete. It is reported that the one-act play *The Hermit and the Harlot (Bhagavadajjuka)* requires thirty-five days to perform, from the introduction of the first character to the completion of the act.

Moral Instruction

In some theatres, the *kūṭiyāṭṭam* is preceded by a *kūttŭ,* which consists of a recitation of verses from sacred texts, like the *Rāmāyaṇa, Bhagavad Gītā,* and *Mahābhārata,* and improvisation on them by the clown. At the Śiva Temple of Trichur forty-one days prior to the beginning of the annual *kūṭiyāṭṭam* performance in October, Mādhavan Cākyār, the actor-teacher of the Iriñjālagada Temple and more recently the Kerala Kalamandalam, performs selected verses for about two hours every afternoon between three and five. These moral discourses couched in a humorous vein are popular, sometimes more popular than the *kūṭiyāṭṭam* itself.

Kūṭiyāṭṭam in Performance

The annual *kūṭiyāṭṭam* performance at the Vaṭakumnāthan Temple theatre of Trichur starts on Vijayādaśtamī Day, an auspicious occasion in the Hindu calendar of events. Every year Mādhavan Cākyār and his party of performers from the town of Iriñjālagada come to Trichur to perform an act of a play. Between October 14 and 20, 1975, they produced "Tornayūdhāṇkam," Act III of Bhāsa's *The Consecration of Rāma (Abhiṣekanāṭakam),* a six-act drama (Bhāsa 1968). Only two acts of the play are still in the repertory of the Cakyar families, the first act entitled "Bālivadhāṇkam" and the third act.

During my first year of study in Kerala, which began in late 1974, I saw the same party perform "Bālivadhāṇkam" at the Trichur temple as part of a cycle of acts dealing with events from the *Rāmāyaṇa.* And although I took copious notes and examined the stage manuals of the act before the show, through translations generously provided by my colleague and friend L. S. Rajagopalan, I was ignorant of the many elaborate and subtle details which are characteristic of a *kūṭiyāṭṭam* performance. When I saw "Tornayūdhāṇkam" a year later, after having studied *kūṭiyāṭṭam* with my teacher Kalamandalam Rāman Cākyār and L. S. Rajagopalan, I was much better equipped to understand the Sanskrit and Malayalam materials, the gesture language, the drumming patterns, and the multitude of subtle ritual actions inconspicuously scattered throughout a performance. The following account highlights the production, as I saw it.

Bhāsa's *The Consecration of Rāma* deals with events drawn from the

Rāmāyaṇa. In particular it begins at the point after Rāvaṇa, the demon King of Laṅkā, has abducted Sītā, Rāma's devoted wife, and taken her to his palace in Laṅkā (the modern Sri Lanka). The events set in motion in Act I, the alliance of Rāma with a band of monkeys led by Sugrīva and Hanumān, culminate in the eventual overthrow and death of Rāvaṇa and the reunion of Rāma and Sītā in Act VI. Act I establishes Rāma's divinity as the reincarnation of Viṣṇu and his prowess as a mighty warrior. He kills the monkey King Bāli so that Sugrīva may forge the monkeys into a well-disciplined and faithful army to serve him in his imminent conflict with Rāvaṇa. In Act II Hanumān, Rāma's monkey general, flies to Laṅkā, discovers Sītā in Rāvaṇa's beautiful garden, observes Rāvaṇa's fruitless attempt to seduce her, and appears before Sītā and assures her that Rāma will soon come to free her. The act concludes as Hanumān joyfully sets out to destroy the garden.

In Act III we learn from Śaṅkūkarṇa, one of Rāvaṇa's attendants, that the garden has been destroyed. He fears that the king will fly into a rage when he hears the news. Hearing the report Rāvaṇa, as expected, is furious. He orders various guards and soldiers to capture, bind, and bring Hanumān to him. Many attempts are made but all fail. Finally Hanumān allows himself to be taken captive so that he may see the famous ten-headed demon king. Before the monkey enters the king's presence, Rāvaṇa speculates that the destruction of his garden is probably the result of a curse laid on him when he shook the very foundations of heaven and disturbed the god Śiva and his wife Pārvatī residing there. Rāvaṇa's brother Vibhīṣaṇa begs him to release Sītā so that the kingdom may be saved from destruction at the hands of Rāma and his mighty army of monkeys. Rāvaṇa arrogantly rejects the idea and orders Hanumān to be brought forth. Hanumān enters and proceeds to insult Rāvaṇa in various humorous ways. Boastfully he predicts the fall of Laṅkā at the hands of the monkey hordes. As a punishment for his insulting remarks, Rāvaṇa orders that Hanumān's tail be set afire. Vibhīṣaṇa renews his pleas that Rāvaṇa relent and send Sītā back to her husband. Vibhīṣaṇa is banished and elects to join Rāma and the side of righteousness. He predicts Rāvaṇa's downfall and his own rise to the throne in order to rebuild the kingdom and restore Laṅkā to its former glory. The remaining acts of the play demonstrate how Rāvaṇa is defeated and Rāma and Sītā are reunited.

Performance Procedures—*Tornayūdhāṇkam*

Day One—October 14, 1975

The entire performance is devoted to the entrance dance of Śaṅkūkarṇa, Rāvaṇa's attendant. Preparations begin in the theatre late in the afternoon, with the placing of ritual offerings to the left of the lamp and a full measure of rice to the right. Stalks of banana trees with bunches of unripe bananas and thick saffron colored coconuts are attached to the pillars to the right and left of the lamp. Decorative strips of palm fronds hang gayly below the stage roof. The whole effect is simple, natural, and charged with ritual significance. After the daily rites in the sanctum sanctorum have been concluded, about 9:30 P.M., a young apprentice of one of the drummer families tones up the wicks burning in the oil lamp and the tuning of the drums commences with special rhythmic patterns. Short religious songs follow, sung by the Nangyar, seated in their regular place upstage right. Then an attendant lights a third wick of the lamp and tones up all the wicks to indicate that the play is about to begin. He recites a special verse in Sanskrit and briefly outlines the story in old Malayalam and sprinkles water and flowers stage center in honor of Brahmā, the god of creation. About 10:00 P.M. the curtain is held behind the lamp and Śaṅkūkarṇa enters to the alternating acceleration and deceleration of the drums. He holds his headdress as though to indicate that something dreadful has happened. After circling the stage several times and sprinkling holy water on his face, he crosses to the curtain and takes his position for his entrance. The curtain is removed and the actual entrance *(purapad)* begins. What follows is based on the introductory scene from Act III of the staging manuals. The Sanskrit text is translated as follows:

Śaṅkūkarṇa: Hello! Who is on duty at the "Golden Gate Entrance" *(torṇayūdha)*?

Portress: (Entering) Sir, it is I. Vijaya. What shall I do for you?

Śaṅkūkarṇa: Oh, Vijaya, convey this message to His Majesty, the Lord of Laṅkā. The garden is almost destroyed. For Mandodarī, our Lord's chief queen, although fond of ornaments does not pluck the sprays out of kindness; wherein even the Malaya breezes do not blow out of fear; and whose plants are untouched by the hand; that garden of Indra's foe is destroyed. Let the matter be reported.

Portress: Sir, I have never seen a person who is always in attendance on the king show such fright. How did this happen?

Śaṅkūkarṇa: Lady, this is an urgent matter. Please convey the message to the king, at once.

Portress: Sir, I shall. (Exit)

Śaṅkūkarṇa: (Looking in front) Lo! Here is His Majesty, the Lord of Laṅkā, coming this very way. And he, with eyes wild and resembling white lotuses, with blazing golden torches going before him, full of fury, he is rushing forward in haste like the sun engaged in ending an Age *(yuga)*. (Bhāsa 1968, 86–88)

Although the exchange is short, probably requiring less than two minutes to perform in a realistic style, the actor playing Śaṅkūkarṇa requires two hours to complete the scene. In order to focus all the attention on Śaṅkūkarṇa, the lines of Vijaya are spoken by the Nangyar-caste performer from her place stage right. Because she is not participating in the acting of the scene she does not wear a costume or special makeup. In the traditional fashion, the actor playing Śaṅkūkarṇa, who incidentally is not the best actor of the Iriñjālagada Temple theatre, chants a short passage of dialogue articulating the separate gestures for each word. Then he repeats the gesture text at a slower pace exaggerating the facial expressions which are appropriate for the mood of each word. This part of the action is accompanied by drums. Finally he repeats the entire passage a third time gesturing and chanting the text as before.

Several points in the text are expanded through the gesture language, based on instructions in the staging manuals. For example, when Mandodarī, Rāvaṇa's chief queen, is mentioned, Śaṅkūkarṇa digresses from the story by taking the role of the queen and her maidservants. He mimes the ladies going to the garden. The maidservants unfold the queen's long black hair, then they tie it up again in a knot, and apply vermillion to the center parting to symbolize that she is a married woman. But neither of them is pleased. Something is missing. They decide that they need to pick a fresh leaf from the garden to adorn one side of her hair. But then they conclude that Rāvaṇa will become very angry if they dare to pick it. Mandodarī starts to pluck the leaf then she hesitates and resolves, "No, if I pluck it, it will fade." This section is acted by Śaṅkūkarṇa to indicate that the garden is so jealously guarded by Rāvaṇa that even his chief queen is afraid to adorn herself with the slightest fragment of the beauty it has produced.

At another point in the scene Śaṅkūkarṇa elaborates on a verse to show that even the sun is afraid to harm the garden. It begins when Śaṅkūkarṇa takes the part of Rāvaṇa talking with his ministers at court. He persuades them to come with him to the garden to enjoy its pleasures. When they arrive they find the leaves of the trees have withered. Rāvaṇa shouts for his gardeners and demands to know why the plants look so poorly. The trembling gardeners tell him that the rays of the sun have caused the leaves to wither. Rāvaṇa becomes angry and draws his sword and forces Sūrya, the Sun God, to fall at his feet and beg Rāvaṇa's forgiveness. Rāvaṇa extracts a promise from him never to shine on Laṅkā and impolitely kicks him aside. The brief digression ends at the point when Śaṅkūkarṇa reiterates that "such a garden has been destroyed." The day's program ends when the actor turns around three times and touches the stage and then his head three times as a sign of respect. As the drums play a special rhythmic pattern to indicate that the program has concluded for the evening, the hundred or so spectators that have gathered to watch the event slowly rise and disperse. There is no applause. It is now 11:30 P.M. Only hushed exchanges among friends and relatives and the buzz of hundreds of crickets that populate the temple grounds break the silence. The actors and musicians hastily take off their costumes and makeup and make their way to the cramped living quarters provided them during their stay in Trichur.

Day Two—October 15, 1975

When I arrived at the theatre about 9:00 P.M., Śaṅkūkarṇa had not completed his makeup. A few elderly ladies and men were scattered about the auditorium. Some of them were fast asleep on the floor. At 9:10 the first drum sounds were played and around 9:30 Śaṅkūkarṇa entered. Korchukuttan Cākyār, another actor in Mādhavan Cākyār's troupe, plays the role this evening. All the ladies stand when the actor enters, as though to show their respect for his character.

This is the first day of the elaboration of the story *(nirvahaṇa)* based on extraneous verses taken from the staging manuals. The primary aim of Śaṅkūkarṇa's elaboration is to enact the events which led up to those concerned with Act III of the play. Emphasis is placed on stories from the life of Rāvaṇa—his birth, the attainment of his boon of "unkillability," how he frightened Kubera, the god of wealth, into leaving the city of Laṅkā, how Rāvaṇa became master of Laṅkā, the elaborate description of the beauty and majesty of the city, Rāvaṇa's coronation, the preparations of Rāvaṇa and his demon companions for a hunt, how he met Mandodarī in the forest, his marriage to her, and finally how he made love to her.

The actor follows the usual pattern for performing the verses and dialogue with an elaborate gesture language. The only thing unique about the performance is that the female cymbal player recites the extraneous verses as the actor performs the appropriate gestures. The performance is also somewhat unusual in that the actor remains seated on a stool during most of the performance. When he depicts the preparations of the demons for the hunt he rises and does various movement patterns reminiscent of those used in the martial art tradition of Kerala.

The performance ends about 11 P.M. with the actor reciting a silent prayer facing in the direction of the temple deity. The ladies in the audience quickly rise as a sign of respect when the actor makes his exit to the dressing room. The small crowd disperses rapidly, probably because the next day is a working day.

Day Three—October 16, 1975

The elaboration continues. The role of Śaṅkūkarṇa is played by Parmeswaran Cākyār, the father of my teacher. All the stage decorations have been removed. The festive atmosphere of the first few days is now gone. About 9:30 Śaṅkūkarṇa enters, sits on the stool, and begins to perform. He tells more stories from the life of Rāvaṇa. They relate how Rāvaṇa refused to listen to the good advice of Kubera, his brother, how he killed Kubera's messenger, the fight between them and the eventual insults Kubera was forced to bear, how Rāvaṇa rides in the aerial cart Puṣpaka and bumps into the Kailāsh mountain on which Lord Śiva sits, his description of the size and shape of the mountain and of the love scene between Pārvatī and Śiva just prior to being disturbed by the jolt of Rāvaṇa's aerial cart, the lifting of the mountain by Rāvaṇa, how Śiva pushes the mountain down with his little toe to the dismay of Rāvaṇa, and finally, the naming of Rāvaṇa, "the demon with the roaring cry."

After the elaboration has been completed for the evening, the actor silently prays facing the direction of the temple deity, touches the stage and then his head three times as a sign of respect, and exits. The performance ends about 12:30 A.M., three hours after it began.

Day Four—October 17, 1975

This is the third day of the elaboration. Tonight Korchukuttan Cākyār, the youngest performer in the company, plays Śaṅkūkarṇa. The performance begins about 9:30 P.M. and concerns the following events: how Rāvaṇa refuses to accept the boon offered by Śiva's wife, the curse she utters, "Oh, Rāvaṇa, your destruction shall be caused by a woman," how Rāvaṇa was also cursed by Naṅdī, the bull, to be defeated by a monkey, how the other gods took flight when Rāvaṇa attempted to pick a fight with them, and the battle between Rāvaṇa and Yama, the God of Death, who is eventually defeated in the conflict. The performance ends about 10:30.

Day Five—October 18, 1975

This marks the end of Śaṅkūkarṇa's elaboration and the entrance of Rāvaṇa. The performance begins about 9:15. Śaṅkūkarṇa describes how Indra is defeated, how the trees of Indra's garden were stolen from heaven and planted in Rāvaṇa's garden. Śaṅkūkarṇa finally comes to the part in the story in which he acts out, "such a garden has been destroyed." He retires to the dressing room. About 11:05 he returns and performs all the text that was recited and acted on the first day. About midnight Rāvaṇa makes his entrance from behind the curtain. Mādhavan Cākyār, the leading actor of the group, portrays the demon king, and he does so extremely well. His eyes are unusually wide and expressive, showing the intensity and arrogance of the demon king. Torches are held by attendants at both sides of the oil lamp. Oil is poured into the bowl of the lamp and the wicks are toned to provide the maximum visibility for his entrance. The curtain is pulled aside and Rāvaṇa grunts and groans to show his demonic and unpredictable nature. The entrance paints a vivid picture of the arrogant demon king. It comes to a conclusion about 1:15 A.M.

Day Six—October 19, 1975

This is the first day in which the actual *kūṭiyāṭṭam* takes place, that is, in which more than one actor appears on the stage at the same time. The scene opens with Rāvaṇa and Śaṅkūkarṇa. Śaṅkūkarṇa reports the vain attempts of the soldiers and guards to prevent Hanumān from destroying the garden. Śaṅkūkarṇa is played by Korchukuttan Cākyār and Rāvaṇa is acted by Kuttan Cākyār. The performance is short, starting about nine thirty and ending by eleven. At the end of the scene the actor playing Rāvaṇa turns on the stage three times and then touches the stage and his head three times as a sign of respect.

Day Seven—October 20, 1975

This is the last day of the *kūṭiyāṭṭam* performance, the day in which the remaining part of the Sanskrit text is enacted. Mādhavan Cākyār, the senior and best actor of the Iriñjālagada Cakyar family, plays Rāvaṇa, Parmeswaran Cākyār enacts Hanumān, and Kuttan Cākyār plays Vibhīṣaṇa. About three hundred and fifty people assemble to watch the show. There is a general sense of excitement. A light rain begins to fall, pattering gently high overhead on the copper shingles of the theatre roof. Faint thunder is heard in the distance. The air is thick and warm. A full measure of rice has been placed stage left of the lamp and the eight auspicious things lie on a banana leaf stage right. When the performance begins with the entrance of Rāvaṇa about 9:15 P.M., the ladies of the audience stand. Rāvaṇa begins in a thoughtful mood. He performs the following ideas from the text:

Rāvaṇa: Oh, alas!
Laṅkā cannot be thought of even mentally by gods and demons (although) united. Yet a monkey has indeed entered it, defying the ten-necked (me). (Bhāsa 1968, 97)

This portion takes about forty-five minutes to perform; then he acts the defence of Laṅkā, taking the roles of his soldiers preparing to do battle, showing their cocky and proud attitudes toward the invaders. Next he acts verse twelve from the text of the play:

Rāvaṇa: Moreover,
After conquering the triple world with its gods and demons in battle and proceeding proudly to Kailāsh, I, having shaken Śiva together with his queen and surrounded by his *ganas,* obtained a boon from him; but again, a curse was laid on me by Pārvatī and Naṅdī as they were not paid any regard (by me). Could that (curse) be (operating now) on me, through the disguised form of a monkey? (Bhāsa 1968, 97–98)

About 10:45 he begins to act a special, long awaited, section of the show, called the *Kailāsodhāraṇa,* the lifting and throwing of the Kailāsh mountain. This takes Mādhavan Cākyār a whole hour to complete. It is a thrilling tour de force of *kūṭiyāṭṭam* acting in which the actor describes the size and majesty of the mountain using only his eyes. It is one of several superb examples of how the actors use facial expressions to tell a story. The climax comes when the actor mimes lifting, throwing, and catching the mountain. The spectators sit in awe of Mādhavan Cākyār's powers of concentration and his ability to create the impression of a mountain simply through his facial expressions. The second tour de force of the evening follows shortly thereafter when Rāvaṇa takes the role of Lord Śiva sitting on his heavenly throne holding Pārvatī on his lap. Switching back and forth between Śiva and Pārvatī, Mādhavan Cākyār portrays the charming scene of jealousy when Pārvatī sees Gaṇgā, the river maiden, in Śiva's hair. The scene is acted entirely in gesture and contains the following text taken from the staging manuals:

Pārvatī: Oh husband, what is it I see in your hair?
Śiva: (Silently thinking) What is to be said to her? Alright, I'll play a little trick on her. (Aloud) Oh Pārvatī, haven't you heard there is water in my hair?
Pārvatī: Oh husband, I see a face! I see a face! What is the reason?
Śiva: Oh Pārvatī, that's not a face. It's a lotus.
Pārvatī: Oh husband, I see curls of hair. What is the reason?
Śiva: Oh Pārvatī, they aren't curls. They're bees.
Pārvatī: I see eyebrows. Why is that?
Śiva: They aren't eyebrows. They're waves.
Pārvatī: Oh husband, I see eyes! What is the reason?
Śiva: Oh Pārvatī, they're not eyes. They're fish.
Pārvatī: Oh Lord, I see a pair of breasts! Why?
Śiva: Oh, they're not breasts. They're a pair of Chakravaka birds.
Pārvatī: (To herself) He is deceiving me. I'll go to my father's house for sure. (To her maids) Oh maids, we shall go to my father's residence.[3]

Rāvaṇa then shows how Pārvatī becomes troubled by the shaking of the mountain when Rāvaṇa accidentally drives into it with his aerial cart. He stands on the stool taking the role of the frightened queen. Then he shows how Rāvaṇa is exhausted from having thrown the mountain up and having caught it. Rāvaṇa exits to the dressing room.

It is now 1:15 A.M. and the actor playing Rāvaṇa's brother Vibhīṣaṇa makes a brief entrance from behind the curtain. He shows that he is happy to see Rāvaṇa. Then he exits. Rāvaṇa reenters and sits on the stool at one side of the lamp. Vibhīṣaṇa reenters and takes his place at the other side of

[3] Translated by L. S. Rajagopalan from the original, unpublished staging manuals of this play.

the lamp and they act a short scene in which Rāvaṇa refuses to give up Sītā. Both exit. About 1:40 Hanumān enters, hands bound behind his back and accompanied by two guards. The actors who represent the guards have their heads covered with red cloth to show that they are characters, but they are not fully costumed. Hanumān wears a spectacular costume and makeup. His body is almost completely covered with tiny cotton balls; even small bits of cotton dot his face, which is elaborately painted with red makeup. He has a long tail made of palm fronds covered with white cloth. A short tug-of-war ensues between Hanumān and the attendants. He breaks away and shows that he has let himself be bound by the guards so that he might be brought before Rāvaṇa. He smells his long tail, slaps his thighs, and performs various monkey antics to demonstrate his great prowess. Hanumān exits with the attendants. About 2:15 A.M. the stool representing Rāvaṇa's throne is placed stage right center and the stool for Vibhīṣaṇa is placed stage left center. Rāvaṇa and Vibhīṣaṇa take their places and Hanumān enters skipping. He takes his seat on a stool right of Rāvaṇa. Vibhīṣaṇa and Rāvaṇa go through their chanted dialogue, verses, and gestures only once, without the usual repetition of the material and without the accompaniment of the drums. Hanumān chants the following verse and performs the gesture accompaniment:

Hanumān: I am the direct son of the wind-god, born of Añjanā; and am the monkey named Hanumān sent by Rāghava (Rāma). (Bhāsa 1968, 102)

Hanumān counts Rāvaṇa's heads throughout Rāvaṇa's response. The audience seems delighted with this and his other antics. Eventually Hanumān is sent off to have his tail set afire and Vibhīṣaṇa is banished. Rāvaṇa is left alone on the stage. He performs several actions which suggest that he is flying. He concludes the program by reciting and acting the last lines of the text of Act III:

Rāvaṇa: Alas! Vibhīṣaṇa is gone. I shall arrange for guarding the city. (Bhāsa 1968, 113)

It is now three in the morning. Mādhavan Cākyār takes off his headdress and does the concluding rituals. He washes his legs in front of the lamp, performs the symbolic act of bathing, using holy water, and extinguishes all but one wick of the bell metal lamp. Then he falls on his face in prayer facing the temple deity. The spectators stand and fold their hands in prayer, facing the stage. A bit of applause breaks out after the last sounds are played on the drums.

The weary spectators trudge out into the chill night. Drops of rain begin to fall. There is a sudden dash to get home before a shower breaks. And another ritual *kūṭiyāṭṭam* performance comes to a close at the great Śiva Temple of Trichur.

Current State

Many unrecorded changes have doubtlessly taken place in *kūṭiyāṭṭam* during its long history. And yet it has survived precisely because the families of actors have doggedly preserved the traditions in an orthodox manner in the orthodox environment of the temple. Yet forces are at work that may bring about major changes in the manner in which it is performed and that threaten the very existence of *kūṭiyāṭṭam* as we know it. It is not for us to judge the wisdom of the changes that are now taking place, but we should be aware of them and their potential consequences. In subsequent pages of this book we will demonstrate that India's theatre forms have responded in radically different ways to changing social and political conditions and public taste.

Perhaps the first major change that *kūṭiyāṭṭam* experienced in this century was the practice of giving public performances outside the temple theatres. On the surface this may seem inconsequential, but in fact it has paved the way for a number of other changes that are just now affecting the Cakyar families. In the past performances always served a ritual purpose. On the concert stage they take on a new meaning for the spectators and become an artistic expression of the region and the community from which they spring. In the 1960s Padma Shri M. M. Cākyār took a troupe of actors to Delhi after having performed elsewhere in South India. He modified his performance in the capital in an attempt to make it more appealing to the audiences there, thus changing the traditional passages of dialogue spoke in Malayalam to the language of that region—Hindi. The results apparently did not meet with favor. Today concert versions of *kūṭiyāṭṭam* have been given outside the temples by all the major Cakyar families. In a performance given in Trivandrum several years ago, the organizers stopped the show midway through and requested that the actors shorten the play to accommodate the spectator-patrons, many of whom had to keep office hours the next day. The actors obligingly truncated the story, bringing the act to a hasty conclusion in complete violation of the orthodox rule that once an act has begun it must be completely performed to the end. A company of actors also toured Europe and the United States in the 1980s. They chose to perform short excerpts from different plays, fearing they might bore the spectators whom they presumed were not accustomed to all-night programs.

To give life to a dying art, *kūṭiyāṭṭam* was introduced into the training program of the Kerala Kalamandalam, the state academy for the performing arts of Kerala. The late Paiṅkulam Rāma Cākyār was given a post and the state and national governments provided funds for student scholarships.

This was a positive contribution during a time of great need. And yet it resulted in a new set of dilemmas. Because the institution is state supported it is obliged to admit at least a few students who do not come from the traditional actor families. The students of other castes have proven more than capable of mastering the rigors of *kūṭiyāṭṭam* acting. Today some of the most competent performers of the younger generation are not members of the hereditary families of actors. Although highly skilled, they cannot perform in the temple theatres because of temple restrictions which permit only Cakyar, Nambyar, and Nangyar to perform *kūṭiyāṭṭam* there. So the concert engagements offer the only opportunity for the practitioners from other castes to be seen in public, thus reinforcing the urge to arrange even more performances outside the temple, and to truncate performances to meet the audience's need for short performances. The critical question which has yet to be answered is, "Will there be a sufficient audience to support *kūṭiyāṭṭam* once it embarks on this path?"

The work generated at the Kerala Kalamandalam also resulted in other changes. The orthodox practice of repeating certain passages of the text three times was modified and now all the Cakyar have virtually abandoned the practice and normally only recite a passage once. Changes have also been made in the costumes and makeup. The headdress of the female characters has been altered somewhat and the beards for many of the chief role characters which were originally made entirely of rice paste, are now constructed of rice paste and paper. An experiment was even made to construct a metal beard to accommodate an elderly actor, allowing him to apply his makeup easily and swiftly.

For centuries *kūṭiyāṭṭam* has been the duty and right of hereditary families of actors and drummers. It certainly has not been a lucrative occupation even during the best of times. Given the critical economic plight of the actors it could be that the future holds many more radical changes for the art, in order that its participants may sustain themselves and their families.

WORKS CITED

Bhāsa. 1968

Abhiṣekanāṭakam. Trans. Vidyaratna S. Rangachar. Mysore: Samskrita Sahitya Sadana.

Cākyār, M. M. 1975.

Natyakalpadrumam. Cheruthuruthy, Kerala: Kerala Kalamandalam.

ADDITIONAL READING

Enros, Pragna Thakkar. 1981.
"Producing Sanskrit Plays in the Tradition of *Kūṭiyāṭṭam.*" In *Sanskrit Drama in Performance.* Ed. Rachel Van M. Baumer and James R. Brandon. Honolulu: The University Press of Hawaii. Pp. 275–298.

Iyer, S. Subramania. 1984.
Sanskrit Drama. Delhi: Sundeep Prakashan.

Jones, Clifford R. 1967.
"The Temple Theatre of Kerala: Its History and Description." Ph.D. diss., University of Pennsylvania.

———. Ed. 1984.
The Wondrous Crest-Jewel in Performance. Delhi: Oxford University Press.

Panchal, Goverdhan. 1984.
Kuttampalam and Kūṭiyāṭṭam. New Delhi: Sangeet Natak.

Raja, K. Kunjunni. 1964.
Kūṭiyāṭṭam: An Introduction. New Delhi: Sangeet Natak.

Rajagopalam, L. S. 1987.
"Consecration of the Kūttambalam Temple Theatres." *Samskrita Ranga Annual* 8, 1980–1987: 22–40.

———. 1968.
"Music in Kootiyāṭṭam." *Sangeet Natak* 10:12–35.

Richmond, Farley. 1978.
"The Rites of Passage and *Kūṭiyāṭṭam.*" *Sangeet Natak* 50:27–36.

———, and Yasmin Richmond. 1985.
"Multiple Dimensions of Time and Space in *Kūṭiyāṭṭam.*" *Asian Theatre Journal* 2, 1:50–60.

Shulman, David Dean. 1985.
The King and the Clown in South Indian Myth and Poetry. Princeton: Princeton University Press.

Venu, G. 1989.
Production of a play in Kūṭiyāṭṭam. Trichur, Kerala: Natanakairal Publication.

PART TWO

THE RITUAL TRADITIONS

INTRODUCTION

All types of traditional Indian performance are suffused with religious significance and punctuated by ritual practice. As witnessed in the previous chapters on Sanskrit theatre and *kūṭiyāṭṭam*, the classical theatre of India may not be discussed without taking into careful consideration its ritual and religious context and significance. In the eastern and southern regions of India, "ritual performance" has played a central role in the development of some forms of scripted theatrical genres. Some genres of ritual performance and many theatrical genres enact their own versions of dramatic episodes based upon epic and mythological sources. Not surprisingly, as scripted theatrical genres emerged historically, some appropriated from ritual performances extant modes of staging and performed important scenes depicting battles between the forces of good and evil. Before turning attention to this special class of performances which we call "ritual performances," it will be helpful to describe three closely related but distinct relationships between ritual and performance in traditional Indian performance: (1) rituals as performative, (2) rituals within a performance genre, and (3) ritual performances.

Traditional Indian Ritual Practice as Performance

The Vedic path toward liberation identified in the introduction as the "way of action" was centered in sacrificial ritual worship led by a specialized priestly class and in its home or family-centered counterpart. The ancient Vedic sacrifical rituals were characterized by attributes we normally associate with highly stereotypical, codified rituals, such as very specific sets of actions performed by a specialized class of priests governed by rules and conventions covering just about everything from directional orientation, postures, gestures, words, sounds, and recitations, to the use of implements or materials (Gonda 1980). In the performance of these elaborate rituals, gods and men were understood to share responsibility for maintaining the order of both the world and the cosmos. The performance of the rituals was understood to "do" something in a fundamental sense—to maintain earthly as well as cosmic order and harmony. The legacy of ancient Vedic ritual practice survives today in some elaborate forms of ritual occasionally performed in Kerala (Staal 1983 and Gardiner 1976).

As suggested in the chapter on the origins of Sanskrit theatre and also by Byrski (1974), one possible explanation for the origin of Sanskrit theatre itself is the Vedic ritual, which also provided a model for the development of drama as such. This legacy is evident in both the prescribed order in which Sanskrit dramas were performed and in the fact that theatre served as a method of sacrifice to the gods. *Kūṭiyāṭṭam* is still considered a "visual sacrifice" to the deity of the temples in which it is performed.

Through time the way of action originating in Vedic sacrifice eventually gave way in popular Hindu temple and family ritual practice to the primacy of *pūjā,* which replaced most elaborate forms of Vedic sacrificial ritual. *Pūjā* is also ritual worship, but involves the devotee in a personal manner as part of a series of transactions. *Pūjā* means worship, but worship of a special kind, in which the image of the deity is given hospitality through offerings and acts considered pleasing to the deity. Each day the deities are treated as divine guests. The images are bathed, dressed, and given offerings such as sights, lighting of lamps, sounds, and, most importantly, foods considered pleasing to a deity. Recitations of sacred texts or learned commentaries on those texts, performances of music, dance, or drama considered pleasing to a deity may be given daily or on special ritual occasions. Many forms of traditional Indian performances are presented in this specific *pūjā* context as an offering to please the god. Devotees pay for any of these different offerings pleasing to the deity. An offering may be given to fulfill a vow or to receive a wish or boon such as a successful journey, birth of a son, and so on.

Both early Vedic ritual and more recent *pūjā* ritual practice are considered part of the "way of action." In both cases, to perform the ritual is to accomplish something. The series of stereotypical actions (sounds, gestures, postures, and so on) which are performed (done) by the priest collectively constitute a ritual per se. To have completed the performance of the ritual is to have maintained or restored cosmic order, pleased the god, or gained the boon. In this most basic sense, Hindu rituals are "performative"—a series of things done which accomplish something. Ritual practices are understood to establish a mediating bridge between the daily world and the "unseen" and powerful world of the gods. The ritual specialist establishes this bridge, mediating between the tangible daily world and the intangible other world by means of his or her ritual practices. The specific type of mediation and the specific techniques of ritual practice achieving mediation vary according to ritual traditions. Vedic sacrificial practices and *pūjā* practice constitute two related but distinct categories.

While the temple context of many dance, music, or theatrical performances is an overtly sacrificial or *pūjā* ritual context, the discrete performance genres themselves performed within that context may or may not be organized to achieve a ritually efficacious end. The example of *kūṭiyāṭṭam* is an important one. As we have seen the *kūṭiyāṭṭam* is performed within a ritual context as a "visual sacrifice" and yet its performance in itself is primarily an actualization of the classical *rasa* aesthetic. Realization of that aesthetic will please the god for whom the performance is given as a sacrifice. Likewise, there are many other genres which possess an organizational impetus based on either the classical *rasa* aesthetic or on bhakti, the way of devotion, but which are performed in a formal temple ritual context as an offering to please the god. For example, at the Śrī Vallabha (Viṣṇu) temple in Kerala, typical offerings to Vallabha which a devotee may pay for include *payasam* (rice pudding), flowers, or chanting Viṣṇu's name one hundred times, among other things. In addition, *kathakaḷi* dance-drama (chapter 10) may be commissioned for performance as an offering, even though, like *kūṭiyāṭṭam,* it is primarily a classical genre shaped to realize the *rasa* aesthetic. Likewise the devotional dance-drama, *Kṛṣṇanāṭṭam,* which originated in the religious fervor of a royal devotee, is traditionally performed only at the Guruvāyur temple of Lord Kṛṣṇa in Kerala as one temple offering among many. In both these cases, commissioning a *kathakaḷi* or *Kṛṣṇanāṭṭam* performance is usually to secure success in having children or for success in marriage. In these two cases, the specific performance of the dance-drama is ideally assumed in the ritual context to achieve the goal, namely, both to please the god and achieve the long-range goal, to "produce children" or "make a successful marriage," for those who have commissioned the offering.

To summarize, traditional Hindu ritual practice is performed. In popular *pūjā* practice something is done—a transaction occurs, the gods are pleased, blessings or a boon is given, a vow is fulfilled. And in some cases, discrete aesthetic or devotional performances are one type of sacrifice or offering pleasing to the deity of a temple.

Rituals in Performance

Within every traditional Indian performance genre, whether primarily classical, folk-popular, ritual, or devotional, there exist specific *rituals* which serve to punctuate, set off, and frame the performance. Commonly there exist preliminary rituals which remove obstacles in the way of successful performance (usually by making offerings to Ganesha), sanctify the stage or playing space, and honor, praise, and actualize the presence of one's teachers or performance tradition in the person of the performer. And usually a performance is concluded with at least a brief closing ritual, even a simple prayer or dance offering to the gods, asking their forgiveness for any mistakes or anything displeasing in the performance. The extensive preliminaries of the Sanskrit theatre and *kūṭiyāṭṭam* have been discussed above, illustrating the important place of rituals as framing devices in the earliest forms of theatrical performance. Attention will be given to these preliminary and concluding rituals throughout this volume, such as to the devotional songs to Ganesha which begin a *tamāshā* production, or to the elaborate song, instrumental, and dance preliminaries of *kathakaḷi*.

Ritual Performances

Although all Hindu ritual is performed (done) and is considered part of the "way of action," and while rituals are an important part of virtually all genres of Indian performance, there are certain rituals which are best characterized as "ritual performances." As rituals these traditional genres share with sacrificial practice and *pūjā* ritual efficacy as their primary goal and organizational center. These rituals are performed (done) to accomplish a specific efficacious end. They, too, establish a mediating bridge between the divine and human worlds by means of specific ritual practices. What distinguishes those rituals we call "ritual performances" from sacrificial and *pūjā* practice is the degree to which overtly dramatic, theatrical, and performative elements are used to establish the mediating bridge and to accomplish its efficacious end.

The priest of most traditional Hindu ritual ideally functions as a permanently "pure" vehicle through which the ritual action is effected by his careful attention to precisely performing the series of stereotypical ritual actions. He provides access to the divine cosmic world by means of his control and manipulation of ritual acts, gestures, words, and so on which effect the result of the ritual. Therefore, as the "performer"—the one who does the gestures, rings the bell, pours the water, and the rest—he usually remains "cool," never himself interfacing directly with the deity or its power.

In contrast, what we call here "ritual performances" are much more vivid, visual, visceral, and overt visitations of divine power. They are often characterized by a direct visitation of the deity in the form of possession, either of ritual specialists or of devotees. The story or mythology of the god is an important part of the ritual performance and is told, sung, or even partially enacted as a performance in which the god himself appears. His or her appearance in some genres is in the form of a specially created figure whose elaborate costume, makeup or mask, accoutrements, and movements or actions make him or her a most immediate and dramatic vehicle for divine visitation in this world. Momentarily at least the god or goddess is understood to have come to this world in a most graphic and immediate sense, seizing hold of or "riding" either ritual specialists or devotees by possessing them. In the state of possession the priest or devotee is understood to manifest special divine or superhuman powers, such as the ability to walk on white-hot coals without injury, the ability to undergo other mortifications of the flesh such as body piercings without harm, or the ability to prophecy or deliver oracles or messages as the god. The "action" of ritual performances is very immediate.

The traditional place of highest social and ritual purity in the Hindu social order was given to Brahmans. However, in the case of ritual performances the actor-priests are only rarely of the highest castes and in many cases are from the lowest groups in the social hierarchy. For those of lower castes who traditionally perform ritual performances, during the period of their performance of the special rituals, they are treated as the gods who possess them—at least temporarily inverting within a ritual frame the social hierarchy. Whatever their initial place in the hierarchy, actor-priests must undergo a series of purifying rituals which prepares them both for their special ritual status and to receive the god.

Ritual performances occur in two main types of settings: either temples or shrines, or family homes. Many temples or shrines are small, local, village or family affairs, humble in appearance and without much outward display of importance. Yet especially for local villagers, such small shrines may be of great importance, for the power of the deity enshrined there may be considered great.

Ritual performances are most often associated with some type of sakti, the manifestation of the feminine aspect of divine power. The feminine principle generally is subsumed within the all-Hindu hierarchy by association with Śiva, usually as the active or feminine aspect, and takes some form of the mother goddess. The mother goddess appears in a wide variety of forms, some benign but others awesome and fearful. The most vivid example is that of Kāli.

> Kāli is typically shown with a sunken stomach signifying her insatiable hunger and thirst for blood. She lives in the cremation grounds as the symbol of the all-consuming power of death. She is sometimes said to wear infant corpses as earrings and to drink blood from a skull. Jackals and goblins accompany her, and her appearance is unkempt and fearful. She has large, sharp fangs and fills the world with terrifying roars. She vividly illustrates certain inevitabilities of human existence, such as sorrow, sickness, and death, and reminds humans of the fragility of their life and its inevitable end. (Kinsley 1982, 89)

Any ritual performance involving the visitation of the god's power makes it a "dangerous" occasion due to the powerful and actual presence of the deity. Therefore, that manifest power must be contained and controlled by the practices of the ritual performers.

The occasion of a ritual performance may be either a seasonal or yearly festival propitiating the deity, or a specially commissioned ritual performance fulfilling a vow or seeking a boon for a family or an individual. Some larger annual temple festivals, of which ritual performances are a primary part, may attract huge audiences of pilgrims and devotees and often take on the aura of a "county fair" where vendors hawk their wares and markets are temporarily set up for barter of animals or goods.

Especially for larger festivals of which ritual performances are a part, a large cross-section of castes and occupational groups are often involved in the preparation of and participation in both the ritual performance and the larger festival. The interlocking nature of rights and responsibilities of a village's castes may be reflected in the tasks and roles each group within the village is called upon to play during the festival period. Richard Brubaker (1979) describes a typical example of this interlocking set of ritual responsibilities for a village goddess festival (the yearly Mariyamman festival, Kongu region, west-central Tamil Nadu):

> A washerman carries a traditional torch each night of the festival. Members of the barber caste shave others who have ritual responsibilities. The Paraiyans provide the necessary drumming, and before the festival begins a Paraiyan must make a ceremonial leaf-covered arch at the entrance to the village. A potter supplies important ritual pots for holding water and fire, and it is a potter who throws bloodied rice to the evil spirits. A Pandram, Mariyamman's regular priest, is responsible for performing all of the ritual obligations or *pūjās* required and also for speaking for the goddess, when possessed by her, and for carrying a pot of fire around the temple each morning. A person who produces fermented toddy from palm trees sacrifices goats and sheep. And a member of the dominant farming caste 'helps with the felling of an important tree to be used in the ceremonies and receives the first blessings of the god(dess) when the ceremonies are over.'

The precise hierarchical constellation and interrelationship between and among castes or occupational groups vary from region to region, but ritual performances are often seen as reaffirming the traditional social hierarchy, which is considered both sacred and social. However, this typical mode of reaffirmation of hierarchy is rapidly changing today under the pressure of new political and socioeconomic developments.

There are numerous specific types of ritual performances spread across the subcontinent; however, most genres identified so far are found mainly along the eastern coastal region of India, including Sri Lanka (Kapferer 1983). The story or mythology of the deity propitiated in ritual performances is an important part of the event. The central importance of the story lies in the fact that it describes the particular power of the god and the origin of that power. In ritual performances like *gambhira* of the Malda region of West Bengal or *teyyam* of Kerala the story is sung as a prelude to the visitation of the deity (on *gambhira* see Ghosh 1979 and Emigh 1984). In both cases the deity possesses the actor-priest in elaborate costume and makeup *(teyyam)* or mask *(gambhira),* making manifest the power, in particular the female energy, of the deity. In *gambhira* the feminine energy takes the form of Durgā or Kāli (the most typical manifestations), and also of Narasinghee, "half-woman and half-lioness, the *sakti* counterpart for Narasimha" (Emigh 1984, 25).[1] In *teyyam,* as we shall see in detail below, the power takes the form of a wide variety of local and pan-Hindu deities. In both cases, the visitation of female energy is in solo costumed, masked, or made-up figures who do not dramatically enact the story of the god.

In other genres, such as the *Ayyappan tiyatta,* also of Kerala, the story of the god receives special elaboration through a form of visual storytelling prior to the visitations of the deity. In *tiyatta* some actor-priests specialize in mono-acting in which some parts of the god's story are told through semicodified mime. This part of the ritual performance probably is derived from the *kūttŭ,* the tradition of moral instruction and mono-storytelling part of the *kūṭiyāṭṭam.* The illustrated telling of the story is later followed by the visitation of the god as another performer is possessed (in this case without elaborate forms of makeup or mask or costume).

Other genres are overtly dramatic, using multiple performers to enact all or part of a god's story. Such is the case with *Prahlada nataka* of Orissa and *mudiyettu* of Kerala (for *Prahlada nataka* see Emigh 1984; for *mudiyettu* see Vidyarthi 1976). These two genres illustrate a remarkable similarity of both mythological action and performative treatment of mythological materials. In both cases, the ritual performances enact the final confrontation, battle, and defeat of the epitome of demonic, evil power (Hiraṇyakaṣipu and Darikan) by a specially created liminal figure, Narasimha and Kāli. In the enactments of these ritual dramas multiple actors play various roles; however, only those playing the roles of Narasimha and Kāli become possessed at the culmination of the performance. So dangerous is the possession considered in both genres that assistants must be present to attempt to control the power of the god unleashed in the visitation. In yet other ritual-drama forms, like Tamil Nadu's *terukkuttu,* the enactment of dramas is punctuated by various types of visitation in which both actor-priests *and* devotee-audience members are seized by the deity (Frasca 1984).

We have selected two forms of ritual performance for further elaboration

[1] Regarding the presence of forceful manifestations of feminine energy associated with Narasimha, an incarnation of Viṣṇu, Emigh, quoting Eschmann, notes that "Narasimha worship is related to Śaktism in its use of Tantric elements, and, in another context (104), states that the story of Prahlada and his unfailing devotion to Viṣṇu has not only become a heart piece of Vaiṣṇava theology but is an important link between Vaiṣṇavism and Śivaism. Narasimha is the furious *(ugra)* aspect of Viṣṇu *par excellence* and therewith also that aspect of Viṣṇu with the highest affinity to Śiva." (1984, 37–38)

here, the *teyyam* and *Ayyappan tiyatta* of Kerala. *Teyyam* is a form of propitiation of an almost infinite variety of both indigenous Dravidian and pan-Hindu deities performed by low caste priest-performers at village or family shrines. *Ayyappan tiyatta* is a ritual propitiation of the god Ayyappan performed by a relatively high Kerala caste, usually at family homes or at Ayyappan temples.

While we have isolated ritual performances as a sphere or category of performance, we need to remember that it interfaces and overlaps with other spheres. This is nowhere better illustrated than in *kathakaḷi,* where the raucous and lively encounters between demons or evil characters and divine or good characters, and the subsequent bloody enactments of disembowelments of mythological characters (Dussassana and Hiraṇyakaṣipu in particular) are staged in a style which leaves no doubt about their origin in Kerala's ritual performances, *mudiyettu* in particular.

Phillip B. Zarrilli

WORKS CITED

Brubaker, Richard. 1979.
"Barbers, Washermen, and Other Priests: Servants of the South Indian Village and Its Goddess." *History of Religions* 19, 2:128–152.

Byrski, M. Christopher. 1974.
Concept of Ancient Indian Theatre. New Delhi: Munshiram Manoharlal Publishers.

Emigh, John. 1984.
"Dealing with the Demonic: Strategies for Containment in Hindu Iconography and Performance." *Asian Theatre Journal* 1, 1:21–39.

Frasca, Richard A. 1984.
"The *Terukkuttu:* Ritual Theatre of Tamilnadu." Ph.D. diss., University of California at Berkeley.

Gardiner, Robert. 1976.
"Altar of Fire." 16mm film. University of California.

Ghosh, Pradyot. 1979.
"Gambhira: Traditional Masked Dance of Bengal." *Sangeet Natak* 53–54:53–77.

Gonda, J. 1980.
Vedic Ritual. Leiden: E. J. Brill.

Kapferer, Bruce. 1983.
A Celebration of Demons. Bloomington: Indiana University Press.

Kinsley, David R. 1982.
Hinduism. Englewood-Cliffs, New Jersey: Prentice-Hall.

Staal, Fritz. 1983.
Agni—The Vedic Ritual of the Fire Altar. Vols. I–II. Berkeley: University of California Press.

Vidyarthi, Govind. 1976.
"Mudiyettu." *Sangeet Natak* 42:51–63.

ADDITIONAL READING

Babb, Lawrence A. 1975.
The Divine Hierarchy: Popular Hinduism in Central India. New York: Columbia University Press.

Cartright, Paul B. 1985.
"On This Holy Day in My Humble Way, Aspects of Puja." In *Gods of Flesh Gods of Stone.* Eds. Joanne Punzo Waghorne and Norman Cutler. Chambersburg, Pennsylvania: Anima Publications. Pp. 33–50.

Eck, Diana L. 1981.
Darsan: Seeing the Divine Image in India. Chambersburg, Pennsylvania: Anima Publications.

Marglin, Frederique Apffel. 1985.
Wives of the God-King: The Rituals of the Devadasis of Puri. Delhi: Oxford University Press.

Chapter Four

TEYYAM

Wayne Ashley
Regina Holloman

IN THIS CHAPTER WE FOCUS ON A MAJOR RITUAL FESTIVAL TRADITION, the *teyyam* or *kāḷiyāṭṭam* of Kerala in southwestern India. The festival is known as *kāḷiyāṭṭam* and the deity propitiated in the festival as *teyyam*. *Teyyam* festivals are held throughout the northern part of Kerala and in contiguous parts of South Kanara and Coorg in southwestern India. Performed during the months of November through June in both private and community shrines throughout the district, it is often the most important event in the ritual calendar for many Hindu communities and draws an enormous amount of attention and financial assistance.

The major task of the festival is to create a divine "other reality" and to achieve its presence in the human world. This is accomplished by drawing upon aesthetic and theatrical strategies similar to those discussed in previous chapters: drumming, singing of sacred texts, dance movements, the wearing of elaborate costumes and makeup, gesturing, processions, feasting, and the manipulation of various paraphernalia such as flags, lamps, swords, and shields.

One of the major sequences and the raison d'etre for the festival is the dance *(aṭṭam)* of the deity by male members of specific low caste performing communities. Wearing elaborate costumes and makeup, the performer is possessed and becomes the deity in manifest form. At the conclusion of the dance, he is approached by devotees who ask for favors, make vows, and receive blessings.

Festivals are of several types: (1) Large regular public festivals which have fixed auspicious dates and are repeated annually, or every two, three, or five years depending upon the cost of the performance and economic status of the village. The propitiation of some *teyyam* require that the entire community be fed, which often means accommodating thousands of people. The

Grand Festival at Karripoti in 1978 cost the community around Rs. 195,000 ($24,000) and took fifty-five years to collect. (2) Private, individual performances, called a "vow to god," are commissioned after a deity has gratified the wishes of a devotee. For example, in Karivellur village a vow dedicated to the god Muttapan (an incarnation of Śiva) was commissioned by a woman to repay the deity for the safe delivery of her daughter's child. A houseowner cured of leprosy built a shrine to a deity and commissioned a performance annually as repayment. A man in Uduma village who received a job in the merchant marine sponsored a festival at his family's household shrine three years later, when he was able to save the money and take a leave of absence. And lastly (3) *otta kolam,* a performance of *teyyam* commissioned by an entire village to propitiate the deity who guides the destinies of the whole village. This might be done every five years or when the village is stricken with an epidemic.

Teyyam is a colloquial expression which means "god." The god referred to may be male or female and one of a number of spirits, historical figures, ancestors, and other deities associated or linked directly to the Hindu gods Śiva and Viṣṇu and to the goddess Pārvatī. Local deities in the tradition are deified ancestors who are known only to a few small kin groups which propitiate them. Another group of *teyyam* is worshipped within a similarly restricted geographical area but involves historical figures, like Tacholi Othenan, a high-caste Nayar warrior who fought numerous battles but always managed to escape by ingenuity and bravery. A few are restricted to specific communities. Muchilot Bhagavathi, for example, is the community deity of the Vaniyar (traditionally oil pressers) and cannot be worshipped by any other caste.

Performance Space

The ritual festival is tied to a specific place where the deity resides and to which it may be summoned during the festival. It may be a tree, a rock, a sword, a wooden platform, or a temporary thatched hut constructed only for the period of the ritual. Often there is a permanent shrine. These are brightly painted and decorated structures with minutely detailed carvings indicating the various deities propitiated in the shrine. What is special about these shrines is their particular histories which tell how they came to be auspicious places. These historical processes are important to an understanding of the "power" of the festival system and of its particular aesthetic.

When members of a family die unexpectedly, become seriously ill, or start quarrelling, or when a village is inflicted with disease, an astrologer is often consulted to find the causes for the disturbance. Through divination it may be discovered that an unsatisfied spirit or deity has come to reside in the house or village or that the deities residing in an abandoned shrine have been angered and require propitiation. An elaborate and costly ritual is conducted to discover which deities are causing the problem, the mode of propitiation they require, and the history relating how the deity came to the place. Many of these histories are old, originating in the distant past, but some are newly created when new places become sacred.

After the deity makes itself known, a permanent place is newly created or, in the case of an abandoned shrine, renovated and purified. Through another expensive ceremony, the power of the deity is infused into physical, concrete objects (usually a wooden stool or various metal swords). These objects are carefully housed and protected in the inner chamber of the shrine and in the course of the ritual calendar of the community, they are chanted to, prayed to, fed, adorned, offered incense, and bathed. They become more human than mere objects, their regular propitiation considered to be enriching to the sacredness of the particular place. Once a deity is installed, the maintenance of its power may be undertaken by the community through daily rituals and annual festivals.

In the aesthetic of the festival, the place not only derives power from the processes which caused it to be but may also derive power from its particular physical organization and capacity for effecting social communication. Where one is spatially positioned during the performance is a result of who one is and what one does in the social world. In the village of Kuttikol, for example, the performance space is organized to emphasize status and social differentiation: The Brahman, being the top of the hierarchy, occupies a space farther away from the shrine complex. Nayars, next on the hierarchy, occupy a raised platform covered by a tile roof closer to the shrine complex. A special covered platform at the edge of the compound nearest to the shrine is reserved for members of the Maniyani caste, slightly lower than the Nayars and therefore positioned closer to the shrine. Tiyyas, "owners" of the shrine and ritually lower than all of the other three castes, occupy the shrine complex. Vannan and Malayan performers, ritually lower than Tiyyas, occupy space at the back of the compound. Here all preparations are made, the costumes assembled, and faces painted. And finally women, also considered to be potentially polluting, are rarely allowed into the shrine compound.[1]

Having the appropriate person in the appropriate space at the right time is seen as contributing to the "power" of both the event and place. A transgression of spatial boundaries is understood to be polluting and therefore diminishes the power. For example, in Kuttikol in 1978, a person broke into the central shrine of the temple box. What seemed to be more devastating than the loss of the money was the defiling of place by an inappropriate

[1] The menstruation of women is considered to be polluting and, therefore, potentially harmful to a propitious occasion.

individual. A costly ceremony was commissioned to purify the compound and restore the place to its previous status.

Participation

Depending upon which aspects of the festival one attends to, the role of skill, imagination, birth, and divination have varying degrees of importance in determining one's activities. Participation is largely constrained by one's occupational role, caste, and location in a hierarchy of ritual statuses.

The Nayar landlords, who until recently represented the dominant agrarian power in this area, are given a special supervisory title of *koyma.* During the festival they are often called in to settle disputes among the organizing members of the shrine. They also head the planning committee for the festival.

Representatives of the blacksmith and carpenter caste are reponsible for bringing firewood, which will be used in various rituals. Members of the goldsmith community, who also make many of the festival ornaments, come to clean the various ritual implements and weapons of the temple. The village astrologer will be present to monitor the efficacy of the ritual. Members from the dancing castes, Vannan and Malayan, become possessed with the deity and the focus of the festival centers around their performance. And finally Harijans, manual laborers in the ordinary world and lowest on the hierarchy, are responsible for bringing raw materials to the shrine which will be used in preparing the temple space. Muslims bring firecrackers.

Other priestly positions are chosen by an astrologer who puts forth the names of several individuals from a particular lineage and through divination attempts to find a match between the nature of the individual and the nature of the deity he is to serve. Still other posts are filled through divine possession. The deity chooses the individual to fill the role. During a festival when a man from the appropriate caste becomes possessed during the correct time, he is likely to be recruited and assigned that particular role. If no one becomes possessed, the post remains vacant and in some instances may never be filled.[2]

Performers

The right to perform *teyyam* is generally inherited by the male members of several low caste communities called Malayan, Vannan, Kopalan, and

[2] The individual who takes on this role is called a *veliccappad* or oracle. He also becomes possessed during the festival. However, he is thought to be merely possessed by the deity, who "attaches itself and speaks through him," while the dancer is believed to become the actual deity.

Velan.[3] The performer is called *kolakarran,* which literally means "the man who takes the form of god."[4]

In addition to performing *teyyam,* Malayans and Vannans serve their communities in other capacities. Malayans perform exorcisms and Vannans are known to engage in the business of traditional medicine as well as providing purified dress for ritual purposes in temples.

Each family has its own performing territory. Annually performers make rounds to the same shrines. They are well acquainted with the rituals, songs, dances, and invocation of the deities which are propitiated within these boundaries, and they know the variations from one shrine to another. These territories are so well defined and well bounded that competition among performing families for patronage seems to be nonexistent.

Performers make little money. And as Kerala continues to shift from an economy based upon exchange of services to a wage economy, performers are finding it increasingly difficult to make ends meet from performing alone. Those demanding more money have met with hostility from patrons and sponsoring organizations. We know of at least one case in which a shrine discontinued its annual festival altogether over a discrepancy regarding how much performers should be paid. Some performers supplement their income by engaging in menial jobs such as rolling cigarettes and repairing umbrellas. However, as new occupations have become more available to larger sections of the society, Malayans and Vannans have taken up such jobs as tailoring, teaching, and banking, and jobs connected with civil service. But when unemployed, many of them fall back on performing *teyyam.*

Although there are few opportunities to make money, performers may be the recipients of various titles which elevate their status and give them additional rights regarding ritual affairs in the community.

Training

Performers are not very detailed in discussing their training. When asked how they learned the songs, face painting, or dances, most performers answer that they learned by watching. Novices do learn informally by accompanying elders from shrine to shrine during the seven to eight month festival season. A child from a performing caste may spend a considerable number of hours in and around festivals. Young boys sing along when deities are invoked and learn to prepare costumes or receive instruction on

[3] Recently individuals from non-dance castes have voluntarily opted to learn *teyyam* and perform the dance on stage as a mode of entertainment.

[4] The terms come from joining together two separate words: *kolam,* which refers to the physical form of the deity, either in the shape of an idol or the fully costumed performer, and *karran,* which means man.

drumming during the actual performance. Training tends to be informal and personal but involves the deliberate learning of a craft. Training and performance are often simultaneous processes. There are occasions, however, when training is given to the novice in more formalized and organized sessions. K. P. C. Panicker, for example, remembers the first training he received from his father. In the beginning he learned only the narratives that invoke the deity *(tottam)*. He would repeat the sung verses line by line, following his father, or they would be written down on paper for reference and study. Often his parents recited the songs as he was going to sleep and he memorized them simply by hearing them again and again. After learning the narratives of several deities his father taught him the dance steps. Later, Panicker was sent to a village to study with a famous teacher known for his performance of one deity (Viṣṇumūrthi). For six months he trained during the night and early morning.

Panicker described this part of the training as rigorous. In the early morning, he developed basic skills through repetition of specific exercises. The session began with jumps, reminiscent of *kathakaḷi* training (chapter 10). The aim of this exercise was to jump high enough to position the legs out in front of the body and touch the forehead with the toes. When the muscles and joints were loosened Panicker applied coconut oil over his body. He would bend his legs in a low second position and slowly move forward by rotating his feet. Then he would practice the special gutteral yell peculiar to Viṣṇumūrthi, learn to make his arms and hands vibrate, and the various dance sequences.

In the evening he would memorize the list of important places where the deity was worshipped, as this is recited during the performance, and a special language to address temple officials and important village members during the ritual. Learning how to talk properly and behave with devotees is equally as important as the dance narratives. Panicker explained that the special language spoken by the deity (a mixture of Sanskrit and Malayalam) gave him the authority to solve problems that were sometimes brought before him by members of the community at the end of the ritual.

There seems to be no fixed age when a novice can begin performing. Minor deities are given to beginners as young as five, but these require very little technique and often involve no more than wearing a costume and walking about.

Panicker is now a teacher himself. Perhaps of all the performers we met, he was unusually critical and articulate about his craft. When asked about his role as a bearer of tradition, Panicker explained:

> *Teyyam* is a traditional art. It is a creation of the past. It must be sustained. And up to a certain point it can be used for a job. My nephew, for example, is trying to get a better job but until that time he can perform *teyyam*. But people are

> losing belief. I see *teyyam* as an art not as a belief. As far as my technique is concerned, no one can surpass me. No one can tell from my performance that I am not a believer. I am not a believer. I am a good performer. But I never tell anyone that I don't believe.

When asked about his performance techniques, Panicker played down the role of divine inspiration and stressed the deliberateness with which he carried out his performance. Local theories about performance have tended to emphasize the deity's power over what is said and danced in the ritual. Panicker insisted that everything he did, including his possession, came from his own ability, not from an outside power.

Panicker gave several examples. Before performing in a village, he would arrive early and secretly discover what problems were going on in the particular community. When talking to devotees during the ritual, he would use this information to demonstrate the omniscience of the divinity and to confirm their belief in him. Sometimes during the ritual, while pretending to fix something on Panicker's costume, an assistant would whisper in his ear which important members of the community had arrived and which titles to call them. The deity is supposed to know this. As we have already mentioned, these titles are very important. If they are left out, the sponsors are angered. He remembered his father reminding him: "Now you are my son but when you put the costumes on you will be the god and you have to behave like that. You should treat other people like your servants, do not fear anybody. And you must call the correct names for certain people. You should even refer to me by my title and not father." We emphasize these examples not to diminish the power of the ritual, or to imply any dishonesty, but to underscore the idea that even the most sacred situations are artfully constructed and put together, even as they appear unquestionable and transcendent.

Whether or not this attitude is common among other performers is yet to be explored. Other theories exist. For example, Ambu Perumalayan insisted that the power of the deity came to him from recitation of special sacred syllables or mantras which gave him the ability to perform the necessary rituals, dance, and speak to the devotees appropriately.

Several schools now offer more formalized teaching. One such school was set up in 1977 at Kotakkat village. There the Institute for Ritual and Traditional Arts of India (Kalanitekthanam) was organized by local villagers in collaboration with several academics from Calicut University, in an effort to attract both foreign and local interest in various folk arts. In existence for hardly a year, it offered space and a little money to allow inspiring *teyyam* performers to teach regularly the songs, dances, invocations, costume repair, and construction to members of their own caste. A group of foreigners under the auspices of the University of California participated in the Institute, where they were able to conduct interviews, see many festivals, learn some of the dances and face painting, and exchange information with local scholars. Ultimately, the Institute came to an end for financial reasons.

Presently there is a man who claims to be teaching *teyyam* "scientifically." For two weeks out of the year at his own expense, he takes in three or four children at a time and systematically teaches them dance steps and *tottam,* or narrative song. Emphasis is given to differentiating the various singing styles of each *tottam,* a concern which seems to have been borrowed from the teaching of classical music.

Performance (Festival) Structure

A *kāḷiyāṭṭam* festival lasts anywhere from two to five days and nights and sometimes longer. From one to thirty-nine deities may be propitiated. It is a multifocused event, having numerous activities, only one of which is the propitiation of the deity. Other items have included political canvassing, advertising, drama, storytelling, gambling, cock fighting, and a traveling zoo. A festival market surrounds the adjacent area of the shrine compound. This area immediately outside the shrine is scattered with tea shops, fruit stalls, and temporary stores selling cloth, sandals, mirrors, and cakes. Occasionally portable hand-operated ferris wheels are set up and gambling in numerous forms is abundant. Young boys and girls come to watch each other.

Preparations for a festival are rigorous. At Kuttikol village, many days before the commencement of the festival, the temple compound is cleaned. The weeds are burnt away. Each day unmarried males from the three villages bring cow dung to the temple site. This is mixed with water and used to coat the temple grounds, which are then painted with elaborate designs by temple priests and assistants. Meanwhile tube lights, loudspeakers, a microphone, and record player are installed. Throughout the five days of the festival, cinema music and popular religious songs are frequently blasted over the sound system in between rituals. When music is not taking precedence, temple offerings, like bananas, coconuts, and various animals, are auctioned off to collect money for the festival and the upkeep of the shrine.

Each day of a festival consists of several ceremonies dedicated to different deities, and each ceremony progresses through similar stages: purifications, invocations, recitation of narratives, the presentation of various offerings, and finally the central performance in which the dancer is possessed by the deity.

An overview of the five days reveals a dynamic which does not move in a straight line culminating in a climax. Although devotees wander in and out of the event at times almost arbitrarily, certain days of the festival are considered more important and attractive than others and a marked increase in attendance during these times is evident. During the opening rituals, consecration of space, and so on, only temple officials and performers are present. Few people attend the second day of the event, but during the evening of the third day, the entire space surrounding the temple compound is filled with spectators and devotees, most of whom come after sunset and remain well after sunrise to watch that day's featured sequence.

The fourth day marks a noticeable tapering off in attendance but increases once again for the fourth night of the festival, when villagers arrive to receive blessings and make offerings to the most important deity of the shrine. The festival concludes when the performers symbolically return the divine power back into the shrine. The doors are closed. Participants bow toward the shrine in reverence.

This emphasis on sequence and addition rather than upon consequence permits a certain open-endedness in how the festival may be organized and allows for the introduction of novel items and genres into the system: new dramas, the latest cinema music, elaborate decorations and processions, and new technical innovations. For example in 1982 at a festival in the central part of Cannanore District, members of the community participated in a procession around the shrine while swinging long, multicolored neon lights which were attached to car batteries. During the festival, individuals may commission special vow performances to a particular deity, requiring that whole ritual sequences be added or repeated. In some situations a festival may be extended to accommodate the additional rituals.

Certain aspects of the festival are more conservative and precautions are taken to ensure their stability. These include the kind of offerings given to the deity, the *tottam,* and certain rituals. However, even these aspects may be altered and astrology is the usual method for making changes. Throughout the festival, temple officials seek out signs which alert them to an unsuccessful performance: Rituals are not completed; the performer faints from exhaustion and cannot complete the performance; ritual bananas do not ripen in time for the festival. An astrologer is called in and through an elaborate process, discovers the cause for the failure and suggests a remedy. Common causes for an unsuccessful performance are stereotypical: The performer ate meat when he should have eaten only vegetarian meals; the priest entered a house that was polluted by a death or birth; the family members commissioning the performance have been quarrelling and lack unity.

Structure of One *Teyyam*

In the performance of all *teyyam* the structure is sequential. Gestures, movements, and paraphernalia are displayed in a prescribed order, the proper sequence often being more important to the festival aesthetic and to its power than how the sequences are technically carried out.

Although variations in performance structure exist, *teyyam* are organized around a basic six-part sequence: (1) invocation of the deity, (2) recitation of the deity's story, (3) possession of the performer by the deity who then dances, (4) recitation of additional stories, (5) giving blessings, and (6) removal of the crown culminating the ritual performance. As all *teyyam* are understood to be a visitation of the divine in the present, the ritual sequence facilitates this transformation, as it shifts from third-person narrative in which the performer *recites* the story about the deity, to a state in which he *embodies* the deity, speaks in the first person as the deity, and participates in an actual and dynamic world. Costuming and makeup play an important part in marking this gradual transformation. The performer dons only a partial costume for the invocation and recitation of the deity's story. He wears no makeup. A full costume is donned when he appears as the deity incarnate and speaks in first person.

For purposes of clarity we will describe part of one *teyyam,* Viṣṇumūrthi, that we saw in March 1981 in the village of Kuttikol. Viṣṇumūrthi is an incarnation of Viṣṇu. He is worshipped by all castes and has come to be regarded as the savior of the "depressed and downtrodden in Kerala society" (Kurup 1977, 34). One of the central myths about Viṣṇu tells how he transformed himself into a man-lion to kill Hiraṇyakaśipu, a demon king who was plaguing the world and causing chaos. The story is enacted in many performance genres throughout Kerala, including *kathakaḷi,* and is the central theme in the performance of Viṣṇumūrthi. The story is summarized by Richmond (1971):

> In ancient times Hiraṇyakaśipu, a demon king, was said to have gained a boon from Brahmā which made him invincible. He could be killed neither by day nor by night, neither inside nor outside his house, neither by man nor by animal. Armed with this divine protection, Hiraṇyakaśipu proceeded to terrorize the people of the world. He forbade all worship of Lord Viṣṇu. The evil king was so angered by the fervent worship of his own son, Prahlāda, for Viṣṇu that he tried to murder him for speaking Viṣṇu's name. Eventually Hiraṇyakaśipu questioned his son as to the whereabouts of his God. Prahlāda said that Viṣṇu was everywhere, even in a pillar, whereupon Hiraṇyakaśipu drew his sword and slashed open a pillar in the doorway of his palace. Narasiṃha, Viṣṇu's incarnation as a man-lion burst forth and tore out his entrails. Brahmā's boon was cleverly circumvented; Hiraṇyakaśipu was killed in the doorway of his house, at sunset, by a man-lion. Good triumphed and order was restored to the world.

In the *teyyam* version of this myth, Viṣṇumūrthi is Narasimha, the man-lion.

Viṣṇumūrthi (foreground) blesses devotees immediately following his ordeal of firewalking. In the background is Bhagavati, a second *teyyam* appearing at this local village festival. (Phillip B. Zarrilli photo)

Viṣṇumūrthi Teyyam
Five Part Sequence

[Donning partial costume]

Invocation of the deity *(varavilli)*
The performer calls the deity down to the shrine. The recitation is chanted in the nominative case, "You."

[Donning the first small crown and garlands]

Recitation of the deity's history *(tottam)*
Dressed in a partial costume, the performer recites the deity's history in the third person ("He" or "She") which makes the deity present.

[Donning the full costume]

Possession and dance as the deity *(teyyam)*
Dressed in the complete costume of the deity and with full makeup, the performer becomes possessed and dances as the deity.

First person recitation *(mumbasthanam)* and offering of blessings
After completing the dance, the performer recites additional history of the deity in the first person, "I." He questions those assembled and offers blessings as the deity.

Removal of headdress *(mutiyettukal)*
The culmination of the ritual performance comes when the performer removes the crown in front of the shrine.

Invocatory Prayer

A short invocatory prayer is recited in the nominative case ("You") by the performer in front of the shrine. These prayers are chanted to the accompaniment of drums in order to invite the spirit of the deity down to the shrine. A selection from one performer's palm leaf booklet of this invocatory prayer follows:

> Pay obeisance with proffered rice to the sacred weapons and the stand-lamp! Let the prospering Hari be glorious, let fruits be in abundance and the lasting blessings of Guru, long years of life and prosperity and riches.
>
> Come, O! Come!
>
> Viṣṇumūrthi, our household god! I invoke you with the incantation of the *tottam* . . .[5]

Recitation of the Deity's History *(Tottam)*

In front of the shrine, before the commencement of the singing of the deity's history, the performer receives a large banana leaf from the officiating priest. The leaf contains five lighted wicks, an areca nut, five betel leaves, turmeric powder, and a small amount of uncooked rice. Inside the shrine, the priest passes the lighted wicks over the idol of the *teyyam* (the various metal swords or wooden stool) to obtain its power. The lighted wicks transfer this power of the deity from the idol inside the shrine to the performer.

"The five lighted wicks represent the five elements—air, fire, space, water, and earth," explained one performer. "These elements are sakti in a form that people can see and concentrate on."

Assistants begin to decorate the performer with colored necklaces and garlands of flowers, while temple officials build a small fire off to the side. The small crown is attached to his head. In front of the opening of the shrine a drum is set up on a stool and assistants gather around with their drums slung from their shoulders. Taking the stick in his hand, he slowly beats the drum and chants parts of the *tottam*. Musicians accentuate each stanza with percussive rolls and join in the chorus. As the *tottam* comes to an end, the rhythms become increasingly louder and faster. The performer begins shaking. Spectators receive handfuls of uncooked rice as they cluster on either side of the opening of the shrine. His singing stops and his lips move silently as he recites the last section of the song. The drums become piercing.

Inside the shrine the priest ritually transfers the divine power from the idol of the *teyyam* to a handful of smoldering coals that are contained in a small shallow brass pot. He waves the pot in front of the performer. The smoke, now endowed with the power, permeates the environment.

The shaking now becomes more violent. The drums are played even louder. Spectators crowd in closer to the opening of the shrine, craning their

[5] Translated by P. C. Gangahdaran.

necks to see. At the final moment, the performer closes his eyes and falls slightly backwards, as if inebriated. Spectators shower him with rice and assistants clear the way leading to the shrine. His eyes bulge and rapidly dart back and forth. There is an incredible immediacy. Emitting a frightful cry, he springs into the air, kicking and stamping in all directions. Rushing forward to the threshold of the shrine, he drops to his knees and begins mimetically killing the demon Hiraṇyakaśipu. Gesturing with his hands, he slits open the demon's chest and lunges inside. Great elaboration is given to this sequence. He brings his hands up, vibrating them rapidly to evoke the showering of blood. Sticking out his tongue he laps up the blood, while draping the entrails around his neck. Then looking up toward heaven, he shakes his hand threateningly at Brahmā, warning him never to grant such boons to a demon again. Again he gestures, fondly putting his arm around Hiraṇyakaśipu's son, Prahlāda, praising him for his strict devotion to Viṣṇu.

Glaring at the spectators, the performer rises to his feet and runs over to the heap of burning coals previously prepared by officials. He steps into the coals. This is believed to purify him after killing the demon. From the priest, he receives the deity's sword and special bow. Dancing triumphantly at the death of Hiraṇyakaśipu, he bounds high into the air. His steps are firm and percussive, punctuated by short staccato kicks. There is never a pause. There is always an urgency, an underlying vibration which never ceases until the end of the two-hour period. In this heated state, he blesses the devotees by throwing rice at them. The performer jumps into the air, is caught by his assistants and rushed off the performing area.

Donning the Costume and Application of Face Makeup

After the *tottam,* the performer once again returns to his dressing area to don the full costume of the *teyyam* for the final transformation. From a small pouch among the clutter of ritual paraphernalia the performer carefully removes several packets which contain the expensive powders he will make into paint. Throughout the process of mixing the makeup performers say they recite sacred syllables associated with the deity to be performed, "charging" the powders with the god's power by chanting the mantras and literally breathing them into the mixture. He raises his hand to his mouth and repeats the mantras again, "blowing" them onto the tip of his finger that now contains a small swab of the mixture. He dabs the color onto a special area of the face between the eyes and slightly higher than the brow, then rubs it over his entire face.

In this simple action, the performer has moved closer toward transformation by literally "painting" the deity onto his face. Having been charged with divine power, the paint ceases to be merely a physical substance, but becomes a tangible and spiritual manifestation of the deity. He lies down and the remaining work will be completed by an assistant. This makeup process usually takes no less than two hours to complete and requires much concentration on the part of both the painter and the performer.

Nearby other assistants make the costumes. These are intricate constructions that must be newly fabricated for each performance, as they are perishable and spoil shortly after use. Coconut leaves and stems, bamboo, husks from the banana tree, sheaths from the areca nut tree, dried grasses, and flowers are assembled into delicate frames and structures that are covered with colored cloth and gilded papers. Intricate wooden shapes inlaid with colored glass are fitted together into headdresses, some of which will tower twenty feet into the air. Performers embodying the power of female deities wear breasts carved from wood or coconuts and sometimes molded from bronze. Beards woven from jute are often worn by performers embodying the power of male deities.

When performers are fully costumed they will look identical to their small wooden counterparts, which are meticulously carved on the outside of many shrines, or to some of the miniature metal icons housed inside. These wooden carvings represent the major deities propitiated in the particular shrine.

During the ritual the costume, manipulated by the dancer, will become a moving icon: dynamic, three dimensional, and capable of interacting with devotees. What temple officials inside the shrine do to the various static images of the deity (propitiation with flowers, incense, ritual offerings of food, purification, and so on) will also be done outside of the shrine to the transformed performer.

Possession and Dance *(Teyyam)*

When the costume is attached, the drums announce the beginning of the performance. The performer is escorted to the entrance of the shrine and seated. He begins a shaking movement in his legs, an intense quivering that travels upward and inhabits the rest of his body. It is a drawing inward of energy that will eventually explode at the moment of transference to him of the god's power. The final touches are made to the costume: The dress is trimmed and a rich, velvety, red powder is applied to the lips. He is handed his mirror. The shaking becomes more pronounced, the drums more forceful, almost deafening. He plucks a small flower from his costume, whispers mantras into it and raises the mirror to his face. After examining his reflection for several moments, the performer's face contorts and becomes awestricken: "At that moment," one performer explained, "I am no longer seeing my reflection but the face of god peering back at me through the mirror."

His cheeks quiver and his body trembles. He rushes forward to the shrine and enacts the killing sequence of Hiraṇyakaśipu once again. This time the whole inside of his mouth is coated with brilliant red powder to give the appearance of blood. After the victory dance, he grabs handfuls of rice and

A dynamic possession dance of Kuttysasthan *teyyam*—one of the hero *teyyam*. (Phillip B. Zarrilli photo)

urgently makes his way around the compound, pelting the eager devotees with the small white kernels. Other devotees hold out their hand to receive the rice, some of which they place on their head, the rest they throw into their mouth, as if to "ingest" his blessings.

First-Person Recitation and Blessings

Upon returning to the *teyyam* shrine, the deity addresses the patrons and devotees in a monologue that relates additional history of the deity, the places where the deity has traveled, and the location of important shrines dedicated in its honor. During the last section of the performance the *teyyam* makes a second speech in which he addresses each caste in order of its importance. Individuals of various castes come before the *teyyam* and answer to his inquisition. In the past, reported one of our informants, if the performer did not remember the names of important Nayar community members by their official lineage title, he would get fined twenty paise and receive a beating the next day.

The *teyyam* calls out to devotees: "Did you worship me? Have you made sacrifices to me? Have you fulfilled all of your duties to me?" Devotees and priests stand when they are approached by the *teyyam* and make humbling gestures to him. His behavior is often impatient, hostile, and haughty. He is the absolute focus of attention, and the patrons are alert to his every need.

The *teyyam* assures each beneficiary that he will provide assistance and security during times of crisis. Any problems, individual or communal, are now brought up before the *teyyam,* who takes the role of mediator. Today, most conflicts deal with property disputes, organizational and financial disagreements between priests and officials of the shrine, and occasionally, frictions arising among members of different castes. In this way *teyyam* performances do more than just make statements about an ideal set of social hierarchies and relationships. They are sometimes the arenas for real social dramas.

The deity receives the offering prepared for him. A cock is sacrificed. He is approached by devotees who give money in exchange for a small leaf containing turmeric, an auspicious powder which is smeared onto the forehead and can be taken back home to family members unable to attend the ritual.

Removing the Crown

Now the drums sound for the last time, and once again the spectators shower the *teyyam* with rice, as he removes his headdress in front of the shrine. He bows to all in reverence. Assistants disassemble the costumes as quickly as possible. There is talking and laughter. One performer lights up a cigarette; another takes a break to buy tea and a snack at a nearby stall. Spectators gradually drift away. Some stop for breakfast on the way or buy a gift for a child from a toy vendor. Performers carefully pack all their belongings and paraphernalia into their baskets. The offerings made to the deity —rice, bananas, coconuts, chicken—are collected and given to the performer. The patron pays each of them their fee. A stop at the local liquor shop is customary for many performers before moving on to their next engagement.

Current State

To summarize, the festival draws into its sphere many social and political realities of the everyday world and fuses them with the divine. The proper place, a propitious occasion, the appropriate participants, all contribute to a successful ritual. *Teyyam* continues to be performed today in large festival contexts, as "vows to god," and to propitiate deities who effect the destinies of a village.

But *teyyam* is not only performed for festival occasions. It has also been performed during Kerala Tourist week, as entertainment for a biology symposium, as part of the Folk Dance Festival during the Republic Day celebrations, at the opening ceremonies of the 1982 Asian Olympics in New Delhi, and at the Village Art Festival in Kerala sponsored by the Ford Foundation. It is possible to view the performance as "standing available to participants as a set of conventional expectations and associations which can be manipulated in innovative ways, working various transformations and adaptations which turn the performance into something else" (Bauman 1975). There has been a tendency among researchers to view "traditional" performance as closed and bound rather than malleable and open-ended.

We cannot detail the process now, but we do want to sketch out some of the occasions on which this has occurred. In a small village, on May 1, 1981, the Communist Party held a rally which featured *teyyam* dancing after speeches were made against capitalism, corruption, and suppression. The plan to show *teyyam* dancing was a conscious attempt to strip the ritual of its efficacy by demonstrating that it could be performed without rituals, priests, or offerings. The Communist Party hoped to show, contrary to the villagers' beliefs, that there would be no anger from the god, no consequences. *Teyyam* could be performed for fun.

At the end of the dance, instead of calling important high caste members of the audience to come and receive blessings, as the deity would do in the ritual, the speaker called local Communist Party members over a microphone. This brought great laughter from the spectators. From the wings of the stage, both men and women approached the dancer in the typical posture of deference, in which the hand is touched to the middle of the chest and the head is slightly lowered. They gave money to the deity but did not receive the ritual blessings. Organizers wanted to recast the role of the dancer in terms of "wage labor" to deemphasize obligation and ritual reciprocity. *Teyyam* should become a job, a way of making money, and not an act of belief or faith.

At the conclusion of the speech, the dancer told spectators to turn their devotion to Namboodiripad, the general secretary of the Marxist Party, and Nayanar, who was the chief minister of Kerala from 1980–1981. Sponsors of the performance told us they would like to see *teyyam* performed as an art form, as something enjoyable to watch, detached from any kind of religious system. In their view poverty, the continuing presence of a caste, and the manipulation of the masses by an upper-class elite, is intimately bound with the performance and belief in rituals, which keep the proletariat passive and dependent on forces outside themselves.

The Natana Kala Kshetram, a theatre company in Cannanore, has rewritten several sacred texts *(tottam)* of *teyyam* and turned them into popular dance-dramas, complete with sound systems, smoke effects, flashing lights, projections, and painted backdrops. In 1981 one such drama, *Muchilot Bhagavathi,* met with much violent opposition. The patron community of the deity brought the theatre company to court and sued them for stealing the *teyyam* and desecrating it on stage (Ashley and Holloman 1982). Others have been successful entertainments.

These examples are not meant to point out any corruptions or impurities in the *teyyam* system. To us, there is no such thing as a closed and perfect event. These examples are meant to demonstrate the open-endedness of "traditional" material, which must finally be viewed within a much larger performative cluster, noting the various ways of framing and rescripting the ritual. To ignore these processes is to miss possible shifts in the domain of cultural meaning.

WORKS CITED

Ashley, Wayne, and Regina Holloman. 1982.
"From Ritual to Theatre in Kerala." *The Drama Review* 26, 2:59–72.

Bauman, Richard. 1975.
"Verbal Art as Performance." *American Anthropologist* 77, 2:290–311.

Kurup, K. K. N. 1977.
Aryan and Dravidian Elements in Malabar Folklore. Trivandrum: Kerala Historical Society.

Richmond, Farley. 1971.
"Some Religious Aspects of Indian Traditional Theatre." *The Drama Review* 15, 3:123–131.

ADDITIONAL READING

Armstrong, Robert Plant. 1982.
The Powers of Presence. Philadelphia: University of Pennsylvania Press.

Ashley, Wayne. 1979.
"The Teyyam Kettu of Northern Kerala." *The Drama Review* 23, 2:99–112.

Ashton, Martha. 1979.
"Spirit Cult Festivals in South Kanara." *The Drama Review* 23, 2:91–98.

Blackburn, Stuart. 1980.
"Performance as Paradigm: The Tamil Bow Song Tradition." Ph.D. diss., University of California at Berkeley.

Claus, Peter. 1975.
"The Siri Myth and Ritual: A Mass Possession Cult of South India." *Ethology* 14, 1:47–58.

Holloman, Regina, and Wayne Ashley. 1983.
"Caste and Cult in Kerala." *South Asian Anthropologist* 4, 2:93–104.

Kurup, K. K. N. 1973.
The Cult of Teyyam and Hero Worship in Kerala. Calcutta: Indian Publishing House.

Mencher, Joan P. 1964.
"Possession, Dance and Religion in North Malabar, Kerala, India." *International Congress of Anthropological and Ethological Sciences* 7th. 9:340–345.

Stache-Rosen, Valentina. 1978.
Bhutas and Teyyams: Spirit Worship and Ritual Dances in South Kanara and North Malabar, An Exhibition. Bangalore: Max Mueller Bhavan.

Chapter Five

AYYAPPAN TIYATTA

Phillip B. Zarrilli

IN ADDITION TO *teyyam,* the southwest coastal region of India is home to many other forms of ritual performance. Another example of the weaving of elaborate ritual and performance elements into an artistic religious expression is *Ayyappan tiyatta* (also known as *tiyattiyattam*). While in *teyyam* many different deities are propitiated, in this ritual only one deity is worshipped—the god Ayyappan. Lord Ayyappan is one of the most popular deities of Kerala. He is one of three Śiva deities and is believed to have been born of the union of Śiva and Mohinī (Viṣṇu in the guise of an enchantress). According to local legends, Ayyappan played an important role in Kerala history, having taken human form and come to the aid of the Malayalee people in a time of distress.

This particular ritual performance is only given in two places: Ayyappan temples or in the homes of Nambūdiri Brahmans, traditionally Kerala's highest caste. In such settings *tiyatta* may be performed for any number of reasons. Two typical purposes for giving the *tiyatta* are as an offering to Ayyappan for prosperity or in fulfillment of a vow. For example, if a Nambūdiri Brahman marriage has produced no sons after a long period of time, the family might vow to commission a *tiyatta* when a son is born, thus giving thanks to the Lord for answering their prayers.

Ayyappan tiyatta is one of three members of a special group of Kerala ritual performances which share common elements. The other two are *Bhagavati pattu* and *Nagayakshi kalam*. The most important common elements include a floor drawing or painting of a large image *(kalam)* of one or more specific deities being propitiated, an elaborate set of initial ritual worship acts *(pūjā)*, and a closely related set of performances, which can include singing songs of the deity, percussion, music, dance, or quasi-dramatic acting (Jones 1981, 1982). The distinctive features of *Ayyappan tiyatta* include a period of mono-acting in which one of the performers narrates and enacts part of the legendary story of Lord Ayyappan, and a highly energetic dance in which one of the performers becomes possessed by the deity, occasionally culminating in his walking on fire (thus one possible derivation of the name of the ritual, "fire jumping").

Ayyappan tiyatta is a collective ritual performance. It requires three groups of specialists to perform it fully. The major performers and those who organize and bear responsibility for the complete structuring and efficacy of the performance are male *tiyatti* Nambyars, members of the caste of temple servants of Kerala and ranking high in the caste hierarchy. Their performance responsibilities include: (1) contracting for a performance of the ritual, (2) drawing the elaborate floor drawing *(kalam)* representing the deity, (3) singing the songs of the deity while accompanying themselves with percussion instruments, (4) performing the mono-acting *(kūttŭ)* narration of some of Ayyappan's legends, while in a special costume, and (5) performing the possession dance concluding in the delivery of oracles. In addition to the *tiyatti* Nambyars, it is necessary to have a Brahman ritual specialist present to initiate the ritual performance through an elaborate set of purificatory acts. Another set of assistants are the percussion specialists who may be brought in to accompany the *tiyatti* Nambyars' dance and acting performances.

Training

Training usually takes place within the immediate family, the father bearing responsibility for teaching the son all the skills necessary to perform each aspect of the complex ritual. The teaching of the various skills is spread over a number of years. Training often begins as early as five years old, when the father begins to teach the twelve songs about Lord Ayyappan sung in the ritual. The more difficult training in mono-acting and dance is taught only after the young man undergoes the investiture of the sacred thread at the age of twelve. Then he is introduced to the mudras, the gesture language necessary for narrating and enacting the Ayyappan legends. In addition training is given in the basic rhythmic patterns and steps required for both mono-acting and the possession dance. Such training usually goes on for several hours at night in an open area of the family home. Occasionally a father will see that a boy undergoes a period of seasonal massage for fourteen days to help him achieve a more flexible body for better performance of the dances.

An important part of the education process of the ritual performer takes place when the boy accompanies his father to a performance. Here the boy is called upon to assist in various aspects of the performance, especially in making the colored floor drawings *(kalam)*. Some students will be taught the outline forms at home, but knowledge of the design and the process of its creation only comes with the experience of making actual drawings. Subtleties of other aspects of the complete performance are also absorbed as if by osmosis at performances, when the young boy assists his elders.

By the age of fifteen or sixteen the youth will have his first "performance." Here he is required to perform both the mono-acting as well as the possession dance and oracle dance *(veliccappad).* No specific instruction is given to the youth on how to allow the deity to possess him. The dance steps and rhythmic patterns are by now engrained in his body from constant practice. The years of observation certainly play an important role in providing a map of the parameters which circumscribe the possession state and inform the young boy of the proper demeanor to be embodied for the duration of the dance. After his initial performance, a young *tiyatti* Nambyar usually becomes a specialist in one aspect of performance. Some become well-known for abilities as master painters of the floor drawings; others are known for their histrionic abilities in enacting and narrating the mono-acting stories; and still others for the efficacy and complete absorption of their possession states. When sufficient funding permits, the Nambyar in charge of arranging a particular performance may hire the best artists of each element of the complete *Ayyappan tiyatta,* thereby enhancing the possible efficacy as well as artistic dimensions of the ritual.

Representation of the Deity

The making of the "threshing floor drawings" (the central visual image of the ritual) is an important artistic tradition which dates to the sixteenth century, or possibly even to as early as the eleventh century A.D. Utilizing important Kerala design motifs present in the mural painting traditions, the artists use five different colored chalks (white, red, yellow, green, and black) to create a striking visual representation of the deity. There are three different representations of the god Ayyappan which may be used for the ritual. Each of the three illustrates Ayyappan in one of his popular legendary roles. One of the three representations is of Ayyappan with his divine mount, a white horse. A second is of Ayyappan in his role as protector of the forests, accompanied by a tiger (which he tamed in order to extract fresh milk for a cure). The third image is of Ayyappan as a hunter and warrior. In this final image, Ayyappan appears alone without an animal, carries a bow and arrow in his left hand, and in his right a sword or another arrow. In all three cases, however, the basic features of Ayyappan himself are the same. What is unusual about the floor paintings is that certain specific parts of the image, such as the eyes and nose, are three dimensional, which lends the image a more striking and living quality. Indeed such visual painting techniques are ritually important, in that the Nambyars perform an "eye-opening" ceremony as a prelude to the

> later ritual of *jiva pratisththa* or establishment of 'life force' which is the point at which the painting is transformed into a receptacle of the deity's *śakti* or power. From that moment of consecration onwards until the ceremonial destruction of the painting, the deity is ritually 'alive' or present in the image on the floor. (Jones 1981, 71–72)

The drawings take from two to five hours to complete, from the laying down of the first two axis lines, through the drawing of the outline of the image, to the final filling in of the outlines with the colored powders.

Ayyappan Tiyatta in Performance

A performance of *Ayyappan tiyatta* at a Nambūdiri Brahman house compound in 1980 will serve as a typical example of the complete ritual performance.[1] The major part of this particular performance takes place in a spe-

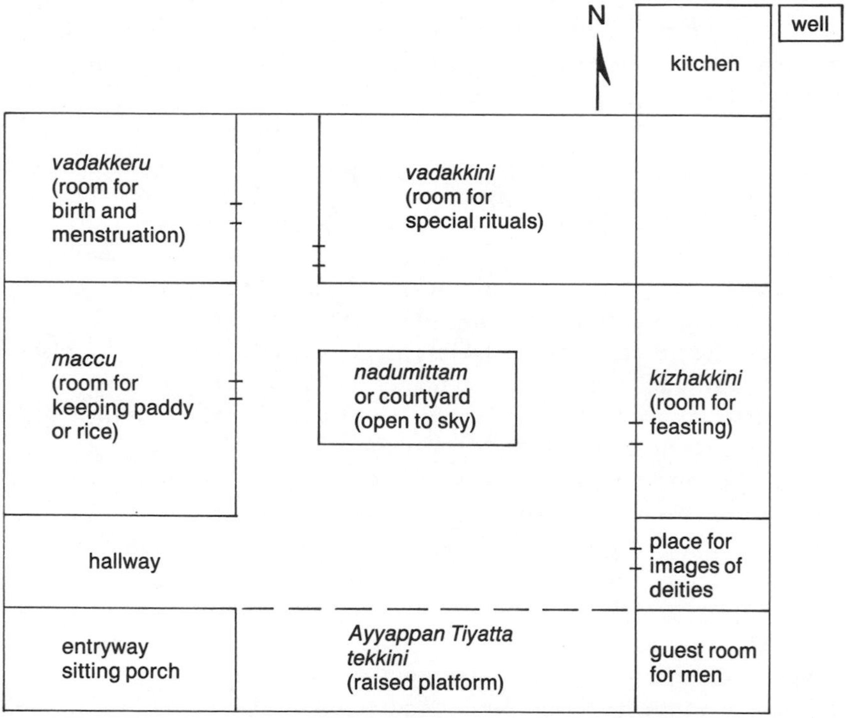

Nambūdiri nalukettu house showing division of space by function and location of the *tekkini* or raised platform where the *Ayyappan tiyatta* is performed.

[1] The times given in this description are approximate and apply only to this one example.

Summary of *Ayyappan Tiyatta* Performance

		Nambyars	Pūjāri or Musicians	Devotees or Patrons	
Preparations preliminary *pūjā* and song	Arranging the materials needed for the ritual (Nambyars)	4:00 PM			(-- Broken line indicates a few members of the family are present from time to time. No constant group of devotees are present until the Keli begins.)
	Ganapadi *pūjā* (pūjāri)		4:40 PM		
	Songs of praise to Ganesha, Parvatī, Śiva, and Ayyappan (Nambyars)	4:45 PM			
	Ayyappan *pūjā* (pūjāri)		4:50 PM		
Creating the image	Drawing of the *kalam*, decoration of space, placing of offerings to Ayyappan (Nambyars)	5:05 PM			
Percussion recital	Percussion music played in the entryway (special musicians)		7:10 PM		
Completion of *kalam*	Drawing fully complete and ready for investiture of deity	7:30 PM			
Beginning worship by devotees	Devotees begin to enter *kalam* area to give initial prayers to Ayyappan			7:50 PM	
Investing life in the *kalam* image	*kalam pūjā* (pūjāri)		8:40 PM		
Songs of praise	Songs of praise to Ayyappan, Viṣṇu, and Śiva (Nambyars)	9:00 PM			
Stories of Ayyappan enacted	*tottam* and *kūttŭ* performed (Nambyars)	9:40 PM			
Purification by fire	Torch passed to devotees for purification (*tiriuzhiccil* by Nambyar)	10:35 PM		10:35 PM	
Beginning of dance	*veliccappad* begins dance in entryway (Nambyar plus special musicians)	10:40 PM			
Procession to *kalam*	*veliccappad* dances to *tekkini* accompanied by musicians	11:00 PM			
Oracles given	*veliccappad* gives oracles to patrons and devotees	11:20 PM		11:20 PM	
Giving of *prasād*	*prasād* of *kalam* powder given to devotees	11:30 PM			

cial raised area on the interior of the main building of the Nambūdiri house. Here the floor painting will be drawn, the rituals conducted, and the major portion of the possession dance performed. This raised area, called the *tekkini,* is located on the south side of the central courtyard of the Nambūdiri house (see accompanying diagram). All of the rooms of a Nambūdiri house have special names and functions and the *tekkini,* where the ritual is held, is reserved for just such special ritual or feast occasions (Moore 1983).

Initial preparations begin at 4 P.M. as the Nambyars prepare the *tekkini* by laying out all the items needed for worshipping the deities and decorating the ritual space. This particular *Ayyappan tiyatta* will last eight and one-half hours, until half past eleven. During the course of this performance only one *kalam* will be painted—Ayyappan with his mount, the white horse. Formerly when funds among Nambūdiri extended families were more plentiful, a full ritual could last for forty-eight hours, during which all three representations of Ayyappan would be drawn in succession.

At 4:40 P.M. the ritual specialist from the Nambūdiri family temple located nearby begins the first act of the ritual. This is a ritual homage to Ganesha, the elephant-headed god to whom one prays or gives offerings before beginning any new undertaking. The homage to Ganesha will ensure that any obstacles in the way of this ritual's success are removed. The Brahman ritual specialist makes use of a variety of particular techniques and offerings in constructing each series of ritual acts. Among the many items included as accessories in the ritual acts of worship are water sprinkled from a special silver conch, sandalwood paste, flowers, incense, brass metal lamps with lit wicks, coconuts, rice, brown sugar, betel leaves, and areca nuts, as well as repetition of mantras. Each offering is purified before being given to the deity.

Included in the series of purifications is consecration of a long piece of black cloth, which the ritual specialist literally throws to the Nambyars, who are not permitted to touch the specialist, and which is used to cover the now sacred, consecrated space in the *tekkini* where the deity's picture will be drawn. In the space where the picture will be drawn, and where the ritual specialist has been performing homage to Ganesha, the Nambyars have constructed a four-posted temporary frame of areca logs. The entire framed area is further decorated with strips of coconut palm leaves and a variety of fresh flowers.

While the Ganesha ceremony is still in progress, the Nambyars gather to the right of the ritual specialist and begin to sing a series of songs of praise to Ganesha, Pārvatī, Śiva, and Ayyappan. By 5:00 P.M. the singing of songs is complete. The ritual specialist goes on to conduct additional obeisances with offerings given specifically to Ayyappan. After consecration, the ceremonial sword (held later by the Nambyar who is possessed by Ayyappan) is taken in procession to a special room where it will be kept until needed later in the ritual. For safety while the deity's image is being drawn, the sword must be kept in a sanctified place and cannot be touched.

By 5:05 the initial rituals have been completed, the space sanctified, and the sword, symbolic of Ayyappan's presence, removed for safekeeping to a separate space. The Nambyars now begin the process of drawing the portrait which will eventually receive the deity Ayyappan. After placing four lamps, and lighting their wicks, at the four corners of the space for the painting (eleven feet by nine feet), the main performer drawing the *kalam* and leading the group faces the southeast corner, where he draws with white powder one small flower. This is his own offering in drawing to Ganesha, further assuring the success of the drawing itself. Now the main axis of the drawing is placed down along an east-west line. The drawing itself will be aligned auspiciously, with the head to the east and feet to the west. The drawing is first outlined by the expert Nambyar, as he deftly uses his thumb and index finger to spread the white powder in constructing the figure. As he proceeds his three assistants fill in the outlines with the colored powders. The image of the deity begins to take shape over the next few hours.

By 7:10 the drawing is nearly complete, and the special percussion orchestra consisting of cymbals, a long cylindrical drum played with two curved sticks *(ceṇṭa),* and a horizontal drum played with the two hands *(maddalam)* begins a recital in the main entryway to the house. The percussion

Nambyar drawing in white powder the basic outline of the *kalam* along an east-west axis. (Phillip B. Zarrilli photo)

The completed *kalam* showing Ayyappan with his horse. (Phillip B. Zarrilli photo)

recital takes place around an oil lamp and is a progressive crescendo of sound, as the musicians move through increasingly complex and faster speeds and rhythmic patterns. While the drumming continues, the image of the deity is finished by 7:30 and the Nambyars proceed to lay out the various offerings to Ayyappan which surround the drawing. These offerings include many of the same items used by the ritual specialist, such as paddy, coconuts, brown sugar, and so on, all neatly arranged and placed on banana leaves.

The percussion concert in the entryway has drawn a number of villagers to the house. Such percussion orchestras often announce performances in Kerala, such as *kathakaḷi.* By 7:50 members of the extended household, as well as some of the villagers, have come into the courtyard surrounding the *tekkini* where the divine image has been drawn. Now that the image is complete the devotees enter and circumambulate it, pray to the deity, and prostrate themselves at the feet of the deity. While devotees begin their worship of the deity, the Nambyars are preparing for the next major part of the ritual: the mono-acting *(kūttŭ).*

By 8:40 the percussion concert has ended and the homage to the drawing begins. The Brahman ritual specialist returns to conduct this ceremony. He goes to the special small room where Ayyappan's ceremonial sword has been kept. Accompanied by drumming and following a lighted lamp, he brings out the sword, circles the courtyard, and passes through the house to the front entryway and back to the *tekkini* and the drawing, where he places the sword on "Ayyappan's seat" (a small stool at the eastern or "head" end of the drawing). The deity Ayyappan is now invested in the image itself. The ritual specialist returns to the foot of the image, takes his seat, and proceeds with the ritual of homage. Again offerings are made, mantras are recited, and the various accessories of worship utilized. Ayyappan is directly propitiated through this homage and offering. The consecrated flowers given to Ayyappan are now taken around and distributed, first to the three brothers who are senior members of the household and patrons of the ritual, and then to the seventy-five to one hundred people gathered in the courtyard area.

At 9:00 P.M. a new phase of the performance begins. The two Nambyars who will be performing the mono-acting and the possession dance have just returned from the temple bathing tank, where they have purified themselves for their part in the ritual. They now join the other two Nambyars in singing songs of praise to Lord Ayyappan, Viṣṇu, and Śiva. They accompany themselves on drum and with cymbals.

By 9:40 the songs of praise are complete and the celebrants begin to move toward the culmination of the ritual. The next section of the performance is the chanting of the twelve parts of the story of Ayyappan (the *tottam*), accompanied by the simultaneous mono-acting of the stories. The twelve stories narrate Ayyappan's life up to his birth, and then after his birth up to the time of his coming to Kerala. In shortened performances today, only one or two of the stories are usually enacted. The performance begins when one of the Nambyars begins to chant an introduction to the stories while the main performer, after praying to Ayyappan, begins to put on his costume at the western end of the floor drawing in full view of those attending the ritual. He puts on a long-sleeved red blouse, red headband, wooden-gilt jewelry, including earrings, necklaces, and bracelets, a small headdress, an everyday cloth piece *(muṇṭu)* wrapped around his waist, and another cloth piece wrapped across his shoulder and tied at the waist. When ready the main performer will enact the role of Nandikeśvara, the servant or gatekeeper of Śiva, who narrates selected stories of Ayyappan. Once ready Nandikeśvara performs a stylized dance at the foot of the floor drawing, accompanied by the two cylindrical drums *(ceṇṭa),* a *para* drum, cymbals, and a shrill horn *(kuzhal).* When the dance is complete, the actor begins to enact, in turn, two stories, the "Churning of the Ocean" followed by the "Birth of Ayyappan."

A few examples of performance from the "Birth of Ayyappan" will serve to illustrate the techniques used by the Nambyar. In brief, the story of the birth of Ayyappan begins with the god Viṣṇu in the form of Mohinī, the enchantress, who appears before a demon who is allured by her beauty. The demon loses control of his senses and destroys himself when he touches his hand. Thus Viṣṇu saved Lord Śiva from the demon but at the same time he was overcome with the beauty of Mohinī, succumbed to her charms, and from their union came Ayyappan, born of the thigh of Mohinī (since she is

The oracle dancer begins his dance in the entryway to percussion accompaniment.

Entering the *kalam* in a possessed state, he begins to destroy the *kalam* and decorations.

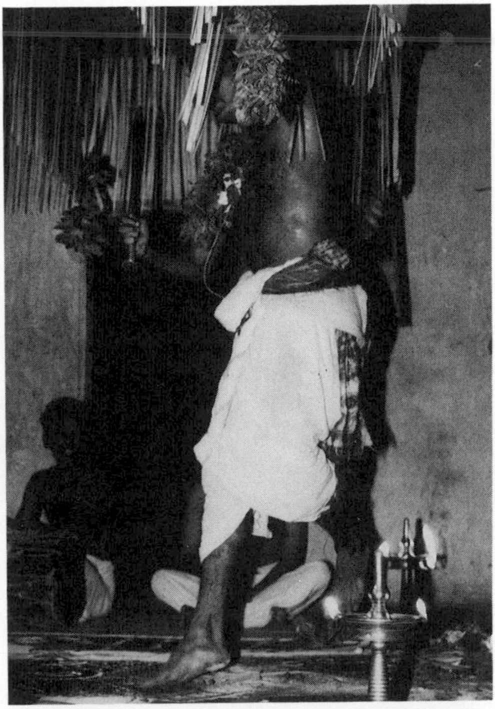

Jumping and cutting furiously, he destroys entirely the image.

Sitting on the stool at the head of the image, he completes his task of effacement.

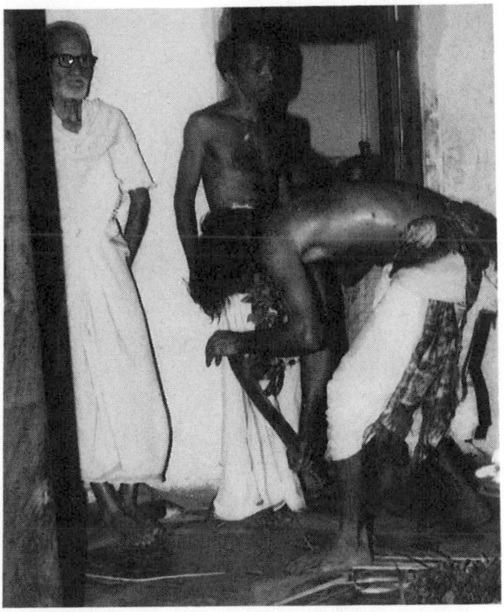

Holding the sword tightly, he gives oracles to the head of the household. (Phillip B. Zarrilli photos)

actually Viṣṇu). In enacting this story the performer sits at the foot of the floor drawing and delivers a short segment of the text in chant, and then rises to enact each portion in turn. It is a form of illustrated storytelling in which, as Nandikeśvara, the actor is always narrating or telling the story. In his acting the performer makes use of mudras in a mimetic telling of the story. The gesture language is not the highly complex, complete grammar of either *kūṭiyāṭṭam* or *kathakaḷi,* but rather a simpler sister art which makes most use of obvious mimetic hand positions and combinations. In describing Mohinī's beauty and her enchantment of Śiva, Nandikeśvara describes her long hair and how, looking up in a garden, she picks flowers. Sitting on the ground Mohinī admires herself in a handheld mirror and prepares her dress, outlining the shape of her voluptuous breasts. After finishing her toilet she begins to play ball. Such elaboration gives the performer some scope for interpretation which must include acting out *(abhinaya),* steps, and total body movement along with the narrative and mimetic gesture language. In contrast to the *kūṭiyāṭṭam* and *kathakaḷi* actor, and closer to the storytelling tradition of the Cakyar actors of Kerala, there is much less scope here for use of the face. Without the lifelong training of the major classical artist, the Nambyars' style of mono-acting is an entertaining but little refined form of story illustration. The telling of this particular story concludes as Viṣṇu-as-Mohinī begins to have labor pains, and the baby is born from his thigh. A final dance, in a fast rhythmic speed, concludes the mono-acting portion of the performance at 10:35 P.M.

On completion of the mono-acting, a few more songs of praise are sung and brief homage is conducted, which concludes with a wick lighting ceremony. The torch is first offered to the deity, and then it is passed among the devotees by one of the Nambyars, to bless and purify the devotees.

With purification of all complete, the final and culminating part of the ritual now begins. In the entryway to the house, accompanied by the special musicians, the oracle dancer *(veliccappad)* begins his steps and perambulations—a prelude and beginning to his possession by the god Ayyappan. His costume is simple—a wrapped *muṇṭu* with a special printed cloth wrapped about his waist and a garland of flowers around his neck. In the entryway the percussionists pass through increasing crescendos of sound, moving into progressively faster patterns, the oracle dancer's steps keeping pace with the increasing tempos and tenor of the drummers. The drums are urging on the dancer's feet as he moves toward a state of possession. By 11:00 the dance is beginning to reach a peak and the performer and musicians move back to the interior *tekkini,* followed by the devotees. The pace of the drumming picks up even more as the oracle dancer circles around the floor drawing, and again a second time around taking hopping steps. By this third circumambulation, the dancer's body has become looser and looser, giving in increasingly to both the rhythm and the possession of the deity, so that finally, as he moves faster and faster, looser and looser, he crosses the threshold into the state of possession and moves then into the space of the floor drawing itself. Explosively, possessed by Ayyappan, the oracle dancer begins to destroy the deity's image and all of the accompanying decorations—he literally tears apart the overhanging ropes and coconut palms, cutting them with his sword, and dances furiously around the drawing, wiping out and effacing the image entirely. He has effaced the image with his dancing feet, except for the face (which he cannot touch with his feet), and here he uses his hands. He now sits on the stool at the eastern ('head') end of the drawing, singing. He places the sword on the small stool in front of him and gives offerings of coconuts. Taking up the sword again, which is alive with the power of the deity, he begins to prophecy, first to the brothers of the house who have commissioned the performance. As the deity, he says whether he is pleased with the ritual. And then in turn he gives oracles to the gathered people. Sweating, panting, and holding tightly to the sword, the oracle's words come in waves and are at times difficult to understand. He tells the head of the house that he is pleased with the ritual. "You will have prosperity and happiness in life. I will be highly pleased if you will perform this ritual again." And when the deity is ready, he decides to leave the oracle dancer. He returns to the stool, the sword shaking violently now. He places the sword on the stool and the deity leaves him as he releases the sword. All that remains of the image of Ayyappan is the grey mixture of once brilliantly colored powders. This is taken up and given to the devotees to mark their foreheads—a sign of their devotion to Ayyappan.

By 11:30 the ritual has ended. The black cloth is taken down from above the sacred space. The oracle dancer takes off his special printed cloth. The Nambyars relax and then slowly begin to gather together their instruments and paraphernalia. The ritual has been a success and brought the pleasure of the god to the household.

Ayyappan tiyatta performances are becoming relatively rare occasions today, with many performers only giving four or five rituals in a year. For many young Nambyar boys, there is little apparent gratification or benefit from taking the time to learn the traditional ritual art of the family. Only a few younger Nambyars are keeping up the performance tradition of their elders today.

Current State

Ayyappan tiyatta is a typical example of the interweaving of ritual and performative elements into a complex whole which simultaneously serves to entertain and fascinate while it achieves its efficacious end. The movement of the entire ritual is from the relatively "cool" preparations and purificatory rituals to the energetically charged or "hot" possession of the oracle dancer.

During the opening preliminaries of the ritual, there is only occasional and perfunctory contact between those performing the ritual and those for whom it is being performed, namely, the patron family and by extension the villagers. In the first rituals, the ritual specialist functions as a solo priest-performer who has minimal interaction with the Nambyars who prepare the image which will receive the deity. While the drawing of the divine image is an artful process requiring great concentration, it elicits only occasional interest among the patron family members. Also there is no necessity of interaction at this point. Up until the beginning of the percussion recital and the completion of the floor drawing, the entire ritual process is purificatory and preparatory—it is a ritualized setting of the stage, as it were, for the visitation of the deity.

The percussion recital serves to announce the performance to the village, and serves as a gathering call to all devotees that the ritual "proper" is about to begin. At this stage there is an air of collective expectation as a small crowd begins to gather. The completed image of the deity now awaits the devotees as they progress to the *tekkini,* visiting the image and paying respects as they would the permanently installed deities of a formal temple. With the homage to the floor drawing and the actual investment of the deity *in* the image, the patrons, devotees, and performers are drawn into closer contact through the mediating immediacy of the deity, now present in their midst in the floor drawing. The chanting of Ayyappan's life stories and their enactment are a pleasant, entertaining, and educational interlude before the culminating "heated" possession. The conclusion of the chanting and enactment of the stories with the passing of the flame to purify the devotees prepares everyone for the culmination of the ritual—the visitation of the deity through possession of the performer. The entire ritual process has built toward this moment and, as the performer crosses his personal threshold in allowing the deity to possess him, the high point of the ritual is reached. He is now able to speak as the deity and to announce the efficacy of the ritual, a public announcement and confirmation that the purpose of the ritual has been accomplished. The departure of the deity effectively closes the ritual but the passing of ritually purified and offered food *(prasāda)* seals the exchange between devotees and deity through the ritual process. It is the collective dimensions of the rich fabric of the performance—the visually striking floor drawing; the use of song, dance, and acting; the narration and enactment of stories; the ritual purification; the moments of joining through ritual acts of spectator-devotees and deity where immediate sensory contact is made via flames, smoke, or possession, and oracles—it is all of these that produce the efficacious result and present immediacy of this ritual performance.

WORKS CITED

Jones, Clifford. 1981.
"Dhulicitra: Historical Perspectives on Art and Ritual." In *Kaladarsana: American Studies in the Art of India.* Ed. Joanna G. Williams. Leiden: E. J. Brill. Pp. 69–75.

———. 1982.
"Kalam Eluttu: Art and Ritual in Kerala." In *Religious Festivals in South India and Sri Lanka.* Eds. Guy R. Welbon and Glenn E. Yocum. New Delhi: Manohar. Pp. 269–294.

Moore, Melinda. 1983.
"Taravad: House, Land, and Relationship in a Matrilineal Hindu Society." Ph.D diss., University of Chicago.

ADDITIONAL READING

Beals, Alan R. 1964.
"Conflict and Interlocal Festivals in a South Indian Region." *Journal of Asian Studies* 23:99–113.

Clothey, Fred. 1969.
"Skanda-Sasti: A Festival in Tamil India." *History of Religions* 8, 3:236–259.

Harper, Edward B. 1957.
"Shamanism in South India." *Southwest Journal of Anthropology* 13, 3:267–287.

Nambiar, A. K. 1979.
"Structure of an Exorcistic Ritual of North Kerala." *Malayalam Literary Survey* 3, 2:48–54.

Neff, Deborah. 1987.
"Aesthetics and Power In *Pambin Tullal:* A Possession Ritual of Rural Kerala." *Ethology* 26, 1:63–71.

Varma, L. A. Ravi. 1971.
"Yatra-kali and Bhadrakali-Pattu." *Bulletin of the Rama Varma Research Institute* 9, Pt. 1:13–32.

Thampuran, M. H. Kerala Varma. 1936.
"Kali Cult in Kerala." *Bulletin of the Rama Varma Research Institute* 4:77–97.

PART THREE

THE DEVOTIONAL TRADITIONS

INTRODUCTION

WE HAVE ALREADY SEEN IN THE CHAPTER ON SANSKRIT DRAMA how the myth of the theatre's origin makes it a creation of the gods and that the ritual nature of Vedic worship makes a direct contribution to theatre through its encouragement of specialization of skills. In the post-Vedic period the Aryan gods were displaced, subsumed, or shouldered into relative obscurity by formerly lesser gods. The period beginning about the eighth or ninth century of the Christian era saw the emergence of a triumvirate of gods who constitute, even today, a triadic Hindu godhead. This triad, represented in sculpture as a single head with three faces, consists of Brahmā, the creator, Viṣṇu, the sustainer, and Śiva, the destroyer. It is to Viṣṇu and Śiva, both in various forms, that the worship of the majority of modern-day Hindus is directed. While Brahmā may be named in prayers, temples to him are practically nonexistent; so for all practical purposes we may divide Hindus into Vaiṣṇavas and Śaivites.

The ways to liberation or salvation (action, knowledge, devotion) discussed in the introduction to this book have tended in time to merge into one system. The *Bhagavad Gītā* accommodates all three but seemingly gives the highest place to devotion.

The type of theatre discussed in this section, the devotional tradition, relates directly to the third way of liberation. In those theatre genres which we have categorized as devotional, the expression of personal love toward and adoration of a particular deity—Rāma or Kṛṣṇa, as the case might be—makes these plays a form of deeply religious expression, as well as entertainment.

Rām līlā and *rās līlā,* the two devotional theatre genres discussed herein, developed out of Vaiṣṇava devotionalism. While there are devotional or bhakti forms of Śaivite piety, bhakti is preponderantly a Vaiṣṇava phenomenon. A part of the reason for this is undoubtedly the nature of Viṣṇu and Śiva themselves.

Śiva is the great ascetic and is commonly depicted in art as seated on Mount Kailash in deep meditation. The signs of his asceticism are his hair, gathered in a knot on the top of his head, the dust of ashes that covers his body, and the leopard skin draped about his loins. His luminous figure tends to inspire awe and mystery rather than warmth and intimacy.

Viṣṇu, on the other hand, by his very nature as the sustainer, projects a feeling of love, acceptance, and help. When the saints are threatened by demonic forces, he enters the world in physical form to deliver those who worship him. So bhakti, especially in North India, is particularly associated with Vaiṣṇavism. According to the Vaiṣṇavas, Viṣṇu has already appeared a number of times. One of the most prevalent traditions is that he has already appeared nine times in various forms. Of the nine manifestations the two most popular are Rāma and Kṛṣṇa. Both of these figures have inspired a rich tapestry of myth, and in different ways have molded the character of the Indian population.

Historically traces of bhakti may be found in the Vedic period when sacrifice was the prevalent mode of worship. It received firm philosophical enunciation in the *Bhagavad Gītā,* which may be credited with turning Hinduism from ascetic rites and self-forgetfulness toward the passionate abandonment of the self to God.

At the end of the sixth chapter which deals with the true yoga, the *Gītā* says:

> The Yogin is greater than the ascetic; he is considered to be greater than the man of knowledge, greater than the man of ritual works; therefore, do thou become a *yogin,* O Arjuna. And of all *yogins,* he who full of faith worships Me, with his inner self abiding in me—him I hold to be most attuned to me [in *yoga*]. (Radhakrishnan and Moore 1957, 126)

The bhakti of the *Bhagavad Gītā* is not yet the bhakti of the later saints. It does not express the lover-beloved relationship which characterizes aspects of later popular devotion. This aspect first finds expression in devotional songs dated from the sixth through the ninth centuries A.D. of Tamil Nadu. These songs express passionate praise of Nārāyaṇa and other incarnations of Viṣṇu. Following the songs, the tides of devotional religion flowed so strongly that the entire religious outlook in the Tamil region was affected and its impact was felt on philosophical Hinduism as well. Rāmānuja (eleventh century), one of India's most important philosophers, succeeded in harmonizing the bhakti attitude with Upaniṣadic insights. In so doing he gave bhakti an intellectual respectability it had not previously enjoyed.

Both of the forms discussed in this section emerge in their present form between the fifteenth and seventeenth centuries of the Christian era. By that time Vaiṣṇava bhakti had spread from the South and flooded into North India. On the great tide of devotion directed toward Rāma and Kṛṣṇa, *Rām līlā* and *rās līlā* emerged.

During that period Hindus in North India were also feeling great pressure from the Muslim invaders who had gained control of the northern regions of the Indian subcontinent. Some of the Muslim rulers were harshly repressive, and the survival of Hindu society was due to a large extent to the spiritual undergirding of the bhakti movement, which resulted in a great flowering of religion, poetry, music, and art.

While the *Rām līlā* and the *rās līlā* are both direct outgrowths of the bhakti movement, their respective heroes, Rāma and Kṛṣṇa, represent responses to different psychological needs. As the hero of the *Rāmāyaṇa,* Rāma is the ideal son, husband, brother, and king. His rule is one of righteousness, justice, and peace. So the *Rām līlā,* reenacting the deeds of Rāma, makes a strong statement about national life and social integration. It did so against a background of oppression and injustice.

The Kṛṣṇa plays of the *rās līlā,* on the other hand, seem to fulfill a different purpose. Here the worshipper is enabled to develop the emotional satisfaction of an intimate individual relationship with Kṛṣṇa under the image of lover and beloved. This deeply emotional attachment may also have been heightened by the sense of oppression. As oppressive acts multiplied, such as the destruction of sacred images, the feeling of need for a close, secure, personal relationship with the deity was heightened.

As these two forms respond to different human needs, they assume different styles of performance. The *Rām līlā,* responding to the need for national unity and social integration, is expansive and public. Its grand pageantry, which includes processions, competitions, and extensive street decorations, draws the whole populace, Hindus and non-Hindus alike, into the festiveness of the event. By contrast, the *rās līlā* is private, performed for the most part within the walls of a temple or residence, away from the eyes of the merely curious. It celebrates a personal and intimate relationship which only the initiated share. Of the two, the *rās līlā* is the more polished, more professional. The *Rām līlā* is more amateur, put on by many communities in cities, towns, and villages during the autumn festival of Daśsara.

There are a number of other regional forms which are performed chiefly as acts of devotion. It is perhaps not coincidence that dance is an important element in almost all of them, for dance is an accepted act of worship commonly performed before deities. *Kṛṣṇanāṭṭam* ("Kṛṣṇa's dance") is a form of devotional dance-drama which dates from seventeenth-century Kerala. The dance-drama was inspired by Manaveda, a member of the Calicut ruling family, who is said to have had a vision of Lord Kṛṣṇa which prompted his composition of a devotional poetic work in Sanskrit, the *Kṛṣṇagīti.* The *Kṛṣṇagīti* was later staged as a dramatic cycle of eight plays enacting the story of Lord Kṛṣṇa in song and dance. The eight-play cycle is traditionally performed over nine nights, the ninth night being a reenactment of the story of the birth of Kṛṣṇa, with which the cycle began.

Traditionally there has always been *only one* troupe—that first patronized by Manaveda and the ruling family of Calicut, and later associated exclusively with the great Kṛṣṇa temple at Guruvāyur in Kerala. The complete cycles of plays is enacted yearly at the Guruvāyur temple. However, in addition devotees are able to commission one or more of the eight plays in the cycle for performance as an offering to Lord Kṛṣṇa at any time throughout the year. Often the play enacting his birth is commissioned by a family seeking a boon for childbirth.

In performance *Kṛṣṇanāṭṭam* is a fluid and graceful mixture of a special style of traditional Kerala devotional singing, interspersed with dance. As a precursor of the later *kathakaḷi, Kṛṣṇanāṭṭam* bears many similarities to that popular and well-known dance-drama, especially in its use of a stylized and elaborate language of gestures and mudras, costuming, and complex makeup. But it is a distinctive tradition with its own charm. A number of characters, especially some of the demons and animals, appear in unique elaborate full-face masks.

Bhāgavata mela of Tamil Nadu is a commemorative dance-drama played yearly in May before the Narasimha temple in the village of Mellattur. The performances celebrate the birthday of Narasimha, the half-lion half-man incarnation of Viṣṇu. As in *Kṛṣṇanāṭṭam* and *kuchipudi,* dance is a major element in this form. The dance, rich in hand gestures, for the most part

Actor, "possessed" by the mask of the man-lion incarnation of Viṣṇu, is restrained by attendants and accompanied by the temple priest who reads from the sacred text toward the conclusion of this *Bhāgavata mela* production. (Farley P. Richmond photo)

describes and illustrates the text, which is sung or recited, much of it by the actor-dancers themselves. There are, however, insertions of pure dance units unrelated to the story.

A mask of Narasimha and a special headdress are used in the performance. In keeping with the drama being a devotional act, costumes, masks, and accessories are stored in the temple when not in use. The mask of Narasimha, displayed as a holy object, is worshipped by the devotees. As in *rās līlā* and *Rām līlā,* the putting on of the headdress and mask is a ceremonial and sacred act which changes the performer from an ordinary person to a living incarnation of the deity. The putting on and taking off of these objects is thus surrounded by an air of awe and mystery.

The performance takes place on a platform set before the presiding deity. Like the stage manager *(sūtradhāra)* of *aṇkīya nāṭ,* the Bhāgavata (leader) holds the thread of the narration together and introduces each character. In spite of the devotional nature of *Bhāgavata mela,* it has a prominent clown character who makes his chief appearance at the beginning of the play.

Kuchipudi of Andhra Pradesh, discussed briefly in the introduction to chapter 1, springs from the same temple tradition as the *Bhāgavata mela* of Tamil Nadu. Both have been shaped by the Vaiṣṇava devotional tradition and draw their subject matter from the myths and legends of Vaiṣṇava literature. A *kuchipudi* performance combines recitation, singing, dancing, and mimetic action.

The Bhāgavata performs the duties of the stage manager, systematizing and coordinating the entire performance. He is the main reciter-singer and the actor-dancers perform according to his recitation. In addition to his recitation, he may enter the performing area and hold brief dialogue with the main actor. He ties the scenes together and comments upon and advances the action. All roles are played by males.

Although still performed annually in the native village of Kuchipudi as an act of devotion, *kuchipudi* dance migrated from its rural beginnings to the urban areas and has been elevated to the level of a classical dance style and is frequently seen in solo concerts in many of the world's cities. The style includes both mimetic and pure dance. *Kuchipudi* is performed to the South Indian, or Karnatic,[1] style of music, and the chief musician is the one who recites the dance syllables while keeping the beat with a pair of brass cymbals. Three other musicians, a *mṛdaṅga* (small two-headed drum) player, a clarinetist, and a violinist, compose the orchestra.

The *rās līlā* of Manipur in the far corner of northeastern India is quite distinct in style from the *rās līlā* of Braj in Uttar Pradesh. The two share a

---

[1] There are two systems of Indian music: Karnatic (southern) and Hindustani (northern). The two differ substantially in theory and the classification of ragas or melody modes.

The famous *kuchipudi* dancer Vedanta Satyanarayana Sarma in a festival performance on the stage of the training school in Kuchipudi village, Andhra Pradesh. (Farley P. Richmond photo)

common object of devotion—Kṛṣṇa—and are energized by the same *force*—bhakti, devotion to Kṛṣṇa. In Manipur, as in Braj, the play is not understood as entertainment but as an act of serious devotion.

The major difference between the two forms is in the styles of dance. While the Braj dances are thought to be forerunners of the lively, vigorous Kathak classical style of North India, the Manipuri *rās* dances are, for the most part, slow, graceful, liquid, and sinuous. They may be thought of as expressing the sentiment of *lāsya* in style. Perhaps this feminine style is accounted for by the fact that, except for the individual who plays Kṛṣṇa, all the roles are taken by women and girls. Kṛṣṇa's role may be played by a

In this *aṇkīya nāṭ* production Kṛṣṇa and his brother Balarama, right, discuss strategy with their monkey general. The stage manager, center, follows the action closely in the text. (Farley P. Richmond photo)

young boy. Kṛṣṇa is the center of attention for the dancers, and the emphasis which they put upon poses and positions, combined with the slow pace, gives the performance the effect of successive tableaux.

As also indicated in the introduction to chapter 1, *aṇkīya nāṭ* is another form devoted to the stories of Kṛṣṇa and his exploits. The plays have a high literary value and introduce song and dance into his worship. The form, then, is a combination of fine poetry set to music and accompanied by dance. *Aṇkīya nāṭ* has been described as "a feast of colour, music, dance, romance and battles—leavened over with piety and prayer which could not have been reproduced in a setting other than that of the community of devotees" (Mathur 1964, 63). In fact temple and ritual are the usual context of the performance of these plays. In performance the stage manager sings the narrative, and other members of the troupe dance and sing.

The forms discussed in this section share a common "bondage to the gods." The source of their inspiration is devotion to a deity who has been personalized in an earthly manifestation. In varying degrees performances of these dramatic forms are understood as offerings to or worship of the deity Viṣṇu in the form of Kṛṣṇa or Rāma. Clearly Kṛṣṇa has inspired a preponderance of these forms.

In conclusion it is safe to say that a strong current of religious devotion continues to flow in Hindu India. Out of that stream have come many expressions in art, poetry, music, and dance. It is not unrealistic to expect that this strong religious current will continue to feed the theatre.

Darius L. Swann

WORKS CITED

Mathur, Jagdish Chandra. 1964.
Drama in Rural India. New York: Asia Publishing House.

Radhakrishnan, S., and C. A. Moore. Eds. 1957.
A Sourcebook in Indian Philosophy. Princeton: Princeton University Press.

ADDITIONAL READING

Dimock, Edward C., and Denise Levertov. 1967.
In Praise of Krishna: Songs from the Bengali. Garden City, New York: Doubleday.

Iyer, K. Bharata. 1966.
"Krishnattam." *Times of India Annual.* Pp. 71–80.

Jones, Clifford. 1963.
"Bhagavata Mela Natakam, A Traditional Dance-Drama Form." *Journal of Asian Studies* 22, 2:193–200.

Kothari, Sunil. 1979.
"Bhagavata Mela Nataka." *Quarterly Journal of the National Centre for the Performing Arts* 8, 2:33–45.

Naidu, M. A. 1975.
Kuchipudi Classical Dance. Hyderabad: Andhra Pradesh Sangetta Nataka Akademi.

Panikkar, Kavalam Narayana. 1977.
"Krishnanattom." *Malayalam Literary Survey* 1, 1:33–41.

Rao, S. V. Joga. 1964.
"The Dance Dramas of Mellattur." *Aryan Path* 35, 7:310–315.

Richmond, Farley. 1974.
"The Vaisnava Drama of Assam." *Educational Theatre Journal* 26, 2:145–163.

Singh, Guru Bipin. 1974.
"The Rasleela of Manipur." *Quarterly Journal of the National Centre for the Performing Arts* 3, 3:27–36.

Chapter Six

RĀS LĪLĀ

Darius L. Swann

WALKING BY THE WALLED TEMPLE COMPOUND IN VRINDABAN you may hear music and that distinctive chink-chink of ankle bells *(ghuṅgharū)* and mentally note that a dance is being performed. Unless you are a total stranger you would also know that behind the walls a performance of *rās līlā* was taking place.

The *rās līlā* is a devotional dance-drama that is a distinctive product of the Braj region, a ninety square mile area of Uttar Pradesh province which borders on Rajasthan, about ninety miles south of Delhi. It is the special preserve of the people of Braj, for it is devoted entirely to the exaltation of the love of Kṛṣṇa and Rādhā and the earthly exploits of Kṛṣṇa. Kṛṣṇa is himself a child of Braj: He was born in Mathura, and Vrindaban, seven miles away, is a city sanctified to Kṛṣṇaites by its association with him. The pilgrims who come here walk barefooted over the very ground that he is reputed to have trod. Each place is invested with a holy meaning because of its connection to Kṛṣṇa's earthly existence: Mathura, where he was born in prison; Govardhan, where he lifted the mountain; Gokul, where he spent his childhood and youth; and the banks of the Jamuna River, where he danced with the maidens.

It should be clear by now that the *rās līlā* is a dance-drama that falls in the realm of the sacred. Its home is within the temple walls, close to the holy shrine itself; it will not generally be staged in the street, as profane dramas are. It is for the eyes and hearts of believers and its purpose is to make real the living god, to induce a *darśana,* an epiphany or vision of Kṛṣṇa and Rādhā in all their beauty. It is a lyric theatre depending heavily on poetry, song, and dance to make its point.

A performance falls into two parts. The first part is called the *rās* and it expresses the lovemaking of Rādhā and Kṛṣṇa. Kṛṣṇa who is dark, beautiful, and playful is especially attractive to women, and the beauteous Rādhā is his choice among them all. From a religious standpoint she is the feminine

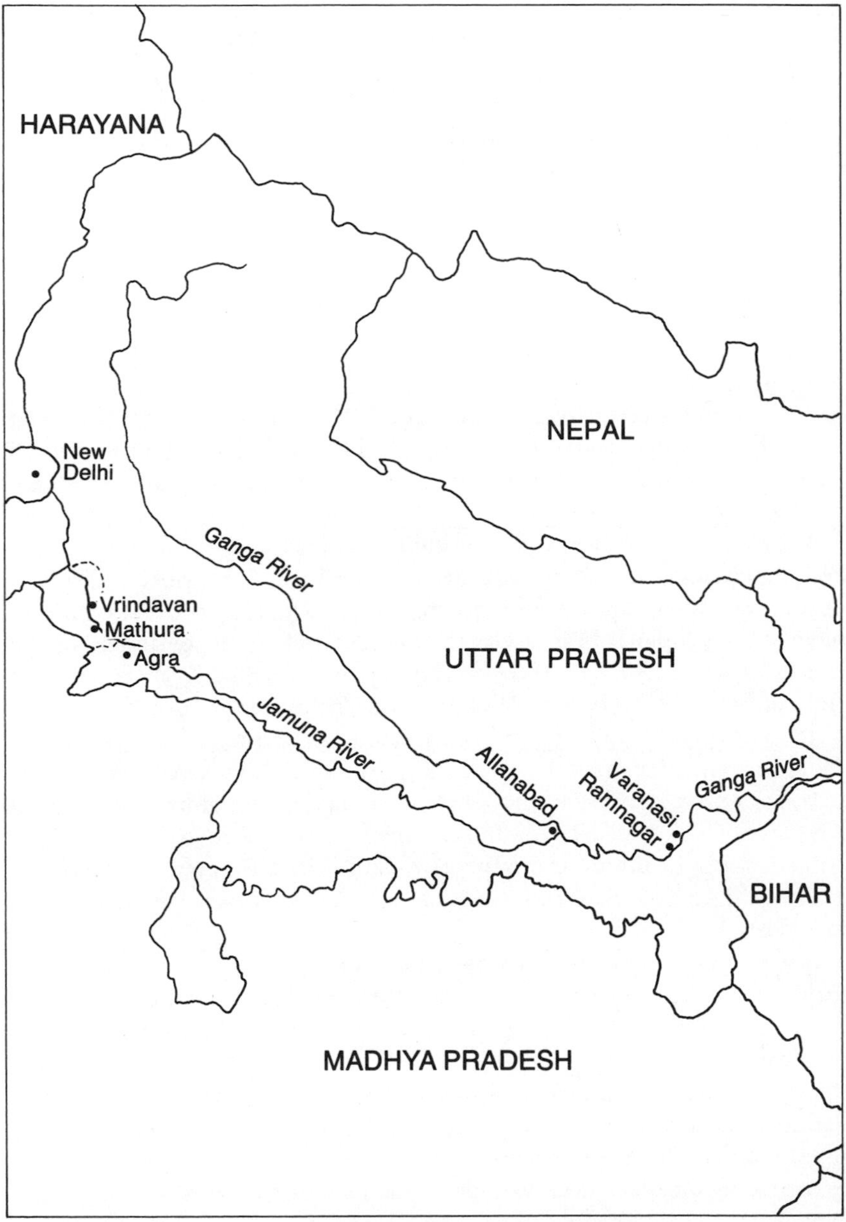
HARAYANA
NEPAL
New Delhi
Ganga River
Vrindavan
Mathura
Agra
UTTAR PRADESH
Jamuna River
Allahabad
Varanasi
Ramnagar
Ganga River
BIHAR
MADHYA PRADESH

Kṛṣṇa and Rādhā on the throne. (Sangeet Natak Akademi photo)

aspect of the godhead, Kṛṣṇa's sakti. The first part of the drama, however, tells us of this relationship in terms of earthly, erotic love.

From the opening curtain, revealing Kṛṣṇa and Rādhā in intimate embrace, through Kṛṣṇa's invitation to Rādhā to dance, through a series of dances and songs which express the passionate love of the couple for each other, the fine poetry of the bhakti poets and the music of the *rās līlā* troupe members combine in a form that is evocative, emotional, and artistic.

The audience is seated in a circular area on the floor around a fairly small dancing area, in intimate touch with the performers. The devotional music, richly imaged poetry, and the dancing of brightly costumed young performers create a moving experience. Here a woman will rise and with eyes closed and arms uplifted dance at her place along with the dancers. Then a greying old sadhu rises, goes to the dancing area, and competes with the young dancers in performing the fast pirouettes. All through the performance, the spectator-worshippers may go forward, bow before the divine pair, and make offerings of money which is passed on to the leader of the troupe (who is usually the main singer).

After an interval the *rās* is followed by the *līlā.*[1] This second part always deals with some incident out of the early life of Kṛṣṇa, such as stealing the butter, holding up the milkmaids and demanding a toll payment, going to Rādhā in disguise, or leaving Gokul for Mathura. In the *līlā* section there is usually less dancing and more song and dialogue.

The performance ends with congregational singing of a hymn. It is repetitive and emotion-building, and people make their final offerings before the couple, who are in a pageantlike setting, and depart.

Origins

The Puranas, especially the *Bhāgavata Purāṇa,* are the sources of Kṛṣṇa's life and exploits. The *Brahmā Vaivarta Purāṇa,* a late work, gives prominence to Rādhā as Kṛṣṇa's favorite. The *Bhāgavata Purāṇa* accounts are the major source of the theatrical *rās līlā* and the primary authority for all bhakti sects, which place it alongside the Vedas as a revealed source of religious truth. In the tenth book of this Purana are the stories of Kṛṣṇa's infancy and youth in Braj and his later life in Dvaraka. Five chapters (29–33) specifically describe the origin of the *rās* dance. Kṛṣṇa, moved by the beauty of the moon and the season, conceives a desire to dance. At the melodious sound of his flute, the milkmaids put aside everything—even the care of their husbands and children—and go to him. They dance beneath the moon on the banks of the Jamuna River. Kṛṣṇa multiplies himself so that there is a Kṛṣṇa for every milkmaid. Then, in order to destroy their pride, he disappears. Disconsolately they seek for him and are finally reunited.

The historical value of the account is difficult to assess. The worship of Kṛṣṇa as deity seems to have developed among a non-Aryan cowherding tribe, the Abhiras. The dance which Kṛṣṇa did with the milkmaids in all likelihood represented a folk dance done among the people of the Abhira tribe. During the Holī holiday season, I have observed in the villages folk dances which may well have served as prototypes of the *rās līlā.* Also in dramatic treatises there are descriptions of minor dramatic forms which correspond to the present *rās līlā.* It was, however, the *Bhāgavata Purāṇa* accounts during the medieval period which supplied the inspiration to the great bhakti saints to institute the *rās līlā* as a ritual theatre of devotion.

This theatre, whose dance is now generally acknowledged as the forerunner of the classical *kathak* dance of North India, began in its present form about the start of the sixteenth century. The tide of bhakti devotion that had

[1] A representation of Kṛṣṇa's acts in his earthly manifestation.

begun in the south was sweeping over northern India. It was the period of the great Moghuls and, experiencing some religious and political repression, Hinduism turned inward. Fervent devotion to Kṛṣṇa was the common factor which drew together all those instrumental in creating the theatrical *rās līlā.*

In the flood tide of the Kṛṣṇa bhakti movement the land of Braj became the mecca for the leading religious spirits of the time. Vallabhācārya came from what is now modern Andhra in 1491. Hitharivaṅs came from Deoban near Saharanpur. Haridās came from a town near Aligarh. Each founded his own sect and each is credited in oral accounts with helping to create the *rās līlā* in its present form. These leaders took an essentially folk and recreational form and converted it into an instrument of devotion, a means by which the believer might realize the presence of Kṛṣṇa and his sakti form, Rādhā.

Although one tradition credits Vallabhācārya and Haridās with beginning the *rās līlā* at Mathura, and another credits Vallabhācārya's disciple, Ghamanddeva, with originating it at the village Karahala, a third names Hitharivaṅs as the founder in Vrindaban. Despite the aura of legend which pervades these accounts, these traditions nevertheless acknowledge the contributions of the several bhakti leaders who may be shown to have contributed historically to the formation of the *rās līlā* stage.

On the basis of the various traditions, it is possible to reconstruct a likely sequence of events: Vallabhācārya and Svāmī Haridās attempted a performance at Mathura, which failed because of some untoward incident. The experiment was then entrusted to Ghamanddeva, disciple of Vallabhācārya, who succeeded in establishing a *rās līlā* stage at the village of Karahala. There the performances were almost certainly of the incarnational *līlā.*

Later Svāmī Hitharivaṅs and Svāmī Haridās established another tradition of *rās līlā* at Vrindaban. Fired by the fervor of the "Rasik Trio" (Haridās, Hitharivaṅs, and Harirām Vyās, the disciple of Hitharivaṅs), the Vrindaban *nitya rās,* celebrating the eternal lovemaking of Rādhā and Kṛṣṇa, outstripped the Karahala *rās līlā.* Whereas the Karahala tradition apparently stressed devotion to Kṛṣṇa (there is one crown and that belongs to Kṛṣṇa) and dwelt on the *līlā,* the deeds he performed in his earthly manifestation, Hitharivaṅs, in what must be some of the most sensuously poetic imagery ever written, gives the premier place to Rādhā, and confines himself to *nitya rās,* that is, to the eternal lovemaking of the divine pair in the eternal realm, of which Vrindaban is the earthly shadow.

> Today Śyāma is beautiful,
> The Crown Jewel
> Among the group of fresh Braj maidens.
> The sweetness of all her parts,
> From head to foot,

Charmed Śyām, her Lord.
The plait of braided hair
Gleams
Over her golden lotus face:
It appears as though Rāhu[2]
In the midst
Devoured Her moon-set curls.
The hair-part on the Beloved's head,
Which is adorned,
Appears like good fortune's essence
in a flowing stream.
Her eyebrows are like Kāmadeva's bows:
Her eyes the arrow,
The lines of collyrium the points.
Her tilak is radiant:
An earring is at her cheek,
A pearl jewel in her nose.
For her teeth like jasmine
The beautiful lips are leaves.
She gives peace to her lover's heart.
O Sakhī, in the middle of her chin
Is a very lovely,
Natural, dark spot!
Bound tightly in her bodice,
Her jewel-box breasts
Are life itself to the Beloved.
Her entrancing arms, like the stems
of lotuses,
Are adorned with shimmering bangles,
Their touch can be compared to moving waters.
It appears as though the Mistress
Has made a beautiful edging
Around the tree that is Śyām's head.[3]
Her navel is as deep as a pond
For Mohan's mind,
Like a fish to play in.
Her waist is very thin.
Her hips are wide and girdled with
a belt of tiny bells.

---

[2] Her plaited hair wound around the back of her head is compared to the mythical dragon Rāhu, which during an eclipse may appear to devour the moon.

[3] Rādhā's arm around Kṛṣṇa's neck is compared to a reflecting pool at the base of a tree.

Her thighs are like the stalks of
plantain trees.[4]
The brilliance of the red dye[5]
Together with the ornaments of
her
lotus feet
Are the protector of the Lover's
heart.
Alluring him in novel ways,
The Female Elephant
Sports with the Male Elephant.
Śrī Hit Hārīvams says,
Praise to the exceedingly spotless
Glory of Śyāma!
Singing and hearing it
Gives pleasure:
It is the crusher of all sins.

(White 1977, 69–71)

In this celestially blissful union there is not even the experience of separation but only the perpetual sporting of lovers. While in the desolation of the milkmaids from whose midst Kṛṣṇa had suddenly disappeared Vallabāchārya symbolized the anguish of the soul separated from the Lord, Hitharivaṅs and Haridās celebrated the blissful conjugal relation of Rādhā and Kṛṣṇa as the epitome of the soul's joy. The author of the *Bhaktmāla* says of Hitharivaṅs: "Who can understand all at once his method of devotion with whom the feet of blessed Rādhā were the highest object of worship; a most staunch-souled devotee; who made himself a page in waiting on the divine pair in their bower of love; who gloried in the enjoyment of the remnants of all that was offered at their shrine. . . ." Hitharivaṅs not only established the *rās līlā* stage in Vrindaban but made the daily *rās,* or dance, an obligatory part of bhakti devotion. Hitharivaṅs created such a loyalty in the devotees toward *rās* that they began believing that through the theatrical *rās līlā* they could experience the presence of Lord Kṛṣṇa and the reality of his deeds. Svāmī Haridās, the second member of the Vrindaban pantheon, whose name appears in several accounts of the founding of the *rās līlā,* was famous as a musician, and it is in this area that his great contribution was made.

After the passing of Hitharivaṅs there was an apparent decline in the *rās* stage. This was inevitable, for Haridās' musical prowess and the poetic gifts

[4] The feminine ideal of beauty in India possesses a thin waist, wide hips, and full breasts.

[5] Dancing girls usually color the soles of their feet and the palms of their hands with red dye.

Rādhā singing in a scene from *The Light of Love,* performed in 1974 in Vrindaban. (John Stratton Hawley photo)

of Hitharivaṅs and Harirāmjī Vyās, combined with the fervor of their devotion, must have taken the *rās* stage to a climax that must have been difficult to maintain. It was about 1545, when the *rās līlā* stage was languishing, that Svāmī Nārāyan Bhaṭṭ appeared on the scene. Growse (1880) gives Bhaṭṭ credit for beginning the *rās līlā,* but it is clear both from oral tradition and the *Bhaktmāla* that the *rās līlā* stage was already in existence.

Bhaṭṭ did, however, make several important contributions to the development of the *rās līlā.* First, he established *rās* stages *(maṇḍala)* at all the spots in the Braj area associated with Kṛṣṇa's earthly manifestations, firmly fixing the theatrical *rās līlā* in the thinking of the people of Braj. He originated the custom of making pilgrimages to all these spots. Going from place to place, he explained the significance of the place to the local inhabitants and stimulated their belief that the places of Braj were indeed vested with mystery and sanctity. He was, as the *Bhaktmāla* describes him, a worshipper of the soil of Braj, and his enthusiasm and faith was a unifying influence among the people of the area. In addition to the five *rās* stages that had been established in Vrindaban by the founders, he established twenty-eight more in the Braj area.

His second important contribution was to add to the *nitya rās,* which had developed at Vrindaban entirely as a song and dance form, the dramatic depiction of the earthly *līlā* of Kṛṣṇa, in which dialogue and mimetic action were important. He was thus able to incorporate in the *rās* the traditions of both Karahala and Vrindaban. Today regardless of the sectarian allegiances of the troupes, the programs of all *rās līlā* troupes follow a common pattern. Through his addition of the incarnational *līlā* Bhaṭṭ popularized the *rās līlā* stage and made it attractive to less sophisticated believers. He also improved the artistic quality of the *rās līlā,* as he was an accomplished musician and furthermore enlisted the help of a friend, a retired court musician and dancer who was living in Braj, to improve the music and dances.

The importance of Nārāyan Bhaṭṭ's work cannot be overestimated. The *rās līlā* today owes its form and appeal largely to his enthusiasm and artistic genius. He both increased the theatricality of the *rās līlā* and strengthened its religious significance.

Though it seems impossible now to distinguish historical fact from the legends that have grown about it, these traditions concerning the origin of *rās līlā* are still of significance. More important for us than the factual accuracy of the details of the tradition is what they imply or state about the motivation for the establishment of the *rās līlā* stage. According to all the traditions the *rās līlā* stage arises from the use of theatrical media (music, impersonation, and mimetic dance) to illuminate reality by evoking a vision of the deity.

In each tradition the purpose of the *rās līlā* stage is to "make present" the *līlā* of Kṛṣṇa. It is this aspect of "making present" that raises the *rās līlā* from mere theatrical spectacle to the status of religious ritual. It is significant that contemporary *rās līlā* performers refer back to the example of the milkmaids in the *Bhāgavata Purāṇa* account of the *rās.* After dancing with the milkmaids in the moonlight Kṛṣṇa suddenly disappears. They search among the trees for him but cannot find him. To console themselves they remember him by miming or acting out the things which Kṛṣṇa did when he was among them. They mimic his walk and flute playing; they act out his miraculous feats. Seeing the intensity of their devotion, Kṛṣṇa returns to them. In the same way today those who perform and see the imitation of his *līlā* will be blessed with the vision *(darśana)* of the Lord himself.

Training

The performance of *rās līlā* involves skill passed on from father to son or teacher to disciple. Usually the performers are relatives of the teacher or children of friends. The *rās līlā* has no training schools or academies such as now exist in various regions of India for the classical styles of dance, in which systematic training is given and a certain standard demanded. The leader of each *rās līlā* troupe is responsible for the training of his performers. The standards of the troupes, therefore, differ widely, depending upon the leader's talents as a musician, teacher of dance and acting, and his mastery of the body of devotional literature upon which performers draw.

The swamis are literate in Hindi but they may not be conversant with the Sanskrit verses which they have to recite in the performance. The boy actors also need to be literate in order to learn their lines. If a boy cannot read, he is taught in the troupe so that he can master the poetic texts of the plays. He may, however, receive little else in the way of education. The resulting imbalance may offer serious problems when the boy is too old to perform *rās līlā* and must find other work.

The boy actors are usually recruited when they are eight to ten years of age, though occasionally one finds performers who are younger. They usually begin by playing the role of a milkmaid. Those who have good voices, good memories, and good looks may aspire to the role of Rādhā or Kṛṣṇa when they reach eleven or twelve. With the onset of puberty and the sprouting of facial hair (usually at thirteen or fourteen) a boy's career comes to an end. At that point some may become a part of the musical ensemble as singer or instrumentalist. The exceptional performer—one with both ability and financial resources—may eventually become a swami and organize his own troupe.

A performer acquires his training by imitating his teacher. He learns roles rather than skills. The son of a *rās* troupe leader, who is around performers and performances from infancy, frequently follows in his father's footsteps. By the time he is able to play the smallest milkmaid, he is already familiar with the role. As a milkmaid he, in effect, understudies the roles of Rādhā and Kṛṣṇa. By the time he is ready to retire as a performer, he knows all the roles well. If he continues as a vocalist and instrumentalist with the troupe, a son is likely to succeed his father as leader. The famous swami Meghśyām, now deceased, was succeeded by his son Rām Svarūp, who has achieved a reputation of his own as one of the two most popular troupe leaders in Braj.

In cases where there are no likely performers within the immediate family, a troupe leader may recruit the talented children of distant relatives, friends, or even strangers. These nonfamily members work on a contractual basis for a monthly wage, which is paid to their parents. They spend the hot, dry months of May and June as a vacation with their parents.

Organization

The *rās* troupe, headed by a swami, is made up of from ten to eighteen persons, all male. Of these six or eight are boys who play the roles of Kṛṣṇa, Rādhā, and Rādhā's milkmaid companions. They range in age from about eight to thirteen. In the *nitya rās* only these boys appear, but in the *līlā* which follows, adult actors also appear in roles such as Yaśodā, Kaṁsa, Śiva, Uddhav, and so on, according to the particular *līlā* being shown. The remainder of the troupe is made up of singers and instrumentalists.

The members of the *rās līlā* chorus are called *samājī*. The *rās līlā* stage apparently took this word from the Vrindaban sects founded by Hitharivaṅs and Haridās. Among these sects the music sung at festivals and on festival days in the temple is called *samāj* (literally, society or community) and the singers *samājī*. This music is powerful and moving, and the use of the *samājī* on the *rās līlā* stage greatly enhances its appeal (Gargi 1956, 117–118). The chorus is made up of several *samājī*, among whom are a leading singer and his assistant, who alternate in the solo singing of most of the verses. The chorus joins in the refrains. Occasionally songs are sung in unison.

The chief singer, who is the leader of the troupe, fulfills the same role as the *sūtradhāra* in Sanskrit drama. Through his singing he maintains the thread of the story and keeps the action of the play moving. Calling upon his knowledge and memory of the devotional literature, he renders an appropriate song at the right moment, subtly creates an atmosphere, and sets the scene for the developing action. On a stage that is without theatrical trappings, he paints the scene against which the dramatic action takes place and, without any break, changes it at the appropriate moment.

The chief singer is also the prompter. By a simple exchange of glances he corrects the actor who has temporarily gone wrong. He shows the actor where to begin again by singing a few words, or he may correct a mistake in pitch by joining the song in the middle of a line or verse, thus helping the actor to recover. In the case of a mistake in dialogue, he may shout "Bali hari maharāj," or "jai jai" (Victory! or Praise!), apparently moved by emotion, but in actuality he is momentarily distracting the attention of the audience from the actor and allowing him to recover and correct himself. Where necessary he directly prompts the actor, giving him the line.

During the intervals when tableaux are being prepared behind the curtain, or when the actors are late coming to the stage, the chorus fills the interval with singing that will heighten the emotional impact of the scene which is to follow. By alternating with the actors in the singing of verses, or by repeating the verses in the manner of a refrain, they afford the actor time to rest. Finally, the chief singer, the swami of the troupe, is the main organizer of the *rās* performance and, at times (though rarely), he must rebuke and discipline the spectators. He is thus the chief link between actors and spectators.

Today's *rās līlā* troupes are professional and perform both in the Braj area and far afield. During the period of Kṛṣṇa's birthday (Janamāṣṭami, the Hindu months of Śravan and Bhadon, or July and August), many troupes are in Vrindaban and give performances at several different hours during the day in many localities. At other times the troupes are contracted to perform outside the Braj area in the homes of wealthy patrons or at large fairs, such as the Kumbh Mela in Allahabad. During the slack season a troupe may perform on any one of the regular stages, or in an ashram or a temple for a very minimal fee plus whatever is offered by the congregation. These performances are offered by the troupes simply as charitable services.

There are some forty-five *rās līlā* troupes operating in the Braj area. Twenty-two are based in Vrindaban; the rest are based at other locations in Braj. Of the Vrindaban group, seventeen are of the Nimbarka sect and five of the Vallabha sect. The former gives primacy to Rādhā in worship while the latter gives first place to Kṛṣṇa. The form of the *rās līlā,* however, is the same for both groups.

Support

Professional *rās līlā* troupes developed as early as the seventeenth century. Some support has come from gifts given by the wealthy to temples and ashrams in Vrindaban. Prior to Indian Independence in 1947, governments of some small princely states, such as Bharatpur and Gwalior in Rajasthan, maintained temples in Vrindaban and provided a certain amount of money for the regular performance of *rās līlā.* With Independence and the absorption of the princely states into India, state support of *rās līlā* was cut off, for the Union government, having declared itself secular, could not offer direct financial support to religious groups. Some troupes perform two or three times daily. In Vrindaban at the places where the *rās līlā* is presented regularly, the troupes are paid a nominal amount by the proprietor of the *rās līlā* stage, usually from about $1.60 or Rs. 12 for troupes of mediocre standard to about $6.67 or Rs. 50 for first-class troupes. In addition the troupe receives whatever is offered by the audience-congregation during the performance. This may range from a few rupees to several hundred, depending upon the quality of the performance and the means, attitude, and mood of the audience. When a troupe is engaged on a contractual basis, it also receives whatever is given in offerings by those present.

Plays

When Bhaṭṭ had finished his work, the *rās līlā* assumed the basic form it has today, a two-part program: (1) the *nitya rās* which has practically no dialogue

Rādhā and Kṛṣṇa swing at the conclusion of *The Stealing of the Butter (Makhan cori līlā),* performed in Vrindaban in 1975. (John Stratton Hawley photo)

but is sung and danced and (2) the *līlā* which has a great deal of singing, considerable dialogue, and less dancing. The first part of the program is restricted in situation, action, and sentiment: Kṛṣṇa and Rādhā sport in endless delight in divine Vrindaban. The only sentiment expressed is the erotic, and the love depicted is exclusively love in union. There is neither development nor variety but a ritual representation of the stable and unchanging state of being of the deity himself. The *nitya rās,* through songs, evocative dances, lyric poetry, music, and rich costuming, suffuses the spectator-participants in the emotion of love.

The *līlā* which composes the second part of the *rās līlā* program is much less restricted than the *nitya rās,* for within its scope may fall any of the well over a hundred legends of Kṛṣṇa's boyhood and youth in Braj. The *līlā* is more the imitation of an action than the *nitya rās,* though the actual development of that action in terms of its dramatic possibilities is rather circumscribed. These *līlā* divide neatly into three parts, each part with its own lyric and dramatic values. First there is the boy Kṛṣṇa, the mischievous prankster who steals Yaśodā's butter, or the precocious child who destroys a giant snake and assorted demons. Then there is the youthful Kṛṣṇa who, with something of the mischievous boy still in him, hides the clothes of the bathing maidens and demands a levy when they take their dairy products to market. He is beautiful and irresistible, the object of the passion of married and single girls alike. Under the full autumnal moon he sports with the cowherds' wives and daughters who have been drawn to the banks of the Jamuna River by the sweet sounds of his flute. Finally there is the heroic Kṛṣṇa who journeys to Mathura for his fateful encounter with Kaṁsa. All three roles have a strong appeal for Indian women, arousing in them by turn the instincts of mother, sweetheart, and wife or daughter.

With two exceptions, only those *līlā* Kṛṣṇa performed in Braj (namely, up to and including the slaying of Kaṁsa) are staged in the Braj *rās līlā*.[6] The Kṛṣṇa who established his throne in Dvaraka (now in the state of Gujarat) and married Rukminī and seven other wives (besides taking countless concubines) is not mentioned in these plays.

Unlike the *nitya rās* the incarnational *līlā* of Kṛṣṇa contain a wide range of sentiments. Only the odious and the terrible are absent. Mostly the erotic sentiment prevails, but there is much of the heroic as well. Kṛṣṇa's departure from his family and friends and his setting out for Mathura provide a much-used pathetic theme, and to a degree surprising for a form so given to pious religious expression, the comic *rasa* also comes into play. The exploits and misadventures of Mansukha, as well as Kṛṣṇa's own pranks, provide this comic element. The overall spirit of the *līlā* of Kṛṣṇa is one of brightness and joyfulness; there is no tragedy or even grave anxiety, for Kṛṣṇa is the divine enjoyer and his devotees find joy in contemplating that enjoyment. Kṛṣṇa is the Beautiful God and his epithet, the Beautiful Dark One, accords with the sensuous loveliness of the face and figure of Kṛṣṇa popularized in calendar art. His amorous play with Rādhā and the milkmaids is the epitome of the expression of his being.

Norvin Hein (1972, 156, 163–178) lists 106 *līlā* performed by Braj troupes and estimates that the total number is probably nearer 150. Among those frequently performed are the following, synopses of which will be given below: *The Play of Kṛṣṇa's Birth (Kṛṣṇa janam līlā), The Play of Śankara (Śankara līlā), The Stealing of the Butter (Makhan cori līlā), The Display of Rādhā's Price (Mundariya chori līlā), The Going to Mathura (Mathurāgaman līlā), The Play of Uddhav (Uddhav līlā),* and *The Great Rās Līlā (Mahārāsa līlā).*

The Play of Kṛṣṇa's Birth tells of the birth of Kṛṣṇa to Vasudeva and Devakī in Kaṁsa's prison. Vasudeva is able to make a miraculous escape

[6] The exceptions are the *Sudāmā līlā,* concerning Kṛṣṇa sends his friend Uddhav from Mathura to Vrindaban with messages for his parents and the milkmaids.

with the child by crossing the river to Gokul. There he leaves Kṛṣṇa with Nanda and Yaśodā who raise him.

The Play of Śankara is a play connected with the birth of Kṛṣṇa. Śiva comes to view the young child, but Mother Yaśodā is afraid that Śiva's terrible appearance will frighten the child and she refuses to let Śiva see him. Śiva refuses to leave without seeing the child and sits down at her door. Finally Yaśodā is persuaded to show the child and Śiva does obeisance to him.

In *The Stealing of the Butter,* although Rādhā is warned that Kṛṣṇa is a thief, she takes a dancing lesson from him anyway. Later her ring is found to be missing and Kṛṣṇa is searched and caught with it. The milkmaids steal Kṛṣṇa's flute, crown, and cloak in retaliation. His scheme for recovering them involves coming to Rādhā in the guise of a girl pining for love of Kṛṣṇa. Rādhā consoles her by donning the crown and cloak and playing the flute. Kṛṣṇa retrieves his property.

The Display of Rādhā's Price tells of Rādhā's dream that Kṛṣṇa has deserted her and is turning his attention to other maidens. When she awakes and finds him gone, she becomes convinced that her dream is true. She sulks and a companion brings Kṛṣṇa, who soothes her pride and jealousy.

The Going to Mathura portrays the pathos of Kṛṣṇa's departure from Gokul. Hearing of the deeds of Kṛṣṇa and his brother Balarām, Kaṁsa sends Akrūra to invite the two boys to Mathura, where he intends to kill them. After a departure from the tearful milkmaids the boys go with Akrūra. While they are resting at the riverside Akrūra has a vision of Kṛṣṇa and Balarām seated in a chariot beneath the water.

The Play of Uddhav tells of the encounter of Uddhav, Kṛṣṇa's philosopher-friend, and the milkmaids of Braj. After the defeat of Kaṁsa, Kṛṣṇa is homesick for Braj and his friends but knows that he cannot abandon his responsibilities to return. He sends his friend Uddhav to Braj with a message for them. Uddhav, who is an Advaitin and conceives of God as the abstract Absolute, is skeptical about the milkmaids' personal and physical attachment to Kṛṣṇa. But their passionate devotion wins over the philosopher and he returns to Mathura a convert to their bhakti form of devotion and reproves Kṛṣṇa for neglecting them.

The Great Rās Līlā is a special reenactment of the dance of Kṛṣṇa with the milkmaids on the banks of the Jamuna under the light of the autumn moon. Kṛṣṇa multiplies himself into many so that there is a Kṛṣṇa for every milkmaid. Some versions of this *līlā* put it into the context of a contest between Kṛṣṇa and Kāma, the god of love. Of course Kṛṣṇa wins; he dances and dallies with the maids without any feelings of lust.

The plots of the *līlā* of Kṛṣṇa that are performed by the Braj troupes derive from several sources. Because of the importance of the *Bhāgavata Purāṇa* to the whole Kṛṣṇaite movement one would expect it to be the chief source. As a matter of fact Norvin Hein could trace only 28 of the 106 he lists (1972, 156, 163–178) to the *Bhāgavata Purāṇa.* Others may be traced to later compositions such as the *Brahmā Vaivarta Purāṇa,* which exalts Rādhā, and compositions of the bhakti poets. And of course writers of the seventeenth, eighteenth, and even the nineteenth centuries continued to add to the Kṛṣṇa mythology.

Four composers deserve special mention because of the prominent place their compositions have in present-day programs of *rās līlā.* The first is Dhruvadās, a seventeenth-century disciple of Hitharivaṅs, who composed forty-two *līlā* which are available under the title *Biyālis Līlā.* The second is Chacha Vṛndābandās, an eighteenth-century writer, who besides composing many verses, wrote *Rās Chhadma Vinod,* a work which performers use as the basis for many *līlā.* Brajvāsidās' *Braj Vilās* (written in 1743) and Nārāyaṇa Svāmī's *Braj Vihār,* a nineteenth-century work, are also much in use by troupe leaders. Besides the compositions of older poets these latter two authors have included their own compositions. Today some troupe leaders use *Braj Vilās* in cantillation style, holding together the mimetic action on the stage with brief passages chanted from this book.

In addition to the above compositions, there is a large stock of fine devotional poetry composed by the poet-saints of the bhakti movement. Poets from all the bhakti sects have contributed to the large storehouse of poetry which is at the disposal of the *rās līlā* performers. Notable among the contributors were Sūrdās, Nanddās, and Parmānand, all members of the "Club of Eight" poets gathered by Viṭṭalnāth (1516–1586), second son of the founder of the Vallabha sect.

The *rās* troupe leader, therefore, has at his disposal a wealth of fine poetry pertaining to Kṛṣṇa's entire career in Braj. Like the composer of the Japanese No play, he uses the poetry of the masters to enhance his work. To this stock of poetry must be added the troupe leaders' own compositions. There is no doubt that a substantial number of the songs used in *rās līlā* performances are the compositions of performers; the size of their contribution cannot be readily assessed since most of these compositions are unpublished.

Language and Imagery

Since the legends of Kṛṣṇa the lover are the main inspiration of the poets of the bhakti movement, the poems are full of the erotic sentiment. The erotic flavor of *rās* poetry is achieved by stimulating the erotic *rasa* set forth in Indian dramatic theory. Recurring poetic images of spring and autumn relate especially to the *rās līlā.* In the poetry describing the spring season the sound of the cuckoo is so common that it virtually becomes a symbol of the season itself. Other common images are the *kusum* flower and the yellow fields of mustard flowers; creepers or vines; and tender leaves and sprouts. In

Kṛṣṇaite poetry the use of cosmetics and unguents is frequently described. Sandalwood, saffron, musk, and various other scents and ointments serve to excite the passion of the lovers. Trees, especially the *kadamba,* groves, gardens, tinkling ornaments, instrumental music, and the dance are other images frequently employed to evoke the erotic sentiment.

Besides these erotic stimulants, there is also very explicit reference to the stimulation involved in physical lovemaking. Embracing, kissing, and fondling are mentioned in the encounters between Rādhā and Kṛṣṇa. Harirām Vyās' poetry contains frequent references to Rādhā's physical endowments,

Rādhā. (Sangeet Natak Akademi photo)

to her breasts, thighs, and buttocks. Bhakti apologists are at great pains to emphasize that what is referred to is not a physical relationship but a symbol of a spiritual one.

Characters

The only characters who appear in the *nitya rās* are Rādhā, Kṛṣṇa, and the milkmaids. Because the situation is unvarying, an eternally blissful union, there is no scope for character development in terms of hidden conflict. The only question which may be raised here concerns the classification of Rādhā as a heroine in the categories of Sanskrit dramaturgy, and the answer is more vital to the *rās līlā* as religious ritual than as good theatre. What kind of heroine is she? The Indian treatises on drama allow for four kinds of heroine: *svakīya,* one's own (wife); the wife of someone else or a maiden; a common woman (belonging to all, namely, a courtesan); and a widow remarried. Rādhā is neither a courtesan nor a widow remarried. The question is whether she is *svakīya* or the wife of someone else. On the face of it one would have to classify Rādhā as a heroine who is the wife of someone else, since it is recorded that she was the wife of the brother of Yaśodā (Archer 1959, 72). However, in the ritual segment *(nitya rās)* of the *rās līlā,* Rādhā is always treated as a *svakīya* heroine. Even in most of the *līlā* she is treated as Kṛṣṇa's own, for all of the Braj sects hold Rādhā to be a *svakīya* heroine.

The range of characters in the *līlā* is wide, including all those personages, from gods to demons, who make their appearances in the Puranic accounts. Because of their importance in the *līlā,* two classes of characters deserve special mention: the milkmaids *(gopī),* female companions of Rādhā, and Mansukha, the amiable clown of the *rās līlā.*

In the *nitya rās,* Rādhā is the center and chief and Kṛṣṇa tries to please her. The milkmaids wait upon the pleasure of the divine lovers and display no individuality at all. In some of the *līlā,* however, they receive more attention but still without significant individual distinction.[7] Of the eight companions of Rādhā, Lalīta is considered the chief. The others are named Viśākhā, Citrā, Indulekhā, Champakalatā, Raṅgadevī, Tuṅgavidhya, and Suderī. In the literature of the Chaitanya sect, each one has her own characteristics, but in the *rās līlā* plays there is little individual development.

After Rādhā and Kṛṣṇa, perhaps the most beloved character is Mansukha, the friend of Kṛṣṇa who has been described as "anxious and daring and stupid." He is the main comic character of the *rās līlā,* and he resembles the

[7]In the *Candrāvalī līlā,* one of the milkmaids, Candrāvalī, is an individual and principal figure in the plot. In the *Dān līlā,* the *Nauka līlā,* and the *Panghaṭ līlā,* the principal action is between Kṛṣṇa and the milkmaids as a group. The plots of the *Vaidya līlā* and the *Brajyātrā līlā* center around Kṛṣṇa and unidentified individual milkmaids.

jester *(vidūṣaka)* of the Sanskrit drama. His misadventures make him the butt of many comic situations.

None of the other characters are sufficiently delineated to be interesting theatrically. Character painting is in broad strokes and lacks the subtlety and shading which would command audience empathy, that quality sought after in the representational theatre. For example, there is enough in the Puranic accounts to suggest that Kaṁsa has some redeeming qualities. But the *rās līlā* account paints him in the hues of a complete villain who, for example, laughs with fiendish pleasure as he destroys Devakī's newborn children. He is not a man of some greatness confronted by a personal nemesis or one who falls prey to his own fears, but a wicked tyrant who relishes his barbarous acts. It is doubtful that any attempt to "dramatize" the characters of these pieces would meet with audience approbation. The *rās līlā*'s appeal does not lie in maintaining suspense about the outcome of an episode, but in the sense of participating in the victory and the joy of the one whom the spectators worship.

Performance Space

The place of performance of the *rās līlā* is called the *rās maṇḍala* (*maṇḍala* literally means circle). The standard *rās maṇḍala* is circular as the name indicates, the shape doubtlessly dictated by the original dance, which was also circular; but the circle, as the symbol of eternity, reinforces the meaning of the *nitya rās.* The lovemaking of lover and beloved is set in the eternal realm and is manifested only to those whose hearts are given in devoted service to their Lord.

On one side of the mandala is the throne, the seat of which is about four feet high, and from it two broad steps lead down to the smooth cement. In the Vrindaban mandalas, in front of this throne, extending into the circular floor area, is marked out (usually by floor cloths or rugs) a rectangular playing area measuring from fifteen to twenty feet in depth and from ten to twelve feet in width. On the side of this playing area facing the throne sit the singers and instrumentalists. Behind them and on the other two sides of the playing area sit the spectators. Printed curtains form a border for the throne and can be closed to hide the throne area from the audience when necessary.

While at the two mandalas in Vrindaban—Topīkūnj and Kishora Van—the circular floors are large enough to accommodate both the players and the audience, at smaller mandalas the audience sits on the ground surrounding the circular floor. At most locations in the Braj area these stages are out-of-doors, wall-less, and roofless. The mandalas at Topīkūnj and Kishora Van have roofs supported by pillars. The roof makes possible performances during the rainy season which is, in fact, the main season for *rās līlā.* At each site the mandala adjoins a temple. At Topīkūnj the throne faces the temple; at Kishora Van, one must pass through the mandala to enter the temple.

Stage decorations and properties are sparse. The throne is usually covered with a brightly colored cloth. The curtain before the throne provides privacy for the actors to change or adjust costumes and to relax between the *nitya rās* and the *līlā*.

The throne with steps is the one indispensable set piece, and may be a permanent masonry construction as at Topīkūnj or devised from a wooden platform on which two chairs or a bench is placed. Otherwise the stage is bare and the audience must largely set the scene with its imagination. Simple personal properties such as a staff, a flute, and a sword are sometimes used in the *līlā*.

Costume and Makeup

The costume of the *rās līlā* has its origin in the Moghul court of the medieval period. Kṛṣṇa wears a dhoti or short skirt and a tunic with a bright colored sash tied around his waist and a stole over his shoulders, or he wears the Rajputāna pajamas of that time with the tunic. Kṛṣṇa wears a highly ornamented crown headdress in which is fixed a spray of peacock feathers. He is heavily adorned with jewelled necklaces, garlands, and a headpiece of braids. The tilt of Kṛṣṇa's crown has a theological as well as an aesthetic significance. Troupes of the Vallabhācārya sect tilt the crown to the right, away from Rādhā, thus emphasizing Kṛṣṇa. Troupes of the Vrindaban sects, which emphasize Rādhā, tilt the crown to the left, toward Rādhā, thus emphasizing the union of Rādhā and Kṛṣṇa.[8]

Rādhā wears a long full skirt with a blouse and a mantle and a veil, another garment derived from medieval Muslim culture. She is adorned with jewelled necklaces, garlands, cotton braids, and an ornate nose ring. Her crown, smaller than Kṛṣṇa's, is adorned with a paisley design. The milkmaids, who wear simple tiaras, are dressed in much the same fashion, but Rādhā's costume is richer and more attractive. Kṛṣṇa, Rādhā, and the milkmaids all wear the dancer's ankle bells.

The faces of Kṛṣṇa, Rādhā, and the milkmaids are made up with stenciled designs, which are applied by an adult member of the troupe. The actor lies on the floor and the stenciled design is traced on his face and covered with glue. Then ground mica or color or both is applied over the glue.

The costumes and makeup of other characters are less fixed and differ according to the resources and ingenuity of each troupe. In a performance of

[8] This explanation was offered by troupe leaders Bipin Bihāri, Hari Krishna Rām Datt, and Kalyāṇ Prasād Kishorī, all of the Nimbarka sect, whom I interviewed in Vrindaban in March 1971.

the *Śankara līlā* on August 16, 1970, Śankara (Śiva) wore a long black tunic and a dull gold dhoti with a green sash. In keeping with his traditional ascetic aspect, he wore long unbound hair and his headpiece included an artificial snake. His assistants, played by small boys, were comically made up with whitened faces. Yaśodā, played by an adult male, wore an ordinary sari with one end completely covering his face.

In several productions of *The Slaying of Kaṁsa (Kaṁsa vadha līlā),* Kaṁsa was made up as a stereotypical Indian villain, with a long black curled mustache. Interestingly his face bore Śaivite markings.[9] Ogres and demons in several productions wore black clothes and white face makeup. Some wore the standard villain's mustache, which bore a striking resemblance to those of the villains of nineteenth-century melodramas of the West.

Music and Dance

Today the music of the *rās līlā* is a mixture of ancient classical and more modern and popular folk music. Few modern performers seem able to master the slow, solemn, classical (Dhrupad) style of singing; increasingly a type of folk tune is being used to achieve greater popular appeal.[10]

Bhakti literature is full of references to the instruments used in the *līlā* of Kṛṣṇa: cymbals, flute, *sāraṅgī* (a stringed instrument of the viol type), *pakāvaj* (a type of drum), and others, but how many of these were ever actually used in *rās līlā* stage performances is not known. Present-day *rās līlā* orchestras contain the *sāraṅgī,* cymbals, and drums, though drums of the tabla or mridanga type have taken the place of the *pakāvaj,* and in most cases the harmonium has replaced the *sāraṅgī.* Today then the typical orchestra consists of two harmoniums, one played by the leading singer and the other by the assistant or second singer, small hand cymbals, and a pair of tablas. Strangely the flute is seldom used, despite its being the instrument which symbolizes Kṛṣṇa.

There is a strong and direct link between the dance of *rās līlā* and *kathak,* the classical dance form which developed in North India. There is now general agreement that *kathak* developed from the *natwarī nṛtya,* the dance of the Braj *rās līlā.* The similarities between the two forms are apparent. In a recital of *kathak* dance in Delhi in February 1971, the outstanding *kathak*

---

[9] Some writers have speculated that the conflict between Kṛṣṇa and Kaṁsa represented a struggle between Vaiṣṇavism and Buddhism or Vaiṣṇavism and Śaivism (Growse 1880, 48–49).

[10] According to L. N. Garg, editor of *Saṁgīt,* "Dhrupad, Dhamar, Holī, and Rasiya are all equally related to Rās, but the kind of song which finds its way into Rās today does not faithfully present the form of this music, but a debased form which lowers the standard of Rās" (Agrawal N.d., 21).

dancer, Uma Sharma, pointed out these similarities, and the following comment on her recital appeared in the press:

> Uma Sharma must be congratulated for reviving the Natwarī Nṛtya or the Rās Līlā of Brindavan, that quaint old form of classical dance which later developed into Kathak. Natwarī Nṛtya is to Kathak what Dhrupad is to Khyāl in North Indian music.
>
> At her recital for the Indian Cultural Society on Thursday, Uma convincingly demonstrated the similarities and differences between the two styles. Her exposition of the original form of Kathak was clearly based on considerable research conducted in Mathura. For instance, the cupped palm of the raised right hand in Natwarī Nṛtya is turned toward the head evidently representing Adiśesha who protected the newborn Kṛṣṇa while being carried by his father to the house of Yaśodā—whereas in the modern Kathak the palm is turned away from the head. (Sharma 1971)

The development of *rās līlā* dance into classical *kathak* is an indication of the contribution which *rās līlā* has made and may still make to an Indian theatre of high artistry.

Audience

The people who gather to witness the *rās līlā* are not spectators who have come to be entertained. These spectator-celebrants are an intimate community of faith, and the action takes place among them. Their attitude of reverence creates an atmosphere in which people respond fervently with the shout "Vṛndāban Bihārī Lāl Kī jai!" (Victory to Bihārī Lāl of Vrindaban), or "Rādhey-Śyām!" (meaning Rādhā-Kṛṣṇa), or are caught up in singing hymns—"Govinda jai jai, Gopāla jai jai, Rādhā Ramanahārī, Govinda jai jai" (Hail to Govinda, hail to Gopāl, hail to Rādhā, the beautiful one). Individuals sometimes stand up and join in the dance, swaying as if in trance. On one occasion an old holy man, grey-bearded, balding, and clad in a single saffron cloth, danced, doing fast pirouettes as though he were a youth of thirteen. The spectators, transformed into participants, urged him on, clapping and singing until the whole occasion took on the atmosphere of a tent revival meeting. As the clapping got faster and faster and the drum rhythms more and more insistent, the emotions of the audience approached ecstasy. Eyes closed, hands clapping rhythmically, and bodies swaying as one, they seemed unconscious of their surroundings.

At another performance a woman stood up in the midst of the spectator-participants[11] and began to dance. Arms raised above her head, she went on

[11] I use the term "spectator-participants" to emphasize that the spectators are not viewers of the *rās līlā;* they believe in and share in the ritual and thus are participants.

dancing long after the musicians had finished their song, seemingly seeing and hearing with her own inward eye and ear the divine dance, its shifting configurations, and its insistent rhythms.

On still another occasion, what was a mimetic theatrical action was indistinguishable from a religious act. The *līlā* being done included the well-known episode of Kṛṣṇa's stealing the butter. When the child actor crawled away with the earthen vessel and sat down to enjoy the contents, the old guru of the temple's patron took him on his lap, and from the earthen vessel the actor playing Kṛṣṇa distributed *prasād* (food that has been offered to an image of a god and, therefore, is specially blessed) to the spectator-participants, who pressed forward eagerly to receive it. To them the actor *was* Kṛṣṇa and the sweets *prasād,* a direct offering from god himself.

This inherent attitude of piety is reinforced by a certain external pressure to maintain an atmosphere of sanctity and devotion. At one theatre the following reminder was displayed prominently on a nearby wall: "*Rās līlā* meṅ shor machnā pāp hai" (Making noise during the *rās līlā* is a sin).

The following conditions laid down by the leader of a certain Vrindaban troupe give an idea of the pressures exerted by the organizers to preserve an air of solemnity and piety:

(1) Those who perform the *Bhagvata līlā* (the actors) should maintain an attitude of devotion themselves.
(2) The place of performance of the *rās līlā* should be the interior of a temple, garden, or private building, a bungalow, or a lodge of a temple, not on the street or at a crossing.
(3) The *rās līlā* ought to be only two and a half hours in duration. To have the *rās līlā* or divine characterization after twelve midnight is contrary to custom.
(4) To sit on a chair or high seat, etc., to watch the *rās līlā* is forbidden and prohibited.
(5) Wearing shoes in the *rās* area, smoking, and making noise are forbidden.
(6) After the beginning of the *rās līlā* changes cannot be made in it. At the end of the *līlā,* with the exception of the putting-to-bed verse, etc., nothing can be added.[12]

The spectators sit on the ground, for sitting on chairs or other elevated seats would show a lack of proper respect for the deities. The wearing of shoes is forbidden, as in any Hindu place of worship. While shouting, clapping, or dancing in response to the performance is permitted, random conversation is not. If the crowd becomes restless and begins to talk, the swami

[12] I have translated this material from a handbill, "Srī Dham Vṛndāban ke Svāmī Baburām Sarma, Master, Adarsha Rās Mandali Ki Niyamavali" (Rules of Svāmī Baburām Sarma of Vrindaban, Master of the Ideal Rās Company).

breaks into the performance to shout, "Say, 'Victory to Bihārī Lāl of Vrindaban' " ("Bolo, Vṛndāban Bihārī Lāl kī jai!"). Everyone joins in, effectively interrupting the conversations. If this fails, the swami or the person in charge of the mandala sternly demands order.

However, the spectators of *rās līlā* are usually attentive, entering deeply and emphatically into the action of the play. At a performance of *The Līlā of the Light of Supreme Love* in Vrindaban the audience was altogether caught up in the pathos of a certain scene. They became exceptionally quiet, a most marked response to pathos, and soon more than half of them were brushing tears from their eyes. As the scene progressed not only the audience but the swami and the actors began to shed tears freely.

Rās Līlā in Performance

Before the performance, the actors playing the role of Rādhā, Kṛṣṇa, and the female companions of Rādhā are made up in a room off stage or in the temple to which the mandala is attached. Sometimes during festival seasons when a troupe performs several times daily, the actors arrive already costumed. When the crowns are fixed on their heads they are considered to have assumed the forms of the deities and from that point are treated with the same reverence and respect shown to an image of the deity. The boys who play Rādhā and Kṛṣṇa are carried in the arms or on the shoulders of one of the troupe and placed on the throne behind the drawn curtain, which may be hung on a wire or held up by two persons. At the same time the musicians and singers take their places. When the actors are in position—Kṛṣṇa seated on the stage right side of the throne, with Rādhā on his left and the milkmaids (usually four or six) seated on the lower steps at each side of the throne—the curtain is drawn for the first tableau, or *jhāṅkī*.

The leader of the troupe, who is also the chief singer, gets up from his place among the musicians, goes forward and touches the feet of Rādhā and Kṛṣṇa, returns to his place, and immediately begins the invocatory song, an example of which follows:

> Homage to my respected teacher; to my gracious perceptor I bow.
> The autumn moon shines in its full beauty and everyone is refreshed.
> Kṛṣṇa stays with Rādhā in Vṛndāban and with the *munis* in Indrajan.
> I bow to Rādhā and Kṛṣṇa, the beautiful pair.
> Shri Rādhā is my mistress; I am her servant.
> Grant that in every incarnation I may reside in Vṛndāban.
> Sing the praises of the prince of Braj, and you will attain the treasure of joy.
> Sing the devotion of the saints of Braj, and you will obtain the riches of Kṛṣṇa.
> *Guru* is Brahmā, *Guru* is Viṣṇu, *Guru* is Śaṁkar.
> I bow to my *guru* who is verily God.

A *rās līlā* troupe on the way to a performance. (John Stratton Hawley photo)

All creatures of the world, wise or foolish, pay homage to the *guru* who gives the vision of wisdom.
I lay my petitions at the feet of Kṛṣṇa who is pleased at the devotion of his worshippers,
Who establishes the three qualities, who fulfills the desires of all,
And who performs the dance in Vṛndāban.

(Agrawal n.d., 157–158)

Then other members of the chorus in turn sing couplets and verses on subjects conducive to an attitude of devotion, such as the glories of Braj, the devotion of lovers, the beauty of Kṛṣṇa and Rādhā, or the tenderness and joy of love.

The swami ends the choral music and begins the *nitya rās* by singing a *dhrupad,* a song in solemn style, sung to a slow time and sober rhythms. As the last line of the *dhrupad* begins and before it ends the milkmaids get up from their seats, come forward, and stand before Rādhā and Kṛṣṇa. The main milkmaid takes a brass tray and performs the *aratī* ceremony, which consists of waving a tray, on which is a lighted lamp, in a circular fashion vertically in front of the divine pair. During this act of worship the couple assumes the intimate pose of lovers; Kṛṣṇa puts his left arm about the neck of Rādhā and with his right hand places the flute, his special symbol, to his lips as if playing it. The milkmaids then sing the *aratī* song, which may be in a form such as one of the two below:

> Praise to Kṛṣṇa, adorned with every virtue,
> Who puts the intellect of man to shame.
> Kṛṣṇa, son of Nanda, who brings happiness to the Yādavas,
> Praise be to you.
> Hail to Rādhā, goddess of the dance of love.
> O Rādhā, daughter of Bṛṣbhānu, grant me my desire.
> Praise to you who practice the arts of love beneath the *kadamba* tree;
> Praise be to you who makes the tinkle of your ankle bells sound in the bower of creepers;
> Blessed be Rādhā and Kṛṣṇa together encircled by hundreds of lovely maidens.
> Perform the *aratī* of Rādhā and Kṛṣṇa with body, mind, and soul.
> Keep in your mind an image of swarthy Kṛṣṇa and fair Rādhā
> Upon whose brow is the peacock crown and at whose lips is the flute,
> On seeing the figure of Kṛṣṇa, the heart becomes joyful.
> Surrender your life at the feet of Lord Kṛṣṇa
> Who makes love in the groves and raised up Mount Govardhan.
> Behold Kṛṣṇa, Nanda's son, bedecked with flowers and garlands.
> Lighting a camphor lamp on a golden tray, all the people of Braj perform the *aratī.*
> Nanda's son, Kṛṣṇa, and Bṛṣbhānu's daughter, Rādhā, unitedly bestow great joy upon all.
> May the *aratī* of Rādhā and Kṛṣṇa which we have sung ascend to heaven and resound there forever.
>
> (Agrawal n.d., 158–160)

At the end of the *aratī* song the milkmaids each touch the feet of Rādhā and Kṛṣṇa. One of the milkmaids then approaches the couple with an invitation, invariably in this form: "O Lover and beloved, the time for your *nitya rās* has come, so please come to the *rās maṇḍala.*" Kṛṣṇa accepts the invitation and the milkmaids sit down in their places below the throne. Kṛṣṇa may first address Rādhā in song from his seat on the throne, or he may at once rise and, offering her his hand, address her with the standard invitation: "O Śrī Kishorījī, the time for your *nitya rās* has come; so please come to the *rās maṇḍala.*" Accepting his hand Rādhā replies, "Very well, beloved," or "Let us go, my love." They rise from the throne and go down into the playing area.

Then follows a series of songs and dances, involving Rādhā, Kṛṣṇa, and the milkmaids, which establishes a mood of romantic and happy love play. At the beginning Kṛṣṇa and Rādhā face each other with the milkmaids, two or three on their right or left, completing a circle. The swami at once begins a song and a dance begins to the same rhythm. At the beginning the dancers do not sing; they only dance. They move slowly in a circle, their hands held in the positions characteristic of the *rās,* keeping time with their feet. The chorus sings a song like the following:

> *Rās* Bihārī is dancing the *rās;*
> All the women of Braj are dancing.
> Tadim, tadim, tat tat thei thei,
> Thungan thungan is its unique rhythm.

This song is first sung slowly, then the tempo is doubled. The instant the fast tempo begins, Kṛṣṇa, Rādhā, and the group of milkmaids, increasing the speed of their foot rhythms, begin to pirouette. After four or five pirouettes, according to the custom of the particular troupe, they kneel down in their original positions, that is, in a circle with Kṛṣṇa facing Rādhā and the milkmaids between them. Through movements of the hands and upper torso done to the rhythm of the instrumental music and through facial expression they express the dance's prevailing emotion, love. Next they all stand in line, Rādhā on the left of Kṛṣṇa and the milkmaids in two groups on either side of them. Then, to the beat given below first Kṛṣṇa dances, then Rādhā, and finally the milkmaids dance in pairs. The swami sings this ancient rhythmic tune: "Tat tata thei, tat tata thei, tat tata thei." The tune is a series of verbal sounds uttered by the dance master. These utterances imitate the various sounds struck on the tabla or mridanga to establish the rhythmic pattern which the dancer is to follow. As this is sung Kṛṣṇa, keeping time with his feet, comes out of the line and advances four or five paces, turns, and stands facing Rādhā. To the rhythm of the music, he hops and jumps. With hand gestures he dances to the following rhythmic tune sung by the swami:

> Tikat tikat dhilang, dhikatak, todim dhilang, takato/
> Ta dhilang, dhig dhilang, dhikatak, todim todim, dhetam dhetam//

Dhilang dhilang dhilang, tak gadagin thei/
Tat tata thei, tat tata thei, tat tata thei//

Kṛṣṇa returns to his place in the line and Rādhā comes forward to the tune:

Tat trang, thun thun to, dhikatu trang, thun thun to/
Tat thun, dhik thun thun, dhik tak, thung thung tak//
Thung thung tak, thung thung thung tak gadagin thei/
Tat tata thei, tat tata thei, tat tata thei//

After Rādhā returns to her place the milkmaids dance, one by one or in pairs, keeping the rhythm with their feet. They go four or five paces, turn and face Rādhā and Kṛṣṇa and with hand gestures and leaping movements begin to dance according to a pattern such as this:

Tatt tuk dam, dhirkit, tirkit, nagam, nagam, tu tu tranto/
Tatt tuk dam, dhirkit, tirkit, nagam, nagam, tu tu tran to/
Ta tring, ta ta tring, tatt thugam thugam tatt thugam thugam, thung thung thung tak, gadagin thei/
Tat tata thei, tat tata thei, tat tata thei//

As soon as "Tat tata thei" is sung, Kṛṣṇa starts again and dances as before according to the rhythmic tune below. At the sound "taddi" he backs up and on "tran tran tran" he gives three leaps, each time ending in a squatting position, after which he stands up.

Taddi taddi taddi taddi, thika tak taddi, tran to/
Taddi taddi taddi taddi, thika tak taddi, tran to//
Tran tran tran// tat tata thei, ta tata thei//
Jijik tatta thei, jijik tatta thei, jijik tatta thei, ta tha/
Jijik tatta thei, jijik tatta thei, jijik tatta thei, ta tha/
Thei ta, thei ta, thei
Jijik tatta thei ta, jijik tatta thei ta, jijik tatta thei ta
Thei thei thei thei ta the the the the the the ta, Triyata triyata,
Tri teg ta, gadagin thei ta/

This is the rhythmic pattern of Kṛṣṇa's most important dance. During the singing of this tune, Kṛṣṇa comes back into the line; then keeping time with his feet (and removing himself four or five paces from the line), he does a somersault. He comes back into the line. Then on the following tune he kneels on one knee and three times expresses his mood with hand gestures.

After Kṛṣṇa's dance, the others join him in a group dance:

Thei thei thei thei thei, tatta thei thei/
Thei thei thei thei thei thei thei ta//

On the last word of the tune all resume their seats, and at this point occurs the most spectacular of the dances, the so-called Peacock Dance, which Kṛṣṇa performs on his knees. Pivoting on his right and left knee in turn, he whirls around in a circle, his head ornaments and skirts standing out in the breeze he creates. When well-executed it is a magnificent dance and usually has an electrifying effect upon the spectators who often shout, "Glory to Bihārī Lāl Kṛṣṇa of Vrindaban! (Vṛndāban Bihārī Lāl kī jai!)."

This climactic dance sometimes ends the first part of the ritual section *(nitya rās)*. But at this point in some performances, while the swami sings a verse such as "Kṛṣṇa is dancing the *rās* (Nachat rās meṅ Rās Bihārī)," Kṛṣṇa comes forward, stands before Rādhā, who is seated on the throne, and rearranges her garments and ornaments. As the song ends he salutes Rādhā with folded hands and sits down beside her on the throne.

The dancers sit on and around the throne and the curtain is drawn. While they rest the musicians sing. Sometimes the dancers are given betel nut to chew and Rādhā and Kṛṣṇa are constantly fanned by attendants. The interval usually lasts five to ten minutes.

After the interval the curtain is opened and Kṛṣṇa comes forward to deliver a discourse. He may speak on a variety of subjects, such as the glory of Braj, the importance of devotion, or the glory of love, or he may give an exposition of his various *līlā,* interspersing his remarks with song. The sermon makes more meaningful and affecting the songs which follow.

The sermon is a fairly recent innovation in *rās līlā,* having been introduced by an ascetic, Śrī Premānand Jī of Vrindaban, within the lifetime of some of the present performers. Some troupes previously featured a short discourse by one of the milkmaids on a subject such as the importance of *rās,* the dance of love, or the importance of a particular *līlā,* but this was never popular or very effective. Kṛṣṇa's discourse, on the other hand, is much liked by the audience and is now included in all performances.

After the discourse the second part of the *nitya rās* begins. The first part is dominated by dance; in the second part dance is subordinated to song. The second part begins with group singing and dancing; sometimes the songs with which the *nitya rās* began are repeated. The group singing is followed by a duet sung and danced by Rādhā and Kṛṣṇa. Then Kṛṣṇa and the milkmaids sing and dance while Rādhā sits on the throne.

While the order of this second part is somewhat less fixed than the first and may be shortened or lengthened at the discretion of the leader, according to length of the *līlā* which is to follow or the response of the audience, the duet of Rādhā and Kṛṣṇa is a favorite with the audience. They may answer each other line by line or verse by verse, but the burden of the duet is the admiration of the lovers for each other, the attractiveness of attire and ornaments, and the beauty of face and figure. While Rādhā and Kṛṣṇa sing and dance, the seated milkmaids may join in the song. They express their love by linking right and left arms, standing back to back, and gazing into each other's eyes. They gently fondle each other's faces, and sometimes they interlock right and left feet as they turn.[13] The *nitya rās* concludes with a group song and dance in which the dancers stand in a line and, keeping time with their feet, advance four or five paces and retreat, all the time expressing with hand movements the emotion of the *rās*.

There remains the very important final tableau, which marks the end of the *nitya rās*. While this is being prepared, one of the milkmaids, usually the smallest, entertains. "She" invariably gets the audience to shout "Rādhey Śyām!" (Rādhā, Kṛṣṇa). She tells them to hold on to the "Rādhey" as long as she keeps waving her finger in a circular movement above her head, and when she makes a deep knee bend, they are to end with "Śyām!" This is pure fun, albeit with a religious purpose; it becomes a contest between the milkmaid and the spectator-participants to see who can prolong the phrase longest without breathing. If preparation for the tableau requires still more time, the milkmaid leads the spectators in singing "Rādhā rāni kī jai, Mahārāni kī jai" (Praise to Queen Rādhā, praise to the great queen), or some other familiar hymn.

In terms of spectacle, the high points are the *tableaux vivants* at the beginning and especially at the end of the *nitya rās*. At the beginning the spectator-participants have a glimpse of Rādhā and Kṛṣṇa seated on the throne in an attitude of happy intimacy, but the final tableau is more elaborate. Rādhā and Kṛṣṇa, or occasionally Kṛṣṇa alone, is seated on the throne. Richly colored silks and diaphanous chiffons, complementing the colors of their costumes, are draped about and around them and held up by the assistants so that the couple appear to be suspended in an expanse of beautiful color.

These tableaux also are the high moments of devotion for the spectators. At this time they press forward in large numbers, sadhus and laity alike, to do obeisance, touching the feet of Rādhā and Kṛṣṇa, placing the feet of the couple upon their heads, prostrating themselves upon the ground, and making offerings of money.[14]

The exhibition of this final tableau may last for five to ten minutes, depending upon how the audience-congregation responds. While members

---

[13] Formerly a stick dance and *jhumar* dance, similar to the *garba* dance of Gujarat, used to be done. The latter was performed with a stick and threads in a manner resembling the winding and unwinding of the maypole. This dance is no longer performed in the *rās līlā*.

[14] The spectators come forward during the performance also, but not in such large numbers as at the time of the tableau.

Gopīs lifting Kṛṣṇa and Rādhā in the *rās* sequence preceeding *The Light of Love*, performed in Vrindaban in 1974. (John Stratton Hawley photo)

of the crowd are going forward the singers continue to sing until the worship and offerings have ceased. The audience joins in the singing of popular devotional songs, such as "Jai Govinda" (Praise Govinda). When people stop going forward the curtain is drawn, the singing ends, and the actors leave the stage.

There is usually an interval of five to ten minutes between the ending of the *nitya rās* and the beginning of the *līlā*. The musicians resume playing and singing and continue until the *līlā* is begun. The *līlā* which follows the *nitya rās* may have as its subject matter any of the events of the childhood or youth of Kṛṣṇa, from his birth to the time when he goes to Mathura to slay Kaṁsa. The two exceptions are *The Līlā of Uddhav (Uddhav līlā)*, summarized above, and *The Līlā of Sudāmā (Sudāmā līlā)*. The latter concerns Kṛṣṇa's sojourn in Dvaraka after being forced by his enemies to leave Mathura. According to tradition, Sudāmā was a native of Braj, and thus the inclusion of this work among the *līlā* of Braj is justified.

A *līlā* is a one-act play made up of elements of dialogue in prose, poetry, and song. In addition to the dialogue of characters on the stage, the leader of the troupe, who is usually the chief singer, often interjects songs full of religious imagery, which serve to build emotion and atmosphere for the action. The actor frequently recites or sings a verse and immediately follows it with a prose paraphrase which clarifies the meaning. Some *līlā* include dance, but it is certainly minor in quantity compared with the amount in the *nitya rās*.

Many of the *līlā* have some comic scenes or characters. In *The Līlā of Śaṁkar (Śaṁkar līlā)*, Śaṁkar's attendants are made up in a clownish manner, and their antics and strange noises bring laughter from the spectators. Adult males also take roles in the *līlā*. They represent a wide range of characters, from demons to holy ascetics. The play usually ends either with the ritual of the waving of the lights *(aratī)* or a tableau.

These *līlā* are usually performed in accordance with the season or festival celebrated. For example, *The Līlā of the Birth of Kṛṣṇa (Kṛṣṇa jaman līlā)* is done on or around Janmastami, Kṛṣṇa's birthday; the *Holī līlā (Horī līlā)* is done during the Holī festival.[15] *The Great Rās Līlā,* sometimes called *The Triumph over Love (Kāmavijay līlā),* is also seen during the Holī festival. Since this festival carries specific erotic and sexual overtones, the connection is obvious. *The Līlā of Śaṁkar (Śiva)* is also done around Janmastami.

Description of a Performance of *The Līlā of Śaṁkar*

Since the *nitya rās* follows a set pattern which has been described in the preceding section, I will only describe the *līlā* part of the performance. This was

[15] In the Braj language the "r" sound is often substituted for the "l" sound.

a performance of Svāmī Rūp Lāl's troupe at Kishora Van in Vrindaban on August 16, 1970.

At the end of the *rās* the swami made the following announcement about the *līlā:*

> Now we are about to present the *Śaṁkar līlā.* Lord Śaṁkar is about to appear before you. This *līlā* which is about to be presented is a very beautiful one. In it you will witness the *tāṇḍava* dance and hear the poetry of the great saints. Listen attentively; it will begin soon and will be finished in a short time.

Śaṁkar enters wearing a long black tunic and dull gold dhoti pajamas with a green sash and stole. He also wears the standard Śiva symbols, long loose hair (in the style of an ascetic) in which a snake is entwined. On the whole his aspect is terrifying. He is played by an adult male and is accompanied by two attendants, played by boys. They are comically costumed and made up. The makeup is clownish and the costumes are shabby and lack dignity. One attendant holds the small two-headed drum *(damarū)* which is one of Śiva's symbols. They jump and tumble about making monkeylike noises. The audience laughs. They sing "Jai Śaṁkar."

Śaṁkar appears before the microphone and declares his intention of going to see the infant Kṛṣṇa, who is lying in a cradle in Yaśodā's courtyard. The attendants beg to go and he gives his permission provided they behave so as not to frighten the baby.

The journey to Yaśodā's house is represented by circling the stage. At Yaśodā's Śaṁkar calls out to announce his presence and sings a song in praise of Kṛṣṇa's birth.

Yaśodā comes out of the house, but ducks back in fright at the sight of Śaṁkar's companions. After reassuring her, he requests a view *(darśana)* of the baby. She refuses. He insists and she offers to give him anything else. Śaṁkar explains to Yaśodā—first in verse and then in a prose interpretation—the real significance of Kṛṣṇa. He tells her that this child is Brahmā, the Absolute, the Creator, Sustainer and Destroyer of the universe, the lord of the three worlds, etc.

Yaśodā continues to refuse him a view of the child and he begins to dance in the *tāṇḍava* style to the timing of the small hand-cymbal. The postures of the dance resemble the familiar Naṭarāja pose of Śiva. The spectators respond with cries of "Victory to Śaṁkar."

Yaśodā continues to refuse to let him see the child, offering instead riches, jewels, wealth, and so on. He refuses all these as inferior to devotion to Kṛṣṇa.

After many refusals, Śaṁkar tells Yaśodā that he will sit outside her door until she brings the child out, even if it takes ten or twenty years. He sits down and sings a long song with the refrain, "Here I sit, waiting for a glimpse of you, O Śyām."

Finally, after another refusal, Śaṁkar starts on his way, sounding the drum. Kṛṣṇa inside begins to cry uncontrollably. Hastily Śaṁkar is called back and Yaśodā, realizing he is not just an ordinary ascetic, lets him see the child. He gives her the blessing of enduring devotion. The spectators shout, "Victory to Kṛṣṇa of Vrindaban."

Current State

The *rās līlā* is by nature conservative; it does not, like the *svāṅg,* or even the *Rām līlā,* open itself to all. Its venue is the intimate circle of believers. This private, almost secret, orientation is partially accounted for by the circumstances of its birth and early development. In the fifteenth and sixteenth centuries the Hindus in North India suffered severe repression by the Muslim rulers. Such was the harshness and repression under Aurangzeb and so furious were his assaults upon the Hindu holy places that some of the famous images of Braj were taken beyond his reach for safekeeping. Some of these have never been returned. Under such conditions it was natural that *rās līlā* should develop a protective veil of secrecy.

When the British became the paramount power in India, they avoided interference in religious affairs as far as possible, and Hindu worship practices were able to continue unhindered. Under their rule the *rās līlā* enjoyed the patronage of several princely states and was able to develop in security under favorable economic circumstances.

With Independence in 1947, the political atmosphere continued to be favorable to the development of the *rās līlā* stage, but the financial backing and encouragement of the rajas of the princely states vanished overnight. Since Independence the consciousness of folk-theatre forms and a desire for their rejuvenation has given a fillip to the *rās līlā* stage. Theatre practitioners and scholars, searching for means to revitalize the theatre of India, are being led increasingly to the traditional theatre. In 1964 the Braj Līlā Kendra (Braj Līlā Center) was founded to study, research, and reform the folk theatre, folk music, and folk arts of the Braj area. The organization concentrated initially on the *rās līlā* because it is acknowledged as the most valuable art of the Braj area. The Kendra's work on *rās līlā* takes several forms: It is collecting ancient verses which are not now used in the *rās līlā* and having them recorded by old masters before they are forgotten; it is conducting an economic survey of the *rās* troupes operating in the Braj area to discover which troupes need help in improving their performance; and it offers aid to deserving troupes which are facing financial difficulties. It organizes *rās* festivals in which many troupes take part, awards are made on the basis of excellence, and constructive criticism for improvement is offered to those that participate. The Kendra also publishes ancient *rās* literature and collects Braj folk music.

While clearly conservative in nature, the Braj Līlā Kendra does recognize that change must come. The changes which have appeared in the *rās līlā* in recent years and are appearing now point in more than one direction. The effects of changes, which we shall note, are to increase the religious emphasis of the *rās līlā,* on the one hand, and its theatricality on the other. Some changes move the *rās līlā* plays toward greater representationalism and a wider popular appeal. The sermon or discourse, a relatively recent feature, increases the religious emphasis of the *rās līlā.* At the same time there are developments in the physical staging of the *rās līlā* that suggest a greater interest in aesthetic than religious expression. The use of electric lighting in the place of the oil lamp was the initial change, from which others are now springing. The introduction of the electric light has modified the appearance and atmosphere of the *rās līlā* performance. The costumes of the players are traditionally bright and colorful; their headdresses sparkle with jewels, silver, and tinsel; their facial makeup is highlighted with sequins and ground mica. In the soft, flickering light of an oil lamp the colors were somewhat muted. The harsh brightness of the naked electric bulb gives the costumes and makeup a certain garishness.

There are now secondary changes following upon the advent of electric lighting. Where most performances are lighted with a few bulbs hanging over the stage, at Kishora Van in Vrindaban the management attempts some elementary stage lighting. A spotlight is fixed above and behind the spectators and focused on the performing area. Color media are used to change the lighting to increase the effect of a scene. At this same place the performers use microphones and amplifiers, effectively and unobtrusively. The use of both spotlights and sound equipment, small developments in themselves, signal a shift toward a greater theatrical emphasis. The direction of both developments is to make the *rās līlā* a thing to be observed and heard rather than an event in which to participate.

Another and potentially important factor is the interest which the *rās līlā* has stimulated among theatre people. It has the necessary elements and the aesthetic quality to provide the basis for a fine theatre, and the search for a base upon which to renew the Indian theatre tradition may force increased attention to it. The gratification that the possibilities of this traditional form are being recognized and supported must be tempered by the prospect that the form itself may be cut off from the primary source of its vitality—faith.

Some troupe leaders are composing *rās*-styled *līlā* on the lives of the founders of the bhakti sects. Hargovind, a leading Vrindaban troupe leader, at the inspiration of Haribābā of Vrindaban, composed a *līlā* on the life of Chaitanya, founder of a new sect of Hinduism. This *līlā* is performed after the *nitya rās,* like any *līlā* of Kṛṣṇa. Rām Svarūp, son of Meghśyām and another prominent troupe leader, composed a *līlā* on the life of Haridās, and this is performed over a period of five or six days. Both of these *līlā* have found wide acceptance and are now performed by other troupes also. The injection of historical material into the *rās līlā* means that it will become less parochial and more open, as its emphasis broadens from a restricted theological appeal to a more broadly human one.

This broadening of content, while still small, is matched by a shift in musical taste. The traditional and sometimes classical styles of singing are beginning to give way to an easier music drawn from folk sources and films. Although the impact of film music on *rās līlā* is much less than upon *svāṅg*, the increase in folk music is quite marked. A recent famous troupe leader, Meghśyām, gave impetus to the the use of folk music through his compositions. He rewrote a considerable amount of bhakti literature, such as the poems of Sūrdās and others, making the language more simple and using folk and modern tunes. The change in taste, as evidenced by the increased influence of both folk and film music, will have various effects. The borrowing of tunes from the folk tradition may serve eventually to revitalize the musical tradition. On the other hand film music may, by increasing prominence, replace the older style.

Compared to other regional forms, the *rās līlā* is in "good health." Performances are regularly held at several places and interest is high. A number of troupes are able to practice their profession. The closeness of the Braj community and the renewed interest in the form suggests an optimistic outlook for its survival and growth.

WORKS CITED

Agrawal, Ram Narayan. N.d.
Braj Ka Ras Rang Manch. Unpublished manuscript.

Archer, W. G. 1959.
The Loves of Krishna. London: George Allen and Unwin.

Gargi, Balwant. 1956.
Folk Theater in India. Seattle: University of Washington Press.

Growse, A. S. Trans. 1880.
Mathura: A District Memoir. 2nd ed. Allahabad.

Hein, Norvin. 1972.
The Miracle Plays of Mathura. New Haven: Yale University Press.

Sharma, Uma. 1971.
The Hindustan Times. February 22.

White, Charles S. J. Trans. 1977.
The Caurasi Pad of Sri Hit Harivams. Honolulu: University of Hawaii Press.

ADDITIONAL READING

Growse, F. S. 1938.
The Ramayana of Tulsi Das. 7th rev. ed. Allahabad.

Hawley, John Stratton. 1981.
At Play With Krishna: Pilgrimage Dramas from Brindavan. Princeton: Princeton University Press.

Hein, Norvin. 1958.
"The Ram Lila." *Journal of American Folklore* LXXI (July–September): 279–304.

Hill, Douglas P. 1962.
The Holy Lake of the Acts of Rama. London: Oxford University Press.

Kinsley, David R. 1979.
The Divine Player: A Study of Krsna Lila. Delhi: Motilal Banarsidass.

Mathur, Jagdish Chandra. 1964.
Drama in Rural India. New York: Asia Publishing House.

Samar, D. L. 1971.
"Rasdhari, Folk Theatre of Rajasthan." *Sangeet Natak* 20:50–56.

Swann, Darius L. 1974.
"Three Forms of Traditional Theatre of Uttar Pradesh, North India." Ph.D. diss., University of Hawaii.

Chapter Seven

RĀM LĪLĀ

Darius L. Swann

IN THE AUTUMN WHEN THE MONSOON RAINS HAVE FINALLY CEASED and the nights are cool and crisp, North India celebrates Daśsara, the great festival of Rām.[1] In village, town, and city over a period of ten to thirty consecutive nights, episodes from the play of Rām—the *Rām līlā*—are enacted. Among all the traditional theatre genres of India the *Rām līlā* comes closest to being a national drama, for it is performed over a larger portion of the country than any other single form. During this great festival there are probably few residents who are not within walking distance of a *Rām līlā* performance. Nearly every village and town has a place for large public gatherings and this is commonly known as the *Rām līlā* grounds, for the *Rām līlā* is the occasion for the largest and most important assembly held in the locality. It is a national drama also because it has been the vehicle for promoting the story of Rām and Sītā, whose images have powerfully molded the Indian ideals of manhood and womanhood and whose mythical rule has come to exemplify the ideal Indian state. Through the *Rām līlā,* a mass education takes place which annually renews in the collective Hindu mind a notion of the integrity of Hindu society and a vision of what the national life might be. The effectiveness of the *Rām līlā* rests partially upon the fact that it is folk theatre—theatre done by, for, and through the support of the people themselves. The plays are almost always produced, acted, and financed by the people of the local communities where they are performed. For that reason the style, length, and organizational support vary according to local traditions. The *Rām līlā,* true to its origin as a community creation, is played on the fairgrounds and in the marketplace. It belongs to all of the people

[1] In this chapter I have used the conventional Hindi spellings of such words as Rām, Lakṣmaṇ, Bharat, and Rāvan, rather than the Sanskrit spellings of Rāma, Lakṣmaṇa, Bharata, and Rāvana, since they convey the way the words are pronounced in North India.

On the shoulders of priests Rām and Sītā, center and right, with Lakṣmaṇ, left, are ready to be carried to the performance area in Rāmnagar near Varanasi. Because *Rām līlā* is a sacred event, it is not thought proper that the incarnation of these gods should walk to the performance area. (Sangeet Natak Akademi photo)

and is enacted where the entire community may gather; it is never far from the profane world. The players enact the *Rām līlā*'s well-known episodes before large and frequently noisy crowds, and sometimes they must compete with the cries of vendors hawking their wares. The *Rām līlā* therefore conveys the impression of a profane theatre in a religious guise.

This view of the *Rām līlā* as a theatre significantly concerned with shaping the secular life of man is not merely a result of present day secularizing tendencies; it was noted by observers a century and a half ago. Heber saw the *Rām līlā* performed in Allahabad in 1824 and noted its nonsectarian tendency even then:

> It being the festival of Rāma and Sītā, all the world was employed in seeing the hero with his army of monkeys attack the giant Rāvanu. Many other hindrances and disappointments occurred, but the delay they occasioned gave me an opportunity of seeing something of the Rāmien festival, which consists in a sort of dramatic representation, during many successive days, of Rām's history and adventures. The first evening I went with Mr. Byrd *to the show, for such it is now considered and so entirely divested of every religious character as to be attended even by Mussolmans without scruple.* [Italics added] (1923, 446)

While it is clearly an exaggeration to claim that the *Rām līlā* is "divested of every religious character," it does project a greater concern for social and political values than for religious or devotional ones. Other early observers also have documented the *Rām līlā*'s orientation toward the expression of national ideals.

In more recent times the overtones of Hindu nationalism in the *Rām līlā* have sparked friction between Muslims and Hindus in some localities, resulting in some instances in the banning of public performances. The present secretary of the Śrī Patharchaṭṭī *Rām līlā* Committee, Allahabad, insists, however, that the *Rām līlā* is a national festival which all Indians, including Muslims and Christians, can and in fact do celebrate.[2] I also have observed this participation by non-Hindus. The *Rām līlā* thus may be said to represent theatrically an important cultural concept of the Indian people (Zaehner 1955, 92).

Origins

Present evidence does not tell us how old the *Rām līlā* is. That which is historically verifiable does not take us back very far. Accounts of Western visitors and travelers testify to a well-established *Rām līlā* tradition in North India in the early decades of the nineteenth century. This is corroborated by Indian sources. The oldest *Rām līlā* committee in Allahabad dates its beginnings to 1836, and the Maharaja of Benares (Varanasi) took the Ramnagar *Rām līlā* under state management in 1805. Both of these events suggest not origins but new ways of strengthening an observance which was well established by that time.

In Varanasi there is an established tradition that Megha Bhagat, a disciple of Tulsīdās, first started the *Rām līlā* at Assi by staging the *Rāmcaritmānas* of his master about 1625. Although there is no documentary evidence at present to support this claim, it seems quite creditable, for fragments of evidence suggest that a *Rām līlā* type of drama existed before Tulsīdās wrote his great work. In the *Rāmcaritmānas* itself there is a reference which suggests

[2] From a taped interview with Śrī Kanhaiya Lal Misra, recorded on October 7, 1970.

that Tulsīdās in his childhood was familiar with performances like the *Rām līlā.*[3] Also the biography of Chaitanya, the great Bengali religious leader, records an incident during his autumn stay in the city of Puri in which scenes from the epic of Rām were acted out. Chaitanya's death and his biography both preceded Tulsīdās' writing of his epic. Finally, a Rāmakrīda is listed among the minor forms of drama, which suggests an early form of theatre dealing with the acts of Rām.

From all this we may surmise that the *Rām līlā* in its present form must have had its beginnings during the early or middle decades of the seventeenth century. However, there were almost surely Rām plays based on the *Rāmāyaṇa* of Vālmīki much earlier.

Organization and Support

The manner of organizing the *Rām līlā* is similar in Mathura and Allahabad, and the pattern of their organization is typical for a large number of cities and towns. Ramnagar is something of an exception because of the interest and patronage of the maharaja. Typically in a city there are one or more committees democratically selected by those considered to be their constituents. These standing committees are responsible for fixing the dates of the celebration, collecting the money to finance it, overseeing the considerable physical arrangements for the performance and processions, and assigning such responsibilities as the training of the players. While the idea that a town should have one committee representing the entire Hindu community has had considerable currency in the past, the larger towns and cities commonly have several committees. Allahabad has five established committees; and in 1970 two other groups sponsored *Rām līlā* performances as well. Likewise in Mathura in 1970, a new group from the Sadar locality produced the Sadar *Rām līlā,* clearly distinguishing itself from the older, established committee which produces the principal *Rām līlā.* A city the size of Delhi has countless groups performing. The folk nature of the celebration accounts in part for the proliferation of committees. New committees arise when people feel a lack of opportunity to participate directly and actively in the celebrations, either because the venue of the existing *Rām līlā* is too far away (this was the reason given by the organizers of the Sadar *Rām līlā* at Mathura) or the size of the constituency makes active participation by many impossible or unlikely.

According to popular tradition the Daśsara festival, the occasion of the

[3] Nisamudd Almed, author of *Tabaqat-e-Akbari,* is cited by an Indian writer as source of the assertion that Akbar himself attended *Rām līlā* performances and was so moved that he ordered the *Rāmāyaṇa* translated into Persian and got his court artists to paint pictures based on it. It is also claimed that in 1575 he made a grant of land in Allahabad for holding the *Rām līlā* in perpetuity.

Rām līlā, is associated with the Kshatriya caste.[4] Actually in Mathura and Allahabad the *Rām līlā* appears to be largely supported by the Vaisyas. The chairman of the Mathura *Rām līlā* committee is the proprietor of an oil mill and in the case of the Sadar *Rām līlā* committee, almost all of the executive committee members are of the merchant caste. The obvious reasons for the involvement of this class are that they have the money to finance the productions and they stand to gain from the business which the festival stimulates.

The *Rām līlā* committees raise most of their budget through subscriptions, many quite small. While the merchants are the staunchest financial supporters of the festival, money is received from a broad cross section of the whole community. A full and careful record of receipts and expenditures is kept and an accounting is given at the end of the *Rām līlā* period. The Mathura Sadar committee, in its first year of operation (1970), raised about $533 (Rs. 4,000). (By contrast the Patharchaṭṭī Committee in Allahabad estimated an expenditure of $4,000, Rs. 30,000.) They spent $133 (Rs. 1,000) on costumes and paid $40 (Rs. 300) more to a professional director for preparing the script and directing the rehearsals through the first few weeks. Some additional income comes from the offerings which people voluntarily make during the *aratī* worship of the actors at the end of the performance. These are mostly small gifts from those who are devout but not affluent. A somewhat more generous gift is expected at the final *aratī* ceremony of the performance which ends the *Rām līlā,* particularly by those who have attended throughout the season.

The *Rām līlā* is performed by amateurs, on a seasonal schedule. During the period of the *Rām līlā,* the actors are given a daily stipend as well as food. At Ramnagar the orchestra-chorus is included in this distribution. In Allahabad and Mathura the *Rām Līlā* committees defray this expense from funds subscribed by the public. At Ramnagar, the maharaja meets this expense from funds set aside for this purpose. The money comes from a central government purse; a sum of $13,333 (Rs. 100,000) is given annually to the maharaja toward the upkeep of temples in the Varanasi area.

In Allahabad the person in charge of the makeup and costuming, the *līlā* master, also does the casting, but this is certainly an accidental privilege related to his contribution of makeup and costume, which his caste group finances. While there is a natural tendency to select boys from the families of those active in the organizing or support of the committee's program, the performers' physical appearance, personality, and ability to speak and sing are important in the casting. In general, the boys are responsible to the *līlā* master, who in some respects fills the role of a director in Western theatre.

---

[4] According to this view the three great festivals are associated with specific castes, according to the nature of the festival and the manner of its celebration. Thus Daśsara belongs to the Kshatriyas, Divali to the Vaisyas, and Holī to the Sudras.

The task of training and rehearsing the actors as well as preparing the script, however, belongs to another, the *līlā* troupe leader. Considering the size of a *Rām līlā* production, the amount of rehearsal seems small indeed. Fifteen days prior to the beginning of the *Rām līlā,* the boys who play the five major roles go to live in the house of the secretary of the *Rām līlā* committee. All Brahmans by caste, they are trained in their roles as *svarūpa,* or embodiments of those divine persons. Actors who play the other roles need not be Brahmans and do not live with the actors chosen for the five principal roles. The latter are always played by adolescent boys and must be recast every three or four years as they mature, but actors in other roles often continue for many years.

Plays

Rām, the subject of the *Rām līlā,* is the seventh earthly manifestation of Viṣṇu, the preserver. Like Kṛṣṇa, Rām entered the world to preserve it at a time when it was threatened by demons, chief among whom was Rāvan, who terrorized the righteous of the earth and the gods themselves. Rām was born at Ayodhya, the eldest son of King Daśaratha and his wife Kauśalyā. The king also had three other sons by his other two wives, Bharat, born of Kaikeyī, and the twins Lakṣmaṇ and Śatrughna, born of Sumitra. Daśaratha, in his old age, decided to install Rām upon the throne, before his death, but when preparations were well underway, fate intervened. Incited by her maidservant, Mantharā, and jealous of Rām and anxious for her son Bharat, Kaikeyī asked for two boons, which the king had earlier promised her. She demanded that Rām be sent into exile and that her son, Bharat, be installed on the throne. King Daśaratha, striken with grief but unable to break his word to her, acceded to Kaikeyī's request.

Taking his wife Sītā and followed by Lakṣmaṇ, Rām proceeded to the forest, where he and his companions visited many ashrams and slew various demons. During the sojourn in the forest Sītā was abducted by Rāvan, demon-king of Laṅkā (Sri Lanka), and Rām, with the aid of the monkey army led by Hanumān, launched an assault on Rāvan's fortress. After considerable combat the hero slew Rāvan and rescued Sītā. Upon their return to India, Rām accepted an invitation to return and ascend his father's throne. He was reunited with Bharat, who had ruled as regent until Rām's return. Rām's coronation usually ends the *Rām līlā* enactment.

With minor exceptions this popular sixteenth-century retelling of the saga of Rām is the source and substance of all the *Rām līlā* dramas.[5] When

[5] In the Mathura-Vrindaban area some use is made of a *Rāmāyaṇa* composed by a modern poet named Rādheśyām. In Allahabad some songs are based on the *Kavitavali Rāmāyaṇa, Gītāvaḷi,* and *Janakī Mangal.*

Tulsīdās chose to write his work in the Hindi vernacular in preference to Sanskrit, the Sanskrit pundits roundly criticized it as a concession to the illiterate masses, but the book quickly won popular favor and established itself as one of the most influential books of Indian literature.

The *Rām līlā,* part of the autumnal Daśsara festival, in most places lasts for a period of ten days. Although from region to region it is celebrated in different ways, the Daśsara festival is interpreted everywhere to symbolize the triumph of good over evil. In Bengal and adjacent areas it is referred to as Durgā Pūjā, for it concentrates on the worship of Durgā, the consort of Śiva in her warlike aspect. Each of the first nine nights is dedicated to one of the aspects of Śiva's spouse. Durgā Pūjā is said to have originated in epic times when Rām invoked the aid of Durgā in his fight against Rāvan. However, in the great central portion of the Indian subcontinent where Hindi and its dialects are spoken, Daśsara means the worship of Rām and the reenactment of his heroic deeds. Here the ten-day cycle is devoted to episodes from the *Rāmcaritmānas.* The choice of episodes is left to the decisions of the organizing committees. The tenth day, however, is universally celebrated as the day of victory, and the defeat of Rāvan is depicted both in stage plays and processional pageantry.

Performance Space and Context

The defining characteristic of the *Rām līlā* is that it is an open-air production inviting any and all to attend. The crowds which gather are large and they cut across all the boundaries of Indian society: high caste and low, men and women, young and old, Hindus and non-Hindus.

The stage for *Rām līlā* varies according to the setting. In places where there are *Rām līlā* grounds, more or less permanent earthen platforms raised three or four feet above the ground are common. In small towns and villages the stages are often simple wooden platforms set up temporarily to accommodate the performances. The stages are covered with canopies that enhance their acoustical properties. In other places, such as Ramnagar and to some extent at Mathura, the sites of the *Rām līlā* episodes are various and the natural topography of each place corresponds as nearly as possible to the setting of the original scene. The action is frequently played on level ground or in a fortress or ashram as the scene dictates. The bare platform stage suggests a nonrepresentational style of performance, and this is generally the case, but in some instances great pains are taken to reenact an incident with as much detail as possible, as the following eyewitness account indicates:

> At one of the places when we saw Hanumān bring down the mountain herbs, a little boy, maybe three years old, climbed a tree. Then he was lifted onto a wooden dolly suspended between two ropes which ran from the tree to the

other side of the stage, maybe some 150–200 feet. Then some men lighted about twenty real candles on a "mountain," passed the mountain to the little boy who was to slide the mountain before him on the ropes. Then the men pulled the boy along from underneath. The whole thing must have taken at least thirty minutes to set up, but what excitement for everyone![6]

Ramnagar Rām līlā

No two communities stage the *Rām līlā* in exactly the same way. It is always a genuine expression of the locale which performs it. The elaborately staged *Rām līlā* of Ramnagar in Varanasi has a national reputation. People come from far and wide to see it. The town of Ramnagar lies across the river from Varanasi and is the site of the palace of the maharaja with whom this *Rām līlā* is closely associated. The name Ramnagar means "Rāma's city," which is an indication of the pious devotion with which the present ruler and his predecessors have regarded Rām. At the beginning of the nineteenth century, Maharaja Udit Nārāin Singh brought the *Rām līlā* under princely patronage, and this support permitted the Ramnagar *Rām līlā* to develop on a scale that would attract national attention.[7]

For about a month roughly spanning the period from mid-September to mid-October, *Rām līlā* performances fill the city of Varanasi and the surrounding localities. In 1970 the Varanasi local newspapers carried daily listings of sixteen or more localities performing the *Rām līlā.* In Varanasi itself one can wander from one part of the city to another, viewing different episodes of the *Rām līlā.* Thus on the night of October 14, 1970, one could witness *Lakṣmaṇa Śakti* at Sadarbazar and *The Meeting of Rāma and Bharata Citrakūt* in Cetganj. The large number of groups performing in no way dampens the zeal of either the performers or the spectators. Rather competition heightens enthusiasm. But the Ramnagar *Rām līlā* remains outstanding because of the color lent by the maharaja's interest and support and the lavish scale of its staging.

The playing areas for the Ramnagar *Rām līlā* are scattered over an area with a radius of about four miles, separated from each other by as much as

---

[6] From a letter to me dated November 24, 1970, by Betty and Peter Madsen.

[7] B. S. Singh, "Rāmlīlā," p. 75. The future of this *Rām līlā* is clouded. Since Independence in 1947, the former rulers of princely states have received annual purses from the Indian government, the amount of which was fixed at the time of their accession to the Indian Union. In 1970 a government bill to abolish these privy purses was narrowly defeated in the upper house of Parliament. Mrs. Gandhi's government then secured a presidential order abolishing the purses, but this action was declared unconstitutional by the Supreme Court. Ultimately the privy purses were abolished and the *Rām līlā* at Ramnagar was seriously affected, since it has been supported almost entirely by the maharaja.

one to three miles. Each locale represents an important place mentioned in the *Rāmcaritmānas:* Ayodhya, Janakpur, Citrakut, Prayag, Pancavati, Rysamuka Hill, and Sri Lanka. The action of the play shifts from site to site, in keeping with the episodes of the story. There is no doubt also that the use of a separate place for each locale fosters a sense of the site as *the* place of an event in the *Rāmcaritmānas.* Except when the action calls for a procession, a day's action is generally confined to one locality. There may be a limited amount of movement within an area, as for example in the scene of the attack upon Rāvan's fortress at Laṅkā. Rām's forces gather at their camp at one end of a football field-sized area and lay their plans. And then with the entire crowd of spectators accompanying them, they surge across the field toward Rāvan's fortress, an impressively high, massive earthen platform, crowned with a "castle." Between Rām's camp and the fortress of Laṅkā, is the arena where the warriors will do battle. For the moment it is easy to believe that the people are not a mere crowd of spectators, but Rām's loyal citizens who will indeed become his army if necessary.

The crowd at Ramnagar is relatively quiet. The presence and demeanor of the maharaja encourages an attitude of faith and devotion. On this occasion, the symbol of secular power publicly displays his humility, his devotion to Rām, and his acceptance of the ideal of his rule.

The maharaja attends the *Rām līlā* almost every day and his presence lends color and pageantry as well as prestige to the occasion. At about four o'clock in the evening, the maharaja emerges from the main gate of the palace in a horse-drawn carriage and, escorted by mounted police, rides down the broad avenue, acknowledging the ovation of the citizenry. The procession makes its way through the town of Ramnagar and proceeds to an area beyond the town where the day's episode will be staged. When he arrives at the place, the maharaja alights from the coach and mounts an elephant. From that vantage point he is able to watch the events of the day.

Rām Līlā in Mathura

The principal Mathura *Rām līlā* cannot compete with Ramnagar's in the elaborateness of its physical staging. It does, however, follow on a limited scale the same principle of assigning the twenty episodes to different locales. Six separate locales, not including places merely passed in processions, are used during the twenty days of performance. Two sites only provide the major setting on seventeen days (on six days episodes are repeated at a second site). Despite this lavish use of space the settings for the stage are, with few exceptions, extremely simple. In many places, a raised stage is not provided, and there are mats for the seating of the spectators.

Rām Līlā at Allahabad

Allahabad can lay claim to an outstanding *Rām līlā,* for people come from considerable distances to see it. Hindus here think of their city as having a special relation to the *Rām līlā* since Rām, Sītā, and Lakṣmaṇ stopped here on the way to and from exile.[8] Here they bathed in the Saṅgam, the confluence of the Ganges and the Jamuna rivers, and the site of the ashram of Saint Bharadvāj is near the present home of the Nehru family.

The Allahabad *Rām līlā* differs from those of Mathura and Varanasi both in form and spirit. The place of performance is a moderate-sized field on one side of which is an open-air earthen stage measuring about two and one half feet in height, one hundred feet in width, and forty-five feet in depth. During performances the stage is sheltered by a cloth canopy. A crowd gathers on three sides of the playing area. Bamboo stakes and ropes separate the audience from the performance area and another similar partition divides the male spectators from the women and children, who form a majority. On the male side of the barrier the first fifteen to twenty rows of spectators are usually seated, but farther back they remain standing and from these ranks there is constant traffic in and out of the *līlā* grounds. There is a continuing roar of conversation which would certainly drown out the performers, were microphones and amplifiers not in use. The loudspeakers and the noisy crowds combine to create a tumult of sound not conducive to an atmosphere of religious devotion; generally the atmosphere here is festive, and on the fringes of the crowd the sweets and peanut vendors do a brisk business. Nonetheless the spectators are aware of what is happening on the stage, for when a particularly touching passage is reached, a hush falls upon the crowd.

The Allahabad *Rām līlā* celebrations include two other features which relate only indirectly to the stage performances but which help to create an atmosphere for them: (1) public processions on the last five days of the Daśsara festival, and (2) float competitions between committees during the ten days of the festival.

During the last five days of the festival, there are *Rām līlā* processions sponsored by the local committees. The first procession on the sixth day is organized by the Civil Lines committee, the most recently established of the five. On the tenth day, the Patharchaṭṭī and Pajāwā committees combine for a spectacular procession through the city. In 1970 this procession included fifty-three floats depicting scenes from Hindu mythology, ten camels, and six elephants. It took six hours to travel its course and was witnessed by an estimated one million people. This procession ended at a large field near the

[8] The ancient Hindu name for Allahabad is Prayag, a name which still designates a portion of the city.

bank of the Jamuna River where, according to established custom, the effigy of Rāvan was burned.

Also during the ten-day cycle observed in Allahabad, the Patharchaṭṭī committee and the next oldest committee, the Pajāwā, stage a nightly float competition. Beginning the first night at about eight o'clock and progressively one hour later each succeeding night, the two committees send carriages decorated according to a prearranged schedule to the heart of the city, where thousands gather to witness this event. The floats are brilliantly decorated in the material chosen for that day—flowers, jewelry, silver, mirrorwork, and so on—and the boys who play the roles of Rām and Lakṣmaṇ, in full makeup and costume, ride on the floats through the festive crowds. The only direct link between these events and the stage performances is that the actors who play Rām and Lakṣmaṇ hold the place of honor in the processions and ride in the carriage competition also.

Audience

It was noted earlier that the *Rām līlā* is a theatre which belongs to all of the people and is enacted where the community at large may gather. It is a theatre whose setting is never far from the concerns of the profane world. The crowds which see the *Rām līlā* are large and heterogeneous, socially and religiously. The spectrum is broad and the commonly held beliefs are few. The atmosphere in all three places is a mixture of devotional, social, and com-

Detail of a *chaukī* (float) decoration, Allahabad. (Darius L. Swann photo)

mercial concerns. Vendors gather on the outskirts of the assembly area and find ready buyers for their wares. The district gazettes published during the pre-Independence period make it clear that the fairs and festivals were of interest to the British administrators primarily as generators of revenue.

This commercial element is present alongside a sincere reverence for the actors portraying Rām, Lakṣmaṇ, and Sītā. The *aratī* ceremony of the waving of the lights is performed, people press forward to touch the feet of the "embodiments," and they shout, "Victory to Rām at his exploits." As in the *rās līlā* there is important preparation of the actors, transforming them into embodiments of Viṣṇu. The spectators then treat the actors portraying Rām, Lakṣmaṇ, and Sītā as actual deities.

Costume and Makeup

The actors playing Rām, Sītā, and Rām's brothers are costumed and made up in a ritual which ends with their crowning. They are then accepted by the spectators as embodiments of deities. There is no significant difference in makeup practice in Allahabad, Mathura, and Varanasi. Indeed the makeup of these five characters is similar to the makeup used in *rās līlā*. The

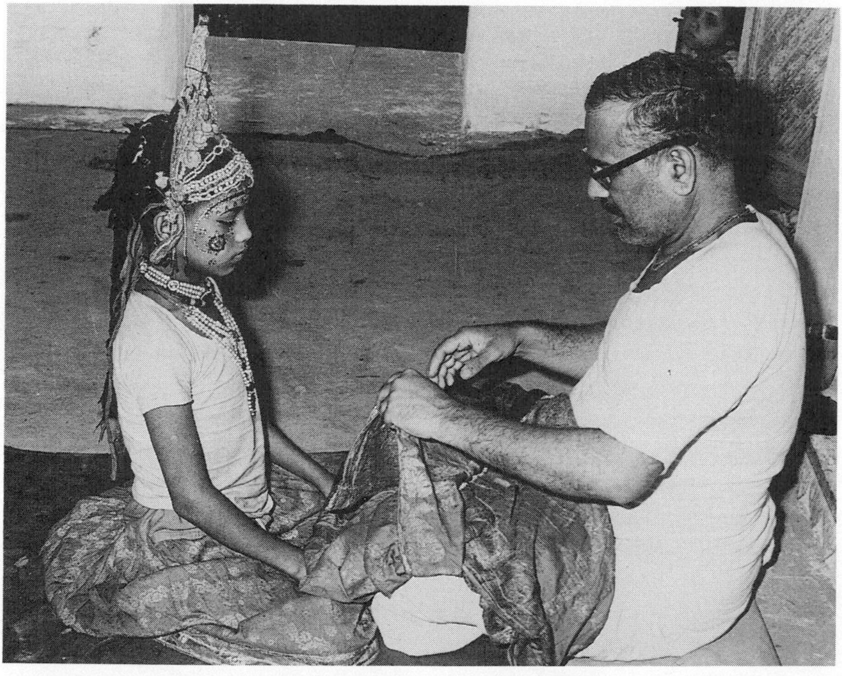

Boy actor playing Sītā is assisted with his costume. (Darius L. Swann photo)

Rām and Lakṣmaṇ fully costumed, Allahabad. (Darius L. Swann photo)

actor lies on the floor while one or more specialists stencil designs on his face and apply makeup. The basic coat of makeup is derived from a soft stone which, when moistened and rubbed, produces a pinkish-white lotionlike makeup. The designs which are then stenciled on the face are abstract, consisting of lines, curlicues, circles, and dots in starlike patterns. Using small brushes and sticks, the makeup artists fill in the stenciled designs with blue and mica. Then using tweezers they apply small colored sequins to the design. With the costumers' help the actors finish their dressing by donning costumes.

Even among groups in the same city or town costume practices vary. In one *Rām līlā* committee's production in Allahabad, Rām and Lakṣmaṇ wore brocaded tunics over breeches which reached just below the knee. The tunics were tied with sashes and the actors' legs were encased in long pink stockings. Another committee dressed its actors in dhotis and *kurta*.[9] Sītā usually wears a sari.

Rām and Lakṣmaṇ always wear a great many ornaments. A strand of pearls around the base of the headpiece, large dangling jewelled earrings, and several strands of gems around the neck are common. The crowns, the most important part of the costume, are generally cylindrical with a halolike ring attached at the back. Groups which have the resources may own several

[9] The *kurta* is an Indian style loose-fitting shirt.

styles of crowns, which the actors may use on successive days. Sītā's crown is usually a coronet.

The makeup and costume of the other characters in the *Rām līlā* are less fixed. Hanumān wears red and he and his monkey cohorts usually wear masks and costumes with tails. When the actor has lines to speak he removes the mask from his face and rests it on top of his head. Rāvan is usually costumed in the tight-legged pajama breeches and long coat reminiscent of Moghul court dress. He usually wears a large mustache and his forehead bears Śaivite sectarian markings. His headpiece is a crown to which is attached flat cardboard cutouts of four heads on either side (Rāvan is ten-headed; the tenth head is at the back of the actor's own). Demons, such as Rāvan's assistants, wear black or dirty-colored garments and their faces are smeared with black makeup.

The Sadar *Rām līlā* committee in Mathura uses a simple color scheme in costuming: Rām and his associates wear yellow dhotis. Rām's associates include Vibhiṣaṇa, Rāvan's brother who defected to Rām. Rāvan and his forces use costumes in which black predominates. In all areas the chief characters are also identified by the props which they carry. For example, Rām and Lakṣmaṇ always carry bows and arrows and Hanumān carries a mace.

The entire act of costuming and makeup takes about one hour. The final act in the process is the investing of the boys with the crowns of the *Rām līlā* and the bows which are the distinctive symbols of Rām and Lakṣmaṇ. Now as divine embodiments they are carried on the shoulders of their costumers and makeup artists through the crowds that have been waiting outside the temple enclosure for a *darśana,* a glimpse of the deity, and are placed in the conveyance which will take them to the *līlā* grounds.

Performers and Roles

The actors in the *Rām līlā* are all amateurs, though some roles, such as Hanumān, may be played by the same actor year after year. Those who play the five principal roles of *svarūpas* (the divine embodiments of Rām, Sītā, Lakṣmaṇ, Bharat, and Śatrughṇa), however, are young boys, usually below the age of fourteen. They may play these roles for three or four years but yield when the onset of puberty is signalled by the sprouting of a mustache. With some scattered exceptions the *svarūpa* roles are always played by boys from respectable Brahman families.

The all-male cast is trained with emphasis on speaking clearly and audibly, and they do so in a declamatory style which is matched by broad, dramatic gestures. The acting generally is unpolished, but some stylization is usually apparent in dueling scenes; here the action is smoother, closely approaching dance. While it is common for a performance to proceed by alternation between cantillation of the *Rāmcaritmānas* by a narrator or chorus and dialogue spoken by the actors, some plays consist entirely of dramatic dialogue interspersed with songs sung by the actors.

The four major characters of the *Rām līlā*—Rām, Lakṣmaṇ, Hanumān, and Sītā—impress upon the spectators of the *Rām līlā* qualities which represent the best in the Hindu view of society. In their bearing and in their response to circumstances, each personifies a quality which makes Tulsīdās' view of society a credible model for modern Indian thinkers. In the *Rām līlā* at Allahabad, Rām had relatively few lines, though he was always present on the stage. If he had no part in the action, he presided from his place stage right. The chief force of the actor's characterization was his dispassionate bearing and his calmness and self-control, a quality shared by the Mathura and Varanasi actors. However poorly the actors might execute their parts otherwise, this basic quality did come through strongly.

This of course is how Tulsīdās paints Rām, as two incidents from the *Rāmcaritmānas* serve to illustrate. Once when Lakṣmaṇ goads to rage Paraśurām, the great destroyer of Kshatriyas, Rām remains calm and self-possessed and soothes Paraśurām. "When the hero of Rāghu's race saw everyone seized with panic and perceived Janakī's anxiety, he interposed; there was neither joy nor sorrow in his heart" (Tulsīdās 1968, 215). This dispassion, triumphing over dualities, is the ideal of Hindu enlightenment.

Lakṣmaṇ, on the other hand, is more passionate, given to hotheaded rejoinders, made bold by his utter confidence in his brother. He also appears more human, for he displays some common human frailties. When the exiles return to Ayodhya and are reunited with their family, Rām and Lakṣmaṇ greet their mothers, including Kaikeyī who was responsible for their twelve years of wandering. There is no indication that Rām evinced any hostility toward Kaikeyī, but Tulsīdās records that Lakṣmaṇ, though he met Kaikeyī again and again, could not rid himself of a feeling of bitterness toward her. Tulsīdās shows him to have one quality above all others; an unwavering loyalty to his brother. It takes him into exile and keeps him happy in the service of Rām and Sītā.

Sītā is the womanly ideal of India. In modesty, fidelity, and uncomplaining acceptance of her lot, she is the classic Hindu wife. There is no suggestion of sensuality about her. Even in the scene of her discovery of her love for Rām and of his love for her, she is chaste and modest. "She surveyed Shri Rāma's beauty from head to foot in the reverse order" (Tulsīdās 1968, 91). That is, she was not bold enough to look first at his face, so her eyes fell first upon his feet.

Hanumān is the model of loyal devotion to Rām. He not only recruits help for Rām in the crucial effort to recover Sītā; he proves his unsurpassed loyalty. In a section of the *Rām līlā,* presented at Mathura in 1949, Sītā makes a gift of pearls to Hanumān, who begins to crack them between his teeth. Finding one after the other without a kernel, he throws them aside.

Hanumān insults Rāvan by standing above him in court. (Sangeet Natak Akademi photo)

When the astounded bystanders ask him why he is destroying the precious gems in this fashion, he replies, "Brother, I am looking in it for the name of the joy-giving Rām. The name of my Lord is not visible in it, brother. That's why I am breaking it." When the argument is advanced that the name of Rām is not to be found in everything, he replies that whatever does not have the name is of no value. "Is the name of the Lord Rāma written even in your heart?" he is asked. "Yes," he replies and rips open his chest to reveal the name of Rāma stamped all over his heart" (Hein 1972, 284–287). This story does not appear in the *Rāmcaritmānas,* but it is known all over North India, and is frequently represented in pictures. Hanumān, the prototype of the ardent devotee of Rām, is himself the object of popular worship in North India and shrines to him are common.

Rāvan, the representative of the demonic, like Kaṁsa in the *Rām līlā,* is without redeeming virtues. Full of wickedness, he terrorizes men and gods. There are hints that he might have been pictured otherwise: As a devotee of Śiva he achieved great spiritual power through practicing terrible austerities. However, this side of his character is not developed.

Performance Structure

Varanasi

When the maharaja, his staff, and his guests are comfortably seated on their elephants, positioned to afford a good view of the entire proceedings, the performance begins. In the Ramnagar *Rām līlā,* and in the Varanasi style of performance generally, there are three components. The entire production is under the control of a *vyās,* who is a pandit, that is, a Brahman scholar of the Sanskrit scriptures. With his open book, the *vyās* takes up a prominent place on the stage behind or beside the actors and openly prompts them in their lines and directs their movements as well. Near the stage or acting area sits a group of men who form a chorus-orchestra. To the accompaniment of small hand cymbals and drums, they chant the *Rāmcaritmānas.* They, too, are under the control of the *vyās,* and at a given signal from him they stop their chanting and the actors speak their lines from the stage. In this manner, alternating singing and spoken dialogue, the performance proceeds, orchestrated by the *vyās.* There is little spontaneity to the performance, as the direction of the *vyās* is particularly conspicuous. The acting takes on the character of a ritual action performed at the instruction of a priest, as indeed it is. The ritual impression is reinforced by the fact that a great part of the crowd cannot hear what is being said. Like a good many *rās līlā* companies, the Ramnagar organizers have spurned the use of microphones and amplifiers. Many of those present, therefore, can see action being performed but cannot hear the dialogue which is spoken. Considering this fact, the spectators are surprisingly quiet and attentive and there is little coming and going.

The performance, which begins at about five o'clock with the *aratī* ritual of the waving of the lights, ends in the same way at about nine. At that time the people show their respect and reverence to the actors as embodiments of deities by performing the *aratī* and making offerings of money. Although it now has a profane orientation, the *Rām līlā* program retains the context of a religious rite. It begins with the worship of the crowns worn by the principal actors, a ceremony performed according to vedic rites, including the reading of scripture, worship, and putting of ornamental or religious marks of vermillion or sandalwood *(tilak)* on the foreheads of the actors. The Ramnagar *Rām līlā* lasts thirty days.

Mathura

Unlike the Ramnagar *Rām līlā,* the Mathura *Rām līlā* does not use a separate orchestra-chorus. The pandit chants the *Rāmcaritmānas,* accompanying himself on a harmonium, while two assistants accompany him on the drums and cymbals. He fulfills, therefore, the role of both the *vyās* and the orchestra-chorus of the Ramnagar production. He seats himself to one side of the stage with a large copy of the *Rāmcaritmānas* opened before him. When he is in place, Rām and Lakṣmaṇ, costumed and crowned with their bows in hand, take their places on the stage. After the performance of the *aratī* ceremony, the pandit begins to sing. The actors mime on the stage what is being chanted from the *Rāmcaritmānas.* At a predetermined point, the pandit pauses and the actors speak in prose dialogue what has been indicated by the pandit's narration. The performance thus proceeds with alternation between poetic narrative passages chanted by the pandit and prose passages of dialogue spoken by the actors. Thus the pandit in Mathura exercises a similar control over the performance as the *vyās* of the Ramnagar *Rām līlā.*[10]

Allahabad

The performance begins at 5:30 P.M., but by 3:00 P.M. the actors who play Rām, Lakṣmaṇ, and Sītā (on the days when she appears) are brought for makeup and costuming to the Rām Mandir, or Temple of Rām, on Hewett Road, about a mile and a half from the *līlā* grounds. There are two temples on the site of the performance, but the tradition of doing the makeup at the Rām Mandir was established at the request of the maharaja of Rewa (formerly a small princely state near Allahabad), who is its patron.

At the *līlā* grounds, the actors are again carried from their conveyance to the stage and are seated on a specially placed throne or chair positioned stage right. From this position they preside, except when they are involved in the action on the stage.

The performance begins with the invocation, followed by that portion of *līlā* which is to be performed. Here there is no direct use of the *Rāmcaritmānas,* as at Ramnagar and Mathura. The dramatic dialogues provide their own continuity. Songs are frequently used, but not for purposes of narration

---

[10] The pandit's part in the *Rām līlā* is evidence of a strong relation between recitation and the traditional theatre represented by the *Rām līlā.* Solo recitation of the *Rāmcaritmānas* is also a common feature of the Daśsara season. During this festival these reciter-singers perform in the streets to small and large groups.

and continuity; they serve rather to reinforce sentiment and for exposition of scenes. These songs are based on the *Rāmcaritmānas* and occasionally other sources. By and large the dramatic dialogue provides its own exposition and narration and advances the action of the play. There is no chorus and the actors sing the songs in accordance with the demands of the situation. While much use is made of the traditional *Rāmāyaṇa* style of singing, the influence of popular film music is also evident. The performance lasts about two hours and then the actors are taken back to their residences, where they eat and rest. The performances in Allahabad are done over a ten-day period.

Rām Līlā in Performance

On October 8, 1970, the Mathura Sadar Committee presented *The Wounding of Lakṣmaṇ with the Śakti (Lakṣmaṇ Śakti),* the episode in which Lakṣmaṇ is wounded by Rāvan's son Meghnād, and *The Slaying of Kumbhakarṇa (Kumbhakarṇa Vadh),* the fight with Rāvan's brother.[11] The story is played out as follows:

When the curtain opens Rām and Lakṣmaṇ are seated on stage. Rām's emissary to Rāvan returns with the news that Rāvan has refused to return Sītā and is challenging Rām to battle. The excitable Lakṣmaṇ is ready to accept the challenge, but the peace-loving Rām is not ready to relinquish the hope of a peaceful settlement. Finally, however, Hanumān and Lakṣmaṇ persuade him of the fruitlessness of negotiation and the necessity of war.

Hanumān and the monkey army take the field against Rāvan's ogres. The battle rages not on the stage but over the *līlā* grounds. The major interest is in the encounter between Lakṣmaṇ and Meghnād. After a heated exchange of words, they duel with bow and arrow. Their movements are stylized, resembling dance. Meghnād, being hard-pressed, uses a special arrow which wounds Lakṣmaṇ and renders him unconscious.

The unconscious Lakṣmaṇ is brought to the stage and Rām laments over him. The crowd grows very quiet at the pathos of this scene.

Hanumān brings from Laṅkā a doctor who prescribes an herb that grows on the mountain. Hanumān volunteers to go and bring the herb, which is to be identified by a certain light. While he is going, the curtain rises on Rāvan's court. A thoroughly stereotyped villain, he laughs at the news of Lakṣmaṇ's wound and congratulates his son on his victory. The comic antics of Rāvan's peon enliven the scene. The latter arranges a cocktail party in which Coca-Cola is used. A boy, impersonating a woman, performs a dance. In the meantime, while Hanumān is on his way to the mountain, one of Rāvan's ogres disguised as a sadhu attempts to delay him. A voice from

[11] A comparison with Hein's description of the same scene in Vrindaban in 1949 reveals that this newly established committee follows the tradition and style of the other committee.

heaven warns the monkey of the true identity of the "sadhu," and Hanumān, to the spectators' delight and amusement beats the imposter soundly. Arriving at the mountain, but being unable to identify the herb, he uproots the mountain itself and returns in haste to Rām. Lakṣmaṇ is revived and the spectators joyfully shout, "Victory to Rāmcandra! Victory to Lakṣmaṇ!"

When Rāvan hears that Lakṣmaṇ has been revived he orders that his brother Kumbhakarṇa (Jug-Ears) be awakened and informed that he must fight a battle. This scene is always played for its humor. The ponderous Kumbhakarṇa is sleeping on a cot, his enormous paunch rising and falling in rhythm with his loud snoring. The clown and a few small demons attempt to waken him. They make noise, punch him, jump on him, but he goes on snoring. After about five minutes of this Kumbhakarṇa wakes up. The clown informs him about the war and gives him Rāvan's message. Complaining that he cannot fight on an empty stomach he demands food and wine. After an enormous meal he gets up and prepares for battle with Rām. He enters the field and kills many monkeys, but is finally slain by Rām. The *līlā* ends with the shout, "Victory to Rāmcandra!"

While the Sadar *Rām līlā* production continues many traditions of the Mathura-Vrindaban area, there are some significant departures. The committee, made up of younger men with a liberal bent, does not adhere strictly to the usual custom of choosing only Brahman boys to play the roles of Rām, Lakṣmaṇ, Bharat, Śatrughṇa, and Sītā. Some are chosen from the Vaisya caste. They also depart from established tradition in another way: During the period of exile Rām and Lakṣmaṇ do not wear crowns. Usually these characters are always crowned, but the Sadar group reasoned that this was unrealistic and not according to the spirit of the epic account.

Current State

The *Rām līlā* flourishes. Its popularity can be accounted for by several factors: the popularity in North India of Rām as the manifestation of Viṣṇu, the association of the plays with the popular Daśsara festival, the widespread reverence for Tulsīdās' *Rāmcaritmānas,* and the folk nature of its organization and performance. Whatever the reasons, *Rām līlā* performances are proliferating. In 1970 on a single day in October the daily newspaper listed sixteen separate performances in and around Varanasi. It can be assumed that there were others which were not listed. A Delhi writer estimated that in 1970 more than three hundred groups performed in that city alone.

Also in large urban areas like Delhi the popularity of *Rām līlā* plays has led producers to offer *Rām līlā* in ballet and other dance forms for wealthier high-class audiences able to pay admission fees.

Given its folk nature, the future of *Rām līlā* seems bright. It is a part of a great national festival that integrates a basic religious and political vision of great contemporary significance. Religiously the festival of Rām concretizes for Hindus the struggle of good with evil, and the outcome assures them of the eventual triumph of the good. Politically Rām sets before them the ideal ruler—just, merciful, self-controlled—around whom dreams of the integration of a nation of diverse peoples can gather. Mahatma Gandhi returned repeatedly to the ideal of Rām's rule *(Rāmrāj)* as the goal for which he struggled.

WORKS CITED

Heber, Reginald. 1923.
Indian Journal. London: (publisher not cited). Vol 1.

Hein, Norvin. 1972.
The Miracle Plays of Mathurā. New Haven: Yale University Press.

Singh, B. S. 1963.
"The Ramlila of Ramnagar." *Natraj* 1:74–77.

Tulsīdās. 1968.
Śrī Rāmcaritamānasa. Bala Kanda. Gorakpur: Gita Press.

Zaehner, R. C. 1966.
Hinduism. London: Oxford University Press.

ADDITIONAL READING

Archer, W. G. 1957.
The Loves of Krishna. London: George Allen and Unwin.

Awasthi, Induja. 1979.
"Rāmlīlā: Tradition and Styles." *Quarterly Journal of the National Centre for the Performing Arts* 8, 3:23–36.

Awasthi, Suresh. 1973.
"Rāmacharitāmas of Tulsīdās—An Appreciation." *Quarterly Journal of the National Centre for the Performing Arts* 2, 3:1–8.

Brahmā-Vaivarta Purāṇa. 1970.
Sacred Books of the Hindus. Trans. Rajendra Nath Sen. Vol. XXIV, Part 5. Allahabad: The Panini Office, Bhuvaneshwari Asram.

Baumer, Rachel, and James R. Brandon. Eds. 1982.
Sanskrit Drama in Performance. Honolulu: University Press of Hawaii.

Gargi, Balwant. 1956.
Folk Theater in India. Seattle and London: University of Washington Press.

Growse, F. S. 1880.
Mathurā: A District Memoir. 2nd ed. Allahabad: (publisher not cited).

Jayadeva. 1940.
Gita-Govinda. Trans. George Keyt. Bombay: Sadanand Bhatkal, Kutub-Popular.

Journal of South Asian Literature. 1975.
Vol. X, Nos. 2, 3, 4. East Lansing: Michigan State University.

Mankad, D. R. 1936.
The Types of Sanskrit Drama. Karachi: Urmi Prakashan Mandir.

Mathur, Jagdish Chandra. 1964.
Drama in Rural India. New York: Asia Publishing House.

Mukerjee, Radhakamal. 1957.
The Lord of the Autumn Moons. Bombay: Asia Publishing House.

Schechner, Richard. 1985.
"*Rām līlā* of Rāmnagar." In *Between Theatre and Anthropology*. Ed. Richard Schechner. Philadelphia: University of Pennsylvania Press. Pp. 151–211.

Swann, Darius L. 1974.
"Three Forms of Traditional Theatre of Uttar Pradesh, North India." Ph.D. diss., University of Hawaii.

PART FOUR

THE FOLK-POPULAR TRADITIONS

INTRODUCTION

THE FORMS DISCUSSED IN THIS SECTION as belonging to the folk-popular genre share two important features that distinguish them from other genres that we have considered thus far: (1) Whatever their origins, they depend for patronage upon the masses, and (2) they are given more to entertainment and profane rather than sacred purposes. Devotional forms in addition to their dramatic significance have a symbolic, holy meaning conveyed through spectacle, mimetic action, dialogue, and the like. Folk-popular forms focus their concern on the mundane life of human beings rather than on the gods.

Until recent decades these forms were largely ignored by serious scholars, who turned their attention to the Sanskrit drama and theatre. The importance of these other forms as bearers of the Indian theatre tradition was obscured. Seen as crude, degraded, and vulgar, neither the sources of their vitality nor their links to the classical tradition was sought. Fortunately that has now changed, and from New Delhi to Cape Comorin, playwrights, directors, and performers are examining these genres to recover the basis for a living contemporary theatre that is genuinely Indian.

Where did these forms come from? We cannot yet say that we know. In their present forms, none may be traced back much farther than the sixteenth century, that is, sometime after the Sanskrit theatre went into decline. The relationship, if any, of these forms to the Sanskrit theatre is an unsettled question. Several theories have been put forward and may be summarized as follows:

1. The Sanskrit theatre developed from early prototypes of folk/popular/devotional forms.
2. These forms represent "degraded remnants" of the Sanskrit theatre which went into decay.
3. The Sanskrit theatre and these popular forms developed separately but in parallel streams, neither having much influence upon the other.
4. The Sanskrit theatre developed from some early popular forms, and after its decline, existing popular forms sprang from its ruins.

There is little hard evidence to support any one of these theses but certain facts do suggest a connection between the elite Sanskrit theatre and the popular theatrical entertainments of the masses, perhaps in some combination of ideas from numbers three and four above. First, the mythological account of the origins of theatre as given in the *Nāṭyaśāstra* clearly describes it as an art for all castes, including the Sudras. Since the latter were barred from access to Sanskrit, the sacred language, forms in the vernacular must have existed for their enjoyment. Second, the curse which reduced actors to the status of Sudras resulted from their parodying of the life of high caste society for popular entertainment (Ghosh 1961, 33–41). One would naturally assume that an audience which enjoyed the ridicule of the upper classes was probably made up of lower caste people, since the upper classes hardly enjoy ridicule of themselves. Third, the popular forms almost universally employ a clown figure resembling, in various degrees, the *vidūṣaka* of the Sanskrit plays. Fourth, the context of a performance, especially the preliminaries, exhibit marked similarities among almost all the forms, including the Sanskrit, devotional, and folk-popular. These include drumming to announce the performance, tuning of the instruments, an invocatory song to the deities, and, in several cases, the ritual marking off of the stage as a sacred area. Fifth, early treatises on drama list minor forms that may provide a link between the Sanskrit and the folk-popular theatre. Existing descriptions of some of these minor forms resemble some present-day devotional/folk/popular forms. It can and has been argued that these minor forms along with the simpler *nāṭya* types, represent the popular tradition of the masses. These forms may be seen as stages in the evolutionary process which, beginning with the simple forms, culminated in the Sanskrit drama. Finally, as the Sanskrit theatre emerged and developed, some continued to practice these minor forms as before and they became a parallel line of development. In their more primitive form they persisted as popular entertainment for less sophisticated audiences to which the Sanskrit theatre did not cater.

There are several genres which resemble in important respects the two regional forms described in detail in this section. Each region has its own particular variety, and forms which are essentially alike may be known under different names from one region to the other. It is also apparent from historical accounts that a performer or composer of one form may borrow from another form whatever features he chooses, to enhance the appeal of his art. The result is several forms which differ only slightly from each other. Such is the case with *nauṭankī, khyāl, mānch,* and *bhagat,*[1] all of which are variants of *svāṅg*. The latter is a generic name for that form of North Indian theatre which places primary emphasis on singing; it is operatic and the predominance of the musical element is indicated by the fact that people speak of going "to hear" a *svāṅg* rather than to see one. *Svāṅg* does not differ in any

[1] *Svāṅg* and *nauṭankī* are widely performed in Uttar Pradesh, Punjab, and Rajasthan. *Khyāl* is prevalent in Rajasthan and *mānch* in Madhya Pradesh. *Bhagat* is localized in a section of Uttar Pradesh.

important way from *nauṭankī,* which is described in detail in this section. *Bhagat* also closely resembles *svāṅg* but is devotionally oriented. We shall look briefly at some of these other forms which belong in this category.

The *khyāl* of Rajasthan is a combination of song, dance, and drama and is thought to have originated in the early eighteenth century. The word *khyāl* may be translated "imagination" and the early *khyāl* were more extemporaneous poetry competitions than dramatic pieces. Although several styles of *khyāl* have developed, the form is basically similar to *nauṭankī* in its elements, style of staging, and subject matter. The connection with *nauṭankī* is made quite explicit in the story of Alibux, poet-saint, born in Alwar, Rajasthan, about the middle of the nineteenth century. Smitten when he was quite young with fascination for the company of artists, poets, musicians, and dancers, he haunted the places where *nauṭankī* was performed. Being rebuked and challenged to form his own group, he proceeded to do so, and performed his first *khyāl* on the life of Kṛṣṇa. Descriptions of his productions indicate a basic similarity to *nauṭankī.* They were heavily weighted toward singing and dancing. His work is distinguished by a strong devotional bias and the dancing is said to bear some resemblance to *kathak,* which we know to be related to *rās līlā* dance. It should be noted that the Kanpur style of *nauṭankī* was heavily influenced by poetic recitation such as early *khyāl.*

Mānch, literally "stage," closely resembles *svāṅg* and is native to the Madhya Pradesh region. It probably originated in the seventeenth century and has close links with the *khyāl* of Rajasthan, *nauṭankī* of Uttar Pradesh, and *bhavāi* of Gujarat (Parmar 1962, 78). With these forms of theatre *mānch* shares a number of characteristics: Song and music are dominant in its performance; preliminary ceremonies honor the gods; and it is played on an open-air stage with a minimum of theatrical accessories. The stage is unique in its height, which may be as much as twelve feet. *Mānch* shares with *bhavāi* a ceremonial dedication of the stage space, and it shares with *nauṭankī* a repertory of stories.

There are two other important regional genres which share the basic forms of those already discussed, *jātra* and *bhavāi.* Both of these dramatic types employ music and dancing as important elements of performance. The home of *jātra* is Bengal but it is also performed in the neighboring states of Bihar and Orissa. The etymology of the word *jātra* suggests that it was originally an open-air drama, though performances are known to have been given in halls specially made for theatrical performance. The root of the word *jātra* is *jā,* to go. In common parlance *jātra* means a journey, a going, a march, or procession. This suggestion of open-air performance is strengthened by the fact that the primary early musical accompaniment was the *khol,* a deep-toned drum more suitable for open-air activities than an enclosed theatre.

By all accounts the *jātra* in its traditional form had a preponderance of songs and music. It has been described as "sacred opera." Like *nauṭankī*, song dominated and spoken dialogue was imperfectly developed. There was a kind of representation in which improvisation played a considerable part. It was common practice for the author to sketch only the "business" and leave the dialogue to be improvised by the actors and the chorus.

The traditional *jātra* stage was a temporary affair. It consisted of a carpet or canvas spread on the ground. The audience sat on all four sides, only leaving a narrow corridor through the crowd to allow the actors to come from the dressing room to the playing area.

The traditional *jātra* were produced during the three annual festivals in honor of Kṛṣṇa, but they were also performed throughout the year on all festive occasions, religious or secular. Most *jātra* have as their theme incidents in the life of Kṛṣṇa. This is to be expected as *jātra* developed in the wake of the bhakti movement that swept Bengal in the sixteenth century and set its adherents singing and dancing in street processions. Chief among the devotees was the Vaiṣṇava saint Chaitanya Dev (1485–1533), who sang and danced himself into ecstasy. By the eighteenth century *jātra* had attained great popularity with its plays full of religious sentiment and historical romance. In the nineteenth century love themes, erotic stories, and legendary heroes diluted the religious fervor and changed *jātra* to a more secular character. The form has continued to change. Modern *jātra* show every sign of the impact of Western play theory. The songs have almost disappeared

Jātra actors sitting on their wardrobe trunks applying their makeup in the dressing room during a rural performance. (Farley P. Richmond photo)

and prose dialogue dominates. The form has been adapted to make telling comments on the contemporary social and political situations.

Traditionally all roles are played by male actors. In recent years, however, some women have been included in *jātra* companies. In addition to the actors, some of whom specialize in feminine roles, the orchestra is made up of two types of drums (the *pakāvaj* and *dholak*), the violin, cymbals, and flute. A clarinet and trumpet may also be included.

Two innovations have changed the *jātra:* the introduction of the *juri* system and the creation of the *vivek* (Conscience) character. The *juri* (double) describes the system, introduced in the mid nineteenth century, of allowing singers at the four corners of the stage to sing the songs which are a part of the actor's lines, thus allowing actors who could not sing to perform. The *vivek,* introduced in the early twentieth century, is a character, who as Conscience can appear anywhere. He is always a singer who comments on the action, externalizes the character's feelings, or puts questions to him or her.

Today *jātra* has changed from what it was traditionally. It has regained some respect in the last couple of decades, during which it has become a predominantly prose form addressing social and political concerns of contemporary life in the cities and villages of Bengal.

Bhavāi consists of a series of playlets of varying lengths and on a variety of

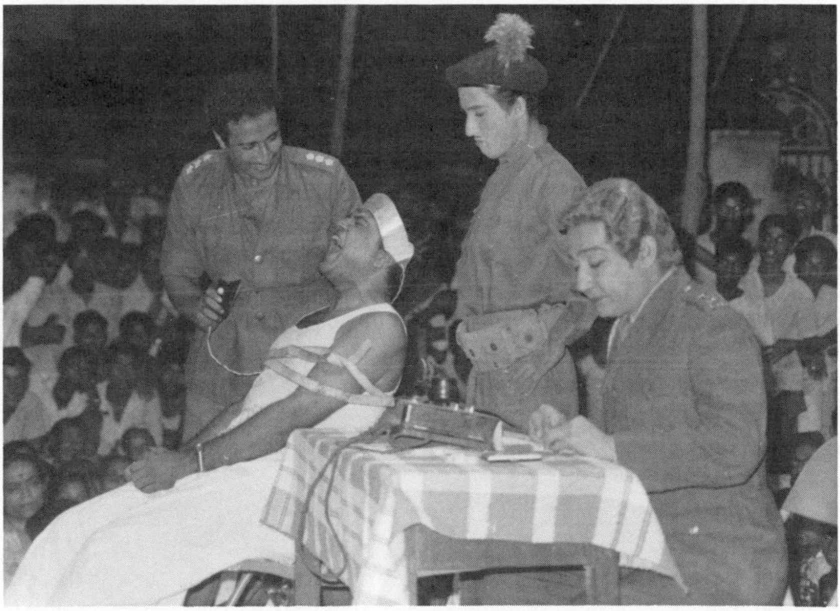

Jātra actors depicting the torture of an Indian patriot during colonial days. Electric shock treatment is applied by enthusiastic British officers. (Farley P. Richmond photo)

themes, which are performed through acting, dancing, and song. Like *nauṭankī* and *svāṅg* in North India, this Gujarati form is traditionally performed out of doors at a crossroads, near the bank of a river, or at some other place of public intercourse. The stage is a circle about ten feet in diameter, drawn on the ground and consecrated during the preliminaries to the performance.

The *bhavāi* form, which dates back to the early fourteenth century, was originated by a Brahman who was expelled from his caste for violating its rules in helping to secure the freedom of the daughter of his lower caste patron, who had been abducted by a military officer of the Muslim conquerors of Gujarat. He ate with her. The Brahman, who was an accomplished poet and singer, turned to writing and performing playlets. From his work sprang a new community of professional performers who devote eight months of the year to touring from village to village. During the other four months of the year they farm their own lands. They are supported by contributions from the villagers.

A *bhavāi* troupe usually consists of twelve to fifteen persons, including the leader, actors who specialize in either male or female roles, and the clown. Also included are the instrumentalists who play the two *bhungals* (long-stemmed trumpetlike instruments which sound like a bugle), two drums (tabla or *narghan*), and two small brass cymbals *(manjīrā)*. The *sāraṅgī,* which was formerly used, has given way to the harmonium.[2] A cook and laborer round out the troupe.

A *bhavāi* performance, consisting of several playlets loosely linked together by the leader, is an all-night affair, and an engagement continues for three or four days. As the makeup of the troupe suggests, song and dance predominate over prose dialogue. A variety of ragas are used and the tala, the rhythmic timing marked by drums and cymbals, is important.

The unadorned playing area traditionally is lighted by oil-fed torches. This lighting is augmented by small torches carried in the hands of certain characters. The costumes vary from simple to ornate depending upon the

[2] The harmonium is a Western instrument introduced into India through the Portuguese. It is incapable of reproducing the tones of the Indian musical scale. William Dye in *A Primer of Hindustani Music* (No publisher or date, p. 4) has explained why. "These latter instruments [Western piano or organ] are tuned according to what is known as 'equal temperament', that is, the octave is divided into twelve semitones, each of which is exactly the same as another. This really involves a slight flattening or sharpening of natural intervals. The Indian scale does not have this rigid uniformity and the exact intervals between the same swars [notes] may slightly differ in different rags and both may differ from the Western intervals. This is one of the reasons why many Indian musicians are opposed to the use of the small harmonium as being unable, as the Indian stringed instruments like the sitar, etc., to reproduce the correct intervals. The moveable frets of the latter enable any intervals to be secured. . . . What we must always remember is that with the 'equal temperament' instrument what we are getting is an approximation only."

characters. The makeup is fairly simple, consisting mainly of vermillion, lime, sandalwood paste, soot, saffron, wax, gum, and oil from the lamps. This type of makeup is enhanced by torchlight.

Most of the plays are on social, mythological, or historical themes. The majority now reflects social conditions and, as in other folk forms, have definite moral overtones. Early *bhavāi* apparently had a religious basis growing from the worship of the Mother Goddess. *Bhavāi* suffered a decline which lasted through the first half of the twentieth century, but in recent years there has been a renewal of interest in the form.

Three other forms of folk-popular theatre are prevalent in South India. Though from a different cultural and linguistic area, *burrakathā, cavittu nāṭakam,* and *veethi nāṭaka* share important common characteristics with forms already described. *Burrakathā* is a form which is popular in Andhra. Like other forms described in this section, its performance includes a combination of singing, acting, and dancing. The name *burrakathā* is a clue to the nature of the form itself. *Burra* is a long-necked, pumpkin-headed, stringed instrument which is used by the leader to accompany his singing and dancing. *Kathā* means "story" and it refers to a form of recitation or storytelling in song which is widely popular in India. So this form bears close association with recitation and storytelling and may be thought of as a form which exists on the border between the latter and true drama. The small size of the troupe underlines this. The lead singer is also the chief actor and dancer. He embellishes his ballad singing with dramatic gestures and movements. The two companions of the leader play two-headed horizontal drums slung from cords around their necks. They also assist the leader in singing. The subject matter of the *burrakathā* play is suitable to its nature; it is stories of heroes, patriotism, and legendary chivalry and courage.

Cavittu nāṭakam is a Christian dance-drama which dates from the later half of the sixteenth century. It was probably initiated by Jesuits working with Catholic converts as a means of education and proselytizing. It is still performed by a few companies in central Kerala. The name literally means "foot stamping drama," a reference to the vigorous, strong, high arching steps that pound the traditional wooden platform stage when male characters dance. *Cavittu nāṭakam,* like many other folk-popular genres, combines song, dance, and acting in dramatizing its stories. The traditional stories enacted are the great epics and myths of western Christendom—Charlemagne and St. George and the Dragon are the most important. The troupe leader serves as an onstage stage manager, directing the action, encouraging performers, prompting forgetful actors, and seeing that all-night performances keep moving. In a traditionally structured performance, the comic character serves as commentator, translator, and often takes roles in the plays. All roles were played by males until twenty to thirty years ago, when it became acceptable for women to appear on the stage. *Cavittu nāṭakam* is usually performed by troupes of amateurs for Catholic feast days, weddings, or other major celebrations during the dry season.

Veethi nāṭaka, which means "street drama" (*veethi* = street, *nāṭaka* = drama), is the most popular type of traditional folk drama in Telegu, the language of Andhra. Like *terukkuttu* in Tamil Nadu and the *bayalatta* of Kannada, it is an open-air show which may date back as far as the twelfth century. In the course of their development these plays may have been influenced in content by the Vīra Śaivite cult and in style by the *kuchipudi* Brahman Bhagāvatārs. Stories from Śiva legends and the Puranic tales make up the content.

During the period of the Vijaynagar empire (1336–1565) *veethi nāṭaka* performers appear to have had royal patronage. After the decline of that empire in the sixteenth century, performers migrated south to Tanjore and Madhura where, under the influence of *yakṣagāna, veethi nāṭaka* was given a new orientation and blossomed in the seventeenth century.

Originally *veethi nāṭaka* was characterized by dialogue, action, and costume, but under the influence of the Tanjore kings who became its patrons, it became a kind of musical drama. While the early plays were religious in subject matter, the later plays used many secular themes. Romance, satiric comedy, and farcical events from contemporary life became common features. *Veethi nāṭaka* plays are full of poetic verse and songs of great metrical variety; they also make use of dance in performance.

In summary, the folk-popular forms discussed here are characterized by a number of striking resemblances which mark them as being of and for the common people: (1) They integrate in varying proportions vocal and instrumental music, dance, and mimetic action. (2) All of them give a significant place to the comic sentiment and many of them have stock comic figures. (3) They show evidence of having originated as open-air performances, open to whomever wishes to attend. (4) While staging is simple, costume may be simple or elaborate. (5) Although the forms may vary in their position in the sacred-profane continuum, all are set within the sacred context, as indicated by some form of religious preliminary.

Today these forms continue to attract large audiences in some locations, especially in small towns and villages where the full impact of the cinema and urban living has not yet been strongly felt. The impact of cheap and accessible movies has undercut the appeal and support of these arts, and with their decline in popularity, the skills of the performers have also begun to show erosion. Encouragement and support from the central and state governments in recent years has slowed the decline in some cases, giving hope for a renewed, solidly based theatre in India.

Darius L. Swann

WORKS CITED

Ghosh, Manmohan. 1961.
Nāṭyaśāstra. Ascribed to Bharata. Vol. 2. Calcutta: Artistic Society.

Parmar, Shyam. 1962.
"Mānch: Lyric Drama." *Nāṭya.* Vol VI, 4:76.

ADDITIONAL READING

Bhanawat, Mahendra. 1979.
"Overview of the Folk Theatre of Rajasthan." *Sangeet Natak* 53–54:26–32.

Chandarvaker, Pushkar. 1973.
"*Bhavāi*: A Type of Folk Drama of Gujarat." *Folk-lore* (Calcutta) 14, 6:217–223.

Chummar, Chundal. 1984.
Christian Theatre in India. Trichur: Kerala Folklore Academy.

———. 1978.
"Medieval Religious Drama of Europe and Chavittu-nāṭakam of Kerala." *Malayalam Literary Survey* 2, 3:76–85.

Dash, Dhiren. 1979.
" 'Jātra' People's Theatre of Orissa." *Sangeet Natak* 52:11–26.

Desai, S. R. 1972.
Bhavāi: A Medieval Form of Ancient Indian Dramatic Art (Nāṭya) as Prevalent in Gujarat. Ahmedabad: Gujarat University.

Emigh, John, with Ulrike Emigh. 1986.
"Hajari Bhand of Rajasthan: A Joker in the Deck." *The Drama Review* 30, 1:101–130.

Farber, Carole Marie. 1979.
"Prolegomenon to an Understanding of the Jātra of India: The Travelling Popular Theatre of the State of West Bengal." Ph.D. diss., University of British Columbia.

Kambar, Chandrasekhar. 1985.
"Folk Theatre As I See It." *Sangeet Natak* 77–78:39–42.

Mitra, Manoj. 1985.
"The Theatre of Kinu Kahar." *Sangeet Natak* 77–78:33–38.

Raphy, Sabeena. 1969.
"Chavittu-Nāṭakam, Dramatic Opera of Kerala." *Sangeet Natak* 12:56–73.

Richmond, Farley. 1969.
"Bhavāi: Village Theatre of West India." *Papers in International and World Affairs.* Michigan State University 2:13–28.

Chapter Eight

NAUṬANKĪ

Darius L. Swann

IN THE QUIET NORTH INDIAN NIGHT the sound of the *nakkārā* drums summon the spectators to a performance of *nauṭankī*. In town or village the clatter of the drums is all that is necessary to announce that a performance is about to take place, for the sound of the *nakkārā* carries for miles through the night air, even above the voices of the city street. *Nauṭankī,* also referred to as *svāṅg,* has been for decades a popular form of theatre in the northern regions of India—Uttar Pradesh, Rajasthan, Punjab, Hariyana, and Bihar. It is characterized by lusty singing and spirited dancing. It is sometimes lewd and slightly disreputable. In large cities like Agra and Kanpur, a largely male audience fills the tent or courtyard to hear the singing of the traditional tunes of this operatic theatre form. They are also attracted by the presence of attractive women dancers who sing the popular filmsongs and mimic the romantic-erotic dances of the filmstars. Without a doubt, the popularity of films has left its impact upon this traditional form, especially in the cities where the two forms compete for audiences. In the villages the audience is likely to be composed of both men and women and sometimes children. While the dancing girls may still be present as a part of the troupe, they are relegated to a less prominent role as befits family entertainment.

Nauṭankī plays have a strong storyline. Tales taken from the great epics, popular legends, historical events, and contemporary society are played before audiences of diverse religious backgrounds. The form is nonetheless secular in spirit in that its objective is primarily entertainment rather than sectarian teaching on cultic celebration. *Nauṭankī* is narrative in structure, operatic in style, and secular in spirit. It is performed by men and women who are semiprofessionals. The performers in the past supported themselves by their earnings, but few are able to do so today. When there are no performances, they supplement their income with other work.

The *nauṭankī Amar Singh Rathor.* (Sangeet Natak Akademi photo. Courtesy of Kathryn Hansen)

Origins

The *nauṭankī* form of theatre is also known as *svāṅg* and by several other related terms. All recent play scripts (roughly those published since 1940) carry the title *saṅgīt,* for example, *Saṅgīt Indal Haran (The Play of the Abduction of Indal Haran),* or *Saṅgīt Patī Bhakti (The Play of the Devoted Wife),* but the term *saṅgīt* is never used in oral references to this theatre. On the other hand, *nauṭankī* is widely used in oral references outside the

Hathras area, but this term appears neither in the scripts themselves, nor in the titles or the advertising material that is frequently included within the books. *Svāṅg* and *sāṅg* are used interchangeably in the scripts and script titles, and the difference seems to be only one of regional pronunciation.

The origin of the term *nauṭankī* is unknown. Theories abound but none has been proven. The most plausible and widely accepted theory, however, is that an exceedingly popular *svāṅg* gave its name to the entire genre. Nauṭankī was a beautiful princess, and the story of her wooing and winning achieved such popularity that all plays of this genre began to be dubbed *nauṭankī.*

The earliest *nauṭankī* scripts that I have found go back only to the last half of the nineteenth century, but the form is certainly much older than that. There is a reference to *svāṅg* in the work of the poet Kabir which, though brief, shows through its description of the nature of *svāṅg* performance and the things associated with it that a theatrical genre similar to the one now existing was popular in the sixteenth century. An earlier reference to *svāṅg* or *sāṅg* is found in a ninth-century folk song sung by women of the Dom subcaste, whose special occupation seemed to be performing *svāṅg.*

Some scholars believe that *nauṭankī* derived from *bhagat,* a form of religious or semireligious theatre which is now localized in the cities of Agra, Mathura, and Vrindaban. There are obviously strong links between *svāṅg* and *bhagat. Bhagat* troupes are organized on the same system as those of the Hathras style of *svāṅg. Bhagat* and *svāṅg* use the same musical instruments and the same song forms and the stage manager performs an identical function in both forms. However, *bhagat* has not been shown to be older than *nauṭankī,* though the two clearly are of a common genre.

Bhagat retains a more religious orientation, and there are several rituals accompanying its performance, including the rite for the construction of the stage, the lighting of the ceremonial lamp, preliminary prayers by the performers in the dressing room, the bidding farewell to the gods and goddesses, and the extinguishing of the lamp. The major difference, however, is that *svāṅg* is performed by professionals and *bhagat* by amateurs.

About a hundred years ago, Captain R. C. Temple published his *Legends of the Punjab* (1883–1886). Among the kinds of bards which he noted, and from whom he collected material, was the priestly bard who "with his company sings Svāṅgs, those curious semi-religious metrical plays that are partly acted and partly recited, and are of such unconscionable length." These bards, he asserts, were called in, on payment always, to perform at various stated festivals such as Holī in the spring or Daśsara in the autumn. He also lists two other types of bards. Professional ballad singers would accompany dancing girls and sing for hire at various joyous ceremonies connected with marriage and other festive occasions. These balladeers, according to Temple, were invariably disreputable rascals, and their materials ranged from fine

Front cover of the *nauṭankī Prahlād Sāngīt* by Lakshman Singh dated 1866. (The British Library, London, photo. Courtesy of Kathryn Hansen)

national legends to the filthiest dirt. Finally there were those who in imitation of the priestly reciters of the *svāṅg* performed at feasts and festivals of the low caste.

The scripts and traditions which now exist offer evidence of the continuation of elements of all three traditions. *Saṅgīt* scripts inculcate material drawn from the *Rāmāyaṇa* and *Mahābhārata,* Rājput legends, Persian and Arabic stories, and melodramatic situations from contemporary life, including some which have been the basis of successful movies. The dancing associated with *svāṅg* cannot be traced to any of the classical or folk forms of dance, but relates to the tradition of the *nautch* girls, those professional female entertainers who appear in the descriptions of a number of foreign visitors to India. This, indeed, seems to be the style of dance of those accompanying the ballad singers about whom Temple writes.

The *nautch* girl does a variety of *nṛtta* dances, which please by their beautiful and graceful movements while displaying in a very modest fashion her physical charms. Mimetic action is absent. Modern *nauṭankī* dancers, whether women or female impersonators, intersperse their singing with bursts of dancing; they improvise routines which are graceful and not infrequently erotically suggestive.

Although the earliest reference to *nauṭankī* indicates that it was, in some instances, at least, performed by women by the end of the last century, it was clearly a male preserve. It remained so until women began to perform in the 1930s. The best dancers were boys who were made up as girls. The testimony of old *nauṭankī* performers is that before the advent of women on the stage, the dancing was more serious and sustained. The skilled boy dancer was much sought after, and he commanded a good salary.

The texts of the *svāṅg* which Temple describes provide evidence of different styles of performance. "This is the play of Puran Bhagat as made by Qadarya. Some sing it in verse (or some sing it seated), some sing it to drums and fiddles" (Temple 456.) That is to say, one troupe may perform it as a stage play with orchestra and singers, and another as a solo recitation. The flexibility in modes of performance is due in part to the different strands of tradition that have gone into the making of this genre, and is also related to present-day differences in style.

Performance Space and Structure

Nauṭankī is performed on a variety of occasions and in diverse settings. The sound of the *nakkārā* can be heard at religious festivals, religious and secular fairs, weddings and other private occasions, and during slack periods in the agricultural season.

Troupes perform in a variety of places and spaces. Although the *nakkārā* has a traditional association with open-air ceremonies, such as processionals and congregational activities, *nauṭankī* performances today commonly occur in large tents and closed halls. As admission by ticket has become more common, indoor performances have increased. At expositions and religious festivals companies set up large, fully enclosed tents, admission to which may easily be regulated. In many places lacking such facilities, semienclosed areas are used. This usually consists of a platform stage with a canvas roof and a high canvas fence around the audience area. Performances for private occasions, such as weddings, may be held within the grounds of the host's residence or possibly in a nearby open space.

The stage is usually a simple, raised, rectangular wooden platform with a plain or painted backdrop from behind which the performers enter and exit. The backstage area, curtained off, provides dressing rooms and a greenroom for the actors. In situations in which the audience surrounds the stage on all four sides, the platform is devoid of decoration of any kind. The size of the acting space may vary considerably depending upon the resources of the company.

The lighting has few subtleties. Bare electric light bulbs hang above the stage in plain view. Where electricity is not available, petromax pressure lamps are used for illumination. It is rare to find a company that attempts the use of color or light control.

The beginning of a traditional *nauṭankī* performance is announced by an extended period of drumming on a set of one large and two small *naḳḳārā.* Although these kettle drums have no device for tuning, the tension of the membrane and thus the pitch is altered during performance by continually dampening the head of the larger drum and heating the head of the smaller. The *naḳḳārā* player sits by a small brazier of coals, and in intervals between accompaniment, he dampens the large drumhead with a wet cloth and heats one of the two small drums before the fire.

Other instruments in the *nauṭankī* orchestra are the harmonium (sometimes two are used) and the *dholak,* another drum with two heads of equal size played with the hands. The *naḳḳārā* player, however, dominates the music, and a performance without him would be unthinkable.

After the preliminary music by the orchestra, which is seated on a low platform at the front of the stage, the performance begins with an opening prayer, either the traditional invocation of the Hathras school or the choral prayer used in Kanpur.

The opening prayers tell us something about the audience the author had in view, for the theological language in them may be Hindu, Islamic, or inclusive. The following prayer, preceding a play based on the *Rāmāyaṇa,* is Hindu in outlook:

> River of grace, shelter of the shelterless,
> benefactor of the humble, Son of Śambu Śiva,

treasure house of virtues, Lord forever, give
health in thy kindness. O helper of the
helpless, you are the deliverer of the dead.
O forest dweller, continually cast the shadow
of the favor of God upon our hearts. O merciful
knower of men, take the boat of Indradas across.
This is the request of Nathārām along with
Rūprām; O good and omniscient one, make
this *Saṅgīt Rāmāyaṇa Uttarkānd* [*The Play
of the Uttarkānd of the Rāmāyaṇa*] a success.
(Gaur, *Rāmāyaṇa Uttarkānd*)

The recurring use of phrases referring to refuge, the protector of the defenseless or shelter of the shelterless, and to taking the boat across (the ocean of samsara), establishes the prayer as a part of the Hindu tradition, and the assumption must be that it was a Hindu audience for which the performance was intended.

More Islamic in language and outlook is the following prayer: "There is none besides thee whom we acknowledge as ruler. Light shines from Thee who art its source. Thou art the kingly and merciful one; Thou are the powerful compassionate one. Lord do not forget me" (from *Sultānā the Bandit* [*Sultānā Dākū*] by Nathārām Śarmā Gaur).

Other prayers obviously anticipate a mixed audience or audiences, for the prayers assert the oneness of god though worshipped under many forms, such as this prayer from *Family (Khāndān):*

> Becoming Rām thou causest men to worship thee in the temple. By thy mercy men worship thee in the mosque; in the churches thou showest mercy, morning and evening. Thou are gracious to all—Hindu, Muslim, Christian, Sikh, all worship thee. All acknowledge thee only. There is none more powerful than Thee.

Samples of the choral prayers made popular by Śrī Kṛṣṇa Pahalvān's company are given below:

O Mother Durgā, guardian of our way,
Protect our path, O Mother.
Kṛṣṇa Murāri Girdhardharī,
Uphold my honor and preserve my reputation,
O Lord of the world.

When the opening prayer is finished, the stage manager immediately begins the story of the play, except when there is a preliminary variety show consisting of song, dance, novelty numbers, and comic sketches. The actors make their entrances on cue and the play proceeds as essentially an operatic performance. After each stanza of a song, the sound of the *nakkārā* fills the interval and signals the singer to begin anew. The drumming rhythm varies according to the meter and mood of the song. If there is a change in mood, the tempo of the drumming announces this also.

While music predominates in a *nauṭankī* performance, there is also dialogue. In most cases actors improvise dialogue between songs, but some scripts, especially those dealing with contemporary domestic situations, include sections in prose designated as "drama," which are intended as spoken dialogue. These passages notwithstanding, dialogue is minor in proportion to sung passages. Singing is what the audience comes to hear, and a good *nauṭankī* performer puts on an impressive demonstration of voice control and endurance.

Three or four comic interludes, which generally are not written into the script, are standard features of any performance. These interludes ordinarily are improvised and are the preserve of members of the company who specialize in comic sketches. The comic's costume and makeup are usually outlandish, like clown's attire and makeup everywhere. Slapstick, double entendre, misapprehension, mistaken identity, boasting, cowardice, stupidity, and gluttony are the subject matter of comic routines.

Dancing is a common feature of *nauṭankī.* It is done by the female characters, whether played by women or well made-up female impersonators, and by the clown figures. The latter usually insert burlesque imitations of well-known types into their routines. The female characters frequently express situations in which dance is appropriate and relevant. At other times the dance seems utterly inappropriate, giving to the scene almost a Brechtian air of alienation. Old performers lay responsibility for this latter development on the prostitutes who came into *nauṭankī* and used it to further their profession. They advertised themselves by dancing, whether or not appropriate for the character or relevant to the action.

The performance proper usually begins about eleven o'clock at night and goes on through the early hours of the morning, finishing as day begins to break. Several decades ago, before microphones and amplifiers came into use at outdoor performances, the audience sat on all four sides of the stage. The actors were obliged to sing each line four times, once on each side of the stage. Because the crowds were large—ten to twenty thousand people—the actor needed a strong voice and good projection. The challenge of reaching this large audience created a powerful style of singing which still characterizes *nauṭankī*. Nowadays most troupes, no matter how poor, operate with microphones and amplifiers, but the tradition of lusty singing continues. A singer is appreciated either for dramatic strength or sweetness of voice. In either case a *nauṭankī* performance requires singing at full voice for a five or six hour stretch and is an enormous feat for any performer.

Plays

Although the content and themes of *nauṭankī* vary, the structure of the plays is always epic or narrative. The *raṅgā* (derived from *raṅgāchār,* stage manager), who plays a central role in the plays, is literally a reciter who assumes roles. At the beginning of the play, he verbally sets the scene and time of the action, introduces the main character and situation, and sometimes indicates the moral which the play will illustrate. He maintains the thread of the story through a large number of short scenes which may be set in diverse places and may include a large number of characters. In this respect, he is the functional descendant of the stage manager of the Sanskrit drama, pulling together all the threads of the performance, but he is even closer to the ancient but continuing tradition of the Indian storyteller. In North India the recital or storytelling is still common and popular. The reciters, choosing their material largely from the epics and the Puranas, narrate their stories, interspersing them with songs and from time to time interrupting them to point out a religious moral.

Immediately following the opening preliminaries, the *raṅgā* sets the scene and introduces the main character, who is painted in broad bold strokes:

Sultānā the Bandit (Sultānā Dākū). (Sangeet Natak Akademi photo. Courtesy of Kathryn Hansen)

> In the province of Uttar Pradesh, there is a district named Bijnor and here was born a bandit named Sultānā. He was a very sharp, clever and brave man who made an occupation of robbing the rich and helping the poor. There was a band of some three hundred bandits who lived with him. (From *Sultānā the Bandit*)
>
> In the city of Yaman, there once lived a king who was famous in all Persia, Khudādost Sultān. He was a good man and a true servant of God. He walked in the way of God and had great wealth. He was merciful, just and compassionate to the poor. (From *Sultān Khudādost*)

The story begun, the *raṅgā* provides continuity which holds together short scenes and abrupt shifts of locale. The setting shifts from palace to battlefield with the stage manager's simple announcement: "*Here* in the palace there is great mourning and wailing, and *there* [on the battlefield] Yudhiṣṭhira swoons repeatedly." "*Here* from confounding the enemy comes Prince Vali; *there* Mandodarī speaks to Rāvaṇa."

Occasionally the *raṅgā* also paints the scene in which the action is occurring. "Taking the hand of Bhoja, he leads him into the dense forest. As they are going, the sun sets and darkness is all around them. The birds have gone to their nests in the tops of the trees."

Exposition through dialogue is not a feature of *nauṭankī* plays, so the *raṅgā* identifies and introduces new characters in the play. Characters frequently are on stage briefly and direct identification allows the story to flow smoothly. Within the *raṅgā*'s lines are also clues to the movement and internal state of the character: "Wringing his hands he reached the palace," or "Batsraj stood thinking this in his heart. . . ."

The structure is narrative, but there is great flexibility as to the manner of presentation. As the advertisements on the covers of some plays suggest, they may be enjoyed as recitation *(kathā)* or as plays *(saṅgīt)*.

Sources and Themes

Nauṭankī has gathered its material from many sources: the *Rāmāyaṇa* and *Mahābhārata*, Rājput stories, Puranic and other Indian legends, Arabic and Persian tales, historical incidents and characters, and movies and fictional material based on contemporary life. Little need be said about the epic material, except that in the case of the *Rāmāyaṇa* it is usually Tulsīdās' sixteenth-century work, not Vālmīki's fourth-century B.C. epic, which forms the basis of these plays. For example, the blurb on the cover of one of Gaur's *nauṭankī* plays based on the *Rāmāyaṇa* reads: "The unparalleled work of the great poet Tulsīdās which is not easily understood by the man in the street the author has put into meaningful and beautiful language."

The exploits of Ālhā and Udal, two Rājput brothers of Mahobā, and the fortunes and rivalries of three Rājput states of the twelfth century in India, namely Delhi, Kanauj, and Rathor, are the subjects of a well-known cycle of ballads which used to be sung by unlettered bards all over northern India. These singers made a profession of reciting the "Lay of Ālhā," passing the tradition on orally from generation to generation. Only in the late nineteenth century were the ballads written down. This saga of Ālhā and Udal, who after the heroes of the *Rāmāyaṇa* and *Mahābhārata* are the most popular subjects among Hindus throughout the middle and upper Doab and Bundelkhand, exalts Rājput chivalry and valor.

There are few *nauṭankī* plays based on Kṛṣṇa literature. Perhaps this is because the composers of *rās līlā* have preempted this subject. Other plays feature political figures of recent history as their heroes. Nathārām of Hathras has published a script whose hero is Subhās Chandra Bose, who led the Indian National Army against the British during World War II. Love stories like *Shirīn and Farhād (Shirīn-Farhād), Lailā and Majñū (Lailā-Majñū),* and tales like *King Khudādost (Khudādost-Sultān)* bring material of Persian and Arabic origin into the *nauṭankī* repertory. The breadth and variety of *nauṭankī* subject matter, drawn from both Hindu and Muslim traditions, insures its appeal to a wide cross section of the Indian public.

Because the men, and in a few cases women, who wrote the *nauṭankī* plays were active performers, the scripts are performance-oriented. Indeed it would be strange if it were otherwise, for even the poets in India are performance-conscious. Poems are not simply read, they are performed. Because they were conscious of the need to create plays that would appeal to a diverse audience, they introduced into *nauṭankī* a variety of situations and language. For a predominantly Hindu audience, the language would be Hindi and the subject one that was popular and acceptable to them; whereas for a Muslim gathering the language would be Urdu and the theme appropriate to the audience's taste.

Because it tends to be nonsectarian, *nauṭankī* concentrates on entertainment. Even so many of the ostensibly secular plays offer strong doses of moral teachings that reinforce the traditional roles of men and women in Indian society. A frequent subject is the erring husband and the faithful, forgiving wife. In *Beggar Woman (Bhikārin)* or *Wife (Bahu Begum),* the rich, idle hero becomes enamored of a prostitute who, with the help of her mother, proceeds to swindle him out of his wealth. The prostitute in these scripts is not the Western cliché woman with a heart of gold, but a heartless, money-loving, grasping woman. This is made clear in the opening narration.

> Dalal frequents the brothels where he takes golden ornaments and is surrounded. The beautiful prostitute is at this time the bank bill of exchange. Whoever brings notes from his iron safe will be beaten and chased away. The one who today lovingly presses him to her bosom, gives herself to whomever has gold. . . . As soon as the gold is finished, the prostitute looks elsewhere. The

poor man exclaims, "Now life is miserable. This is the business of prostitutes. Do not fall into their snare." (From *Beggar Woman* by Śrī Kṛṣṇa Pahalvān)

Again in *The Devoted Wife* the hero, led astray by a companion, becomes entangled with a prostitute who wangles from him the promise of a golden necklace. He attempts to steal a necklace belonging to his wife, but she discovers him in the act. When she learns what has happened she gives him the costly necklace to redeem his honor. Her act puts her firmly in the tradition of the good Hindu wife who is faithful in spite of the lapses or shortcomings of her husband.

In *Beggar Woman* the erring husband turns his wife out of the house because she rebukes him for the neglect brought on by his infatuation with a harlot. Disguised as a servant, she worms her way back into the household and is there to save his wealth at the critical moment when the prostitute, laughing villainously, is making off with it. Likewise in *The Devoted Wife* the wife saves the husband by taking the blame for a murder of which he is wrongly accused. Her innocence is proved at the last minute and the repentant husband is restored to his wife. Thus the marriage bond is upheld and prostitution is condemned, not because of its effect upon the women who serve in brothels, but because it is a threat to the institution of marriage.

As one might expect, the plays based on traditional Hindu heroes reinforce the moral teachings of that faith. One of the oldest of the stories in this genre is that of Harīścandra, the famous king whose integrity, like that of Job, brings him to the brink of disaster. The god Indra, seeing the uprightness of Harīścandra, king of Ayodhya, becomes jealous. He sends the sage Viśvāmitra to tempt him from the path of honesty and goodness. In the disguise of a holy man he asks for Harīścandra's help. The unsuspecting king encourages him to ask for anything, big or little. The sage asks for the key to the treasury. Claiming the entire treasury for his gift, he demands sixty times this amount as the gift which a student is obliged to offer to his preceptor. The king, unable to keep his word and fulfill the demand, offers himself, his wife, and his child to be sold into slavery. His wife is sold to a Brahman and is given the job of bringing fresh water daily from the Ganges. His son brings fresh flowers each morning for obeisances. Harīścandra is sold to a sweeper and is given over for crematory work. He collects money from those who come to cremate their dead. After many other hardships sent to test his faith, he is sent to kill his wife, who has been falsely accused of eating her own son, who died of a snake bite. As he raises the sword to strike, God appears to him and stops him. His son is restored to life and the king is restored to his throne. There he rules many years, and God blesses him abundantly.

Another model of integrity and uprightness is the hero of *Pūran Mal*. Pūran Mal is a young lad who becomes the object of his young stepmother's desires. Like Joseph (or Hippolytus in *Phaedra*), he resists all her efforts and in revenge she accuses him to his father. He is cast out and suffers greatly, but finally his uprightness is proven and his virtue recognized.

This story also points up another popular theme, the evil of marrying a young maiden to an old man. This was a lively concern, for the practice of child marriage was the object of attack by reformers, both Hindu and foreign, especially during the late nineteenth and early twentieth centuries. The custom of early marriage seems to have arisen out of a concern that a girl might become unmarriageable due to premarital relations with other men, or because some husbands sought an early control over their prospective brides. Not infrequently very young girls were wed to men several times their age. Not only was the match an unequal one, but in the event of the husband's death, the young girl suffered all of the disabilities of a Hindu widow. The abuses of child marriage were somewhat mitigated by the Sarla Act of 1929, which prohibited the marriage of girls below the age of fourteen, but the scripts of that period indicate that child marriage was still a problem.

Śrī Kṛṣṇa Pahalvān's *Trick of the Eye (Ānkh kā Jādū)* (1920–1921), which deals with this problem, ran for twenty-seven days in the Bareilly district. Nathārām's play, *The Play of the Husband's Murder (Saṅgīt Katle-Shauhar)*, begins in this uncompromising fashion:

> O my friends very evil times have come,
> India's boat is sinking in the sea of sin,
> Those who covet wealth nowadays have no fear of sin.
> Old men are wedding young virgins.
> Some, already wealthy, are coveting wealth
> And are marrying off their young daughters in childhood.
> From this mismating what will the future result?
> Many will suffer the sad fate of child widows.
> And some will become prostitutes to be sure.
> But living itself will be a great misfortune.
> Whoever gives his daughter in such a match is her enemy.
> He never thinks of honor nor reputation.
> In this connection I will tell you a story . . .

The scripts borrowed from Persian, Arabic, or other Islamic cultural contexts provide an interesting variant to the traditional Hindu moral outlook. The stories of *Shirīn and Farhād* and *Lailā and Majñū* (Lailā-Majñū) are both accounts of overpowering but illicit love. In the end the lovers are united, Shirīn and Farhād in heaven. This introduces a romantic element into the plays which is largely absent from the traditional Hindu cultural context. In their preoccupation with buttressing the sanctity of marriage, particularly in

The *nauṭankī Laila-Majñū.* (Sangeet Natak Akademi photo. Courtesy of Kathryn Hansen)

regard to the woman's duty to her husband, the authors tend to pass over romantic love, except where it occurs outside the marriage bond. In the traditional Hindu story such as Rām and Sītā, Śākuntala and Duṣyanta, Savitri and Satyavan, the romantic attachment is a secondary concern of the plot, which develops instead around the continuing fidelity and truth of the relationship. In *Shirīn and Farhād, Lailā and Majñū,* and others from a Persian-Arabic context, the romantic element receives full expression and is the main element of the plot.

These plays are probably popular because they answer the need for the element of romance that is largely absent in both Hindu and Muslim marriages, which are arranged by the families of the couple. If a romantic attachment develops between the man and woman, it develops within the context of marriage, for seldom are they acquainted with each other before. In spite of the moralizing of *The Devoted Wife* and *Beggar Woman,* Indian literature makes clear that the romantic element in a man's life is sometimes found in an extramarital relationship.

It should perhaps be expected that a form with the flexibility of *nauṭankī* should also be adaptable to a political message and orientation. In a number of instances, the opening prayers exhibit a conscious effort to promote unity and national integration. Since religion is the major source of divisiveness in India, national unity is sometimes promoted through propagating the oneness of the object of worship of all men.

> Thou art Iśvar, Thou art Dawar, Thou are called Rām. Thou inspirest worship in temples and mosques. With garland and rosary men murmur Thy name; Thy virtues are sung in the *Brahmanas,* the *Gītā* and the *Koran* . . . in churches and congregations Thou art the compassionate giver. By thy power incarnations, messengers, and prophets arise whom Thou graciously cause to be sent for our guidance. (From *Chitralekhā* by Śrī Kṛṣṇa Pahalvān)

Śrī Kṛṣṇa Pahalvān of Kanpur goes far beyond expressing such uncontroversial ideas in his writings. Coming under the influence of the ideas of patriots like Lokmānya Tilak, he became active in the movement for national independence from British rule. During the Gandhi-led, noncooperation movement of 1920–1921, one of his plays entitled *Non-Cooperative Pickles (Asahayoga Chatnī)* was widely distributed in North India at a few cents per copy. He also wrote and staged in Kanpur his play dealing with the British massacre of Indian nationals at Jalianwala Bagh. This he entitled *The Senseless Massacre (Khune Nāhak).* The impact of his writing and productions was such that the British placed him under strict surveillance; refusing to be intimidated, he staged the play again in Najivabad. Finally, by order of the district officials, he was forced to leave that area.

Context

The important centers which have shaped the style of *nauṭankī,* namely Hathras and Kanpur, are both in the state of Uttar Pradesh which, geographically and ethnically, is the heart of India. With the exception of its mountainous regions, this state lies in the great central Indo-Gangetic plain, formed by the basins of the Indus, Ganges, and Brahmaputra river systems. This plain is one of the greatest stretches of flat alluvial soil in the world; it is largely agricultural, supporting a dense population scattered in hundreds of villages. There are, however, seventeen towns with populations in excess of one hundred thousand, and five cities with populations numbering more than four hundred thousand (Kanpur, Agra, Lucknow, Allahabad, and Varanasi).

Although Uttar Pradesh has nearly double the number of institutions of higher education of any other state in the Indian union, its rate of literacy (17.6 percent) places it fifteenth among the eighteen states. Hindus constitute 84 percent of the population and Muslims 14 percent. Christians,

Sikhs, Jains, and Buddhists account for the remaining 2 percent. The language and culture of modern Uttar Pradesh reflects the blending of Hindu and Islamic cultures.

The characteristics of the population are reflected both in the audience and the form of *nauṭankī.* Its patrons are not the educated elite; they are rather the villagers and the lower economic ranks of the town and urban dwellers. They are culturally conditioned by the oral traditions of verses recited to ragas made familiar by usage. Nonetheless there are afficianados among them who are literate in the material and connoisseurs of the form and styles.

The Muslim rulers, particularly from Bābur (1483–1530) onward, were builders and patrons of the arts. Over the next three hundred years the tastes of the foreign rulers seeped down into the life of the people, giving birth to a hybrid language and culture reflecting both Hindu and Muslim elements. The Persian language of the rulers mingled with the Hindi of northern India to form Urdu (literally, "language of the camp"), which is commonly referred to as Hindustani. Hindi supplied the syntax and common words, Persian the higher vocabulary and highflown forms. During the period of Muslim domination and even down to the period of the struggle for Indian independence from the British, Urdu was the cultural language of the northern India area.

Kanpur and Hathras, centers of the two major styles of *nauṭankī,* are about as different as they can be. Kanpur is a large industrial city, and Hathras is a small town dominated by rural concerns. Kanpur had its beginnings as a sizeable city when the British East India Company made it an important military station about 1778. Before that it was a mere village named Kanhapur. The British probably chose it because of its central location in the plain of the Ganges. As an important military station, its economy developed to reflect colonial interests. Today it is a major industrial city noted particularly for cloth, shoes, and electrical and industrial products. It is not, nor ever has been, distinguished for architecture, culture, or religion. Like industrial cities everywhere, it has large slum areas which house those migrants seeking jobs in its mills and factories.

In sharp contrast with Kanpur, Hathras is a small town with virtually no industry of any kind. The one cloth mill which the town once boasted has been shut down for a number of years. Whatever commercial importance the town has derives from its position as a rail junction. The broad-gauge line from Delhi to Tundla and the narrow-gauge line from Mathura to Kathgodam intersect here.

The Hathras and the Kanpur styles of *nauṭankī* are distinguished by both artistic and organizational differences. In Hathras the songs are generally higher pitched and the singer holds on to the notes, elaborating and ornamenting them. In the Kanpur style the music is subordinated to the dramatic requirements of the play. The manner of singing is less demanding: The pitch is generally lower, and there is little ornamentation in the singing. The Hathras style requires a great deal more genuine musical skill. Like opera anywhere, Hathras *nauṭankī* is hard to understand because of the ornamental style of singing, but Kanpur-style songs can be followed easily, a consequence of Śrī Kṛṣṇa Pahalvān's background in reciting poetry.

As might be expected from a man who came to *nauṭankī* from a background of poetic competition, Śrī Kṛṣṇa's Kanpur style is distinguished by its emphasis on clarity and correctness of diction in rendering the language of the songs. Śrī Kṛṣṇa himself worked hard to master Urdu as well as Hindi when he discovered that among Muslims (the major patrons of poetic competitions), Hindus were recognized and disparaged because they usually substituted "s" for "sh" and "j" for "z."

Because of the dissimilar circumstances under which the two styles of *nauṭankī* developed, their organizations are also different. The differences, in an incidental way, also illustrate the nature of the pressure for change on the traditional forms. The Hathras style, the older of the two, developed in the school made famous by Indarman and Nathārām. These two men drew together a group of composers and performers and established an *akhāṛā* which became famous throughout northern India. The *akhāṛā* was a training school where aspiring, young performers learned and performed under the guidance of masters of the art. At the heart of the *akhāṛā* system were discipline and exclusiveness. It was a kind of closed trade union, jealous of its secrets. There was an oral and direct transmission of the skills and secrets of the profession from the teacher to the student. Having once entered the *akhāṛā,* one was bound to it forever. The student could neither offer nor agree to perform with any other troupe; he could perform only with his own *akhāṛā*. The teacher-student relation which this setup implied was a traditional vehicle for high artistic achievement. It assured the maintenance of high standards of performance and tended to conserve the traditional form and style of the art. At the same time, it served as a brake on the development of new troupes, which could find no trained, experienced performers for their productions. It also discouraged innovation and experiment.

From passages included in some of the Hathras scripts there emerges a picture of a large, well-ordered group in which each individual through his specialty shared in the corporate tasks of teaching and performance under the leadership of a chief *(khalīfā)*. The senior and most accomplished members were acknowledged as the teacher-preceptors of the whole *akhāṛā*. Others were recognized for their specialties in performance, either as singers, comedians, or composers of songs. Clearly members were at different stages of their career. They are variously described as famous, established, in the process of establishing reputations, or as beginning students. For example:

"The fame of Govind and Chevañjīlāl is established throughout the world."
"Lekrāj, Parshādilāl and Nārāyana are establishing their reputations."
"Benārsī, Bihārī, Cunuā, Cindā and Anta are singers."
"Caube and Cajjulal prescribe medicine for clearing the throat."
"Parshādīlāl teaches all the boys showmanship; he criticizes their acting when it is pompous or tawdry."

In such an account from about 1910, thirty-two living persons are actually named, and the author indicates that there are others: "To mention all the names would make a big book. I have described it [the *akhāṛā*] in brief." (Gaur 1967, 110).

The first troupe leader mentioned is Indarman, by whose name his *akhāṛā* is known. Indarman is linked to Nathārām as teacher to student. Nathārām began his career as a boy. His melodious singing and artful dancing in feminine roles were one of the chief attractions of Indarman's troupe. Indarman was succeeded by Totārām and Totārām by Govindrām. Eventually about 1910 Nathārām became the troupe leader and the fame of the troupe spread over the northern provinces. Nathārām augmented his fame by the ownership of a printing press through which he printed and distributed *nauṭankī* scripts, printed on cheap paper and sold for a few cents per copy in the market. According to contemporaries still living, many of the plays attributed to Nathārām were written by others, particularly by his teacher Indarman, who wrote the scripts and sold them to Nathārām who printed and distributed them. The financial return on *nauṭankī* scripts comes from their sale and not performing fees, since many people buy them to read or recite. The seller of the script, through his imprimatur, usually becomes more closely identified with the script than the author. For while the author in traditional fashion identifies himself in the script at the beginning and the end, the seller places his name, picture, seal, and address on the front cover and some identifying mark on each page.

The Kanpur school of *nauṭankī* established by Śrī Kṛṣṇa Pahalvān approached the matter of organization somewhat differently. When the young Śrī Kṛṣṇa Pahalvān made his entry into *nauṭankī* about 1913, he found that the *akhāṛā* system had a stranglehold upon *nauṭankī* development in Kanpur. Having moved to *nauṭankī* from his interest in *shaiyar,* a kind of poetic competition in which he had won considerable local fame, he was first encouraged by the local Arya Samaj in 1912 to turn his poetic talents to the writing of *nauṭankī*.[1] His first competition in this genre, *Hakikatrai,* was a play which had as its subject a nationalist leader. When he

[1] Śrī Kṛṣṇa's style may have been influenced ultimately by the *khyāl,* an operatic form of drama performed in Rajasthan. There are similarities in style, and the *khyāl* is known to have developed from sitting poetic contests among Rajasthan performers about a century and a half ago.

decided to hold performances himself the next year, he came squarely up against the *akhāṛā* system. So firmly was the system entrenched that even his own employees would not perform his compositions. Śrī Kṛṣṇa, therefore, determined to break the system. With another outstanding poet, Rasikendra, he conspired to destroy the system of *akhāṛā* control. In order to achieve their aim, the two men substituted for the traditional invocation in which homage is always paid to god and gurus, a chorus sung by the entire cast in a very simple meter. This chorus proved so popular with the spectators that they soon began to join in with the troupe in singing it. Other *akhāṛā*s in Kanpur began to follow the lead of Śrī Kṛṣṇa's company and the *akhāṛā* system was broken.

The number of persons in a troupe will vary with its circumstances, but staging most plays will require at least ten or twelve persons, including the musicians. It is not uncommon for the troupe manager to enlist outside performers to help in staging a show.

Training

The results of Śrī Kṛṣṇa's attack on the *akhāṛā* system were mixed. On the positive side, it opened up *nauṭankī* to a greater number of performers and to new ideas. At the same time it made the matter of training more difficult, for it removed an element of control over artistic quality and perhaps rendered the traditional form more vulnerable to outside pressures, such as the appeal of the movies.

The Hathras *akhāṛā* system, based on the traditional guru-disciple relationship, had training built in. The neophyte learned by imitating his teacher. Śrī Kṛṣṇa Pahalvān at Kanpur solved the problem by establishing three companies, one of which gave training to young, inexperienced players. His method apparently included three basic elements: (1) imitation of the teacher, (2) learning specific roles rather than isolated techniques, and (3) self-discipline, including sexual abstinence and control of diet. This much of Śrī Kṛṣṇa's method fits comfortably in the traditional Hindu way of teaching and learning. However, because Śrī Kṛṣṇa chose to break with the *akhāṛā* system, he lessened the emphasis on the guru's authority. He personally denies having any guru in the art of singing and claims his accomplishments are the gift of God. At the same time, he acknowledges that he had a guru in wrestling and another in poetic composition, though he admits to disobeying the latter.

Most *nauṭankī* performers probably begin their training early in life. In a country where skills and crafts are usually passed on from one generation of the family to the next, many performers are children of performers and begin to master their art in their adolescent years or earlier. Śrī Kṛṣṇa began at sixteen. However, the testimony of old performers indicates that it was quite possible for one skilled in singing to find his way into *nauṭankī* even in adulthood.

Because of the heavy emphasis on singing, training appears to have concentrated mainly on this aspect of presentation. The neophytes were introduced to the melodies, versification, and rhythms that are common to *nauṭankī*. From both Hathras and Kanpur there is evidence that the aspiring performers came under the close scrutiny of those considered masters. Śrī Kṛṣṇa's system formalized the training somewhat more than the Hathras group; the special troupe for training apparently spent two or three hours a day in training and practice.

A frequent concern in training was overcoming the problem of adolescent change of voice. To overcome this difficulty, the neophyte was instructed to sing into a large earthen jar or inside a temple with a domed ceiling. In these ways he was able to hear his own voice and train it until it found its permanent register.

Neither in Hathras nor Kanpur was much attention given to physical movement on the stage. Actors are often quite stationary while they sing. Even dance, which is an important feature of *nauṭankī*, received little emphasis. Apparently, the dances were learned informally, and what was done seems to follow no set pattern. Each performer adapted routines which pleased his audience. Much of the female dancing today is patterned after dance sequences from popular films. In the past, the dance must have resembled the so-called *nautch* dance, which seems to derive from the dances of the courts.

The *nakkārā* drum being a distinctive feature of *nauṭankī*, the drummer is an important performer. In training, the traditional Indian way of passing on knowledge and skills through kinship and communal groups again prevails. Almost all the *nakkārā* players are Muslims.

Today's *nauṭankī* troupes are struggling to survive. They are not in demand as in the past and many performers supplement their income by working at other things such as farming, factory work, or business, depending upon their location. The players are called together when there is an engagement to fill. Under these circumstances training suffers, for the troupe cannot be kept together and training cannot be offered in a disciplined, systematic way.

Support

There are three ways in which *nauṭankī* troupes are supported: (1) through the patronage of well-to-do individuals, (2) through communal effort, and (3) through the sale of tickets.

In the past when rajas and princes abounded in India, it was not uncommon for them to engage a troupe to perform, especially for special occasions such as marriages. The performance, more often than not, was open to the ruler's subjects. The prince might himself witness at least a part of the performance and, if pleased, make a handsome gift to the performers. Since Independence, the Indian princes have fallen on lean days and many are impoverished. There are still, however, wealthy individuals who invite and finance performances of *nauṭankī*.

Another traditional and continuing means of support is through communal subscription. Villages or neighborhoods collect money from their citizens and invite a troupe to perform for a number of days. The troupe is compensated out of the collected funds, and performances are open to the public. Performances are sometimes used as fundraisers for community organizations or projects.

Finally more and more *nauṭankī* are performed on a ticketed basis. Śrī Kṛṣṇa Pahalvān claims credit for first presenting *nauṭankī* on the basis of the sale of tickets in 1913 at the famous Takiya Melā (fair) in the town of Unnao. This method is especially successful at fairs, festivals, and expositions, which bring large numbers of people together for several days at a time. At Allahabad, for example, at the Magh Melā, which continues for approximately a month and during which several hundreds of thousands of people camp in tents on the site, two or three companies perform.

The better companies travel widely throughout northern India. Before partition they went as far as cities in what is now Pakistan. Tours may last from a few weeks to six months. Śrī Kṛṣṇa's troupe played in Karachi for eleven months.

It is hard to estimate the earnings of these performers. However, old performers estimate that at today's rate of exchange a community would collect fifteen hundred to two thousand dollars, Rs. fifteen to twenty thousand, before inviting a troupe. They estimate that fifteen years ago the popular performers earned from two to four hundred dollars, or two to four thousand rupees, per month.

Whatever the means of compensating the troupe, some additional income can be anticipated from special offerings by the spectators for numbers that are especially pleasing. The money is usually held up by the donor while the performance is going on and collected by a member of the company who drops it on the harmonium. The leader of the company immediately and publicly acknowledges the gift: "Mr. X of (place) has given (x amount) rupees in appreciation of the fine singing of (name of actor). We thank him sincerely." Some performers will render their thanks in a song improvised on the spot.

Nauṭankī in Performance

On June 4, 1970, a performance of *The Curd Seller (Dahiwala)* or *The Devoted Wife* was staged by the Bharati Kalā Nambardār Theatrical Company of Kanpur at the Agra Exposition. This exposition began on April 5,

1970, and continued for six weeks. During this entire period the Nambardār Company nightly performed a *nauṭankī* from its repertory. During that run I witnessed, in addition to *The Devoted Wife, Gangā and Jumnā (Gangā-Jamunā), Shirīn and Farhād,* and *The Wife (Bahu Begum).*

These performances took place under a large tent in one corner of the fairgrounds, which large numbers of people visited each night to see the various exhibitions. Admission to the performances was by cash payment at the gate. The three or four rows of seats which were nearest the stage were comfortable chairs and cost $.70, Rs. 5.25. Three other sections of less comfortable chairs, increasingly distant from the stage were priced at $.50, Rs. 3.75; $.27, Rs. 2.00; and $.17, Rs. 1.25, respectively.

The tent seated approximately one thousand and each night that I attended the house was full. The audience was made up almost entirely of males. On one occasion I saw a couple of women in *burkha* (the black garment worn by Muslim women which covers them from head to toe when they go out of the home).

The stage was a temporary one made of earth. It had two levels, the higher one for the action of the play and at the front a lower level for the orchestra, which consisted of the *nakkārā*, a *dholak,* two harmoniums, and an electric vibraharp. A charcoal fire was built on this level to aid in tuning the drums. At the rear of the stage was a painted backdrop depicting Western style buildings. The backdrop remained the same for all the plays. Essentially it was a proscenium arch stage with entrances and exits from the wings.

The performance on stage began with a choral prayer by the entire company. This included the ten or so female dancers and the actors who appeared in the play proper. As soon as the prayer of invocation was done, the female dancers, hardly losing a beat, went into their hip-shaking dance routines. A group dance to a film song was followed by a large number of individual numbers interspersed with three comic routines. The dancers all performed to recorded film music, in most cases mouthing the words as they performed their dance routines. The dances were erotic and suggestive and there was constant interplay between the dancers and the men in the front rows. One, two, and five rupee notes were offered in appreciation of the performance. These were received by the dancers and placed on the harmonium. This "variety" entertainment continued for about three hours. The play proper began at eleven P.M.

The Devoted Wife concerns a young husband who, led astray by a companion, becomes infatuated with a prostitute who wangles from him the promise of a golden necklace. He attempts to steal his wife's necklace to give the girl, but his wife discovers him in the act. When she discovers what has happened, she gives him the costly necklace to redeem his honor. Further, when her husband is accused of murdering the prostitute, the wife confesses to the crime which in reality was committed by another man. At the eleventh hour, however, her innocence is proved and the repentant husband is restored to his wife. A subsidiary plot concerns the husband's sister, who falls in love with a once rich but now poor servant.

The play began with the *raṅgā*'s introduction. The *raṅgā* then moved to the role of Madanchand, the husband, and the play moved through a number of scenes. The performance proceeded in operatic fashion, with the main dialogue and actions conveyed in song. Brief passages of dialogue were included and the play was divided by three interludes, composed of short comic skits unrelated to the play's action and a few "variety numbers." The *rasa* was mainly erotic with some pathos included. At about four o'clock in the morning the performance ended.

Current State

The *nauṭankī* troupes continue to suffer from the inroads of a large movie industry, which appeals to its traditional audience. It cannot compete well with the spectacle, glamorous stars, and enormously popular film music offered cheaply at movie houses all over the northern part of India.

It is the Kanpur and urban-based troupes which have suffered most, for they have felt most strongly the pressure to compete with the glamor of the movies. The most readily available weapons for this competition are technical innovations in staging and female glamor. Both are now being used extensively. The Hathras companies have also been forced to follow, but they continue to preserve a good deal more of the artistic integrity of the *nauṭankī* of the past. In rural areas, change is slower and the audience demands are less sophisticated.

Films appeal to the Indian sense of novelty in portraying not only the sense of place but the concrete details which the *nauṭankī* stage could only conjure up in the imagination. A film moves with equal facility inside or outside, from hut to castle. Indian films generally make much of this appeal to the eye; they portray not only the varieties of daily existence, but the wealth of a colorful imagination as well. For example, in films with a romantic element—an overwhelming majority of all films made—there is an inevitable scene of the hero's pursuit of the heroine around and among some fantastically beautiful settings of natural scenery. In traditional *nauṭankī*, the stage manager would have set the scene verbally and the actor would have had but a bare stage with which to work. Some *nauṭankī* troupes have begun to use curtains and scenery. The stage, which was formerly open to all sides, is now usually curtained on at least one side. At home and on the road, for example, one Kanpur-based company uses a set with a painted backdrop of an interior scene which might be in any large city in Europe or in some other place in the Western world. This company also uses various novel stage effects in some of its plays, such as scrim scenes and smoke screens for change of scene. Some of this influence, of course, comes from Western stage practices, since in Kanpur the better-known touring troupes were frequently booked into halls for performances and thus became acquainted with a closed stage. The transition from an open-air stage to a closed hall represents more than a change in staging; it also marks a trend away from *nauṭankī* as a community entertainment toward a private, individual amusement.

The really important effect of film has fallen upon the music of the *nauṭankī,* which is its heart. While the traditional meters are still dominant, increasingly the audiences demand and get "*filmigit,*" that music with the distinctive character of the film, Indian but with Western instrumentation. Indian film tunes have an enormous popularity and exposure. Since the films or movies are the major recreational outlet for city dwellers, film music has a wide hearing. The songs that prove popular are played on radio day after day and are heard blaring forth from loudspeakers set up in the streets on special occasions. The film songs are catchy and easy to sing and increasingly film tunes are being used in *nauṭankī*. In some recent *nauṭankī* scripts, these film tunes are indicated by the designation "theatrical," as prose dialogue is designated "drama."

Women began to appear in *nauṭankī* productions in the late nineteen

A scene from *Sultānā the Bandit (Sultānā Dākū).* (Sangeet Natak Akademi photo. Courtesy of Kathryn Hansen)

thirties. Their presence on the stage produced considerable excitement and strong reactions—for and against—among *nauṭankī* practitioners and patrons. Śrī Kṛṣṇa gave up active participation in his production company in protest. Once a few companies discovered that the presence of women brought spectators and assured financial success, however, the rest were bound to succumb. In the female performer, it seemed, they had found an answer to the challenge of the cinema. The glamorous stars of the silver screen, or their equivalents, were now a few feet away on the stage. Their simple presence caused excitement among the spectators, especially in villages where the spectators had never seen women bold enough to show their faces on the public stage.

The entry of women onto the *nauṭankī* stage also encouraged the trend toward film music. With rare exceptions, these actresses have not mastered the traditional *nauṭankī* music and their repertory is restricted to popular film tunes.

The nature of the female performer's act on stage is affected by and affects the composition of the audience. In Kanpur, where the spectators are usually all male, the performer uses all of her physical charms to captivate and excite the spectators; the songs are bawdy and the dancing erotically suggestive. Members of the audience respond by offering money as a gift to an individual performer for a specially fine performance of a number. (This, of course, is also done in the case of the male performers.) A disproportionately large part of the performance time is devoted to the variety acts of the female performers, that is, to song and dance unrelated to the play. In the Hathras area where the audiences often include women and children, the use of the female performers is more limited, and what the performers do is more suitable for family entertainment.

The malleability of *nauṭankī* is an important factor in its continued vitality. All through its history it has shown a great capacity for borrowing and absorbing foreign elements to its particular needs and style. It has borrowed tales of faith and devotion from the lives of the saints; it has taken elements of the style of the ballad singers of the past; it has made use of stories of romance and heroism from the Arabic-Persian and the Rajput traditions; it has adapted its form to social and political concerns; and now it is borrowing music and stories from films. It has clothed the whole collection in its robust style of singing and added its own earthy and sometimes satiric comedy. Some Indians who are concerned about tradition note the influence of films upon *nauṭankī* with regret, fearing the loss of the integrity of the form. They particularly fear the dying out, without heirs, of the old performers. While this cannot be discounted as a possibility, past history offers grounds for hope that the present influence of movie films may also be absorbed to the ultimate enrichment of *nauṭankī,* and present interest in the traditonal theatre offers hope for the renewal of this form.

WORKS CITED

Gaur, Natharam Sarma. 1967.
Bahoran Ka Byah. Hathras.

———. N.d.
Ramayana Uttarkand (The Uttarkand of the Ramayana).

———. N.d.
Sangita Atha Ka Byah.

Samar, D. L. 1962.
"The Traditional Theatre of Rajasthan." *Natya,* Folk Theatre Number 18. See also pp. 25–32.

Temple, R. C. 1883–1886.
Legends of the Punjab. 3 vols. Bombay: Education Society's Press.

ADDITIONAL READING

Awasthi, Suresh. 1977.
"Nautanki—An Operatic Theatre." *Quarterly Journal of the National Centre for the Performing Arts* 6, 4:23–36.

Gargi, Balwant. 1956.
Folk Theatre in India. Seattle and London: University of Washington Press.

———. 1965.
"Folk Theatre-5: The Nautanki and Nagal." *The Illustrated Weekly of India* May 9, 1965:31.

Mathur, Jagdish Chandra. 1964.
Drama in Rural India. New York: Asia Publishing House.

Ojha, Dasrath. 1970.
Hindi Natak, Udbhav aur Vikas. 5th ed. Delhi: Rajpal and Sons.

Swann, Darius L. 1974.
"Three Forms of Traditional Theatre of Uttar Pradesh, North India." Ph.D. diss., University of Hawaii.

Waterfield, William. Trans. 1923.
The Lay of Alha. London: Oxford University Press.

Chapter Nine

TAMĀSHĀ

Tevia Abrams

Tamāshā IS THE PRINCIPAL FORM OF FOLK THEATRE of the Marāṭhī-speakers of Maharashtra in central India. It emerged in the Deccan plain in the late sixteenth century from earlier entertainments, and it served as a bawdy, lascivious diversion for both the occupying Moghul army and the opposing Marāṭhā forces trying to free the territory. Although the bawdy, "raw" strain is still popular today, recent refinements by some of the artists have brought this folk form closer to the "wholesome" family tastes of the middle and upper classes. This refinement has led to the development of a sophisticated variety of *tamāshā* called people's theatre *(loknāṭya).*

Estimates suggest that there are today about 450 itinerant professional troupes in Maharashtra, a state of about three hundred thousand square kilometers and a population of sixty-two million people. Since these troupes regularly tour the state's cities, towns, and most of its thirty-eight thousand villages, *tamāshā* theatre serves as a medium of communication capable of reaching large numbers of people. This inherent outreach capability is particularly important in rural areas—beyond the frontiers of literacy and the effective reach of the mass media—where both government and nongovernmental organizations have employed a number of the troupes in development-oriented programs.

Modern *tamāshā* troupes are of two varieties: song troupes *(saṅgīta-bārī)* which specialize in song-and-dance entertainments; and folk-drama troupes *(dholki-bārī)* which offer more substantial theatre fare, including dramatic presentations *(vāg),* as well as songs and dances. A song troupe typically comprises five or six female dancers and singers and several musicians. The folk-drama troupes take their name from a cylindrical, two-sided drum *(dholki),* slung from the shoulders, which provides the most characteristic rhythms in *tamāshā.* An average folk-drama troupe has a leading male actor; six to eight additional male actors, who double as choral singers; one or more female dancer-singers; and several instrumentalists. Both troupes fea-

ture a stock comic jester character, a comic jester *(songādya)*, who serves as improvisational punster and master of ceremonies. The well-known itinerant troupes in Maharashtra include some 250 song troupes and 200 folk-drama troupes, but additional troupes are often formed for special occasions from among village residents.

Tamāshā theatre is characterized by a loosely arranged mixture of elements. A performance might include an opening devotional song *(gāna)*;

Farmer's dance performed in typical *tamāshā* style by members of Shahir Amar Shaikh's troupe in a 1965 production of *Wherever We Go We Eat (Jau Tethe Khaoo)*. Typically a *dholki* drummer is always close to the action. (Rajdatt Arts Photos)

traditional songs and dances; farcical skits, notably the *gaulan* segment evoking the playful antics of the young Kṛṣṇa and the milkmaids *(gaulan);* and a full-length dramatic folk-play *(vāg)*. There is freedom as to the employment and ordering of these elements; however, their content must generally express the comic *(hāsya)* and romantic *(śṛñgāra) rasa.*

The philosophical and aesthetic scheme of *tamāshā* incorporates three basic elements: (1) the entertainment tradition, expressed through love songs *(lāvanī)* and dramas and evoking very often the romantic and comic *rasa*s; (2) the more serious propagandistic tradition, extolling the *rasa* of bravery *(vīra),* through strongly masculine ballads *(povāda)* performed by the great poet-singers *(shāhirs)* and their accompanists; and (3) the devotional tradition, steeped in the bhakti transcendentalist movement, which inspired folk troupes to express moral truths through witty songs and dialogues.

Origins

Several origins have been offered for the *tamāshā* entertainment form. One traces a line of development of popular, low-class entertainments, in the vernacular languages, running parallel to the sophisticated classical Sanskrit theatre. According to this view, nonclassical folk entertainment forms—

comic pantomimes, music, dance, and circus-type acts—developed, blossomed, decayed, and in general muddled along until they congealed into the *tamāshā* form in the sixteenth and seventeenth centuries.

Another suggestion, with a better basis in fact, claims that *tamāshā* developed among the Marāṭhā people in the sixteenth century from decaying remnants of the literary Sanskrit dramatic and linguistic traditions, which had never been very strong in the Deccan in the first place and which had been declining steadily following the invasions by the Moghuls early in the fourteenth century. These remnants in particular included two entertainment forms, one-act skits *(prahasana)* and musical sketches *(bhāṇa)* (Konow 1969, 48), which responded to the popular and rustic tastes of the Marāṭhās. Both were secular forms and both provided openings for crude humor and satire appealing to the entertainment-starved audiences.

The one-act skits are thought to have originated in the twelfth century. They concern social foibles and are laced with spicy comments and puns. The form was popular among Sanskrit-speaking audiences down to the fifteenth century and, as the vernacular languages replaced Sanskrit in western India, the skits passed into the Marāthī culture as a literary device, and were later incorporated by poet-singers in the *tamāshā* presentations.

The musical sketches, on the other hand, are solo, improvised musical pieces, containing a mixture of love poetry, humor, wit, music, and song. The oldest known example dates from the end of the fourteenth century, but the form goes back at least to the classical period and possibly even to an earlier tradition of mimes from the preclassical era.

A variety of musical sketches, called *misrabhāṇa,* is worth mentioning here because of its direct influence upon *tamāshā.* A medieval example of *misrabhāṇa* is known to have offered a secular look at the frolicsome adventures of Lord Kṛṣṇa and the milkmaids, in a manner quite reminiscent of the later *gaulan* segment of *tamāshā.*

It may reasonably be supposed that *tamāshā* actually developed from the decaying remnants of both the Sanskrit and Prakrit traditions, and from the Moghul entertainments—the vigorous *kathak* dances and the *kavalī* and *ghazal* songs—that were brought to Maharashtra from the seat of imperial power in the north of India.[1] The indigenous Marāṭhā theatrical forms may be broadly categorized as rustic and either religious or secular in inspiration. A few of these forms survive today, but performances are rare. They include puppet shows, musical operas *(dashāvatāra),* dramatic poetry recitals *(bhārud),* and festival entertainments.

Tamāshā theatre has more in common, in form if not in subject matter, with the musical opera, which originated in the seventh century, than with

[1] Moghul rule continued in the Deccan for more than 350 years, from 1309 to 1674, until it was broken by the stunning victory of the Marāṭhā warrior, Śivājī the Great.

any of the other early Marāṭhā folk forms. Two specific musical opera elements influenced *tamāshā:* skits *(kala)* similar to the *gaulan* segment of the later *tamāshā* plays, and the employment of a clownlike stock comic character resembling the comic jester of the *tamāshā* troupes. The musical opera itself declined in popularity over the centuries and all but disappeared after the early eighteenth century, about the time the Marāṭhā Peshvas[2] became involved in the series of fatal wars that culminated in defeat at the hands of the British. The secular *tamāshā* entertainments quickly filled the vacuum with the *gaulan,* heroic ballads, and love songs.

Religious inspiration was also important in the development of *tamāshā.* The dramatic poetry recitation *(bhārud),* a form created by the Mahar untouchable community, later proved effective for devotional propaganda by the Maharashtrian poet-saints who represented the bhakti cults of Hinduism. The saints were reformers, and their goal was to break down social barriers, especially those of caste. The sensual beauty of their songs and dialogues appealed naturally to the poet-singers, who later shaped their own poetic conceits into a more secular kind of entertainment which became part of the *tamāshā* performance.

From the dramatic recitals came more sophisticated and elite plays of the gods *(lalīta)* that served as court entertainments during religious festivals. Because it was such a rarefied entertainment, serious writers of the nineteenth century experimented with these entertainments (as well as with minstrel songs and musical operas) in their efforts to establish a sophisticated and thoroughly urban Marāṭhī theatre tradition (Das Gupta 1961 and Marāṭhī Natya Parishad 1961, 1–8). The work of Vishnudās Bhave (b. 1819 or 1820), which is partly based on the *lalīta,* is cited as the beginning of urban Marāṭhī drama.

Marāṭhī minstrel songs *(ghondals)* in praise of the local mother goddess are performed at festivals or at the request of individuals for private celebrations, such as weddings. One variety gave to *tamāshā* theatre something of its present troupe structure, including a narrator, an accompanist who provides the humor, and two instrumentalists on the *damarū,* a small hour-glass shaped drum,[3] and the *tuntuni,* a single-stringed drone instrument which is even now associated with *tamāshā* performances. The minstrel songs also lent to *tamāshā* its sense of troupe inventiveness and improvisation, as well as its itinerant performing tradition.

To these early forms must be added a one-man, hour-long musical sermon

---

[2] A line of prime ministers that ruled the Deccan from 1707 until the British takeover in 1818.

[3] The *damarū* is a two-headed drum. A small ball attached to a string strikes the drumheads alternately when the player rolls the instrument from side to side, producing rhythmic beats. It is a popular instrument of Indian jugglers, wandering minstrels, and monkey trainers.

(kīrtan), which may feature devotional songs *(bhajan)* performed in unison with gathered spectators. Because of their flexible nature, these sermons provided the narrator-singer with an opportunity for introducing a wealth of contemporary social considerations into the performances. The inventive and supple use of language, especially in its narrative and anecdotal double-entendres, influenced the later *tamāshā* form.

Although the forms discussed here are unique in themselves and some continue to be performed separately on special occasions, they have essentially all given way in popularity to *tamāshā*. Most of the elements and features now associated with *tamāshā* presentations were incorporated early in the seventeenth century, about the time male *kathak* dancers were being sent from the Moghul court at Delhi to entertain the imperial armies in the Deccan. Eventually local acrobats and tumblers from certain outcaste communities picked up the northern dance styles and either joined the troupes or created their own. For the Marāṭhī poet-singers, meanwhile, *tamāshā* became an effective outlet for their own compositions and songs.

There is no actual historical record of the early emergence of *tamāshā,* because it was so much a part of the unwritten story of the lives of the untouchable classes and outcaste communities. Artists apparently picked up elements from the living oral traditions—the love songs and ballads then in popular demand—and imaginatively surrounded them with dances, improvised skits, and music. When the dramas were added in the nineteenth century, they quickly became the "soul of *tamāshā*" (Sathe 1957).

To recapitulate briefly, the opening devotional song of the *tamāshā* performance was known to performers of older forms and was probably incorporated in *tamāshā* as part of a natural transition. The *gaulan* segment seems to have evolved out of the musical opera skit, as did the stock comic character, the comic jester. Other elements of the format, as well as character types, were borrowed from different folk dances, song forms, and devotional dramas. The foreign elements of *tamāshā,* such as the Urdu song forms and the *kathak* dance styles, were directly influenced by the Moghul camp entertainments. The most recent addition to *tamāshā,* the drama, derived its scenarios and plotlines from the historical and mythological lore of kings, princes, and gods. The early *tamāshā* plays dealt with masculine themes revolving around battles, bravery, and war, while harsh elements of raw, bawdy humor and suggestive dance gestures were thrown in for the amusement of the battle-weary soldiers. The later refinements of the more peaceful and civilized Peshva period resulted in the introduction of the gentler themes of love and religious devotion.

The Poet-singer (Shāhir) Tradition

A word on the great poet-singer tradition must be added, since it is so closely identified with the history of *tamāshā* entertainments. The poet-singer was acknowledged by the people as their troubadour, balladeer, and chronicler of important events and trends in society. During the seventeenth century, the best of the poet-singers would generally become leaders of their own *tamāshā* troupes.

The first in the line of great poet-singers was Agindās, whose nationalistic ballads extolled the bravery of Śivājī the Great. His best-known works date from 1645, and were composed in a style reserved for times of war. He aimed to stir the people against Moghul rule, and his verses were characterized by a lack of refrains, a stylistic feature continued by poet-singers until about 1731.

During the Marāṭhā kingdom, the poet-singers used their talents to perform in enemy camps in order to learn their military secrets. They also helped to inspire the Marāṭhā people to resist the enemy. Their awareness and understanding made them a mirror of society and conscience of the people. Even illiterate peasants knew the histories of their communities through the poet-singers' ballads and other entertainments.

The Peshva period (1707–1818) witnessed the refinement of the compositions by poet-singers. Court patronage was largely responsible for this flowering of talent, as emphasis shifted from battle cries to composition and performance of more artistically complex narrative ballads with refrains, and to love songs. This period was the golden age of *tamāshā*.

Most revered of the poet-singers of the Peshva period were Ānant Phandi (b. 1744), Prabhakar (b. 1754), Parshurām (b. 1754), Honāji (b. 1754), Rām Joshi (b. 1762), Sagan Bhāo (b. 1778), and Haubatti (b. 1794). Phandi lived most of his life in Pune. He wrote many love songs and ballads, and performed in *tamāshā* troupes. Later in life he turned from pure entertainment to devotional songs, for which he also gained wide fame. In a moment of despair, he wrote the following lines in a ballad:

> Oh, how the times have reversed themselves
> The servant won't listen to his master
> They have all become proud
> The World's in such a mess
> It's plunging into nothingness
> (Joshi 1961, 194)

With the start of British rule in 1818, Peshva patronage came to an abrupt end. The fortunes of performers and poet-singers declined, and *tamāshā* troupes were forced to rely upon the rural peasants for support. However, just when the fortunes of the poet-singers and the other performers appeared to reach their lowest point, a new group of socially committed artists began to breathe new life into the *tamāshā* form, starting in the 1930s. This regeneration can be seen in the writings, compositions, and performances of such poet-singers as Sunbe, Naniwadekar, Gavankar, Amar

Shaikh, Sathe, and Bhandāre—all activists and all concerned with effecting social or political change. This impulse reached its fullest expression in the years immediately preceding Indian Independence, and was inherited in the post-Independence period by Ātmarām Patil, Shahir Sable, Shahir Phrande, Shahir Hinge, and others.

The seeds for the twentieth-century renewal may be found in the developments around 1870, when Jotirao Phule, founder of an anti-Brahman movement, used the ballads to disseminate ideas of social reform. Phule's followers, the Truthseekers, continued to utilize ballads to preach to the populace. The great Tilak, father of anti-British resistance, also turned to the methods and styles of composition and performance of the poet-singers when he created the Ganesha festival in 1893.

Ballad singers worked unceasingly in the late 1930s through the 1940s in pursuit of an independent India. They sifted through the writings of Tilak and Gandhi, and brought them vividly before the people. The more committed of the poet-singers were jailed for their anti-British propaganda work.

The Communist cause produced the most eloquent and persuasive team of poet-singers, including D. N. Gavankar, Amar Shaikh, and Annabhau Sathe. They performed individually at first and later teamed up to create a hard-hitting *tamāshā* troupe.

After Independence, other causes caught the attention and the talents of the newest breed of poet-singers. These causes included linguistic rights for Maharashtrians, the Free Goa movement, the 1962 Chinese invasion of India, and the Indo-Pakistani wars.

The late Shahir Amar Shaikh, effective propagandist, who experimented extensively with the *tamāshā* form beginning in the 1940s. He is seen here in 1968, a year before his accidental death. (Rajdatt Arts Photos)

Looking back upon the long line of poet-singers, it is possible to discern three kinds of compositions: (1) ballads and people's theatre works addressing political, social, and educational subjects with a revolutionary zeal and flavor; (2) compositions to glorify history and to propagandize the mythological base of Hindu society (*Śiva-śakti* works); and (3) sensuous love songs, performed by *tamāshā* troupes in villages and cities. Of the three types, the first appears most in favor today, as social awareness and the modernization process develop. However, the poet-singers of history and myth still survive, singing ballads about Peshva times. The sensuous tradition, though, has languished over the years. Pathe Bapurao (1865–1945) was perhaps the last great poet-singer of sensuous *tamāshā* songs and dances.

As a result of a growing sense of concern, hundreds of poet-singers pooled their efforts in 1969 to establish a *Mahārāshtra Shahir Parishad* (Association of Poet-Singers of Maharashtra). The following year, a conference of 328 of these artists was held to inspire the poet-singers, who once inspired the people.

Performers and Training

Two untouchable communities are closely linked to the early history of *tamāshā* entertainments: the Kolhati and the Mahar. The Kolhati were among the first to be recruited into entertainment troupes for the amusement of the warring Moghul and Marāṭhā forces in the seventeenth century, while the Mahar carried *tamāshā* from the military camps to the villages. By the late nineteenth century, the Mahar artists had become widely known and praised for their folk-drama troupes and their repertoire of folk dramas. The Mang are another untouchable community long associated with the folk form.

These communities were landless and dispossessed people, free from taboos respected by the higher castes and the upper social and economic strata of society. Eventually a small group of determined and dedicated Brahman poet-singers became associated with *tamāshā* troupes, an eighteenth-century development that obliged the upper strata of society to take notice of the form.

The art of *tamāshā* performance has largely been passed down from generation to generation. The method of training is not so much a consciously developed structure as an apprenticeship. It is essentially a profession based upon heredity. Early in childhood, the sons and daughters of *tamāshā* performers begin to model themselves after their parents. They are often seen dancing and singing backstage while a performance is in progress, and by the time they reach their teens many are already accomplished artists. Often children are discouraged from pursuing the career of a *tamāshā* artist, as parents are very conscious of the desirability of sending their children to school, in the hope that they will do better in life. It is therefore not uncommon for artists to make great economic sacrifices for the education of their children. This process is selective and therefore weeds out a significant number of potential *tamāshā* performers. Of those who remain with their parents, many continue through years of "on-the-job" training, until they are ready to join the troupe or to move on to some other troupe. Depending upon the level of artistry in a troupe, a child of one of the members may develop into a very accomplished performer by virtue of this apprenticeship system.

Concerned about the low level of professionalism in *tamāshā* troupes during the 1950s, scholars, journalists, and *tamāshā* enthusiasts prevailed upon state government authorities to help in raising standards of living for the artists and in launching training programs to improve the quality of artistry. While some economic relief measures were introduced and annual festivals and conferences of *tamāshā* artists were established to generate awareness of the needs of the profession among artists and in society, little attention was actually paid to the improvement of training methods as a means of strengthening the artistry. In the mid-1970s, however, plans for training camps for young *tamāshā* apprentices, covering costuming, singing, dancing, and acting, were finally drawn up by the cultural authorities of the state government.

Support

With the exception of the sophisticated people's theatre troupes, which have cultivated large followings among the middle classes, many of the professional itinerant *tamāshā* troupes earn a subsistence living for their members. A large number of professional *tamāshā* performers are illiterate, and they are often exploited by the theatre impresarios who book their tour programs in the cities, towns, and villages.

Tours through the rural districts occur in winter, the time of outdoor fairs and religious festivals. Audiences of five to six thousand may be anticipated on a typical winter evening. In the monsoon months—June to September—the *tamāshā* scene shifts to the indoor theatres in the cities and larger towns. The monsoon provides the city folk the opportunity to see the best troupes in performance.

Methods of payment to troupes vary: An unsophisticated song troupe may be paid on a share system, while artists in a refined folk-drama troupe are generally paid a fixed daily wage, in cash. Shares for the song troupe are divided after such common expenses as travel, food, and lodging are deducted from the gross income. Extra money may be earned from gifts paid by patrons during performances.

The uneven fortunes of the artists, in both unsophisticated and refined troupes, the exploitation by sometimes unscrupulous impresarios, and the inability of many performers to rise above a subsistence income level were major factors in the decline of *tamāshā* troupes from the turn of the century until relatively recent times. These problems were compounded by the fact that many artists grew up in economically deprived castes and classes.

Since the 1960s conscious efforts have been made to rebuild the profession, strengthen its artistry, and bring some measure of welfare relief and economic stability to the artists and their families. These efforts include government welfare and pension schemes, exemption of performances from long-standing and crippling entertainment taxes, creation of a Maharashtra *tamāshā* association to focus periodically on the problems common to all the artists, and the occasional holding of training camps and workshops to help improve the professional quality of the artistry. These measures have yet to be proven effective on a broad scale, but today the best and most famous troupes do exceedingly well, and some have been known to donate significant sums from their profits to charitable causes such as homes for the disabled, schools for the poor, and scholarship funds for the needy.

Dramatic Sources

Tamāshā skits, farces, and dramas were originally unscripted and drawn from traditional sources in Hindu devotional mythology, secular history, prehistorical legends, and contemporary social issues. In a typical *tamāshā* production, the *gaulan* segment is the first piece of dramatic material presented to the audience. The source of the *gaulan* is the oral tradition surrounding the mirthful antics of the young Lord Kṛṣṇa, the *gaulan* or milkmaids (notably Kṛṣṇa's beloved Rādhā), Kṛṣṇa's friend Pendya, and the old auntie *(mavshi)* who acts as the protective chaperon for the milkmaids. The oral tradition surrounding the efforts of the milkmaids to get past Kṛṣṇa in order to sell their containers of milk in the town of Mathura is rich in anecdotes and provides fine openings for the improvisational talents of *tamāshā* artists. With the scenario set firmly in the minds of audiences, the artists may freely interpret the content and, depending upon the social or entertainment concerns of a troupe, the *gaulan* segment offers excellent opportunities for multilevel communication with the audience. In the hands of professional dramatists working with sophisticated troupes, the *gaulan* has been scripted with devastating comical and satirical effect. Among such writers are Shankar Patil, Vasant Sabnis, and Vijay Tendulkar.

The main dramatic piece performed by a folk-drama troupe is the full-length drama, which originated in the last century from unscripted entertainments, based upon scenarios from mythology, history, and social concerns. These dramas were produced for a variety of propaganda purposes, as well as for pure entertainment needs. Here again, opportunities for improvised puns and social comment abound.

A traditional drama deals typically with mythological or pseudohistorical characters; but contemporary writers for the sophisticated troupes have long since broken through this convention. In 1958 noted Marāṭhī writer Vyankatesh Madgulkar wrote a brilliant comic drama entitled *Chaos All Around (Kunācha Kunala Mel Nahi)*. The piece served as a critique of the contemporary political system. A simple uneducated washerman *(dhobī)* is given a few impressive words to memorize. He is then propelled into a position of political power, with embarrassing results. The effect was a farcical comment on the inane, high-sounding speeches of typical politicians.

Fulfill My Desire (Vichyā Mājī Purī Karā), which opened in 1965 and continued with occasional performances through the mid-1970s, established Vasant Sabnis as a comic writer of great note, and made an overnight star of Dada Kondke, who played the comic jester character. The storyline was very thin but its relevance in performance over the years was kept timely and fresh by the clever wit of Kondke.

The scenario of *Fulfill My Desire* concerns the troubles at the court of a mythical king—problems of corruption, petty thievery, and nepotism. At the outset the king discusses matters of state with his minister and the police inspector. News is brought of the death of the chief minister and the king retires to his harem, seeking consolation. In a scene between a guard and the minister, it is learned that according to custom the replacement for the dead chief minister should be the police inspector. However, the minister is determined that his own brother-in-law will have the post, as a means of placating his own domineering wife.

The brother-in-law assumes the vacant post but he is clearly out of his element. As a cowherd, he acts the uncouth boor, insulting people and abusing his authority. He also fancies the police inspector's sweetheart, who happens to be a *tamāshā* dancer and who brightens the show with some song-and-dance numbers. The inspector and his girlfriend devise a plot for ridding themselves of the cowherd. By encouraging the boor to engage in petty thievery, the king himself is obliged to take the initiative of deposing the chief minister. The inspector is offered the post, he marries the dancer, and the work ends on a happy note, with praises for the virtues of truth and justice.

Some of the satire of the work is conveyed in the opening lines:

KING. What is the condition of our Kingdom today?

GUARD. Everything is fine. No need to worry.

KING. Have there been any thefts lately?

GUARD. No thefts, only thieves stealing.

KING. Any murders?

GUARD. Generally no, but. . .

Vasant Sabnis' *Fulfill My Desire (Vichyā Mājī Purī Karā)* owed a great deal of its success to producer and main character, Dada Kondke (here at left). Kondke's improvisations and witty lampoons of local social and political figures and situations were enormously popular. (Rajdatt Arts Photos)

KING. What about the percentage of murders?

GUARD. Two-point-five.

KING. What?

GUARD. This is government language so that people shouldn't understand.

(Abrams 1974, 113, 114)

Among the truly socially committed artists were a group of Communist *tamāshā* performers who were very active in efforts in the 1940s and 1950s to rally the populace to their views. Their work helped to sharpen *tamāshā* performance as a propaganda tool and refined it as people's theatre, making it acceptable for the urban working classes as well as the middle classes.

The work of Shahir D. N. Gavankar with the Red Flag Cultural Squad troupe *(Lalbawata Kala Pathak)* is worth mentioning in particular. The group's first production in the early 1940s was Gavankar's own full-length drama *Bandya, the Accountant (Bandya Divan),* which attempted to expose black-marketeering by following the crooked efforts of Bandya, the village accountant, who grew rich hoarding scarce government-controlled grain for later resale at illegal profits. A brief moment of dialogue illustrates the bitter insights of the author:

BALU. . . . Do you know what the moneylender's asking for grain?

TATYA. I guess you haven't heard that there's government control on grain prices.

BALU. Hah! Controls! Once the village leader and the inspector are paid off a little, then all your government control goes straight to the moneylender.

The Red Flag Cultural Squad was the most exciting theatrical phenomenon of the 1950s. Two other major talents of the group were the poet-singers Annabhau Sathe and Amar Shaikh. After India gained its independence, the Communist front fragmented, and this affected the committed *tamāshā* artists, who shifted to illustrating issues that did not directly confront government authorities. But this bold experiment in the 1940s in propaganda was the start of a long process of regeneration, which may have saved the *tamāshā* form from its slide in the direction of oblivion.

Performance Space and Context

Tamāshā performances may be presented under a variety of outdoor and indoor conditions. In small villages, the performing space could be a temporary, raised wooden platform, set up in a large clearing, especially for the event. Or the space could simply be a suitable area marked out on the ground. The performing space must be at least ten by fifteen feet, to accommodate a minimum of six and as many as twelve or even eighteen performers. An audience is likely to be seated on the ground, fanned out on three sides of the stage. An undecorated backdrop would adorn the rear of the stage area, and often there would be a front curtain. In the cities indoor theatres might feature backdrops with paintings of colorful outdoor pastoral scenes. With the increasing availability of electric power, lighting is provided by electric bulbs strung over the stage, above the heads of performers, as well as by one or more floodlights affixed to posts at the sides of the stage. Sound amplification would also be provided with the aid of microphones and loudspeakers.

A large and prosperous village might make a permanent outdoor stage facility available to a visiting *tamāshā* troupe. This would likely consist of a sturdy raised platform, boxed in proscenium style, facing the audience frontally rather than on three sides. Technical facilities would essentially be the same as those available in smaller villages. The audience could range from several hundred to two or three thousand.

The very successful *tamāshā* troupes may conduct village tours without regard for the inconveniences of travel and the lack of facilities that plague most troupes. These successful groups have elaborate arrangements for transporting in their own vehicles their own stage and technical equipment, costumes, props, and instruments. Some have purchased their own buses and a few have mobile stages.

Productions in towns and cities are generally held at indoor stages. The unsophisticated *tamāshā* troupes are admitted to the poorer theatres in the poor working-class districts, while the sophisticated people's theatre troupes can command the best and most modern stage facilities in the large commercial theatres. The chief urban centres for *tamāshā* performance are Bombay, Pune, Nagpur, Nasik, Ahmednager, Kolhapur, Sholapur, Satara, Sangli, Belgaum, and Aurangabad.

Costume and Makeup

Tamāshā artists use traditional Maharashtrian dress for costuming. As a rule, the female singer-dancers wear brightly colored nine-yard saris that are gathered and tucked in at the waist, and pinned to allow freedom of movement, especially for dancing. The borders of the saris are highlighted with silver or gold threads that glisten during movements about the stage.

Costume jewelry for the female performer may include bangles, sparkling earrings, noserings, and necklaces. Her costume is complete once she winds a few heavy strands of tiny linked ankle-bells *(ghuṅgharū)* about each ankle. Dances and other stage movements are performed in bare feet, and therefore each step makes a characteristic jingling sound. Makeup for female artists is minimal. It consists of highlighting the eyes, painting the lips, and rouging the cheeks.

While the male performers also use traditional dress on stage, they are permitted some variety: An actor or musician may wear a white pajama outfit or a Nehru shirt, dark grey jacket, and a large colorful turban wound around the side of his head. He may also wear earrings. Male performers too use little makeup, mostly highlighting of the eyes and a little rouge on the cheeks. Sometimes a false moustache or beard may be used to enhance char-

Intense moment of confrontation between exploiting money lender, left, and activist peasant leader, is captured in the *vāg* or dramatic part of Shaikh's *Wherever We Go We Eat.* (Rajdatt Arts Photos)

acterization for such roles as chief minister or a wise old man or, possibly, an evil protagonist.

Costuming and makeup are minimal in both unrefined and sophisticated *tamāshā* productions. The latter productions may, however, call for special costumes for male characters such as a king, prince, policeman, wise man, government official, or moneylender. The lack of insistence upon elaborate costuming or makeup in a *tamāshā* performance is matched by a minimal reliance upon props, sets, and other trappings of stage decor. The focus of interest is therefore placed squarely upon the performer, as human instrument.

Music and Dance

Music is an integral part of any *tamāshā* presentation and mention needs to be made of the instruments used in performance. Chief among the instruments employed is the *dholki,* a cylindrical, two-sided drum that provides the essential rhythms for the variety of song-and-dance forms that go into a *tamāshā* program. Twenty-one inches long, the drum is slung from the play-

Typical instruments used in *tamāshā:* center is the large circular *daf* percussion instrument; immediately to its left is a standing one-stringed *tuntuni,* which is partly hidden by a two-sided, barrel-shaped *dholki*—itself partly hidden by a smaller *daf* or *halgī* resting on the foreground. Slightly to the rear and right of the large *daf* are the two drums that look like *tabla.* To the right is another *tuntuni.* The tiny drum in front of the large *daf* is called a *kanjīrī* and the jangling instrument strung to wooden rods is the *lejim.* Lost in the foreground, and to the left of the *lejim,* are the small cymbals or *thal.* (Rajdatt Arts Photos)

er's shoulder on straps. It rests at hip level. At one end, the striking surface is eight inches across, while at the other end the diameter is just six inches. The *dholki*-player sets both the pace and mood of a *tamāshā* performance. He is called upon to provide the required rhythms for performers and he often plays counterpoint rhythms to accentuate a dancer's gestures and movements. During stretches of dialogue, he may help to underline dramatic moments with mood-creating drum patterns.

The next most characteristic instrument used in the folk form is the *tuntuni,* a single-string drone instrument that is plucked at regular intervals to produce a fixed and continuous note. The curiously shaped instrument is twenty-three inches long, and it has a mechanism by which the string may be tightened.

Other instruments include the tiny brass cymbals *(manjīrā),* which normally accompany devotional singing; a single-faced tambourine-shaped instrument *(daf),* about eighteen inches in diameter, which is beaten in sharp staccatto manner with a tiny stick; a smaller type of tambourine, the *halgī,* which is just ten inches across and is beaten by hand; a metal triangle with six-inch sides (the *kade*); an instrument resembling buttons strung like beads on wooden rods and producing jangling sounds (the *lejim*); and the harmonium, a boxlike accordion. In addition some song troupes also use a variety of drums, including the tabla, the *dagga,* and a tiny one-sided cylindrical drum which is only four inches deep (a *kanjīrī*). All female dancers moreover wear strings of ankle-bells to accentuate their movements on stage.

Musicians form a small group on the stage, playing in close relationship to the dancers, singers, and actors. In particular the *dholki* player works intimately with individual performers, moving with them, leaning into their activity as if interpreting and enriching the performance through the rhythms of the drum.

Tamāshā dance styles reflect both local and foreign influences. As the Deccan is culturally and geographically at the midpoint between North and South India, there are traces of classic *kathak* dances from the north, as well as elements of the major southern dance form *(bhārata nāṭyam)* and the *kathakaḷi* dance-drama. *Kathak* influence is seen in the vigorous stamping footwork of the *tamāshā* dancers, while the southern forms are vaguely recalled by their hand gestures, head and body movements, and the rolling of their eyes.

It should be stressed that *tamāshā* performance reflects only traces of the classical forms. The dance steps and gestures, as well as the lyrics of the songs, are not structured for the employment of the balanced system of *rasas*, but are bent to the evocation of easily attained sensual expression. The dance steps, moreover, do not follow set forms or patterns; they are determined by the music only, in free interpretation.

Tamāshā song forms include sensual love songs, interpreted through singing and dancing. These songs are called *lāvanī,* after the Marāṭhī word for transplantation. *Lāvanī* originally referred to the transplantation of rice, and is derived from the Sanskrit *lapanika,* an adjective describing sensual beauty, with a second meaning of harvest song, referring to the rice harvests. Early love songs were indeed work songs, but the form was gradually absorbed into the bardic traditions, and during the Peshva period it evolved as a major poetic song form in *tamāshā* entertainments. One type of love song *(bhedik)* was developed to express devotional elements of Vedantic philosophy.

An example of the love song from the Golden Age of *tamāshā*, during the Peshva reign of Baji Rao II, was written by the poet-singer Honaji (b. 1754). It describes the sadness of the lonely, separated lover:

> My love has flown away from me.
> Should I poison myself?
> How long can I control my sad heart?
> If you don't return soon
> I think that I may die.
>
> (Joshi 1961, 222)

Until the end of the nineteenth century, love songs were performed by male singers and dancers dressed as women. Today the form is practiced by professional dancing girls, richly clad in nine-yard saris and wearing ankle-bells to call attention to their footwork.

Another important song form is a poetic dialogue *(chakkad)* that simultaneously employs singing and mime. The singer is called upon to mime and act out states of feeling and action suggested by the lyrics of the song. The following brief selection from a poem by the great romantic poet-singer Pathe Bapurao (d. 1945) illustrates the sensual appeal that this form may evoke:

Man

Oh, pretty girl. Stay where you are.
Come and talk to me awhile.
I'm wild about you, you know.
Don't spurn me.

Woman

Behave yourself! Always after me.
Why do you persist? My husband will come.
Somebody might come and somebody might see,
And they'll surely tell my brother-in-law,
And my husband will take it out on me.
(Joshi 1961, 172–173)

Serious dramatists and contemporary filmmakers in Maharashtra have often recognized the unique effect of mixing song, dance, and poetic dialogue. Both love songs and poetic dialogues have been included in urban stage presentations as well as films in order to distract and entertain audiences. Some of the most popular Hindi and Marāṭhī film songs are refined performances based on the rhythms and styles of presentation of the love songs. Many of these film songs eventually gain such popularity that lesser versions of them are often presented in *tamāshā* performances—an ironic twist of the original creative impulse.

Other song forms used in *tamāshā* entertainments include the poetically evocative Urdu *kavalī* and *ghazal,* which are performed in an intimate manner by a female singer seated on the stage; the ballads used by poet-singers for hundreds of years; and the question-and-answer riddle form *(sawāl-jabāb)* set to music in the eighteenth and nineteenth centuries by poet-singers engaged in philosophical competitions with each other.

Performers and Roles

Tamāshā actors receive no formal stage training or direction. However, through long apprenticeship they manage to achieve a particular style of performance, characterized by a tendency to focus body, gesture, and speech in the direction of the audience. Focusing upon the stage and on other actors is reserved for the most intense moments of dramatic conflict. The style is further defined by a rigid gesturing during speech delivery. In view of the late addition of drama to the *tamāshā* form, it has been suggested that the rigidity of gesture and the general downstage focus may have evolved from the use of microphones for sound amplification. While the directional focus and the gesturing suggest a sense of awkwardness, this is offset by additional features of the acting style: vivid facial gestures, especially eye movement; moments of mime and stage business that do, after all, focus upon the stage; and the rich and pungent torrent of improvised dialogue. Exceptions to this style of acting are to be found among the handful of sophisticated people's theatre troupes that have adopted the conventional naturalistic style of the urban Marāṭhī stage. Even here, however, the comic jester is left free to play directly to the audience.

While acting in a *tamāshā* performance may lack finesse and objective standards, as well as formal stage direction, audience taste still serves as the ultimate judge of excellence. In this respect performers gain fame, adoration, and respect not from the excellence of their acting talent, as defined by the legitimate Marāṭhī theatre, but from their establishment of personal rapport with audiences. The comic jester role, with its special relationship to both audience and other performers, is thus a critical one for any troupe, as an audience will judge a troupe by the excellence of its jester.

The comic jester may have a part in the *gaulan* segment of an evening's performance, teasing the actor playing Lord Kṛṣṇa, as well as the women playing the milkmaids. Later he might turn up in the farce segment, and once again in the drama. His task clearly is to wander in and out of the dramatic action, interrupting sometimes tedious proceedings with unscripted jokes, witty remarks to other actors, or asides to bored or impatient spectators. As the troupes often work from brief scenarios and plot ideas, their performances depend on the quick wit of actors in the creation of lively dialogue, and the comic jester may need to look sharp if he is to rescue his troupe on an "off" evening.

Other fixed roles are found in the *gaulan* segment—Kṛṣṇa, his beloved Rādhā, his friend Pendya, the auntie, and the milkmaids she must watch over. During a folk-drama segment, a troupe's featured female singers and dancers will often retain their functional roles in any dramatic scene. Thus, a female artist playing a queen or a romantic lead will take time out during the dialogue to execute some song-and-dance routines.

Stage Conventions

A *tamāshā* performance places no physical boundaries on time and space, and realistic and naturalistic stage settings or props are unnecessary for such suggestions. By a variety of gestures, movement, mime techniques, and word images in the dialogue, an actor may convincingly convey to the audience any kind of setting in any time and any place in heaven or on earth. By accepted convention, the *tamāshā* actor is himself the instrument of all stage illusion.

When an actor playing a king in a drama looks around and "sees" a temple, the audience is expected to see it too. If the king then acts out entering the temple, where he is approached by a group of temple dancers, the audience is also fully expected to accept that the scene has shifted to the interior of the temple.

It is also an accepted convention that actors may step in and out of character, and that they can switch roles as needed. In this way, a few actors may easily play a wide variety of characters. Such arrangements are helped by the fact that there is very little employment of costuming and makeup.

Another convention pertaining to illusion is the actor's quick turn around the stage, which can tell an audience of a long trip carried out and of a new city or country reached. The successful employment of these stage conventions is one of the marks of a good *tamāshā* actor.

Involvement of the audience in two-way contact with the performers is an especially important convention of *tamāshā* acting. This involvement may take the form of teasing or joking exchanges between spectators and artists. The informality of onstage proceedings is conducive to such involvement, and often results in brilliant and memorable moments of improvised humor. One convention associated with the unsophisticated song troupes represents a physical form of artist-spectator involvement: It consists of the payment of sums of money by spectators for special encores or favored requests of song and dance performances. This convention, the *daulat-jadda,* developed from the practice during Moghul times of offering gifts to performers. Today, however, the practice has degenerated to thrill-seeking contact with the artists, particularly with the women singer-dancers.

Performance Structure

A *tamāshā* production normally opens with a devotional song *(gāna)* to Ganesha, the elephant-headed god and patron of the arts. Song troupes and folk-drama troupes alike open their programs with such a song. There are two kinds of these devotional songs: those giving prominence to Brahmā and Lord Śiva the destroyer; and those giving prominence to love and sakti, the reconciling aspects of Śiva (Joshi 1961, 126). The poet-singers who com-

The practice of presenting money for audience requests is called *daulat jadda* and serves as an important moment of contact between artist and spectator. (Rajdatt Arts Photos)

posed these songs traditionally competed with each other for supremacy in the eyes of the audience. Poet-singers who invoked Śiva were called *turewāla,* while those who invoked sakti were called *kalgiwāla.* The competitions, which also involved other *tamāshā* song forms, including love songs and question-and-answer riddles, reached their height in the nineteenth century (Joshi 1961, 126–129).

Modern devotional compositions are less theologically involved, and more concerned with praising Ganesha in the hope of gaining artistic inspiration and reward, as the illustration below demonstrates:

Ganesha, I'm praying to you.
Listen to me,
Come to us in human form
And bless us.
You're fond of art.
And this is just for you.
I hope it's appropriate.
Please inspire us.
The bonds between us are immortal.
We are ready to serve you.
Just support us always.
This is what we ask.
(Abrams 1974, 277)

The opening invocation is most often followed by the *gaulan*—an improvised set of irreverent and saucy songs, dances, and sketches centered about the young Lord Kṛṣṇa, his friend Pendya, his beloved Rādhā, and the old "auntie" called Mavshi. Mavshi is always played by a male actor dressed as a woman, and "her" role is to steer the milkmaids away from Kṛṣṇa, who is himself generally disfigured and who is always teasing them. Mavshi tries to keep the milkmaids on the road to Mathura—the holy city of the Hindus—where they plan to sell milk and butter. Kṛṣṇa typically attempts to exact a tax from the group.

The following is a brief sample of dialogue:

ALL MILKMAIDS. (In unison) You tell Kṛṣṇa our pots are heavy with curds and milk. The pots are new and they're leaking and our saris are getting all wet. Please let us go. (Jester gives the message to Kṛṣṇa, who turns a deaf ear to the plea.)

RADHA. We won't pay him! We'll teach him a lesson. (To Jester) Go and tell Kṛṣṇa that if he's brave enough he should come and collect the tax himself. (Jester passes the message back to Kṛṣṇa)

KṚṢṆA. (To Milkmaids) What are you waiting for? Is this a marketplace?

MILKMAIDS. We're going to the market.

KṚṢṆA. Without paying my tax?

RADHA. You're not going to get it.

KṚṢṆA. Then you can't pass. (Pause) By the way . . . the rule is that people can pay what they like.

(Joshi 1961, 164–165)

The dialogue goes back and forth in this manner until the milkmaids agree to pay their tax. Contemporary and socially committed *gaulan* segments of *tamāshā* performances include inspiring propaganda messages on such themes as milk scandals, language rights, and problems of social injustice.

The *gaulan* segment is most often performed by folk-drama troupes, and less frequently by the song troupes, which generally avoid dramatic elements in favor of such purely crowd-pleasing fare as the traditional sensuous love songs, poetically evocative Urdu *kavalī* and *ghazal,* and popular film songs. An evening of song troupe entertainment may feature half a dozen troupes, each performing for about half an hour, and each climaxing its brief appearance with singing and dancing. On special occasions, such as village festivals or on weekends in the cities, a folk-drama troupe would complete the night's entertainment with a two-hour folk-drama. If a folk-drama troupe is on stage for a full evening of entertainment, it will follow up on the *gaulan* segment with its own interlude of sensuous songs, dances, and poetic dialogues.

In a full-length performance by a folk-drama troupe, the program segment devoted to sensual songs is an interlude. The next part of a typical production is the farce, which serves as a prelude to the folk-drama. In the farce, laughter is the primary aim, not the evocation of sensual awareness. Situations from daily life—ill-matched marriages, prostitution, educational difficulties, economic and social problems—are the typical subject matter. The farce derives from earlier examples brought to India by British theatrical troupes in the eighteenth and nineteenth centuries, which were themselves influenced by the Italian *commedia dell'arte* tradition.

The folk-drama is a nineteenth-century outgrowth of the earlier improvised *tamāshā* skits and other bits of dialogue. Today it is the highlight of a

Every good *tamāshā* troupe is rated by the talents of its main character actor. For a time, Raja Mayekar served as one of the mainstays of Shahir Sable's troupe. He is seen here in the 1968 production of *One Night in Hell (Yama Rajyat Ek Ratra)*. (Rajdatt Arts Photos)

typical night of Maharashtrian folk entertainment. Traditionally the dramas were created by *tamāshā* troupes on the move around the countryside, in bullock carts and later in buses and trains. Dramas were by nature unscripted pieces based upon short storylines and scenarios designed by the troupe leader and his actors. The actual dialogue was created upon the stage during performance.

For color and variety the dramas mix dialogue, improvised humorous asides by the jester to the audience, out-of-context byplay between artists, and songs and dances—mainly love songs but occasionally ballads. The unscripted language of the drama is simple and direct, so as to be accessible to rural folk and to the urban working classes alike. Increasingly, however, the newer dramas are fully scripted, with refinements in dialogue and wit created to appeal to the middle and upper classes. Themes and subjects for the dramas cover mythology, history, nationalism, government, social evils, new ideologies, propaganda for various causes, and entertainment for entertainment's sake.

The drama has its own particular format. It begins with a male chorus chanting poetic lines of reportage that help the audiences grasp the plot. This chanting in a high pitch *(mhani)* is featured at key points in the drama to keep the plotline in focus for the audience, especially where extended improvised dialogue may have rendered the story difficult to follow. Highest notes in the chanting are most often carried by the "note-players" *(surte),* who sing while playing tiny cymbals *(manjīrā)* and the single-stringed *tuntuni,* which produces a fixed continuous note. Other members of the chorus stand shoulder to shoulder, each performer cupping a hand over one ear while singing at a near shout. Leaning into the group are the *dholki* player and the *daf* player, both of whom fill the moments between each line of the opening chorus with wild beats and rhythms.

A traditional drama may open with a chant about some legendary king called Vijay:[4]

King Vijay ruled the land.
He was a very brave and handsome leader.
His subjects were happy everywhere.
One day he went out to hunt.
Look, now! Here he comes on horseback,
He is riding through the forest.
Look at him ride!

[4] The example cited is a composite of several dramas of the same genre, dealing with fictitious accounts of legendary figures. It is included here to help the reader visualize the form and its staging conventions.

Having set the scene, the chorus withdraws to one side, or it may exit, leaving the performing space clear for an encounter between the king and his mistress. The beautiful girl is concerned that he may not return; but the king is reassuring. He will return to her soon, he says. The girl exits; the king gallops away on his make-believe horse. He does a few turns around the stage to indicate that he has traveled far. He stops, looks around, and remembers he has left his bodyguards behind at the court.

Gazing off in the distance, King Vijay sees a temple. He decides to rest there and in a moment he is inside. A quick turn around the stage, the accepted staging convention to overcome limitations of time and space, permits the king to appear inside the temple. The chorus returns to chant more details and thereby advance the plot. Interestingly the king may join in the singing, since his makeup is minimal and the audience is unlikely to be disturbed if an actor moves in and out of character. The chanting describes the king's chance meeting with a temple dancer. Another girl enters: the temple dancer. She looks to the audience in a very matter-of-fact manner, pouts disdainfully, and turns amorously to the king. From the chorus, the audience learns that this temple dancer is only making a pretense of falling in love with the handsome king and that, in reality, she is a wicked witch busily casting her evil spell over him. The chorus withdraws again and the dancer-witch sings and dances a beautiful and tender love song to beguile the king.

Eventually, the spell of the witch is broken by the appearance of a faithful guard who, as it turns out, had wandered into the forest in search of the king, after being informed by the king's mistress of fears for her lover. The king is restored to his senses and there is a happy reunion back at the court. The good have prevailed; the evil-doers are crushed. There might now be a concluding song performed in chorus. There are no prescribed rituals at the close of a drama.

Tamāshā in Performance

Pune's Āryabhushan Theatre is a focal point for *tamāshā* activity. It is a necessary stopover for itinerant troupes, most of which are of the unsophisticated song troupe variety. For devotees of the folk form, it is a gathering point, a veritable institution, and for the community in the immediate vicinity of the theatre, it is a thriving economic center. There are tea stalls, restaurants, and musical instrument shops that actually depend upon *tamāshā* artists and the theatre audiences for survival.

The Āryabhushan is also the center for a Pune-based clique of *tamāshā* lobbyists—mainly politicians and civic leaders—some of whom have exploited the artists to gain political influence among working-class and rural audiences. This kind of influence is considered to be most important just before city, state, and national elections.

The atmosphere at the Āryabhushan is extremely relaxed and informal. The backstage area, behind the backdrop, serves as a tiny camping ground for the performing troupes and their families. There is also an outdoor courtyard that holds the spillover of artists and their instruments, their families, and their personal belongings, including bedding, bundles of clothing, and cooking utensils. Evidence of the poverty in which the majority of artists live is especially apparent during the daytime hours. Night and darkness cover up its traces during the performances.

The Āryabhushan's stage is worn smooth, if uneven, along its boards—clear evidence of many years of barefoot dancing. The auditorium seats five hundred persons, but there are concrete perches down both sides of the hall, and these are capable of holding hundreds more. Red-colored flags and a plain backdrop mask the back walls of the stage area.

Unlike a typical outdoor village production that may feature just one song or folk-drama troupe, the Āryabhushan engages a large number of troupes for display each night. There is a regular turnover of performing groups and after a few months of regular attendance, it is possible for the discerning among the audience to gain an excellent overview of the best performing folk talents in Maharashtra.

Habitués of the theatre claim that there is no other *tamāshā* stage with such a peculiar flavor of informality. Perhaps the atmosphere may be communicated to some degree through the following notes I prepared during one of many visits to the Āryabhushan.

It is early on a Saturday evening, about nine thirty. A dozen song troupes and a folk-drama troupe are scheduled to perform. We take our seats just in time to see one song troupe finishing its performance; another troupe is preparing to make its entrance upon the stage. As the dancing and singing continue, spectators file to the edge of the stage with offerings of rupees for special requests. The troupe in action is concentrating upon film songs, and while this is certain corruption of *tamāshā* traditions, the songs nevertheless attract a lot of rupees from the audience. The musical numbers are short and brisk, and the *dholki* player, setting a fast pace, provides good rhythmic support to the dancing girls. The girls for their part demonstrate intricate footwork and they seem to be making the most of their ankle-bells, through the vigorous stamping of their feet. Suddenly a bell rings in shattering fashion, putting an end to the proceedings. The troupe's allotted performing time is over. Taking its cue the troupe switches from a secular lascivious song to a closing devotional number, *Jejunicha Khanderaya.*[5] Their exit is thus made to appear chaste and pure.

---

[5] *Jejuni* is a village in Maharashtra; *cha* means "belonging to"; *Khanderaya* is the name of the local deity. So the title indicates a devotional song to the local deity (Khanderaya) of the village of Jejuni.

In this way one troupe follows another at twenty-minute intervals. The fast pace is maintained. There are some troupes which perform better than others, and there are a handful of individual artists who stand out from the rest. Throughout the evening performers and audience interact warmly. One patron, for example, comes forward to present a ten-rupee note to a dancer. Her ankle-bells tinkling, body wrapped in folds of her traditional nine-yard sari, the girl shuffles down to the edge of the stage and bends low to receive the note, asking, "What does this ten-rupee note say?" The patron replies, "It says that you should sing the song you just sang again, from the beginning." The dancer obliges to the great delight of the benefactor and the rest of the audience.

Later a spectator approaches the stage in a drunken haze, and a scuffle ensues between him and a dancer. There is some misunderstanding about the man's request and a tug of war over his rupee note follows. The furor subsides peacefully, however, when the fellow manages to explain that he wants his favorite song performed by the dancer in seated position—a fairly common request.

In response to another request, an artist sings and dances a number wearing the end of her sari over her head, like a shawl. This is considered to be a very intimate and personal presentation. During her song the girl winks seductively, turns aside shyly, smiles wantonly, and suddenly looks sad—almost in tears. The entire play of emotions is directed only to the man who requested and paid for it.

One song troupe features a fine comic jester who interacts so well with the members of his troupe and the spectators that one of the members of the audience is moved to present him with a stick of candy as a token of appreciation. The actor, a natural-born jester, calmly removes the wrapper, sucks momentarily on the candy, and then sings a duet with one of the female artists. To judge by the interaction, warm audience contact and extra rupees offered as tips, this troupe comes off the best of all the song troupes.

By contrast, the next troupe is a disappointment. It consists of a group of ungainly, unpretty girls, all of whom perform badly and without much enthusiasm. Little money is offered by spectators, and what is given is done out of pity and sympathy.

Just after midnight, the folk-drama troupe makes a powerful entrance, with two *dholki* players beating away furiously and singers chanting in high-pitched voices the opening lines of the play. It is a pseudohistorical drama in traditional style, about a king, his son, and a wicked minister who plots unsuccessfully to do away with the young prince. The production features a melodramatic struggle between the forces of good and evil, some witty and humorous asides, and a little social commentary to update the significance of the drama. An hour later the harsh neon house lights are turned up and the curtain drops heavily to the stage. The forces of good have triumphed.

The audience applauds half-heartedly for a moment, then rises and rushes outdoors to the dark, quiet street with its shuttered tea stalls, restaurants, and musical instrument shops.

Current State

Currently only the wealthy people's theatre troupes can afford to play the major urban theatres, which cater to middle and upper class entertainment tastes. These productions attract the attention of theatre critics and the Marāṭhī intelligentsia, who follow the continuing evolution of *tamāshā* as a durable and by now respectable entertainment form suitable to urban interests. The refinements in music, singing, dance, and drama in the people's theatre troupes have catapulted some artists to fame, and sent others on to greater stardom in Hindi and Marāṭhī films.

Fortunately fears that cinema and television would exploit and subsequently ruin *tamāshā* theatre have not been borne out. If anything, the borrowing of the tradition's vibrant inspiration by the mass media has helped to focus the attention of cultural authorities and artists themselves upon the need to pursue vigorously the efforts begun some years ago to provide training for the perfection of skills and talents.

This message has also gotten across to many of the unsophisticated folk artists, who have now been made conscious of the fact that they represent the well-spring of the *tamāshā* tradition and that they must press government authorities as well as other interested elements of society to help them overcome conditions of poverty and cultural deprivation. Only through improved economic conditions can these less economically privileged artists continue to develop and fulfill their historical functions within rural and proletarian urban society: providing durable entertainments, bringing awareness of new ideas and perceptions of community needs, and recalling the historical and cultural traditions of the past.

In addition to performers in the refined people's theatre and the unsophisticated song troupes, there are small numbers of artists who have found a temporary sense of economic security devoting their talents to development-oriented communication experiments on behalf of both state and central governments.[6] Activity of this kind, modest though it is, has been traced back to the 1950s. There are indications that it is bound to develop and grow, and that much of it will be transposed to the mass media, which commands an impressive outreach to broader sectors of the society. In the process, the possibility remains that the traditional forms will be changed. Indeed this transformation is already noticeable; however, government plan-

[6] Abrams 1974 and Abrams 1975 offer a comprehensive treatment of the use of *tamāshā* troupes for propaganda purposes.

ners are sensitive to such dangers and they have been attempting to exercise care in their dealings with *tamāshā* performers.[7] Fortunately, and despite earlier grandiose plans to expand the government-sponsored use of folk troupes in Maharashtra, only a handful of performers are involved in this kind of work. Therefore, to draw meaningful conclusions from government-assisted folk-media activity would be erroneous.

There is certainly keen awareness within Maharashtra today both of the sociocultural value of *tamāshā* theatre as a relevant and lively form of interpersonal communication, and of the ever-present danger of its disappearance or destruction through neglect or, worse, overzealous experimentation and exploitation. Such awareness offers hope for the survival and further development of the *tamāshā* tradition.

WORKS CITED

Abrams, Tevia. 1975.
"Folk Theatre in Maharashtrian Social Development Programs." *Educational Theatre Journal* 27, 3 (October):395–407.

———. 1974.
"Tamasha: People's Theatre of Maharashtra State, India." Ph.D. diss., Michigan State University.

Das Gupta, Hemenchanath. 1944.
The Indian Stage. Vol. 3. Calcutta: M. K. Das Gupta.

Joshi, V. K. 1961.
Loknatyachi: Parampara (The Tradition of Folk Theatre). Poona: Thokal Prakashan.

Konow, Sten. 1969.
The Indian Drama. Trans. S. N. Ghosal. Calcutta: General Printers and Publishers.

Marathi Natya Prishad. 1961.
The Marathi Theatre: 1843 to 1960. Bombay: Popular Prakashar.

Sathe, Annanabhau. 1957.
"Guidelines for Tamasha." In *Nava Yug*. October.

ADDITIONAL READING

Awashti, Suresh. 1973.
"Dadu Indurikar." *Quarterly Journal of the National Centre for Performing Arts* 2, 4:21–40.

[7] Program planners in both the Song and Drama Division of the Information and Broadcasting Ministry in Delhi and the Publicity Department of the Government of Maharashtra have on numerous occasions issued statements to this effect, most notably during the 1974 New Delhi Seminar/Workshop on the Integrated Use of Folk Media and Mass Media in Family Planning Communication Programmes, which was supported by Unesco and the United Nations Fund for Population Activities.

PART FIVE

DANCE-DRAMAS AND DRAMATIC DANCES

INTRODUCTION

THE TERM DANCE-DRAMA has often been used as a convenient modern label for those Indian performance genres which are neither clearly dance forms nor purely dramatic forms. The English language terms dance and dance-drama are recent classifications developed by urban, Western-educated Indians and Western dancers or scholars of the Indian performing arts. Forms which are considered primarily dance include many diverse styles from every geographical region of India, such as Tamil Nadu's now well-known *bhārata nāṭyam,* a renamed modern recreation of the temple dance tradition of South India; Kerala's lesser-known *Mohiniāṭṭam* (the "dance of the goddess Mohinī"); the *Odissi* (or *Orissi*) dance of Orissa in northeastern coastal India; *Manipuri* dance on the frontier region of eastern Assam in extreme northeastern India; and *kathak,* the primary form of North Indian classical dance associated with the cities of Lucknow in Uttar Pradesh and Jaipur in Rajasthan. Some of these dance forms *(bhārata nāṭyam* and *Odissi)* are known to have originated as devotional temple dances performed by women given in service to a temple (Marglin 1985). The recent revival of these devotional dance genres has reconstituted each dance style and transformed it for performance on the modern dance concert stage. Today, these dance forms are considered "classical"; that is, in their development, they are said to be dependent on the principles and forms of movement first discussed in the *Nāṭyaśāstra.* But as Marglin points out regarding *Odissi,* "The term 'classical' does not really translate any indigenous term. . . . The adjective classical reflects the Western model of the reformers: Indian Classical Dance connotes a status on a par with Western Classical Ballet" (1985, 2). Many genres, like *bhārata nāṭyam, Mohiniāṭṭam,* and *Odissi,* are traditionally performed by women, although in some periods men have been the primary teachers or there have been closely related male styles of dance. Another shared characteristic of all these dance forms is that they are primarily performed by individual dancers with choreography which is either pure dance *(nṛtta)* or interpretative dance *(nṛtya).* Until recently, these dance forms did not usually stage source materials (usually devotional songs) that required multiple performers. For this reason we have chosen to focus here on dance-dramas and dramatic dances, genres which are more overtly dramatic and in which multiple performers play roles enacting either a complete dramatic text or story.

We have chosen to focus on two representative types of Indian performance which are *both* overtly dramatic *and* which give primary or equal emphasis to dance when enacting a scripted drama or dramatic story. Genres which are usually called dance-dramas include those which freely intermingle pure and interpretative choreography with the playing of individual roles enacting the drama or story. With the exception of opening or closing pure dances *(nṛtta)* which are part of the ritual preliminaries pleasing to the gods and which frame the performance, movement and choreography are determined by dramatic context—pure and interpretative dance elements are subsumed within and shaped by the drama *(nāṭya)*. Movement styles and choreography appropriate to each character are set according to each dramatic moment. Movement supports and fills out the playing of roles in the drama.

Like solo dance forms, the major dance-dramas include a variety of genres from nearly every region of India. Genres often labeled dance-dramas by modern scholars and journalists include *yakṣagāna* of Karnataka, *bhāgavata mela* of the Melatur area, *terukkuttu* of Tamil Nadu, *kuchipudi* of Andhra

Terukkuttu entrance dance on an earthen stage in a rural area of Tamil Nadu. (Farley P. Richmond photo)

Pradesh, the *rās līlā* of the Braj region of Uttar Pradesh, and *Kṛṣṇanāṭṭam, kathakaḷi,* and *cavittu nāṭakam* of Kerala. In all these forms stylized movement and solo and group choreography are important modes of dramatic enactment. The primary impulse in the development of many of the early dance-dramas was the popular devotional bhakti movement, discussed in Part Three. Forms such as *rās līlā* and *Kṛṣṇanāṭṭam* have remained primarily devotional performances, where dance is a vehicle for establishing devotional union with Lord Kṛṣṇa. In contrast to the devotional tenor of these two forms, the *terukkuttu* is primarily performed as a ritual propitiation of village deities or as a ritual marker in important rites of passage. While *kathakaḷi* possesses roots both in the devotional *Kṛṣṇanāṭṭam* and in ritual forms of propitiation common in Kerala, it developed under the watchful tutelage of elite patrons and therefore possesses a closer tie to the refinements associated with the "classical" tradition.

Given the variety of contexts within which dance-dramas are performed, the various genres encompass widely varying choreographic traditions and quite different degrees of stylistic refinement. *Kathakaḷi* is usually considered primarily a classical form since it has borrowed much from the earlier Sanskrit temple drama, *kūṭiyāṭṭam,* and possesses a highly varied, often refined, choreography in which virtuosity is expected. From *kūṭiyāṭṭam, kathakaḷi* developed its highly complex and refined codified system of gesture language. Other genres such as *cavittu nāṭakam* of Kerala and *terukkuttu* of Tamil Nadu are stylistically much less codified and exact, and by contrast with the "classical" virtuosity of *kathakaḷi,* are often labeled "folk."

The dance-dramas differ markedly in historical and social respects, each having a unique place in the history of its region. *Kathakaḷi* performers were supported by the landed political and cultural elite of Kerala, who provided sufficient patronage to allow the performers to devote their full attention to their art. In contrast *yakṣagāna* troupes were sponsored by temples. However, during the six-month performance season wealthy landholders sponsor local performances open to the community. Outside of the performance season the performers must have regular jobs to support their families.

One common feature of dance-dramas is that each enacts a scripted text. Since most are based on episodes from the great epic stories, the dance-dramas are closely related to other modes of narrative communication—to storytelling and puppet theatre traditions.[1] In some dance-drama forms like *yakṣagāna,* there appears an onstage narrator/stage manager/chief singer who narrates and sets the context for dramatic scenes, which are enacted by actors playing individual roles who speak either scripted or improvised dia-

[1] In both *kathakaḷi* and *yakṣagāna,* puppet theatre companies developed which enact complete dramas as close to the dance-drama style as is possible with puppets.

Mysore rod puppet demonstrated by an urban expert. (Farley P. Richmond photo)

logue. A peculiar historical characteristic of *kathakaḷi* which differentiates it from the other textually-based dance-dramas is that the lines a character "speaks" are not delivered by the actors or dancers themselves. The actors "speak" only with their hands, their "lines" (in first person) being sung by the onstage vocalists. One reason often suggested for this historical innovation has been that giving lines to vocalists freed the actor-dancer to integrate more dance movement and gesture language into playing dramatic roles, thus making dance movement more central for actors than in other genres.

Dance is central to the entire dramatic enactment, and involves (1) elaborate forms of stylized entry (often with imaginative use of a hand-held curtain) that immediately identify a character and set the appropriate mood for the character type; (2) stylized forms of gait, walk, and general stage deportment considered appropriate for a particular character type; (3) choreographic patterns by which characters move about the stage; (4) choreo-

Aṇkīya nāṭ actor illustrates the gesture for "lotus." (Farley P. Richmond photo)

graphic passages of varying length, which literally punctuate or accentuate a dramatic moment, concluding or highlighting a scene; and (5) group choreography used for enacting high points of action, most spectacularly battle scenes.

From among these various dance-drama forms, we will focus on the well-known *kathakaḷi. Kathakaḷi* is a dance-drama which calls upon the performer to be both a virtuosic and inventive dancer *and* actor. The *kathakaḷi* performer must have the ability to enact and sustain a role through an all-night performance. He must be able to suffuse that role with creativity under the watchful eyes of an educated, critical audience of patron connoisseurs. Simultaneously he must be a consummate dancer who transforms set choreographic patterns into evocative statements colored by the dramatic role and context of the story.

The second form on which we will focus is *chau,* a generic term for three closely related, yet highly individualized forms of performance found in the Bihar, West Bengal, and Orissa triangle of northeastern India. While *chau* has usually been discussed as a "dance-drama," like the other genres above, it is best characterized as a "dramatic dance" (Awasthi 1983, 76), since it neither possesses an inherited dramatic text nor sustains lengthy performances of its stories. The *chau* forms clearly originated in pre-Hindu tribal dance of the region, and only later were transformed into miniature dramatic dances, many of which enact stories from the great Hindu epics. One form of *chau,* the Seraikella, bases at least some of its recent choreography on abstract themes and ideas. While clearly nonscripted dance forms, *chau* genres are highly dramatic, and the organizational, choreographic impetus is a dramatic scene. In *chau* performances individual dancers take a different role in each of the mini dance-dramas staged as part of a composite performance. *Chau* performances emphasize movement and dance. They do not require their performance to "play a character" in a long, sustained, scripted drama. With its roots in tribal culture, the styles and vocabularies of movement in the three *chau* forms are noticeably different from those whose origins lie in the *Nāṭyaśāstra.*

Phillip B. Zarrilli

WORKS CITED

Awasthi, Suresh. 1983.
"Traditional Dance-Drama in India: An Overview." In *Dance and Music in South Asian Drama.* Tokyo: The Japan Foundation.

Marglin, Frederique Apffel. 1985.
Wives of the God-King: The Rituals of the Devadasis of Puri. Delhi: Oxford University Press.

ADDITIONAL READING

Ashton, Martha Bush. 1974.
"Of Music, Bells and Rhythmic Feet: The Dance of Yaksagana." *Anima* 1, 1: 40–55.

———. 1975.
"The Rituals of Yaksagana Badagatittu Bayalata." *Journal of South Asian Literature* 10, 2–4:249–274.

———, and Bruce Christie. 1977.
Yaksagana: A Dance Drama of India. New Delhi: Abhinav Publications.

Balasaraswati, T. 1973.
"Music and the Dance." *Quarterly Journal of the National Centre for the Performing Arts* 2, 4:41–45.

———. 1976.
"Bharata Natyam." *Quarterly Journal of the National Centre for the Performing Arts* 5, 4:1–8.

Bhavnani, Enakshi. 1967.
The Dance of India. Bombay: D. S. Taraporewala Sons.

Bowers, Faubion. 1967.
The Dance of India. New York: AMS Press.

Devi, Ragini. 1972.
Dance Dialects of India. Delhi: Vikas Publications.

De Zoete, Beryl. 1953.
The Other Mind: Dance and Life in South India. London: Victor Gollancz.

Jones, Betty True. 1972.
"Mohiniyattam: A Dance Tradition of Kerala, South India." *CORD Dance Research Monograph One,* 7–27.

Karanth, K. Shivarama. 1974.
Yaksagana. Mysore: Institute of Kannada Studies, University of Mysore.

Khokar, M. 1979.
Traditions of Indian Classical Dance. Delhi: Clarion Books.

Kothari, Sunil. 1974.
"Kathak: North Indian Dance." *Asia Society Monographs on Music, Dance, and Theater.* New York: Asia Society.

Naidu, M. A. 1975.
Kuchipudi Classical Dance. Hyderabad: Andhra Pradesh Sangeeta Nataka Akademi.

Patnaik, Dhirendranath. 1971.
Odissi Dance. Bhubaneswar, Orissa: Sangeet Natak Akademi.

Rao, Vissa Appa. 1959.
"Kuchipudi School of Dancing." *Sangeet Natak Akademi Bulletin* 11–12:1–8.

Sathyanarayana, R. 1969.
Bharatanatya: A Critical Study. Mysore: Varalakshmi Academies of Fine Arts.

Vatsyayan, Kapila. 1956.
"Kathak." *Journal of the Madras Music Academy* 27:74–88.

———. 1974.
Indian Classical Dance. New Delhi: Publications Division, Ministry of Information and Broadcasting.

Chapter Ten

KATHAKAḶI

Phillip B. Zarrilli

Kathakaḷi DANCE-DRAMA IS PERHAPS THE BEST KNOWN of India's "classically" influenced performance genres. More has been written about *kathakaḷi* and more Western audiences have had opportunities to see *kathakaḷi* than any other style of Indian performance. In part, *kathakaḷi*'s international popularity comes from its exuberant, heroic, *tāṇḍava* style, which colors *kathakaḷi*'s blending of dance, acting, and music. This characteristic vigorous style has been joined with a language of hand gestures and facial expressions, as well as with colorful costuming and makeup, to create larger than life characters for the *kathakaḷi* stage. These characters are selected from the host of heroes, heroines, demons, gods, sages, and common folk who are found in India's great epics. The name *kathakaḷi* literally means "story play" and refers to the dramatization of stories drawn by playwright-composers from the epics—first the *Rāmāyaṇa,* then the *Mahābhārata,* and later from the *Bhāgavata Purāṇa.*

Kathakaḷi was born in the seventeenth century in Kerala (the same area where *kūṭiyāṭṭam, teyyam, Ayyappan tiyatta,* and *Kṛṣṇanāṭṭam* are found), from a confluence of historical and cultural circumstances. *Kathakaḷi* has always been both a popular and accessible form of theatre open to village communities, as well as a virtuosic genre appealing to connoisseurs and patrons of the art—those educated in the most specific nuances of the form. Members of the higher castes in Kerala were the traditional patrons, until the early twentieth century. Since the 1920s and 1930s troupes have been subsidized by a variety of sources, including both private industries and the government.

While traditionally *kathakaḷi* performances are staged outdoors in a family compound or near a temple, in recent years performances have been given on Western-style proscenium stages in major cities. *Kathakaḷi* performers in the past were drawn from one of the higher local Hindu castes, but again, recent changes have opened training to a wider spectrum of young students.

Closing scene of the *kathakaḷi* play *The Killing of Bali (Bali Vadham)*. Bali, left, has been shot by Rāma's arrow. Tara, his wife, stands to the left. Angada, his son (wearing the monkey mask), weeps at his side. His brother Sugrīva, at right, repents and confesses his wrongdoings and asks Rāma to care for Tara and Angada. (Phillip B. Zarrilli photo)

While *kathakaḷi* dance-drama has maintained continuity and integrity in its aesthetic and performance style over the years, it has always been in a process of constant change. The forces of change and modernization in recent years have brought increasingly diverse pressures on *kathakaḷi*. Some innovators have attempted to update and change *kathakaḷi* to meet what they feel are styles better suited to the modern world, while others have attempted to preserve the most traditional aspects of the form and to allow as little change as possible.

In this chapter, we will survey the most important aspects of *kathakaḷi* dance-drama, from the rigorous training of its actors through the contemporary situation in which *kathakaḷi* exists today.

Origins

By the seventeenth century, Kerala's performance tradition included the well-established Sanskrit temple drama, *kūṭiyāṭṭam,* as well as a wide variety of ritual performances *(Ayyappan tiyatta, mudiyettu,* and *teyyam),* and the newly established *Kṛṣṇanāṭṭam* devotional dance-drama. The exact process by which elements of classical, ritual, and devotional performances were melded into a new form of dance-drama is difficult to determine. What follows is a reconstruction of the birth of *kathakaḷi* based on what is part legend and part historical fact.

The most important and immediate ancestor of *kathakaḷi* dance-drama was probably *Kṛṣṇanāṭṭam.* Under the patronage of the ruler of Calicut, *Kṛṣṇanāṭṭam* developed as a devotional dance-drama enacting a cycle of eight plays based on the life of Lord Kṛṣṇa. A widely circulated legend in Kerala offers one plausible explanation for the early development of what eventually became known as *kathakaḷi.* The story relates that

> soon after its (*Kṛṣṇanāṭṭam*'s) debut on the stage, Kottarakara Thampuran (Vira Kerala Varma) . . . made a request to the Zamorin to depute his *Kṛṣṇanāṭṭam* troupe to Kottarakara to give a few performances. For certain considerations—maybe political, maybe personal—the Zamorin turned down this request and Thampuran, in a state of offended pride, decided to compose a new art form by himself, more or less on the same model. The result was the emergence of *Rāmanāṭṭam,* which later came to be known as *kathakaḷi.*

This local legend reflects the type of petty jealousies prevalent in medieval Kerala among the various rulers of the many principalities dotting the fractured political landscape of the period. It is certainly possible that the intrigues, bickering, and hostility so much a part of political life of the fifteenth through the eighteenth centuries had their counterpart in cultural life. We may thus assume that this story serves as the basis for the beginning of *kathakaḷi.* Although scholars disagree, the *Rāmanāṭṭam* plays were probably composed toward the close of the seventeenth century, somewhere between 1660–1680.

These *Rāmanāṭṭam* plays were a cycle of eight plays based on the *Rāmāyaṇa,* reflecting the fact that they were probably modeled on *Kṛṣṇanāṭṭam*'s eight play cycle. The change in name to *kathakaḷi* came later, as *Rāmanāṭṭam* expanded to include other plays outside of the *Rāmāyaṇa* and as the dance-drama evolved artistically and aesthetically. In part the growth of *kathakaḷi* must have been the result of competition among Kerala's chieftains, who vied with one another in developing the art.

The devotional, largely third-person Sanskrit of *Kṛṣṇanāṭṭam* gave way in the *Rāmāyaṇa* plays to a literature which contained less third-person narrative and more first-person dialogue in the local language. Significant changes occurred during the formative years of *kathakaḷi*'s development. In *Kṛṣṇanāṭṭam* the emphasis upon dance lessened the attention given to facial expression and hand gesture. *Kathakaḷi,* however, also came to incorporate some of the more virtuosic dramatic techniques of *kūṭiyāṭṭam,* including its emphasis on face, hand, and eye gestures.

Other innovations followed later. The speaking or singing of the text became divorced from the acting. While in *Kṛṣṇanāṭṭam* the actors deliver their own lines, *kathakaḷi* developed its distinctive energetic choreographic style, where the entire text is given to the vocalists, freeing the actor-dancers for the vigorous choreography and complex gestural interpretation of the script. Further changes occurred in costuming and makeup. In *Kṛṣṇanāṭṭam* masks had been used for characters like Brahmā, Narakāsura, Murāsura, and Yama. In *kathakaḷi* all but a few of the characters made use of elaborate facial makeup similar to that used in *kūṭiyāṭṭam*. The emergence of a wider range of performance techniques, the consolidation of *kathakaḷi*'s vigorous, heroic, strong style, and the standardization of costuming all combined to make *kathakaḷi* a highly popular yet virtuosic genre by the early to mid-seventeenth century.

Training

> I always used to be in the greenroom watching. It was so colorful—the costumes and the makeup . . . that was in my village where they would have occasional *kathakaḷi* performances. I was fascinated by this even from an early age. . . . I thought it was something great. I was content just to sit there and watch, even though I couldn't really understand anything. Then I knew I wanted to become a *kathakaḷi* actor.

For any child the first fascination of *kathakaḷi* is its color and the exciting synthesis of movement, light, and sound which creates a special world. At any *kathakaḷi* performance children crowd around the greenroom, watching the makeup process. On the stage itself Hanumān (the monkey god) or Jāṭayu (the bird) with their stylized, yet so mimetically enlivened embodiments of a man-monkey, or man-bird, capture the child's imagination and attention for a remarkable length of time.

Many children may have that same thought—the desire to become a *kathakaḷi* actor—but only a handful will be selected to enter training. Of those selected, few will become well-known master actors. Of those selected, none will fully realize the rigors of the path set before him. It is a long and arduous path because there are no shortcuts to perfecting a technique which calls for intricate and independent movement of muscles which have never been asked to work in this particular way before. It will take time—at least six, eight, or ten years to conquer the basics. It will take even more time—an entire lifetime—to become a master. With good reason actors generally state that the individual only reaches his prime as a performer at the age of forty. Beyond this age one sees the seasoned, mature, virtuosic actors.

To reach that goal—to become a master—the student must pass through a process which gradually reshapes his body and perfects techniques so that each movement, each rhythmic pattern, becomes a part of his body-consciousness, part of his onstage language of creation and expression.

In the past, *kathakaḷi* actors were trained in the guru-disciple system. Students were usually from a performer's extended family, and once accepted took up residence at the teacher's home. While living with his teacher the student trained and fulfilled any task the teacher might ask of him.

Twentieth-century economic pressures and a breakdown in the old patronage structure has brought the creation of contemporary schools. While an occasional student may train today under the old system, the vast majority of students train with a specific company or school and receive a small subsidy from either the government or private sources. In the present school context, the traditional bonds between teacher and student are preserved as much as possible.

At some schools students study primarily with one teacher, while at others they pass from one teacher to another with each year of training. At the Margi southern-style *kathakaḷi* school in Trivandrum, there is one regular junior teacher. He has responsibility for the day to day training of the students. Senior students who have been studying five to six years help teach first and second year students. They also have their own special studies at advanced levels. Four times per month the senior teacher (in 1980 Kalamandalam Krishnan Nair) comes to the school. He is a well-known and respected actor and training under him even four times per month gives the students additional status in the outside performance world.

In contrast at the Kerala Kalamandalam, there are specific teachers for each year of training. Teachers concentrate on first year, intermediate level, or advanced and postgraduate students. This specialization is a relatively recent development. The most senior and well-known actor-teachers take the highest level students.

In addition to full-time training for the professional, there are students within Kerala and throughout India, Western Europe, and the United States who study as "part-time" students. In Kerala today government-supported public schools occasionally hire actors to teach after-school cultural enrichment courses in acting or drumming. These students study thirty minutes to one hour per day, from one to three days per week. They occasionally perform for amateur school programs or continue their training for personal satisfaction. Students include both males and females.

Selection of the Full-Time Actor Today

In recognition of the importance of at least minimal public education, training today begins at the age of twelve to fourteen instead of seven. The "ideal" age to begin is while the young boy's body is still flexible and easily adapted to the rigorous physical training which reshapes the body to fit the aesthetic form.

Today's schools give public notice of "auditions" to fill their quota of first year students. At major institutions receiving at least a partial government subsidy, formal applications are reviewed by a committee consisting of teachers, members of the governing board, and administrative personnel. Students are then called for interviews and auditions. Major criteria for selection include:

(1) *Physical Features:* Is the student's body flexible and healthy? How good are his facial features? Will these features be suited to a particular role or character type?
(2) *Sense of Rhythm:* Does the student have an inherent sense of rhythm? (The student may be asked to keep time to various rhythmic patterns to test his abilities.)
(3) *Sincerity of the Student:* Does the student have a genuine desire to become a *kathakaḷi* actor?

Three innate requirements are looked for: possession of a good physique, facial structure, and natural sense of rhythm. Without these basic qualities there is little chance for a boy to become a *kathakaḷi* student. Teachers must recognize during the short interview period those students who possess these innate qualities as well as the desire to learn. As one teacher stated, "In trying to teach rhythm to a student, all we can do is improve upon his basic sense of rhythm. If it's not there in the first place, then there's little hope for the student ever achieving a good sense of keeping rhythm in performance, even with all the years of training."

Courses and Techniques of Training

Formal full-time training begins with the onset of the cool monsoon season in June. This is considered the ideal season for vigorous physical conditioning. This idea is derived from its martial precursor and ultimately from the Ayurveda, the indigenous medical system, which holds that vigorous exercise is only to be taken in the appropriate cool season, otherwise an imbalance in the three bodily humors will result and illness will be likely.

The first year student begins by giving symbolic gifts to his teacher—usually betel leaves, areca nuts, and a few coins. In return, the teacher presents the student with the loin cloth in which he will train, and utters a prayer and blessing for the student. These simple first-day rituals illustrate the reverence and dedication of the student for his teacher and of the teacher for his own teachers.

The largely ceremonial opening of training begins a yearly cycle which continues for at least six years of formal training in most schools. Today's training may be divided into four basic elements (see accompanying chart):

(1) yearly preliminary body preparation;
(2) basic training (first year);
(3) intermediate training (second and third years);
(4) advanced training (fourth through sixth years and postgraduates).

With the onset of the monsoons all students, whether beginning or advanced, begin the training season by undergoing preliminary body preparation. This preliminary body preparation is derived from martial techniques and is designed to render the body supple, flexible, and controlled through the repetition of a series of vigorous physical exercises joined with complete body massage. The yearly repetition of these exercises prepares the student each season for the rigorous course to be followed over the next ten months and, through time, literally reshapes his body to fit *kathakaḷi*'s basic physical mould. It is equally important for the first year beginner and the advanced student, who needs this refresher course to increase his body flexibility and to further embody the correct psychophysical forms.

The rigorous early morning exercise and massage continues throughout the monsoon season from June through August. It lasts approximately two to three hours and is confined to the cool predawn period of the day. Basic exercises include a series of leg exercises, body circles, body control exercises, kicks, jumps, and *kathakaḷi*'s basic footwork patterns. The student's completely oiled body moves through the vigorous workout, culminating in a full body massage where the teacher literally "walks" on his body with his feet. The difficult training places primary emphasis on mastery of the body. Once the body is prepared, techniques of expression are taught through progressively more difficult stages. With each year of training the student improves his mastery over details of physical expression, and increases precision of movement, body suppleness, grace, and flexibility. All this is accomplished through repetitious and exact imitation of the teacher.

In addition to learning the beginning body preparation exercises and undergoing massage, the first year student concentrates on the rudiments of techniques in gesture, choreography, dance, steps, and rhythm, learning all the basic skills needed to perform *kathakaḷi*. Techniques are broken down into their most minute segments, introduced as independent sets of exercises, performed repetitiously and in direct mimicry of the teacher. To perform the particular hand or facial gestures needed to portray a character, the student first masters independent sets of muscles: cheeks, eyelids, eyebrows, fingers, and so on.

There are exercises for the eyes performed in nine directions and at three

Year	Preliminary Body Preparation (During Monsoon Season)	Early Morning Class (non-Monsoon period)	Morning Class	Afternoon or Evening Class
One	Physical training: jumps body control exercises footwork patterns massage post-massage exercises Eye training (not always done today)	Eye exercises Footwork patterns Parts of sections of *kalāśams* or pure dance patterns	(Continue learning physical exercises in first weeks of training) *Curipp:* body circles *Tōṭayam:* pure dance *Puṛappāṭu:* pure dance *Iḷakiyāṭṭam:* eight ways of showing *mudrās* putting together simple *mudrās* with choreography for the first time Study of minor roles	*Mudrās:* hand gestures *Rasābhinaya:* facial gestures Exercises for hands, wrists, and upper body; arm exercises *Tāla:* rhythm patterns learned and repeated Learning *mudrās* in story context Beginning study of texts
Two and Three	Same as above	Eye exercises *Kalāśams* Footwork patterns Pure dance sequences such as sari or women's dance	Repeat above for the first few months as review Learning minor roles (Music often added for first time here)	As above, but learning more texts and more roles with increasing complexity (By end of third year should have learned all minor roles in the syllabus)
Advanced	Same as above	Eye exercises Pure dance sequences such as *kēki* dance and *pada puṛappāṭu* or choreography for battles	Story practice Minor and major roles rehearsed with musicians	Review morning mistakes *Mudrās* learned for text in rehearsal Some discussion of stories, characters, sources, etc.

Stages of training for *kathakaḷi* actors.

Preliminary *kathakaḷi* training exercises: A complete back bend helps to develop an arch in the small of the back. Boys circle the body around and around to develop fluidity necessary for performance. (Phillip B. Zarrilli photo)

different speeds, for the hands and wrists, for single hand gestures, and for all facial muscles (cheeks, lips, eyebrows, eyelids). These independent exercises are gradually combined in more advanced exercises, including, for example, a turning of the body accompanied by face and hand gestures. The student also learns combinations of hand gestures and through them how gestures create meaning. Facial gestures are also introduced. Students combine the use of specific facial muscles with eye movements in order to embody emotional states and convey meanings. Students also begin to learn

Kalamandalam Gopi, well-known *kathakaḷi* actor, demonstrates "tiger," incorporating appropriate gestures and eye and facial expressions. (Niels Roed Sorensen photo)

basic rhythmic sequences and the four footwork patterns. Footwork patterns are taught in each rhythmic pattern, and are performed at three basic speeds: slow, medium or doubled tempo, and fast or quadrupled tempo.

Face and hand gestures are the bases of the "actor's art," the ability to embody moods and convey meanings in a dramatic context. Rhythmic patterns, footwork, and choreography are the bases of the "dancer's art," embodying a character's moods and conveying meaning via the rhythm and flow of dances, which elaborate on or illustrate the dramatic context.

The combination of these elements eventually create the consummate *kathakaḷi* performer. Even in the first year of training the student begins to combine these at first independent pieces. Such composite training comes by learning preliminary dances. The student performs a piece of set choreography with no dramatic context, requiring use of various rhythmic patterns, speeds, footwork patterns, and hand and facial gestures.

The first year student may actually perform a preliminary dance during his final months of first year training. Suddenly the novice is thrust onstage, in costume and makeup for the first time. The bulk of the costumes, the fear of disturbing the facial makeup, the sweat of his body and face on a warm night, all combine for what is often an initially harrowing performance experience.

Finally the first year student begins to learn a few simple minor roles. This opportunity requires the student to put together his basic skills within the theatrical context of a story.

Kathakaḷi students learn texts by memorizing the entire play. Each student must master every role in each play which is part of his particular school's or teacher's syllabus. The syllabus at the Kerala Kalamandalam consists of eighteen plays covered during the regular six year acting course. These eighteen plays are only about one half of the active repertory. The current syllabus of any school introduces the student to the full range of character types and choreography demanded for the performance of any play. The individual actor, by the end of his course of study, should be able to take up any role, even if he has not directly been taught a particular role or play.

The student's "typical" day is long:

Early Morning Class: approximately 5:00 A.M. to 7:30 A.M.
Morning Class: approximately 8:30 to noon
Afternoon or Evening Class: either 3:30 P.M. to 5:30 P.M. or early evening

The older student playing Hanumān demonstrates the flexibility characteristic of trained *kathakaḷi* actors. (Phillip B. Zarrilli photo)

During the monsoon season the early morning class is when preliminary body preparation and eye exercises are practiced. For advanced students, it is a time for repetition of pure dance patterns and choreography. The major morning class is usually devoted to practice of roles from specific texts, while the afternoon or evening class is devoted to sitting quietly, reviewing rhythmic patterns, texts, hand and facial gestures, and so on.

During the second and third years, the intermediate student learns additional minor characters, texts, and dramatic contexts in which to apply his basic skills. By the end of the third year, the student usually has learned all the minor roles in the syllabus.

Advanced training is the culmination of the formal process. Major and minor roles are rehearsed with musical accompaniment, as the teacher leads students through an entire story and all roles in a play.

During the intermediate and advanced years, students have a variety of opportunities to perform with their company. Intermediate students usually perform a preliminary dance or minor roles. Senior and postgraduate students play intermediate roles.

Plays

The plays in the *kathakaḷi* repertory were traditionally written or composed by members of the highest castes. The texts are in the regional language, Malayalam, but contain a high proportion of Sanskrit and therefore are difficult for many in the audience to understand. Texts include much poetic imagery, which gives the actor scope for interpretation. For example, in *Naḷa Caritam* by Unnayi Warrier, Naḷa is in a flower garden pondering his love for Damayanti and their separation:

> This is the headquarters of my
> powerful foe Madana (the god of love): the
> trees on the banks of the lake are the tents,
> the flowers his arsenal, the songs of
> the birds (Koil) his bugle and the scent-laden
> sephyr, his warriors; this is indeed a dread-
> raising place for separation-sufferers. (1977, 71)

Such passages are characteristic of *kathakaḷi* love scenes and give the actor scope for demonstrating his virtuosic mimetic, emotive, and expressive abilities.

The two most basic textual units used by the playwright in constructing his play are the *śloka* and the *pada*. As used in the context of *kathakaḷi* plays, *śloka* are verse forms, usually written in the third person, that narrate what happens in the dialogue portion of the play. They are composed in particular metrical patterns and set the context for the "action" of dialogue scenes. *Pada* are used to create the "dialogue" portions of the play. They are usually written in the first person, as if the actor (who never speaks) were actually speaking the lines.

Since both narrative and dialogue portions of a text are sung by the onstage vocalists, the *kathakaḷi* playwright must also be a composer. Original texts indicate the specific melodic mode and rhythmic pattern in which each portion of the text should be sung. Melodic mode, rhythmic pattern, and speed of performance are selected according to what is appropriate to the dramatic context and mood.

Most of the plays in today's repertory were written by the close of the nineteenth century. Most playwrights authored only one or two *kathakaḷi* texts, and only five authors wrote more than two plays. Unnayi Warrier is hailed by connoisseurs as the most expressive author. He created a cycle of four plays, performed on four different nights, based on the love story of Naḷa and Damayanti.[1] Warrier's *Naḷa Caritam* is considered by most exponents the highest gem of literary expression in the repertory, and the role of Naḷa is considered by most present-day actors as the most complex and difficult of all *kathakaḷi* roles. *Naḷa Caritam,* like all traditional plays, is based on one of the epics, the *Mahābhārata.*

In recent years, new plays have been written and there have been several nonepic stories dramatized and performed on the *kathakaḷi* stage, including a Christian play based on the Bible, a Muslim play, and even an adaptation of Goethe's *Faust.* These experiments have usually had only one performance.

Of greater importance are what might be called "composite" plays. As *kathakaḷi* troupes have reached a wider audience in the past twenty to thirty years, composite plays enacting an entire epic have been constructed. For example, during the late 1960s the Kerala Kalamandalam constructed a composite *Mahābhārata* play by taking selected scenes from the traditional repertory and joining them together. This composite play has a great deal more action than a series of single plays that concentrate a full night on a specific episode of an epic. Composite plays provide a vast panorama of character types, relatively short action-packed scenes, and less of the leisurely unfolding of serial plays. Such plays are more accessible to non-Kerala audiences in Indian urban areas or on the international tour circuit.

Performance Space and Context

Today the *kathakaḷi* world is a multifaceted one, with performances held in many places, including the traditional outdoor setting within a family com-

[1] For a complete translation see Warrier 1977.

pound, a village temple setting, a stage in a large city, or even a temporary outdoor stage on the beach in Los Angeles, California. The places where *kathakaḷi* is performed have multiplied with the revival of interest in *kathakaḷi* and the spread of interest outside of its place of origin.

Traditional outdoor performances are usually held within a compound of a family house or just outside a temple compound. In both cases, the outdoor stage space is the same. A simple rectangular space approximately twenty to thirty feet square is cleared on the ground. Four poles are inserted at each corner of the rectangle. Over and behind the poles long pieces of cloth are spread to create a defined acting area. The audience gathers on three sides, although the largest concentration is directly in front of the stage space. Women traditionally sit to house right and men to house left. Around the outer periphery of the performance area vendors set up tea stalls or offer other items for sale. The patrons, guests of honor, and connoisseurs sit closest to the stage.

The atmosphere of the traditional performance is relaxed and festive. The tea stalls usually carry on a bustling activity through the night. Some of the audience remain through an entire performance, while others leave early if they work the next day. If audience members become tired, they simply stretch out, take a nap, and perhaps have a friend awaken them if they wish to see a scene they especially enjoy. Children are always present during the long makeup period prior to the beginning of a performance and usually stay awake through the opening scenes of the evening. Many children eventually fall asleep but awake for the big battle scene as dawn breaks.

Kathakaḷi performances in villages are most often sponsored by temples as one part of their annual festival. Temple performances are paid for by the temple committee. Circulars announcing the festival, as well as the *kathakaḷi* performance(s), are distributed several days before the event. Such performances are often a high point of the celebrations and as many as a thousand may turn out for the all-night performance.

One unique temple context for *kathakaḷi* is the Śrī Vallabha Temple in Tiruvalla, Kerala. At this particular temple, a devotee may commission a *kathakaḷi* performance as an offering to the deities of the temple. The cost for a performance runs between $83 and $100 (Rs. 1,000–1,200)—an extremely expensive offering within the means of only the most wealthy devotees. In this context *kathakaḷi* serves a function similar to that of *Kṛṣṇanāṭṭam,* given as a regular offering at Guruvāyur Temple.

In more recent years, *kathakaḷi* has appeared on the regional stages in Kerala's major urban areas. As cities have grown in Kerala, clubs have been organized of traditional patrons and connoisseurs of the art. These clubs usually sponsor a monthly *kathakaḷi* or, occasionally, a *kūṭiyāṭṭam*. Most of the larger cities have regional proscenium theatres used by local modern drama groups. As multipurpose modern stages, the playing space is large compared to the traditional outdoor stage space. Most often the background is an upstage neutral colored curtain on which the club's banner is hung to indicate sponsorship of the event.

The relatively large playing space and the general illumination from electric lights spreads out the acting area, especially for entrances and exits. While the traditional illumination for an outdoor performance was the centrally placed large brass oil lamp, even outdoor performances now use neon tubes or electric lights.

At the home of the Kerala Kalamandalam, the Kerala state arts school, a recently completed theatre represents a contemporary attempt at combining the architectural principles outlined in the *Nāṭyaśāstra* with Kerala's traditional style of theatre architecture. As seen in chapter 3 above, *kūṭiyāṭṭam* is still performed on *kūttampalam* stages in Kerala temple compounds. The designers and architects of the new Kalamandalam stage sought to meld classical principles with the regional style. The result is a graceful structure in which many performances of *kathakaḷi* (and occasionally *kūṭiyāṭṭam*) are given today.

A final performance context deserves mention in today's changing world. Most foreigners who travel to Kerala know about *kathakaḷi* and are often interested in seeing at least one performance. In Ernakulam, Kerala, one of the major tourist centers of the state, *kathakaḷi* performances are given six nights each week, all year around, catering especially to foreign and Indian tourists. Performances are given each evening at seven, under a thatched shed. A small raised stage is used for performances, which last approximately one and one half to two hours and consist of an introductory lecture followed by brief selections from a *kathakaḷi* play. Intended solely for tourists, the performances have little of the aesthetic or artistic merit of full-fledged performances for a traditional audience.

Costumes and Makeup

Kathakaḷi's highly colorful costuming and makeup transform the actor into a wide variety of idealized and archetypal character types. The bulbous shape of the layered skirts of most male characters and the relative enlargement and exaggeration of features through use of elaborate headdresses and facial makeup, when combined with the basic stance, combine to create a wide variety of good and evil epic figures. For the audience educated in *kathakaḷi*'s costuming and makeup codes, the basic character types are easily identifiable. From a character's first entrance the audience knows the general character type and what sort of behavior they can expect from the character.

There are six basic makeup types to account for the wide variety of *kathakaḷi* characters. The colors used in costuming and makeup are bright and bold, ranging from green, red, black, a warm yellow-orange, and white, for basic colors, to more occasional use of yellows for accent. The white of the makeup is usually used for framing either the entire face or as design motifs applied to part of the face through use of rice paste. The thick white border framing the entire face from "ear to ear" and inherited from *kūṭiyāṭṭam* is called the *cuṭṭi.*

The basic costume for male characters consists of a long-sleeved upper jacket tied in the back, a series of heavily starched cloths wrapped around and around the waist to give the character bulk, a midcalf outer skirt or cloth

The makeup process is slow and meticulous. The actor begins his own makeup—here the *karutta tāṭi* or "black beard" type. (Phillip B. Zarrilli photo)

wrapped around and over these undercloths, and finally, decorative accessories, including stylized crowns, bracelets, breast plates, and long pleated cloths worn around the neck. Most crowns and accessories are carved light wooden frames decorated with a variety of materials, including gold-leaf foils, mirrors, and small colored imitation stones. In addition silver is used on the special crown worn by the character Kṛṣṇa. Finally most male characters wear long black wigs which hang down behind their large crowns.

Female costumes are less abstract and bulbous than male costumes. There is slight padding of the hips so that the female figure appears to have the ideal large, rounded hips. Male actors playing female roles wear breastplates to give shape to the upper body, as well as false hair buns attached to the head, around which the head cloth is wrapped to cover the hair. Finally various accessories, such as stylized earrings and bangles, are added to adorn the figure.

Brahmans and holy men make up another general group of characters with its own basic costume. Holy men wear a special crown built of a wooden frame shaped to give the impression of the traditional holy man's look of hair piled up on top of the head. Sandal-paste markings cover the body and, again, various adornments partially cover the holy man's bare chest above his bright yellow body wrappings.

While some details have changed over the years, *kathakaḷi*'s basic makeup and character types have remained constant. Each is described below.

Green (Pacca)

This class of characters includes divine figures, kings, and epic heroic characters such as Rāma. The most refined of any type, a character in this class will be upright, moral, and full of a calm inner poise. The white *cuṭṭi* makeup frame sets off the green base, reflecting the type's basic inner refinement. The stylized mark of Viṣṇu is painted on the forehead with a yellow base and markings of red and black. The soft curving black of the eyebrows and the black underlining of the lower lids extended to the side of the face frame the eyes. The lips are set off in brilliant coral red.

The most characteristic colors of outer garments for the Green characters are the red upper and white lower skirts with orange and black stripes. Two side panels of red carry through the red motif onto the lower body. The entire picture is dignified, with elaborate use of upper body accessories.

While the majority of characters in this class wear a highly jewelled, medium sized crown, a few wear a special kind of vase-shaped crown, decorated with silver, and with a short tuft of peacock feathers on top. This special crown is worn by Kṛṣṇa, Rāma, and Lakṣmāṇa.

Kṛṣṇa and others wearing the silvered crown are most often costumed in

Pacca makeup for Rāma is depicted here. (Phillip B. Zarrilli photo)

different colors. Most usual for Kṛṣṇa is an upper garment of blue (the color traditionally associated with Kṛṣṇa) and a skirt of bright mustard-yellow. Accessories are identical to those of other Green characters.

Knife (katti)

These characters are arrogant and evil, yet they have some redeeming qualities, usually a streak of nobility in their blood. They wear the same *cuṭṭi* or face frame as the Green characters, as well as the same size and shape crown. The makeup base is green, indicating that they too are high born, but their arrogance and evil are illustrated through an upturned red moustache framed by white rice paste. This same motif is carried through by a red pattern above the eyes and eyebrows, again sharply lined and set off by white rice-paste frame. The final indication of their evil nature are two protrusions on the face, white bulbs attached to the nose and forehead. While the Knife character's makeup illustrates his evil nature, his costume is identical to that of the heroic Green.

Beard (tāṭi)

The identifying characteristic of characters in this class are the beards that all wear. The trimmed beards are set in the colors appropriate to the three different subdivisions of this class.

White Beard (veḷḷa tāṭi)

White Beards represent a higher, divine type of being. Hanumān, the monkey king, is the main character in this group. A monkey face is suggested by the red, white, and black patterns of the delicate design. When the face is in action, the slightest gesture is accentuated, especially the cheeks and eyes, perhaps the most distinguishing features of a monkey's expressive face. The small patch of green on Hanumān's nose illustrates his pious and virtuous nature. But most easily identifiable are his white beard and furry white coat matched by his wide-brimmed headdress. Hanumān's lower costume and accessories are very similar to the heroic Green characters, with the addition of chest binders of gold.

Red Beard (cukanna tāṭi)

Red Beard characters are extremely evil, vicious, and vile. The red beard frames the neck while the base makeup is a matching brilliant red. The eyes are encased in black and framed by a white double moustache which extends up to the ears. Black lips set off a ferocious mouth, while the nose and forehead knobs are even larger than those of the Knife characters. Perhaps the most distinguishing characteristic of the Red Beards are their huge crowns. While the basic shape and decoration is similar to that of Green and Knife crowns, the Red Beard crown is much larger and framed with red on the outside border. While the colors and accessories are similar to the Green type, the upper garment is a heavier, furry material indicating the grosser nature of this class.

Black Beard (kaṛutta tāṭi)

These Black Beards are equally as evil as the Red Beards. In addition they are usually schemers. The makeup is very close to that of the Red Beard except that the lower part of the face is black instead of red and the face is framed by a black beard matched by a black upper shirt and contrasted with a blue lower skirt. An unusual bucket-shaped headdress is another identifying feature, as is the "flower" on the nose of such characters. These are primitive beings often associated with the forest.

Black (kari)

In this class are female demons, such as Surpanakha. Similar to the Black Beards, these demons also are dressed almost exclusively in black and wear the bucket-shaped headdress, but then they add unusual touches such as comic false breasts. Their jet-black faces are dotted red and white. These are the grossest and most grotesque of the *kathakaḷi* characters.

Shining (minukku)

This is a special class in which are included characters who are gentle and have high spiritual qualities. The costumes and makeup are relatively close to real life and are somewhat simpler than other types. Included here are heroines, women servants, and female demons in disguise as beautiful maidens. Also included here are male characters, including messengers, charioteers, sages, holy men, and Brahmans.

The base makeup for all in this class is a warm yellow-orange. The heroine's makeup and costume are a stylization of everyday practice. The holy men wear the typical saffron yellow and special crown. Brahmans, on the other hand, wear a simple cloth over their heads.

Special (tēppu)

The final category is a catch-all class which includes approximately eighteen characters who do not fit conveniently into the usual character types. Here are included the special bird-style makeups and costumes of Garuḍa and Jāṭayu; Haṃsa the swan in *Naḷa Caritam;* the grotesque Bhadrakāli of *Dakṣa Yaga;* and the fantastic man-lion makeup of Narasimha (appearing in *Prahlāda Caritam*).

Masks

In addition to the regular makeup types and the special characters, there are some characters who wear masks or who, in the course of a transformation scene, reappear in a mask. In *Dakṣa Yaga,* Dakṣa at the end of the play is beheaded by Virabhadra and Bhadrakāli. His head is thrown onto the sacrificial fire. Brahmā asks Śiva to forgive Dakṣa his oversight and to return him to life so that the sacrifice may be completed. Śiva agrees and has a goat's head placed on Dakṣa's body to restore his life. This transformation is accomplished by having the actor playing Dakṣa remove his crown and place a carved, wooden goat mask on his face. Once life is restored, Dakṣa prays for forgiveness, which is granted, and the sacrifice is completed.

Performers and Roles

Kathakaḷi makeup creates a broad range of types, from the most refined to the most vulgar and gross. The various makeup and character types may be arranged along such a continuum:

Most Refined
- Green (heroic characters)
- Shining (women, Brahmans)
- Knife (arrogant characters)
- Beards
  - White
  - Red
  - Black
- Black (primitive beings)

Least Refined

The Green roles are the most refined of all. The degree of refinement is reflected not only by a statuesque and symmetrical plastic mask but also by the type and quality of movements the actor playing such a role may exhibit in performance. Green characters are never permitted to make a sound onstage. They are perfectly self-possessed and in control of every action—such is the ideal heroic figure. The actor playing such roles must manifest this ideal of self-control. If he is playing a love scene it must be played with the subtlety and nuance expected of a hero and, therefore, with no trace of lust. If he is going into battle it must be a journey and confrontation characterized by a self-possessed assurance of his role as hero. The upper body, even in the most vigorous moments, must be qualitatively more refined than those of more vulgar characters.

The Shining characters, especially most females and Brahmans or charioteers, are next in degree of refinement. Just as the makeup and costumes are a stylized version of everyday models, so the acting of such roles is characterized by a stylization of typical everyday gestures. For example, when in distress female characters often hold their hands to their chest, one hand over the other, and then reach out in a gesture of supplication—both movements based on a stylization of everyday gestures. Yet the performance of such "everyday" gestures must be refined. For the Shining characters, as for the Green, no sounds are permitted.

The Knife roles are next in degree of refinement. In keeping with their general nature, Knife characters are permitted to make some noises, perhaps best characterized as grunts of approval or disapproval. The actor's movements and physical playing should be more exaggerated than those of the Green. The somewhat "grosser" appetites of a Knife character are reflected in his somewhat more vulgar action.

With the Beard types we move closer and closer to the gross and vulgar end of the spectrum of behavior and role playing. As a White Beard character, Hanumān is a higher type of divine being, who is pious and virtuous. He is permitted to make monkey sounds and, in his improvisatory sections, often mimics to the special delight of children in an audience the actions and movements of a monkey. But his mimed action, like the stylizings of female characters, is a stylization of "everyday" monkey gestures. Hanumān's playful general nature is reflected in the actor's playful attitude, exhibited in his mimicry. Relative to the other Beards, Hanumān is the most refined of this lot of characters and must always reflect a divine aspect as part of his portrayal.

The Red Beards are nearing the gross end of the spectrum. Their makeup is even more exaggerated than that of the Knife characters. Out of the Red Beard's mouth can come protruding fangs at a moment of great fury and rage. And also from his mouth come wild cries of enraged sound, illustrating his evil and vile nature. The large bulbous extensions of the nose and forehead are more exaggerated than on the Knife characters. The huge circular crown accentuates the larger-than-life nature of the Red Beards and adds to their imposing stature during their wild "curtain looks," explained below. The actor playing the Red Beard roles is usually the tallest of the *kathakaḷi* actors, and from him is required some of the most violent and vigorous movement. When he makes his entrance his steps and stamps are extremely vigorous and large—the shock of his movements is often manifest throughout his body, while the more refined movements of a Green character keep his basic posture on a steady base.

When we get to the Black characters, we arrive at those closest to primitive beings—female demons, forest dwellers, and so on. Here the primitive nature of the characters is clearly seen in the emphasis on the gross blackness of the base makeup, overexaggerated breasts, protrusions of fangs, and the fact that such characters often brandish branches of trees, illustrating their association with nature in its primitive and most frightening state. As might be expected, the "pooii, poooiiii" cries of the hunter are a vocalization which capture the primitive nature of this class of characters. The sounds are matched by the most exaggerated movements performed by any *kathakaḷi* characters. Large sweeping movement characterizes the playing of these broadly represented characters.

Properties

The most important stage property in *kathakaḷi* is the hand-held multicolored curtain. Two stage attendants usually hold this front curtain just behind the central brass metal lamp, to conceal character entrances or exits. The curtain is usually made of multicolored rectangular bands, often with an emblem of the company.

Kathakaḷi's simple stage can become a palace or a forest at a moment's notice. Through the text, hand gestures, and physical action visual images are painted for the audience of any setting desired. The only "set piece" to assist the actor is a small square wooden stool. Here the king can sit on his "throne," holding audience and receiving guests. For the monkey-god, Hanumān, the stool may become an extension of his physical presence, as he suddenly shows his "divine" superhuman form for his brother, Bhima. Hanumān hops onto the stool and physicalizes his superhuman size, "growing" before the audience's eyes.

Hand properties are rarely used. A chariot is created through the mimetic action of the actor-dancer as he rhythmically physicalizes the action of the chariot through conventional patterns of movement. The charioteer's whip is mimed as his right wrist displays the laying of the whip onto the chariot's horses while his left hand holds the reins.

Like the whip, many other objects are created mimetically. The most consistantly used hand properties are weapons. Stage weapons include a large mace, bow and arrow, sword, small club, and sword and shield. All these weapons are made of lightweight wood and are painted, usually red and gold.

The other important piece of stage apparatus is an overhead canopy. This colorful canopy is held over the heads of actors during initial entrance tableaux, most often for love scenes.

Stage Conventions

The use of the *kathakaḷi* stage is governed by several important factors. In the past when a large metal oil lamp was the only means of illumination, the center of the stage immediately in front of the lamp received the best light. Characters holding the stage alone concentrate their action at this center stage position.

When two characters are onstage together, the use of the stage is generally governed by the socially accepted preeminence and cleanliness of the right side over the left. On the *kathakaḷi* stage the right side (stage right to the audience's left) is always the side of respect. Normally the character of higher status will be on stage right.

There are a number of different methods used for entering or exiting the stage. Dramatic context, character type, and function within the performance determine which method is used. The first method is direct entrance from upstage right or left without curtain or special effects. A second method is entrance through the audience. These are highly theatrical entrances, usually just before a battle, and accompanied by torches. A third technique involves the of the curtain. In the simplest use of the curtain, it is merely dropped to reveal the character or characters onstage. A more decorative use of the curtain is a partial lowering to give the audience a glimpse of a character about to make a first entry. This is usually used for the heroic character types. An important use of the hand-held curtain is the "curtain look," which is reserved for entrances of partially or totally evil characters. This is a highly vigorous piece of set choreography during which the curtain is manipulated by the actor, moving the curtain back and forth, up and down, until first one part of him, then another is revealed until, finally, there is a full revelation of the figure.

Hanumān (white beard) in the play *Kalyana Saugandhikam.* (Phillip B. Zarilli photo)

Dance

As a dance-drama *kathakaḷi* depends equally on the performer's skills as an actor, able to embody and play characters within each archetypal makeup type, and as a dancer, able to perform the full range of complicated footwork patterns, pure dance endings, and a wide variety of choreographic patterns. *Kathakaḷi*'s basic wide stance places the feet just beyond shoulder width, the knees bent and splayed to the sides, and the upper body a one-frame unit from the hips through the shoulders, centered over the lower, wide frame. The upper body frame should be capable of moving as a unit while the legs operate almost independently, moving through various footwork patterns. The upper torso provides the stable frame from which the arms and hands gesture, literally communicating the text through the gesture language.

Kathakaḷi dance is based on four basic footwork patterns performed at three different speeds. From the basic wide stance, the performer uses the outsides of the feet with the big toe extended and turned upward. The basic curve and bowing of the legs (with the knees splayed out) presents a circular body line reemphasized by the curved foot position.

The most characteristic movement of the body is circular. One of the basic training exercises is a circling of the upper body frame over the low center of the basic stance. Most of the delivery of the gesture language is through movements based on these various fluid circling motions of the upper body.

If the basic body movement is often circular, *kathakaḷi*'s floor patterns alternate between rectangular, circular, and diagonal or straight line patterns. From the beginning *kathakaḷi* actors learn to move through a series of exercises while tracing a basic rectangular pattern on the floor. Characters in dialogue scenes often move in rectangular floor patterns. Circles and diagonals are most characteristic of more vigorous choreography, especially battle scenes. Characters challenge one another across the stage area, charge forward and back toward one another, and finally circle as they lock and engage in stylized combat.

Kathakaḷi choreography includes a set of pure dance endings or patterns that punctuate the performance of the dialogue portions of the text. These pure dance endings are part of the student's basic training and are one of the most characteristic features of *kathakaḷi* performance. When dancing them there is no vocalization. They vary in length and complexity, some taking fifteen to thirty seconds and others lasting substantially longer. They reemphasize the mood of the scene just enacted.

In addition to dance endings there are much longer pieces of set choreography inserted in particular plays. One example of many beautiful pieces of *kathakaḷi* choreography is the "peacock dance" performed as a part of *The Killing of the Demon Narakāsura (Narakāsura Vadham).* In this play the main character, Narakāsura, has been describing to his wife the beauties of the various birds they see before them in a garden. It is a typical *kathakaḷi* love scene between a partially good–partially evil Knife character and his wife. As he points out the "beautiful dances of peacocks," he begins to dance for her these patterns to which he refers. In this piece of choreography, which lasts for fifteen to twenty minutes, the performer playing Narakāsura "becomes" a peacock. He begins to stretch out his wings mimetically, preens and cleans his feathers, and begins to strut and dance about the garden. When the actor completes the "peacock dance" (which is performed while the vocalists sing one portion of the text line over and over again), he returns to where he left off in the performance text and completes his description of the other birds in the garden for his wife.

Kathakaḷi dance consists of both pure dance patterns, like the endings or the opening dances prior to the beginning of a performance, and "dramatic dance." The dramatic dances range from the beautiful, graceful minetic re-creation of a peacock, to vigorous, strong battle choreography. Initiating movement from the low center in the region below the navel, the performer in battle scenes is capable of performing jumping kicks and turns. The wide, bulbous *kathakaḷi* skirt, held out by the starched underskirts, becomes a mass of flying motion and color in these vigorous battle scenes. The dancer takes his weight on his right foot and, gathering himself through his low center, leaps high into the air as the right leg kicks up, raising the skirt in a tremendous *tāṇḍava,* full-body gesture.

The wide variety of moods created by *kathakaḷi* dance and choreography is of course integrally linked with the rhythm, speed, and mood created by the orchestra and vocalists. But the creation of the delicate choreography of a woman's dance is equally as satisfying to an audience as is the turbulent din of a battle.

As a relatively popular dramatic form of Kerala, *kathakaḷi* also has spectacular scenes in which the use of torches, battle choreography, and realistic effect combine to produce striking results. In the staging of battles between the forces of good and the demonic forces of evil, we discover the roots of *kathakaḷi* in the Kerala performance and literary heritage, which gives graphic life to vivid and often bloody epic combats. As described in the introduction to Part Two, some ritual performances enact the victory of the goddess Kāli over the evil demon Darika, by presenting at dawn the killing of Darika in which the demon's abdomen is ripped open and the avenging goddess drinks his blood. She adorns herself with the garlandlike entrails of the demon (Pandeya 1961, 25). Virtually the same scene appears in Kerala's literary heritage before the birth of *kathakaḷi*. Ezhuthachan, the most widely read and influential poet of sixteenth-century Malayalam literature, describes Bhima's slaying of Duryodhana in his abridged regional language version of the *Mahābhārata* epic as follows:

At the conclusion of the play *Pṛahlāda Caritam,* Narasimha (the fourth incarnation of Viṣṇu and a special makeup type) feasts on a demon's entrails. (Phillip B. Zarrilli photo)

He stood astride and grabbed his feet
and tramped on them, and then firmly
mounted himself on him, and when
unnumbered devas and men looked on
he took his sword and split his breast
and with his nails did break his bones
and crushed and pulverised them to naught
and guzzled the hot red gushing blood
which like a mighty torrent rose,
and roared, and lying prone on him
filled his mouth with all that blood
that surged again like rising floods
and pulling out his entrails decked
his neck in them as with garlands

> and stamped and raised dense clouds of dust
> and whacked his thighs and rocked the earth.
> (Nair 1967, 73–74)

Ezhuthachan's account as well as ritual performances of such disemboweling were both present as sources for *kathakaḷi*'s original staging of such scenes. In several *kathakaḷi* scenes disembowelment of the evil character takes place following a protracted, stylized, and choreographed fight. Cloth entrails are dipped in realistic stage blood. The actor keeps these hidden until, at the final climactic moment as the drummers are creating a din of sound, he dips his hands into the victim's stomach and mimes eating his victim's entrails. The actor raises his head from the victim, displaying to the audience his bloodied hand, with entrails streaming from his mouth. In such final, graphic stage displays between the forces of good and evil, *kathakaḷi* reveals part of its roots in ritual performance.

Music

The ragas of *kathakaḷi* music are created by vocalists who sing the entire text. There are no melodic instruments per se in the *kathakaḷi* orchestra. Rather the entire orchestra is made up of a variety of percussion instruments. So diverse and versatile is this percussion orchestra that the various instruments are capable of creating a complete sound environment, with rhythmic patterns and percussive accents to accompany the smallest nuance of an actor's performance.

As noted earlier, the playwright-composer in his original text indicates the specific raga and tala for each section of the text. Each is selected on the basis of how well a particular raga or tala will capture the emotion or sentiment appropriate to the dramatic context. There are six different rhythmic patterns in *kathakaḷi* music. Each may be played in one of three different speeds: slow, medium, or fast. Medium speed is a doubling of slow speed and fast is a doubling of medium speed. A sudden change in the basic speed of a rhythmic pattern, or a change from one pattern to another, indicates and signals both onstage characters and audience of a change in mood or sentiment. Although something of an oversimplification, it is still generally the case that certain of the major moods or sentiments are associated with particular speeds in playing rhythmic patterns. For example, slow speed is generally associated with the erotic sentiment, medium speed with the heroic, and fast speed with the furious.

Kathakaḷi's vocal music is sung in its own unique vocal style. The lead singer sets the mood and tempo of the entire performance. He functions as an onstage "stage manager" since he controls the rhythm of the performance through his hand-held gong. His gong is made of bell metal and he keeps the steady rhythmic patterns with a stick held in his right hand. The second vocalist, as well as drummers and actor-dancers, take their cues from the lead singer. As their voices overlap, the lead and second singer create dynamic waves of melodic sound, reinforcing the emotional content conveyed by the text.

Vocalists sing both the primarily narrative sections and dialogue portions of the text. However, it is in singing the narrations that the vocalists have more scope for elaboration within the constraints of the vocal style. The narrative portions are sung *without* background percussion and therefore with no strict adherence to a particular rhythmic time structure, allowing the vocalists great freedom of interpretation outside the constraints of rhythmic pattern and speed. The narrative portions provide the vocalists with the opportunity to display their capabilities. Unfettered by restrictions of rhythmic patterns, they have the freedom to interpret by elaborating on any long or stressed syllables. But this freedom is always within the bounds of the dramatic context they are attempting to create through their singing. It should also be noted that approximately eighty percent of the time narrations are sung without actors onstage. The singers are indeed narrating and preparing the context for the dialogue portions which follow.

While narrations are performed without the constraints of rhythmic pattern and a set specific speed, the largely dialogue, first-person portions of the text are set in a specific raga, tala, and speed. These "dialogue" sections are the substance of a *kathakaḷi* play and bring together the entire performance ensemble, including vocalists, percussionists, and actor-dancers.

The percussion orchestra, which provides the various rhythmic patterns, speeds, and accents of performance, includes not only the gong of the lead singer but also a wide assortment of drums and cymbals. The second singer assists the lead singer in keeping the basic rhythmic pattern. The three drums include the *maddalam, ceṇṭa,* and *iḍakka,* all played by specialists.

The *maddalam* is a two-headed barrel-shaped drum. When played the approximately three-foot-wide drum rests horizontally across the player's thighs, held in place by a cloth strap wrapped around the waist. With the drum resting below the waist, the hands of the player extend to comfortably meet each drum head to the left and right. The right head is made of ox hide. The performer wears on his right hand thick rice-paste and lime finger coverings used to give his drumming tremendous resonance and a sharp, deep sound. The left head of the drum is made of buffalo hide and is played by the left hand and fingers. The *maddalam* is the major drum in the *kathakaḷi* orchestra and is used to accompany any character or situation onstage.

The second drum, the *ceṇṭa,* is a cylindrical double-headed drum played most often with two curved sticks. Occasionally the drum may be played with one stick and one hand. A long cloth allows the drum to rest on the shoulder, with the main drum head vertical. Both heads are made of cow hide. The drum may be tuned through the series of cords holding the drum heads together. The *ceṇṭa* may be used when any male character is onstage. It is a versatile drum and is most obvious during battle scenes or scenes of great excitement, where the expert drummer through lightning-quick rolls creates thunderous cascades of sharp sounds. At times from two to four or more *ceṇṭa* are brought onstage to create the din of a great battle, usually at dawn as the performance ends.

In contrast to its sharp loud voice, the *ceṇṭa* is also capable of "weeping." The drummer, by slightly wetting the rim of the drum and altering the tension of the head with a free hand, rubs with the stick across the head and makes the drum "weep" in scenes where pathos predominates.

The third drum is the *iḍakka.* This small hour-glass shaped drum is used in *kūṭiyāṭṭam.* A fragile drum whose sound is altered by the tension of the strings pressed in the free hand, the *iḍakka* has a wide range of relatively muted and melodious sounds. It is used exclusively to accompany female characters.

The final instrument of the *kathakaḷi* orchestra is the conch shell, used for dramatic effect, especially the entry of certain characters.

Members of the music ensemble are onstage throughout a performance. The vocalists are usually upstage center left, and the drummers center to the right. At least one vocalist is always onstage, keeping the basic rhythmic pattern, and is accompanied by at least two drummers (always the *maddalam,* plus either the *ceṇṭa* or *iḍakka*). There are at least two *ceṇṭa* and *maddalam* players and vocalists. This is a practical necessity for all-night performances so that musicians can relieve each other, alternating through the night.

Performance Structure

In former times *kathakaḷi* performances usually lasted all night, from the opening drum call at dusk announcing the performance, to dawn when the closing prayers and dance culminate the performance. The percussion announcement and performance preliminaries take up approximately the first two to three hours of an all-night performance. The play proper begins somewhere around 10:00 P.M. and takes seven to eight hours to perform. The leisurely pace set by the preliminaries serves several purposes. The early announcement at dusk gives villagers notice of the upcoming performance and ample time to gather at the house or temple where a performance is to be held. The lengthy preliminaries serve to give the audience time to settle down and make ready for the beginning of the performance. The first preliminary dance gives students, early in their training, a valuable opportunity for onstage practice, one of the most important pieces of training choreography. The singing of prayers provides an opportunity to seek the blessings of the gods for a good performance. By the time the second preliminary dance is performed, the audience should be close to settled. This dance is the second important piece of training choreography for young students. It also serves a dramatic function. The two characters who appear in the dance are supposed to be the two main characters of the play being performed. While this is not always the case, it does serve to introduce these characters to the audience long before the actual performance begins. The long vocal and percussion composition given just prior to the beginning of the text's performance provides vocalists and percussionists ample opportunity to display their artistic skills for the audience, especially the connoisseurs and music lovers. A truly exciting composition, it allows for enough free improvisation that music lovers are drawn into the rhythmic variations of the percussionists as much as jazz lovers are drawn into free improvisation in the West. The second pure dance and this final composition really serve to "warm up" the audience for the beginning of the play.

As *kathakaḷi* has had to adjust to changes in recent years, this traditional order and time of performance has been substantially altered. While there are still performances where each of these items is included, many of these preliminaries, as well as entire sections of plays, are cut in order to shorten performance time. Of the preliminaries, the first pure dance is most often left out today. The final vocal and percussion composition is often either shortened or completely left out. Even in the shortest programs, however, the lighting of the lamp, percussion interludes, and prayers are always kept. Through these cuts the preliminaries can be shortened from three hours to fifteen minutes.

Most texts were originally written for all-night performances. During the past thirty years two important methods arose for altering an all-night performance of a single play. The first is cutting entire sections of plays so that emphasis is upon the most popular scenes. It has become fashionable to make all-night programs consisting of several scenes from different plays performed one after the other. This is comparable to taking three major operas, selecting scenes for which famous performers are known, and having these favorite scenes played one after the other in the course of one evening's night at the opera.

The second method of alteration is simply an extension of the first. As the demand for shorter performances has become greater, especially in cities, cuts made to accommodate the performance of favorite scenes have created ready-made performances of two to four hours. With shortened preliminaries a full performance of a shortened play may take place between 7:00 P.M., when a city *kathakaḷi* program most often begins, and 10:00 or 11:00, allowing people time to get home to have a night's sleep before work the following day.

Whether a *kathakaḷi* performance is a traditional all-night affair or a shortened three-hour version, preparations begin early on the day of performance. Costumers and makeup artists must make sure everything is prepared, including cleaning, washing, and starching of the literally hundreds of yards of cloth, skirts, and so on required to outfit a company for a performance. The immediate process of making up and dressing begins approximately three to four hours before "curtain"; most often today, the first entrance being the second preliminary dance. The long makeup process takes place in a "greenroom," a room or temporary shelter set up near the stage area. The costumers hang most of the costume pieces and crowns from ropes suspended above the floor area where the makeup process goes on. Makeup is the joint responsibility of both actors and specialized makeup artists. Each actor draws the basic shape of his makeup pattern, and the makeup artist applies the delicate frame or *cuṭṭi*. Later the actor "fills in" various colored areas of his face to complete his makeup.

The atmosphere of the greenroom is quiet and subdued. Children often watch the "transformation" from man to beautiful heroine or demonic forester. Actors may think about their characters, have a cigarette, sleep, or drink a cup of tea or coffee. At all-night performances the makeup and costuming process is also an all-night affair, as the vast array of characters needed for a play must all receive their turn under the hand of the makeup artist. Each actor before going onstage completes his immediate preparations by saying a prayer to his teachers and to the gods for the success of his performance. Then he dons his crown, the final part of the three to four hour process of preparation.

Support

As mentioned earlier, traditional patronage came from the highest and most wealthy of Kerala's castes. Members of families who traditionally patronized *kathakaḷi* usually constitute today's connoisseurs. For today's actors their most gratifying performances are given when a large number of appreciators of the finer points of the art are in the audience.

The *Nāṭyaśāstra* discusses, at length, the importance and responsibilities of the audience in the success of a performance. Connoisseurs of *kathakaḷi* are able, in varying degrees, to understand and appreciate its most refined moments: the highly Sanskritized texts, the nuance of vocal inflection made by a vocalist, or even most of the actor's gesture language. This is true of both men and women of the higher castes. Some women who attend *kathakaḷi* performances gather socially to sing *kathakaḷi* texts and therefore often come to performances knowing the vocal style and text.

Connoisseurs are interested in seeing the mature and best-known actors play roles for which they have become well known. To see Ramankutti Nair of the Kerala Kalamandalam Company perform in a Knife role like Rāvaṇa or Keechaka is a performance a connoisseur would not want to miss. Or the chance to see Padmanabhan Nair perform the role of the Brahman, Santanagopalan, or Gopi Asan as Naḷa will surely bring a good crowd to a performance. These appreciators will be watching for the nuance of detail in a mature actor's performances: What changes, if any, will he make in the playing of this role tonight? How well will he identify with the role and fill it out? What small improvisations will he make at this point in the text as he expands on the character's mood or situation? For the actors this is their ideal audience.

Kathakaḷi in Performance

A Kerala village, 1976
The Complete Rāmāyaṇa (Samporṇa Rāmāyaṇanam)

Members of the P. S. V. Natyasangam Kathakaḷi troupe have just finished their afternoon meal. At one they climb aboard the troupe bus, already laden with large boxes filled with the costumes, properties, and makeup needed for the evening's performance. The "major" troupe is performing this evening so the bus fills quickly with nineteen members—eleven actors, three singers, four drummers, and two makeup artists. As the bus leaves Kottakkal in North Central Kerala, some members of the company try to sleep while others talk or attempt to read. The bus, lurching over the narrow, traffic-laden, winding Kerala roads, makes sleeping or reading difficult. The road is leading toward Palghat to the west, to a small village in the western Ghats. The Ghats are the beautiful range of mountains which rise along Kerala's eastern border. These mountains have historically served as a kind of protective ring around the state.

It is October 8th, still early in the performance season that began in September, as the monsoon rains were beginning to decline. This will be one of seventy-five or more performances that the Kottakkal company will give during the season, lasting through the end of May. The members of this company are fortunate. This is a well-patronized troupe, long established and recognized in Kerala as one of the best performing companies. The P. S. V. Natyasangam Kathakaḷi troupe was organized in 1939 by the late Vaidyarathnam P. S. Varier. He was the founder of the Kottakkal Arya Vaidya Sala, a hospital, training facility, and factory of indigenous *ayurvedic* medicines and treatments. Because of its reputation as a performing company and because of the generous subsidy established by P. S. Varier, the actors are relatively well-paid for their duties as teachers and performers.

Tonight's performance in a small village is typical of many *kathakaḷi* performances today. It is being held just outside a Hindu temple compound where the annual temple festival is being held. This evening's performance has been commissioned by the temple festival committee who will be paying (in 1976) $87 (Rs. 700) plus travel and hospitality for an all-night performance by the company. Temple sponsorship has become a major source of income for many *kathakaḷi* companies.

The bus finally grinds to a halt about four hundred yards from the entrance to the temple. The three-hour bus ride has taken us over the rugged foothills of the Ghats, just to the edge of some of the major mountains. It is a striking setting for an all-night performance. The Ghats rise up majestically, forming an imposing backdrop behind the temple and the cleared ground where the performance will be held.

The nineteen members of the company disembark from the bus and are graciously greeted by the temple festival committee. Some laborers have been gathered to tote the heavy boxes down the dirt road to the temple compound. The actors head for a nearby tea stall to take their afternoon tea; it is now four.

While the actors and musicians are having tea, the two makeup men and their assistants prepare the greenroom. For each performance a special greenroom is set up as close to the performance area as possible. In this case, a conference-cum-storage room has been turned over to the makeup artists. They are busy hanging ropes, opening the large trunks, and setting out the piles and piles of starched undercloth (for a kind of petticoat), formal costume pieces, crowns, accessories, and properties—all of which will be needed for the evening's performance.

Outside the greenroom, the festival committee has cleared and swept a large area beside the wall of the temple compound. They have hired local help to set up the bamboo poles, four of which have been set up to form the frame for the stage area.

As both stage and greenroom preparations begin, the actors drift back to the greenroom area. It is 4:45. In fifteen minutes the first of the actors scheduled to appear onstage for the all-night performance will begin putting on their makeup. The makeup artists have already begun to grind the various stones and plants into pasty substances, rich in bright colors, to be applied to the actors' faces.

As the first actors begin their makeup at 5:00 P.M., the festivities of the temple program intensify. The image of the deity of the temple has been taken out of the inner shrine of the temple compound and around the village on the back of a caparisoned elephant. This is a modest temple, and so only one medium elephant has been hired for the procession. A crowd of about fifty people, including festival committee members and priests, follow the elephant and the temple deity in its circumambulation of the village area. As the elephant returns to the temple and passes the performance area, vendors begin to appear around the periphery of the performance area. These vendors—tea stalls, sweet sellers, one-man variety stores with small toys for children, and so on—set up shop on the outside of the large performance area where the audience begins to gather for the performance.

At 5:30 the musicians gather in the greenroom and prepare their instruments for the opening "announcement" of the performance. The drummers put on their cleanly pressed white *muṇṭu,* the white cloth wrapped around the waist that is the typical daily wear of the Malayalee men. They begin the *kēḷi,* the announcement of the evening performance, by gathering at the performance area. There the *ceṇṭa, maddalam,* and cymbal players go through several cycles of rhythmic patterns, beginning with the slowest and gradually building to the fastest rhythm. The *kēḷi* is a chance for the musicians to display their skills, as well as an immediate call to the villagers to come to the performance.

The makeup artists see that everyone begins his makeup so that each will be ready for their entrance on stage. The makeup crew acts as backstage manager for each performance. Since the play is an all-night performance, some actors won't begin their makeup until 1:00 or 2:00 A.M. Other actors may be completely finished with their responsibilities in the play after the first scene or by about 1:00 A.M. Whatever the particulars, the greenroom is busy all night long.

By 6:15 P.M. the *kēḷi* is complete and the crowd has begun to gather. To the west the sun is beginning to set. Already two hundred people have arrived and are beginning to find a place to sit, crowded around three sides of the stage. The early arrivals sit close. Some have brought blankets or towels to spread on the ground. Men are seated to the right and women to the left. Those sitting closest will have the best view of the slightest nuance of the actor's movements, gestures, and facial expressions.

As backstage preparations continue and the sky grows deep orange with the glow of the sunset, the audience continues to grow in size. The sense of expectation continues to rise as more people arrive. Many children have come this evening—a contrast to city performances where audiences are 99 percent adult. The children entertain themselves around the periphery of the performance and audience areas.

At eight, a stage attendant and a *maddalam* player come downstage center where the large Kerala oil lamp is located. Other musicians come onstage at this time. The stage attendant pours oil into the bowl of the large lamp, places the cloth wicks, and lights the lamp. The *maddalam* player immediately beats out several measures and then moves back to his place upstage right as the stage attendants in plain white *muṇṭu* enter to hold up the curtain.

At this point the singers deliver prayer verses invoking the deities. These verses are immediately followed by the entrance behind the curtain of two actors in Kṛṣṇa makeup and costume. They are there to perform the *puṛappāṭu* (literally, "going forth"), which is a pure dance and part of the performance preliminaries. These are the two students who began their makeup at 5:30 and are the first to enter the stage this evening. The students are excellent performers.

As the *puṛappāṭu* draws to a close and the two students leave the stage, the musicians take over. For about forty-five minutes the musicians hold the stage, performing the *melappadam,* the opening percussive-vocal composition. Tonight the *melappadam* is an elaborate composition drawn from the *Gītā Govinda* of Jayadeva. This is the premiere occasion for the musicians as musicians to show off their skills to the audience. The vocalists sing the text while the drummers *(ceṇṭa* and *maddalam)* provide the accompaniment. But it is more than mere singing with accompaniment. The *melappadam* is a complex competition among the musicians themselves, a chance for them to literally "play" with one another's talents. They push and challenge each other to greater and greater heights in singing and drumming. The musicians sense each other's rhythmic improvisations, picking up on nuances of inflection. The *melapaddam* might be compared to jazz musicians jamming within a framework of rhythmic and vocal variations.

By the time the *melappadam* is complete, it is 9:10 P.M. The preliminaries are over and the performance of tonight's story is about to begin. The conclusion of the *melappadam* brings a change in mood, from the fast-paced and loud drumming to the melodious voices of the musicians singing the opening verses of the play, occasionally interspersed with the accompanying voice of the *maddalam* drum. The two curtain holders reappear and again spread the brightly colored curtain.

During the *puṛappāṭu* and *melappadam* those members of the audience closest to the stage area are most attentive, watching the young students perform with keen interest. Many of the children, after sitting and watching the dropping of the curtain to reveal the two Kṛṣṇas dancing the introductory choreography, quickly lose real interest and go back to explorations around the periphery of the performance area. Likewise during the *melappadam,* many in the audience talk casually and don't really pay attention to the onstage musical activity.

By performance time the audience has grown even larger. There are eight hundred to a thousand gathered in this cleared space of about one hundred and fifty square feet and spilling over onto the accompanying roads. Even as the performance is about to begin, the temporary tea stalls are doing a brisk business. In the clear and crisp evening air people begin to settle in, seated on the ground, women wrapping their saris or *muṇṭu* sets over their shoulders and heads and many men wrapping towels around their shoulders or over their heads to keep out the slight chill of the air. The electric lights set up by the temple committee fully illuminate the stage and the periphery of the performance area. It is harsh and grating to my eyes but the combination of neon tubes and bare bulbs is standard lighting at any public function today in Kerala.

Tonight's play, *The Complete Rāmāyaṇa,* was arranged and written by Shri C. A. Varier. It was first performed in 1969 by the P. S. V.

Natyasangam company of Kottakkal and was written for this particular troupe to perform. Since that time it has become a part of the troupe's standard repertory and is often in demand, especially at temple festivals. Part of the reason for the popularity of this story, even though a recent addition to the repertory, is that it is based on the *Rāmāyaṇa* and enacts the *entire* story.

Another reason for the popularity of *The Complete Rāmāyaṇa* at temple festivals is that the play-in-performance moves rather quickly for a complete all-night *kathakaḷi* event. Divided into many shorter scenes, rather than having a few long scenes, this version of the complete *Rāmāyaṇa* introduces the audience to a vast number of diverse characters in the course of the night, as well as keeping the "action" at a relatively fast pace, at least compared to many other *kathakaḷi* plays and performances. The shorter scenes keep the audience interested even though most are not connoisseurs. It is a play which appeals to a mass audience.

With the preliminaries complete, the audience settles down for the beginning of the performance proper. The first scene takes place in the Palace of Ayodhya. The colorful curtain is lowered to reveal King Daśaratha. He, like all "good and heroic" characters, is made up in Green. The musicians perform the opening narrative of the play, in which King Daśaratha conveys his sadness over having had no children by any of his three wives.

When King Daśaratha has completed his soliloquy conveying his sadness about having no heirs to his kingdom, he approaches his great teacher, Vaśiṣṭha, for advice. Vaśiṣṭha appears onstage by entering from upstage left. He is in the typical Shining makeup and costume of sage or saintly characters. Vaśiṣṭha informs the king that four sons will be born to him. However, in order for his sons to be born, he must perform a great sacrifice.

On the advice of Vaśiṣṭha, King Daśaratha immediately makes preparations for the sacrifice. During the sacrifice the God of Fire appears to King Daśaratha in the form of a child, played by one of the Kottakkal students. He gives *payasam* ("pudding") to the king, and in turn this is given to the three queens. The singers complete the first scene by narrating the effect of the sacrifice: Eventually all three of the wives become pregnant and give birth to four children: Rāma, Bhārata, Lakṣmāṇa, and Śatrughna.

The second scene picks up the action of the *Rāmāyaṇa* story by introducing the episode of Viśvāmitra and the sage's arrival to see Daśaratha. After a warm greeting, Daśaratha finds that Viśvāmitra has asked him to send his two young sons, Rāma and Lakṣmāṇa, with him into the forest to keep the religious performances safe from attacks by demons who roam the forest disrupting holy activities. At first Daśaratha refuses and offers himself as protector; however, Viśvāmitra refuses the offer and becomes angry. Vaśiṣṭha arrives with the two sons and advises the king to send them. On his advice Daśaratha parts with his sons.

Viśvāmitra, like Vaśiṣṭha, comes onstage in Shining makeup and in the sage's typical costume. Rāma and Lakṣmāṇa, played by two of the older Kottakkal students, are in Green makeup and costume, but wear the special silvered crown typically worn by Kṛṣṇa. The roles of Rāma and Lakṣmāṇa are particularly vigorous roles, usually played, as is the role of Kṛṣṇa, by relatively young junior actors or older experienced students. These are vigorous dance roles in which lengthy, fast-paced *tāṇḍava* choreography must be performed.

With twenty-four scenes performed in approximately eight hours, each scene lasts between ten and thirty minutes. In other plays, scenes may last as long as one to two hours. By the time these two scenes are complete, it is almost 10:00 P.M. The audience follows the production with interest. The atmosphere is attentive but casual. Those closest to the stage are most attentive, while those at the periphery of the performance area are less so.

The third scene is very short. Viśvāmitra, with Rāma and Lakṣmāṇa accompanying him, is on his way through the forest when Thataka (a demoness) attacks them. Thataka is wearing the Black character makeup and enters using the "curtain look" convention. She reveals herself to the audience through a set of conventionalized grabs, pulls, and looks over the curtain. The battle is quick and Rāma kills Thataka with an arrow to complete the stylized battle choreography.

The action continues through the night following the various major episodes of the *Rāmāyaṇa.* Some of the major events depicted onstage include Rāma's stringing and breaking of Lord Śiva's bow; the marriage of Rāma and Sītā; then Queen Kaikeyī's servant, the aged Mantharā, persuades the queen to ask for her two wishes, including the demand to send Rāma to the forest for fourteen years; Bhārata rejects his mother's offer of the kingdom and leaves for exile with Rāma; Bhārata is persuaded to return and rule the kingdom; Lakṣmāṇa rejects Surpanakha's advances and cuts her breast and nose; Rāvaṇa becomes angry with the actions of Rāma and his brother; a demon comes in the form of a deer; there follows the deer scene with Sītā; Jāṭayu fights Rāvaṇa over Sītā and receives a fatal wound; Rāma and Lakṣmāṇa find the dying Jāṭayu; in turn they search out Sītā, meeting Sugrīva; the battle is staged between Bāli and Sugrīva; Hanumān leaps across the mighty ocean to Laṅkā; Hanumān becomes a prisoner; he sets fire to Laṅkā with his tail; Rāma and his army march on Rāvaṇa; there ensues the great battle in which Rāma kills Rāvaṇa; the return to Ayodhya after exile; and finally the crowning of Rāma as the King of Ayodhya.

From this exhaustive list it may be seen that nearly all of the major events of the *Rāmāyaṇa* are enacted. In contrast to this mass of characters passing across the stage in one evening of performance, the play *The Killing of Bāli (Bālivadham),* one of the original *Rāmanāṭṭam* stories, is also an all-night performance; however, the "action" of the story is confined to the abduction of Sītā by Rāvaṇa, Jāṭaya's attempted defense, Rāma's meeting with

Sugrīva, and the battle between Bāli and Sugrīva in which Rāma's arrow kills Bāli. What occurs in *The Killing of Bāli* in the course of one night occurs in *The Complete Rāmāyaṇa* in four of twenty-four scenes.

The compressed action of this particular play keeps the pace of the performance moving quickly all night long. There are over twenty characters in this story, an unusually large number for a *kathakaḷi* play. The backstage organization for the production must be perfect. Some of the actors who perform small roles early in the evening return later, with complete makeup and costume changes, to take another role only performed in the last few scenes of the play. It is a truly epic production of an epic story.

By about 5:00 A.M., the sun is just beginning to lighten the eastern sky. The performance is in its last few scenes. Scene 22, "The War Field," is just beginning at 5:15. Rāvaṇa arrives onstage to fight with Rāma. In the fight that follows, Rāma kills Rāvaṇa as the sun peeks over the western Ghats to the east. The sky glows a golden orange and the green of the surrounding paddy fields becomes visible in the early morning light. The performance continues with the installation and blessing of Rāma as King of Ayodhya. It is 5:45. Finally the closing dance is performed by Rāma, the last actor leaves the stage, the music stops, and there is only the shuffle of feet and the quiet talk of the audience as it departs. There is no applause but there is appreciation felt by the audience for the performance.

About four hundred audience members have stayed the entire night. Those who remained go to tea shops or local inns for the morning meal, or return home.

Backstage the makeup artists began packing the costumes about 4:00 A.M. As each actor finished his role, they began to put away the crowns, accessories, and costumes for the trip home. Some actors sleep. Others, just offstage, must go through the quick process of shedding the many yards of cloth in which they've been wrapped and then remove their complex makeup, using coconut oil. While the makeup and costume process lasted three to four hours or more, getting out of costume and makeup takes barely fifteen minutes. Other actors and musicians head for local tea shops, smoking a cigaratte and looking forward to some food.

Another performance is over for the Kottakkal troupe. By 7:30 the bus is loaded and packed and the actors have climbed aboard. The festival committee bids the company goodbye and congratulates them on a good performance. The members of the festival committee ask me to take their picture in front of the *kathakaḷi* stage area. Their job is complete, the festival is over. The story of the *Rāmāyaṇa* has been enacted as a part of the yearly festival. Only the final clean-up of the cleared performance area remains. Next year they will again have the Kottakkal company for the festival.

Most of the troupe sleep on the way home. By 10:30 A.M. they arrive in Kottakkal. They immediately depart for home, most sleeping the day away.

Tomorrow the training of the young students will resume for the three days until another performance, this one in a city theatre, will momentarily disrupt the formal training cycle of the young students in the company. But their education in *kathakaḷi* occurs both in the classroom and on the stage.

Current State

Like many of India's cultural arts, during the early twentieth century *kathakaḷi* faced a bleak future due to the crumbling of traditional patterns of patronage and loss of interest. At the height of British rule, many disparaged their own cultural traditions. *Kathakaḷi* was not immune to naive criticism offered by those with a British education. But a rejuvenation of interest in *kathakaḷi* was kindled within Kerala by the poet Mahakavi Vallathol Narayana Menon. Vallathol had a vision of creating a performing arts academy where *kathakaḷi* could be taught and preserved for future generations. By 1930 he had established a small institution first in Kunnamkalam and later (1936) in Cheruthuruthy village, the home of the now internationally known Kerala state arts academy, the Kerala Kalamandalam. Since Vallathol founded the school, *kathakaḷi* has become world famous.

Today there exist a number of well-organized and well-managed *kathakaḷi* troupes. These troupes are also teaching institutions which receive subsidies from a wide variety of sources. The Kerala Kalamandalam receives the most substantial support from the Kerala State Arts Council, while other smaller teaching and performing institutions receive a small portion of their total operating budget from the state. The P. S. V. Natyasangam Kathakaḷi troupe, as noted above, receives its subsidy from a major *ayurvedic* medical hospital and factory. Another company in central Kerala receives a subsidy from a major chemical and fertilizer company. State government, private nonprofit arts councils, and private industry all provide means of support for today's *kathakaḷi* troupes.

Outside of Kerala many of the major internationally known art schools, like the Kalakshetra of Madras, teach courses in *kathakaḷi*. The teachers at Kalakshetra, or schools in Calcutta, New Delhi, or other Indian centers, have usually been trained in *kathakaḷi* at one of Kerala's major schools.

Kathakaḷi, like all of India's performing arts, has always been adapting and changing, but usually in rather subtle ways. For example, the rice-paste and paper facial frame, the *cuṭṭi* of the heroic characters, during the twentieth century evolved from a small thin rice-paste frame to the very wide, curved facial frame of today. This alteration may seem minor but in forms where nuance is the essence such changes are significant and show that the form has always been adapting and changing.

More important perhaps are the pressures which have been brought by many of Kerala's own self-appointed innovators and creators of art. The early interest of dance "artistes" who received only minimal training in *kathakaḷi* led to the development of *kathakaḷi*-style performances for urban audiences throughout India. These performances kindled wide interest in *kathakaḷi* and other traditional Indian performance genres. Guru Gopinath was one of the leading figures in attempts which began in the 1930s to transpose *kathakaḷi* into a new form of dance with appeal beyond the Kerala region. In Gopinath's early programs with dancer Ragini Devi, they performed *kathakaḷi*-style dances, including the "Hunter," "Peacock," and "Garuda," all adapted from original *kathakaḷi* choreography for the concert dance stage. Such uses have led to the incorporation of *kathakaḷi* in composite forms of twentieth-century pan-Indian dance and dance-dramas. Largely confined to urban areas, these composite dances are choreographed by contemporary artists whose training is in several genres and whose style of choreography is eclectic, making use of bits and pieces of various Indian traditions. Feeling that regional arts like *kathakaḷi* can never have national or truly international appeal, artist-teachers, such as Gopinath, want to see *kathakaḷi* change to please a wider audience.

While Gopinath is one force at work on *kathakaḷi* today, others want the traditions and aesthetic of the form to remain as "pure" and fixed as possible. But subtle nuances continue to change any traditional form, and *kathakaḷi* is no exception. Performances on proscenium stages subtly alter the use of the playing space, spreading out the performance, creating a chasm between audience and performers. It is likely that *kathakaḷi* will continue to exist as an adaptable performance art able to adjust to multiple contexts and please distinctly different audiences. Each context will continue to exert its influence on the future of *kathakaḷi* and will continue to have its own appreciators and detractors.

WORKS CITED

Nair, P. K. Parameswaran. 1967.
History of Malayalam Literature. New Delhi: Sahitya Akademi.

Pandeya, Gayanacharya Avinash C. 1961.
The Art of Kathakali. Allahabad: Kitabistan.

Warrier, Unnayi. 1977.
Nala Caritam. Trans. V. Subramania Iyer. Trichur: Kerala Sahitya Akademi.

ADDITIONAL READING

Bolland, David. 1980.
A Guide to Kathakali. New Delhi: National Book Trust.

Boner, Alice. 1935.
"Kathakali." *Journal of the Indian Society of Oriental Art* 3:61–74.

Chaitanya, Krishna. 1970.
"The Aesthetics of Kathakali." *Sangeet Natak* 15:5–10.

———. 1971.
A History of Malayalam Literature. New Delhi: Orient Longman.

———. 1961.
"Costumes and Accessories in Kathakali." *Census of India, 1961, Vol. VII: Kerala* Part VIIA:26–74.

Iyer, K. Bharata. 1955.
Kathakali: The Sacred Dance Drama of Malabar. London: Luzac and Company.

Jones, Betty True. 1983.
"Kathakali Dance-Drama: An Historical Perspective." In *Performing Arts in India.* Ed. Bonnie C. Wade. Berkeley: Center for South and Southeast Asian Studies.

Jones, Clifford R. and Betty True. 1970.
Kathakali: An Introduction to the Dance-Drama of Kerala. New York: Theatre Arts Books.

Menon, K. P. S. 1957.
Kathakali Rangam (Malayalam). Kozhikode: Mathrubhumi Printing.

Namboodiri, M. P. Sankaran. 1982.
"*Bhava* as Expressed in the *Vacikam* and *Angikam* aspects of *Abhinaya* in *Kathakali.*" In *CORD Dance Research Annual.*

Omchery, Leela. 1969.
"The Music of Kerala—A Study." *Kalamandalam Annual.* Pp. 7–15.

Rajagopalan, L. S. 1969.
"Damayanti in *Nala Caritam Attakatha.*" *Sangeet Natak* 14:30–39.

Rajagopalan, L. S., and V. Subramanya Iyer. 1975.
"Aids to the Appreciation of Kathakali." *Journal of South Asian Literature* 10, 2–4:205–210.

Warrier, Unnayi. 1975.
"Nala Caritam Attakatha." *Journal of South Asian Literature* 10, 2–4:211–248.

Zarrilli, Phillip. 1977.
"Demystifying Kathakali." *Sangeet Natak* 43:48–59.

———. 1979.
"Kalarippayatt, Martial Art of Kerala." *The Drama Review* 23, 2:113–124.

———. 1983.
"A Microanalysis of Performance Structure and Time in *Kathakali* Dance-Drama." *Studies in Visual Communication* 9, 3:50–69.

———. 1984.
The Kathakali Complex: Actor, Performance, Structure. New Delhi: Abhinav Publications.

———. In press.
"A Tradition of Change: The Role(s) of Patrons and Patronage in the Kathakali Dance-Drama." In *Patronage and Performance in India.* Ed. Joan Erdman.

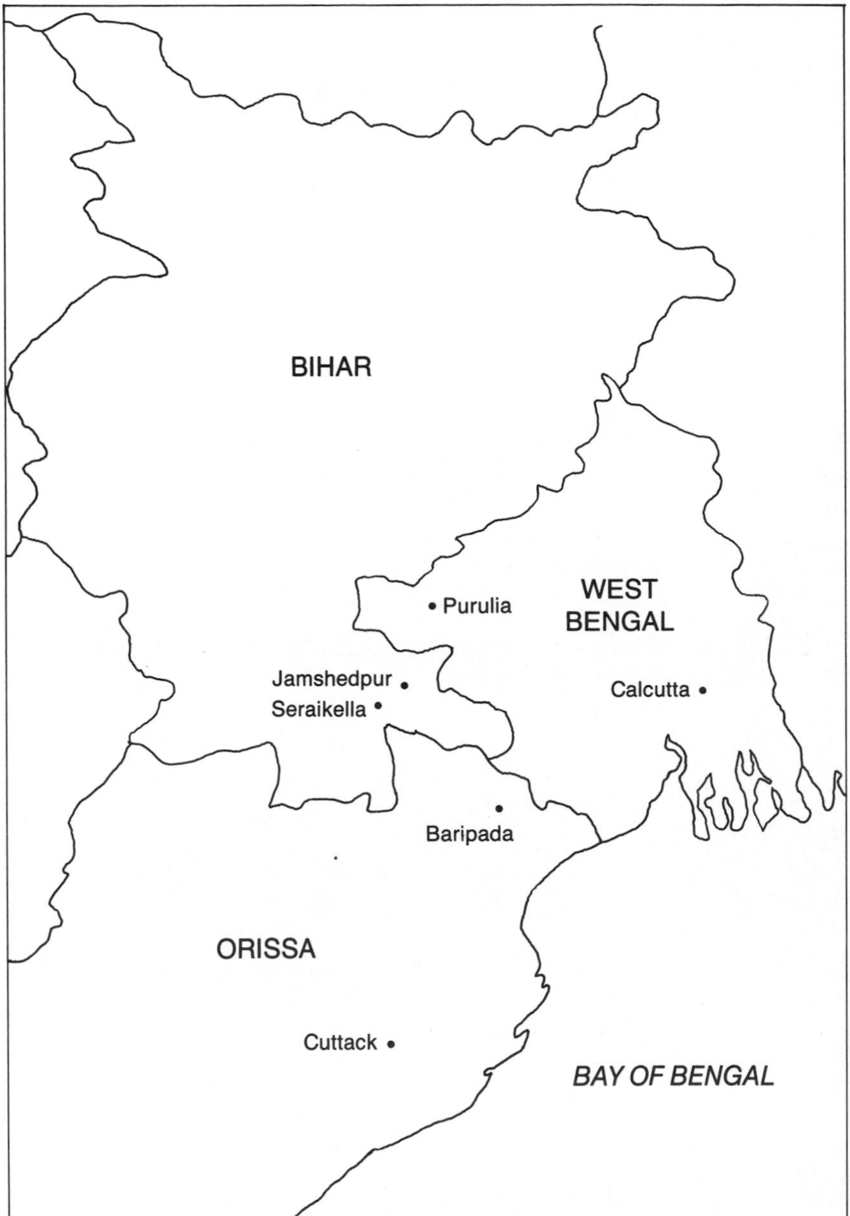
BIHAR
WEST
BENGAL
Purulia
Jamshedpur
Seraikella
Calcutta
Baripada
ORISSA
Cuttack
BAY OF BENGAL

Chapter Eleven

CHAU

Andrew Tsubaki
Farley P. Richmond

HEADING STRAIGHT WEST BY EXPRESS TRAIN FROM CALCUTTA, in five hours or so you reach Tatanagar, the railway junction for the sizeable steel city of Jamshedpur. From there you may take a bus or minibus to arrive at Seraikella, almost an hour's ride further west. Bounded on the west by the Kharkai River, Seraikella is a subdivision of the district of Singhbhum in the southern part of Bihar. Seraikella became the center of *chau* dance because of the patronage and performing activities provided by the local princes and, more recently, due to the presence of the Government Chau Dance Center.

Around Seraikella, a rather arid and flat land dotted by low-lying hills, two other forms of *chau* are popularly practiced—the Purulia *chau* of the state of West Bengal and Mayurbhanj *chau* of the state of Orissa.[1] The names of all three forms are derived from the districts where the *chau* is performed, and all three districts are geographically linked (see map). Today it takes about three hours by bus to travel from Jamshedpur to each of the other two localities.

Even though *chau* is spread over these three states, the art form is essentially confined to one contiguous geographical region. And yet the travel time among these districts, which not long ago was counted in days, not mere hours, must have been significant enough for three distinctly different styles of *chau* to have emerged.

In the following pages we will focus on the two forms that we know best—the Seraikella *chau* and the Purulia *chau*. However, a word or two is in order concerning the contrasting characteristics of all three forms. The *chau* is part

[1] *Chau* in colloquial Oriya, the vernacular of the Seraikella and Baripada or Mayurbhanj areas, means an armor or the act of hunting stealthily. Various other sources, however, have said the term means "shadow," "disguise," or "mask." *Chau* may also be spelled as *chhau,* although in this essay, we have preferred the first spelling owing to the way the natives of Seraikella pronounce the word today.

of the ritual and religious celebrations of the people of all three regions of the country, and as such is not considered a professional occupation. Except for the artists employed by the Seraikella maharajas, most *chau* artists eke out a living in the city or as common laborers in the fields. Although their training may be as rigorous as that of a professional artist, the form is practiced by amateurs.

Masks are used in Seraikella and Purulia, even though the style of their construction, general features, and colors differ considerably. Mayurbhanj performers do not wear masks. The characteristics of the movements in all three forms are uniquely different. Seraikella *chau* emphasizes small ensemble numbers. Rarely more than two or three dancers at a time enact short narrative stories or abstract pieces. Mayurbhanj *chau* is known for its bold group choreography, in which two parties of dancers contrast their abilities as though they were competitors for public attention. A solo dance is also frequently performed in Mayurbhanj. Of the three forms, the Purulia *chau* has the most vigorous movement patterns and masculine emphasis, hinting at its tribal origins. Purulia *chau* also claims to lay more emphasis on dramatic narrative and storytelling. All three forms have techniques derived from the martial arts of their respective regions. In musical accompaniment and costuming they have their own unique features. A significant characteristic of all three forms is the absence of dialogue between characters. In this respect, as indicated earlier, *chau* is a dramatic dance, but like the ritual forms examined in Part Two, it demonstrates a strong theatrical character.

Seraikella *Chau:* Origins

Little of the historical background of Seraikella *chau* is known to us today. What is clear is that the region of its birth remained relatively quiet and free from outside hostility, from the signing of a treaty with the British in 1820 through the merger of the region into the modern Bihar state in 1947. This period of prevailing calm produced an atmosphere in which generations of rulers of the princely state became intimately associated with a religious festival, the Chaitra Parva, as well as with *chau* dance, which was a part of the festival. For several generations members of the royal family became *chau* dancers themselves and took an active role in shaping and reshaping the art form, its repertoire, and the style and variety of masks used in performances. Such long-term royal support of the *chau* and its festival context contributed to molding the Seraikella style into its present distinctive features: its relative refinement, sculptural and sustained or elongated movement, and its clear-featured, relatively plain, simple but uniquely stylized masks.

The direct involvement of members of the royal family undoubtedly altered the nature of Seraikella *chau*, although the exact nature of such alterations through time have yet to be precisely documented. When queried about the nature of such changes in the form, members of the royal family maintain that Seraikella *chau* is "classical," often denying any possibility of tribal origins for the form. Despite such enthusiastic convictions on the part of royal family members, the fact remains that Seraikella *chau*, like its close relatives in Mayurbhanj and Purulia, has retained many of the folk and tribal elements of its origin, even if these elements have been reshaped into a more polished, refined, and even abstract dance form. Such mundane roots are evidenced by the *chau* practiced in many of the smaller outlying villages surrounding Seraikella itself, where the influence of the royal family has been much less direct.

Even with the coming of the era of royal family involvement in Seraikella *chau*, members of the agricultural, tribal, and traditional Kshatriya caste continued their participation in either the dance or the Chaitra Parva festival. During the heyday of royal family patronage and involvement, the palace maintained its own exclusive performance troupe and training program. The radical shift in economic conditions precipitated by Independence and loss of the privy purse led to the disbanding of the permanent troupe and training program. What *does* continue to exist is a small core group of *chau* performers loosely constituting the present palace "troupe." A member of the royal family is still in charge of organizing the *chau* performances presented as a part of the Chaitra Parva festival. Some of these performances are danced by the core members of the troupe, but the majority of programs are presented at the invitation of the royal family by various village troupes from the neighboring area.

In recent years the most visible and organized center of training for both dancers and musicians has been the Government Chau Dance Center, established in 1964. With funds from the Bihar and Central Indian governments, a modest two-room building is provided along with salaries for a director, an assistant director, two musicians, a caretaker, and a few modest scholarships for college-age students of dance. The center, with its core of "faculty" and students trained there, constitutes a second troupe capable of organizing and giving performances. However, their performances occur on individual occasions, not as part of the traditional Chaitra Parva festival.

The two core groups of performers at the palace and center constitute almost rival groups, which vie with one another for precedence and recognition. In spite of this rivalry, they often share ancillary performers when organizing a particular set of performances, since their core groups are so small in numbers.

In addition to these two most recognized groups, there are also little-known village troupes from outlying villages around the Seraikella area. Some are invited to perform at the palace in conjunction with Chaitra Parva, but all of them also offer their own performances in their own villages at the time of the festival. Little study has been made of these less centrally located groups.

Training

Given the centrality and visibility of the Government Chau Dance Center, this discussion of training will focus on the process and techniques of training under the leadership of the first and current director of the dance center, Guru Kedar Nath Sahu.

In any given training season, there is a progression from the rather low-key initiation of beginners to the ongoing training process, through to an intensive period of final rehearsals, as the date of the great Chaitra Parva festival draws near in April. The reason for this intensification is quite simple. The regular ongoing training teaches beginners ranging in age from young boys of fifth-grade elementary school age to young adults—college-age dancers receiving a stipend for their studies. All these "regular" students in any given year are joined toward festival time in the training-turned-rehearsals by dancers who have received previous training and currently hold regular jobs in town or who have left the area for higher degree studies.

The regular training takes place in afternoon sessions, the most convenient time for students coming after their regular school hours. (Foreign students desiring additional study have recently been accommodated in additional morning classes.) From February on the pace of training accelerates and nightly sessions are added to accommodate the schedules of workers and students returning home. By March the intensive heat makes late morning or midday training impossible. With the rise in intensity in the training-rehearsals, the center is packed with onlookers.

The fundamental benefits imparted during the regular training may be divided into two major classes: the building of physical strength and skill through *parikhanda* exercises (*pari* meaning "shield," and *khanda*, "sword"), and the dance technique itself, consisting of steps, movements, and choreography. A drummer and flutist accompany the training sessions. The dance master frequently joins by playing the harmonium. If an additional musician is available, he joins in playing a kettle drum.

The *parikhanda* exercises are generally accepted as the origin of *chau* dance technique. The early martial origins of the genre are traced from a number of sources. Awasthi cites "*parikhanda-khela*," the play of shield and sword, as the name used in Mayurbhanj to identify the early stage of *chau* dance. In addition, the earliest dance number was known as *Ruk-mar* (defense and attack) (Awasthi 1983, 74). Both in Seraikella and Mayurbhanj village warriors existed. This tradition of the village warriors was gradually transformed and taken over by dancers. Thus even in today's practice, the basic posture and position of the hands gives the appearance of holding a sword and shield.

The *parikhanda* exercises naturally express and embody a martial spirit, manifest in a chest thrust forward, outstretched legs, and uplifted face and hands. These martial exercises were meant to foster alertness and preparedness to counter attacks and to enable immediate and split-second responses with the agility of a panther.

While the *parikhanda* formed the early basis of *chau* technique, essential for the correct fundamental body position and dynamic movement of the torso and lower body, the specific footwork of the form is derived from routine tasks of the Oriya housewife. Such tasks include sweeping, collecting and throwing stones, picking up cow dung, mixing dung with water, grinding rice to make paste, cleaning a bracelet, and so on. A third part of the essential movement vocabulary is derived from activities of birds and animals.

As in other forms of Indian dance, training progresses from the fundamental and basic sets of movements and steps through increasingly complex sets of movements and steps, choreographed in linked chains set in progressively faster and more difficult speeds. And in Seraikella *chau*, of course, the fundamental training process culminates with the teaching of specific dance roles from the repertory or in learning roles newly created for the festival period.

Context and Support

The performance of Seraikella *chau* is traditionally nested within the context of the Chaitra Parva festival. Chaitra is the Hindu month that extends from the middle of March to the middle of April, while *parva* indicates a time for rejoicing (Kothari 1968, 12). The season of performance clearly places this spring festival (Chaitra Parva) within the agricultural cycle. Śiva and his consort Śakti are the principal deities propitiated during the festival. The most celebrated series of *chau* performances take place both in Seraikella and Mayurbhanj during the evening, immediately following the completion of the specific rituals performed on each day of the festival. However, *chau* dancing is restricted to the final three or four days of the festival.[2] In recent years the period of the festival appears to be getting shorter. Nevertheless what is most important for our purposes is recognizing that Seraikella *chau* originated in a ritual festival context and is still performed in this context, even with the creation of an ancillary and relatively new secondary context of performances *separate from* Chaitra Parva.

The date for the beginning of the festival was traditionally determined by

[2] The exact length of the festival is difficult to determine since various sources are contradictory. Kothari (1968) gives the ritual as thirteen days. On the other hand, Khokar (1982, 75) lists the festival as lasting four to five days, and Vatsyayan (1980, 68) represents the festival as lasting twenty-six days.

A *chau* teacher demonstrates an intricate basic step. (Daniel J. Ehnbom photo)

the royal astrologer who, by consulting the ruler's horoscope, found the day in April when the stars were favorable for the commencement of the festival. The formal inauguration of the festival is marked by hoisting the ritual banner pole. This tall, green bamboo staff with a red banner and mango leaves attached at the top is freshly made each evening during the festival. The ritual flag is assembled at the royal bathing place on the banks of the Kharkai River and is taken in procession from the river to the principal Śiva temple in the heart of the village square, accompanied by drums and a *shenai* (a simple oboe-like instrument). The procession continues to the courtyard of the palace where the ritual flag is deposited for the night in the Raghunath temple of the palace, access to which is limited to members of the royal family. The same procedure is repeated each day of the festival.

Once the festival has been initiated, each day is marked by its own particular set of specific acts of propitiation. While there currently exists confusion in reports over the exact length of the festival and over the features of ritual practice associated with each particular day, an outline of some of the major practices of a few of the most important ritual events of the festival will provide some idea of the context in which *chau* is performed.[3] The first day of the festival features both a set of afternoon rituals and a series of evening rituals. The afternoon ceremonies consist of a series of ritual acts carried out by women, including the carrying of holy water, dancing, trances, offerings of fowl, and the return of the body of each bird to the offerer for a special feast. The evening rituals begin with a procession by a male devotee, in red makeup and clothing, carrying a small earthen pot. He represents a manifestation of the goddess Śakti. The pot is filled with water from the Kharkai River. The carrier of the pot begins to dance, and eventually enters a state of possession. Offerings of sheep, goats, or lambs are made for propitiation or as thanksgiving.

The second day of the festival marks the observance of *brindahani.* On this day the monkey-god Hanumān is presented. Here a monkey, played by a devotee, is decorated with bamboo leaves and dances at the urging of his handler, another devotee.

On the third day, the *garia bhar* ritual is presented. A man with blackened face and dressed in a long black costume carries in a procession two pots wrapped in red fabric and filled with river water. He is accompanied by two men dressed as women, representing the milkmaids who appear with Kṛṣṇa, who is portrayed by a young lad. After completing their procession route, the performers watch the *chau* and then visit every house in town offering as *prasād* some of the sacred water they carry.

During the 1983 festival, videotaped by Braja Bhanu Singh Deo (Rajkumar of Seraikella), an additional ritual was performed immediately following the *garia bhar.* This additional ritual began with three dancers performing a hopping-step dance on the palace grounds. A ritual obeisance followed in the corner of the palace compound. Finally the performer who had carried the river water in procession, having removed his black costume and makeup, was carried in procession on a triangular scaffold about five feet high. During the procession he stepped on two rusty swords attached to the base of the scaffolding, sharp edge up.

---

[3] For discrepant accounts of the variations and differences in the festival, see Kothari (1968), Khokar (1982), and Vatsyayan (1980). It is certainly possible that through time there may have been considerable alterations or adjustments made in the ritual duration and activities, although only further research will determine what has happened over the years.

The fourth day includes the enactment of *Kalika ghāṭ,* the most solemn part of the festival. A performer here represents the forbidding goddess Kāli, another manifestation of Śakti. The action of the ritual parallels the earlier evening ritual of the first day in that a dancer carries, secured on top of his head, a pot of sacred water. The performer representing Kāli appears in black costume and makeup, embodying Kāli's awesome countenance. He visits all of the typical spots along the processional route, blesses devotees, and sanctifies sacrifices; however, in this particular ritual, the performer does not enter the palace courtyard, since it is taboo for the royal family to set eyes on the form of Kāli. The procession this day ends at the Śiva temple and the pot is removed and buried ceremoniously, to be removed the following year when it will serve as the basis for divination and oracles based on the nature and amount of water remaining in the pot.

During the 1983 festival, *chau* performances were held each night following the completion of the ritual events. On the fourth night when the enactment of *Kalika ghāṭ* is complete, the solemnity of the occasion of the representation of Kāli and her ritual propitiation is *supposed to preclude* any performance of the *chau*. However, interestingly enough a performance of *chau will* be permitted if the ruler pays a fine for the "defilement" of the occasion by calling for a *chau* performance. The prohibition against *chau* on this evening, the payment of the "fine" (Rs. 1.25, or about $.10), gives the performance, when it occurs, added enthusiasm. This night of "prohibited performance" is actually the final night on which the *chau* is presented! Thus the quality of the dance and the size and enthusiasm of the audience reaches its climax at this point in the festival. In 1983, as customary over the past few years, the Government Chau Dance Center held its own government-sponsored dance program during the Chaitra Parva festival. However, these rival performances have been held only on the fourth night, the last night of the officially sanctioned performances.

The conclusion of the festival comes on the fifth day with the performance of the *pat sankranti* ritual. In the *pat sankranti* the principal devotee lies on a plank of wood and, simulating death, is covered with a red sheet. The ruler visits the "dead" body. He reaches out and touches the "corpse" with his hand, thus instantly reviving the "dead" man. The ritual act symbolically indicates the ruler's divine power. No *chau* performances are held on this final evening following the completion of the ritual and the conclusion of the festival.

The close association of Seraikella *chau* with the Chaitra Parva festival raises the question of whether *chau* should be considered as separable from this important context of performance. First and foremost, the long-term association of *chau* with the festival has made the dance performances a prized part of the festival ambiance. For the local populace, Chaitra Parva without *chau* performances would be unthinkable! However, the long-term association of the palace with *chau*, and the years of refinement given to its technique and choreography, have rendered it, at least during the twentieth century, a form of dance which is appreciated outside the ritual and local context. Thus, the passage of *chau* from the festival stage to the modern dance stage is not a great distance for Seraikella *chau* to have traveled, given its recent history. The following discussion of the repertoire, movement quality, and essential performance features of these dances should provide ample evidence of the ease of this transition of contexts.

Performance Structure

The repertoire of Seraikella *chau* ranges from a depiction of the epic themes of the *Mahābhārata* and Puranas to purely lyrical pieces. For example, there is the dramatic dance of the encounter between Bhima and Duryodhana in the "Durjayadhana" or "Duryodhana" episodes in *Urubhangam (The Broken Thighs),* based on the final encounter between the two warriors at the culmination of the *Mahābhārata.* This piece of choreography is one of the most overtly "dramatic" in the repertory since it is based on a mace fight. It is staged as a choreographed combat, each of the performers wielding a light mace in this enactment of the killing of Duryodhana. On the other hand, there is also much more lyrical and abstract choreography in which characters taken from nature, birds or animals, are presented on stage. The lyrical and abstract characters and themes of the Seraikella style vastly expand its interpretative range beyond the more limited thematic content of Mayurbhanj and Purulia *chau* which rely solely on traditional sources. In fact, one of the most distinctive features of the Seraikella style is its repertoire, which encompasses virtually anything or any topic in the cosmos as a possible source of inspiration. Seraikella *chau* must have been one of the first traditional forms to incorporate the ongoing creation of *new* choreography based on individual interpretation of thematic materials. In its creative choreography, Seraikella *chau* is distinctive.

It is possible to group the dance pieces into three categories. The first and simplest dances, frequently performed by children either with or without masks, reveal rudimentary *chau* techniques. In the second category the choreography closely follows the theme selected. Such dances include "Offering Lights" *(Aratī),* "Hunter" *(Sabar),* "Archer" *(Eklabya*—based on the *Mahābhārata),* and "Fisherman" *(Dheebar).* The third and most intriguing, as well as most typical, dances of the Seraikella style are those which possess beneath the outer layer of movement an inner, allegorical, and philosophical interpretation, which is symbolically suggested through the figures of the dance. These include such dances as "Peacock" *(Mayura),* "Boatman" *(Nabik),* "Tragic Love" *(Chandrabhaga),* "The Ocean" *(Sagar), "Hara-Parvati,"* and "Swan" *(Hansa).* In these dances stylization pre-

The boatman in *Nabik,* performed by the Government *Chau* Dance Center in Jamshedpur. (Daniel J. Ehnbom photo)

Masks created for use in Seraikella *chau*. (Farley P. Richmond photo)

dominates. It is a stylization composed of inner restraint "employed in the execution and the slow, gradual build up of the theme" (Vatsyayan 1980, 73). In addition to these traditional types of choreography, there exist several pieces of "modern" work. "Passionate Love and Devyani" *(Koch-O-Devyani),* based on Rabhindranath Tagore's poem "Bidya-Abhisap," is the most celebrated.

Costumes and Masks

The unique lyrical charm displayed in Seraikella *chau* movement is greatly enhanced by the now widely known Seraikella style of masks. Indeed it is the masks that determine the nature and patterns of choreography when it is first composed. The expression the masks bear is not as sharp as that of the Purulia *chau* masks. In Seraikella each facial feature is drawn painstakingly and colored in pastel shades to preserve a lyrical, luminous, almost otherworldly quality. The characteristic expression of the mask, which may be described as dreamy, lyrical, or even transcendental in the case of some deities, is attained through distinct and consistent stylization. The masks tend to be round like the full moon and are endowed with elongated eyebrows and eyes—a reflection of the elongated stretches of fundamental body movement and movement of the body in space.

The lyrical beauty of the masks, however, itself "masks" the impracticality of their use. The stylized features make them difficult to wear and

The late Prasanna Kumar Mahapatra applying final touches on a female mask. (Daniel J. Ehnbom photo)

extremely difficult to use for extended performances. The eye openings on the mask do not usually match the location of the dancer's eyes. The mouth is generally closed and is only indicated by attractively drawn, stylized lines painted on the mask. Thus, with only nostril and eye apertures provided for breathing, the performer's ability to sustain a performance is rendered difficult at best. Most Seraikella *chau* dances are relatively short, lasting little more than seven or eight minutes.

It is reported that both earthen and wooden masks were worn by dancers in earlier periods. They were said to be heavy and created difficulty in performance. The refinement of the Seraikella masks took place around 1933, when Maharaja Aditya Pratap Singh Deo endowed the mask-making artisan family of Mahapatra. The most respected maker in modern times, Prasanna Kumar Mahapatra, was a descendant of this family, which has a mask-making lineage dating back at least three generations. He died in 1983 at the age of 75. Today some of the finest masks in Seraikella are made by Khanai, who learned his trade from the late Mahapatra.

The basic facial color of the masks varies from white (used for Lord Śiva), light pink (used for Pārvatī), and brown (for tribal men, such as Eklabya), to blue (for Kṛṣṇa). The surface has a matte finish, in contrast to the glossy finish of the Purulia masks. Some female masks have painted hair, while a warrior mask like those used for Bhima and Duryodhana in *Urubhangam* has a mustachio, curled up at the ends. Matted hair is employed as a wig for sages, a particular male character, Nabik, and in a brown hair version for Śiva. Frequently the masks are adorned with headgear or crowns that create a touch of elegance with jewels, beads, artificial pearls, and silk cloth woven or embroidered with silver or other metal thread, thus presenting a restrained figure.

Costumes are similar to those used in the Mayurbhanj style. For the lower portion the male character wears a dhoti or a pair of trousers contoured and sewn like a dhoti in the traditional Indian style. For the top a snug-fitting shirt may be worn, either half- or full-sleeved, or a simple bare top. The material for these garments is cut from a silk sari for dignified characters and a cotton sari for commoners. Female characters wear a sari wrapped around the legs like the dhoti, but with the long end brought up to cover the front part of the tightly fitted shirt and draped over one shoulder onto the back. A cummerbund and pair of stringed ankle-bells are worn by all dancers both in practice and performance. Jewels and beads are used along with simple hand properties such as oars, spear, sword, and shield. The exposed part of the body is painted light pink, as in Mayurbhanj. The palms and lower side of the feet are painted red, as in many other forms of Indian dance.

Music

Rhythmic patterns and melodic modes are selected to suit particular dances. As the tala changes, so does the raga. The music, however, remains essentially in the background. Vocal accompaniment is minimal in all the *chau* forms, but especially so in Seraikella. Instrumental music dominates. Although *chau* musicians select compositions of famous Oriya poets and folk songs as well, after selection the words are discarded and only the tunes are kept, to be played as accompaniment. The selection of such familiar, deeply embedded tunes from the Oriyan countryside gives them an immediate emotive association in the audience.

Performance Space

The outdoor space where Seraikella *chau* is presented usually has a large canopy covering the entire acting area. Aside from the practical value of protecting the performers from the elements, it adds color and gaiety to the performance. The performance space is used quite differently than in many other forms of Indian dance. For example, in *kathakaḷi* choreography (with the exception of battles or traveling steps) pure dance segments are choreographed for a very small area, with little lateral or diagonal movement from the performer. In contrast, one of the distinctive features of Seraikella *chau* is its use of space. Here interpretative choreography predominates. And with interpretation comes an elongated, stylized line so that *chau* dances make use of virtually the entire stage space. The elongation of the mask lines, as well as their soft, flowing curves are matched by the elongation and subtle curves of the dancers' body lines as they move through space. As lengthening movements are performed, the dancers often pass laterally through space, or extend and curve slowly upward—unusual and unique movement characteristic of the Seraikella style. Qualitatively in the best performances these long and curving lines are achieved through a constant, subtle, sustained flow of energy.

Current State

At the height of royal patronage in the mid-1930s, the best performers were recognized through annual competitions sponsored by the royal court. The maharaja presided over the function, awarding trophies to the winners. Competitors were drawn from the eight gymnasia into which the town had been divided for purposes of the *chau* competitions.

In those same years Seraikella *chau* first traveled out of the country. In 1937–1938, the royal troupe toured Europe. Since that glorious period Seraikella suffered the vicissitudes of changing patronage, but then again began to attract wider audiences, both in India and abroad, through performances such as those in Bombay in 1963 and Delhi in 1965. Since that time numerous foreign visitors have gone to Seraikella to study the style and observe the festivals.

What remains distinctive about Seraikella *chau* today is its freedom to exist in both the festival and nonfestival context, its heritage of new and creative, dynamic choreography, its lyrical and often dreamlike quality, and its beautifully sculpted masks, with their soft, elongated lines.

Purulia *Chau:* Origins

Purulia *chau* is the descendant of tribal war dances performed by the Kurmi, aboriginal and semiaboriginal people who inhabit this area of West Bengal.

The Kurmi still refer to their dances as *chau yuddha,* or "*Chau* war." Up to the early 1940s Purulia *chau* was patronized by the rajas of Baghmundi, powerful local chieftains who had converted to Hinduism centuries earlier. In order to proselytize their new faith, the rajas encouraged the Kurmi villagers to modify their war dances by incorporating choreographed interpretations of popular religious stories from the *Rāmāyaṇa, Mahābhārata,* and Puranas. The short war dances performed today between dramatic segments of the Hindu epics are a remnant of *chau*'s origin.

Since the abolition of the zamindari system of land ownership, the rajas of Baghmundi have not patronized Purulia *chau*. It has survived with minimal changes and flourished entirely through the support of faithful villagers, who can ill afford the luxury of sustaining the art when they themselves live in abject poverty. Until recently Purulia *chau* was hardly known outside the western region of Bengal. It was not seen in New Delhi until June 1969, and a U.S. tour by a company of dancers in the late 1970s first exposed the form to the Western world.

Today about five hundred troupes of dancers are said to perform Purulia *chau*. Every village has at least two companies and this lends a spirit of healthy competition to the annual festivals. Like most troupes of villagers that perform traditional dance and dance-drama, however, the artists of Purulia *chau* do not expect to earn a living at the art of dancing, and so they live by cultivating the arid, unprofitable land or working as menial laborers in the district towns.

Performance Space

Performances of Purulia *chau* take place in any open space in a village that is large enough for crowds of spectators to gather. The performance area is simple, the bare earth swept clean and demarcated by four poles of bamboo or wood, which form a square or rectangle. The spectators sit on the ground around the playing area, leaving only enough room for the dancers to enter along a narrow pathway to one side. Scenery is not used to suggest locale. The dancers alone create the place and atmosphere of the dramatic conflict. All attention is focused on them and their performance.

Dance

The physical movements of the dancers are characteristically masculine and extremely vigorous. Masculine movements and gaits typify its choreographic structure. It is one of the very few forms of traditional dance-drama in India where one may see Rāma, the epic hero of the *Rāmāyaṇa,* portrayed as a virile warrior. When Rāma makes his entrance in Purulia *chau*, he shakes his shoulders proudly to show his prowess. His gait is wide, punctuated by leaps, swirls, and twists as he symbolically rids the countryside of demons during his exploits in exile. Even the epic heroines, such as Sītā and Draupadī, seem masculine in temperament when portrayed by the male dancers. The graceful movements and gaits commonly associated with female characters of other forms of dance-drama, such as *kuchipudi, bhāgavata mela,* and *manipuri,* are rarely seen in Purulia *chau*.

During its long history an elaborate system of dance steps and poses has evolved, according to the type of character portrayed. Generally all characters may be classified as one or the other of two basic types, heroic characters or divinities and demons. Corresponding to these divisions are two basic gaits, the "gait of the gods," appropriate for use by dancers playing heroic mortals and divinities, and the "gait of the demons." Special movements

Deep knee bends of a heroic character. Note drummer at rear. (Farley P. Richmond photo)

are prescribed for the head, shoulders, and chest, as well. Even jumps, twists, and turns are conventionalized according to a character's basic temperament.

Fights between opponents symbolizing good and evil are staged in a way similar to those in other forms of traditional theatre throughout India. The dancers circle the playing area several times, pausing only long enough to fire imaginary arrows at each other and brandish their swords threateningly. It is a highly stylized competition meant to convey the idea of a struggle. No actual blows are struck, for that would be entirely too realistic and out of character for the conventionalized pattern of the dance. In some conflicts, particularly those in which an extremely crude demon participates, the dancers roll in the dirt and throw stones at each other. At such times the spectators are as likely to be the object of wrath as the demon's opponents.

Music

Music plays a vital part in Purulia *chau*. As in *kathakaḷi,* there would be no dramatic action without music to guide its progress. The largest and most resonant percussion instrument is the giant *dhamsa* drum (better known as the *nakkara* or *nagara* in some areas), measuring approximately three feet in diameter and played on one end with short thick wooden sticks. Sometimes as many as half a dozen *dhamsa* accompany the dancers. The favorite percussion instrument among village musicians is the *dholak,* which is hung loosely across the shoulders and played just below the waist. It is usually struck on the left end by a thin wooden stick and on its right end by hand. A *shenai,* a wind instrument played in the manner of an oboe, provides the ragas suitable to conveying the mood and sentiment appropriate to a particular scene. The ragas and their accompanying talas in Purulia *chau* are similar to those used in classical Indian music, although they are interpreted with their own regional flavor. The musicians always assume a lively part in the proceedings. Like the *kathakaḷi* musicians, those of Purulia *chau* flank the performers. The *dhamsa* players sit on the ground at one side of the dancing area. The *dholak* drummers, along with the *shenai* player, stand in the playing area and mingle with the actors as they dance. A unique characteristic of Purulia *chau* is the active part that the *dholak* players take in introducing the dancers. After a short introductory song, the drummers recite verbal time patterns, repeated on the drums. Gradually as the patterns accelerate in tempo, the *dholak* players rush toward the entrance of the passageway and stop short in a wide knee-bend at the completion of each time pattern. Sometimes they appear to be seized by a frenzy during which they compete with each other for supremacy in unrestrained passages of virtuoso drumming. When the dancer finally appears, the drummers charge headlong toward him as though to entice him into the playing area, much as the

In the dressing room the horned demon with wild matted jute hair prepares to make his entrance. (Farley P. Richmond photo)

Spanish do at Pamplona when the bulls are herded through the village streets to compete in their bloody struggle with the matadors.

Masks

One of the more striking features of Purulia *chau* is the masks, which are worn by all of the dancers. The high quality of workmanship of these masks speaks well for the village craftsmen, who continue to ply their trade in Charida village, the major site in Bengal where the masks for Purulia *chau* are made. About forty families consider this their hereditary trade. Since this is a family business, the women and children assist the male members at different stages in the process. Each mask is carefully wrought of papier mache modeled on a clay form. All are painted in vivid colors and patterns to symbolize the rank and temperament of the characters. The craftsmen are said to follow the Krishnager School of Art, which originated in Nadia District, West Bengal, during the eighteenth century. In general, the range of colors used to symbolize character types is consistent with that used in other forms of traditional Indian theatre. Masks of heroes and heroines are white with delicate designs of blues and greens painted along the jaw line and on the forehead, somewhat in the same manner as the elaborate makeup designs applied to the faces of young actors who portray Rāma and Lakṣmāṇa in *Rām līlā* or Kṛṣṇa in *rās līlā*. In Purulia *chau* Rāma's mask is painted

Finely designed and painted mask of a heroic warrior. (Farley P. Richmond photo)

pastel green, as is that of Arjuna. The mask of Kṛṣṇa is pastel blue over which white designs have been carefully applied.

All heroic characters in Purulia *chau* wear elaborate headdresses, which are structurally a part of their masks. These ornate headdresses are composed of fingers of silver beads strung on wires which protrude in profusion from the base of the mask. Dangling from the tip of each finger are clumps of colorful feathers and yarn. Silver tinsel paper is cut and pasted in elaborate patterns to cover the crown of the headdress. Feathers of many colors adorn the extremities. The slightest movement of the dancer causes the headdress to shimmer. If he shakes his shoulders or chest, the headdress responds with a dazzling display of reflected light.

Masks of the popular Hindu deities usually follow customary designs. Śiva's mask is crowned by a serpent. Ganesha, the elephant-headed god,

Śiva mask with snake hair knot and Gaṇga, the river maiden, peeping out. (Farley P. Richmond photo)

sports a long trunk, tusks, and floppy ears. The mask of Durgā, the mother goddess of the Bengali people, is usually painted white with a benevolent smile and refined features. The goddess Kāli is a frightening creature in black, with stylized patterns of blood dripping from her gaping mouth. Her eyes are bloodshot and protrude from her taut skin. Long flowing black hair made of jute fiber dyed black gives her an unkempt appearance.

The lions which attend Durgā and Kāli are realistically depicted, with yawning jaws from which rows of fanglike teeth protrude. Their manes are made of natural jute fiber. Bears, birds, and monkeys are also depicted with stylized features. Sugrīva, the monkey king, wears a mask with pinkish skin, although his facial features resemble those of a human more than they do those of a monkey. A mop of flaming red hair crowns his mask.

The *pièces de résistance* of Purulia *chau* masks are those of the demons. The masks may be painted green or red. Invariably they have distorted facial features—blazing bloodshot eyes, wide dilated nostrils, and wrinkled skin caused by their open mouths, from which two fangs jut out from the upper jaw. Unkempt black hair protrudes from the base of the mask. The male demons wear thick black mustaches and beards.

Demon mask with matted hair. (Farley P. Richmond photo)

Costumes

The costumes worn by the dancers are dictated by years of conventional usage. Heroes and villains alike wear black pants baggy at the hips and tapered to the ankles. Almost invariably the pants are decorated with strips of pleated red and white cloth, stitched in diagonal designs around the legs from the hips to the ankles. The pants are held tightly about the ankles by strings of brass bells. Through the influence of troupes of urban actors in the early twentieth century, the dancers of Purulia *chau* now wear black or dark blue velvet short-sleeved jackets which hang loosely at the waist. They also wear wide belts of black velvet, from which panels fall over the stomach and to the sides of the body. The bodices and belts are covered with heavy silver embroidery, creating the impression of thick armor.

Performance

A typical performance of Purulia *chau* begins when the preliminaries honoring Ganesha are concluded. Heroes and demons alike move slowly and with great dignity to the dancing area. At the entrance the dancers pause in deep knee-bends. Each step they take is accented by a tattoo of drums. Once a heroic character has made his entrance, performed a simple dance to suggest travel, and taken his position on the playing area, his adversary appears. Usually this character introduces conflict which can be resolved only by a battle or some act of violence. For example, when Rāma accompanied by his wife and brother enters the playing area on his way through an uninhabited forest, he is ambushed by a vicious demon. The scene opens as the heroic characters move slowly from the entrance to the opposite end of the acting area. After they assume set poses, the demon enters. He wears a mask that accents the crude details of his distorted features. Ugly fangs protrude from his gaping mouth and his skin is painted green. As he enters he pauses, shaking his shoulders vigorously with arrogance and pride, daring anyone to challenge him to a fight. Sometimes the actor portraying a demon grasps one of the poles near the entrance to the playing area and shakes it violently, during which he may do bodily harm to himself. In a performance witnessed at Amba Forest Village near Purulia, an actor playing a demon ripped open his arm on a piece of barbed wire jutting from a post. Rather than attending to his wound, the dancer continued in an even greater frenzy than before, cheered on by the expectant crowd. After the demon reveals his true identity to Rāma through his dance, a battle ensues in which he is routed. Once again the forces of evil are defeated and good triumphs.

Current State

Like other forms of theatre and dance that have enjoyed little exposure outside their rural area of origin, and which were designed for specific regional and communal purposes, the Purulia *chau* is faced with major dilemmas as it gains greater exposure to outside audiences, especially to those in India's urban areas and in the Western world. Should it make concessions to the taste of those who commission it in places like Delhi and Calcutta? Should it aim to please by "improving" the form by modifying its choreographic structure and continuity? Should it attempt to become an art for the concert stage? Although firsthand knowledge of these issues has not been available to researchers for a dozen years, rumor has it that changes are now taking place among Purulia *chau* artists who have toured beyond Bengal and that changes have been made to "modernize" the form, perhaps at the expense of valued old traditions. Whatever is now happening in the villages, young theatre artists and dancers of Calcutta in 1986 were talking about adopting ideas from Purulia *chau* for their own experiments on the modern stage, and many of them reported making special trips to this region to get ideas for their productions. Full-blown research on Purulia *chau* is yet to be undertaken, although in recent years numerous researchers have explored selected social and artistic aspects of it.

WORKS CITED

Awasthi, Suresh. 1983.
"Traditional Dance-Drama in India: An Overview." In *Dance and Music in South Asian Drama: Chhau, Mahakali pyakhan and Yakshagana, Report of Asian Traditional Performing Arts 1981*. Ed. Richard Emmert, et al. Tokyo: The Japan Foundation. Pp. 64–77.

Khokar, Mohan. 1982.
"Chaitra Parva Rituals—Chhau Dances." *Marg* 34: 3.

Kothari, Sunil. 1968.
"Chhau Dances of Seraikella." *Marg* 22, 1:5–27.

Vatsyayan, Kapila. 1980.
Traditional Indian Theatre: Multiple Streams. New Delhi: National Book Trust.

ADDITIONAL READING

Arden, John. 1971.
"The Chhau Dances of Purulia." *The Drama Review* 15, 3:64–75.

Awasthi, Suresh. 1979.
"Chhau Dances: Tradition and Style." In *Arts of Asia*. Hong Kong: 40–46.

———. 1979.
"Seraikella Chhau: Talking to Guru Kedar Nath Sadhu." *The Drama Review* 23, 2:77–90.

———. 1983.
Drama: The Gift of Gods; Culture, Performance, and Communication in India, Performance Culture, No. 2. Tokyo: Institute for the Study of Languages and Cultures of Asia and Africa, Tokyo University of Foreign Studies.

Bhattacharyya, Asutosh. 1972.
Chhau Dance of Purulia. Calcutta: Rabindra Bharati University.

———. 1983.
"The Social Background of the *Chhau* Masked Dance of Purulia." In *Dance and Music in South Asian Drama.* Ed. Richard Emmert, et al. Tokyo: The Japan Foundation. Pp. 95–106.

Blank, Judith. 1972.
"The History, Cultural Context and Religious Meaning of the Chhau Dance." Ph.D. diss., University of Chicago.

Hasumoto, Isumi. 1983.
"Musical Aspects of the Chhau Dance of Purulia." In *Dance and Music in South Asian Drama.* Ed. Richard Emmert, et al. Tokyo: The Japan Foundation. Pp. 107–126.

Khokar, Mohan. 1973.
"Seraikella Chhau." *Journal of the National Centre for the Performing Arts* 2, 2:25–32.

Konishi, Masarochi A. 1983.
"Masks and Masked Performing Arts in South Asia, with Special Reference to *Chhau* of East India." In *Dance and Music in South Asian Drama.* Ed. Richard Emmert, et al. Tokyo: The Japan Foundation. Pp. 78–88.

Mahapatra, Sitakant. 1978.
"Chhau Dance of Mayurbhanj." *Journal of the National Centre for the Performing Arts* 8, 3:31–44.

Matsumoto, Chiyoe. 1983.
"Movement and Symbol: A Comparative Analysis of *Chhau* Dance Styles." In *Dance and Music in South Asian Drama.* Ed. Richard Emmert, et al. Tokyo: The Japan Foundation. Pp. 144–156.

Ohtani, Kimiko. 1983.
"An Analysis of the Structure and Movement of 'Chandrabhaga' in the Chhau of Seraikella." In *Dance and Music in South Asian Drama.* Ed. Richard Emmert, et al. Tokyo: The Japan Foundation. Pp. 136–143.

Pani, Jivan. N.d.
"Chhau Dances of Mayurbhanj." *Marg* 22, 1:30–45.

———. 1969.
"Chhau—A Comparative Study of Seraikella and Mayurbhanj Forms." *Sangeet Natak* 13:39–43.

Singh Deo, Juga Bhanu. 1973.
Chau Dance of Seraikella. Cuttack: Srimati Jayashree Devi.

Singh Deo, Rajkumar Suddhendra Narayan. 1983.
"Expression and Movement in Seraikella Chhau Dance." In *Dance and Music in South Asian Drama.* Ed. Richard Emmert, et al. Tokyo: The Japan Foundation. Pp. 127–135.

Vatsyayan, Kapila. 1975.
"The Chhau Dance of Mayurbhanj." *Journal of the National Centre for the Performing Arts* 4, 4:1–13.

PART SIX

THE TRADITIONS OF MODERN THEATRE

Chapter Twelve

CHARACTERISTICS OF THE MODERN THEATRE

Farley P. Richmond

MODERN THEATRE IN INDIA IS URBAN, NOT RURAL. It is created by and primarily for people who may be regarded as middle and upper middle class. The plays run the gamut from serious to comic, political to frivolous. As the reader will soon see, various complicating forces create hardship for the production of plays and yet, in the face of seemingly insurmountable odds, live theatre survives, and in some regions of the country even flourishes.

To Western theatre students, much of what is presented in the following pages should have a ring of familiarity. Modern Indian theatre has characteristics similar to those in many Western countries and yet it has features which are uniquely Indian. Like the Sanskrit theatre of ancient times, modern theatre is an all-India phenomena. Although there is no national theatre movement, there is a national character to the urban theatre. And like the colorful regional theatre forms discussed earlier, urban theatre has a personality all its own.

Origins

Modern theatre in India owes its origins to the growth and development of large urban centers, such as Calcutta, Bombay, and Madras. Beginning in the eighteenth century, British soldiers established fortifications in widely separated regions of the country. These were constructed on behalf of the East India Company as a means of assuring a firm foothold on the Indian subcontinent, as part of a worldwide colonial expansion in anticipation of eventually establishing a pipeline to the China market (Said 1979). Having established safe and secure centers of trade by the mid-nineteenth century, the British were ready to introduce the English system of higher education and soon founded three major universities: Calcutta University, Bombay

University, and Madras University. The spread of English education led to the spread of British ideas, tastes, values, and morals among the Indian intelligentsia, along with a genuine love and abiding knowledge of British drama and theatre. In these early days plays were performed in English by Englishmen in proscenium arch playhouses modeled along the lines of similar structures in London.

Drama written in Indian languages and performed on the stage by Indian actors was not to emerge until the last quarter of the nineteenth century, when private theatres were constructed for the amusement and edification of the rich, particularly those who lived in Calcutta. Eventually these early attempts led to the construction of public theatres appealing to the taste of a wide variety of castes and classes of people, presented in the language of the region. Enterprising producers with nationalistic tendencies soon employed theatre for a purpose for which it was well suited—as a forum for social and political ideals designed to influence opinion and raise social consciousness. Seemingly unbeknownst to the British rulers of the time, theatre quickly became a powerful weapon to promote social and political reforms.

By the late nineteenth century, the British had firmly established a policy of indirect rule of India and were very much aware of theatre's potential to

English actors being dressed and served by Indian servants of the Bombay theatre in the early nineteenth century. Indian spectators look on. (*British Social Life in India*, 1938. Courtesy of Dennis Kincaid)

contribute to social unrest. They had the immediate example of a production of *The Mirror of Indigo Planters*, or *The Blue Mirror (Nildarpana)* presented in the North Indian city of Lucknow in 1875, in which a white planter was depicted as raping an Indian peasant woman. An enraged band of Europeans stormed the stage and stopped the show. The district magistrate hustled the actors off to the railway station and sent them packing back to Calcutta from where they had come. This event, and other political developments elsewhere in the country, soon led to a strict enforcement of censorship rules, which were imposed on the theatre through the enactment of the Dramatic Performances Act of 1879. The act gave the government the power to prohibit public performances suspected of being scandalous, defamatory, seditious, or obscene. Subsequently political and social protest was forced underground and Indian producers had to pass it off under the thinly veiled guise of historical and mythological subject matter. Frustrated by the harsh restrictions, many playwrights turned their attention to exposing the corruption within Hindu society and addressed a host of social injustices. Common themes included the immolation of widows on the funeral pyres of their husbands, child marriages, the dowry system, the restrictive role of women at home and in society and politics, and love marriages, to name but a few of the more popular issues of the day that were addressed on the stage.

Standing apart from the main stream of Indian theatre and yet bridging the nineteenth- and twentieth-century developments is the well-known Bengali poet, playwright, and actor Rabindranath Tagore. Tagore is best known in the Western world for his contributions to literature. He won the Nobel Prize for literature in 1913 for his poems *Gītāñjali* and *Gītāli*. He made several lecture tours of the United States, in which his ideas about what it means to be human received serious attention on college campuses. Indians remember him for his poetic contributions and for the fact that the national anthem of India is his handiwork. And in Bengal and principally Calcutta, this native son continues to be eulogized for his contributions to the theatre. However, in truth, Tagore has never really had much influence on the professional or amateur theatre, either in playwriting or in staging. According to Kironmoy Rahu, "His plays—and his ideas of theatre—developed along lines divergent from the general direction of development of Bengali drama and theatre. They had little influence on other playwrights and his attitude to the theatre in Calcutta was cool, distant, or, at best, ambivalent" (1978, 105).

Born into an extremely wealthy and artistic family in North Calcutta in 1861, Tagore is responsible for writing and staging many plays, most of which were presented by his large extended family, who played all the roles. The plays were mounted in a special theatre constructed in a comfortable massive bungalow in North Calcutta, Jorasanko House, which is now preserved as a museum and doubles as quarters for Rabindara Bharati Univer-

Chaiti Ghosal and Sombhu Mitra in Tagore's *The Post Office.* (Bahorupee photo)

sity. Tagore first appeared on the stage at the age of sixteen in a play directed by his elder brother, and he was seventy-five when he last appeared in one of his own works in 1935 at Santiniketan, a unique university in rural Bengal dedicated to the arts, an institution, incidentally, which he founded. He died in 1940 having written an impressive body of work, including plays, dance-dramas, poems, songs, and novels. Among his better known plays are *Rājā* (1910), *The Post Office* (*Dakghar,* 1913), and *Red Oleanders* (*Raktakarabi,* 1924).

The development and widespread popularity of the Indian cinema in the early twentieth century had an enormously adverse impact on live theatre. Owing to the drop in patronage, many famous commercial companies shut down. Some theatre halls closed their doors for good, others were converted to cinema houses. Actors, directors, and technicians abandoned the stage to seek careers with film companies.

When Independence finally came to India in 1947, the theatre was struggling to survive. Today just as theatre has begun to regain some of its lost ground, India is experiencing the rapid development and growth of television and the home-video industry, which poses a serious threat to the health of live theatre.[1]

The modern theatre of today boasts a number of unique characteristics, including commercial ventures, various grades and qualities of amateur

[1] Detailed historical surveys of the modern Indian theatre and drama may be found in Rangacharya and Gargi.

work, limited attempts at experimentation, and determined effort to establish and sustain school and college theatre programs. In the following pages, I will examine urban theatre in key and contrasting areas of the country—Calcutta, Bombay, Madras, Delhi, and the state of Kerala.[2] As in the preceding chapters, our format is designed to discuss various topics of interest, concluding with descriptions of selected live performances.

Organization

Commercial

In India as in much of the Western world, the main objective of the participants of the commercial theatre is to make money, no matter what the quality of the product. Indeed although they may wish to derive their living from theatre, many theatre artists consider it an insult to be called "commercial," and prefer instead to be labeled "professional."[3]

Considering the size of the population, India has comparatively few commercial theatres. Relatively few companies are able to make a living exclusively from the theatre. Calcutta has more commercial theatre activity than any other city of the subcontinent, and commercial theatre in Calcutta is confined almost exclusively to the region of a few city blocks in North Calcutta, the center of the Bengali community. The Star is the best-known commercial house in the city. Built in 1888 the Star is operated by a wealthy proprietor-manager whose family has investments in a variety of other business concerns, from jute production to film distribution. Actors who work at the Star are paid a run-of-the-play contract, unless the management gives them a twenty-one day notice. Well-known Bengali actors and actresses of stage and screen appear in the productions. Generally a senior actor stages the plays with the proprietor-manager offering his advice at his own discretion.

To act at the Star means steady employment. The Star runs at least five

---

[2] Material for this chapter was gathered beginning in 1980 during a field trip to the areas concerned and then updated in 1986 during another field trip. For logistical and pragmatic reasons, many areas of the country were not included in this survey, among them Bangalore, Ahmedabad, Pune, Allahabad, Lucknow, Hyderabad, Chandigar, Srinigar, and Gauhati, to name but a few of the more important cities with modern urban theatre companies and unique characteristics of their own.

[3] *Professional.* The term professional has been used variously in the Indian theatre to describe both the commercial and amateur theatre. It is sometimes used synonymously with commercial theatre to indicate that those who participate in it make a living by it—that theatre is their profession. However, many members of the amateur theatre in India refer to their work as "professional" to distinguish it from what they derisively refer to as the commercial fare. Still others think of professional theatre as the companies of India's village actors which tour a region, such as those in North Mysore state that make a living from theatre and that rarely perform in the large urban centers of Bangalore and Mysore.

performances a week, once on Thursdays and twice a day on Saturdays, Sundays, and holidays. Better-known actors earn a good living and those that have the time and energy perform other jobs during their off hours to generate additional income. The house has a paid staff of ticket sellers, ushers, stage and lighting technicians, makeup artists, and property and costume personnel. The entire operation seems to run smoothly and efficiently. The main objective is to provide the public with the kind of fare it has come to expect. A play runs as long as there is a profit to be made by the management. Generally a new production is opened every season.

Calcutta boasts of other commercial houses in the theatre district, as well. Circarena, the only major arena theatre building in India, is one of the most recent additions to the district. Other commercial theatre houses in Calcutta include Rangmahal, Biswaroopa, Minerva, Rangana, Bijon, Tapan, and Muktangan.

By contrast in Kerala the commercial theatre is scattered about and has a diverse character depending on the philosophy of the groups involved. The Kalanilaya Vistavision Dramascope Company has an office in Trivandrum but the company spends most of its time on the road traveling about the state. Founded in the early 1970s by Kalanilaya Krishna Nair, this group rents or leases a plot of land on the outskirts of a large town or city and proceeds to erect a large temporary theatre of thatch and bamboo, seating about a thousand patrons. This temporary home has the character of the temporary rural cinema houses of Kerala. A manager travels with a company of paid actors and backstage artists, arranging the food and living accommodations and organizing the schedules of nearly seventy-five individuals. A repertory of plays is produced and once audiences begin to dwindle or expenses are not met by the box office receipts the company strikes camp and moves on. Wages are paid according to the grade and level of the actors and technicians. Top rank or "A" grade actors are said to receive about $61 (Rs. 750) per month. Actors and scenic workers at the apprentice grade receive $18 (Rs. 225) per month. Because the company tours regularly and since the theatre personnel are producing plays nearly every day of the week, it is not possible for anyone to engage in other employment.

The Kerala People's Arts Company (KPAC) and Kālidāsa Kalakendra, the two major Communist commercial theatre groups in Kerala, usually mount only one new play a season to add to a repertory of productions the groups are capable of performing virtually at a moment's notice. Like the Kalanilaya, these two groups have permanent homes. The KPAC has a small plot of land on which is located a modern office complex and living quarters, in a beautiful rural area where the company rehearses plays during the monsoon season (June, July, and August). When the theatre season begins in earnest in September two companies tour in modern vans, on top of which scenery is stored, performing primarily for sponsoring organizations throughout all

Headquarters of the Kerala People's Arts Company. (Farley P. Richmond photo)

the regions of India in which Malayalam is spoken. The group performs for a flat fee per production. By contrast Kālidāsa Kalakendra is located in the suburb of a medium-sized city and operates its business on a telephone request basis. After nearly four weeks of rehearsal, a new production tours in a company-owned van different regions of the state.

Commercial theatre in Madras is virtually dead, with one exception. Manohar's National Theatre is one of the best-organized and slickest commercial operations that one may find anywhere in urban India. Although not a modern theatre in the sense that the plays deal with contemporary issues (the National continues to produce historical and mythological works using wing and drop settings in the style of the nineteenth century), the company still has a strong appeal for a segment of the theatre-going public of Madras and elsewhere in India where Tamil is spoken. Details concerning the work of the National are described elsewhere in this chapter.

By contrast the thriving metropolitan center of Bombay is relatively poor in commercial theatre. In Bombay only a few actors and directors are able to eke out a living producing and performing plays. Many of Bombay's leading theatre personalities do manage to survive by performing in theatre, films, and on radio. But a company in which theatre is the sole support of its members, and theatre houses that are regarded as commercial, are not features of the Bombay theatre scene. Perhaps the high cost of theatre rental, advertisement, and production expenses prevent theatre from developing into a viable commercial venture in this city of many millions of people.

Delhi is in far worse shape than Bombay. Yatrik, an English-language group, attempted to organize a professional repertory company during the mid-1970s but failed to consolidate all the forces that were necessary to bring about its success. The attempt came to an early end but was heavily subsidized by state funds, otherwise it could not have survived on box office revenues alone. And in the early 1980s the Sri Ram Centre, a building supported by a wealthy family of industrialists, inaugurated a paid company. Yet for all its splendor as the capitol city of India, Delhi theatre is still in its infancy.

Amateur

Most of India's modern theatre may be categorized as amateur; that is, theatre in which the majority of those who participate do so with little expectation of earning a living. They do so for a multitude of reasons: love of theatre, enjoyment, as a means of gaining self-confidence, to meet people, as a stepping stone into cinema and TV, and so on. The quality of amateur theatre is often extremely high, in some instances higher than the quality of the commercial ventures, and some of the participants may even make a good part of their living from amateur theatre. There is a wide range of amateur groups, too—those that are totally independent entities, those that are appendages of larger social organizations, and those associated with colleges and other educational institutions. Typically an amateur group has a dynamic leader or small corps of leaders surrounded by a band of devoted followers and a large body of peripheral individuals whose participation fluctuates depending on the reputation and fortunes of the group. Historically most amateur groups depend on the vision and guidance of a strong director. The very life of the group may be in the hands of one individual who brings a sense of unity and purpose to the activities of the group. However, there are some variations in this basic pattern, as we shall see below.

Calcutta is said to have over three thousand registered theatre groups. Enthusiastic supporters refer to some of the amateur organizations as "group theatre." The so-called group theatre of Calcutta is distinguished from both the commercial theatre and college theatre primarily by its choice of fare. Group theatre prides itself on performing plays that generally have a serious content, many of them satiric, and that espouse mild to strong political messages, some of which are highly partisan. Each group has developed a reputation for its work and the leadership cultivates that reputation by sustaining the kind and level of offerings with each passing season. Although most of the workers in Calcutta's group theatre do not earn a living participating in productions, they do pride themselves on the quality of their work. Indeed some of India's finest productions and best individual performances are to be seen on the Calcutta stage. Bahorupee's productions of *Red Oleanders, Rājā,* and *Oedipus;* the Little Theatre Group's *Coal;* and Nandikar's *The Three Penny Opera* and *Antigone,* as well as performances by Sombhu Mitra, Tripti Mitra, Utpal Dutt, and the late Asutosh Bhattacharya, to name but a few, are etched in my memory as superb examples of the group theatre tradition. It should be noted that Western plays in translation or adaptation provide a considerable part of the repertory of many of the companies. In fact group theatre tends to stress the importance of performing work similar to that of the festival and repertory theatres of the United States and the municipal companies of Europe.

Bombay also has its share of amateur theatre. It is said that there are nearly five hundred amateur theatres that function in the city and a total of about twenty-five hundred groups in the state of Maharashtra. As in Calcutta the groups range from organizations with long-standing reputations for high quality work to college theatricals from which many of the local theatre organizations draw promising young talent. Theatre in Bombay is somewhat complicated in that a number of languages are spoken in the city; thus, theatre groups have sprung up to accommodate different language constituencies. As the capital of Maharashtra and the largest city of the state, Bombay is the center of Marathi theatre. It is said that a Marathi theatre group, even in the neighboring city of Pune, must first make its mark in Bombay before it attains any standing elsewhere. Like the people of Calcutta, the Maharastrian middle class loves theatre, and yet complicated economic factors prevent a full-time professional theatre from developing. Despite the restrictions, some of the directors and actors of the Marathi theatre make a living producing plays. Generally they do so by participating in a wide variety of jobs, including acting in Marathi and Hindi language films and on All-India Radio and TV. An individual with many irons in the fire in Bombay or Pune has the potential of making a living. However, no one can be sustained by performing only one play at a time or solely by directing. As in Calcutta theatre in Bombay depends on strong personalities and teams of dedicated workers.

Theatre organizations are either autonomous bodies or they are extensions of larger cultural organizations. For example, Kamalkar Sarang and his wife each run separate groups. Both groups produce plays on a regular basis. Besides directing and acting in the work of their own groups, the Sarangs also perform in the plays of several other organizations. In contrast, the Goa Hindu Association, founded in 1919, is a social organization which has many enterprises. Among them are a diagnostic center, a cooperative credit society, and a music school. In addition to these, a theatre wing was founded in the early 1950s. A board of directors chooses plays, commissions directors and actors, and generally runs its productions with the intention of earning enough profit from the theatre to help defray the expenses of its other social operations. The size and dedication of the membership of the various Marathi theatre groups depend on the reputation of the organization and the benefit the members derive from their participation. Bombay has a lively theatre in Gujarati, Hindi, and English, not to mention theatre in several South Indian languages. As a cosmopolitan commercial center attracting large populations of individuals from throughout the country, Bombay supports a variety of amateur theatres with ease. But still none of them can muster enough support to provide a living for all members of the groups.

The Indian National Theatre (INT) is a cosmopolitan theatre organization sponsoring theatre productions in Marathi, Gujarati, Hindi, and English. However, the leadership of the group is primarily Marathi- and Gujarati-speaking and most of the productions have been in these two languages. The INT has a large support staff, a separate office with business managers, secretarial staff, and telephones, a small library, a research wing, and space for conducting workshops, building scenery, and so on. Through the returns on its productions and grants from the state and central government, it is able to carry out all its diverse functions. Founded in 1944, the INT has been instrumental in bringing Bombay residents a consistently high standard of entertainment for adult plays and children's shows, from folk-inspired productions to translations and adaptations of Western plays. One of the longest running plays in the history of the Bombay theatre has been the Gujarati version of *Pygmalion* (called *Pūnarānī*) presented by the INT. The show had a phenomenal run of several thousand performances over a decade of its history. As with other groups, the INT depends on a corps of dedicated leaders and a large group of enthusiastic workers.

Hindi theatre has a much smaller audience base to draw from but several nationally known personalities have led the fight to nurture a Hindi theatre in Bombay. In 1944 Prithvi Raj Kapoor, a Pathan by birth and one of India's most famous film stars, founded a company (the Prithvi Theatres) and produced several remarkable plays in Hindi in an attempt to attract audiences to the Hindi theatre. The effort did not result in a permanent movement, however, and he was soon heavily in debt. Ebrahim Alkazi organized the Theatre Group in 1953 and as part of a broad range of offerings produced numerous plays in Hindi. On leaving Bombay for his post as director of the National School of Drama (NSD) in Delhi, the Theatre Group fell into the hands of Satyadev Dubey, a very capable actor and director, who has sustained Hindi theatre in Bombay virtually single-handed until recent years, when several other groups have emerged to foster Hindi-language plays.

Theatre in English has a long and impressive history in Bombay dating back to the mid-eighteenth century, when British plays were first performed by English actors for the entertainment of British soldiers and merchants and eventually to the delight of local citizens. After Independence in 1947, an

Vijaya Mehta, Yasmin Richmond, and Alaknanda Samar in Theatre Group's *Dead Water* written by Pratab Sharma. (Gurmeet Singh photo)

English-language theatre produced by Indian actors and directors actually grew in size and influence, partially because English remained a major medium of communication. Alyque Padamsee, one of the English-language theatre's leading directors, recently observed that the English-speaking population of the city is even growing and that there is now a greater demand for more plays in English than ever before. At the forefront of the groups that produce plays in English is the Theatre Group, organized in 1943 by Sultan Padamsee. Since that time, the Theatre Group has provided a wide range of plays on a regular basis to a corps of devoted members and spectators.

For a city of its size and importance Delhi has relatively little amateur theatre. At the very most about fifty groups function in Delhi, primarily in the city of New Delhi. Because it too has large populations of individuals from many different regions of the country, it is possible to find amateur theatre in almost every regional language. However, there are more groups in Hindi and Punjabi because a large percentage of the population speaks one or the other of these two North Indian languages. As in Bombay and Calcutta, a typical amateur theatre group in Delhi is composed of a few prominent personalities and relies on a corps of active fringe members. As one disgruntled director recently observed, "Younger members of the fringe of a group tend to develop their talents and once they have gained a bit of confidence they form a splinter group keeping Delhi theatre groups in a constant state of flux."

According to the State Academy for Music, Dance and Drama, Films and Folk Arts (Tamilnadu Eyal Isai Nataka Manram), Madras has about fifty registered theatre groups, most of which perform plays in Tamil, the language of Tamil Nadu. As I discuss further, a unique feature of the Madras theatre is the control sponsoring organizations exert over the economic viability of the amateur organizations and the choice of productions. Except for these unique features the organizations and function of Madras theatre is similar to that of amateur groups elsewhere in India. As late as 1965 Madras also boasted one of the oldest English-language organizations in the world, the Madras Amateur Dramatic Society (MADS). For all practical purposes the group came to an end as an active producing group about this time. Today the Madras Players continue to produce plays in English, serving a small but dedicated patronage.

The theatre groups of Kerala are either commercial organizations or they are linked to educational institutions. College amateur theatrical activity is the primary mode of furthering the cause of theatre in Kerala. There are some exceptions, which we shall discuss in connection with experimental theatre. Unlike the activities elsewhere in India, Kerala does not sustain a thriving amateur theatre apart from that associated with educational institutions.

School and College

Dramatic societies in the schools and colleges of the nation serve as a chief training ground for would-be directors, actors, and technicians. Following in the footsteps of the English system of education, India has not experienced the phenomenal growth of academic (educational) theatre that has occurred in the United States. Later in this chapter I will discuss theatre training as it applies to departments of drama and theatre. School and college amateur dramatic societies are really places for members to participate in performances, rather than to study the theory and practice of performance and theatre history in depth. And yet many of India's major urban theatre figures have emerged from this background. Dramatic societies of Saint Xavier's College, Calcutta; Elphinstone College and Saint Xavier's College, Bombay; St. Steven's College, Lady Irwin, and Miranda House, New Delhi; and Women's Christian College, Madras, have provided some of the finest talent that may be found in the commercial, amateur, and experimental theatre of India today.

Experimental

Experimental theatre in India may be considered a branch of the amateur theatre, but in some instances the objectives of the groups and their approach to producing plays are quite different from that of the general run of amateur groups. Calcutta has the reputation of being the foremost center of experimental theatre in the country. The unofficial leader of the experimental theatre is Badal Sircar, well-known playwright, director, and actor. In his book entitled *The Third Theatre* (1978), Sircar describes some of the major characteristics of experimental theatre. He says it can survive on a shoestring and by so doing attempts to break away from the system that so many commercial and amateur theatre groups find themselves locked within, such as the rental of expensive theatre houses, costly advertisement in local newspapers, dependence on expensive lighting, scenic, and sound equipment, playwrights suited to more conventional staging techniques, and actors struggling to make a living performing theatre. Sircar derides the commercialism of all Indian theatre and proposes that the only way to produce new works is to break away from the old system and establish a different one. He has done this to an extent with his Satabdi group, which usually performs a show every Friday evening, often at any site found suitable for the production, such as a simple, open, unfinished hall with no lighting equipment, using simple costumes and properties, and presented to the general public at a low uniform price. Another group, the Living Theatre of Khardah, located in suburban Calcutta, has produced its works in a tiny school hall in the middle of a rice paddy field, borrowing electrical connections from an adjacent cigarette shop at the charge of eight cents (Rs. 1) a night. Sometimes no more than a dozen spectators witness a work, which often consists of little dialogue and frequently a combination of human and animal sounds. Critics and enthusiastic supporters of this experimental work are willing to travel nearly an hour by train from the heart of Calcutta just to see this kind of theatre. In recent years other groups have emerged along similar lines around Calcutta's congested suburbs. As yet the "Third Theatre" has not become a vital movement, nor has it changed the prevailing pattern of amateur theatre in this theatre-loving city.

Unconventional theatre in Bombay goes by the name of "experimental theatre." The recent home of this branch of the amateur movement is the antiquated third-floor hall of the Chabildas School in the heart of the Marathi-speaking district, near Shivaji Mandir, one of the most popular Marathi theatre buildings in the city. During the day the hall is used by school children. At night a large common room doubles as a theatre, where an enterprising brand of theatre workers swiftly converts the space into a makeshift proscenium theatre with a curtained stage and lighting equipment. The whole setup is struck after each performance so that the school may use the space during the day. Numerous groups use the facility, paying a nominal fee for rental to Avishkar, the group which leases the hall from the school on a yearly basis. Many shows play to packed houses night after night in this theatre, indicating that the desire for unconventional theatre does exist in Bombay. The only restriction seems to be the lack of available reasonably priced space. To meet the need for a small, well-equipped theatre space, the Prithvi Theatre was constructed at Juhu Beach in North Bombay in 1979. Although its location is somewhat out of the way for individuals who must travel by public conveyance, the Prithvi operates a year-round program of performances by numerous small theatre groups producing plays in Marathi, Hindi, Gujarati, and English. The theatre is run by Shashi Kapoor, one of Raj Kapoor's sons and a motion picture star in his own right. The Prithvi boasts of being the only three-quarter round theatre in Bombay and one of the best little theatres in India. In 1983 construction began on a "black box" theatre in the heart of the commercial and tourist district of Bombay. Located on prime land amid the impressive facilities of the National Centre for the Performing Arts, the Experimental Theatre opened in 1985. One day soon it may become one of Bombay's most popular facilities for the presentation of experimental productions.

Until his death in 1972, the playwright Mohan Rakesh ran an experimental workshop in New Delhi which attempted to break new ground for the production of unconventional, nonrealistic plays written in Hindi. His group of enthusiastic young people attempted to develop productions with a focus on physical movement, gesture, and sounds rather than be ruled by the dictates of a script. Unlike the lines which are clearly drawn in Calcutta and Bombay between the amateur theatre and the experimental theatre, it is more difficult to make the distinction in Delhi, a city with relatively little theatre and where almost anything seems new and different. As the capital of the country, Delhi audiences have been privileged to witness a host of performances of traditional rural theatre, often presented in quasi-authentic settings, as well as tours by theatre groups, both modern and conventional, from around the world. In this respect, unique theatre which stresses unconventional means of production has found its way into the theatre life of the capital. Much of the experimental theatre in Delhi is performed in the intimate basement theatre of the Sri Ram Centre.

Madras and Kerala are quite different from Calcutta, Bombay, and Delhi.

Experimental theatre hardly exists in Madras, a city locked into a rigid pattern of survival. Only two groups have earned the reputation for experimentation in Madras in recent years. Today only one is still active. With no tradition of experimentation and no major theatre personalities dedicated to promoting new work, the experimental theatre in Madras is at a standstill. Except in Trivandrum where Kavalam Narayana Pannikar doggedly continues to produce works heavily influenced by ideas from traditional theatre forms, such as *kūṭiyāṭṭam, kathakaḷi,* and folk dances and music, and the work of G. Shankaran Pillai for the new repertory company[4] of Calicut University's School of Drama, Kerala may claim no experimental theatre tradition outside attempts by directors of various colleges and universities to produce works in an unconventional style and manner.

Plays

In the modern Western theatre, the text usually serves as the guide to the production concept. Generally you must first have a text before a production concept emerges. And once the text is available, a variety of production concepts emerge as possibilities, depending on the latitude the script allows and the imagination and ingenuity of the director, actors, and designers. Modern Indian theatre is similar to Western theatre in this respect, in that it depends on the creative interpretation of the playscript. The Bombay director Satyadev Dubey somewhat begrudgingly admitted, "Today's theatre is still play oriented and not performance oriented." Indeed, it may be said that this is one of the things which distinguishes urban theatre from the traditional forms of theatre that we have examined thus far—the importance that is given to the text of a play. For centuries smug urbanites have frowned on the devotional and folk-popular forms and the dance-dramas because they did not stress the text in performance.

However, there is some question, as there always has been, as to whether the playwright is the dominant force in the urban theatre of India. Another equally well-known Bombay director has said, "The urban theatre of the recent past was dominated by playwrights, whereas now it is controlled by

[4] Although some groups think of their work as repertory, there is no true repertory system functioning in urban India. Generally a group produces a work and runs it for as long as it can afford to or as long as a profit may be made from it. Sometimes a theatre organization has a number of plays that may be performed on very short notice over a period of many years but there is no repertory, in the Western sense of a system in which a regular rotation of plays is part of a series of presentations by a theatre organization. Nonetheless the term is used to describe the National School of Drama Repertory Company and the Sri Ram Centre Theatre Repertory in New Delhi and Rangmandal in Bhopal. Perhaps only the village theatre troupes may claim to operate a true repertory system in which they produce their works regularly on a rotating basis with the same company of performers.

actors." Although many other theatre workers in this giant metropolis believe that this is true for the amateur theatre, they claim that directors dominate the experimental theatre. The truth probably lies somewhere in between. It usually requires a working combination of playwrights (or makers of plots), directors, and actors to produce modern theatre. The way this happens in contemporary India is outlined in the following pages.

Hundreds, perhaps thousands, of plays are written every year in Indian languages. Authorities of Bombay's theatre group report that the Sultan Padamsee Playwriting Competition annually attracts several hundred new scripts composed by Indian writers in English. Few are ever produced and fewer still are ever published. It is simply remarkable that so many works may be created in English, since the language is spoken by a fraction of the total population of seven hundred and fifty million. One may only imagine that the writing must be prolific in languages such as Marathi and Bengali, with extensive population bases, and a long history of modern theatre.

Considering the extremely large number of plays that are performed every year in India, it is not possible to make definite statements concerning trends or characteristics. However, it seems from reports of theatre personnel that contemporary Indian playwrights are concerned with a multitude of themes that center on the family, social life in general, the plight of the individual in a modern mechanized society, and contemporary political and social events. This is particularly true of the Marathi playwrights of Bombay. Works which satirize social institutions, particularly the government and politicians, are popular in Bombay. The problems and lifestyles of the middle class are also portrayed by local writers. Until the establishment of the Left-Front government in Bengal, Calcutta writers seemed obsessed with political issues, such as the injustice and authoritarian behavior of the police force, central and state government, political parties, business, and industry. Corruption and mismanagement of resources have been common themes explored by Calcutta playwrights. Even comedy has a barbed, bitter edge in Calcutta. In Madras one may find plays that are concerned primarily with family and social issues. The generation gap is a favorite theme among Madras playwrights. Many of the contemporary plays show older, tradition-bound parents attempting to come to grips with the new lifestyles and changing values of their children.

Some theatre groups perform plays which expound views which are synonymous with those of certain political parties. The Kerala People's Arts Company (KPAC) is believed to be a political organ of the Cultural Wing of the Communist Party of India (CPI), which is pro-Soviet, and the Kālidāsa Kalakendra, a splinter group of the KPAC, expounds the dogma of the CPI (M), the Marxist branch of the Communist Party which is pro-Chinese. Both groups employ well-known Kerala playwrights who are sensitive to the subtle differences between the political philosophies of the parties and who are aware of the current political trends in India. The KPAC and Kālidāsa Kalakendra survive because of their party affiliations. A few years ago when Utpal Dutt of Calcutta, perhaps India's best-known left-wing theatre spokesman, discovered that his plays were expected to echo the philosophy of the Marxist party of Bengal, whenever the party's views happened to change, he refused to do so. But by then it was too late. He had already alienated a large segment of his original supporters by agreeing to echo the views of that political party in the first place. When the CPI (M) disowned him for failing to toe the party line, he alienated his political supporters, as well. His plight has served as a harsh object lesson to all theatre artists of Bengal: Never jeopardize your career by unequivocal affiliation with any political party. In order not to offend anyone, local company owners of *jātra* parties, Bengal's most popular form of rural theatre, have portraits hanging in their Calcutta offices of the major political figures of both East and West, from Lenin to Reagan, from Mao to Mohammed.

The sources of modern works in India run the gamut from original ideas to adaptations of short stories, novels, films, and plays in other languages. Foreign plays have provided a wealth of inspiration for many authors. Critics

Utpal Dutt's *Titu Meer.* (Utpal Dutt photo)

of the Gujarati theatre of Bombay accuse it of being nothing but "Xerox" theatre in which plays are churned out like carbon copies of Western works. Gujarati directors have often been accused of plagiarizing bits and pieces of various plays to suit their own needs, creating so-called new works from among the parts of several Western plays.

By Western standards, most contemporary Indian plays are long, taking anywhere from two to three hours to perform. In Madras when Manohar reads out a new work to a close band of faithful followers, he keeps a stop-watch handy and allows only so much time for the dialogue, so much time for action and scene changes, and so much time for songs, music, and dances. He claims that today's audiences will not sit through a show that runs for more than two hours. Only a few decades ago, audiences in Madras and elsewhere in India expected, even demanded, plays that ran at least three and a half hours.

Today plays composed by Indian authors tend to have a multitude of scenes arbitrarily interrupted by a short intermission or two. Very often the scenes are written as though they were composed for a film, each having a limited purpose with regard to the overall dramatic action. (Elsewhere I will discuss how plays with short scenes may tax a production concept, especially when realistic detail is demanded in props and setting.) None of the playwrights I interviewed said that they were influenced by or even interested in films. However, some of the writers have recently engaged in scripting feature-length films and TV serials and there may be no doubt that films and TV have captured the public imagination, while theatre may claim only limited public appeal. In structure and form, many modern Indian plays simply echo the cinema.

Realism seems to dominate the settings and dialogue of most plays, even though scenes may be strung together in a theatrical manner. Occasionally a playwright introduces a novel twist, such as a narrator or dialogue spoken by groups of characters. Occasionally also songs or segments of dance are introduced, which suspend the flow of the dramatic action and provide variety to the proceedings. Many playwrights today are turning to highly theatrical gimmicks, such as "stop action" over which the recorded thoughts of a character are played.

In the 1960s a small corps of playwrights from every corner of the country became enamored with the traditional village theatre forms of their region. They attempted to wed some of the techniques of rural theatre to their own writing. The results promised to lead to an awakening of the consciousness of urban theatre people to the potential of the rural theatre. The experiment was short-lived, however. None of the writers felt comfortable borrowing styles of composition from forms of theatre that were not a vital part of their own tradition. In the early 1980s producers and directors were encouraged to try similar experiments through grants from the Sangeet Natak Akademi

(National Academy of Music, Dance, and Drama) in Delhi. These efforts have begun to pay dividends in which a number of young artists have emerged and their work has been seen in regional festivals and workshops, climaxed by an annual national gathering in Delhi.

Modern plays seem doomed to remain in the language in which they were created. Today Bengali or Marathi plays are rarely translated into other languages. English-language or Hindi plays by Indian writers rarely make the transition into other languages. In the 1970s, the work of a small corps of writers was translated into Hindi and then into other regional languages or English. Works by Utpal Dutt, Badal Sircar, Girish Karnad, and Vijay Tendulkar, to name but a few of the more popular writers, were adapted into languages other than those in which they were written and received recognition from more than the regional audiences for which they were intended. This trend, too, has been somewhat retarded in recent years, perhaps owing to the resistance of theatre groups to select works they do not view as surefire successes with their audiences.

Very few people earn a living writing plays. In Kerala N. N. Pillai earns his living writing for his own company. Most writers have other occupations and write plays only as part of their leisure time. Jaywant Dalve is a barrister and playwright in Bombay. C. L. Jos of Trichur, Kerala, writes plays on the side while he engages in his major occupation, assistant manager of a busy office. Vijay Tendulkar has a multitude of activities connected to writing; plays are but a part of his various activities. Badal Sircar of Calcutta was an architect who gave up his profession to write for and work in the theatre. In recent years he has given up playwriting in favor of working as a director and actor. Between film engagements, acting jobs, and directing, Utpal Dutt writes plays for his theatre group. Indeed there are no clear cut patterns of success among India's playwrights. Most writers need to make a living and at the same time they also feel the need to write.

A few playwrights compose works exclusively for their own companies. Kavalam Narayana Pannikar writes for Sopanam, his current group in Trivandrum. Utpal Dutt writes for the People's Little Theatre (PLT) of Calcutta, and the Tamil playwright Cho creates his works exclusively for the Viveka Fine Arts Club, the Madras group with which he is affiliated.

More often than not, a playwright produces a work and then has a director or actor take a look at it. Better-known writers are commissioned to write plays for a group; they may be given so-called pen money in the range of $407–$813 (Rs. 5,000–10,000) to produce a play within a fixed period of time. Besides directing his own works, Thopil Bhasi writes for pen money in producing plays for Kerala's KPAC. The managers of Calcutta's commercial theatre may have an idea for a play that they think will appeal to a general audience. They will assemble some of the leading actors of their company and talk over several ideas. Then they employ hack writers to compose various sections of the work for their scrutiny. After evaluating the results, they complete payments for the script. In Madras Manohar describes a similar process for the development of one of his historical dramas. He selects the story, title, and writes a scenario. Then one of his hack writers composes a "treatment." (The vocabulary of the cinema is telling!) With that in hand Manohar deletes or adds to the plot, depending on the need for scenic effects. After he approves this, then the writers complete various portions of the script. One writer handles the comic episodes, another takes care of the serious sections, and so forth. Manohar holds the rights over the entire script and gives each of the writers a fee based on a verbal contract. If a film is made from the script, the writers have some interest in the sale, which is negotiated by Manohar.

Many playwrights receive royalties from groups that perform their works. The amount varies considerably depending on the reputation of the playwright. In Bombay it is said that the playwright receives approximately $8.10 (Rs. 100) per performance. A long-running work may net a handsome royalty income for a popular playwright. Some authors have done very well by publishing their works. C. L. Jos writes social dramas meant to be produced by college theatrical societies and amateur groups in Kerala. His plays are published in Kerala by the National Book Society (NBS) in lots of five thousand copies. Royalties on the book net a substantial additional income for the author. Several years ago, when sales waned for one of his scripts, he discovered that it wasn't being bought because the title page implied that a royalty fee would be charged if the play was produced. Since then he has not bothered to ask for royalties for play productions, and now his book sales are high and some of his works are even used as texts in Malayalam literature classes. One of his plays was broadcast simultaneously on All-India Radio in all the major Indian languages.

It is common to find plays at book shops and on railway platform bookstalls throughout Kerala. Modern Bengali plays are published but not widely circulated, except along Calcutta's College Road. Only a few book shops in Delhi and Madras handle plays in Indian languages. But Cho confided that plays are usually published in Madras' so-called theatre periodicals. Coupled with a few news items and articles, the periodicals are sold for a minimum price of about eight cents (Rs. 1), whereas if they were published alone in paperback or hardcover editions, they would cost more than forty cents (Rs. 5) each and the publisher would not realize a return on the investment. Overall Indian plays of the urban theatre are hand-crafted pieces, even though they often borrow themes from past successes. They appeal to the theatre public by their novelty. Unlike many of the rural theatre forms, prefabricated works do not attract urban Indian playwrights.

Performers

Directors and Directing

Historically the artistic control of theatre in rural areas of India has been in the hands of actors. True, some actors were also designated for other jobs in the theatre companies. The *Nāṭyaśāstra* outlines the various duties of the stage manager, who was to serve as manager of the theatre company as well as one of its principal actors. But the stage director, in the modern sense, owes his origin to the changing conditions of nineteenth-century urban India, which followed English patterns of theatrical organization, at least through Independence in 1947.

There is some question whether things have changed all that radically since the nineteenth century. Many of today's directors serve a multitude of roles. The majority are actors with distinguished careers to their credit. Some directors also write plays, plus design scenery, lighting, and costumes. It may be more proper to describe the director in the modern Indian theatre as an individual capable of performing a multitude of functions and doing most of them as well or better than most of the other theatre personnel with which he or she associates.

To begin with, it is necessary to note that the commercial theatre companies of Calcutta and Kerala usually do not employ the talents of a stage director. Responsibility for the blocking and stage compositions is shared among the major actors. They also have a hand in making decisions about the setting and costumes, along with the producer or company manager. In some theatres of Kerala the playwright may serve as the director, articulating his views about the interpretation of his characters and line readings but rarely planning and conceiving of the production concept, as a Western director might do.

More commonly directors are found among the amateur theatre organizations of all the cities in the country. The very life of many organizations depends on one and only one individual—the stage director. Many well-known groups have disappeared, virtually overnight, when their director quit. Considering the hardships that many Indian theatre directors must endure, it is no wonder that a group's survival remains in the hands of one individual.

Stage directors in India have enormous power and responsibility. One old hand in Bombay is quoted as saying, "You have to be crazy to direct a play today. Most of us work a full nine-hour day and then on top of that we take on the hassles of another nine-hour job by directing for a local theatre organization!" Group members look to the director to make all the major and many of the minor decisions connected with a production. The director's

Rudra Prasad Sen Gupta, right, the well-known actor-director with his wife Swatilekha Sen Gupta in an adaptation of Ibsen's *A Doll's House*. (Nandikar photo)

artistic guidance sets the tone of the production and generally goes unquestioned, unless an equally strong personality emerges from the group to challenge for power and authority. When that happens the result is likely to be the formation of a separate theatre group. Directors depend on the cooperation of a team of diverse personalities who must be forged into a unified company of actors and technicians. Considering the financial problems most organizations face, the director is expected to keep the company solvent without sacrificing the artistic integrity of the group. This means choosing plays that are appealing to the actors as well as to the audiences that come to see their work. A string of box office failures may spell the end of a budding career, unless the director can convince the other members of the group that the public doesn't understand the work and that the production has merits which have not yet been recognized. In success or failure, the director must be in a position to command respect from the troupe membership. Indeed the individual must be able to delegate authority when needed and to make hard decisions at the right moment.

Modern directors are more than managers and psychologists. They are often called upon to organize and conduct workshops in various aspects of theatre for the benefit of less experienced members of their organization. Workshops often pay dividends, in that fresh talent may be spotted and nurtured. It is also for these reasons that directors produce plays for and with local college students. A freelance director in Delhi admitted, "There is a demand for directors among the college dramatic societies. We fill that void."

Either a director works exclusively for one theatre organization or does freelance work, engaging in whatever projects pay sufficient wages and have a suitable appeal or challenge. The following thumbnail sketch traces the career of one of India's most prominent directors: Ebrahim Alkazi. Elk, as he is familiarly known among his friends throughout the country, completed his school and college days in Bombay in the 1930s and 1940s. He sought a career in painting after graduation from college and spent time in London pursuing that goal. Frustrated by the teaching methods of the Royal Academy of Art, he shifted to theatre, another of his interests, and studied for some time at the Royal Academy of Dramatic Arts. Returning to Bombay in 1951, along with several other organizing members of the Theatre Group, one of the city's oldest and best known English-language theatre organizations, he began to produce plays. Eventually after serving his time with the Theatre Group he formed the Theatre Unit. The objective of the Theatre Unit was to produce Western classics, in a charming rooftop arena theatre overlooking the Arabian Sea. Part of his apartment below the rooftop was designed as an art gallery and the Theatre Unit soon became a center for art and theatre in Bombay, as well as a sponsor of chamber music concerts, recitals, poetry readings, and eventually a center for the production of plays in Hindi. Alkazi's reputation grew steadily during the 1950s and early 1960s, as he was invited to conduct theatre workshops for the state and national government throughout the country. When the post of director of the National School of Drama (NSD) became available in New Delhi, he was offered the position. Through many years of continual labor he brought leading theatre personalities from India and abroad to New Delhi to teach, direct, and lecture. He assembled a talented faculty and was responsible for building one of the best theatre libraries and slide collections in the country.

Ebrahim Alkazi's production of Girish Karnad's *Tugluk* for the National School of Drama Repertory Company, New Delhi. (National School of Drama Repertory Company photo)

Although the NSD emphasizes both English and Hindi as the medium of instruction, all the major productions were and continue to be in Hindi, and so most of Alkazi's productions, since he assumed the directorship, have been in Hindi. During these years many handsome and critically acclaimed productions have been produced by Alkazi for the NSD.

A magnificent production of Girish Karnad's *Tuglak* was mounted among the ruins of the medieval Muslim fortifications of New Delhi. During the political turmoil in New Delhi in the late 1970s Alkazi resigned his post as director of the NSD to take up the management of a well-known art gallery and to resume his interest in his old love—art.[5] Few Indian directors have had the luxury of handsomely funded productions, the resources of a national theatre school, and the influence that such a position brings on forming future generations of top-notch talent; and few have had the headaches or the heartaches that such a post brings. Although Alkazi's career is unique, it does illustrate the potential that is available to Indian directors, once they are given positions of responsibility and authority in modern Indian theatre.

Among India's leading directors are also the following: Cho, Utpal Dutt, B. V. Karanth, Bansi Kaul, Manohar, Vijaya Mehta, Arun Mukerjee, Kavalam Narayana Pannikar, M. K. Raina, B. M. Shah, Rudra Prasad Sen Gupta, Habib Tanvir, Ratan Thiyam, Alyque Padamsee, and Pearl Padamsee.

Actors and Acting

It goes without saying that actors are the primary ingredient of the theatre—without them, there would be none. Urban Indian actors differ from their village counterparts in several essential respects. City actors belong to a variety of different castes, communities, and religious groups. Acting is not a hereditary occupation for them as it is for many rural artists. But the taint that is associated with actors around the world is also attributed to modern Indian actors—accusations by the public of loose morals, high living, alcoholism, and drug abuse. Many actors come from wealthy or influential families, some of which see acting as a short step away from prostitution, although more than likely, actors are no better or no worse than other members of the society from which they come.

Urban Indian actors certainly have a different lifestyle from rural performers. Like other city dwellers, they are tied to the urban economy, subject to the pressures of making a living one way or another in an inflationary economy, pressed and pummeled in overcrowded commuter trains, queuing up to wait an hour or more for public buses, living in high-rise apartment com-

[5] For a more detailed exploration of Alkazi's background, see the "Journal of South Asian Literature Interviews: Ebrahim Alkazi" 1975, 289–325.

plexes, and attracted to and sometimes able to afford the luxuries of modern life out of reach of the majority of India's masses.

Relatively few theatre people are able to earn a living as actors. Most of them, even some of the leading artists, have an occupation in government, business, or industry which provides a steady income to support their family and style of life. In India acting is considered a risky business. A lucky few are independently wealthy or are supported by a family business which provides them with the leisure to participate in theatre. Since urban actors subsist on an income earned through other means, they may be considered amateurs. But many of them are in every other way professional in their outlook and their level of performance, comparable to the best actors of any other country in the world. But because they do not earn their living from theatre, they are often not taken seriously in India or by visiting artists from abroad. Yet they have strong convictions about the level of their competence and a frustration bred out of the attribution of the label "amateur."

Actors in Calcutta's Commercial Theatre have a written contract with the theatre management for the run of a show. Top-ranked actors, usually older performers with more experience or those who have made a reputation as film stars, command salaries of about \$813–\$1,626 (Rs. 10,000–20,000) per month, or approximately between \$58 and \$102 per show. A comparable actor in Bombay, referred to as an "A" grade actor, may earn \$41 (Rs. 500) per show. The Bombay actor works without a written contract and has to travel wherever the show is being performed, inside or outside the city. In Bombay medium-ranked actors ("B" grade) earn between \$16 and \$24 (Rs. 200–300) a show. There are said to be a large number of them in the city. Actors with little experience may earn only \$2.85 (Rs. 35) a show. By comparison the lowest-ranked commercial actor earns a paltry \$4.85 (Rs. 60) a month.

As indicated earlier, at Calcutta's Star Theatre an actor or the management may give three weeks notice before termination of a contract. The actors are obliged by the terms of the contract to remain in the company at least a hundred nights. The contract also provides opportunities for taking short leaves of absence due to illness. The Star also provides bonuses for actors if a show is doing particularly well at the box office. Meals (called *tiffin*) are also provided. In general the actor's backstage life is made easy by permanent dressing rooms and the service of bearers who bring them tea or coffee or buy them cigarettes. Although the wages of a commercial actor are not royal, they are steady. Besides the contract only obliges the actor to perform a set number of shows, usually no more than four per week. The remainder of the week may be spent performing other jobs. A particularly enterprising actor may work on TV or radio, perhaps in TV serials or reading the news, make radio or film commercials, or act in Hindi and Bengali films. Indeed aggressive actors manage to diversify their activities and organize a schedule which keeps them busy the entire day. Since India has no professional agents to represent actors' interests, they must look out for themselves.

Unions have been formed by actors in Bombay, Calcutta, and Madras but they have not been particularly active or influential in improving the wages or working conditions of performers. Apparently the profits of theatre groups have not been so enormous that actors feel they may bring pressure to bear on the management to increase their wages.

The position of actors is somewhat unique in many parts of India. In Kerala and Madras, for example, an amateur group is made up entirely of actors who are not compensated for their efforts, yet the women must be paid and are considered "commercial" artists. More than one director has complained that competent actresses cannot be found to play the female characters in a play. In a society in which women have only recently begun to perform on the modern stage, it is still considered suspect for a woman to appear on stage with men, often in front of an audience usually more than half of which are men. Tripti Mitra, one of India's leading actresses and long a reigning star of Calcutta's group theatres, confided that none of the members of her family were actors. Indeed most contemporary actors come from families which have had little or no previous contact with the theatre. Ms. Mitra came to the theatre more through conviction in the principles associated with the social and political changes of the 1940s than out of any love of acting. In a sense she is the first of a generation of actresses who consider acting a serious art, even if they do not earn a living at it.

In some areas of the country, the leading actresses of a group are the wives or female relatives of actors or directors. If an actress is not related to someone in the group, she is usually accompanied on tour by a member of her family. Company managers and directors are always wary of the possible troubles that a noncompany member may cause on tour, and complain bitterly of unfortunate incidents concerning relatives who travel with actresses.

Many things prompt actors to participate in India's amateur and commercial theatre. Despite frequent protests to the contrary, younger actors see the theatre as a stepping stone to a career in films. In India film stars have glittering careers and earn reputations, real or imaginary, in the numerous film magazines that are published in every major language. The dream of many young stage actors is to break into the Hindi film industry in Bombay, which is the largest in India and one of the largest in the world, or to be hired to play in a TV serial. Fresh talent, in or recently out of college, may get an unexpected break when a film director or talent scout spots him or her in a theatre production. Theatre directors tell harrowing stories of the productions that are devastated by an actor who quits a group or company at a moment's notice when offered a part in a film. Without the protection of a contract, many of the amateur groups have no other recourse but to rehearse a new actor in the role and to carry on as best they can.

The temperament of actors also plagues many directors. A well-known Calcutta director said that he preferred to work with new and fresh talent because so many young people have visions of stardom and if they get critical acclaim for a role they begin to dictate terms to the directors, even if they have only played one or two roles in their career. On the whole, however, directors enjoy a good working relationship with their actors, perhaps because their struggles are so great in the trying world of the urban theatre.

The predominant style of acting in India is realistic. Actors are very much aware of the principles of the West's so-called method acting and Stanislavski's observations about acting. Foreign critics cannot help but notice a slightly melodramatic tone to much of what they see on stage, perhaps because India is a land of sharp extremes in emotional relations. The exaggerated and often melodramatic situations of many indigenous plays may also explain the melodramatic tendency of this style of acting. Owing to the historical and epic material used by Manohar's National and Kerala's Dramascope troupes, the acting styles of both groups border on the melodramatic. Directors who have experimented with unconventional styles of staging, such as Kavalam Narayana Pannikkar, M. K. Raina, and B. V. Karanth, have adapted stylized conventions from rural theatre forms, which requires their performers to use stylized gestures and vocal patterns.

It is difficult, if not impossible, to single out actors among the realistic school for their acting talent, but certainly some names are familiar to the theatre personnel and audiences throughout the country. In Calcutta, Sombhu Mitra, Utpal Dutt, Rudra Prasad Sen Gupta, and Tripti Mitra have enjoyed a consistent reputation for excellence in acting. They have all received awards from the Sangeet Natak Akademi of New Delhi for their contributions to the field of acting. In Bombay, Vijaya Mehta, Usha Katrak, Pearl Padamsee, Dina Gandhi, Dr. Sriram Lagu, Lalan Sarang, Yashwant Datta, and Nana Patekar are some of the major actors in various languages. In Delhi, Om Shivpuri; in Madras, Cho, Manohar, and J. V. Sekhar; and in Kerala, T. R. Sukumar Nair, Kunyandi, Premji, and Gopi have distinguished themselves for their acting talent.

A unique distinguishing feature of modern acting is the presence of the ubiquitous microphone, which has taken over the theatre to such an extent that *not* to use it is considered a thing of pride by some organizations. In general the actors of Calcutta have resisted the mike and continue to place emphasis on a good resonant speaking voice that can project to audiences of several thousand. Only in Bengali villages when crowds may exceed ten to twenty thousand do actors actually require microphones. However, the amateur Marathi theatre of Bombay is dominated by the microphone. One disgruntled theatre director confided that when his group decided not to use microphones for a production, the spectators complained so loud and boisterously that they were forced to mike the show, even though the voices of the actors could be heard clearly at the back of the house. It is almost as though the tinny sound of the voice over the microphone has become a necessity to the spectators in most theatres. Bombay's English-language theatre groups pride themselves that they never use mikes. And the experimental theatre of the city has resisted the temptation, for the most part.

In Madras and Kerala, where the drone of the ceiling fans and the air-conditioning serves as a healthy competition for attention, the mike reigns as king. In a small rehearsal hall not more than twenty by twenty feet in diameter, a Communist theatre group even sets up the microphone to conduct rehearsals, just to give the recording artist practice adjusting the sound levels of each voice.

The backstage routine of urban Indian actors differs little from their Western counterparts, with one exception. No matter what their religious beliefs, most actors perform or participate in some ritual offering prior to performing a play. Sometimes the rituals are elaborate and conducted by a priest, as with the obeisances performed about five minutes prior to the opening of Manohar's National productions. Sometimes they are simple offerings in the dressing room of fruit, flowers, and incense to a framed picture of Ganesha, the elephant-headed god of good fortune, and the pinning of garlands of flowers on the front curtain and the distribution of bits of coconut to the actors. Although a performance is not viewed as a ritual or religious act, the rituals associated with bringing good luck to the proceedings and warding off the evil eye are still very much a part of many contemporary theatre groups. In this the modern theatre companies are similar to traditional theatre companies and to those of ancient India.

Training

We have already explored the various training processes of selected forms of theatre elsewhere in this book. It may be helpful to summarize the various processes as an introduction to this section. Traditional theatre in India is passed down from father to son, relative to relative, and guru to disciple. It is also gained through observation of performances from early childhood through old age. In more recent times, training may also be obtained through formal education in institutions devoted to instruction in the traditional art forms. With all of these methods, some form of active participation becomes a key element in the learning process.

The avenues of training in modern Indian theatre are three: observation, informal training and experience, and formal training and experience. Participation is still an essential part of the process but, unlike the traditional forms of theatre which demand long years of discipline and participation by the adherents, the modern urban theatre makes less stringent demands on its participants. Training is generalized rather than particularized. Theory and analysis become an essential part of the training process for modern urban theatre people.

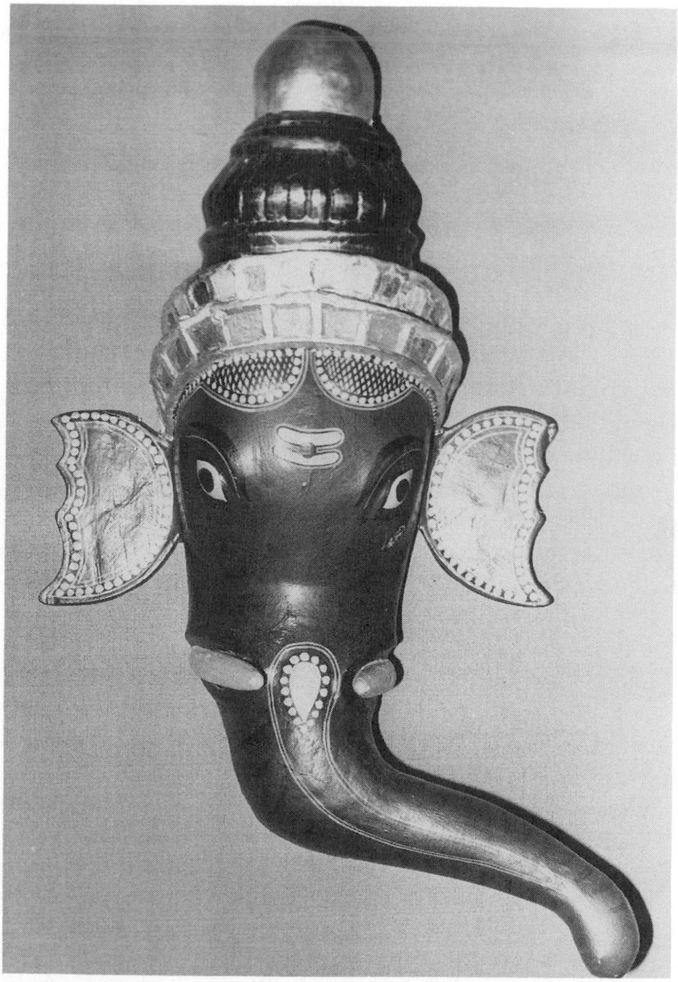

Mask of Ganapati, elephant-headed god of good fortune. (Farley P. Richmond photo)

The transformation of individuals from one side of the footlights to the other is a subject which deserves special attention, much more than may be given here. Yet it must be noted that many individuals have been "turned on" to theatre through critical exposure at some early stage in their lives and that the urge to act (to imitate?) has encouraged participation.

The vast majority of urban theatre participants receive some informal training and experience. This comes in a multitude of ways but generally it may be characterized by the absence of a regularized routine of activities resulting in the completion of a well-defined set of goals. The most common informal training is through participation in college dramatic societies or amateur theatre organizations. In both cases the goals of the group are centered around the production of a play or plays rather than training participants to understand more than the rudiments of the theatre. In recent years there has been a growing trend for student leaders of college dramatic societies to seek guidance from experienced, trained, and well-known directors from the community. By doing so they hope the members of their organizations will learn something during the process of participation, even if the experience is not designed to teach formal, focused lessons.

There are both long-term and short-term avenues for formal training of theatre personnel in India. The majority of individuals receive short-term instruction. The elite of Indian theatre are those rare individuals who have an opportunity to receive formal instruction in theatre over a considerable length of time.

Short-term instruction is usually given to students in workshops and drama camps. Some of the amateur theatres of Bombay, such as the Theatre Group, Indian National Theatre, and Avishkar, conduct workshops primarily for their membership and also for any individual that has an interest in theatre and that the leadership believes may prosper from the instruction. Workshops are usually focused on playwriting, acting, and technical areas, such as lighting and scene or costume design. Usually there is a beginning, middle, and end to the training and the end often culminates in a performance project. This project is usually not open to the public but only to invited guests and friends, unless the length of time and intensity of the instruction is such that public performances are warranted. Even then more emphasis is placed on what is learned than on the production itself. In recent years the workshops principle has become so popular that the National School of Drama of New Delhi has hired a special faculty member just to organize and conduct workshops around the country. Along with a colleague he has traveled the length and breadth of the country giving formal training in theatre. The training is described as three years of experience crammed into two and a half months of intensive instruction. The teacher carries along a mobile library, sound and lighting equipment, and color slides. The objective is to expose the students to a wide variety of specialized areas of theatre and to explore ways to develop indigenous solutions to problems of production rather than to rely on expensive equipment and mechanical devices that may not be available to the participants of the region. In the process the teacher learns as much as he can about the traditional theatre practices of the region in order to show students how relevant materials from it may be incorporated into their final projects. Some well-known workshop leaders now and in the recent past have been Ebrahim Alkazi, Vijaya Mehta, Badal Sircar, Habib Tanvir, Alyque Padamsee, Bansi Kaul, and M. K. Raina. Over the last twenty years, countless individuals have been exposed to a high level of instruction in focused areas of theatre and have improved the general level of performance and playwriting throughout the country.

Long-term formal instruction in theatre is limited but is slowly gaining in popularity. The National School of Drama in New Delhi is the undisputed leader primarily because it has an enormous budget (allocated by the central government) for programs and performances, the potentials of attracting highly qualified students from throughout the country, and a faculty with a national reputation for excellence.[6] The MS University of Baroda's College of Indian Music, Dance, and Drama has an old and well-established program of theatre instruction, in a state which has precious little rural or urban theatre activity. In Calcutta, a city which seems to have an insatiable appetite for theatre, the excellent newly appointed faculty of the Department of Theatre of Rabindra Bharati University have to fight an uphill battle to dispute the reputation of being a relatively inferior institution compared to the high level of commercial and amateur theatre available. The Department of Theatre of Punjab University at Chandigar is one of the newer departments of theatre in the country and, despite its remoteness from the center of modern theatre activity, is developing a solid program of training. The Department of Theatre of Calicut University in Trichur, Kerala, is located on the estate of Dr. John Matthai, a well-known politician and writer, who donated the land for theatre studies and history. Cramped for space and remote from the centers of urban theatre activity, the faculty valiantly provides solid instruction to enthusiastic and qualified students. Along with the Visvabharati University at Santineketan, the Punjab University of Patiala, Marathwada University at Aurangabad, Bangalore University, the University of Andhra at Waltair, and Osmania University of Hyderabad, these are the only major centers for formal theatre instruction in India.

The institutions share many of the same characteristics. Enormous power is invested in the directors. To a great extent the fate of the institutions rests in the hands of the directors or heads. An individual with little or no vision who is incapable of maximizing the potential of faculty and students may lead the institution into blind alleys or, worse yet, to certain failure.

Among the institutions only the National School of Drama is not affiliated with a university. All the others are extensions of larger bodies which influence the philosophy, direction, and management of the theatre organization. All the institutions administer courses, taught by instructors ranked according to a salary scale, to students given marks for each course which they take. Advancement toward graduation is carefully plotted out and highly structured. There is little flexibility in the curriculum for a student to choose a variety of options. A fixed syllabus of course content is prescribed in all the institutions and covers a broad range of theatre subjects. Students are expected to have an all-round knowledge of theatre and to have specialized in one aspect of it before graduation. Unlike traditional training, which stresses a specialization, modern theatre education attempts to give the stu-

---

[6] An intensive and extensive study of the subject may be found in Gilbert 1971.

dent a theoretical base as well as a comprehensive theatre education. Unlike many of the curricula in the colleges and universities of the United States, students are not expected to complete a broad range of courses in subjects which are irrelevant to their theatre training.

The institutions are strictly governed by rigid rules of admission, which normally stress that the institution may not discriminate on the basis of caste, yet a certain quota of admissions is reserved for members of the so-called Scheduled Tribes and Castes (tribal groups designated by the government of India to receive special concessions and privileges in education, employment, and so on to help integrate them into Indian society more rapidly). There are rigid standards of admission, expectations, and demands. Because of the clamor for entrance, usually students of the highest calibre are available to fill the places every year.

Depending on the strength of the institution, training consists of a balance of both limited and public classroom theory and performance. In its own way each institution attempts to answer the questions "What is theatre?" and "How does it function?" In general Indian students exhibit a greater knowledge of Western theatre than they do of that of the rural areas of their own country. Libraries are stocked primarily with books published in the United States and England. Few comprehensive or specialized texts have been developed in any Indian language. For some languages there are no texts in the native language of the students. Knowledge of theatre is disseminated primarily through articles and periodicals. The theatre practices and forms of China, Japan, and Southeast Asia were for long virtually unknown, except perhaps at the National School of Drama, although directors of some institutions have expressed a concern for the ignorance that Indian theatre students exhibit of their Asian neighbors.

Usually students graduate with diplomas and not degrees in theatre. Theatre is still not recognized as a reputable branch of higher education. In recent years this trend has begun to be reversed, by dedicated individuals who believe in the value of top-notch theatre education at the college level.

A dreary picture presents itself to most graduates with diplomas or degrees in theatre. Since educational theatre is virtually unknown in India, there are few teaching jobs to be had. High schools follow the lead of the universities and treat theatre as an extracurricular activity. Commercial theatre offers little scope for a graduate, because the type of fare that is offered is considered trite and shallow by most young graduates. Virtually the only avenue of expression is in the various amateur theatre groups around the country. Either a student sets out to establish his or her own group and gives training to peers in the hope that their fortunes will eventually lead them to a situation in which they may become self-supporting, which is highly unlikely, or they join already well-established groups and cope with the politics of conflict that invariably confront an outsider with high ideals and relatively little experience in the local organization.

The situation was so critical for theatre students in the late 1960s that graduates of the National School of Drama formed a company of actors in New Delhi and began to produce their own plays. The repertory has managed to sustain itself and its actors with a meager living, and that too through a state subsidy and not through box office revenues.

The avenue which has appealed to most theatre graduates is the same one that attracts students in Western theatre schools—films and television. The vast cinema business, principally in Bombay, and particularly the experimental work which has developed a demand for "art" films in recent years absorbs some of the graduates of theatre institutions, and the slowly expanding government-controlled TV industry also presents alternative career avenues. The only problem has been that specialized courses in TV and film are not offered to theatre students in the institutions from which they graduate, and consequently they are not exposed to the special demands of these disciplines. Only in the last year have courses such as these been considered as possible additions to the curriculum of the National School of Drama.

Support

The actors, their interpretation of the material, the space, and the audience—these are the major components of theatre. There is a marked contrast between the audiences for modern plays and the audiences for the rural the-

Audience at a Goa Hindu Association production, Bombay. (Rajdatt Arts Photos)

atre forms, yet no detailed sociological studies have been undertaken to attempt to understand the cultural implications of this fact. The following remarks highlight the observations of some of India's leading theatre critics and theatre personalities and my own views about Indian audiences of the urban theatre.

There is a general consensus that modern Indian theatre is geared to appeal to the middle class. Plays are designed to appeal to the joys and sorrows and problems and potentials of this small but influential segment of Indian society. India's middle class, unlike that in Western countries, constitutes a very small percentage of the total population, but it is growing rapidly and it has begun to exert increasing political and social power. Closely connected with urban concerns, the middle class prides itself on the symbols of modern life—a job, however small, in government, business, or industry and the potential for upward mobility and none of the perceived constraints of the traditional lifestyles of that 80 percent of India's population that still resides in villages. It is generally believed that individuals ranked in the upper class are either not interested in theatre or they attend the English-language theatres and concerts of dance, music, or theatre performed by Western artists touring from abroad. And then there are said to be the intellectuals, who are college-educated and generally left-wing in their political views, who support the experimental theatre and to some extent the amateur theatre. For all practical purposes, the intellectuals may be considered as part of the middle class or upper class elite.

The lower social classes, by far the largest single segment in urban areas, are said to prefer films, particularly those in Hindi, or indigenous forms of entertainment such as the *jātra* of Bengal, the *tamāshā* of Maharashtra, the *nauṭaṇkī* of Uttar Pradesh, and peculiar to the urban regions, the *terukkuttu* of Tamil Nadu.

Undoubtedly urban theatre attracts some crossovers among these social groups. Not all middle class people in India like theatre; many prefer films or TV. There are those who like a good *tamāshā* or who will go to a touring production of the Old Vic. But generally it is believed audiences follow class lines, that certain classes are attracted to plays that probe appropriate values, are produced in a similar manner, and are performed in a particular location in a city.

In Calcutta the theatre personnel speak of the differences between audiences for commercial theatre in North Calcutta as distinguished from those who attend the group theatres of South Calcutta. A leading newspaper critic and keen observer of theatre of all kinds has expressed the opinion that audiences for commercial plays come from the suburbs or from small towns near Calcutta, that they are nouveau riche, that they can afford to pay high prices for tickets, and that they take in the sights, such as the aquarium, the planetarium, the zoo, and the museum in Calcutta during the day, see a play, and return home by rail in the evening.

Audiences for the group theatres are made up primarily of Bengalis drawn from the so-called homogenized south side of Calcutta, which has a large minority of Punjabis and Gujaratis living among the dominant Bengali community. This audience may differ in composition depending on the appeal of the theatre group. The older, well-established groups like Bahorupee seem to appeal to an older, well-dressed audience. Nandikar's productions appear to be geared to people in their teens, twenties, and early thirties. Experimental plays in Calcutta attract a cross section of the middle class of every age, but they generally appeal to the young.

Although it has not been ascertained, it is said that very few individuals attend plays other than those in their native language. Marathi-speaking audiences do not attend English-language plays or those in Gujarati or Hindi. Audiences of Hindi plays in Delhi rarely see English-language plays or Punjabi plays. Bengali-speaking individuals usually attend plays in Bengali. Tamil plays attract Tamil speakers, and so forth.

"Why do people attend theatre?" Without probing the complexity that such a question raises, the standard answers to this question found elsewhere in the world also apply to Indian audiences. People attend modern plays in India to be entertained, as a social occasion, and perhaps for prestige (one of the amenities of urban life) and to reinforce social or political convictions. We have already implied that urban audiences of various classes in and near Calcutta are attracted to certain kinds of theatre. We have not spoken of the motivations that prompt people to attend which have to do with reinforcing their beliefs. No doubt the KPAC and Kālidāsa Kalakendra of Kerala attract many spectators with beliefs which are similar to the political beliefs that both groups espouse. And yet the spectators may simply go to see performances for their entertainment value. In Calcutta Utpal Dutt's plays are thought to draw audiences who support leftist causes. IPTA productions in Bombay are still designed to appeal to individuals who see social reform as a crying need in urban society. Some critics view beliefs such as these as the province of intellectuals but little has been done to confirm this observation.

A subsidiary but not a major reason audiences may attend theatre in the hot season is to enjoy the air-conditioning. Yet this should be considered an added bonus rather than a central motivation. There are many other air-conditioned spots to which people may be attracted during the hot season.

Considering the amount of money that is expended in newspaper advertisements, it would seem that the newspapers are the major form of advertising a production. But in reality most newspaper critics and members of theatre organizations place a great deal of importance on word of mouth advertising. It is believed that however devastating newspaper reviews may be, a production succeeds if it has good word of mouth publicity.

Theatre audiences behave in much the same way in urban India as they do in the West. They laugh, cry, jeer, and applaud during a play. Except for an occasional unruly child or a belching teenager, a production proceeds in respectful silence. One unique feature that the urban theatre shares with that in rural areas is the absence of applause at the end of acts and at the conclusion of the play. There are some exceptions, of course. English-language audiences generally applaud at the end of acts and at the conclusion of a play. However, one may see productions of Bengali or Marathi plays in which the actors stand on stage, hands folded in a respectful show of greeting and thanks, as the audience files out of the theatre. The absence of the reward of applause may be particularly disconcerting if the production seems to merit a show of appreciation, and leaves a Western viewer feeling that the actors have been robbed of their moment of glory. Yet the box office receipts and longevity of production often indicate a different conclusion.

Most theatres provide a tea stall or two, usually conveniently located on every floor of the theatre to satisfy the vociferous appetite of Indian patrons. Stalls usually serve coffee and tea premixed with milk and sugar, soft drinks of every description, various fried and seasoned snacks, mixed nuts, and chocolate bars, to name but a few of the more popular eatables.

Performance Space

With few exceptions, India has wholeheartedly accepted the Western conventions of proscenium arch stages. A quick survey of the country reveals that most of the buildings are relatively new, having been constructed within the last forty years or so and almost all of them are in the hands of landlords who employ a manager to rent the facilities. A few are owned by state governments who, with the help of a manager and a board of trustees, conduct the business of the building.

The theatres of North Calcutta are located in the congested heart of the Bengali section of the city, all within the radius of a few city blocks. Conveniently situated on or very near the tram lines and a large suburban railway station, the theatre buildings of North Calcutta tend to service the commercial theatres rather than the group theatres. It is possible for a hearty patron to catch an afternoon matinee in one of these theatres, wriggle through the throngs of late afternoon pleasure seekers, and take in an evening show at another theatre only a few short blocks away.

South Calcutta is the home of most group theatres. The buildings in South Calcutta are handsome, modern in appearance, and located amid parks, gardens, and spacious avenues of trees. One of the busiest theatres in the area is the Academy of Fine Arts, which is part of a museum and library complex situated amid flower gardens, fountains, and trees. Until recently transportation to and from the South Calcutta theatres has been somewhat disrupted by the construction of a subway system that has created gaping ditches and holes in the public streets that many cars and buses and pedestrians must cautiously maneuver around. Heavily traveled buses and minibuses connect patrons of the South Calcutta theatres with the suburbs or with railway terminuses which service the suburbs. As mentioned earlier the experimental theatre of the city has attempted to break away from the conventional pattern of renting proscenium arch stages in favor of using found spaces. For this reason it has not established a permanent home; rather it favors using incomplete office and commercial spaces, school rooms, and parks, all of which have periodically been employed for its performances.

Bombay is a city built on a chain of islands gradually connected by landfill over its relatively brief three hundred year history. Like New York City, its long corridor connecting the northern with the southern tip of the city is jammed with skyscraping offices and apartment complexes. In appearance Bombay has the look of Miami Beach, with its snow-white structures glittering in the warm tropical sun, fringed by coconut palms and bright blue sea. Theatre construction in Bombay started in the Fort area, at the southern tip of the city, beginning in the eighteenth century. As the population grew and began to push northward along the Arabian Sea in subsequent centuries, theatre buildings began to be constructed along the way. The only exception to this pattern has been the construction of the impressive complex of theatres for the National Centre for the Performing Arts in the heart of the financial and commercial district of the Fort area. At the opposite extreme of the city, well to the north, almost two hours by commuter train, is the new and impressive Gadkari Nangayatan in the suburb of Thane. This new structure, located at the edge of an artificial lake with gardens and lawns, indicates to what extent the Maratha community and the Marathi theatre has moved away from the congested heart of the city. The building is fast becoming one of the major centers for the performance of Marathi plays in Bombay. Because of its geographic configuration, Bombay may never have a theatre district like Calcutta or New York. Bombay theatre is a theatre of the road. All the major houses stretch north and south on or near the railway arteries of the city, conveniently near the lines of the Eastern and the Western railways. And all are connected to the suburbs by the most reliable bus system in all of India, the B.E.S.T. lines. Experimental theatre in Bombay is confined primarily to the antiquated Chabildas School Hall, near the Western Railway's busy Dadar Station, to the small, modern, and new Prithvi Theatre of Juhu, near the Sun and Sands and Holiday Inn beach resort hotels, and to the Experimental Theatre of the National Centre for Performing Arts, in the financial district.

Most of the theatre halls in New Delhi are clustered in the radius of a few city blocks within walking distance of the Sangeet Natak Akademi and the National School of Drama. Large, impressive, and modern structures, the proscenium halls of New Delhi are linked to the hub of the new city by bus, auto, rickshaw, and taxi. Since Delhi, like Los Angeles, is a metropolis which sprawls over a relatively flat land area, patrons are keenly aware of the

Sapru House, New Delhi. (Farley P. Richmond photo)

necessity to schedule their attendance at the theatre so that they may not reach home too late at night. Unlike Bombay and Calcutta, night life in Delhi closes down early in the evening. There is not a lonelier feeling than to leave a play late at night and to search the broad tree-lined avenues of the theatre district for a cab or an auto rickshaw, and then to suffer the indignity of paying an outrageously inflated fare just to get home.

Except for the jewellike nineteenth-century Museum Theatre, theatre buildings in Madras, South India's largest city, are large, modern, and impressive structures dotted over the city. Most of the halls are located near a convenient point of public transportation, so patrons are able to find a way home, provided the play does not end too late, for Madras, like Delhi, tends to go to bed early.

Almost every city of any size in Kerala has at least one theatre hall that serves for the performance of modern plays. But the state is a gigantic version of Bombay, stretching up and down the Arabian Sea coast like one extended village, connecting larger pockets of population with less populated areas. Therefore the theatre organizations usually produce their works outdoors or in temporary structures constructed for other events. Although Trivandrum has a few new and impressive theatre halls, the experimental organizations of the city prefer to find a space for their work which doesn't demand such a high rental fee. Until IBM decided to locate its offices there, Kavalam Narayana Pannikar's Sopanam group used the courtyard of the palace of the maharaja of Tritavillinar. Now like many other experimental groups around India, this one is searching for a new home.

Museum Theatre, Madras. (Farley P. Richmond photo)

Theatre rental charges are relatively high throughout the country, especially when compared with the running cost of most productions, which averages between $97 and $245 (Rs. 1,200 and 3,000) per day. Indeed the excessive rent is a major budget item for most commercial and amateur theatre groups. The reason for the high rent is simple. Like other urban centers around the world, the value of property has soared in recent years in India. Landlords have sought to keep pace with these trends by raising their rents. Since many of the halls are located on prime land in the heart of a city, it is no wonder that the rental charges continue to soar. There is no evidence to suggest that the trend will be reversed in the near future. All of India's big cities are showing phenomenal, if not suicidal, rates of growth in population. Pressure for more living space, for shops and offices, has followed suit. Unless and until the trend stops, the cost of renting a theatre building in the urban centers is likely to continue to rise.

For many years now leaders of the smaller amateur and experimental theatre groups have argued publicly and privately for the need to construct small- or medium-sized theatre buildings with seating capacities between 250 and 600 persons. Since they believe the appeal of their fare is not likely to exceed this level, they argue that the rent would be considerably less for these halls and their budgets would not be so severely strained. This plea has not been heeded by the government and only minimally by private initiative. Exceptions are the Prithvi Theatre and the Experimental Theatre of the National Centre for Performing Arts in Bombay, and the basement theatre of the Sri Ram Centre and the outdoor and studio facilities of the National School of Drama in New Delhi. Just as the Off-Broadway movement once did, the Indian theatre groups are forced to search for inexpensive space that may be converted to their production needs.

Next to paying the rental charges, selecting a theatre and booking the space are the most important considerations for most of the theatre organizations. In Calcutta the Star is regarded as the best commercial house in the city. Playing in the Star, even with the disadvantages of performing in a theatre nearly a hundred years old, has its prestige value. Groups clamor for an opportunity to book the facility, even though it may be the most expensive theatre in all of India and not necessarily the best equipped either. The group theatres generally arrange individual bookings with theatres throughout the city, on first come first serve basis.

In Bombay a Marathi theatre company must make a success at the Shivaji Mandir before the public will pay any attention to its work. Therefore booking dates at the Shivaji Mandir are held at a premium.

To bring some order and a bit of control over the bookings of theatres in Bombay, some of the major theatre groups in the city have formed the Marathi Professional Dramą Producers Guild (Marāṭhī Natya Byawasaik Neermata Sangha). The guild now has about forty-five member groups. About twelve are extremely active, with shows running throughout the city on a continual and regular basis. Until the system broke down last year because of internal conflicts among its members, the guild negotiated a three month agreement with some of the leading theatre managers to commit 60 percent of their dates to guild members. The remaining dates were kept open to nonmembers for a fixed period. After a hiatus of a year the guild has begun to mend fences and to renegotiate an arrangement with the theatre managers.

According to some the major theatre buildings in Bombay for the production of Marathi plays are Shivaji Mandir, Sahitya Sangh, Ravindra Natya Mandir, Dinanath Mangeshkar Hall, Gadkari Rangayatan, and Balagadhagandharya Natya Mandir (in Pune). When the guild was operating all six theatres agreed to its demands. A list was published quarterly with categories for the date, month, and theatre group and divided into morning, afternoon, and evening slots. From the list it was easy to tell what group was scheduled to perform in what space. Due to government restrictions the Ravindra Natya Mandir and the Mumbai Marāṭhī Sahitya Sangha, which are both popular theatre halls operated by the state government in Bombay, could not officially participate in the agreement with the guild members, but on an unofficial basis they made the same arrangements with the guild. They just did not publish a list. The system also permitted groups to exchange dates with one another and even to buy another group's dates as long as the hall was booked and paid for. This meant that it was possible for some theatre groups to make money selling their dates without ever producing a play! After a certain agreed upon period of time had elapsed, the managers negotiated with the guild members and booked what remained of the 40 percent of the dates. This proved especially advantageous to groups that had a successful show on their hands.

The Bombay experiment was the only one of its kind in India and helped to hold down the cost of theatre rentals, as well as serve as a means of bringing order to a complicated system of booking.

Expenses, Income, and Government Support

As might be expected, estimates of the cost of production differ considerably from group to group, from city to city, depending on the type of production, demands for scenery, props, lighting, costumes, and music, and accessible storage and supplies. Some general patterns emerge, however. Theatre production is expensive everywhere in India. In those areas where the cost of living is high, production costs are exorbitant. In areas where the cost of living is relatively low, the cost of play production is still comparatively high. It is risky to produce plays everywhere in the country and nowhere is the risk greater than in Bombay and Calcutta, where the cost of living is judged to be the highest in India.

In general, dialogue drama in Bombay or Calcutta demanding only one set is said to cost between $1,225 and $2,500 (Rs. 15,000 and 30,000), and this in a country in which the average per capita yearly income is $164 (Rs. 200). A multiset play may run anywhere between $3,250 and $5,700 (Rs. 40,000 and 70,000). In Calcutta's commercial theatre, a play demanding costumes of a historical period could run between $97,500 and $130,000 (Rs. 1,200,000 and 1,600,000). In contrast the production costs in South India and in New Delhi are considerably lower.

A dialogue drama produced by one of the amateur theatres of Madras may cost as little as $250 and $400 (Rs. 3,000 and 5,000) or as much as $3,250 (Rs. 40,000). In Delhi a straight play produced by a local amateur group would average around $500 (Rs. 6,000). And in Trivandrum between $250 and $1,600 (Rs. 3,000 and 20,000) is required to produce a play. Obviously groups that have their own stock of scenery, costumes, and lighting equipment require less capital. The officials of Bahorupee, one of Calcutta's oldest amateur groups, estimate that a new production of their group may cost between $1,220 and $1,625 (Rs. 15,000 and 20,000), provided there is a considerable reliance on existing stock scenery and costumes kept in the wardrobe of the organization.

Many factors enter into the general cost of a production. In all the theatre organizations surveyed, officials estimated that the major items of play production are theatre rental, advertising, and settings and costumes. As indicated above, experimental theatre groups attempt to circumvent these expenses by advertising by word of mouth and by seeking free advertisement in local newspapers, finding a cost-free space to perform in, and minimizing the cost of settings and costumes. Even then some notable experimental productions in Bombay are estimated to cost the producers as much as $815 to $1,220 (Rs. 10,000 to 15,000).

Whenever a group produces a musical, production costs spiral. For example, Manohar's National Theatre of Madras and even the local amateur groups in the city estimate that a musical will run nearly $8,130 (Rs. 100,000) to mount. A Marathi or Western-style musical in Bombay or a Bengali musical in Calcutta sends the cost of production soaring, well over the Rs. 100,000 mark. And yet musicals are still produced in India, perhaps for the same reason that they are in the United States, because the returns are likely to be equally impressive.

Although it is difficult to estimate the exact daily running cost of a straight play or a musical, some say it ranges between $122 and $400 (Rs. 1,500 and 5,000) per show. This includes theatre rental, advertisement, transportation, scenery and costumes, gratuities to the cast and crew, payment to actresses, and transportation for some of the actors. In a commercial venture like the Circarena of Calcutta, the proprietors estimate that it requires $9,750 (Rs. 120,000) a month to keep a play going, or nearly $487 (Rs. 6,000) per show, at sixteen shows per month. So in this respect the commercial and amateur theatres are very costly and similar in expense.

In fact the commercial and amateur theatres share many of the same problems where production expenses are concerned. The only difference between them is that commercial organizations often have substantial backup capital should a production fail. Amateur groups that have struggled for years to make ends meet and have protected their capital in long-term savings accounts and in investments cannot afford too many mistakes at the box office.

There is an unusual twist to the financial picture in Madras which warrants discussion at some length here. It is the direct result of the Sabha system. According to one of Madras' leading amateur actors, "Sabhas are commercial bodies whose main business is to make a profit." A Sabha makes a profit by selling a subscription to its members in exchange for monthly programs of music, dance, and drama. In Madras city there are said to be nearly fifty Sabhas in operation.

The Sabha system was unique to the Madras theatre scene until the last few years when it began to take root in the neighboring state of Kerala. The concept of organizations catering to the artistic taste of its members is centuries old in India. However, the modern Sabha system originally developed in Madras in this century as a means of sponsoring programs. At that time amateur and professional theatre groups functioned independently, struggling to make their own way financially. Then in the late 1950s the Sabhas entered the picture in a dynamic way and began to sponsor plays as part of their monthly subscription season. This started a trend which had some initial advantages for the amateur theatre groups. It assured them of a ready-made audience for their productions. No longer was it necessary for the group members to sell tickets from door to door and to rely on the vicissitudes of the box office receipts for their survival. The Sabhas took over the function of paying for production costs, including the advertisement. This reduced, if not eliminated, the high risk of production in this large metropolitan center, with its escalating inflation rate. The Sabhas assumed the risk on the strength that a carefully planned and produced play by a competent theatre group would appeal to its members as part of a season of varied entertainment and might even turn a handsome profit. In the 1950s, this had the immediate advantage of encouraging many groups of young amateurs to produce plays.

It also had some unforeseen disadvantages. In the late 1960s and early 1970s it became apparent that a theatre group needed the Sabhas in order to survive. The Sabhas monopolized the business of amateur theatre. The theatre groups were forced to cater to the whims and tastes of the Sabha office bearers and their membership. Plays with controversial themes or productions with unique or unusual themes or staging techniques were out of the question because they did not appeal to the tastes of the Sabhas and threatened to jeopardize their small but significant investments. Experimentation came to a standstill in the city. The tail now wagged the dog. And yet theatre groups had to continue to produce plays to remain in the eye of the public, otherwise they might lose whatever reputation they had gained in the 1950s. Thus they continue to produce plays no matter how trite their content or how low the standard of the production.

Among the other hidden disadvantages, the Sabha system hastened the demise of the old-style commercial theatres of Madras. To survive famous professional companies like the TKS Brothers, Seva Stage, and Rajamanikam Company that had been influential in Madras theatre life for years needed the support of the Sabhas with their ready-made audiences. But the high overhead and the cost of production of the professional companies could not compete for sponsorship with the low production costs of the amateur groups. And eventually the only commercial theatre that was able to withstand the pressure was Manohar's National Theatre, organized in the mid-1950s—a group which catered, to an extent, to the changing tastes of its audiences and the demands of the Sabhas.

The way the Sabha system works is described as follows: An amateur group produces a play which may cost on the average of about $400 (Rs. 5,000). Once the production is ready, the group writes to the Association and Federation of City Sabhas, a combination of organizations set up to promote the interests of the Sabhas, and asks that a fee be set for the show. Better-known theatre groups are often approached by the Sabhas and asked to produce a play for the association. The president, secretary, and committee members of the association meet and decide whether to sponsor the show and what payment should be made. Payments range from $45 to $122 (Rs. 550 to 1,500) per performance for amateur groups and may run as high as $250 (Rs. 3,100) for the National Theatre. Once the price per performance has been set, the word is circulated among the member Sabhas of the association so they may make arrangements with the group for scheduling shows in an appropriate theatre building convenient to the subscribers. In recent years two and sometimes three Sabhas have banded together to sponsor one show, thus cutting costs, reducing risks, and sharing the profits, if a production is successful.

The financial success of the theatre groups varies considerably. For one performance a small, little-known amateur group whose production I saw in 1980 at a better-known theatre hall in Madras was paid $65 (Rs. 800) by a local Sabha to cover the cost of the stage technicians and the fees for the actresses. After expenses the group realized a small profit of about $12 (Rs. 150). A well-known amateur group in the city may command a fee of $122 (Rs. 1,500) per performance. The initial cost of its productions are borne by the group and made up through profits above the expenses, which are somewhat greater than those of a lesser-known group. In contrast to the profits of the theatre groups, it is said that a sponsoring Sabha might make $490 (Rs. 6,000) at the gate on Saturdays and between $245 and $325 (Rs. 3,000 and 4,000) during other days of the week in a hall seating 920 and costing $98 (Rs. 1,200) per day to rent. In other words the profits for the sponsoring organization are far greater than they are for the producing group, despite the high risk to the producers.

According to the State Academy for Music, Dance, Drama, Films, and Folk Arts (Tamilnadu Eyal Isai Nataka Manram) Madras has about fifty registered theatre groups, about five of which are said to be professional. In recent years these groups have attempted, without much success, to band together into an association called the Drama Academy to negotiate more favorable terms with the Association of Sabhas. However, internal conflicts among participants have prevented any constructive reforms in the present system and so the groups continue to find themselves locked within a system which dictates the content and governs the profits of every organization.

As with other theatre groups elsewhere in India, those in Madras may realize considerable financial rewards for their productions, only if they tour to smaller towns and cities in the region. As I will elaborate further, touring is the only means by which a substantial profit may be realized by a theatre organization.

Among the many ways theatre organizations produce revenue, the most common is through ticket sales. Normally this is on a ticket-per-performance basis. Hardly any groups sell a season subscription.

Generally throughout India ticket prices have held the line against inflation, especially among organizations where there is a large audience potential. Commercial theatre in Calcutta, for example, has a wide range of ticket prices beginning with choice front row seats at $1.20 (Rs. 15) and decreasing to forty cents (Rs. 5) for a relatively poor balcony seat. By contrast the group theatres of Calcutta have kept their highest priced seats somewhat lower still, at eighty-one cents (Rs. 10) per ticket and a trifle below the bottom priced commercial seat at twenty-four cents (Rs. 3). The experimental theatres of Calcutta pride themselves on extremely low ticket prices—rarely charging more than eight cents (Rs. 1) per ticket for any seat in the house. Compared to the price of a film in Calcutta, which ranges from sixty cents (Rs. 7.50) to five cents (60 Pice), a ticket to an experimental play is a bargain.

Bombay ticket prices vary widely among the language groups in the city. The Theatre Group, the major English-language organization in the city, offers top priced seats at $3.65 (Rs. 45). Sponsored shows presented elsewhere in India with film-star talent command the astronomical sum of $8.10 (Rs. 100) per seat! The lowest priced seats are eighty-one cents (Rs. 10). Top price seats for Gujarati plays in Bombay begin either at $2.50 or $1.50 (Rs. 25 or 15) per seat and bottom out at fifty cents (Rs. 5) per seat. These relatively high ranges compare unfavorably with ticket prices for the popular Marathi theatre, which begin as do the group theatres of Calcutta with $1.21 (Rs. 15) and sometimes even eighty-one cents (Rs. 10) for choice seats and extend as low as eight and sixteen cents (Rs. 1 and 2) per ticket for balcony seats. Even then the theatre is a relatively expensive form of amusement to the patrons who may attend a Hindi or Marathi cinema that charges sixty cents (Rs. 6) for a reserved seat or levies a twenty cents (Rs. 2) charge for the cheapest seat in the house. Experimental theatre in Bombay is relatively costly by Calcutta standards, with groups offering forty cents (Rs. 5) top choice tickets and eight cents (Rs. 1) for the worst seat in the house. When individual seats are sold for amateur productions in Madras, they begin about $2.00 (Rs. 25) and bottom out at fifty cents (Rs. 5). As we indicated earlier, the theatre organizations in Madras depend on sales through the Sabha system.

Although it is not common to sell a subscription season, Trivandrum's Sopanam group did so for a few seasons, offering three plays for $8.10 (Rs. 100) a ticket, a rather steep price for urban theatre anywhere in India. However, the audience potential for this experimental theatre group is low and those to whom it appeals are in a position to pay this steep charge for a season subscription. Still compared to the range of ticket prices for the commercial theatre of Kerala, the price is very steep. Commercial theatre in the state offers an eighty-one cent (Rs. 10) seat and a low bargain ticket at twenty-four cents (Rs. 3).

Since very few theatre groups own or manage their own buildings, groups often place tickets with ticket sellers at strategically located box offices throughout the sprawling metropolitan area of a city. For example, Rhythm House in Bombay, a local record shop, keeps a table for selling theatre tickets. Many organizations make advance sales at the multiple windows of the box office of the Fine Arts Academy in Calcutta. Advance sales are also possible in some popular theatre halls, such as Calcutta's Star and Bombay's Shivaji Mandir. Volunteer members of the theatre organizations usually man the box offices at peak hours during the day and early evening. Sales at the door prior to performance comprise a substantial percentage of the counter sales for a production. Popular shows are sold out well in advance of performing dates, and as already discussed shows for the amateur theatres in Madras, and now to a growing extent in Kerala, are marketed through umbrella organizations.

Many amateur theatre organizations depend on two other means of support. Some distribute a special souvenir program, which they usually print once a year. The program is filled with advertisements and often includes short articles about various aspects of theatre in general or historical information about the group. These programs often provide a substantial income for organizations that would not survive on ticket sales alone. The ads are used as a tax deduction by the contributors. And programs are relatively easy, if somewhat time consuming, to organize. Cost-cutting measures virtually prevent all theatre groups from printing a program which could be handed out to the patrons as they enter a theatre. As a substitute some groups announce the names of the cast and crew over a public address system prior to the show or during intermission. The late Adi Marzban, a successful Bombay director of Gujarati and English-language plays, was unique in that he personally introduced the members of his cast to the public at the end of many of his productions.

Some amateur theatre groups are able to make ends meet by securing grants from the central government. Through exemptions from many of the taxes that are levied on the commercial theatres and cinema businesses, the amateur theatre groups couple this with a grant for running the box office and business side of the theatre. Some groups secure small grants of $406 to $1,220 (Rs. 5,000 to 15,000) for individual projects from the Sangeet Natak Akademi. Added to small supplementary grants from state governments, these often make the difference between the survival and the demise of a local amateur organization. However, as in the United States, government support of the arts is only a "Band-aid," short-term remedy. Once the organizations secure a grant, they are forced to busy themselves preparing applications for renewing the grant each year rather than focusing their attention on the business of producing plays and nurturing the creative talents of their groups.

Relatively little is known and virtually nothing is published about the government support of theatre, or for that matter of any of the arts in India. Considering the vast population of India, the multiple demands of contemporary and traditional theatres, India's political complexity, and limited financial resources, it is no wonder that the public has little information about the extent to which the central and state governments support the arts. The more enterprising theatre groups have made it their business to explore the potential resources of funding and have managed to tap what little wealth there seems to be for the benefit of their organizations.

The Ministry of Culture provides several categories of grants. One category is for salary grants to help maintain organizations which have been established ten years or more. The Indian National Theatre of Bombay and Nandikar and Bahorupee troupes of Calcutta and several other prominent amateur groups have received grants of this type over the years. The grants are said to have averaged about $50,000 (Rs. 615,000) per year.

Grants may also be made to support a particular production of an organization. Scholarships are provided to students who attend institutions that focus on traditional and modern art forms or to those who wish to study with a particular teacher. For example, students of the National School of Drama receive a monthly stipend of about $40 (Rs. 500) during their three years of training.

The Ministry of Culture also budgets the National School of Drama. The grant is said to have exceeded $268,300 (Rs. 3,330,000) in 1979–1980.

To oversee this whole operation, a position was established for an undersecretary of culture, a post which until recently has been held by Dr. Kapila Vatsyayan, a forthright, knowledgeable visionary who is intimately familiar with the affairs of a wide range of cultural organizations around the country. A board of prominent individuals from throughout the subcontinent oversees the progress of the schemes that have been sanctioned and reviews grant applications and considers recommendations for awards of merit and various positions of honor recognized by the central government.

Two other arms of government, the Sangeet Natak Akademi (the National Academy of Music, Dance, and Drama) and the Sahitya Akademi (the National Academy for Literature), are both located in New Delhi. The latter is an institution which publishes collections and individual plays as part of its literary program. From the point of view of the theatre, the former is the more important organization. Founded in 1953, the Sangeet Natak Akademi makes awards of recognition and cash to individuals who have distinguished themselves throughout the year, holds national and regional conferences on various aspects of theatre, publishes a journal and bulletin, and serves as a repository for the collection of tape recordings, films, and slides of conferences and activities deemed important in the preservation of materials on Indian music, dance, and theatre. The Sangeet Natak Akademi also provides small grants in aid to institutions for focused projects and to students for fellowships to attend various academies and institutions which provide training in the arts. In 1983 a scheme was devised by the Akademi specifically to assist young theatre workers. Essentially it encouraged directors throughout the country to develop productions inspired by village theatre forms. This led to a series of zoned festivals (North, South, East, and West) sponsored by the Akademi to which selected productions were invited. Out of the sixteen plays presented at the zoned level, eight were staged in a national festival held in New Delhi in December 1984. Although it has had its detractors, the zoned idea continues to grow. In 1984–1985 twenty groups participated in the initial festival and the following year twenty-four groups participated at a cost to the Akademi of $48,750 (Rs. 600,000).

Some thirty Fellows serve as members of the Sangeet Natak Akademi. Fellows receive no cash awards but consider the honor more valuable than money. Usually elderly individuals receive this honor toward the end of their careers. A board supervises the affairs of the Akademi and a secretary and staff oversee the daily chores of the institution. Most states have an equivalent of the Sangeet Natak Akademi which is funded with state and national resources. The effectiveness of these organizations often depends on the local leadership and the extent of the support given by the government. The more effective organizations sponsor conferences, give small awards to distinguished individuals and grants-in-aid to students, and publish periodicals.

The impact of the state governments on the theatre may be great and often a crucial part of its survival. For example, the government of Maharashtra, through its directorate of cultural affairs, sponsors an annual drama competition among amateur theatre groups in the state, many of the participants of which are college or university students. With a budget of nearly $285,000 (Rs. 3,500,000) at its disposal, the directorate funds thirteen centers to hold regional competitions. The winners of the regional competition are brought at government expense to Bombay, where they present their productions. Theatre organizations in the city are very much aware of the importance of these competitions as a means of identifying fresh and potential actors and directors and particularly for spotting new plays and playwrights.

Through its own resources the Theatre Centre, a local group theatre in Calcutta, sponsors a small-scale competition in Bengali to provide fresh amateur talent in outer-lying cities in Bengal with exposure to Calcutta audiences.

To an extent state governments individually support the theatre by exempting amateur groups from the entertainment tax that is usually levied on commercial theatre organizations and cinema houses. Although the extent of the savings cannot be measured accurately, it is clear that it might constitute a considerable part of the budget for most of the organizations, if it had to be paid.

Another vital institution with regional centers throughout the country grew up in the 1950s, but has virtually come to an end today in most cities: the Bharitya Natya Sangh. Organized through the efforts of Smt. Kamladevi Chattopadhyaya, who is regarded as the grand dame of Indian art and culture and who has written several important books on Indian arts and crafts, the Sangh published an important periodical in English, entitled *Natya.* With the emergence of the Sangeet Natak Akademi as an active force in the support of all of the arts, the Bharitya Natya Sangh is now only a page in the history of Indian theatre.

Season and Selection Process

Although play productions go on all year round in urban India, November through July is generally regarded as the prime theatre season. Except for parts of Kerala and Madras which have a second, less intense, monsoon season in September and October, these are the months which are free of heavy rains and when the weather is relatively mild. Toward the end of the regular season, the weather becomes considerably hotter and parts of India are dry and parched. Whenever the weather is hot, audiences are said to rush to the box office to claim a seat in an air-conditioned theatre hall. Theatres that do not have air-conditioning provide large ceiling or wall fans that clatter and hum throughout a performance and generally interfere with the ability of the audience to concentrate on the play.

One of the most important decisions to be made by any theatre organization is the choice of the plays to be produced. As in the United States many options lie open to the would-be producer depending on a multitude of factors, such as the personal taste of the director, the philosophy of the group, financial and technical considerations, the availability of qualified performers, expected audience response, and so on. Considering the great amount of work and the high cost of production and risks involved, it is no wonder that choices must be made judiciously.

In Calcutta's commercial theatre a primary consideration is to assure good audience response and steady, if not phenomenal, income. No one wants to lose money in the commercial theatre. Therefore investors look for a formula that seems to work. Plays are developed which usually have a love theme, a bit of conflict, sensationalism, sentimentality, humor, and a happy ending. The formula and the way it is devised reminds one of the fare often dished up on commercial television in the United States. The Bombay commercial theatre uses virtually the same formula.

Family dramas or plays that stress social concerns are usually the fare of Calcutta's group theatres and the amateur theatre in almost all of India's cities. As indicated earlier, Calcutta's group theatres are unique in that they stress obvious political messages, as well. Relevance coupled with entertainment is usually their objective. Plays which have serious or satiric content are favored over those works which are seen as pure entertainment.

Directors and officials of theatre groups are constantly reading plays in search of works that suit their needs. Because Western plays are often readily available in the large urban centers through book shops or the libraries of Western cultural organizations, they are frequently consulted and translated. Some are even liberally adapted. Brecht's *The Three Penny Opera* has been successfully produced in Calcutta and recently a version appeared in Bombay under the title *Teen Pysa Tamāshā,* earning the director a national award for his efforts. The liberal and sometimes outrageous plagiarism of some works is recorded in C. C. Mehta's two-part *Bibliography of Stageable Plays in Indian Languages* (1963). The editor reports that out of Shakespeare's twenty-seven plays nearly two thousand adaptations and translations have been created in Indian languages. Since international copyright laws have not been strictly enforced, it is possible for Indian language versions of a Western play or combination of plays to be produced and even published.

Casting, Auditions, and Rehearsal

Theatre organizations throughout urban India usually cast their plays without auditions. Rarely, if ever, are open auditions held for roles. A director or casting committee usually selects actors from among the ranks of the group members. The talents of older members of the group are well-known to the directors of every organization and the abilities of newer members are often assessed through school or college productions.

Great care is taken in casting. A poorly cast play may easily result in a box office failure, a fate a group may ill afford. Actors who have gained some recognition from the audience are likely to get major roles. New talent is worked into a group through workshop sessions or by trial and error in small roles.

Groups that advertise open auditions for roles report that hundreds of applicants usually apply, indicating that there are many people that fancy themselves to be actors and who hope for a chance to appear on the stage, particularly if the group has a positive reputation in the community.

In *Theatre In Southeast Asia,* James Brandon (1967) describes Western theatre productions in Southeast Asian countries as hand-crafted, hand-tooled, each with its own unique characteristics. This description also aptly characterizes the productions of modern urban plays in India. During the rehearsals the director may convey the production concept to the cast. And gradually a unique production of a play emerges. There is little in this process that has a unique Indian flavor, unless the production concept revolves around themes which are relevant to contemporary Indian audiences. Individual directors have their own way of handling actors and forging a team of theatre workers into a united production unit.

External factors which affect rehearsals are location, time, and duration. Rehearsals usually require a three to four week rehearsal period. Depending on the problems presented by the play and the experience of the cast, some directors prefer to take several months to rehearse. In general directors of experimental theatre groups do not like to set deadlines for the opening of their productions. Preparations for a production have been known to take as long as a year. Without the pressure of deadlines, the directors feel the process of development is less inhibiting and there is more room for exploration not possible with limited rehearsal and a production deadline.

Rehearsals often begin after office hours, around 6:15 or 6:30 in the evening, and continue until 9:00 or 10:30. Since most of the participants in the contemporary theatre are amateurs and hold jobs during the day, they often lack sufficient energy to rehearse late into the evening. Considerate directors usually serve tea or coffee and snacks to the actors before and during a rehearsal in order to keep up their energy level. Since the actors are rarely paid for their efforts the treats are a welcome gesture.

The length of a rehearsal is always limited by the dinner hour, which in India tends to be rather late. Fortified with a late afternoon tea and snack, many Indians usually prefer to eat dinner around nine. A rehearsal which extends past this time does not give the actors a chance to find their way home until well past the dinner hour.

Of major concern to most theatre organizations is the problem of rehearsal space. Since theatres do not own their own facilities and rental of the building for rehearsals is prohibitive, they must locate an adequate rehearsal space. Many of the groups use the largest room in the apartment of the director or a cast member. Considering the rush for transportation after office hours, this often means that actors come late and sometimes do not appear at all, if the space is inconveniently located. The logistics of finding a convenient rehearsal space have kept many a potential director from working in India.

In cities like Madras and in Kerala some of the theatre organizations strike a bargain with managers of schools or local marriage halls. Since there are many such facilities, groups are often able to locate an inexpensive hall that is conveniently situated for most of their actors, provided school is not in session and the marriage season has not begun. A shady lawn in a garden compound has sometimes provided rehearsal space, if the space does not attract the curiosity of passersby who might stop to watch a rehearsal and tend to disrupt the proceedings.

A Calcutta director of group theatre productions confided that he meets

Othello, performed by the National School of Drama Repertory Company, New Delhi. (National School of Drama Repertory Company photo)

individual cast members in the large Maiden Park across from Chowringee Road in the commercial heart of the city and rehearses them under the trees after office hours. When the production time nears, the actors take sick leave and work around the clock in his apartment in order to complete the final preparations.

If these arrangements seem somewhat makeshift, it should be remembered that virtually none of the contemporary theatre groups own their own facilities, that the theatre organizations are generally amateur and not commercial, and that the actors hold down other occupations. So the rehearsal space is bound to present a serious stumbling block to the success of most productions.

Scenery and Properties

To a great extent theatre architecture dictates the production style of the modern Indian theatre, and since the vast majority of the urban theatre buildings use proscenium arch stages, the production style of much modern theatre is wedded to the staging practices of the proscenium theatre. Most of the theatre groups surveyed do not own their own theatre building. The lucky ones have a business office, which is too small for constructing scenery; therefore, they either commission local carpenters to build sets based on sketches or plans prepared by the director or a designer or they commission a professional company which specializes in the building and carting of scenery. For a fee Ramaswamy Naidu and Sons of Madras will provide local groups with scenery, transported to and from a theatre building, and will store it for future use by the company. Perhaps as a result of the pressure brought to bear on the theatre managers by many organizations, some of the major theatre houses now provide a set of black flats which are used in varying combinations to create a neutral background. Groups with little or no capital have relied heavily on these black flats, coupled with simple wood or rope outlines, to suggest sets and furniture. Well-established organizations such as Calcutta's Bahorupee, one of the group theatres, and commercial houses like the Star and Madras' National have a large stock of scenery from which different settings may be constructed.

Scene design in urban India is almost nonexistent. The most tawdry scenery may be used to suggest locale. Often box settings are inconsistently combined with wings and drops to suggest place. The condition of the settings is often poor due to the heavy wear and continual cartage from one theatre to another. This makes scene design the least well-developed art of the modern

Theatre Group's production of Brecht's *The Measures Taken* directed by Pearl Padamsee, Bombay. (Pheroza Shroff photo)

Indian theatre. And yet there are some exceptional directors who manage to produce plays with remarkably effective settings. Ebrahim Alkazi, founder of Bombay's Theatre Unit and past director of the prestigious National School of Drama, and Alyque Padamsee of Bombay's Theatre Group have distinguished themselves for their interesting and polished settings, as well as for their exceptional directing talents. Both men have put cyclorama, platform, and staircase units to good use.

India is one of the few countries in the world where one may still see multiple scene changes accomplished with painted wings mounted in grooves and shutters and backdrops. Techniques developed in Restoration England for producing marvelous scenic effects to astound the eye of the beholder are still in vogue in the southern states of Tamil Nadu, Andhra Pradesh, Karnataka, and Kerala. The most polished and tasteful of these is produced by Manohar's National Theatre of Madras. Plays requiring fifty to sixty scene changes in the space of a two-hour production are arranged with the most primitive equipment of bamboo, wire, and rope and superbly executed by a tightly knit team of synchronized backstage workers, who seem to be the last of a vanishing breed. The remarkable thing about Manohar's Theatre is that it is designed to tour from theatre to theatre within the city and on the road and must be flexible enough to make use of a wide variety of theatre facilities and adapt to the most challenging conditions. The process of design and execution is organized down to the last detail. Once a play has been chosen, Manohar commissions Ganesan, his designer, a local commercial artist, to sketch the setting in black and white based on historically accurate details adapted from various books and magazines. The sketches are then photographed and the photographs are laid out and pasted on thin board and cut out to resemble wings, drops, and shutters. The "setting" is then hung in a small model, which has a false proscenium containing space for three wings and several shutters and backdrops behind. Manohar reads the play scene by scene with the setting before him and contemplates possible scene changes. Models for all of the settings are tested in this way.

Once the costumes have been developed and the fabric chosen by the director, the color schemes for each of the settings are selected and the job is given to the company scene painters, who construct and paint the scenery in the spacious shop facilities in a second-story garage studio located in one of the fashionable residential districts of Madras. In the meantime the director and his assistants plan the process by which the scene changes will be accomplished, carefully numbering all the flats and determining which will be pulled out of the grooves in what sequence and which flats will replace them. The effectiveness of changeable scenery is that it occurs quickly and seemingly without effort to the amazement of the spectators. A theatre is engaged for one month prior to opening. For the first fifteen days the stage crew rehearses the scene changes over and over again to develop a speed, accuracy, and smoothness that eventually seems so effortless to the audience and which would be the envy of many Western scene technicians. During the next ten days the actors are brought in for the only staging rehearsals of the play, with their lines already learned. The final three days before opening are spent in dress rehearsals with full scene shifts.

Most of Manohar's productions have special effects, such as a flood scene, the appearance of a giant monster or snake, decapitations, swords flying through the air, and so on, all calculated to deceive and impress the eye—"trick shots," as they are described in the local newspapers. The means that he uses to accomplish these special effects are nothing short of miraculous, considering the limited technical equipment of the theatres in which he works. Kerala's Kalanilaya Vistavision Dramascope is a hyped-up version of Manohar's National with less taste and often using a clumsy combination of scenic effects. But the scene painting on the flats is just as impressive, even if the artistic taste is wanting. Sometimes Dramascope uses bits of film integrated with sections of changeable scenery to add variety. Usually the film sequences are less impressive than the changeable scenery. In its production of *Rāgam Tānam Pallavi,* a play about the life of a famous South Indian musician, the chief character plays a musical instrument with such force that a fire is produced on stage, concocted in a firebox trap up center. To display his own virtuosity, the musician's teacher plays so well that he produces a thunderstorm and a deluge of rain which douses the fire. Both effects are visually stunning examples of the extremes to which the scenic arts go to appeal to the taste of some contemporary audiences.

Turntable stages gained currency in Calcutta during the 1930s, when they were introduced at the Rangmahal Theatre by Shatu Sen, a Bengali who first saw them in New York. Turntable stages were then introduced to all of the Calcutta theatres—to the nineteenth-century Star and to the new and largest theatre in the city—the Tagore. Considering the cramped backstage space of the Star, a turntable stage is a necessity, if fast scene changes are to be effected. The turntable stage has even been adapted for use in the Circarena, Calcutta's only arena theatre, which is a modified version of the Arena Stage of Washington, D.C. The twenty-foot diameter Circarena stage is built on a hydraulic lift that descends into the cellar of the building to permit scene changes. A black cloth is mechanically whisked across the pit to mask the activities in the basement while transition scenes are enacted on a four-foot wide ring around the circumference of the pit. It is remarkable that proscenium arch staging techniques have been adapted even in an arena setting without losing their essential flavor. Although the attempts are sometimes clumsy, they can result in some exciting and appropriate dramatic moments. For example, at the end of the melodramatic scene from Ajit Ganguly's *Samadhan* performed on August 10, 1980, as a villainous theatre manager falls dying of a heart attack, the stage begins to whirl and descend into the pit suggesting a whirlpool drawing the forces of evil into its depths. Suggestive lighting effects accentuated this symbolic scene and helped to salvage the play from total vulgarity.

To make quick transitions between scenes, most of the Bombay theatres rely on scenic units mounted on wagons. The turntable stages of Calcutta have not had any influence on the scenic traditions anywhere else in the country.

Items to be used as stage properties for most Indian productions may be had at a local market in the Thieves (Chor) Bazaar, where antiques may be found and bargained for. Historical furniture and properties representing periods in European, English, and American history are far more difficult to obtain and often demand that a substitute be located. Carpenters may still be found for hire to reproduce historical items for a nominal sum. India is one of the few countries in the world where skilled craftsmen will build wooden properties from scratch for a nominal fee.

Lighting

Watching a contemporary Indian production unfold one cannot help but notice that lighting instruments are used sparingly and that in most theatres they are positioned in rather unconventional locations backstage and out front. Stage lighting in India may not be as technically advanced as it is in

Bharat Bhavan production of *The City Dies* based on the Bhopal gas tragedy, directed by Alaknandan. (Bharat Bhavan photo)

the West but as far as design it has a style and character all its own. This may be attributed primarily to the work of one man—Tapas Sen. Little has been written about Tapas Sen, yet his work is respected and imitated throughout the Indian subcontinent. In a lecture he delivered for the Bombay Institute of Engineers in 1978, Sen pointed out that India was behind most Western countries in physical facilities. It still relies on indigenously produced variable transformer dimmers and tungsten halogen lamps, fresnels, and spotlights. Colored gels are still imported from abroad and are jealously guarded by lighting technicians. But India has adapted what equipment it has to its own needs and has given stage lighting a decidedly Indian flavor.

Sen has introduced the notion that only a few lighting instruments need be used to produce striking visual effects. In many of the theatre facilities for which he has served as lighting consultant, he has advocated the construction of platforms about eight feet high, behind and to the right and left of the proscenium arch, on which spotlights are mounted and operated. Coupled with a few fresnels hung from battens above and behind the proscenium arch and several floodlights and lekos mounted on the right and left walls of the house or on a balcony railing, lighting designers may cover all areas of the stage sufficiently to illuminate a production.

Since the rental charges of most theatre buildings include the use of a few house instruments, it is usually possible for a theatre organization to light a play without renting additional equipment. To an outside observer, the intensity of the light is not particularly dazzling but a skilled designer may produce a myriad of appropriate effects with what is available.

Because the work horses of most Calcutta theatres are the spotlights behind the proscenium arch, the best acting areas are those up right, up center and up left. By contrast the downstage positions are considerably weaker because the light thrown from floodlights or lekos at the front of the house takes longer to reach the stage and results in less intense light downstage. Spotlights are even used in a special cage above Circarena's round stage in Calcutta, following Sen's principle that actors are the center of the theatre and not the scenic environment.

Sen maintains that light should paint pictures and that it should ebb and flow with the dramatic action. It is not possible to tell whether the cinema has influenced playwrights to compose multiscene plays or whether Sen has influenced the writers to produce plays which have a cinemagraphic flow. But the multiple transitions required by most plays produced by contemporary Indian authors blend remarkably well with the lighting designs created by Sen and exponents of his method. Sombhu Mitra and Utpal Dutt in Calcutta, Ebrahim Alkazi in Delhi, and Derek Jefferies in Bombay have developed their own special method of integrating stage lighting into their artistic productions, but Tapas Sen stands alone as the chief architect of the Indian method. Today he has his own private company which hires out his services and those of his son and his other employees to theatre organizations throughout the country. After consultation with the director and careful survey of the play and the theatre facilities, a light plot is developed to suit each production. It is possible to identify Tapas Sen's unique stamp on any production he undertakes to light. He has proved that it is not necessary to use vast numbers of instruments to produce creative lighting effects. In this his methods are well suited to the Indian situation and the financial limitations of most theatre organizations. Because of his contribution to this branch of technical theatre he was the first Indian theatre technician ever to be honored by the Sangeet Natak Akademi in a special award granted in 1975.

Costumes

There is nothing particularly unique about the approach that is taken to the costuming of most modern urban plays. Actors often use their own clothing or buy appropriate clothing from the city markets under the watchful supervision of a director or costumer. But the historical costumes of a period or country require special attention. The director does the necessary research or hires a designer to do so and produces a sketch or watercolor which is translated into a costume, usually by a professional tailor. Since the services of tailors and shoemakers are still relatively inexpensive in India they are used by groups with sufficient capital.

Except in a few educational theatre institutions, costume shops are virtually unknown in India. Yet some fabulous costumes are produced for historical Indian plays by groups that can afford that luxury. Historical and mythological productions in Madras, Bombay, Delhi, and Calcutta rival any of those abroad for their sumptuousness and attention to detail. Obviously it requires a tasteful director or designer to bring off a miracle, but the range of Indian fabrics and colors in silk and cotton is vast and the potential for splendid visual effects is great.

Advertising

Besides the rental of a performance space and the cost of scenery, theatre organizations spend more money on advertising than on anything else. Newspapers provide the best access to the theatre-going public. Papers in English and the regional languages make daily contact with hundreds of thousands of potential patrons. Although the newspaper critics and the theatre personnel claim that reviews do not have much influence on attendance patterns, all agree that ads are the best way to notify the public of when, where, and by whom a production is to take place. Most agree that the cost of the ads is unusually high.

In New Delhi the manager of the Sri Ram Centre indicates that he spends an average of $7.30 (Rs. 90) per column centimeter in the English-language dailies, such as the *Hindustan Times,* the *Statesman,* the *Times of India,* and the *Indian Express,* and approximately the same in the Hindi language dailies, such as *Nav Bharat Times, Hindustan,* and *Jan Satta.* This results in a cost of nearly $56 (Rs. 700) per month.

In Calcutta theatre organizations place ads in various local papers, such as the *Statesman, Jugantar, Amrita Bazar Patrika, Ananda Bazar Patrika,* and, depending on the philosophy of the group, the left-wing political weeklies. The policies regarding theatre advertisement differ from paper to paper. Calcutta's *Statesman* is said to charge $1.46 (Rs. 18) per line, perhaps the cheapest advertisement space in the city. But since the vast majority of the audiences for Bengali plays read the Bengali language papers, commercial and group theatres use those papers to advertise a play. One estimate sets the cost of placing an ad per day in a Bengali paper at $14.15 (Rs. 174) per three centimeter columns, approximately one inch by three inches. Regular use of several papers might easily bankrupt a theatre organization. It is no wonder then that one commercial theatre group estimates it may easily spend $4,900 to $6,500 (Rs. 60,000 to 80,000) to advertise just one production prior to opening night!

Bombay's Producers Guild has attempted to hold down the cost of newspaper ads by negotiating lower rates with the press. To an extent this has worked. It is said that it costs $1.20 (Rs. 13) per centimeter column to advertise in some Bombay papers. But considering the charge of $400 (Rs. 5,000) to advertise in the newspapers for one week, the cost of newspaper ads in this metropolis are still exorbitant. Bombay's theatre-going public consults papers like the *Maharastran Times,* the *Times of India, Lok-Satta,* and the *Indian Express* to get news of theatre events.

Outside the larger cities of the North, the cost of advertising is not quite so steep. Yet one estimate places the cost of a column line of copy in Kerala at eighty cents (Rs. 10).

Many organizations have resorted to other means of advertising. Because Bombay's Theatre Group directors work in or are connected to the advertising industry, the Theatre Group is able to secure valuable billboard space along the busy thoroughfares of the city. Normally the cost of billboards is prohibitive for most theatre organizations. Some groups resort to printing posters and tacking them up at strategic shops and offices around the city. It is said that this form of advertisement works particularly well in Bangalore. Even then the cost of producing posters may run as high as $40 (Rs. 500). Postcards mailed directly to patrons advertising a show are also used by some groups. But the rising cost of postal rates, printing, and paper has jeopardized this as a means of reaching potential audience members.

Theatre periodicals in various languages carry word to subscribers of the titles, time, and place of the various performances in key urban centers of a state. And magazines placed in many hotels, such as "What's Happening in Bombay" "Delhi" and so on, advertise a few productions that may appeal to a curious traveler or tourist.

Show Times

The timing of plays, like rehearsal schedules, normally takes into consideration the trend in India to dine around 8:30 or 9:00 P.M. Therefore most plays begin between 6:30 and 7:00 and rarely finish later than 9:00. In the early part of this century, urban plays are said to have run three to four hours to accommodate the expectation of spectators who demanded that they get their money's worth from this form of entertainment. Today only the film industry seems to have continued the tradition of long productions.

In Bombay the experimental theatre often performs shows twice a day, at 6:30 and 9:30. Normally only patrons who live nearby are able to attend a late show, since most forms of public transportation shut down after midnight. On weekends some theatres book one or two matinees, as well as an occasional morning show. Bombay's Shivaji Mandir is so heavily in demand that theatre organizations vie with one another for any booking. A typical weekend day at the Shivaji Mandir might see as many as three different theatre organizations setting up, performing, and striking their productions from early morning to midnight.

Touring

"The road" conjures up romantic images for most theatre people. It was virtually the life blood of the nineteenth-century American actor, who portrayed a famous role or played shows in repertory from town to town, all across the United States—the legendary grist of many books and films. For an Indian theatre organization taking to the road may make the difference between survival and failure. For some the quality of survival is questionable. In this section we will examine some of the motivations that prompt theatre organizations, particularly amateur groups, to tour.

Conditions and practices differ widely from one region to another. The commercial theatres of Calcutta generally do not tour, principally because if not permanently, at least for a relatively long period of time they have control of a single theatre building to which audiences will flock to see a good production; therefore, for them touring is not a necessity. Commercial groups in Kerala consider touring a natural consequence of producing plays. Kerala audiences are spread about the state in remote clusters, so touring has always been a way of life. By contrast the amateur theatre organizations of Delhi rarely expect to produce a play for a long run and the audience for their work is concentrated in or near New Delhi, so they play in a single theatre building for a short period of time, perhaps for no more than several weekends in a row, as long as the demand is perceived and the theatre bookings are available. The situation is completely different and certainly more critical for Calcutta's group theatres and for most of the amateur organizations of Bombay and Madras.

As a well-known theatre personality in Calcutta put it, "The pace of Calcutta theatre is suicidal. We produce plays here which travel from theatre to theatre, sometimes on the same day. Then we get a 'call' booking outside the city. The money is good outside. And the only way we can keep our group afloat is to take a booking outside. Even if it disrupts the lives of our members." The seeds of potentials and problems are found in these remarks. In Calcutta, Bombay, and Madras amateur theatre organizations cannot sustain performances in a single theatre for a long period of time because of the competition for performance space and because they have no control over any theatre building. This means that the booking schedule for most amateur groups is a complicated affair, requiring that orders be given to cart scenery to a theatre, supervise its setup in a short period of time, perform, strike the sets, and cart it to another theatre or to storage to wait for the next booking. In a place like India where stages differ considerably from one building to the next, the settings must be designed to accommodate almost any possibility. What must the problems be outside the familiar terrain of the city?

Tours outside a group's home base are referred to as "call" shows, which means a theatre organization has been "called" or summoned to play at a particular time and place by the manager of an organization—sometimes for a religious occasion, like a fair or festival designed to earn money and respect for a church or a temple, for a political rally that organizes entertainment for its members to promote the party, for a factory or school, and so on. When a theatre organization is called, a flat fee is set which covers specific payment to the actors, the directors, the technical personnel, and a small return for the organization. The sponsoring organization also pays the cost of transportation and generally the gratuities, such as meals, tea, coffee, and snacks. Theatre organizations accept "call" bookings because they provide a predictable source of revenue.

Why then do groups perform in the city at all if call shows are so reliable a source of income? As one theatre personality put it, "We play in Madras only to establish our reputation outside the city. If the production is a success in the city, outside parties will call us." Without first establishing the credibility of a production, it is not very likely that a call show will be forthcoming. The initial risk must first be undertaken. Once that has paid off, a tour usually follows.

Touring in India is not easy. Most members of amateur theatre groups hold regular occupations which provide them a steady income. Their work hours give them little free time to act, other than half days on Saturdays, all day Sunday, and holidays. Even then a persuasive director may be able to convince the cast to journey outside the city even on a weekday, after office hours, arriving several hours later at the destination to set up, play, and strike, and then to return to the city in time for office the next morning. Love of the theatre and loyalty to the group has more than once taxed production teams to the limit for weeks on end. In places like Calcutta, where it is possible to travel to the potential "call" show market within a matter of hours, actors and technicians have been willing, particularly if there is a good financial incentive. Usually the rewards are attractive. The director of one theatre organization predicted that in ten days on the road actors will make as much as their regular monthly salary. Since payments are made in cash, they are not normally reported as income and therefore are not taxed. For an actor who can endure the strain, touring is a positive financial, as well as artistic, incentive.

Many amateur groups own their own vans, which allow a greater degree of flexibility and comfort on the road. Scenery is either loaded on top or carried in a truck hired to accompany the tour. A tragic traffic accident in rural Maharashtra in the late 1970s killed several prominent members of an amateur theatre organization, prompting some members of the local press to question the wisdom of touring. But as one avid supporter put it, "Indian theatre has always been on wheels. I suppose it always will be."

National and even international tours have also been undertaken by several commercial and amateur theatre groups. Obviously these are meant to meet the demands of large groups of people living far from home and desiring to hear their native language spoken, as well as to be entertained by some of the best talent of their home region. The Marathi theatre wing of the Goa Hindu Association recently toured the United States, playing mostly for Marathi-speaking audiences, and Calcutta's Chetna, an experimental organization, and Tripti Mitra, a famous Bengali actress, have also performed there. It is doubtful that many Western theatre audiences came into contact with these organizations, and so critical evaluation by the Western press is wanting. But there is no evidence to suggest that tours of this kind will not continue, particularly when there is a demand for indigenous entertainment among the resident aliens of the United States and other parts of the world.

Criticism

Theatre people, newspaper critics, and audiences alike agree that there are no uniform standards by which to evaluate modern Indian theatre. Performances in Calcutta are geared to meet the taste and demand of Bengali audiences; performances in Bombay are designed to reach Marathi audiences, Gujarati audiences, Hindi-speaking audiences, or those interested in English-language plays. Plays in Punjabi and Hindi are chosen and produced to suit Delhi audiences. How then may one compare a production in Calcutta with similar productions in Delhi, Bombay, or elsewhere in India, particularly if production conditions and objectives differ so radically from one city and one region to another?

Perhaps the only way to establish standards is for critics to arrive at a system which is suitable to the conditions and taste of each region. Yet newspaper critics and theatre personnel alike agree that newspaper reviews have little or no influence on box office receipts or determine the success or failure of a production, and rarely help to raise the standards of a group's work. The opinions of a professional theatre artist from the West are likely to carry more weight with a group than the reviews of a local newspaper critic. So many groups operate on the principle that their work is a success or failure compared to a real or imagined knowledge of standards of excellence in Europe, England, and America.

Unfortunately no critic has emerged who commands the respect of the Indian theatre personnel. One experimental theatre group in the South has encouraged a respected professor of literature to observe rehearsals and to offer opinions. To an extent this critic has become a resident dramaturge and has attempted to articulate the philosophy of the theatre group, helping to formulate a standard of taste among the actors and the director of the company. But a system has not yet been devised whereby serious criticism sets the standard for the theatre in any region, much less for the country as a whole.

This is not to say that there are no commonly held beliefs. Certain regions are thought to produce better theatre than others. It is common knowledge among Indians that the Bengalis think of their theatre as superior to the theatre of other regional languages. This belief is shared by audiences and theatre personnel outside Bengal, as well. Many Marathi-speaking people view their theatre as the best in India. Among the theatre personnel it is common knowledge that the two hubs of the modern Indian theatre movement are Calcutta and Bombay. Southerners like to debate which southern city has the best theatre. When pressed to provide a rationale for why the theatre in one language is judged better than that in another, it usually does not boil down to a question of taste but to the bulk of activities. In India success is frequently measured by the numbers of productions that are presented. Groups often speak of their productions according to how many performances they have played. For example, the Goa Hindu Association of Bombay now boasts that it has produced over four thousand performances of thirty-five plays in its thirty year history, with one production hitting the eight hundred night mark. Since 1952, Kerala's KPAC has performed eighty-five hundred performances of twenty-five plays, with the box office success *You Made Me a Communist* playing over thirty-five hundred performances and still going strong today. As mentioned earlier, the longer the run the better chance there is for a production to realize a profit on the initial investment and to build the resources of the group. Commercial theatres usually judge the success of a work not by any standard of excellence but by the total number of performances it has played. Amateur theatre groups also reflect this same thinking. Usually commercial and amateur groups estimate a point at which performance above that number may show a profit.

Experimental theatre groups are more likely to brag that the production experience is more important than the number of performances played or the box office receipts. Badal Sircar, one of India's leading experimental theatre experts, argues that the test of success is how relevant the work is to the people before whom his group performs and to what extent the rehearsal and production experience has been valuable in re-educating his actors to a philosophy of theatre that serves the people and not the economic system of the city, state, or nation.

Durgi, produced by the Goa Hindu Association, Bombay. (Rajdatt Arts Photos)

Modern Theatre in Performance[7]

Bombay

Durgi, written by the well-known Marathi novelist and playwright Jaywant Dalve, was presented on Friday, July 4, 1980, in a matinee show at Shivaji Mandir, Bombay's most popular theatre house. The production was sponsored by the Goa Hindu Association, a commercially oriented organization whose aim is to collect money from play production to use as contributions to its various charitable activities. *Durgi* is based on a novel composed by the same author. It concerns the attraction, developing relationship, and eventual union of an elderly man and woman, both of whom are widowers. A leading actor of the company described the moral and central theme of the story as "What will people say?" In his view widows and widowers, especially in Hindu society, are normally not expected or encouraged to remarry. Society dictates that they spend their advanced years in solitude and prayer rather than enjoying the company of members of the opposite sex. The title role and heroine of the piece is a widow. In the opening scenes she wears a pure white sari symbolic of widowhood and resides near a local temple. Her hair has turned silver, although she is not particularly old. The man who falls in love with her lives in depressing surroundings, eats unappetizing meals from vendors' stalls, or brings home food parcels wrapped in old newspapers. As their relationship matures they begin to dye their hair, wear cleaner and neater clothes, and convey a sprightliness in their walk and conversation. All goes well but various relatives and friends attempt to dissuade them from seeing each other, fearing that people will talk and that they would bear the brunt of public scorn. Eventually after several touching and wistful scenes between the elderly couple, interspersed with raucously humorous scenes between the older man and his friends and relatives, the couple decide to marry and those who once derided them wish them well.

As acted by the Goa Hindu Association Theatre Wing, the play is divided into three acts and thirteen scenes. The production required numerous scene changes back and forth between the seedy room of the old man, a garden near a temple, and the veranda of a bungalow. The matinee of July 4 was

[7] The following reports of selected productions is but a small sample of the rich variety of the modern theatre movement. It includes commercial and amateur efforts. It is not meant to represent the major or best works in the 1980 theatre season, by any means. Those who prefer a particular type of modern theatre work are likely to be disappointed, for I have attempted to represent the field rather than to suggest that modern theatre is exclusively made up of one kind of product. There is much that has been published in recent years about modern theatre of a particular kind. For these views I suggest the reader consult *Enact, Sangeet Natak,* and the *Journal of the National Centre of the Performing Arts.* A selection of plays in translation is provided in the Additional Reading section which follows.

the eighty-first performance of the show and so the scenery had become a bit tawdry with excessive shifting, carting, and storage. Wagons and drapes were used to change scenes from one locale to another, often in rapid succession. Considering the cramped backstage facilities of the Shivaji Mandir Theatre, the changes were made quickly and quietly.

Shivaji Mandir seats a thousand persons and the house was packed for the matinee, with gaily dressed people of all ages wearing what appeared to be their "Sunday best." The seats in the theatre are comfortable, although they are nearly threadbare with excessive use. The stage has a twenty-six foot wide proscenium, which is about fifteen feet high at the center. Although the house has a limited dimmer capacity which is operated behind the proscenium arch, stage right, the Goa Hindu Association brought in a bank of its own dimmers and sound equipment and mounted them in the orchestra pit in full view of most of the patrons.

The total performance experience lasted about three hours and ten minutes, which is a fairly common length for Marathi productions in Bombay. As the ushers seated the chattering crowd which rapidly gathered in the house, a bell rang backstage as part of the ceremonial blessing of the stage behind the crimson front curtains. At the end of the ceremony one of the stage hands hung garlands of white flowers about chest height on one edge of the front curtain. At 4:00 P.M. the house began to dim and a voice boomed over the loudspeaker announcing the play, author, list of characters, and actors. Announcements such as these have become standard practice throughout India as a way for the theatre groups to cut down the cost of producing printed programs. Then the stage lights came up on the opening scene, which was set in the tawdry room of the chief male character. The play was performed entirely in Marathi. The only English spoken was "Keep quiet, this is not any of your business," which the old man shouts at his son in the last act.

A typical feature of most Bombay theatres today is the use of microphones, which project the actors' voices over loudspeakers. When the actors in this production spoke too loudly the microphones gave off a tinseled ring.

Durgi used very few special effects. One effect repeated throughout the show and seen in other productions throughout India during the research period, was a dream sequence. Stage lights dimmed and several colored lights came up on the character, whose thoughts were revealed by tape-recorded voices over the loudspeakers. Sometimes music or special sound effects accompany the inner thoughts of the characters. In *Durgi* the director chose to use the breaking of glass as a convention to suggest that whenever the mood of the male character was broken there was the sound of breaking glass to suggest that his illusions had been shattered. To cover the many scene changes in the show, music bridges were used liberally.

Even though the play ended happily and on an energetic, upbeat note, the audience rose and filed out of the theatre silently, without applauding the actors. Indeed none of the scenes or act breaks were acknowledged with applause.

As the house was being cleared the stagehands busied themselves cleaning and striking the scenery and properties to make ready for the evening show scheduled in the hall by another company. Shivaji Mandir is reputed to be the most popular theatre in Bombay and in order to maximize its profits the management encourages as many productions as it may book into the hall.

Not far from the Shivaji Mandir, Vijay Tendulkar's delightful and popular Marathi satire *The Right Person for the Right Job (Pahije Jatice)* was presented by the Avishkar theatre group at Bombay's Chabildas School Hall the evening of July 10, 1980. Although then in its hundred and forty-second performance, the play attracted a capacity crowd of about three hundred people to the tiny headquarters of the experimental theatre of the city. The excellence of both the play and the production have undoubtedly contributed to the success of the venture.

The Right Person for the Right Job is a biographical study of a friend of the playwright. The plot centers on a young man who hails from one of the lower Hindu castes. In his opening monologue, the chief character relates something of his past history—how he barely squeaked through his M.A. exam, how he was removed from his first job as a clerk for a small newspaper because he was considered to be overqualified, and his vain search to find employment elsewhere. He attributes his problem to the fact that he only had a "pass" class ranking in college and he does not know anyone from his community with influence that could get him a job. As the story progresses the young man breaks into short scenes with the other actors to illustrate his point. Finally he has an interview for a teaching job in a small town. In the state of Maharashtra, members of the so-called Sugar Lobby, a band of individuals who all hail from the Maratha caste and who virtually control the price of sugar in the country, have taken control of the educational system. The young man is interviewed for his teaching job by the Sugar Lobby representatives in an unnamed town, rather than by the principal of the school. Because he is the only applicant for the job, he is given the position. As the play progresses the young man relates and acts out a few of the memorable days in class, explaining how he won the friendship and respect of the disobedient gang leader of the school and how he eventually brought order into the classroom. At the end of act 1 a young and appealing woman is introduced to his classes, to whom he is immediately attracted. In act 2 we learn that the woman is the niece of the chairman of the local Sugar Lobby and that she has obviously gotten as far as she has in her education because her parents have paid off all the teachers along the way. At the play progresses, the young man figures out that the board of education intends that the girl should get a degree and replace him in his job. He decides to seduce and marry the girl and become the son-in-law of one of the wealthy owners in order that he may keep his position. When the principal of the school and the chairman of the board find out that he is in love with the girl, they provide her an escort in the person of a tough old aunt who makes sure the couple are never alone together. He plots with his friend, the school gang leader, to abduct the girl so that they can marry in secret. The plot misfires when he ends up on his wedding night with the recalcitrant old aunt. In desperation, he decides to use the girl's love letters as a bribe. The girl comes to him and from all appearances she has turned into a robot. She tells him, "You're from a lower caste, therefore we cannot marry." All the apparent feelings she had for him are now gone. She warns him that he will be killed if he tries to marry her. The young man tears up the letters, quits his job, and leaves town as the play draws to a close.

Under the mask of light comedy and slapstick humor, which the play liberally evokes, the playwright seems to have a serious point to make—there are those who rule and those who are being ruled. All they need do is to change costumes to revert to the opposite viewpoint. The cynical point of view of Tendulkar, the playwright, is also evident in his best-known works, such as *Sakharam Binder* and *Silence, the Court is in Session.*

Avishkar's production of the play did justice to the rapid-fire humor and bitter seriousness underlying the piece. The production was staged in front of a vertical set of wings and drops. The chief actors addressed the audience directly, establishing a close rapport from the beginning. Simple props and scene pieces were used to establish locale. Freezes were used to stop action and focus on the monologues. The show moved at a galloping pace, keeping the audience delighted and amused, never giving them a moment to get bored or weary. The cast displayed a fine range of talent, from older actors who were character types to young actors, one of whom was the playwright's daughter and played the young girl with verve. A particularly handsome youth portrayed the gang leader. During intermission I learned that he has become something of an overnight sensation in the Hindi film industry and planned to leave the company in order to keep a tight shooting schedule for a new picture.

Audience members who come to the Chabildas School Hall to see a play always undergo something of a hardship, according to one of the local experimental directors. Suburban trains are always crowded when they call at the Dadar Railway Station a few blocks away. The street is jammed with pushcarts; hawkers line the pavement selling their wares. The narrow sidewalks barely allow passage between the temporary stalls and the dozens of cloth shops and goods shops that line the streets. It is always risky to negotiate the street because of the heavy traffic of buses, trucks, pushcarts, and stray cattle. In the evening the place is ablaze with flickering kerosene lamps, neon lights, and light bulbs hung out everywhere, calling special attention to the goods being sold. People always seem to be pushing and shoving to go one place or another. Less than three blocks away from the railway station Chabildas School is located on a dead end street. Late at night in the monsoon, the street is awash with muck and paper and rats playfully scour the ground in search of morsels of food dropped by neglectful school children. An inconspicuous sign board announcing the play stands at the doorway to the building.

The building is quite old. Once you purchase tickets from the women seated behind a small table in the hallway, you negotiate a rickety wooden staircase, worn thin with age and use, and wind up in a big open room with bleachers lined with metal chairs. Carpets separate the proscenium from the bleachers, providing a comfortable space for the spectators to sit cross-legged on the floor and witness the show. There is hardly any lobby, except in the narrow hallway outside the entrance and the rickety veranda along one side of the building, flush against the back of a lower-income row of flats where one may see the lives of the occupants openly revealed.

This production began at 8:30 P.M. with the ringing of the buzzer used by the school to announce the beginning and end of classes. The show was over at 11:05, just in time for spectators, who had to travel by train, to take the midnight coaches home.

Because the actors had missed their dinner that evening, they were treated to a simple meal of potatoes and a thin lentil soup served on leaf plates. A feeling of camaraderie, so often necessary to the survival of theatre, was in the air as the actors chatted and helped each other to strike the set and props and restore their temporary theatre home into a school hall once more.

Calcutta

The matinee of the Star Theatre's *Samadhan* on August 10, 1980, was the three hundredth performance, an occasion of celebration for the management, which considers three hundred shows a positive assurance of the financial success of the initial investment. Everything beyond that figure is considered pure gravy for all concerned. This contrasts with the run of approximately fifty to one hundred performances for most plays of the group theatres of the city.

Samadhan was written by Ajit Ganguly, a freelance writer who was commissioned by the management to create a play based on a well-known 1968 film entitled *Dadu*. Since the film had done good business at the box office, it was believed that the same story could be modified to appeal to the middle-class audiences that patronize the Star. And it seemed a true prediction. Although the top priced tickets of $1.50 (Rs. 15) went begging, the less costly seats in the house were packed by enthusiastic spectators. The Star is located in the heart of the Bengali-speaking section of the north side of the city, and spectators were dressed in the saris and dhotis typical of Bengalis in a holiday mood.

Prior to the show religious ceremonies were performed in the main dressing room honoring important saints and past dignitaries of the Star, not the least of which was the famous Girish Chandra Ghosh, one of Bengal's most famous actor-managers. Everything backstage seemed neat and orderly from the individual dressing rooms for the production's star players to the stage manager's office, the greenroom, and the narrow aisles separating the large stocks of scenery in the nearly hundred-year-old house from the scenery used for the current play. Wrinkled, elderly men who had been employed in the theatre since boyhood waited patiently in the wings to perform their tasks as scene changers, musicians, lighting technicians, and so on. A general air of calm, assured professionalism abounded. The manager and his assistants lounged in a comfortable, air-conditioned room built along the fly gallery. A charming balcony off the office overlooked the outdoor snack bar in the courtyard adjacent to the side of the famous house.

The matinee performance began promptly at 3:00 P.M. The story centers on Dadu, the central figure in the piece, who is the grandfather of the leading characters. Throughout the show he offers sage advice, counsel, and direction to the younger people whose lives seem perpetually tangled by love intrigues. The plot centers on a quiet, unassuming granddaughter who secretly loves a local doctor, played by a current movie idol. Her sister is also in love with the same young man and in every way she is her antithesis—dressed in gaily colored saris, wearing clog shoes, she carries a transistor radio, dances to provocative disco melodies, and generally creates the dramatic excitement of the play. Eventually after scenes of farcical humor juxtaposed with scenes of convincing sentimental emotionalism not unlike those which abound on T.V. soap operas, the retiring girl and the doctor are contracted in marriage and the gay young woman wishes both of them well.

In general the playing style was realistic, with convincing portrayals delivered by all the actors. Live piano music was used to heighten the mood of many scenes. Recorded film music provided additional life as the actors mouth the words in what are commonly referred to as "playback" songs. Scenes were shifted frequently between the drawing rooms of several houses, bedrooms, a doctor's office, and exteriors of a bungalow. These changes were made swiftly by a revolving stage located at the center of the proscenium, employed no doubt because there was no room to move large pieces of scenery on and off stage. The lighting from the battens above the stage and from portholes at the sides of the proscenium provided the various moods demanded by the different scenes and locales.

The show ended at 6:10 P.M. when the front curtain was rung down on a colorful wedding scene. An evening show followed closely on the heels of the matinee, allowing the actors only a few moments to have tea and snacks.

Down the street from the Star, at the other end of the active theatre district of North Calcutta, is the Circarena, whose evening show August 10 was *Samrat-o-sundari.* Then in its four hundred and fiftieth performance, the play boasted of several sensational features, to which newspaper critics attributed its enormous popularity.

Madras

Ottakkoothar was presented by Manohar's National Theatre at the Music Academy Hall on July 26, 1980. The National is the only surviving commercial theatre company in the city and its productions are a carryover from the work of older generations of theatre groups, such as the TKS Brothers, Seva Stage, and Rajamanikam Company, all of which retained vestiges of the nineteenth-century scenic and acting tradition until economic pressures and poor audience response dealt a death blow to their efforts.

The whole atmosphere of the Music Academy Hall exudes a feeling of newness in the city, located in a fashionable district with spacious grounds, plus carpets and seats and boasting of the latest signs of modernity—a digital clock located in a conspicuous spot directly to the left of the proscenium arch broadcasting the hour, minute, and second throughout the performance. The hall rents for $170 (Rs. 1,700) a day, the highest priced space in the city. It seats eleven hundred patrons. *Ottakkoothar* and the Sabha which sponsored the show packed the hall.

Women with expensive silk saris strolled casually in the spacious lobbies. Men wearing snow-white Tamilian wrapped dhotis and shirts or suits and ties accompanied them. Flower vendors outside the theatre did a brisk business selling foot after foot of fragrant white and orange blossoms, linked in chains, to ladies and young girls to adorn their hair knots. Fast-food vendors kept pace by distributing cups of coffee and tea, snacks and savories to thirsting and hungry crowds as they began to gather in the fading evening light.

About twenty minutes before the show started, an elaborate sacrifice *(pūjā)* was offered by a Brahman priest at the center of the stage, behind the front curtain. A large picture of Ganesha and various gods and goddesses and teachers had been arranged. The sacrifice was performed in an elaborate manner by the priest using the sacred items—a large bronze bell, conch shell, water, flowers, incense, burning camphor sticks, garlands of fresh flowers, and fruits. The priest sat on a deerskin and after passing a light among the actors, in the *aratī* ceremony, he prostrated himself on the floor before the sacred pictures. The actresses stood stage right in a row, some of them with partially made-up faces and bobby pins in their hair. They could be seen muttering their silent prayers as the sacrifice proceeded. Some of the men touched the drop curtain reverently with their hands and said their own special prayers. Some touched the fire of the sacrifice tray and then their eyes, asking for the blessing of the God of Fire, who presides over the sacrifice and over the pure flames, whose smoke is said to feed the gods in heaven. After the sacrifice the sacred items were removed and returned to the dressing room, where they are kept in a hallowed place.

The stage itself held many wonders—special contrivances for creating marvelous scenic effects, numerous slots and grooves for sliding wings, and drops and shutters and wires and ropes in the flies for special effects such as flying swords and the decapitation of imaginary figures. Chalk marks on the stage indicated the placement for some of the stars of the show so that they might be hit by the correct light for a particular scene. A chalk center line indicated the correct placement for the wings. Each set of wings required three people to operate it. Nine stagehands in all were required for each side of the stage just to handle the wings.

The show opened at 6:40 P.M. with special effects that produced a swirling of stars and flickering light focused on the company name and insignia. In and of itself the effect was extremely impressive. The company, like so many in other parts of India, relies on microphones to project the actors' voices. An unusually large number of lighting instruments were needed to produce the many special lighting effects. A corps of seven musicians in the orchestra pit provided most of the instrumental music and accompaniment for several of the songs used in the show. Additional sound effects, both orchestral and electronic, were produced by tape recorders and amplifiers.

The plot of *Ottakkoothar* is simple. It is the tale of the miraculous events surrounding the life of a famous historical figure who had a very human side and who is thought to have been favored by the goddess Saraswatī. The events are related through two acts and nearly fifty scenes. Like so many of the plays of this genre, the plot includes generous opportunities for comic interludes, sentimental and tearful scenes, heroic scenes of gallantry, songs, and mysterious and atmospheric environments, in addition to the abundant miraculous events which are emphasized by special effects, such as swords flying through the air, heads reuniting with human bodies, a disastrous flood, a demonic snake with flaming eyes, and so on. Costumes appeared to be sumptuous, many of them having elaborate beadwork and spangles. Some scenes required over twenty actors costumed in elaborate court regalia. Painted perspective scenery highlighted the general atmosphere of the space.

Spectators seemed transported into a mythical and historical world beyond the one in which they live. There is little doubt that the objective of the show was to emphasize the spectacle and to entertain.

At the conclusion of the play around 9:30 P.M. the actors assembled on stage. A lighted lamp in a coconut shell was passed in a clockwise manner in front of each actor, the audience stood out of respect but there was no applause. The front curtain closed in silence as the crowd burst forth into the cool evening, getting into limousines, taxis, and rickshaws waiting impatiently along the broad avenues beyond the Academy gates. One wondered how long this finely tuned, well-executed vestige of the past would survive the rapid changes of modern India life.

WORKS CITED

Brandon, James R. 1967.
Theatre in Southeast Asia. Cambridge: Harvard University Press.

Gargi, Balwant. 1962.
Theatre in India. New York: Theatre Arts Books.

Gilbert, Eddie Reid. 1971.
"The National School of Drama Contributes Significantly to Theatre Training in India." Ph.D. diss., University of Wisconsin.

"Journal of South Asian Literature Interviews: Ebrahim Alkazi." 1975.
Journal of South Asian Literature X, 2, 3, 4 (Winter, Spring, Summer): 289–325.

Mehta, C. C. 1963.
Bibliography of Stageable Plays in Indian Languages. 2 vols. New Delhi: Bharitya Natya Sangh.

Rahu, Kironmoy. 1978.
Bengali Theatre. New Delhi: National Book Trust.

Rangacharya, Adya. 1971.
The Indian Theatre. New Delhi: National Book Trust.

Said, Edward W. 1979.
Orientalism. New York: Random House.

Sen, Tapas. 1978.
"Stage Lighting: Indian Style." Bombay: Bombay Institute of Engineers. December 8 and 10.

Sircar, Badal. 1978.
The Third Theatre. Calcutta: Badal Sircar.

ADDITIONAL READING

Benegal, Som. N.d.
A Panorama of Theatre in India. New Delhi: Indian Council for Cultural Relations.

Bharucha, Rustom. 1983.
Rehearsals of Revolution: The Political Theater of Bengal. Honolulu: University of Hawaii Press.

Kidd, Ross. N.d.
"Domestication Theatre and Conscientization Drama in India." In *Tradition for Development: Indigenous Structures and Folk Media in Non-formal Education.* Eds. Ross Kidd and Nat Colletta. Berlin: International Council for Adult Education and German Foundation for International Development.

Mahanta, Pona. 1985.
Western Influence on Modern Assamese Drama. Delhi: Mittal Publications.

Mukherjee, Sushil Kumar. 1982.
The Story of the Calcutta Theatres: 1753–1980. Calcutta: K. P. Bagchi.

Panikkar, Kavalam Narayana. 1985.
"*Karimkutty.*" *Asian Theatre Journal* 2, 2:172–211.

Perumal, A. N. 1981.
Tamil Drama, Origin and Development. Adaiyarum Madras: International Institute of Tamil Studies.

Richmond, Farley. 1973.
"The Political Role of Theatre in India." *Educational Theatre Journal* XV, 3 (October): 318–334.

AFTERWORD

Farley P. Richmond
Darius L. Swann
Phillip B. Zarrilli

WHILE MUCH OF CONTEMPORARY INDIAN THEATRE HAS ABSORBED, adapted, and been profoundly affected by Western theatre, some of the West's most perceptive and creative theatre artists and theorists have, on their side, been deeply influenced by the theatre arts of India and other Asian countries. Three of the most prominent are Bertolt Brecht, Antonin Artaud, and Jerzy Grotowsky.

Although Brecht drew primarily from the Chinese theatre, the features he admired in that tradition are also present in several Indian theatre genres. His actual borrowings from Chinese theatre are substantial, even though it is believed he never actually traveled to China. Most fundamental are the spirit and style of the storytelling. His plays, like their Chinese counterparts, are straightforward and uncomplicated in plot, directly presentational in their exposition, narrative in style, stereotypical in character depiction, and symbolic in conventions. Brecht's plays thus exhibit characteristics that closely parallel those of some Indian theatre forms; indeed, interested observers may find in these Indian forms illustrations of how some of Brecht's theories work. This is particularly true of *nauṭankī* and *tamāshā,* among others.

At typical village performances in India, for example, the audience is seated on all sides of a simple platform stage or a bare playing area. This nonillusionistic use of playing space deemphasizes the physical setting and restores to the actor the central focus. This broad Brechtian principle is also seen in Chinese *jingxi* (Peking opera) and Japanese No. To be sure, the latter two do make use of elegant costumes, but the costumes become aspects of the actor's persona—they add to the actor's presence rather than distract from it. Further, the majority of the Indian theatre forms illustrate how effective a Brechtian structure can be. Their narrative, episodic structure bears strong resemblance to the epic form that Brecht promoted. The Indian plays, story centered, do not press implacably to a climax; their sometimes meandering pace allows the spectators to savor the sentiment *(rasa)* which a particular scene evokes.

While the savoring of the sentiment may be contra-Brechtian, there are in some Indian theatre forms the equivalents of Brecht's alienation devices, which keep the spectators aware of the distinction between real life and the stage. For example, in *nauṭankī* the dances done by the performers in the intervals between verses of song are quite foreign to the characters portrayed. Again, the freedom with which spectators come forward to express appreciation by making offerings and contributions while the performance is in progress and the immediate acknowledgment by the performer in *nauṭankī* and *tamāshā* underscore the fact that this is a performance, not real life. Likewise, the comic interludes, unrelated to the play's story and performed between scenes of the play, also serve as an alienating device.

There are at least three other ways in which Brechtian principles can be observed in Indian plays. (1) Simple stereotypical characters can be effectively used: The basic character does not unfold but is established in broad strokes at the outset—for example, the wicked king, the grasping whore, and so on—and the action of the play is a justification of that characterization rather than a revelation of it. (2) Like Brecht's, many Indian plays are given to didactic moralizing. Generally, their teaching undergirds traditional social values, but some forms—for instance, *tamāshā, bhavāi,* and even *kūṭiyāṭṭam* performances in the which the clown appears—make use of satire to expose and correct social ills. (3) The potential of theatre for social comment and political agitation became particularly evident in the struggle for freedom from British rule. *Nauṭankī* in the hands of Śrī Kṛṣṇa Pahalvān was an effective propaganda weapon against the British. Contemporary Calcutta *jātra,* moreover, deals with highly politicized issues.

If Brecht wished to keep us from empathizing too deeply in order to engage our rational faculties and thus stimulate change, Antonin Artaud set a different goal for his theatre. He wanted the theatre to arouse in us the same acute sharpness of feeling that primitive human beings experienced. Artaud, whose ideas have strongly influenced contemporary Western theatre, also drew his inspiration from Asian theatre performance, particularly Balinese, which he apparently never saw in its original environment. Much of our recent fascination with ritual theatre is directly traceable to Artaud, although he himself did not call for a theatre of ritual. In some ways our Western conception of ritual as patterned actions worn smooth by repetition and emptied of the emotions that called them forth is the opposite of what Artaud intended. He asks us to go to the experience behind the ritual, to be primitive men and women for whom the universe functions as the result of mysterious and awesome forces. His word for this is not ritual but magic.

> The question we must now ask is whether in this slippery world which is committing suicide without noticing it, there can be found a nucleus of men capable of imposing this superior notion of the theatre, men who will restore to all of us the natural and magical equivalent of the dogmas in which we no longer believe. (Artaud 1958, 32)

What Artaud suggests is the recapturing of a fundamentally religious experience. He uses the word "magic" probably because he wanted to indicate an experience much more potent than the pallid practices of Christianity that surrounded him. His writings in fact reflect important parallels with the Hindu beliefs that underlie many of the theatre forms we have described, particularly the dramatic rituals and dance-dramas. The masks, and masklike makeup and costumes, of Hindu gods, goddesses, and demonic beings in *teyyam, Ayyappan tiyatta, chau, kūṭiyāṭṭam,* and *kathakaḷi* conjure up the mysterious, shadowed, and irrational forces that underlie the myths and dances, however polished the form has become. Thus, while Brecht addresses technique, Artaud speaks to spirit, and it is indeed into a different spiritual world that Indian traditional theatre invites us.

Whether or not Artaud's limited exposure to Balinese theatre prepared him correctly to understand the nuances of Asian theatre is not important; the fact is that he grasped another world view, one closer to Asia than to Europe. His manifesto called for two things that he saw present in Asian theatre. (1) He sought a theatre not dominated by dialogue and, therefore, not dominated by text. In his vision of theatre there is a physical language of signs, gestures, and mimic actions which defy expression in logical discursive language and which contain a force that is quite inaccessible to thought. (2) He wanted in theatre a shift of focus from the human psyche to the cosmic forces in the universe. Human beings in this drama are conceived as something higher, a part of creation, though not its lords. The world view expressed in Indian theatre, demonstrably in *kūṭiyāṭṭam, kathakaḷi, chau, rās līlā,* and *Rām līlā,* resonates to Artaud's prescriptions.

The third theorist upon whom the Asian impact is clearly evident is Jerzy Grotowski. Unlike Brecht and Artaud, Grotowski experienced India firsthand, if only for a limited time. While Grotowski has concentrated his attention on actor training, he shares with Artaud a reliance on the primal myths and motivations that lie behind the smooth surfaces of everyday existence to spiritually energize his "holy actor." Grotowski thus emphasizes nonverbal means of communication. The theatre experience is to emerge out of the actor's struggle for self-revelation; to Grotowski, "the personal and scenic technique of the actor is the core of theatre art" (Grotowski 1969, 15).

Grotowski acknowledges his indebtedness to *kathakaḷi,* and to *jingxi* and No. His actor training methods specifically incorporate techniques in breathing and theories of the human anatomy learned from Indian yoga. Very clearly he believes that a theatre that is poor in stage scenery and the gadgets of modern technology may still be rich if there are "holy actors" committed to their vocation.

In sum, both Artaud and Grotowski seem to be saying that the path to vital theatre may well involve an extensive journey through the spiritual and philosophical understandings in which these materials have their roots. And Brecht and Grotowski continue to remind us that the structure and technique of all performance may be creatively utilized as one important means of generating incisive commentary on political and social realities.

More recently, explorations in the field of live performance have helped to expose Western audiences to Indian and Asian-inspired materials and have prepared the way for a more ready appreciation of Asian techniques and perceptions. Contemporary channels of communication, travel, and trade have certainly assisted in this process. As a result, the plays of Brecht are valued in India, particularly in Bengal; the theories of Artaud and the experiments of Grotowski, Eugenio Barba, Peter Brook, and Richard Schechner, among others, are as familiar to urban theatre artists in India as they are to us in the West. Dramatic changes have therefore begun to take place. The way Indians view their own performance traditions has begun to lead in new directions, and the way Western theatre practitioners and scholars are implementing and writing about Indian traditions is also undergoing change. In particular, contemporary Indian theatre workers are exploring the dilemma of coping with contemporary sociopolitical and economic realities in the midst of a culture with centuries-old traditions. The transition to a marketplace economy, the imposition of institutional structures foreign to the usual ways of organizing life, and the formation of a modern nation-state have brought on social, personal, and artistic crises for many. Playwright Girish Karnad recently summarized the dilemma:

> My generation was the first to come of age after India became independent of British rule. It therefore had to face a situation in which tensions implicit until then had come out in the open and demanded to be resolved with apologia or self-justification: tensions between the cultural past of the country and its colonial past, between the attractions of Western modes of thought and our traditions, and finally between the various visions of the future that opened up once the common cause of political freedom was achieved. (Karnad 1989, 93)

These tensions have led contemporary theatre practitioners to a reexamination of their own performance traditions, including those discussed here, in order to "confront what is 'Indian' about our own culture" (Bharucha 1984, 258). A recent publication of *Sangeet Natak* (1985) with articles by Deshpande, Pannikar, Jain, Kaul, Mehta, Mitra, Nath, Raina, and others amply illustrates the range of differing views on whether and how contemporary Indian theatre should return to its cultural roots.

In the West, the aftershock of colonialism in South Asia has meant both a reassessment of our orientalist constructions of India (Inden 1986) and a realization that research and cultural exchange between India and the West must now be mutually beneficial rather than an unequal partnership (Zarrilli 1986). This reexamination of colonial influence has led to a series of important new studies on the history and context within which the "classical" traditions, especially *Odissi* and *bhārata nāṭyam* dance, have been recreated in the twentieth century. The pioneering work of Marglin (1985) on *Odissi,* and more recently Kersenboom-Story (1987) and Meduri (1988) on *bhārata nāṭyam,* helps us ask new questions about the roots, performance, and audience reception of modern stage versions of these dances performed throughout the world today.

Finally, scholars awakening to the richness of anthropological, folklore, and performance-studies methods in field research and writing have begun to analyze Indian performance with new purpose and resolve. Richard Schechner and Linda Hess' panoramic study of the Rāmnagar *Rām līlā* (1977) awakened area studies scholars to new, complex, and evocative issues in the study of Indian performance. This and subsequent versions of Schechner's essay (1985) explore the multivocality of public festival performances and have helped lead a new generation of scholars to innovative ways of studying traditional Indian performance. Joyce Burkhalter Flueckiger's recent essay, "He Should Have Worn a Sari," for example, discusses a "failed" performance of a central Indian oral epic because studying a failure brings "to light certain aspects of successful performance" (Flueckiger 1988, 159).

On the eve of the twenty-first century, it is apparent that even more dramatic changes lie ahead both for India and for the West, perhaps linking our cultures even closer together than they ever have been in the past. Such a prospect brings us the opportunity to explore more deeply the rich potential that cross-cultural contacts offer, and it is our hope that this volume will prove to be useful to those setting out toward that goal.

ADDITIONAL READING

Artaud, Antonin. 1958.
The Theatre and Its Double. New York: Grove Press.

Bharucha, Rustom. 1984.
"A Reply to Richard Schechner." *Asian Theatre Journal* 1, 2:254–260.

Blackburn, Stuart H., and A. K. Ramanujan. 1986.
Another Harmony: New Essays on the Folklore of India. Berkeley: University of California Press.

Emigh, John, with Urlike Emigh. 1986.
"Hajari Bhand of Rajasthan: A Joker in the Deck." *The Drama Review* 30, 1: 101–130.

Flueckiger, Joyce Burkhalter. 1988.
" 'He Should have Worn a Sari' A 'Failed' Performance of a Central Indian Oral Epic." *TDR The Drama Review: A Journal of Performance Studies* 32, 1: 159–169.

Grotowski, Jerzy. 1969.
Toward a Poor Theatre. New York: Simon and Schuster.

Hiltebeitel, Alf. 1988.
The Cult of Draupadi, I. Mythologies: From Gingee to Kuruksetra. Chicago: University of Chicago Press.

Inden, Ronald. 1986.
"Orientalist Constructions of India." *Modern Asian Studies* 20, 3:401–446.

Karnad, Girish. 1989.
"In Search of a New Theater." In *Contemporary Indian Tradition.* Ed. Carla M. Borden. Washington, D.C.: Smithsonian Institution Press.

Kersenboom-Story, Saskia G. 1987.
Nityasumangali: Devadasi Tradition in South India. Delhi: Motilal Banarsidass.

Kumar, Nita. 1988.
The Artisans of Banaras: Popular Culture and Identity, 1880–1986. Princeton: Princeton University Press.

Marglin, Frederique. 1985.
Wives of the God-King: The Rituals of the Devadasis of Puri. Delhi: Oxford University Press.

Meduri, Avanti. 1988.
"*Bharatha Natyam*—What Are You?" *Asian Theatre Journal* 5, 1:1–22.

Schechner, Richard. 1985.
"Ramlila of Ramnagar." In *Between Theater and Anthropology.* Ed. Richard Schechner. Philadelphia: University of Pennsylvania. Pp. 151–211.

——— and Linda Hess. 1977.
"The Ramlila of Ramnagar." *The Drama Review* 21, 3:51–82.

Zarrilli, Phillip. 1986.
"The Aftermath: When Peter Brook Came to India, An Interview." *The Drama Review* 30, 1:92–99.

GLOSSARY

This glossary is designed to aid the reader in defining the meaning of important terms used with some frequency throughout the text. The list is not meant to be exhaustive. Theatre forms, personal names, place names, and words used infrequently have been excluded.

abhinaya. Literally, "to carry forward," ***abhi,*** 'toward,' ***ni,*** 'lead'; 1. acting as defined in the ***Nāṭyaśāstra.*** 2. mime; in dance, the imitation of human actions or the telling of a narrative through gesture and movement.

adbhuta. Wonder; one of the eight major sentiments (***rasa***) to be savored by the spectators of a classical Sanskrit play.

aratī. A worship rite in which lighted lamps are rotated before deities or actors in a clockwise direction.

Bhagavad Gītā. A philosophical poem placed in the ***Mahābhārata*** but probably written much later than the rest of the epic. It is an important source of Indian philosophical thought, especially that which pertains to ***bhakti.***

bhakti. Devotion; a religious movement stressing worship through devotion to a personal deity; one of the three paths to liberation or salvation in Hinduism.

bharata. 1. an actor; the term is said to have been derived from a tribe of the same name. 2. the reputed author of the ***Nāṭyaśāstra.*** 3. also, ***Bhārata*** is the brother of Rāma in the ***Rāmāyaṇa.***

bhārata nāṭyam. Classically based South Indian solo dance art recreated in the past century and based on the earlier tradition of temple dancers.

bhāva. An emotion or state of being. According to classical Indian dramatic theory the actor presents ***bhāva*** through acting (***abhinaya***) within the framework of the character and the play. In the ***Nāṭyaśāstra, Bharata*** describes eight fundamental emotions and thirty-three transitory emotions or states.

bol. A series of nonsense syllables called out by the dance master that describe the rhythmic pattern for the drummer to play.

Brahman. The priestly caste, highest of the social order in the ancient hierarchy.

Cakyar. A subcaste of temple servants in Kerala who are the hereditary actors of *kūṭiyāṭṭam*.

ceṇṭa. A large cylindrical drum played with two sticks in *kathakaḷi, kṛṣṇāṭṭam*, and *yakṣagāna*.

cuṭṭi. The built-up facial frame of makeup used in various forms of theatre in Kerala.

darśana. Sight or vision; the goal of worship of a personal god; philosophy.

Daśsara. An autumn festival which in North India celebrates the triumph of Rāma over the demon Rāvaṇa.

dholak. A kind of drum with two heads of equal size, played with the hands.

dholki-bārī. A *tamāshā* troupe which performs dramatic pieces as well as songs and dances. Performance is characterized by vigorous drumming on the two-headed drum (***dholak***) slung by a string from the shoulders.

dhoti. Lower garment worn by males throughout most of India; usually an unsewn white piece of cloth, at least five yards in length, wrapped and tied.

gāna. 1. a devotional song sung as a preliminary to a performance of *tamāshā* and other types of folk theatre. 2. the demi-gods.

gaulan. Literally, "milkmaid"; one of the girls with whom the youthful Kṛṣṇa sported.

guru. Teacher or spiritual preceptor; one who teaches and initiates his disciples in the teachings and traditions of his sect.

jarjara. Literally, "one who crushes"; the god Indra's flagstaff, or banner pole, which was used in the first dramatic production in the heavens to drive away evil spirits. Its ritual presentation became an essential element of stage preliminaries.

kala. Speed or tempo of rhythmic patterns.

kalam. Floor drawings or paintings, which become embodiments of the divinities they represent.

kaḷarippayaṭṭu. Martial art of Kerala.

kathak. A form of Indian classical dance which originated in North India; the dance shows the influence of both the *rās līlā* of the Mathura-Vrindaban area and the entertainments of the Moghul court.

katti. Literally, "knife"; *kathakaḷi* makeup type in which are combined arrogance and evil and redeeming, noble qualities.

kīrtan. A type of devotional song sung by a leader and congregation as chorus. The style is associated with **bhakti** preaching and public presentation; in *tamāshā* a one-man musical sermon.

Ksatriya. The warrior caste, preservers of the order of society and particularly of the sacrifice of the ***Brahman*** priests.

kūttampalam. A theatre building attached to a temple in Kerala and designed for performances of *kūṭiyāṭṭam*.

kūttŭ. A performance in Kerala in which the clown or jester (***vidūṣaka***) expounds on Puranic stories and takes the roles of various characters, while accompanied by a drummer.

lāsya. The graceful or sensuous style of dance and drama.

lāvanī. A style of song in *tamāshā* often given to expressing erotic sentiments, interpreted through dancing as well as singing.

līlā. Literally, "sport," "play," or "deeds" of the deity; in *rās līlā* the dramatic reenactment of a deed or exploit of Kṛṣṇa during his earthly manifestation.

loknāṭya. Literally, "people's theatre"; a sophisticated or refined form of *tamāshā*.

Mahābhārata. One of the two great Indian epics. The ***Mahābhārata*** is the extended story of the great war fought between the Pandavas and the Kauravas, who were cousins, over their kingdom.

mandala. A movement sequence made up of a succession of gaits to represent a fight or battle in Sanskrit theatre.

mantra. Single or combined syllables or sounds, the recitation of which gives the reciter access to special powers.

mohiniāṭṭam. Literally, "dance of Mohinī," the enchantress; classically-based female dance of Kerala, also closely linked to earlier tradition of female dancers.

mudra. Symbolic hand gesture used in classical Indian theatre and dance, and in many forms of regional theatre.

Nambyar. The drummer in *kūṭiyāṭṭam;* a member of a subcaste of temple servants.

nandī. The benediction at the beginning of a Sanskrit play; one item of the preliminaries.

Naṅgyār. A female singer and actress in *kūṭiyāṭṭam;* a member of a subcaste of temple servants.

naṭa. In classical Indian theatre, the generic term for actor, pantomimist, or dancer.

nāṭakā. The most important of the ten major play types of Sanskrit drama. Ideally it had four to ten acts, a legendary figure as a hero, and either the erotic (***śṛngāra***) or heroic (***vīra***) as the dominant sentiment (***rasa***).

nāṭya. 1. in classical Indian dramatic theory, dramatic art, as distinguished from rhythmic dance (***nṛtta***) and mimetic art (***nṛtya***). Its essential characteristic is its ability to arouse or evoke sentiments (***rasa***) in the spectator. 2. more broadly, "all theatrical activity." 3. also referred to as dance-drama; dancers enact a story through hand gestures (**mudra**) and acting (***abhinaya***). Music, songs, and occasionally dialogue accompany the performance.

Nāṭyaśāstra. Literally, "the dramatic scripture"; the most ancient and authoritative treatise on dramaturgy and the theatrical arts.

nirvahaṇa. 1. a conclusion; the fifth and last juncture of action in a classical Indian play. 2. in *kūṭiyāṭṭam,* a recapitulation of the events that precede the play being enacted, by one actor playing many roles.

nṛtta. Literally, "pure dance"; nonmimetic dance that emphasizes rhythmic footwork, body movement, and hand gestures for their beauty of form. Described in detail in the ***Nāṭyaśāstra.***

nṛtya. Pantomime, or emotion-laden storytelling with bodily movement in Indian theatre.

pacca. Literally, "green"; a makeup type in *kathakaḷi* and *kūṭiyāṭṭam* in which the face is painted a rich green. It is used for noble, virtuous, and heroic characters such as Rāma or Kṛṣṇa.

parikramaṇa. Literally, "walking around"; a conventional acting technique in which an actor suggests a journey from one locale to another, within the same scene, through a stylized walk around the stage.

prahasana. A one-act play which combines comedy and farce and deals with lowly worldly characters. One of ten major types of classical Sanskrit plays.

prasāda, prasād. Food that has been blessed by being presented to a god and then returned to the giver and those who partake of its ritual purity.

pūjā. Literally, "sacred offerings"; in all traditional Indian theatre, a play is preceded by offerings to various deities of flowers, incense, music, song, and sometimes dance, and prayers asking for a successful performance.

pūjārī. Ritual specialist or priest.

Purana. Classical sacred works which are collections of wisdom and stories and often serve as sources for plays, especially the life of Lord Kṛṣṇa.

purapad. See: ***puṛappāṭu.***

puṛappāṭu. Literally, "the going forth"; in *kathakaḷi,* a pure dance sequence, the third section of the preliminaries before a play.

raga. The basic unit of organization of classical Indian music, combining mode and melodic pattern. A contemporary term.

Rāmāyaṇa. One of the two great Indian epics; the ***Rāmāyaṇa*** recounts the life and exploits of Rāma.

Rāmcaritmānas. A retelling in Hindi of the Rāma epic by Tulsīdās in the sixteenth century.

Rāmnagar. Literally, "Rāma's city"; a section of the city of Benares (Varanasi) where the *Rām līlā* is staged under the patronage of the raja of Benares.

raṅgā, raṅgāchār. 1. the stage manager of the *svāṅg* performance; roughly the equivalent of the ***sūtradhāra*** in Sanskrit theatre. 2. broadly, in ancient India any public place for presenting shows or performances. 3. a stage.

rās. A dance expressing the lovemaking of Rādhā and Kṛṣṇa in the heavenly sphere; the first section of a *rās līlā* performance.

rasa. Flavor, color, and residual essence, or the joyful consciousness which a spectator experiences while witnessing a dramatic performance. ***Rasa*** is the major aesthetic goal of classical Indian theatre and many regional theatre forms as well (*kathakaḷi, kūṭiyāṭṭam, kuchipudi, rās līlā,* and so on). Usually translated "sentiment," ***rasa*** is evoked by the actor's appropriate depiction of various emotions (***bhāva***) by means of a codified system of determinants, consequents, and transitory feelings.

rāsdhārī. A member of a professional troupe which performs *rās līlā;* the leader of a *rās līlā* troupe.

Ṛg Veda. The oldest book of hymns of the ancient Indo-Aryan civilization that inhabited India after the first civilization had come to an end (about 2000 B.C.); still considered the most sacred book of the Hindus.

Sabha. Literally, "assembly," an organization of like-minded people; cultural organizations in Madras city (and Kerala) that sell subscription seasons of cultural programs, including plays, to its membership. In ancient India a place where theatrical performances were held.

sādhu. A hermit; a holy man.

sakhī. A female companion or friend; a friend or companion of Rādhā in the *rās līlā.*

śakti. Divine power, particularly in its feminine aspect, often personified in the form of a goddess, especially Śiva's wife or the Divine Mother goddesses who take several manifestations, such as Durgā, Kāli, and so on.

sari. An unsewn garment worn in different styles, regarded as the "national" dress of Indian women.

śloka. Metrical verse composed in stanzas.

śṛngāra. Literally, "love"; in classical Indian dramatic theory, the erotic or romantic sentiment (***rasa***) which is aroused in the spectator by experiencing the enacted emotion of love in the play. The most important of the eight sentiments.

Sudra. The lowest of the four castes of ancient India, identified with service or labor.

sūtradhāra. Literally, "string holder"; 1. possibly a puppeteer in ancient shadow theatre. 2. in classical Indian theatre, the director-manager of a theatre troupe. Described by Bharata as the person responsible for all aspects of performance—forming the troupe, training the actors, casting, directing, producing, making offerings to the gods (***pūjā***), supervising building a theatre, and appearing before the audience in preliminaries to the play.

swami. Literally, "master, lord"; the proprietor of a *rās līlā* troupe.

svarūp, svarūpa. Literally, "shape, form"; the young actor who impersonates the deity, such as Kṛṣṇa, and is considered his temporary embodiment.

tabla. A pair of drums played with the hands, used to accompany Indian classical music, dance, and some drama forms.

tala. Literally, "palm, indicating drum beats"; a rhythmic pattern that controls the beat of drums, cymbals, song, and dance (***nṛtta, nṛtya***) in all types of Indian theatre. The dancer's footwork especially is tied to the rhythmic pattern (**tala**) being used. One of three elements of theatre music.

tāṇḍava. Style of dance characterized by strong, vigorous movement; masculine dance style.

teyyam. The deity propitiated in Kerala festivals known as Kāḷiyāṭṭam.

tottam. Songs narrating the story of a deity, ancestor, and so on.

vāg. A full-length dramatic folk play from the *tamāshā* repertory.

vidūṣaka. A jester or fool; a traditional character type in classical Sanskrit plays. Portrayed as fat, ugly, uncouth, and greedy, but always a **Brahman.** Equivalent character types are found in most forms of folk-popular theatre.

vīra. Literally, "heroism"; one of eight principal sentiments (***rasa***) to be experienced by spectators of Sanskrit plays. It is aroused by the enacted emotion of energy.

yajña. A great or major sacrifice to be performed by elaborate rites and rituals recreating the primordial self-immolation and resurrection of the primal man.

INDEX

Abhinaya, 40, 66, 162
Abhira tribe, 180
Academy of Fine Arts (Calcutta), 424
Actors and acting: auditioning in modern India, 438–439; illustration of nineteenth-century English performers, 388; in *kūṭiyāṭṭam,* 88, 89–92, 102–104, 115–116, in modern theatre, 412–416; and photos of actors, 91; in *Rām līlā,* 228–229; in Sanskrit theatre, 37, 39, 40–43, 44; in *tamāshā,* 283, 294. See also *Abhinaya*
Actor training: in *kathakaḷi,* 318–326, in *kūṭiyāṭṭam,* 91–92; in modern theatre, 416–421; in *nauṭankī,* 265–268; and photos of *kathakaḷi* training techniques, 322, 323, 324, 325; in *Rām līlā,* 219–220; in *rās līlā,* 186; in Sanskrit theatre, 37–38; in *tamāshā,* 283–284, 294. See also *Ayyappan tiyatta,* performer training in; Seraikella *chau,* training in; *Teyyam,* training for
Advertising: in modern theatre, 446–448
Akbar: and *Rām līlā,* 218n
Akhāṛā. See Actor training, in *nauṭankī*
Alaknandan (director), 444
Alexander the Great: and Sanskrit theatre, 30
Alkazi, Ebrahim (actor, director), 396, 409–412, 418, 442, 445
All-India Radio, 395, 406
All-India Television, 395
Amar Singh Rathor: production photo of, 250
Amateur theatre: in modern India, 394–398
Amrita Bazar Patrika (Calcutta), 447
Ananda Bazar Patrika (Calcutta), 447
Aṅka, 22, 67, 72
Aṇkīya nāṭ, 14, 23, 43, 44, 173; origin and characteristics of, 22, 175–176; production photos of, 175, 311
Antigone (Anouilh), 395
Aratī, 202, 226, 231
Arena Stage (Washington, D.C.), 443
Aristotle, 35
Artaud, Antonin (director, theorist), 463, 464, 465
Āryabhushan Theatre (Pune), 300
Aryan, 7, 28
Aśoka: and origin of Sanskrit theatre, 30–31
Association and Federation of City Sabhas, 431–432
Aśvaghoṣa (Sanskrit playwright), 53, 54, 57
Atharva Veda, 25
Aṭṭam, 131
Audience: in *kathakaḷi,* 346–347; in *kūṭiyāṭṭam,* 88, 94–95; in modern India, 421–424; in *nauṭankī,* 264; photos of, 23, 421; in *Rām līlā,* 225–226; in *rās līlā,* 198–200; in Sanskrit theatre, 46–48; in *tamāshā,* 284; in *teyyam,* 134
Auditorium: consecration of, in Sanskrit theatre, 51–52; in *kūṭiyāṭṭam,* 95–96; in modern India, 424–429, photos of, 426, 427; in Sanskrit theatre, 49–50, 51
Avishkar theatre troupe (Bombay), 400, 418, 455, 456
Ayurvedic, 347, 354
Ayyappan tiyatta, xii, 127–128, 315, 316, 465; current state of, 163–164; definition and overview of, 151–152; performance example of, 154–163; performance photos of, 160–161; performer training in, 152–153; and summary of performance events, 155

Babur (king), 264
Bahorupee (Calcutta), 395; audience, 423; government assistance to, 435; production expenses of, 429; production photo of, 59; scenery for, 441
Balagadhagandharya Natya Mandir (Pune), 428
Bāli, 31; *kathakaḷi* performance photo of, 316
Balinese theatre, 464, 465
Bandya, the Accountant (Gavankar), 288

Production Notes

This book was designed by Roger Eggers. Composition and paging were done on the Quadex Composing System and typesetting on the Compugraphic 8400 by the design and production staff of University of Hawaii Press.

The text typeface is Garamond No. 49 and the display typeface is ITC Garamond Light.

Offset presswork and binding were done by Vail-Ballou Press, Inc. Text paper is Glatfelter Offset Smooth, basis 60.